HOW TO DRINK AUSTRALIAN

An Essential Modern Wine Book

HOW TO DRINK AUSTRALIAN

Jane Lopes & Jonathan Ross

with Kavita Faiella, Mike Bennie
and Hannah Day

Original maps by Martin von Wyss

murdoch books

Sydney | London

Contents

Introduction 10

NEW SOUTH WALES

Introduction 26
Hunter Valley 30
Central Ranges 52
Southern New South Wales 72
Other New South Wales 92

VICTORIA

Introduction 100
Yarra Valley 104
Mornington Peninsula 122
Geelong 138
Macedon Ranges 152
Gippsland 166
Heathcote 180
Western Victoria 194
Beechworth 212
Rutherglen 226
Other Victoria 238

TASMANIA

Introduction 254

SOUTH AUSTRALIA

Introduction 284
Barossa 288
Clare Valley 320
Adelaide Hills 336
McLaren Vale 356
Coonawarra & Wrattonbully 380
Other South Australia 398

WESTERN AUSTRALIA

Introduction 408
Margaret River 412
Great Southern 432
Other Western Australia 446

QUEENSLAND

Introduction 456

Conclusion 470
Thanks 472
Glossary 474
Bibliography 478
Index 482
Index of Producers 489
Conversion Charts 495

WINE REGIONS OF AUSTRALIA

Spanning 33 degrees of latitude (10°S to 43°S), with a land mass about as large as the continental United States, it is impossible to generalise anything about Australia. The growing regions are largely confined to the bottom half of the country and within a couple of hundred kilometres of the coast: everything else is too hot and/or humid. Wine regions find respite from the country's heat in three ways: proximity to the coast, elevation, and/or a higher latitude (being further away from the equator). Access to a major water source — like the regions on the Murray River, dividing Victoria and New South Wales — has also been an establishing factor for several wine regions.

Less than 0.35% of the delineated area of Australia's wine regions is planted to the vine; coupled with the amount of suitable land that has yet to be designated as a wine region, Australia has exponential possibility for new growth. As excellent and established as many of its wine regions are, plenty of people believe that some of the country's best sites have yet to be discovered. Invest in learning Australia's wine regions now, and you'll be rewarded with continual opportunities for exploration and wonder in the decades to come.

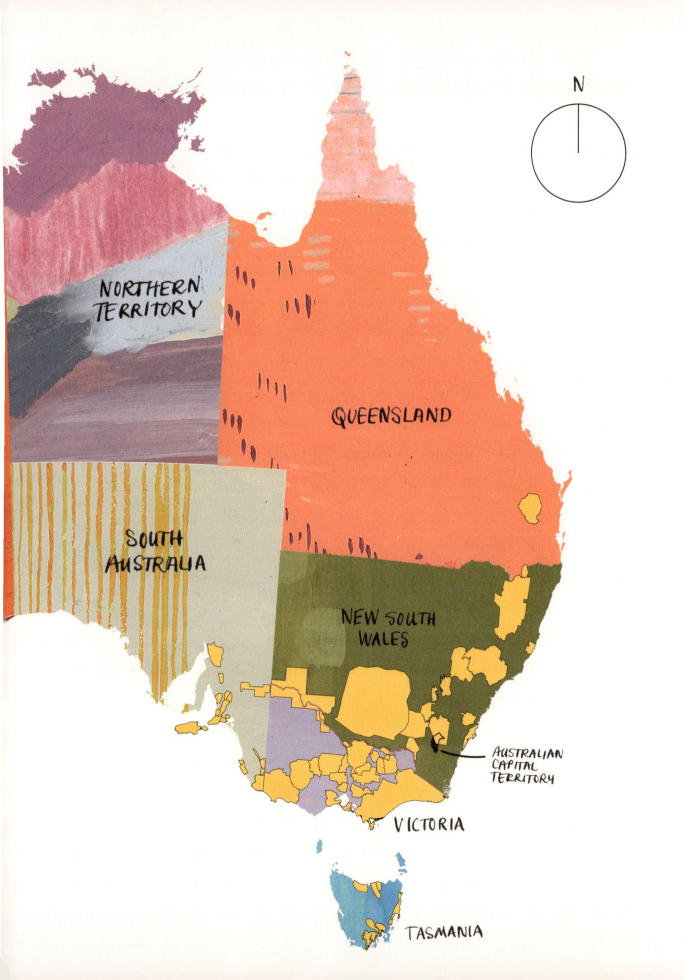

Introduction

There are plenty of options out there when looking for a bottle of wine to drink. We think you should choose Australian. This book will show you how to go about learning Australian wine — and why.

The landscape of Australian wine is cracking with both new energy and historic traditions that make it one of the most exciting (we think *the* most exciting) wine-producing countries in the world right now. But the scholarship on Australian wine hasn't always matched the output. Think of the dozens (hundreds?) of books that exist on France's Burgundy alone, a region that could fit inside many of Australia's individual appellations. Australia hasn't been afforded the same attention in the world of wine, especially by those living outside its borders.

How to Drink Australian is an insider's and outsider's guide to Australian wine, both perspectives offering something important to the conversation. The value of the insider's view is easy to calculate: this book will provide insight on the culture, nuances and happenings of each wine region — told by the important players themselves. The history, growing conditions, wines produced and leading personalities are detailed to distinguish what makes each wine region of Australia unique and captivating.

From this perspective, this book will seek to provide a narrative of the regions: not just a timeline, but a digestion and interpretation of the pertinent facts to draw observations on the historical patterns, current events and future developments that make each wine region unique. While we aim to be as objective as possible, there is some inherent subjectivity, and potential for generalisations, in this process. We find this to be the lesser of two evils; the worst thing an insider's view can do is not give insight on what's actually going on.

The value of the outsider's point of view, on the other hand, is not as obvious. But it does carry one important facet in relaying information: enthusiasm.

One of the greatest things about Australians is their humility, verging on self-deprecation. While this is an endearing trait, it is not always a helpful one in selling premium wine. Rob Mann, a prominent Western Australian winemaker, said: 'If you want to be thought of as making the best wine in the world, you've got to be able to stand up in front of people and tell them that. And that's not something we're particularly good at as a culture, as Australians.'

Michael Hill Smith, of Adelaide Hills' Shaw+Smith, concurs: 'The major challenge for Australia, in its entirety, is we need to be better at selling our fine wine.' He goes on to say, 'Australian wine has never been so exciting as it is now. I honestly believe we make the very best wines. And if they are truly exciting, we'll win in the end.'

So, as a partial team of outsiders, we'll be the ones who stand up for Australia and say: Australian wine deserves to win. They're making the best wine in the world. Keep reading (and drinking), and you'll discover why.

Cheers,
Jane & Jonathan

We encourage those who drink and sell alcohol to do so in a responsible and considered manner; wine is a beverage that can bring much joy and prosperity when consumed in moderation.

The Team

JANE LOPES

Having spent most of my career selling and drinking European wine at top spots across the US, I was wholly unprepared for what Australia had to offer when I moved to Melbourne from New York in 2017. Almost immediately, Australian wine replaced European favourites in my arsenal of go-to sips, and I knew that most of the world was missing out on some of its very greatest wines. Importing wine to the US, and writing this book, is all part of my grand plan to let everyone else in on this secret. With my work in fine dining across the world, boots-on-the-ground experience in the vineyards of Australia, completion of studies with the Court of Master Sommeliers, and authorship of a previous wine book, I finally feel confident to stand up and say: Australia is making the world's most exciting wine. And that is what we hope this book shows.

JONATHAN ROSS

I've had a lengthy career working with wine in the final moment of a bottle's life: when it is being consumed and enjoyed. That career includes stints in some of the US's most celebrated dining rooms, culminating in passing the Master Sommelier exam. My 2017 relocation to Melbourne, though, opened my eyes to connections with wine I had yet to make; the distance that had grown between me and what makes wine special disappeared as soon as I landed in Australia. I was awestruck by how much joy the people and the wines expressed. My excitement and curiosity about wine has never been fuller, and the natural and human beauty of Australia is to thank for that. This is our love letter to Australia.

KAVITA FAIELLA

Originally from Sydney, Australia, I have spent over half of my 20 years in wine living and working as a sommelier overseas, mainly throughout Asia. From the busy bustling cities of Hong Kong, Tokyo and New Delhi to remote villages in Bhutan and the islands of the Maldives, I always felt a distinct pride when opening and talking about Australian wine in the far-flung corners of the world. Using wine as a medium to discuss some of what I would consider the most unique and special places on earth is my great privilege. Today I am even more proud to have contributed to this book, which will see these vinous stories, along with those of First Nations people, the traditional custodians of this great land, travel far and wide.

MIKE BENNIE

HANNAH DAY

MARTIN VON WYSS

I'm from Sydney, Australia and fell into wine while finishing a dual university degree in law and media. Originally, I worked in radio news and current affairs, but the lure of wine hooked me in and I ended up working, then running, Australia's leading corporate fine wine merchants, which cascaded into the kaleidoscopic array of work I do now between writing, presenting, co-directing an avant garde wine merchant, inventing festivals, curating events, consulting and winemaking. It's been an extraordinary benefit working in possibly the world's most diverse wine community, where rules are few and creativity is rewarded. To work on a book like this that mainlines not only the historical backdrop of Australian wine, but its contemporary mores in such detail, and with such care, is a once in a lifetime project and indeed a celebration.

If you'd asked me two years ago what wines and stories I most wanted to share with my guests, you most likely would have heard a blend of 'MoselBaroloBurgundyChampagne' eagerly flutter off my tongue. It has taken contributing to this book about the wines of my homeland to bring me back to my roots. As a journalism student-turned-cabaret artist-turned-sommelier-turned-winery hand, I have a fierce obsession and unquenchable fascination for wine – and for communicating about it. I have been lucky enough to have worked at some of Melbourne's most sought-after dining destinations and I hold very dear the opportunities I have had to share the wines that are created in this country – we are so lucky to be driven by such passion and innovation. It took me a moment to realise, but it is truly the most exciting wine scene to watch, and I cannot wait to weave my own piece into the story.

When I arrived in Australia in 2005 with cartography tools and plenty of curiosity, I set about mapping the vineyards and wine regions of my new home. My first Australian publication, a big wine map of Victoria, garnered a positive response from winemakers and consumers, fuelling my passion until it became an obsession. I have mapped wine-related information in all sorts of formats from paper to 3D-printed to web-based animated maps. But I never lost sight of the fascinating central character, wine, which is why I've now opened a bottle shop in Melbourne, whose organising theme – of course! – is the geography of wine. But for all my vinous travels to the far-flung corners of the world, I find that Australia has it all and never fails to amaze.

An Acknowledgement of Country

Australia is often referred to as being a 'New World' wine region, meaning that its wine story is relatively young when compared to European wine (the 'Old World'). This makes sense, especially since wine is a European system of agriculture based on vine species native to much of Europe and Western Asia.

However, when looking at Australia from a sociological and geological point of view, it is one of the oldest worlds in wine.

Australia is home to the oldest earth material known to humans: zircon, a 4.4-billion-year-old particle found in formations in Western Australia. The Porongurups, in Western Australia's Great Southern, are the oldest mountains on the earth's surface today.

When we speak in terms of soils and geology across the wine world, we reference France's Massif Central: a granite plateau that formed the Rhône Valley 350–300 million years ago. Or it's the alpine Langhe region of Italy (15 million years old), the majestic slopes of the Douro (500 million years old) and the steep cliffs of the Mosel (400 million years old).

Crossing the ancient terrain of Australia, we reference a geological history as young as our current epoch, the Holocene era, which started after the last ice age, and as old as the Porongurup foothills, formed 1.2 billion years ago – and everything in between.

To walk among the vines in the Barossa Valley is to step on rocks that were created 760 million years ago, when Melbourne and Sydney were at the bottom of the ocean. The geo-formative history of Australia is one that spans the supercontinents of Rodinia, Gondwana, Pangaea and the continental organisation we see today when we think of the globe.

While we often talk of the geo-formative landscape of a region in the world of wine, we rarely talk about its socio-formation – the humans who shaped and cared for the land before it was planted to the vine.

The history of the arrival of humans on the island continent of Australia has continued to become clearer as the nation begins to unite under the common goal of reconciliation. Archaeological evidence shows that the earliest humans – all of our ancestors – first lived in Africa. The 'Out of Africa' migration theory, based on further archaeological evidence, shows early humans moving into Asia between 2 and 1.8 million years ago, and north into Europe between 1.5 and 1 million years ago.

While less concrete, it is thought that *Homo sapiens* akin to the modern-day human evolved by about 130,000 years ago, from ancestors who remained on the African continent. They too migrated out of Africa and spawned the modern-day spread of humanity by way of the same path their ancestors took: east to Asia and north to Europe.

This migration took place during the last ice age. 'Ice age' conjures visualisations of the entire globe frozen over, though the more formal name, Last Glacial Period (LGP), paints a better picture. The **Quaternary** Glaciation, which lasted for over 2.5 million years and ended some 11,700 years ago, was when the Arctic Cap formed. This resulted in much of the earth's water being frozen in the Northern Hemisphere and the sea level across the world being lower.

Today, over 25,000 islands sit in the Maritime Southeast Asia area, though during the LGP they were connected via land bridges and shallow waters. The average global temperature was only 6°C cooler than that of the past decade, setting the stage for continued human dispersion.

The north coast of Australia was accessible by land bridges that now lie beneath the sea. Humans arrived on the Australian continent via two paths: either through what's now known as Arnhem Land, in the north-central expanse of Australia, or through the Torres Strait Islands, off the northern coast of Queensland, through a land bridge that connected the country to Papua New Guinea.

There is archaeological evidence that proves humans have lived in Australia for at least 65,000 years, and have occupied the entirety of its landmass for at least 30,000 years.

The First Peoples of Australia, like many early civilisations, have often been mislabelled as primitive and uncivilised. While Torres Strait Islanders farmed their island gardens, mainland

The traditional application of fire to cleanse and invigorate Country is central to physical and spiritual life. The antiseptic oils of eucalyptus and emu bush are retained in the smoke produced, and are often present when a mother gives birth, for example, to prevent infection.

Aboriginal peoples have long been portrayed as hunter-gatherers who didn't work their land in a way to make it work for them. They were framed as people with basic technologies and temporary dwellings who lacked ecological foresight and complex social structures. This is what has traditionally been taught in Western school curriculums and recorded in literature, a distortion that is not specific to the First Nations of Australia, but has been applied to many Indigenous peoples and cultures throughout the world.

What has become clear, however, is the colonial and racial bias underpinning this way of looking at Aboriginal society. Increasingly, it is apparent that what Aboriginal people achieved in Australia was just too big, too complex, for the early settlers to appreciate. Early colonists recorded their observations of a land so uniquely and proficiently cared for that they thought the entire country looked like a 'gentlemen's garden'. Yet they couldn't reconcile this observation with an acknowledgement of Aboriginal custodianship.

Despite the tourism campaigns and settler mythologising, the environment those first colonists saw had in fact been shaped and sculpted by Indigenous custodianship over thousands of generations. Principal technology of that sculpting was fire, which was applied to

Increasingly, it is apparent that what Aboriginal people achieved in Australia was just too big, too complex, for the early settlers to appreciate.

ecosystems seasonally at small scales, but systematically across the continent, to remove old growth, regenerate species and stimulate cycles of ecological succession. This strategic 'farming with fire' has shaped the flora, fauna and human balance of the continent.

Introduction

15

The ancient fish traps in Brewarrina, New South Wales, are made of thousands of carefully placed stones, reflecting the elegance and genius of Indigenous land management. The current of the river feeds the races with fish that are trapped by rock walls before being pulled out of the water with a net. Known as Baiame's Ngunnhu, the traps are a part of Wailwan Country, and continue to provide sustenance for many local Nations.

Always Was, Always Will Be

For those unfamiliar, an Acknowledgement of Country is a formal practice that pays respect to the traditional custodians, past and present, of the country known today as Australia. It is practised by non-Indigenous people in Australia, and will often open a meeting, event or occasion by honouring the specific caretakers of that place and naming the traditional people and First Nation of the land.

This practice is informed by Welcome to Country: one of humanity's oldest traditions. Australia is home to over 500 First Nations. Aboriginal and Torres Strait Islander culture and society was underscored by a coexistence among all things – especially with one's neighbour. While sharing with neighbours was a critical part of social and ecological security, protocols needed to be observed. You didn't just walk onto someone else's Country and take what you wanted: you needed to be invited, and the Welcome to Country protocols reinforce this cultural principle.

The pursuit of learning more about Aboriginal and Torres Strait Islander culture is at times riddled with mental barriers of our own Western culture. In this book, in the effort to make proper and accurate acknowledgements for land now planted to the vine, we found ourselves looking for *the* nation or people that belonged to *this* piece of land – as if it were a finite, delimited object in the way we view wine appellations.

Across tens of thousands of years of uninterrupted existence, natural landforms changed, and so did the people who cared for them. As Sue Bell of Bellwether (p. 394) in Coonawarra teaches, the 'boundaries of these First Nations are fluid, and changed with the land, with people, and their relationship to both Country and each other. It is our Western culture that creates the vision that boundaries are stagnant, permanent and have an everlasting meaning.'

While acknowledging these naturally blurred boundaries and the fluidity of human experience through time, caring for Country is also a very specific concept across Aboriginal cultures. Leading up to colonisation, Aboriginal Australians and Torres Strait Islanders had amassed tens of thousands of years of knowledge about the specific places they looked after. Their purpose was to care for this land – to help it flourish so that in turn it would support their own flourishing, and that of the generations to come.

Complex systems of land care were employed, observing every nuance of place.

As mentioned, custodians would prescribe burnings in specific types of Country at specific points of the year based on the season. We see 'controlled burnings' today as fire prevention, as avoiding catastrophe but, in Indigenous wisdom, fire was always employed to stimulate the prosperity of Country. Aboriginal and Torres Strait Islander culture shows that fire breeds life, and it can be applied in nuanced and complex manners to do exactly that. In his 2020 book *Fire Country*, Victor Steffensen writes: 'The original application of Aboriginal fire knowledge requires you to learn about the country. To activate the landscape in a way that opens the doors to many other practices and opportunities.'

All this knowledge of land would be passed down through generations by 'Dreamtime' stories or 'the Dreaming'. These are stories of creation, unique to each language group across Australia, which contain within them inherent information on each group's rituals, society, ethics, morality, relationship to the land – and much more. According to Common Ground, an Indigenous advocacy group, 'the Dreaming' is considered 'a vastly inadequate translation of a concept which is difficult for non-Indigenous people to understand due to its complexity, non-linear and non-finite nature'. 'The Dreaming' is not mythology, but a worldview: a system of stories in which ecological and cultural values are preserved and passed between generations.

We see 'controlled burnings' as fire prevention ... but, in Indigenous wisdom, fire was always employed to stimulate the prosperity of Country.

A Brief History of Colonisation and Indigenous Sovereignty

At the time of colonisation, it is estimated that there were approximately 750,000 people living on the continent of Australia. The date 26 January 1788 is memorialised as Australia Day, and marks the landing of the First Fleet in Sydney. But this day is known to Aboriginal and Torres Strait Islanders, and a growing number of non-Indigenous Australians, as Invasion Day (or Survival Day). It is the day when the 65,000-year Indigenous custodianship was interrupted, and Australia's path radically changed.

Though some early relations were peaceful, conflict began as Europeans started to occupy land in ways that disrupted the balance the First Nations had developed with Country. Land was taken, forcibly, and the influx of European agriculture drastically changed the ecosystem. The planting of wheat invaded native species that were once food for local game animals like kangaroo. Irrigation schemes dried up rivers and streams, causing the disappearance of fish, abalone and birds.

Grazing sheep and cattle became the only animals in sight. When these animals were speared by native communities for sustenance, violent confrontations ensued. Fences went up, Indigenous children and women were taken, and the introduction of novel diseases like smallpox quickly decimated the local population. By 1840, numerous nations had lost over 90% of their population. By 1900, it is estimated that there were fewer than 100,000 Aboriginal and Torres Strait Islander people on the continent, and fewer than 75,000 in 1933. Though the word is often reserved for despotic regimes rather than colonialism, this begins to look (statistically at least) like attempted genocide. In places like Tasmania, where government policy was to eliminate the local populations, there is no other word for it.

By the 1960s, Indigenous advocacy began to take root. In 1962, Aboriginal and Torres Strait Islander people became a part of the voting population. The next 10 years brought the end of the 'Stolen Generation', whereby children had

The High Court ruling in Mabo v. Queensland (1992) overturned the legal fiction of Terra Nullius (the premise of 'nobody's land' that predicated so much colonisation) and acknowledged that Indigenous people had been living in Australia for thousands of years prior to colonisation.

been systematically taken from their families between 1871 and 1969 by government agencies and church missions for the purpose of 'eradicating Aboriginal culture'.

In 1993, the Australian Parliament passed the Native Title Act, which 'recognises the rights and interests of Aboriginal and Torres Strait Islander Peoples in Land and Waters according to their traditional laws and customs'. This was the result of the High Court ruling in Mabo v. Queensland (1992) that overturned the legal fiction of Terra Nullius (the premise of 'nobody's land' that predicated so much colonisation) and acknowledged that Indigenous people had been living in Australia for thousands of years prior to European arrival.

Subsequent laws were passed in all Australian states to further such reconciliation. Though the motives may have been genuine,

part of the problem is that the European and colonial-derived government controls the re-establishment of Aboriginal and Torres Strait Islander land and water rights. The missing piece of the puzzle is self-determination.

Aboriginal Corporations are legal entities, which can receive government funds to serve Aboriginal and Torres Strait Islander communities: supporting education and housing needs, securing land, seeking greater recognition, providing legal assistance, developing infrastructure, and promoting art, music and culture.

These corporations are also the bodies that work to have their native title claims codified by state governments. To gain a native title claim, a group needs to prove their historic and continued existence on the land. In many cases, this is quite difficult considering that entire language groups and nations were decimated by colonisation, and their continuous relationships to Country interrupted by a stream of government policies and practices.

By 2021, the population of Aboriginal and Torres Strait Islander people had grown to resemble their pre-1788 size of nearly 800,000 people, though it still constitutes only 3.2% of the Australian population. Australia has a long way to go to facilitate a justice-oriented future for its Indigenous communities, but there is more attention now than there has ever been to this outcome.

Caring for Country

Land care – learning from, acknowledging and making space for the First Nations of Australia and their relationship to Country – has become an important topic, not the least among Australia's vintners. Bruce Pascoe concludes in *Dark Emu*, one of Australia's most important books on Indigenous culture and society, that 'farmers have always been crucial to land conservation, and have always had a more practical approach to soil conservation than most of their critics, but it is the reliance on European plant and animal domesticates that has caused them the most conflict with this continent'.

Today, we are on the precipice of the realisation of this concept in Australia's wine industry, as well as a seemingly universal focus on the specificity of place, and how best to care for it. This sense of place – 'terroir' to Europeans and most of the wine industry – is a familiar notion to members of Australia's First Nations.

In Kaurna Country – the traditional lands of Adelaide and its environs – the word *pangkarra* describes the characteristics of a plot of land, but speaks to more than just the physical properties. *Pangkarra* encompasses all that is connected to that place: the life it gives, the life breathed into it by the cosmos, and the animals, plants and people that belong to it. *Pangkarra* is terroir, but it is also the whole story of the connection between people and place, beyond the elements we typically associate with the word, like climate, soil and topography.

Wine, or more importantly wine growing, is a European system of agriculture. Along with its introduction to colonised nations came other systems like raising sheep or cows and growing wheat. These systems require few people to operate but support a large community, thus removing the need for that community to have a relationship with the land.

Wine, however, was not born an efficient agriculture system. It requires unparalleled levels of manual labour. While technology has been able to shift many aspects of the industry to heightened levels of efficiency, it is still quite labour intensive. At the premium end of the spectrum, most (if not all) of the work is done by hand.

At its core, wine is a communal effort. It takes many to look after a vineyard and its produce. A viticulturist's job is to promote the health and balance of a vineyard. To know each vine. There are numerous conversations about the future of wine in Australia, the future of people in Australia, and the future of land in Australia that seem to be finding a path towards each other, with the goal of finding a sustainable future for all.

Gary Green, a Kamilaroi man and the proprietor of Mt Yengo (p. 48), a new estate on Wonnarua Country in today's Hunter Valley, sees how those paths can come together: 'Some of the oldest winemakers in Australia have their own European-style Dreamtime story that's been handed down from generation to generation to generation. So wouldn't it be lovely if Mt Yengo can go back and help intertwine and infuse our cultural footprint into those Dreamtime stories so that when they grow together from this point onwards, they grow together as one.'

The Australian Geographical Indication System

All wine regions have their appellation systems: officially delimited areas that guarantee provenance and authenticity, help us understand where wines are made in relation to others and, sometimes, geographic commonalities that unite that region. Australia's system is the 'GI' system, abbreviated from 'Geographical Indication'.

Australian wine writer Jeni Port, in a 2007 article in *The Age*, gives a succinct and useful summary of how the utility of GIs was envisioned: 'When the Australian Wine and Brandy Corporation first looked at the problem of defining local wine regions it came up with a formula that was supposed to ensure critical mass and the economic survival of regions. A region would comprise an area with a minimum of five vineyards of at least five hectares each and producing at least 500 tonnes. How the lines were drawn on a map was left up to individual winemaker groups to decide. Some chose shire or municipal boundaries, some longitude, some altitude and some chose soil types.'

Wine Australia is responsible for administering the GI system, though it's the GIC (Geographical Indications Committee), an independent decision-making body, that considers applications pertaining to the establishment of GIs. Historically, the relevant legislation referred to GIs as being either Zones, Regions or Subregions to guide the GIC as to the degree of 'uniformity and distinctiveness' that ought to be considered for a new GI to be established. Since 2018, there has been no such distinction for the purposes of legislation: legally, a GI is just a GI, not a Zone, Region or Subregion. However, colloquially, GIs are still categorised as one of four tiers – in order from broadest to most specific: State, Zone, Region and Subregion – and we still use these terms throughout this book (as does Wine Australia in their literature), as they help the reader understand the relative placement of different GIs.

State GIs share borders with Australian states: New South Wales, Victoria, Tasmania, South Australia, Western Australia and Queensland are the wine-producing ones. Occasionally wines are labelled by just their state (and exclusively in Tasmania, where there is a single GI for the entire state), but typically winemakers will seek to label by a more specific region.

Zones are the next tier down, almost always within a single state, and usually housing several GI regions within them. Limestone Coast, for example, is a zone within South Australia that holds a number of regions within its borders. A producer could blend grapes from multiple of these regions and label the wine 'Limestone Coast', or could source from vineyards outside of the boundaries of any individual region within the zone and label by the zone name as well. This does happen (especially in more notable zones, like the Limestone Coast), but it's rare.

There are a few exceptions to this rarity: Gippsland, a zone with no regions within it, is treated more like a GI region in how it is referenced. The South-Eastern Australia zone is often featured on labels as well. It's a 'super zone' that encompasses the wine-growing regions of South Australia, Victoria, Tasmania, New South Wales and Queensland, allowing wineries to source grapes from multiple states and still have an appellation more specific than Australia, which is required for a wine to carry a vintage for export. Barossa is another commonly labelled zone, allowing producers to blend grapes from both the Barossa Valley and the Eden Valley in the same wine.

After zones comes GI regions, and this is where the meat of labelling designations lie. Barossa Valley, McLaren Vale, Coonawarra, Margaret River, Yarra Valley and Mornington Peninsula – among many, many others (65 of them) – are all GI regions. With a few exceptions, most of the chapters in the book focus on an individual GI region.

Subregions are the fourth and final tier: only 14 of them exist in Australia and have been used to designate important areas of distinction within GI regions. In general, subregions are worth paying attention to, and do tend to be areas of concentrated production, notable quality and/or unique traits. Few subregions have supplanted their larger region in terms of name recognition, but it does happen – think Nagambie Lakes in Goulburn Valley or Frankland River in the Great Southern region.

Unofficial subregions are permitted to be labelled on bottles. This practice is quite common throughout Australia – an acknowledgement of Australia's immense **regionality** that goes beyond the 100-odd official geographical indications.

For labelling, it's the 85% rule: if a wine is labelled by a GI, 85% of the grapes must come from that GI. Labelled by grape, it must be composed of 85% of that grape. And labelled by vintage, it must come 85% from that vintage.

Structure of the Book

This book is divided into six sections based on the six wine-growing states of Australia: New South Wales, Victoria, Tasmania, South Australia, Western Australia and Queensland. While states are defined by somewhat arbitrary political boundaries, each one has some overarching commonalities, whether it be related to ancient or modern history, geographical and climate features, or the development of wine-related identities over the years.

Each state section has an introduction covering these common features, as well as the various wine regions within that state. The most significant wine regions will have their own chapters within the state sections. The end of each state section will have a chapter devoted to regions that didn't get their own chapter; these regions aren't to be discounted! Many are up-and-coming or revolutionising their quality output. We expect quite a few of these to warrant their own chapters in years to come.

Regional chapters and state introductions will have varying degrees of information on First Nations history, depending on whether the information is more specific to the state or a smaller region, and the level of information available.

Two states do not have any further regional chapters within them: Tasmania and Queensland. For the others, each chapter within the state sections will cover either a region, collection of regions, or zone.

The body of each chapter is split up into four sections: Introduction, Evolution of Wine, Lay of the Land and Hubbub. The introduction sets the stage, including information often on the socio-formative origins of the region, in addition to an overview on the important facets of the region. The Evolution of Wine details the origins of wine in the region, and how it has developed over time; Lay of the Land explains the natural features of the region, and how those factors influence wine styles; and Hubbub gathers the inside scoop, pressing concerns and current events in each region.

Within each chapter is a series of tables with the viticultural footprint and climate data for the region at hand. The data shown in these boxes is sourced from Wine Australia. It can be found using their GI Dashboard, available to the public for free. This information is given as an overall figure for the GI in question. Within each chapter, where relevant and applicable, data for more specific locations is given. When it is, the information is collected from the Australian Bureau of Meteorology's website.

The first row in the Climate Data box, **Heat Summation** (Growing Degree Days/GDD), is calculated by adding the number of degrees the daily average temperature exceeds 10°C for each day within the defined growing season (1 October to 30 April); 10°C is chosen as the

Winkler Scale

REGION	CELSIUS	FAHRENHEIT	NOTABLE INTERNATIONAL WINE REGIONS
Region 1a	850–1111	1500–2000	Champagne, France; Leelanau Peninsula, Michigan; Kremstal, Austria; Okanagan Valley, Canada
Region 1b	1112–1389	2001–2500	Burgundy, France; Tokaj, Hungary; Willamette Valley, Oregon
Region 2	1390–1667	2501–3000	Barolo, Italy; Douro Valley, Portugal; Columbia Valley, Washington
Region 3	1668–1944	3001–3500	Rioja, Spain; Sonoma, California; Cornas, France
Region 4	1945–2222	3501–4000	Napa Valley, California; Châteauneuf du Pape, France; Alentejo, Portugal
Region 5	2223–2700	4001–4900	Lodi, California; Jerez, Spain; Patras, Greece

threshold, as grapevines do not experience any growth below this temperature.

The total of these daily average temperature surpluses is then plotted on a scale to index the warmth of a growing area's climate. The scale was developed by A.J. Winkler and Maynard Amerine at UC Davis in the 1940s, and is often referred to as the **Winkler Scale**.

There are, of course, limitations to this scale. It doesn't consider any other important climate attributes, like **diurnal swing**, sunlight hours, latitude, rainfall, durations of high temperatures, seasonal variations, fog, humidity and extreme weather events – which, of course, can impact how a climate is experienced. We find it useful, however, as a snapshot of temperature (and temperature changes) in a region: one good metric to consider among many.

The second row in the Climate Data box is Annual Rainfall and Growing Season Rainfall. Growing season rainfall is an indicator often used to classify a region's climate: for example, when a majority of a region's rainfall occurs in the winter, leaving the summer dry, it is an indication of a climate heavily influenced by the proximity to water (often Mediterranean climates). Continental climates, on the other hand, experience more of their rainfall in the warmer months.

The third row in the box is Warmest Month Average Temperature – for Australia, that's mean January temperatures – and is a basic metric used to further define how warm a region gets in the height of its summer.

The figures are given across three periods: the average of the years 1960–1990, the average of the years 1991–Present, and then the 2019/2020 growing season separated out. This season was, for many, one of extremes, resulting in the worst bushfires Australia has on record. This singular vintage could replicate in the future, as climate patterns become more variable. It's the kind of year that Australia's extensive research into climate change is hoping to mitigate in the future.

Each regional chapter's map zooms in on important vineyards and producers, and has been treated uniquely to best showcase what makes that region tick. In some regions, elevation will be the highlight. In others, it's the unofficial subregions. In yet others, it's soil type and geological formations. Keep an eye out for 'How to Read This Map' to really understand how each region operates, and the factors that are of the most importance to the resulting wines.

The maps display the exact vineyard area that is planted, which is only possible because of the work of Green Brain. Green Brain recently merged with GAIA (Geospatial Artificial Intelligence for Agriculture), and together they integrate satellite scans of vineyards (and other farmland), irrigation scheduling and weather monitoring with artificial intelligence. The result is a precision viticulture tool that will undoubtedly improve predictive capacity of irrigated agriculture in Australia. And it's a tool that has allowed us to show, with the finest detail, exactly where vineyards are planted in each of the GIs we profile (current as of 2021).

While some information on producers will be woven into the body of each chapter, it has been separated out for the most part, both for emphasis and for ease of access. At the end of each regional chapter, there is a directory of producers, with a blurb that illuminates the qualities of each. This is not an exhaustive list of every producer in every region, but more of a jumping-off point; there are many great wineries that we didn't have the space to list. The ones we've chosen are the ones we believe have had the most significance to the region and/or have been personally meaningful to us. Producers may be accompanied by one or more icons to further explain their significance in the region.

On this point, we want to recognise that each author has some investment, in one way or another, in various Australian wineries: whether it's producers that we import to the United States (in Jane and Jon's case, see p. 481), a winery we work for (in Kavita's case, for Shaw+Smith), a label we co-own (Mike's Tasmanian project Brian), or producers that we stock on our shelves or sell off our wine lists (for Mike, Martin and Hannah). We have relationships with all these wineries because we believe that they are significant and they are featured in the book because of that significance, not because of any intentional favouritism. But we do recognise there is subjectivity inherent in selecting these profiles, and hope to add more and more in future editions.

New Guard – These producers, whether young or more mature, represent a departure from traditional norms of their regions. This can appear in many ways: eschewing oak and ripeness, usage of uncommon grape varieties, experimentation with alternative aging vessels, varying levels of skin contact (more for white wine, less for red), lack of fining/filtration, low **sulphur** usage, and even paying more attention to farming techniques, environmentalism and **regionality**.

 Environmental Hero – A producer that has outlined and implemented significant practices to have a positive impact on the environment, including (but not limited to) organic and **biodynamic** farming, regenerative farming, renewable energy, water management, carbon neutrality, resource recycling and climate change action. Many wineries are doing their part for sustainability, but this icon will only appear next to the wineries truly making the most significant impact.

 Rising Star – A producer that has less than 15 vintages of wine released, who is finding their voice and gaining recognition, and in the process generating lots of buzz. An ascending winery; one to watch.

 Legend – A producer that has not only been influential to the development of their region, but also impactful to Australian wine as a whole.

 Regional Stalwart – A producer whose wines have helped define and fortify their region, contributing to its overall reputation and style.

 Must Visit – A winery that offers a superb experience and top-notch tourism amenities alongside great wine.

 Cult Following – A producer whose wines inspire fanaticism across Australia and are often highly sought after and sometimes hard to come by. Often this also applies to a personality at said winery who has garnered a loyal following.

 Historical Estate – A producer who was instrumental in the early development of their region. For regions with significant lulls in production, these will often be the wineries associated with modern redevelopment.

Within the producer directories, we have included a feature called 'What We're Drinking', for when one of the authors has a specific wine or style they want to recommend from a particular producer.

We hope you enjoy the book and it prompts you to seek out the great Australian wines that align with your palate and values – they're out there, no matter what you enjoy drinking. Australia has been making some of the world's best wines for decades – at every price-point, in every style – and it's time that this reality is reflected in its international reputation.

NEW SOUTH WALES

Hunter Valley 30

Central Ranges 52

Southern New
South Wales 72

Other New
South Wales 92

Arriving via plane in Sydney (the capital city of New South Wales), it's easy to see why the British First Fleet landed there in 1788 — its breathtaking coastline, an intricate pattern of turquoise-clear water and red-blonde sand, is a welcoming sight. The landscape sent a beacon that this area provided life, as it had done for the Eora Nation and its numerous language groups for thousands of years prior.

Led by Captain Arthur Phillip, the First Fleet had embarked on its 20,000-kilometre journey from England under the promise of Captain James Cook's theory of Terra Nullius ('land belonging to no one'). Cook had landed on Wangal Country – today's Botany Bay, just south of Sydney – in 1770, naming it New South Wales and claiming the land for King George III. According to the Aboriginal Heritage Office, 'His failure to even attempt to gain the consent of the natives began the legal fiction that Australia was waste and unoccupied'.

Wine culture developed early in the colony of New South Wales. The vine was immediately introduced by the British, with plantings at Sydney Cove the same year the fleet landed. The first winemaking efforts were in and around Sydney, though long-term wine-growing had its real hook in the Hunter Valley, 250 kilometres north of Sydney.

It's in the Hunter Valley that some of Australia's most significant wine history took place. And it's a region that also points to the defining geographic feature of New South Wales: the Great Dividing Range. The Great Dividing Range spans the length of the east coast of Australia, from Queensland to Victoria, throughout the entirety of New South Wales. Most of the state's wine regions sit on the continental side of the Great Dividing Range, its elevation providing protection from all manner of humidity, heat, rain and weather extremes. The Hunter Valley is singled out as the sole fine wine region left exposed to these coastal vagaries. To study the climate and pressures of the Hunter Valley against regions like Canberra District and Orange is to understand the significance of the Great Dividing Range.

Proximity to major tourist cities, predominantly Sydney, has been a boon for many of the wine regions of New South Wales – in a sense. These regions have a long history of the vine and enjoy constant local and tourist trade. But this proximity has also crippled development in some regions because the demand has historically been for inexpensive, serviceable wines (and great tourism amenities), with an interest in excellent, site-driven wines remaining more niche. Of the 138 wines in **Langton's Classification**, only seven are from New South Wales. That's 5% of the list, out of a state that supplied 28% of the harvest in 2021. Though this classification is not the last word in fine wine, it is an accurate depiction of market trends and what people are buying for their cellars; people aren't spending serious money collecting New South Wales wine.

New South Wales certainly has the stuffing to assert itself more forcefully onto the great wine lists, retail shelves and cellars of not just Australia, but the world. As **regionality** becomes a greater focus in the world of wine, surely New South Wales' regions will benefit. Besides Hunter Valley and Canberra District, which have led the pack, there are many names – Orange, Mudgee, Cowra, Hilltops, Tumbarumba, Gundagai, New England Australia, Riverina and Murray Darling among them – that will undoubtedly be explored further in the years to come and found to offer abundance.

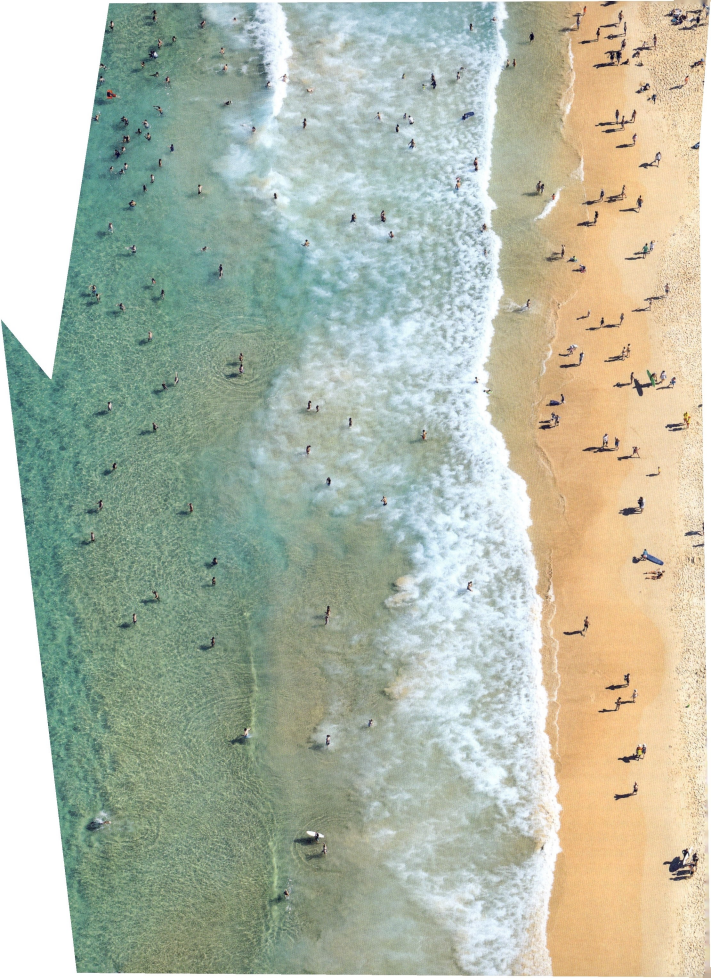

New South Wales Geographical Indications

ZONE	REGION	SUBREGION
Big Rivers	Murray Darling Perricoota Riverina Swan Hill	
Central Ranges	Cowra Mudgee Orange	
Hunter Valley	Hunter	Broke Fordwich Pokolbin Upper Hunter Valley
Northern Rivers	Hastings River	
Northern Slopes	New England Australia	
South Coast	Shoalhaven Coast Southern Highlands	
Southern New South Wales	Canberra District Gundagai Hilltops Tumbarumba	
Western Plains		

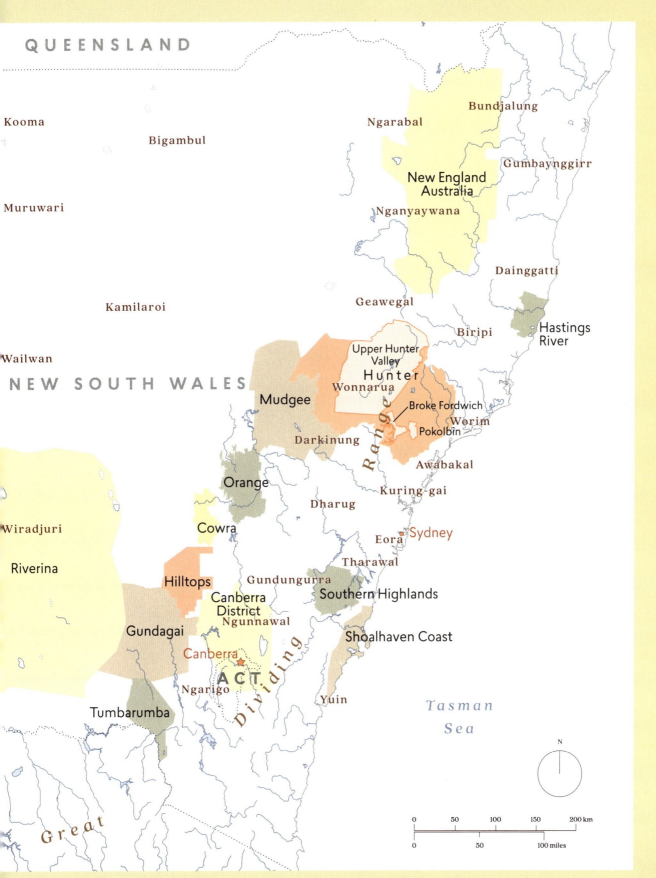

Hunter Valley

Introduction

Hunter Valley is the name of the GI zone; Hunter is the name of the region within it. Their boundaries nearly match, though, and the names are used synonymously. The vineyards and wineries of the Hunter region broadly sit on the traditional lands of the Wonnarua and Geawegal people. This Country finds the Hunter River at its core, surrounded by the vast, mountainous woodlands of the Great Dividing Range. At the lower reaches of the Hunter Valley, closer to the coast (where there are no vineyards), sit the traditional lands of the Awabakal Nation, centred around Lake Macquarie. The Wonnarua and Geawegal people often traded with the Awabakal people, each recognising the bounty each other's Country provided.

The Hunter, despite this physical bounty, is by all measurements an unusual wine region. It is the only fine wine region situated east of the Great Dividing Range, which creates a unique (and challenging) set of growing conditions. Its warmth and moisture – historic benefits to the region – have provided modern-day vintners with a narrow range of possible grapes and styles.

The grape that the region has become most famous for, though by no means its only success story, is semillon. Hunter semillon is a specific style – early-picked, low in alcohol, high in acid, benefiting from bottle age – because that is what the climate allows. Bruce Tyrrell, the custodian of one of the Hunter's great lineages, describes it like this: 'One of the features of Hunter semillon is that it is flavour ripe at lower alcohols ... it can be drunk young, but maintains good acid and pH so it has the inherent ability to live and develop over time'.

Historically and today, the Hunter Valley's proximity to Sydney (about a two-hour drive north) have helped buoy the wine industry. The Hunter has become a serious tourist attraction, now built up with all manner of fine accommodation, restaurants, concert grounds and wedding venues. Though there is a fringe culture of alternative grapes and experimental styles, the Hunter largely sticks to what it does best: semillon, chardonnay and shiraz.

But behind the difficult conditions, the unique semillon and the tourism flurry, the Hunter is the oldest continuous grape-growing region in Australia. Its historic lore and modern culture have permeated all layers – across all regions – of the Australian wine industry. It's a region that has caught its fair share of flak (more on this later), but has banded together to promote its wines and face its challenges. Most Australians either love it or leave it when it comes to the region's signature style, but no one can argue that the Hunter isn't an impressive testament to resilience, community and identity – and, by most standards, and against all odds, a source of some excellent wine.

Evolution of Wine

A whole book could be (and a few have been) written about the vinous history of the Hunter. It is a region flush with well-documented vineyards, winemakers, pioneers and stories. Some triage was necessary when writing the paragraphs to come, with the goal of offering a streamlined narrative of a region that is one of Australia's most historic.

The Hunter contains some of Australia's first vineyards and has continuously produced commercially designated wine for nearly 200 years. In 1797, British Lieutenant John Shortland happened upon the Hunter Valley while tracking escaped convicts from the penal colony of Sydney. Soon after Shortland's 'discovery' (the Wonnarua and Geawegal people had been in the region for at least 50,000 years prior), the Hunter Valley became an important source of timber and coal for Sydney's bustling ports. British settlement followed shortly after, along with western agriculture, and by the 1820s grapevines were planted in the region.

James Busby, dubbed 'the father of the Australian wine industry', was important to the Hunter Valley's development – though the case for his single-handed parenthood of the entire industry has been overstated.

A Scottish-born immigrant to Australia, Busby studied wine in France before setting sail for Sydney in 1824 at the age of 22. Busby's father secured a land grant in Branxton, about 20 kilometres north of Pokolbin, in the heart of the modern-day Hunter Valley area. They named this site Kirkton, after Busby's Scottish birthplace. According to Julie McIntyre's 2018 book *Hunter Wine*, 'it is possible – *but not proven* – that James Busby planted grapes from the [Sydney] Botanic Gardens at his father's property of Kirkton in 1830'. Busby's encouragement of the Hunter wine industry is often centred around Kirkton, though the extent of his hands-on involvement in the region is unknown.

But Busby 'does deserve credit for promoting the idea of wine-growing' in Australia, according to McIntyre. He published three works on viticulture and winemaking in his early days in Australia; he set up a program for colonists to get free vine-cuttings from the Botanic Gardens at Sydney; and he brought back 'many hundreds' of cuttings from an 1831 trip to Spain and France.

There are numerous other individuals who were instrumental in the development of the Hunter. George Wyndham planted Dalwood vineyard, also near Branxton, in 1830. Among the first grape varieties planted at Dalwood were 'Madeira' (verdelho) and 'Hermitage' (shiraz) –

the first commercial shiraz plantings in Australia, and some of the country's longest continuously productive shiraz vines (though they have since been replanted). Perce McGuigan bought the Dalwood vineyard from Penfolds in the 1960s and renamed it Wyndham Estate.

James King was another seminal figure in the early development of Hunter viticulture. King, a Scottish immigrant, established his vineyard in 1832 at a site he called Irrawang, about 50 kilometres east of Pokolbin. King frequently communicated with European scientists, who advised him of the region's ability to prosper with the right labour force. As a result, records show at least 43 coopers and 'vine dressers' (people skilled in vine **pruning**, training and cultivating) were brought over from Europe to help foster the fledgling wine region. King also started the Hunter River Vineyard Association, to organise and mobilise the grape-growing efforts in the region.

In this era, two white grapes emerged as being particularly successful in the Hunter. The first was verdelho, an import from Portugal's island of Madeira – a natural fit for the Hunter, as both regions experience a humid and rainy subtropical climate. The grape was valued for its moisture-hardiness and primarily used for **fortified wines** in the early days of the Hunter.

The second grape was semillon (pronounced sem-a-LONN by some locals to this day). James Busby catalogued 'semilion' in his 1833 treatise *Journal of a Tour Through Some of the Vineyards of Spain and France*. He speaks of the grape in reference to the other white grapes of

Bordeaux and notes, 'it is recommended that this variety [semillon] should occupy a proportion of two thirds of the vineyards in which the other five varieties are cultivated'. High praise.

There is evidence, however, that semillon predated Busby in Australia. Many believe that semillon came over on the First Fleet with Captain Phillip in 1788, acquired as 'green grape' (or *groen druiwe* in Afrikaans) on a stopover in South Africa. A horticulturist and nursery-owner, Thomas Shepherd, took a particular interest in the grape in the late 1820s, so much so that it was referred to as 'Shepherd's Grape' or 'Shepherd's Riesling'. At the time, it seemed few (if any) were aware that this grape was the same as Busby's 'semilion'.

In an 1850 essay in *The Maitland Mercury and Hunter River General Advertiser*, Henry Carmichael wrote of his vinous submissions to an exhibition in London. Carmichael maintained a vineyard in Seaham, at the eastern expanse of the Hunter River, called Porphyry. Carmichael waxed poetically about 'Shepherd's Riesling', saying it was 'gratifying the eye by its greenness and health in the midst of an atmosphere which was withering and desiccating every other form of vegetation'. Carmichael recognised the growing challenges presented by the subtropical Hunter Valley and how semillon was able to withstand such challenges, an observation that would continue to be made over the years as semillon's favour grew in the region.

In the years to come, the viticultural industry (and overall agriculture industry) suffered labour shortages due to the gold rush. But a few figures

Shiraz vs. Syrah

Shiraz and syrah are the same grape. Syrah is what the grape is called in most places in the world, including France, where it originated. Shiraz is the term for syrah that Australia typically uses, historically and to this day. So where did the word 'shiraz' come from? Shiraz is the name of a port city in Iran, where syrah was long believed to have originated. The legend went that a lone knight, home from the Crusades, brought the syrah vine back with him from Shiraz and planted it on a hill in the Rhône Valley, where the grape became known as syrah, and the hill as Hermitage. This myth has been debunked through modern DNA testing that puts the grape's origins in France. But at the time that the syrah grape made it to Australia, this was still firmly in the consciousness. In fact, James Busby, who is thought to have brought the first syrah vines over from France, wrote in his journal that 'according to the tradition of the neighbourhood, the plant — scyras [believed to be a misspelling of syrah] — was originally brought from Shiraz in Persia.' The name 'shiraz' caught on and the rest, as they say, is history.

emerged in the latter half of the 19th century who were able to sustain the momentum of the wine industry in the Hunter. Most notable was Edward Tyrrell, an immigrant from England who bought 130 hectares of land in the Hunter Valley in 1858. In 1864, Tyrrell harvested the grapes for his first vintage, and by 1870 his 30-hectare vineyard was planted to mainly shiraz and semillon.

The fifth generation of the Tyrrell family is now working the land. The family has had an enormous impact on the Australian wine industry over the years, pioneering sectors as diverse as direct-to-consumer sales, single-vineyard bottlings and late-released wines. Tyrrell's Vat 1 Semillon – first produced in 1963 – is the world's most awarded varietal semillon and put Tyrrell's on the national and international map for fine wine.

Along with Tyrrell's, many other historic estates took root in the latter half of the 19th century, including Oakvale, Drayton Family Wines, Lindeman's and Audrey Wilkinson. At the turn of the century, the Hunter was experiencing a boom. But with the onset of an economic recession and a national palate turning away from dry wine, the Hunter lost some momentum in the early 20th century.

With the help of a handful of families who continued to wave the flag for Hunter viticulture, the man who is credited with salvaging the **table wine** industry in the Hunter (and Australia really) is Maurice O'Shea. O'Shea, the son of an Irish wine merchant, was born in Sydney in 1897. He spent his formative years studying in France, attending high school there as well as completing advanced studies in agriculture and oenology. O'Shea internalised France's deep appreciation for **table wine** – a style whose popularity was at an all-time low in Australia when he returned there in 1920.

No matter, in 1921 O'Shea and his family purchased a 16.3-hectare vineyard in Pokolbin, which had been planted by Charles King in 1880. They extended the block in 1925 and named it Mount Pleasant, a brand that persists to this day. Keith McWilliam recognised Mount Pleasant's potential in 1932, investing in the estate and later buying it, while retaining O'Shea as the managing director. In the early 1940s, O'Shea added the vineyards Lovedale and Rosehill to the Mount

Pleasant holdings, two vineyards still considered some of the finest in the Hunter.

As a follow-up to Busby's moniker, O'Shea is often referred to as the 'father of Australia's modern winemaking'. At a time when few were seeking out premier sites for **table wine**, he almost single-handedly kept the style alive. Alive and well, in fact: modern-day wine professionals speak of tasting fresh and vibrant (among many more superlatives) 75-year-old Mount Pleasant wines. Iconic wine writer James Halliday has reviewed O'Shea's wines as 'the quintessence of all that is great in the Hunter'; and legendary show judge Len Evans (p. 37) has said that the wines have brought him more pleasure than any others. These are wines that continue to inspire and define the modern era of winemaking.

Despite O'Shea's achievements, it took a long time for interest in fine winemaking to pick back up. The man credited with the upswing is Dr Max Lake, a Sydney hand surgeon who uprooted his life in 1963 to seek out a site for a cabernet sauvignon vineyard after tasting Penfolds Dalwood 1930 cab-petit verdot blend – a wine he called the best he'd ever tasted. Due to his lack of experience in the industry, and grand ambitions, Lake was considered somewhat eccentric, perhaps even foolish, by the other growers of the day, and thus the winery name Lake's Folly was conceived.

The chroniclers and commentators of the Hunter, apparently not ones to miss out on a 'father' sobriquet, dubbed Lake 'the father of the Australian boutique wine industry'. Lake's new plantings launched a boom in wine industry growth in the Hunter and inspired similar projects across Australia.

Plantings in the Hunter rose nearly tenfold over the next decade. Before Lake's plantings, the Hunter had 466 hectares under vine; by 1976 it had amassed over 4100 hectares (a number which has fallen below 3000 hectares today). The upswing of the stock exchange and beneficial tax regulations encouraged hobby vignerons to buy in droves. Bruce Tyrrell explains, with a laugh, that, 'by 74 or 75, if you didn't have a share in a vineyard and lived in Sydney, you weren't socially acceptable'.

The cost of land rose tremendously during this time. Lake bought his land for $42/acre. By 1970, when the land that would form Brokenwood

Looking southwest across the vineyards of Pokolbin towards Mt Bright and the Yengo National Park.

Hunter Valley

Tyrrell's 1923 semillon vine planted in deep alluvial sands.

was purchased, founders Tony Albert, John Beeston and James Halliday paid a record $970/acre, which was triple what they had expected.

Pushing plantings and renown in this era was Lindeman's, who created two sweet, sparkling wines: 'Rhinegold' under the Leo Buring division, and 'Ben Ean Moselle', named after their winery at Pokolbin. Though both wines allude to being made from riesling, they were actually semillon dominant. And while these two wines were inexpensive and commercially scaled, Lindeman's also invested in site-specific and ageable wines in this time period. The most famous of these wines were named with an aspirational nod to the Burgundy region of France – 'Hunter River Burgundy' and 'Hunter River Chablis' – though the grapes were not Burgundian, but what Hunter did best: shiraz and semillon, respectively.

The Hunter would also come to be known for world-class versions of a third grape: chardonnay. Tyrrell's can be credited with introducing chardonnay commercially to the Hunter, and helping to popularise the grape across Australia, rounding out the trifecta of fine wine-producing grapes in the Hunter. Tyrrell's released Australia's first commercial chardonnay in 1971, setting off a national craze for the grape that has yet to abate.

The 1980s and 1990s saw Hunter wine ebb and flow slightly with the trends and concerns of the day: a mild economic recession in the 80s slowed growth, while the 90s saw an upturn, with corresponding corporate investment. But the early history of the region, combined with the new interest of the 1960s and 1970s, protected the region against the fluctuations of the day, and fortified it for long-term success.

Iain Riggs' first vintage at Brokenwood was in 1983. Under his care, what started as a weekend hobby for Sydney lawyers became one of the Hunter's most acclaimed wineries, heralding a new standard for quality in the region. To this day, their Graveyard Shiraz is the only Hunter wine to earn 'Exceptional' status on **Langton's Classification**. And though the 90s saw corporate shifting and a turn toward mass production, it also brought a number of producers who continued to push quality, like Margan, De Iuliis and Thomas Wines.

Today, the Hunter comprises over 120 different wineries, and continues to be a hotspot for Sydney visitors. Naturally, some of these wineries have moved away from any notion of site-specificity in favour of branding and tourism. But the history and soul of the Hunter remain, with many of the region's pioneering names still leading the charge in quality: Tyrrell's, Brokenwood and Mount Pleasant in particular continue to wow consumers and critics alike. And though Hunter isn't known for being avant-garde, several of the region's producers – like Vinden Wines, Usher Tinkler Wines, M&J Becker, Harkham and newcomers Dirt Candy and Sabi Wabi – have brought an energy of experimentation that not only appeals to young wine drinkers, but also allows for dexterity in one of Australia's more difficult winemaking climates.

Len Evans and the Tutorial

Len was a true renaissance man: he worked as a duck farmer, golf instructor, auto muffler producer and script writer before finding his love for wine. He then became one of Australia's most prominent restaurateurs, retailers, commentators, writers and vignerons. He had his hand in nearly every aspect of the wine trade. He was larger than life, the ultimate host, and mentor to many of the current leaders of Australia's wine industry.

When Len was in his 70s, with some extra time on his hands, he came up with the idea of starting a tutorial for show judging (p. 464). Though Len passed away in 2006, his legacy lives on through the tutorial. Each year, hundreds of candidates (winemakers, sommeliers, retailers, distributors, importers, educators and wine writers from across Australia) apply to have a seat at the Len Evans Tutorial: a week-long wine-tasting crash course that benchmarks the best domestic wines against the greats from around the world. And by great we mean the absolute greatest: to this day, the seminar is known for pulling up flights of the best wines of Australia alongside the likes of Coche-Dury, Domaine de la Romanée-Conti, Egon Müller, Haut-Brion, Jamet, Keller, Krug, Lafite-Rothschild, Leflaive, Leroy, Raveneau, Rousseau, Salon, Sassicaia and many more.

Lay of the Land

It is easy to look at the Hunter Valley today and wonder why grapes were ever planted there. Clearly, the results are not in dispute – though surviving some unfashionable periods, the wines of the region have been considered excellent for almost two centuries. But the conditions are difficult: rainy, warm and humid, with risk of hail, tornadoes, flash floods, typhoons, cyclones and bushfires. These hazards are mostly unique to the Hunter Valley among fine wine regions in Australia.

But the qualities that make Hunter challenging (i.e. warm and water-rich) also made it appealing in its beginnings. In a 1969 essay by W.P. Driscoll on the pre-1850 days of the Hunter wine industry, he states that 'conditions for growing the vine were so good, and yields so abundant that, despite the experiments and clumsiness of the early winemakers, enough marketable wine could be made to satisfy the grower and hold out prospects of a good profit as his skill gradually increased'. Colonial history is often told the other way around – with the skilful pioneers triumphing over difficult land – but the land itself was more the hero than is often thought.

Make no mistake, though, the Hunter presents plenty of difficulties, which are more acute now than they were in the 19th century – and set to keep on growing, especially as climate change accelerates.

The Hunter is a transverse valley, carved out of the Broken Back Range, a subset of the Great Dividing Range. At 32 degrees south, the Hunter sits at the edge of the band of latitude considered suitable for viticulture. (This suitable range of viticulture is usually noted as 30–50 degrees in both the Northern and Southern Hemispheres,

Hunter Valley Viticultural Footprint

Total delimited area (km²)	19,970
Total planted area (hectares)	2608
% of delimited area planted	0.130%
Total elevation range	20–1000 masl
Elevation range of plantings	40–220 masl
Number of producers	97

Hunter Valley Climate Data (°C)

	1960–1990	1991–PRESENT	2020
Heat summation (GDD)	● 2070	● 2137	● 2374
Annual rain/GSR	800/537	786/536	658/478
Warmest month avg. temp.	22.4	23.3	25.8

Winkler Scale:

● 850–1111 ● 1112–1389 ● 1390–1667 ● 1668–1944 ● 1945–2222 ● 2223–2700

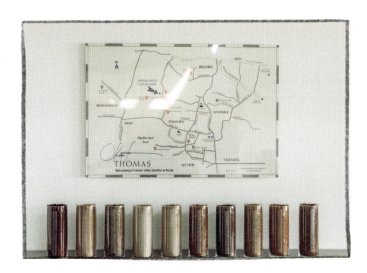

The experience at Andrew Thomas's cellar door dives deep into the nuances of soil and site across the Hunter.

though with climate change, those numbers are shifting upwards – away from the equator.)

The climate is classified as subtropical, with maritime influences from the Pacific Ocean. While most New South Wales east-coast wine regions sit on the continental (western) side of the Great Dividing Range, which effectively creates a rain shadow (or at the very least a boost in altitude), keeping temperatures moderate and conditions dry, the Hunter Valley carves through the mountain range, leaving it unprotected and vulnerable to the coastal weather system.

Wine Australia's Climate Atlas shows that the Hunter has been, and projects that it will continue to be, getting warmer over time, with more precipitation extremes – both greater rainfall and more intense droughts. Though overall the Hunter is considered a wet wine region, rainfall varies drastically across its extremities, with the coast nearly twice as rainy as the interior vineyard areas of the Upper Hunter Valley.

Total rainfall is not really the problem though; it's the timing of the rain, and the attending humidity and moisture, that presents issues. Grapevines tend to prefer rain in the winter and a dry growing season, conditions that help promote growth and yields but prevent against disease. In the Hunter, this pattern is inverted: summer and autumn are the rainiest seasons. This trend continues to grow: rainfall has been increasing in spring, summer and autumn, but decreasing in the winter.

The GI Committee has bestowed three rare subregions upon the Hunter region: Upper Hunter Valley, Broke Fordwich and Pokolbin. Few vineyards exist outside of these three subregions; more than half of the overall GI contains acidic clay soils unsuitable for viticulture. Although not an official subregion, the area of Lower Hunter is often referred to when discussing geographic diversity, and both the Broke Fordwich and Pokolbin subregions are within this general area. The Lower Hunter is the low-lying, downstream area near the outlet of the Hunter River into the Tasman Sea, extending inland past the township of Fordwich.

The Lower Hunter is where the Broken Back Range is at its most influential, providing gentle slopes in its foothills for vineyards to nestle into. Northern and eastern **aspects** are the most common. Yengo National Park acts as the southwestern border of the Lower Hunter, amplifying the boundaries of the valley and pulling in the coastal influence. The two main soil types are sandy alluvial soils, well suited to semillon, and red volcanic loams, considered more shiraz territory. The alluvial soils tend to hug the waterways, while the volcanic intrusions are found closer to tree lines at higher elevations, though most areas have an interplay of both types.

The subregion of Pokolbin is the most densely planted area within the Hunter, and where many of the region's famous producers and vineyards are based. Pokolbin is situated in the foothills of Mt Bright in the Pokolbin State

Hunter Valley

HOW TO READ THIS MAP

99.87% of the Hunter Valley has never seen a grapevine planted, so this map is zoomed and centred on two of its subregional GIs: Pokolbin and Broke Fordwich. Vineyards are set against a hypsometric display of the elevation changes across the region. Note that while the region's formations breach 600 metres in elevation, vineyards are exclusively planted below 220 metres.

1 Audrey Wilkinson
2 Bimbadgen Estate
3 Mt Yengo Wines
4 Briar Ridge Vineyard
5 Brokenwood
6 Dalwood Estate
7 De Iuliis
8 Dirt Candy
9 First Creek Wines
10 Gundog Estate
11 Hart & Hunter
12 Keith Tulloch
13 Lake's Folly
14 Leogate Estate
15 Lindeman's Hunter Valley Cellar Door
16 Margan Wines
17 McLeish Estate
18 McWilliam's Wines
19 Meerea Park
20 Mount Pleasant Lovedale Vineyard
21 Mount Pleasant Rosehill Vineyard
22 Mount Pleasant
23 Pepper Tree Pokolbin Creek Vineyard
24 Silkman Wines
25 Thomas Wines
26 Tulloch Glen Elgin Estate
27 Tyrrell's
28 Usher Tinkler Wines
29 Vinden Wines
30 Whispering Brook

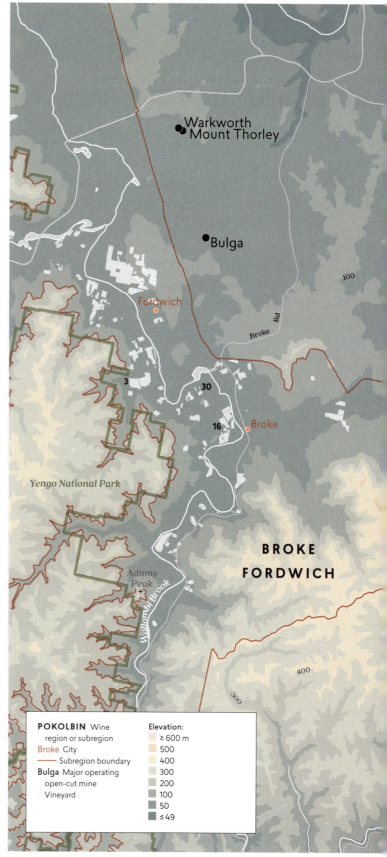

New South Wales

40

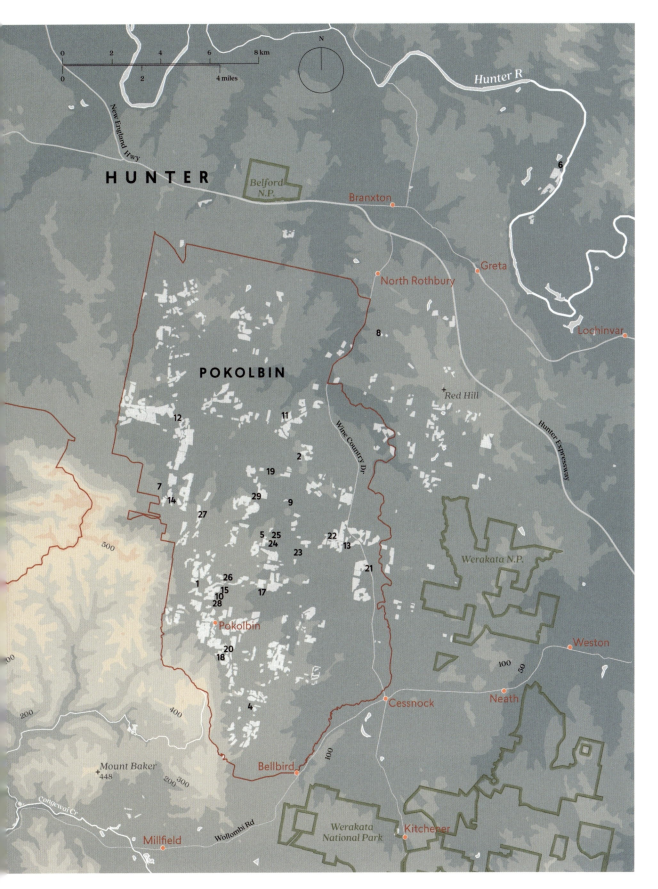

Hunter Valley

Forest, sprawling across a sloping valley that generally faces northeast. Vineyards tucked under the tree line of the forest reach up to 220 metres in elevation, though it's the hillsides that trail away from these peaks that are the most densely occupied by vineyards.

Pokolbin has been the destination of choice for many of the region's most famous vignerons: Mount Pleasant, Lindeman's, Drayton Family, Tyrrell's, Tulloch, Brokenwood, Scarborough, De Iuliis, Usher Tinkler, Vinden Wines and many others. The region's success, despite the challenges of the Hunter Valley climate, is largely attributed to its shelter on three sides by the neighbouring mountains, and the moderating easterly winds it receives. The gentle hills of Pokolbin are considered to produce much of the finest semillon, shiraz and chardonnay in the Hunter Valley.

Broke Fordwich, the second most densely planted subregion after Pokolbin, encompasses the vineyard land of two municipalities: Broke and Fordwich. It's a small **mesoclimate** that sits protected within the hillsides of the Putty State Forest. A narrow, finger-like valley meanders into the hills along the Wollombi Brook, with vineyards never cresting 140 metres in elevation.

A unique soil type runs through the region, named the Fordwich Sill. It is a red volcanic clay, replete with basalt and iron, which was formed from subterranean volcanic eruptions. 'Most growers accept,' according to Brokenwood's Iain Riggs, 'that there were no volcanoes at Pokolbin, but at least three at Broke Fordwich'. These soils are said to express wines that are both richer and softer in style, and favour red grapes like shiraz and cabernet sauvignon over semillon. Sandy alluvial soils can be found along the Wollombi Brook, quite similar to those nearest the Hunter River in Pokolbin; these are often more heavily planted to semillon.

Broke Fordwich was originally planted in the 1960s by Lindeman's and Saxonvale, though it didn't flourish until the 90s, with the launch of wineries like Margan, Krinklewood and Poole's Rock. Semillon is the most planted grape, followed by shiraz, chardonnay, verdelho and merlot.

The Upper Hunter – surrounding the upper stretches of the Hunter River – occupies a large swathe of the region, approximately half the delimited area. Plantings are concentrated along the banks of the Hunter River at the town of Denman, and only reach about as far inland and north as the town of Muswellbrook, leaving nearly the whole top third of the appellation unplanted. Along the upper reaches of the Hunter River, dark, silty loam soils sit atop a layer of alkaline clay and create a small amount of area suitable for viticulture. But much of the delimited Upper Hunter Valley GI includes state forests and national parks, which will never be planted to vineyards.

The legacy of Bob Oatley's Rosemount Wines began in the Upper Hunter, which would grow to be Australia's largest family-owned winery. After its sale to Southcorp in 2001, the production of Rosemount shifted to South Australia, and much of the Hunter land was sold off to become a buffer zone for coal mining. The Upper Hunter today, though not densely planted, is known for its affordable semillon and chardonnay, as well as serving as a volume source for commercially oriented wines.

Single vineyards and single sites have always been meaningful to the Hunter. 'It does change that quickly,' Bruce Tyrrell says, referring to the capricious topography. 'Within a block, it can change quite a bit ... you can go 50 metres, and go from the best shiraz soil to the worst.' Attention is being brought to these nuances, and the land of the Hunter is being cared for in a more informed and thoughtful way than ever.

The Hunter has on occasion tried to fight its nature – like attempting the powerhouse Barossa-style shiraz, even going so far as to add brawny juice from McLaren Vale to its leaner-styled reds. However, as it matures, the region tends to stick to what thrives in the conditions: early-picked, long-lived styles of semillon; more robust chardonnays, though still fresh and acid-driven; and red wines of moderate body and intensity. A younger generation has found more play and experimentation among less common varieties – including tempranillo, gamay, fiano, alicante bouschet, barbera, graciano, chenin blanc, vermentino, albariño and cinsault – all with a sustained reverence for tradition and the past.

Hubbub

The potential concerns for the wineries of the Hunter reads like a laundry list of all viticultural (and many non-viticultural) concerns known to humankind – rain, humidity, heat, hail, tornadoes, flash floods, typhoons, cyclones, bushfires, climate change, **phylloxera**, labour shortages, coal mining, trendiness, market position ... oh my! Dorothy's lions, tigers and bears have nothing on the Hunter Valley.

The dominant critique of the Hunter Valley is that it has no business being a wine-growing region, and the leading thinkers of the region don't disagree. Jim Chatto, long-time McWilliam's group winemaker, believes that, 'if you started from scratch, looking at a map and looking at climate, you probably wouldn't plant grapes in the Hunter today'. Brokenwood's Iain Riggs agrees: 'We're all trying to eke out a living in a region where we shouldn't be growing grapes.' (Pokolbin, appropriately, loosely translates from Polish to 'hell hole'.)

But when asked about the pressing concerns of the region, very few winemakers detail the punishing growing conditions. It's almost old hat to them at this point. They've been dealing with harsh weather patterns and severe climatic threats for so long, they know how to manage them. While other regions are scrambling to adapt to new climate-change scenarios, the Hunter Valley is unfazed about their weather.

So what does faze them? **Phylloxera** is a concern, mainly because of the old vines that the Hunter houses. The Hunter Valley has 11 hectares of vines that were planted before 1900, and another 108 hectares planted between 1900 and 1968 – all on original rootstock. 'We've got these amazing old vines – that's heritage,' says Angus Vinden, of his family's eponymous estate. 'I need to make sure I can pass them onto the next generations'. An outbreak of **phylloxera** would be devastating to this historical bounty.

But the region is equally worried, maybe even more so, for the future of these vines for another reason: lack of skilled labour to look after them. As many of the older-generation viticulturists retire, there is a dearth of trained vineyard workers to replace them. Education is an important part of the equation, where few viticulture students today are getting the practical, hands-on training needed to be successful in the vineyards (a problem by no means unique to the Hunter). Bruce Tyrrell tells a story of how 10 recent graduates came to work at Tyrrell's, and 'the first thing they asked our chief winemaker was which computer was theirs'. (The chief winemaker took the students out of the lab, gave them shovels and brooms, and said, 'Fire that up. And when you can operate that, we can talk about going to the lab.')

Coal mining presents another threat to the region. From the coastal city of Newcastle through to Cessnock and surrounds, underground mining has been widespread, though is increasingly becoming more limited; whereas from the town of Broke and further north, open-cut coal mines have scarred the landscape, such projects continuing to expand. In 2015, all coal seam gas licences in the area were cancelled, following strong opposition to gas projects in the region.

The wine industry doesn't have a clear consensus on where they stand on open-cut mining. Some believe that the best sites aren't threatened, and that it's better to work with the government and coal industry rather than against them (and even, that Australia as a source of 'clean coal' is better than the alternatives found around the world). Others, like Iain Riggs, count coal mining as one of the greatest threats to the region,

While other regions are scrambling to adapt to new climate-change scenarios, the Hunter Valley is unfazed about their weather.

and to the environmental protection of Australia in general: 'We're currently fighting an open proposal for a coal mine exploration in the Broken Back Range … we have to raise hundreds of thousands of dollars to fight. It's a national park for goodness' sake. It's just rubbish, absolute rubbish', he laments. The region is watching closely to see if the mining will infringe on viticultural land, all the while experiencing increasingly bad air quality, traffic and pollution in correlation.

In addition to the challenges related to the land, the unfashionable nature of the Hunter Valley over the years has not helped with its national and international reputation. Though the Hunter is one of Australia's major tourism attractions, with over 8.2 million visitors from March 2021 to March 2022 (and that was a year without many international visitors), the region's wines tend to be less popular beyond the borders of New South Wales. The rest of Australia has not gotten behind Hunter semillon in great numbers, despite its unique style and history.

This litany of challenges has had a positive outcome, though – banding the region together. 'Collegiate' is the word used again and again to describe the culture of the Hunter Valley. As Chris Tyrrell says, 'Everyone is ultracompetitive, but everyone is working together and always thinking about putting the Hunter first rather than their own winery.'

This culture has also acted as an incubator for winemaking talent across Australia. As neighbouring vintner, Tom Ward of Central Ranges' Orange, puts it: 'The best winemakers in Australia either work in the Hunter or have done training in the Hunter because, you know, talk about tough. They really know what to do in tough years. They know how to make great wine.'

Acclaimed winemakers across Australia today have had long stints in the Hunter Valley – Samantha Connew (Stargazer, Tasmania), Jim Chatto (Chatto Wines, Tasmania), Sarah Crowe (Yarra Yering, Yarra Valley) and Simone Steele (Medhurst, Yarra Valley) among them – and dozens (maybe hundreds) more have trained or worked isolated harvests in the Hunter – often tacked on to the beginning of harvest in another Australian region because of the Hunter Valley's early picking dates.

The Hunter Valley also brings in a dozen rising-star wine professionals to its precinct every year for the Len Evans Tutorial (see p. 37) – a tradition founded on the idea that tasting the great wines of the world is an important part of professional development in the wine industry. 'If you're going to make great wine,' says Chris Tyrrell, 'you need to know what great wine looks like'.

So, despite all the criticism and all the trials, the Hunter has the last laugh. It's a region so accustomed to adversity that not much bothers it. There is always a good drop in their glasses – whether it's a local semillon or grand cru Burgundy. They enjoy a vigorous tourism industry that allows wine production to flourish. And, ultimately, they are living up to the true ideals of what makes a wine region fine: being shaped by place. 'What I love about it, it's so *true*, because the climate shapes it, not people, not their ideas,' says Jim Chatto. And Chris Tyrrell adds, providing the ultimate soundbite on the region: 'All of the best wine regions in the world are usually marginal in some way, shape or form. And that's Hunter.'

Options Game

The legendary English-Australian wine personality Len Evans (p. 37) came up with the aptly named blind-tasting game called Options. The idea is to play it at a big gathering of your wine mates. The person who brought the wine (and who knows what it is) comes up with options to ask the group. 'Is this wine from Australia, France or the United States?' Everyone in the group shouts out their guess, and only those who get it right proceed to the next question. 'Is it a gamay, grenache or pinot noir?' The questions go on until there is one guesser standing or the full identity of the wine is revealed.

PRODUCERS

AUDREY WILKINSON

The Wilkinson family bought a plot of land in 1866 and subsequently planted one of the first vineyards in the Pokolbin subregion of the Hunter. When the patriarch of the family died, his son Audrey took over running the vineyard at just 15. Audrey began to develop the estate with cutting-edge technologies for the time, including concrete fermenters and steam-powered crushers. During the early 1900s, the Wilkinsons won many awards around Australia for their **fortifieds** and clarets. In 2004, lawyer Brian Agnew purchased Audrey Wilkinson, maintaining the family's tradition. *audreywilkinson.com.au*

BROKENWOOD

Originally destined to be a local community cricket pitch, Brokenwood's first block was purchased in 1970. The buyers were Sydney-based lawyers, one of whom was a young James Halliday, who went on to become one of Australia's foremost wine critics. The first vintage was a labour of love, with all the partners' friends and family roped in to help. It was 1973 and they picked just a tonne of shiraz and half a tonne of cabernet sauvignon. Iain Riggs joined Brokenwood in 1982 and promptly took on the great Hunter Valley semillon. The wines soared under Iain's careful hand and he developed something of a 'wine university' for up-and-comers. Iain believes in giving back to the industry, and many successful winemakers have developed under his tutelage. After 38 vintages at the helm, Iain has stepped back from his management role, passing the baton to the new generation. *brokenwood.com.au*

DALWOOD ESTATE

Dalwood is the longest-running commercial estate in Australia. George Wyndham planted a large number of trial vines in 1838 – believed to be mostly Iberian varieties – but it was soon discovered that 'Hermitage' (shiraz) thrived. Penfolds bought Dalwood in 1904. However, by the 1960s, the estate was thrust into a period of new owners, changing names (among them, Wyndham Estate) and fractionalisation of land. It wasn't until 2017 that the name Dalwood was restored to the original vineyards, with their purchase by Iris Capital. Senior winemaker Bryan Currie has continued to craft Hunter classics as well as add new plantings to the fold. *dalwoodestate.com.au*

DE IULIIS

Joss and Anna De Iuliis traded careers in the mining industry for a passion for wine, buying a grazing property in the late 1980s, which they planted to vine. The estate started with grape growing, rather than winemaking, selling fruit to the likes of Tyrrell's in nearby Pokolbin. Wine production began at the family vineyard when their son, Michael De Iuliis, finished his oenology studies in 1999. Michael has developed De Iuliis into the benchmark producer it is today; everything from their estate range to the single vineyards feels quintessentially Hunter. *dewine.com.au*

DIRT CANDY

Daniel Payne's wines sit in stark contrast to the majority of what comes out of the Hunter. Where there is acid-driven semillon and mid-weight shiraz, Daniel responds with aromatic, skinsy traminer and a blend of every grape in the valley fermented with the skins of that traminer. Dirt Candy plays with traditional winemaking techniques before tipping them over the edge: semillon is sent sparkling and shiraz gets the old-school Aussie cabernet-blend treatment. Dirt Candy is an experimental and modern lens into the Hunter. *dirtcandy.com.au*

DRAYTON'S FAMILY WINES

One of the classic old-timers of the Hunter Valley, Drayton's was founded in 1853. Six generations later, the winery remains family owned. Tragedy has marked the Drayton family over the years: several family members died of typhus on their 1850 voyage over from England; Barry and Rhonda Drayton died within months of each other from fume suffocation and hepatitis, respectively, in the 1980s; Reg and Pam Drayton died in a plane crash in 1994; and, most recently, Trevor Drayton died in a winery explosion in 2008. But the family has persevered and continues to offer affordable Hunter classics of shiraz, semillon, chardonnay and verdelho, among others. *draytonswines.com.au*

HARKHAM

One of the experimental set of the Hunter, Harkham have been making minimal-input, low-to-no-**sulphur** wines in the region since 2005. The family has winemaking roots going back to the 1950s, when they were among the first pioneers of the Israeli wine region Zichron Yaakov. They farm using organic practices in the Hunter (no small feat with the region's high moisture levels) and make wines that speak of place in a fresh, modern way, with a focus on shiraz, chardonnay and semillon, as well as a few sweet wines (and many Kosher wines – some of Australia's only!). Accommodation and a restaurant on site make for a complete package. *harkhamwine.com.au*

KEITH TULLOCH

As the son of viticultural researcher Dr Harry Tulloch and cousin of Jay Tulloch (see Tulloch Wines p. 49), wine is in Keith Tulloch's DNA. Keith worked at iconic producers Lindeman's and Rothbury Estate before launching under his own name in 1997. Following the success of his first release, The Kester Shiraz, Keith was inspired to pursue another classic Hunter Valley style; in 2008, he bought the Field of Mars vineyard in Pokolbin, with the sandy riverbed soils that are perfect for semillon. He strives to create precise and elegant wines in the most environmentally conscious way possible. In fact, Keith Tulloch was the first carbon-neutral winery in the Hunter Valley. *keithtullochwine.com.au*

LAKE'S FOLLY

Lake's Folly, established in 1963, is widely recognised as Australia's first boutique winery. It began with Max Lake, a young hand surgeon, who decided to plant cabernet sauvignon, armed only with a love of food and wine. Lake's Folly was the first new vineyard to be planted in the Hunter since World War II. To naysayers and sceptics, he said: 'Well if I am a fool, this is my folly.' His folly paid off: the wines were widely acclaimed across Australia and made waves overseas. Despite initially intending to only make cabernet, chardonnay was planted in 1969. The estate was sold in 2000 to Fogarty Wine Group and Rodney Kempe came on as winemaker. Though a giant in the Hunter Valley, Lake's Folly is still a boutique winery in many ways; only the two flagship wines are produced – a cabernet blend and a chardonnay – made on site from estate-grown grapes. And production is limited: when they're gone, they're gone. *lakesfolly.wine*

LINDEMAN'S

Henry Lindeman, an English doctor with an interest in winemaking, immigrated to Australia in 1840 and planted his first vines in 1843 at Cawarra Homestead. Lindeman's began exporting wine in 1858 and found huge commercial success, with an annual production today of 80 million bottles. More vineyards have been purchased in South Australia and Victoria, as well as across the Hunter. Today, Lindeman's is owned by Treasury Wine Estates. *lindemans.com*

MARGAN WINES

Andrew Margan grew up in the Hunter and gained experience near and far before establishing his eponymous winery with wife Lisa in 1996. They have 100 hectares of vineyards across two locations, farmed following regenerative agricultural principles on the ancient red soils of the Fordwich Sill.

Hunter Valley

47

What we're drinking

*The **Mount Pleasant** single-block wines pay tribute to founder Maurice O'Shea. They have been made by some of Australia's best winemakers over the decades. Current custodian is Adrian 'Sparksy' Sparks. These wines should form the backbone of any cellar collection of great Australian shiraz. – **Kavita Faiella***

Plantings today are both 50-year-old traditional Hunter varieties and newly planted, lesser-known grapes; Margan was the first winery in the Hunter to plant barbera in the late 90s. Many of their blends are co-planted in the vineyard and co-fermented in the cellar. Second-generation Alessa and Ollie (viticulturist and winemaker, respectively) have joined the family business and are seeing it into the next era, with particular attention to a new range called Breaking Ground.
margan.com.au

MOUNT PLEASANT

With just basic tools and an old basket press, Maurice O'Shea founded Mount Pleasant in 1921, a winery that would go on to become one of Australia's most important. In 1932, the McWilliam family, who already had a reputation for quality **fortifieds**, bought a 50% stake in Mount Pleasant, and in 1941, they became sole owners of the historic estate, retaining Maurice as managing director. With the additional financial assistance, Maurice expanded the Mount Pleasant empire, planting his Rosehill vineyard to shiraz, and Lovedale to semillon (with chardonnay and verdelho added later). The wines from this era are still as characterful today, a testament to the longevity of what Maurice created. Jim Chatto (Chatto Wines, Tasmania) tasted a Mount Pleasant semillon during his studies and was so taken by it that he applied several times for a job at the winery before starting as chief winemaker of McWilliam's in 2013. He elevated the quality of the Mount Pleasant wines, returning to a familiar O'Shea adage: making great wine starts in the vineyard. In 2021, McWilliam's was sold and now The Medich Family Office (a Sydney-based investment group) owns Mount Pleasant. The wines show no sign of letting up quality though, and are made today by the talented Adrian Sparks.
mountpleasantwines.com.au

Gary Green
Mt Yengo Wines

MT YENGO WINES

One of the few Indigenous-owned wineries in Australia, Mt Yengo was created as a way of bridging the cultural divide between Indigenous and non-Indigenous Australians. Co-founders Gary Green and artist Wayne Quilliam are keen to challenge the negative image surrounding Indigenous Australians and alcohol. They use the platform of Mt Yengo Wines to provide opportunities for Aboriginal communities, with a percentage of bottle sales donated to the National Indigenous Culinary Institute, which offers training and mentorship to aspiring Indigenous chefs. The team at Mt Yengo has found their home in the Hunter by collaborating with Bisous Estate, developing a cultural centre to tell the stories of the local Wonnarua people.
mtyengowines.com.au

SILKMAN WINES

Liz and Shaun Silkman launched their eponymous label in 2013, alongside their day jobs at First Creek. Liz began her career at Brokenwood as a lab assistant before dedicating herself fully to winemaking. Her passion for chardonnay is clear, with their inaugural bottling of the grape winning the James Halliday Chardonnay Challenge in 2015. The couple have also joined the revival of the shiraz-pinot noir blend, with a succulent mix of brooding mid-weight and aromatic red fruit. Silkman is small batch, but they have plenty of scope to play with the facilities and fruit coming in at First Creek. *silkmanwines.com.au*

THOMAS WINES

McLaren Vale-born Andrew Thomas followed a love of Hunter Valley wines to join the winemaking team at Tyrrell's. Over a decade later, with some travelling vintages under his belt, Andrew established under his own label in 1997, making the decision to focus just on semillon and shiraz. He knew of a vineyard in Pokolbin's 'dress circle' – a collection of sites with soils ideal for semillon – which were producing extremely successful wines in the area. The Braemore vineyard, now estate-owned, proved rewarding for Andrew, and his semillon wines from the site are highly regarded. *thomaswines.com.au*

TULLOCH WINES

John Younie (JY) Tulloch accepted an unusual debt settlement in 1895: a property with a couple of hectares of neglected shiraz vines. This sparked an interest in viticulture and winemaking, and by the 1920s he was one of the largest vignerons in the Hunter. The Tulloch business continued to prosper with the development of the profitable Pokolbin Dry Red and Hunter River White labels. The Tulloch family sold the business in 1969, but it was eventually bought back by third-generation Jay Tulloch. The success of Hunter Valley verdelho is in a major part thanks to Jay, a champion for the grape's suitability to the region's climate. *tullochwines.com*

TYRRELL'S

Bruce & Chris Tyrrell
Tyrrell's

Five generations of Tyrrells have produced wine on the family estate in the Hunter Valley, starting with the establishment of semillon and shiraz by English migrant Edward Tyrrell in 1858. Edward's grandson, Murray Tyrrell, took over winemaking just under 100 years later. His tireless work raised the value of their wines and the profile of the Hunter Valley brand. He developed Tyrrell's Private Bin system – where single sites are named after the vats in which they were aged – and started Australia's first mail-order wine club. The first Vat 1 Semillon was produced from Tyrrell's Short Flat vineyard and is now, with little room for debate, Australia's most important semillon. Murray planted chardonnay in the late 1960s to produce Vat 47, the first commercial chardonnay produced in Australia. Murray's son and grandchildren have similarly left their mark on the family business. Bruce Tyrrell has been a lifelong champion of Hunter semillon and its ageability. He proudly works alongside his three children, Jane, John and Chris. *tyrrells.com.au*

> **What we're drinking**
>
> Andrew Thomas of **Thomas Wines** specialises in semillon and shiraz, including an utterly original version of the former: the Six Degrees Semillon is off-dry in style, balancing the long lines and serious acidity of Hunter semillon with a bit of sweetness – a delicious take. **– Jane Lopes**

Hunter Valley

USHER TINKLER WINES

The Usher Tinkler property has been farmed by three generations named Usher Tinkler: a dairy farmer, a cattle farmer and now a winemaker. Usher the winemaker worked his way around well-known Hunter wineries before becoming chief winemaker for his family's estate. For Usher, creativity is the name of the game, and he strives to make wines that are innovative and thought provoking. The standard Hunter Valley varieties are blended to explore new flavours: a semillon-chardonnay, a rosé from shiraz-merlot and a flavourful stab at the increasingly popular shiraz-pinot mashup. Usher Tinkler acknowledges the traditional custodians of their land, Wonnarua Country, on labels.
ushertinklerwines.com

VINDEN WINES

The Vinden family moved to the Hunter Valley in 1990, to a farm that was just four paddocks of weeds. The first vines, planted in 1995, were an unusual combination: shiraz, merlot and the teinturier (red-fleshed) alicante bouschet – the latter rarely found in Australia (or anywhere else for that matter). Angus Vinden took over the family estate in 2015. He has grown Vinden into a hub of innovation that pays tribute to tradition. Angus' reinvention includes organically farming his vineyards (with no use of herbicides, even organic ones), recycling all water on site and bottling some wines with swing tops so the entire package can be recycled. He has an offshoot label, Vinden Headcase, which takes an even more experimental approach to grapes and styles – as well as labels. The Pokolbin Blanc Experimental Release is labelled with his self-portrait, so that with each new release, the bottles can be lined up to show how he has changed, both visually and as a winemaker.
vindenwines.com.au

And don't forget ...
Briar Ridge Vineyard is known for its classic Hunter styles as well as grapes like albariño and verdelho ... **First Creek**, managed by the Silkman family, and one of the busiest wineries in all of Hunter, oversees the bottling of over 100 different labels (some proprietary and some contract) ... **Gundog Estate** sources from some of the best vineyards in Hunter, Hilltops and Canberra District, and holds sustainability paramount ... **Hart & Hunter** is a playful take on the Hunter from two hospitality veterans, serving up the stalwart Hunter trio (chardonnay, shiraz and semillon) as well as fiano, grüner veltliner and a pinot-shiraz blend ... **Leogate Estate**, built around the historic Brokenback vineyard, was planted by Len Evans in the 1960s and is now under the watch of the Widin family ... **M&J Becker** is Meagan and James Becker, a husband-and-wife team making fresh and vibrant takes on Hunter classics off their recently certified organic vineyard in Pokolbin, as well as **piquette**, eau de vie and an agave spirit ... **McLeish Estate** was planted in 1985 by the McLeish family, with wines made under the guidance of talented Andrew Thomas (see Thomas Wines, p. 49) ... **Meerea Park** is particularly known for its chardonnay, with the Eather family lineage dating back to the 1860s ... **Pepper Tree Wines**, who for years had highly decorated winemaker Gwyn Olsen at the helm, releases impressive wines from Hunter, Orange, Coonawarra and Wrattonbully ... **Sabi Wabi** makes some of the more creative wines of the Hunter, turning out **pét-nats**, orange wine and chillable reds, all staying true to its name in 'finding beauty amongst imperfection' ... **Whispering Brook**, based on the Fordwich Sill soil, is known for its richer reds and semillon, now incorporating Portuguese grapes like touriga nacional and arinto.

Angus Vinden
Vinden Wines

Angus Vinden checking in on firm, green semillon berries approaching harvest.

Central Ranges

Introduction

The Central Ranges is a GI zone comprised of three regions – Mudgee, Orange and Cowra – that run northeast to southwest (in that order) on the western slopes of the Great Dividing Range. These three regions connect the Hunter Valley in the north to the appellations of Southern New South Wales in the south – they're central and they're on ranges, a good moniker all around.

The vineyards of the Central Ranges zone lie on Wiradjuri Country. The Wiradjuri Nation has the largest cultural footprint in New South Wales, and the second largest geographically in Australia – an area roughly the size of Greece. About 12,000 people spoke Wiradjuri before colonisation.

The first European colonists stepped onto Wiradjuri Country in 1813 after finding a route through the Blue Mountains, where the Wiradjuri had lived for 60 millennia. Governor Macquarie of the New South Wales colony had a road built through the mountains and journeyed west, establishing the town of Bathurst in 1815, recognised as the first inland colonial settlement. Bathurst populated slowly as Macquarie was hesitant to start conflict, and it seems that the Wiradjuri were tolerant of this slow growth and peaceful relations.

After Macquarie resigned in 1821, relations turned sour. Land grants were expanded, European diseases were introduced, natural resources became strained and sacred sites were destroyed. Soon violence broke out, culminating in a massacre and a war known as the Bathurst War of 1824, which decimated the local Wiradjuri population. That violence and loss of culture cannot be undone, and the traditional Wiradjuri place names that remain today serve as daily reminders of the reconciliation work that needs to be done: there's Narrandera, named for the spiny lizard that inhabits the area; Cootamundra, derived from the word *guudhamang*, meaning turtle; and Murrumburrah, or 'two bark canoes' for the area's trees that support life in many ways.

The region's winemakers, especially the younger generation, want to acknowledge, learn more about, and give back to Wiradjuri Country. Nadja Wallington, of Cowra's Wallington Wines and Orange's ChaLou, acknowledges the Wiradjuri Nation on her labels and platforms. She says this type of recognition is not necessarily commonplace in the region yet, but attests: 'I think it's coming. And I think there's an interest for it.'

The mentality of the long-term custodianship that comes with caring for a vineyard, though, is common throughout the region. While the Central Ranges has long sold its wines to locals and tourists – maybe getting them as far as Sydney, up to a four-hour drive from any given point in the Central Ranges – vintners are starting to recognise that the quality of their land (especially in the higher and cooler pockets of the zone) deserves to be spoken about beyond the borders of New South Wales. In terms of Australian GIs to watch – the wine regions that will assert themselves in the fine wine space in years to come – Central Ranges is close to the top.

Evolution of Wine

By 1850 the Hunter Valley was teeming with commercial vineyards, and by 1858 this activity had trickled into the town of Eurunderee, just 40 kilometres over the current border of the Hunter Valley GI. These 1858 plantings – part of the modern-day Craigmoor winery – are recognised as the first in Mudgee, and the first in the larger Central Ranges zone.

By the end of the 19th century, up to 55 producers had been established in the Mudgee region. As the century turned, a trifecta of difficulties impacted Australian wine: economic recession, **phylloxera** and shifting tastes toward **fortified wine** (and away from **table wine**). Though Mudgee did not fall prey to the root louse **phylloxera**, it could not avoid the other challenges; plantings and production nearly came to a halt.

During the ensuing period of relative dormancy, one planting of note did occur, giving rise to one of the most legendary controversies of Australian wine. In 1918, Craigmoor (then named Rothview) received chardonnay cuttings from James Busby's original collection at Kirkton (p. 31) and began cultivating them. The vines were forgotten for half a century when a French ampelographer named Denis Boubals visited the estate in 1969 and identified the vines as chardonnay – and a unique disease-resistant **clone** at that.

The next year, a Dutch immigrant named Pieter van Gent started as the head winemaker at Craigmoor and took interest in the chardonnay vines on the property. In his words: 'I was told to forget about making white wine in Mudgee and stick to the reds. I made chardonnay in 1971, but there was only one hogshead which was not enough to bottle … this was the first time the chardonnay grape was made into a wine in Australia.'

Here's the catch: the Hunter Valley's Tyrrell's lays claim to this feat too. According to their website, in 1968, 'Murray [Tyrrell] plants the first Chardonnay vines on the Tyrrell's property using cuttings from the Penfolds-owned HVD vineyard. The resulting wine, Vat 47 Chardonnay, becomes Australia's first commercial Chardonnay when it is released three years later.' The Tyrrells' timeline puts their first release of chardonnay (labelled 'Pinot Chardonnay' at the time) in 1971, the same year that van Gent claims to have made Australia's first chardonnay wine.

This is a sticking point for many, and numerous articles and essays have been written about the great Mudgee vs. Hunter Valley chardonnay race. But even if Mudgee didn't release or make the first Australian chardonnay, the region was still of enormous importance in incubating and identifying the grape, and initiating its commercial significance across the nation. And it is beyond argument that Craigmoor's chardonnay, when it was first released in 1972, came from vines that outdated those of Tyrrell's by decades – this is the

Food-grade hoses ready to transfer wine from tank to barrel and to bottle, a common sight at wineries around the world.

magic of Mudgee's dry, moderate climate, which allowed chardonnay vines to survive for 50 years with little tending.

Mudgee can also lay claim to Australia's oldest certified organic vineyard. Botobolar was founded in 1971 by Gil and Vincie Wahlquist. This winery launched a tradition of organics and preservative-free wine in Mudgee, long before those practices were in vogue in Australia (or the rest of the world). The Wahlquists sold Botobolar in 1994, and the winery had its last vintage in 2017, citing a series of droughts as razing the **dry-farmed** vineyard. Robert Stein winery was also established in the 1970s, and along with Craigmoor and Botobolar, helped relaunch the small but ambitious wine scene of Mudgee.

Though neighbouring Orange saw Australia's first real gold rush, with 300 colonists breaking its ground by May 1851, its early wine history was much less illustrious. An old muscat vineyard or two in the 19th century was the extent of it. It wasn't until the second half of the 20th century that any significant winemaking took root in the region, following the reinvigoration of Mudgee. In 1952, a state-employed viticulturist planted a trial vineyard of cabernet sauvignon and shiraz in Molong, in the modern-day Orange region. But it would take almost another 30 years for grape growing of any commercial significance to take hold.

The 1980s were big for Orange. Wineries like Nashdale, Sons & Brothers, Bloodwood, Cargo Road Wines, Forest Edge, Canobolas-Smith, Highland Heritage and Ibis were all founded, and cool-climate winemaking was on the rise across Australia. Orange was also attracting local farmers, as well as nationally experienced winemakers, to its high-altitude vineyards.

Bloodwood and Canobolas-Smith in particular were early icons of quality in the region. But neither was great at marketing themselves and received little attention from media and consumers. With plantings as early as 1989 (owned by Rosemount at the time), and the first commercial vintage in 2004, Philip Shaw has been the estate that has done the most to promote the GI's name – which is finally, though still slowly, beginning to receive its due.

Cowra, with neither the history of Mudgee nor the cool climate of Orange, has made fewer inroads than either. Viticulture was established in the early 1970s with the aim of providing fruit for

Central Ranges Viticultural Footprint

	MUDGEE	ORANGE	COWRA
Total delimited area (km²)	9740	3420	1460
Total planted area (hectares)	1899	1075	932
% of delimited area planted	0.195%	0.310%	0.638%
Total elevation range	227–1242 masl	600–1390 masl	262–527 masl
Elevation range of plantings	450–1180 masl	600–1150 masl	262–400 masl
Number of producers	35	32	6

established regions, namely Mudgee and the Hunter Valley. There was some early buzz about Cowra chardonnay (Adelaide Hills' Petaluma used Cowra chardonnay for its first few vintages), but as a region of growers, and few actual wineries, Cowra had a hard time furthering its reputation.

In the 1990s, a push to establish a national profile for the Central Ranges attracted big corporations like Orlando and Southcorp. Cowra, and to a lesser extent Mudgee, with greater ability for yields and ripeness, were the main targets. But by 2010, most of the corporations had pulled out. Central Ranges had not built up enough of a profile to justify the production cost, which was greater than in neighbouring Riverina. The bigger companies that did stay (like Casella, of Yellow Tail fame), rarely released wines with a Central Ranges-branded GI on the label; there just wasn't enough of a draw.

Although corporate divestment caused some trauma in Mudgee and particularly Cowra, an ethos to become more self-reliant emerged. As vintner Tom Ward says, 'when the big companies come in to buy fruit, when it becomes tough, they'll retreat … you've got to create your own DNA in the region and have wineries there'.

And indeed, a new generation of wineries has emerged in the 21st century that are committed to building regional identity. There is a distinct feeling that these regions, though in parts historic, are just getting started.

Although corporate divestment caused some trauma … an ethos to become more self-reliant emerged.

The tablelands of the Great Dividing Range, long overdue for imminent summer rain.

Lay of the Land

The Central Ranges of New South Wales are the fading, western slopes of the Great Dividing Range, separated from the coast by Mt Yengo, the Blue Mountains, and the Wollemi and Goulburn River National Parks.

Vineyard areas are all nestled within the north-south oriented striations of small mountains and ranges; Central Ranges is reminiscent of a collapsed accordion, telling the story of the continental folding that created the Great Dividing Range. These valleys have been bisected and carved by rivers that originate in higher elevations to the east and flow inland to the west, shrinking into creeks that either ultimately flow into the Murray River or terminate at dried-up lakes turned salt flats.

The result is a gently undulating topography of vineyards, sheltered by hills and mountains, cooled by elevation and watered (though imperfectly) by rainfall and available ground moisture from the rivers, lakes and streams nearby.

Many wines claim 'Central Ranges' as the origin on their labels – more than is usual for an Australian zone. There are a few reasons for this: it allows blending across the three disparate regions of Orange, Cowra and Mudgee, the freshness of cooler sites balancing the ripeness of warmer ones; it accommodates sites outside the three regions, including vineyards displaced from the Orange GI for not meeting its elevation requirement (more on that later); and it allows three regions that have not yet established strong brands of their own to band together.

However, as the world of wine craves greater regional specificity, the individual regions of the Central Ranges are diverse enough to grant it.

Mudgee shares its eastern border with the western border of the Hunter Valley, though planted areas in the two are separated by various mountains and national parks. The major distinguishing factor between the Hunter Valley and Mudgee (along with the rest of the Central Ranges) is the way in which the Great Dividing Range protects the latter from challenging coastal conditions. Thus, the Hunter Valley experiences a subtropical climate, while the Central Ranges are dry and often cooler, with temperatures moderated by elevation.

Mudgee is planted along the Cudgegong River Valley, where most vineyards range in elevation from 450–600 metres above sea level. The delimited area includes peaks that breach 1200 metres, but almost no vineyards lie among the heavily forested upper hills – with exceptions near Rylstone and Nullo Mountain, where vineyards have been planted upwards of 1100 metres above sea level.

Inland elevation creates a stark continental climate. Although there's no subtropical moisture, as in the neighbouring Hunter Valley, this climate brings summer heat spikes, occasional hail, frost risk and a steep **diurnal shift**.

Soils in Mudgee are generally fertile and have a higher **nutrient load** than the average ancient soils of Australia. Sandy loams derived from the weathering of volcanic earth sit atop sandy clays that drain freely, with veins of gravelly ironstone and quartz.

Mudgee is a town of about 11,000 people. Compare that to Orange's 41,000 and over half a million in the Hunter District, and the lack of local consumers is clear. Mudgee has tried to compete with these two neighbours on tourism as well, but has not reached the heights of either region's draw. Of the three Central Ranges regions, though, Mudgee has probably done the best job with robust and structured styles of shiraz and cabernet sauvignon – Orange is a little too cool and Cowra a little too warm. In particular, cabernet sauvignon has become the signature grape of the region, a unique specialty for New South Wales.

Orange – named for an indirect affiliation with William of Orange, not anything to do with the colour or fruit – sits southwest of Mudgee. The majority of the planted area, and the town of Orange itself, sits between the Mullion Range in the northeast and Mt Canobolas (an extinct volcano) in the southwest.

Approximately 13–11 million years ago, Mt Canobolas formed at the end of a large chain of volcanic activity that created a low-profile shield volcano, with continued basalt lava flow forming both undulating hills and rocky cliffs. This younger volcanic formation creates the elevation of Orange.

Unusual in Australia (and the world, for that matter), the GI of Orange is based upon a minimum required elevation of 600 metres above sea level. Vineyards in Orange are planted on slopes and hillsides to avoid the frigid air channels at the base of valleys. But within the hierarchy of the slopes, temperatures drop drastically with elevation. The mean January temperature at Mudgee (454 metres) is 23.5°C; at the lowest elevation of Orange (Molong, 600 metres), it's 21.5°C; and at one of the higher elevations in Orange (Millthorpe, 960 metres), it's 19.15°C.

While the elevation creates temperature drops, it also promotes mild summers and cold winters, and serves to increase sunshine. In a sense, the elevation acts like a rain shadow, not only promoting dryness, but collecting sunlight as well. Most sites generally face north as south would be too cold.

The region is generally humid, which can relieve the pressure on vines as they lose transpiration at the hottest and driest parts of the year. Precipitation is fairly consistent across the year and increases with altitude. While the average annual rainfall across Orange ranges from 700–950 millimetres, it can break 1000 millimetres at the top of Mt Canobolas, and be as low as 650 millimetres at the lowest parts of the GI.

Central Ranges is reminiscent of a collapsed accordion, telling the story of the continental folding that created the Great Dividing Range.

Because of this increased precipitation, **canopies** tend to be a bit bigger at elevation as well. This can also be helpful for shading fruit, to protect from sunburn late in the season, and doesn't increase disease pressure thanks to the wind.

After climate, the soils in Orange have the most impact on vines – and they adhere to altitude changes just like the climate, with an added dimension of distinction based on whether a site falls on the west side of the GI, surrounding Mt Canobolas, or among the eastern peaks. On the western side of Orange, surrounding Mt Canobolas and above 800 metres, soils are generally defined by

Stephen Doyle surveying his vineyard from a lightweight vehicle, preventing the compaction of Bloodwood's free-draining gravel soils.

Central Ranges

HOW TO READ THIS MAP

Spread across the western tablelands and slopes of the Great Dividing Range, the three regions of the Central Ranges Zone owe their viticulturally suitable climates to their elevation. The colour gradient across the map shows the changes in elevation across the zone.

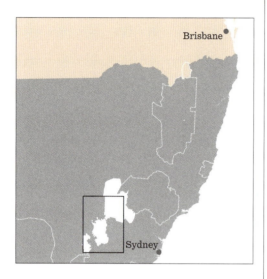

1 10's Estate
2 Angullong
3 Bloodwood
4 Boree Lane
5 Borrodell on the Mount
6 Brangayne Old Forbes Road Vineyard
7 Brangayne of Orange
8 Burnbrae
9 Burrundulla Vineyards
10 Canobolas-Smith
11 Cargo Road Wines
12 ChaLou
13 Colmar Estate
14 Craigmoor/Montrose
15 De Salis
16 First Ridge
17 Gilbert Family Wines
18 Heifer Station
19 Highland Heritage Estate
20 Huntington Estate
21 Kalari
22 Logan
23 Lowe Wines
24 Nashdale Lane Wines
25 Philip Shaw Wines
26 Pieter van Gent
27 Pinnaroo Estate
28 Printhie Wines
29 Renzaglia
30 Rikard Wines
31 Robert Stein Vineyard
32 Rosnay Wines
33 Ross Hill Wines
34 Rowlee
35 Stockman's Ridge
36 Swinging Bridge Wines
37 Tamburlaine
38 Vinifera
39 Wallington Wines
40 Windowrie
41 Yeates

Mudgee Climate Data (°C)

	1960–1990	1991–PRESENT	2020
Heat summation/GDD	● 1879	● 1983	● 2196
Annual rain/GSR	690/432	690/449	586/457
Warmest month avg. temp.	22	23.2	26.1

Orange Climate Data (°C)

	1960–1990	1991–PRESENT	2020
Heat summation/GDD	● 1496	● 1608	● 1812
Annual rain/GSR	813/455	760/445	640/417
Warmest month avg. temp.	20.5	21.6	24.5

Cowra Climate Data (°C)

	1960–1990	1991–PRESENT	2020
Heat summation/GDD	● 2140	● 2168	● 2354
Annual rain/GSR	619/364	603/359	497/338
Warmest month avg. temp.	23.8	24.7	27

Winkler Scale:

● 850–1111   ● 1112–1389   ● 1390–1667   ● 1668–1944   ● 1945–2222   ● 2223–2700

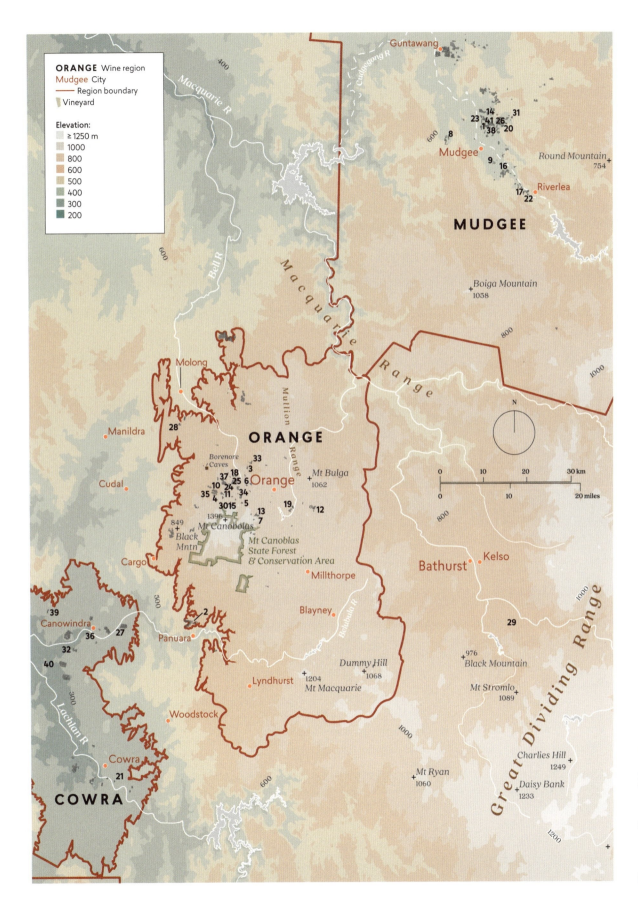

If anything, Cowra's warmth just accentuates how important Orange's altitude is and the influence of Mt Canobolas.

brown-red loams with windblown silts at hilltop sites. These soils are good, fertile hosts for orchards and vineyards.

Surrounding the eastern peaks of Orange, between 700 and 900 metres in elevation, soils derived from older volcanics provide excellent sites with less vigour – though with less rainfall as well, there is a greater reliance on irrigation.

A third soil type resides to the north and west of Mt Canobolas, in a lower elevation pocket of 600–700 metres. This belt is derived from both limestone and volcanic sediments.

While elevation defines climate and soil, it has less impact on grape choice. A variety of grapes are found in a variety of **mesoclimates** across the region, displaying unique characteristics from each. However, there are a few exceptions: merlot isn't found planted above 900 metres because the wind impacts its fruit set and renders it commercially unviable; and pinot noir is not found below 750 metres due to the more favourable cool temperatures at higher altitudes, as well as increased frost risk at lower ones.

Opinions vary about what grapes should be the signature of Orange. Most agree on chardonnay and shiraz (though the latter struggles to market itself against Barossa versions). Cabernet sauvignon, though widely planted by the numbers, is on the fringe of its growing suitability for many sites – the climate is just too continental, and brings the autumn chill too early to ripen its tannins in most years. Riesling is gaining some traction in the region, though remains a fringe grape. And pinot noir, though also less planted, is causing great excitement around the region. More viticultural work needs to be done – namely finding the right **clones** – but pinot noir's future looks bright in Orange.

Cowra, southwest of Orange, occupies a dramatically different landscape than its neighbour. Cowra is much lower in elevation; its highest vineyard reaches just over 500 metres, but most sit between 260 and 400 metres above sea level. This makes Cowra warmer and drier than Orange. Annual rainfall is barely 600 millimetres. Two small elevation gains exist on the western side of the GI, creating slopes where **aspects** range from northeast to east to southeast facing.

The dramatic **diurnal swings** enjoyed by Orange and Mudgee are absent in Cowra. This makes farming easier, though it can impact the quality of the grapes. Humidity sinks into the river

The dam at the bottom of the certified carbon-neutral Ross Hill estate in Orange, collecting rain water to redistribute across the property.

valleys and lowest parts of the region, but it doesn't result in much disease pressure; instead, it helps retain ground moisture. This moisture can be helpful in mitigating the growing season heat spikes that Cowra regularly sees, often exceeding 40°C. True continental climate characteristics abound, including spring frosts, summer hail and consistent rainfall through the year.

Neighbouring Orange calls Mudgee a 'hot' and Cowra a 'very hot' region in their marketing materials, which isn't too far off. Cowra is a high Region 4 on the **Winkler Scale** compared to Orange's Region 2 classification, only a 30-minute drive north – and Mudgee's low Region 4 beyond that. If anything, though, Cowra's warmth just accentuates how important Orange's altitude is and the influence of Mt Canobolas. The lowest-lying, warmest areas of Cowra are only 40 kilometres (straight downhill) from the coldest sites in Orange.

Cowra is defined by two rivers – the Lachlan and the Belubula – flowing from the east to the western lowlands. The Belubula is a tributary of the Lachlan, converging just outside the northwestern corner of the GI (the lowest-lying corner of the region). Vineyards are most concentrated along each river's valley.

Soils in general have a clay subsoil, with brown volcanic loam mixed with alluvial wash from the meandering rivers. Pockets of sand appear, and in general the soils are slightly acidic. At the northern reaches of the region, eroded granitic sand and basalt are common, an influence from the lava fields resulting from Mt Canobolas' formation.

The delimited area of Cowra covers about 1460 square kilometres and is home to over 40 vineyards (most of which are locally, independently owned), covering 932 hectares of plantings. Chardonnay accounts for 50% of the plantings in Cowra, followed by shiraz, cabernet sauvignon, merlot, malbec, petit verdot, semillon, sauvignon blanc and verdelho. The white grapes are generally getting the most attention in the region, with verdelho seeing a similar treatment as it receives in Western Australia's historic Swan Valley (p. 446), producing dry, sweet and **fortified** versions. And semillon is often vinified in a manner to resemble the commercial Hunter style – early-picked, heavily fined and filtered, and aged in stainless steel.

There has been more corporate interest in Cowra than Mudgee and Orange because it is easy to farm – Cowra is flat, temperate and has historically had access to water. These characteristics have also allowed Cowra to emerge as a leader in organics and **biodynamics** too. While the more marginal conditions of Mudgee and Orange (cooler, wetter, higher) make this type of farming much more difficult, Cowra has several certified organic and/or **biodynamic** producers, with the goal for more. The Cowra regional association has recently established the mission 'to produce wine of regional character with the least environmental impact of any region in Australia'.

Hubbub

Of the three Central Ranges regions, Cowra is the least developed; because the region was the target of the most corporate winemaking, vineyards were planted, but few wineries were established. When the corporations were no longer interested in those vineyards, no one was left to promote them. As a result, there are very few actual wineries within Cowra, and none that has attracted wine professionals and consumers from beyond the region's boundaries.

Mudgee, the most historic wine-producing region of the lot, is the next most developed. While some of the historic producers of the region – Craigmoor, Pieter van Gent and Burrundulla – are still active, none has been able to break out as the icon producers of many other Australian regions have – as Clonakilla (p. 86) did for Canberra District or what Jasper Hill (p. 190) did for Heathcote. And Mudgee is not attracting the next generation in the same way that its neighbour Orange is. The wines of Mudgee are generally reliable, if not delicious – especially when they embrace the warm climate that the region is settling into – but national (and certainly international) interest remains tepid.

Orange historically suffered from the same branding woes as Mudgee, with its early bastions of quality unable to reach icon status. But Orange has done a much better job in recent years of building up the quality of its wine and its brand messaging. Though tourism has been a strong suit of the region for decades, 'you still gotta make a great product', Tom Ward says. 'And that's been a huge development. It's probably happened in the last ten years. We're getting winemakers here. We're getting good equipment. Viticulture, now, it's spot on here. We've come a long way.' Between its leaders, its growth and its cool climate, Orange has been able to attract a younger generation who is excited about adding to the conversation.

But rising land prices across all three regions, especially in Orange, are threatening access for the next generation. Nadja Wallington bought land in Orange for her label ChaLou in 2020. In 2021, she acknowledges, 'I don't know if I could buy land this year'. Though this increase in real estate value often accompanies wealth and development in an area, it is not good for the future of wine regions that are still in the process of establishing their identities. Access is paramount, and it's becoming more and more difficult.

As climate changes, the land itself also presents its fair share of perils. Bushfires have historically not affected the Central Ranges dramatically, but the fires of 2019–2020 revealed an unprecedented threat. 'We've never seen anything like it,' Wallington says. 'All our prior research made us think that we wouldn't be affected.' But the Central Ranges were affected and millions of dollars' worth of unusable, smoke-tainted grapes were left on the vines.

The vintners of the region don't know if they'll ever be hit so hard by bushfires again, but at present there is nothing they can do to prevent or mitigate the threat. And insurance only protects against physical damage, not smoke taint, which is the much more dominant and insidious injury. The **AWRI** has been working hard to research mitigation techniques, and continues to lead the global wine community on this topic.

Bushfires are a real concern for the future of the region, but water is the problem that has been continually present. Orange has the greatest rainfall of the three regions, though even vineyards in Orange often irrigate with dam-collected water because the rain doesn't fall at ideal times throughout the year. Rainfall is lower in Cowra and Mudgee, so irrigation is a necessity most years. And the region, as a whole, has experienced prolonged drought seasons – a nearly 10-year drought in the first decade of the 21st century, and a three-year drought from 2017–2020. During droughts, dams dry up and the bore water (access to underground aquifers) becomes so saline as to be unusable. Water has perhaps been the biggest challenge to the development of the GI.

The three regions of the Central Ranges may be at different places in their brand development, though it doesn't mean that any one is more or less capable of making fine wine – all have proved their ability to do so. As Tom Ward says, on how great wines come to be, 'if it was just about the wine, just about the flavour, it'd be a different game. But it's the situations, the whole momentum, that determines who goes on to that icon stage.'

That word, *momentum*, seems particularly appropriate for Central Ranges today. Whether its regions have slowed, stalled completely or are gaining velocity, none has, as yet, harnessed that momentum perfectly to be recognised for the quality of their wines across Australia (and the world). But that momentum seems to be building. It's only a matter of time – and a matter of creating the 'DNA', to harken back to another Tom Ward quote – for these regions to step onto the world stage.

Bushfires are a real concern for the future of the region – but water is the problem that has been continually present.

See Saw Wines' certified organic vineyard facing a cloud-covered Mt Canobolas in Orange.

PRODUCERS

MUDGEE

CRAIGMOOR/MONTROSE

Craigmoor is Mudgee's oldest continuous vineyard and winery. It was planted in 1862 by German settler Adam Roth. Over a century later, the Montrose vineyard was established by two Italian engineers. Today the two are combined under one label, owned by the Oatley wine family. One of Australia's first chardonnays was produced at Craigmoor in 1971, but Montrose has made a name for itself with its Black Shiraz. *craigmoor.com.au*

GILBERT FAMILY WINES

Gilbert Family Wines is both a nod to legacy and a firm step forward into the future. Joseph Gilbert planted some of the first vines in South Australia's Eden Valley in 1842. Simon (Joseph's great-great-grandson) and his son Will are fifth- and sixth-generation winemakers. While their range features some rieslings from the Eden Valley, the core wines for Gilbert come from their base of operations in Mudgee, and the chilly climes of Orange. The father-son duo has continued to make classic single-variety wines and **traditional method** sparklings, but Will Gilbert's effect on the label is clear: convincing his dad to make a couple of **pét-nats** and a highly fashionable **piquette** from a blend of gewürztraminer and sangiovese. Both styles align to make Gilbert one of the most important wineries in Mudgee, and a leader in all of the Central Ranges. *gilbertfamilywines.com.au*

HUNTINGTON ESTATE

Huntington downplays its origin story, telling of a young Bob Roberts, a Sydney lawyer, who in 1969 'shoved a few thousand sticks in the ground and hoped they would grow'. Bob was a champion of Mudgee and, in particular, a champion of cabernet sauvignon in the region, a hunch that has turned out to be prescient. The wines – which don't see widespread retail and restaurant exposure, most being sold directly to consumers – are numerous, with Huntington making everything from grenache to late-harvest semillon, but they are best known for their shiraz and cabernet sauvignon. Current owners are Tim and Nicky Stevens, who were regular customers of Huntington and friends of Roberts before being given the opportunity to purchase in 2005. *huntingtonestate.com.au*

LOGAN

Peter Logan's dad once sat him down and pointed at some land in the distance, asking if he thought grapes would grow there. When Peter said yes, his father mentioned he had bought it in the pub the night before. Perched on top of that hill now sits a spectacular tasting room, overlooking Mudgee's Apple Tree Flat Valley. The wines are crafted from their own fruit, as well as from sites in Orange, at some of the highest altitude vineyards in Australia. The Ridge of Tears wines are made from shiraz, picked at 564 metres altitude in Mudgee and 970 metres in Orange. The rest of Peter's range spans several styles and grapes: think chilled red blends, skin-contact pinot gris, shiraz-viognier and pinot noir. *loganwines.com.au*

What we're drinking

The **Gilbert Family Wines** Blanc is a blend of riesling, pinot gris and gewürztraminer. I'm not generally a lover of the latter, but I particularly like this incarnation. More nashi pear than Turkish delight, it hits the spot, with that taut line of riesling coming through on the finish to leave you salivating and thirsty for more. — *Kavita Faiella*

LOWE WINES

Tinja, the name of the property that has been in the Lowe family for five generations, was first planted to vine in the 1970s. Lowe Wines was founded in 2000 by David Lowe, who began his career at Len Evans' Rothbury Estate. David's vineyards are organically certified, a principle shared across the extensive kitchen garden and farmlands that grow produce for their restaurant and events pavilion. Lowe's iconic wine is made from **bush-vine** zinfandel – an extraordinary combination of concentration, spice and soft tannin (their restaurant is even called The Zin House).
lowefamilywineco.com.au

ROBERT STEIN VINEYARD

Robert and Lorna Stein established their vineyard in 1976. The Steins's grandson Jacob took over winemaking duties in 2009, having completed several vintages abroad, including reconnecting to the vineyards his ancestors worked in Germany eight generations earlier. (The Steins' ancestors were also some of the early farmers in the Camden Park vineyard, an important early site outside Sydney, in the 1830s.) Jacob's passion for riesling is reflected in the highly sought-after wines made from 40-year-old vines planted at 550 metres. **robertstein.com.au**

ORANGE

BLOODWOOD

In 1983, Stephen and Rhonda Doyle planted the first modern commercial vineyard in Orange. Their wines are made only from grapes grown on their property and their website offers creative food pairings and recipes from Rhonda. They make all manner of styles – from sparkling to sweet wines to structured reds – and are considered one of the pioneers of quality winemaking in the region. The Doyles also have a sense of humour about their wines: they make a deep-coloured rosé called Big Men in Tights from malbec, and a cabernet franc that bears the subheading '(Caution, may contain traces of nuts)'. They also write one of the most entertaining winery email newsletters in Australia.
bloodwood.biz

CANOBOLAS-SMITH

Murray Smith founded Canobolas-Smith in 1986, combining his surname and the slopes that made it all possible. Mt Canobolas provides north-facing 850-metre slopes for the vineyard with rich volcanic soil and excellent airflow. Smith worked in Bordeaux, Napa and around Australia before establishing his own winery, which has been one of Orange's most seminal, producing chardonnay, a red Bordeaux-grape blend, and small amounts of sparkling and pinot noir. In 2021, Canobolas-Smith was bought by Jonathon and Limei Mattick, formerly of Handpicked Wines, who are reviving the winery's great legacy.
canobolassmithwines.com.au

Nadja Wallington — ChaLou

CHALOU

With her parents establishing Wallington Wines in Central Ranges in the early 1990s, Nadja Wallington knew she wanted to be a winemaker from a young age. She spent several years making wine overseas before a seven-year stint at Philip Shaw in Orange brought her back home. Alongside her husband, Steve Mobbs, she returned to Wallington in 2017 to help her mum and carry on the family legacy. Steve and Nadja bought their own property, ChaLou, in Orange in 2020 and released their first wines the following year. Also in the ChaLou stable is Steve's label Dreaded Friend and a label called The Somm and The Winemaker, which Nadja makes with her childhood mate and Sydney-based sommelier, Louella Mathews. Between the three labels, Nadja and Steve (and Louella) are making some of the Central Ranges' most compelling wines, including everything from **biodynamic** grenache to off-dry riesling to fragrant arneis, with some exciting chenin blanc plantings on the horizon. *chalouwines.com.au*

DE SALIS

The story goes that Charlie Svenson talked all the time about one day making wine. For his 40th birthday, a mate gave him a **barrique** and told him to 'get on with it'. A microbiologist by trade, Charlie understood and trusted the process of making wine. The first De Salis wine was made in a Sydney garage in 1999, from cabernet franc picked in Orange, and soon Charlie and his wife Loretta bought Lofty Vineyard on the northern slope of Mt Canobolas – which at 1050 metres in altitude, is one of the highest vineyards in the GI. Made from chardonnay, pinot noir, pinot meunier, cabernet sauvignon, merlot and sauvignon blanc, the wines are delicate and elegant, reflective of the altitude and cool climate of Orange. *desaliswines.com.au*

NASHDALE LANE WINES

Nashdale Lane is the culmination of a decade-long search for the right piece of earth; Nick and Tanya Segger fell in love with viticulture while in Italy in 2001 and purchased their vineyard in Orange in 2012. At the entry level, the wines are unique and approachable blends that belong on a bistro table. At the top end, Nick and Tanya hand-select pinot noir and tempranillo to showcase the best vintages. A visit to the cellar door not only yields a taste of these wines, but the property also houses several luxury glamping cabins. *nashdalelane.com*

PHILIP SHAW WINES

A trip to Roseworthy College, one of Australia's foremost agricultural universities, inspired a 12-year-old Philip Shaw's lifelong fascination with wine. He began in the industry as a teenager, washing bottles for Penfolds. His career includes stints as chief winemaker for some of the biggest names in Australian wine, including Penfolds, Lindeman's, Wynns and Rosemount. Philip planted his Koomooloo vineyard in Orange in the late 1980s: 47 hectares of vine on the rich volcanic soils of Mt Canobolas. The reins have passed to his sons, Daniel and Damian, who look after winemaking and management respectively, producing cool-climate classics ranging from chardonnay and pinot noir to Bordeaux varieties, shiraz and viognier. Philip moved on to start a new winery in 2015 called Hoosegg, making minuscule quantities of high-end wines, sometimes with provocative hand-drawn labels. *philipshaw.com.au*

PRINTHIE WINES

Printhie's first vineyard was planted by Jim and Ruth Swift on their family property in 1996. Their initial focus on grape growing expanded to production with the development of their winery in 2004. The reins have now been handed over to their sons, Ed and Dave, and winemaker Drew Tuckwell came on in 2007, cementing Printhie as a real competitor in the region. The team is also paving the way for Orange to be considered among Australia's best sparkling wine-producing regions. *printhiewines.com.au*

RIKARD WINES

Born out of tragedy and built by resilience, Rikard started in 2015. William Rikard-Bell was working at Drayton's in the Hunter Valley in 2008 when an explosion in the winery took him out of action for two years. His recovery gave him the necessary determination to start making wine under his own label. The Rikard block sits at 1050 metres

---

 What we're drinking

Printhie's sparkling wines under the SWIFT label are among some of the most underrated Australian bubbly. Ten years on **lees** *for their flagship blanc de blancs is quite the investment in the future: for Printhie themselves, for the Orange GI and for all the drinkers who get to participate in this patient project.* **– Jane Lopes**

Tom Ward
Swinging Bridge Wines

altitude and is planted to pinot noir and chardonnay. William carefully selects his fruit with multiple passes through the vineyard, making tiny batches of taut, lean whites and complex, brooding reds. *rikardwines.com.au*

ROSS HILL WINES

Peter and Terri Robson planted their Griffin Road vineyard in 1994 – one of a few vineyards in Orange at the time. In 2007, they were joined by their son James and his wife Chrissy, and soon established a winery in an apple-packing shed and planted a second vineyard. In 2016, after a six-year process, Ross Hill became a certified carbon-neutral winery, having offset their emissions and reduced their carbon footprint. A variety of classically made wines are produced: from value blends to the flagship cabernet sauvignon-based The Griffin. The family also makes olive oil from a grove at the Griffin Road vineyard. *rosshillwines.com.au*

SWINGING BRIDGE WINES

The Swinging Bridge tale begins with two related families who had been farming in the area since 1867. The Ward and Payten families established the estate in 1995 at Canowindra, in the Cowra GI. Tom Ward spent several years working at Swinging Bridge as a viticulturist and took over ownership in 2008 after studying winemaking. In order to take advantage of the plethora of grapes that thrive in a cool climate, Tom sold the original vineyard and moved Swinging Bridge to Orange. Tom strongly believes that Orange is at its best with chardonnay and pinot noir, but this hasn't stopped him from branching out. The Hashtag Series has become his playground, where his team can push the boundaries of the classics, including Tempinot, the strange (but effective) bedfellows of tempranillo and pinot, and the first gamay produced in Orange. Swinging Bridge is doing the work to put Orange on the map as one of Australia's best cool-climate wine regions. *swingingbridge.com.au*

COWRA

GROVE ESTATE

Croatian settlers first planted grapes on this property in 1861. Grove Estate was bought by three couples in 1989 and since then, over 50 hectares of vines have been planted. Some of the original cuttings survived, and one of the pickers' huts still stands as the cellar door. Thanks to the diversity of vineyards owned by each couple, Grove Estate has access to a wide variety of fruit. Tim Kirk (Clonakilla, p. 86) and Bryan Martin (Ravensworth, p. 89) – both producers in Canberra District – have produced a number of the wines over the past 15 years. *groveestate.com.au*

ROSNAY WINES

The Statham family has been one of the regional leaders in organic viticulture since establishing their farm, starting in 1995 in Canowindra. In fact, Sam Statham was awarded the inaugural New South Wales Organic Pioneers award in 2012. Sam is a fount of knowledge and curiosity,

Central Ranges

69

and Rosnay's website includes musings on everything from oak usage to indigenous yeasts, solar power, metabolic processes, figs, olives, and – of course – wine. The styles range from traditional cabernet sauvignon and chardonnay to the 'Vin de Garage' series of **pét-nats**, **nouveau** reds and skin-contact whites. *rosnay.com.au*

WALLINGTON WINES

Margaret and Anthony Wallington moved to just outside Canowindra in the early 1990s and began planting vineyards on the 405-hectare property, starting with cabernet sauvignon (Anthony's favourite) and eventually shiraz, chardonnay and other Bordeaux and Rhône varieties. When Anthony passed away, mighty matriarch Margaret raised their four daughters while managing the property and their business, Wallington Wines. Margaret converted the vineyard to organics and **biodynamic** practices. Daughter Nadja and her husband Steve Mobbs have helped run the winery, in addition to running their own label in Orange (ChaLou, p. 67). *wallingtonwines.com.au*

And don't forget ...
Angullong is one of the oldest vineyard areas in the Orange GI, now with 200 hectares under vine and a diversity of offerings ... **Benson and the Mooch**, a **lo-fi** label, is based on the New South Wales coast but sources wines from Central Ranges, including their debut **pèt-nat** made with chardonnay and pinot gris ...

Burrundulla Vineyards, one of Mudgee's most historic vineyards, was originally planted in 1845 ... **Cumulus** is Orange's (and one of Australia's) largest single-vineyards at 508 hectares, with a huge variety of grapes planted, and includes not only the Cumulus wines, but several other (largely value-oriented) brands ... **Pieter van Gent**, the eponymous label of the man who crafted one of Australia's first chardonnays at Craigmoor, this Mudgee winery focuses mainly on reds and **fortifieds**, though chardonnay, müller-thurgau and verdelho are also made ... **Renzaglia**, based in the O'Connell Valley (south of Mudgee and east of Orange) and planted since 1997, produces some classic expressions and has recently launched vermouth production in response to the 2020 bushfires ... **Tamburlaine**, established in 1966 in Orange, has one of the largest single-winery organic holdings in Australia, a **sulphur**-free range and a charitable donation program in place for certain purchases ... **Windowrie** farms 32 hectares of certified-organic vineyards (with another 20 hectares in conversion) in Canowindra, making classics like chardonnay, shiraz and merlot, as well as experimenting with **sulphur**-free wines.

Southern New South Wales

Introduction

It should be called the Snowy Mountains zone. Southern New South Wales zone is a bit of a mouthful and offers up a bland geographic description instead of the real commonality of this area. The Snowy Mountains are a subsection of the Australian Alps (themselves a bio-region of the larger Great Dividing Range), and the highest peaks of Australia, with Mt Kosciuszko reaching 2228 metres above sea level.

The other defining feature of the region is the city of Canberra: Australia's capital. Over the decade following Australia's independence from the United Kingdom in 1901, Canberra was nominated as the newly formed nation's capital. The story goes that neither Melbourne nor Sydney would let the other become the capital, so an independent region between the two had to be nominated. Canberra, coming from the Ngunnawal word *kamberra*, appropriately meaning 'meeting place', was chosen in 1913.

Canberra District GI straddles the Australian Capital Territory (ACT) – an independent territory, controlled by the Federal government, which contains the city of Canberra – and the surrounding area of New South Wales, including the towns of Hall, Murrumbateman and Bungendore. The other three regions of the Southern New South Wales zone lie further inland, to the west of Canberra District, forming a north–south line along the Great Dividing Range, with Hilltops in the north, Gundagai in the middle (adjacent to Canberra District) and Tumbarumba in the south, near the Victorian border.

While Canberra District has long been the marquee region of the Southern New South Wales zone, there has been a collaborative spirit between all four regions, with many of the headlining Canberra District producers making wine from the others. (Southern New South Wales has also been known to welcome Shoalhaven Coast and the Southern Highlands into the greater Canberra area in regional wine shows.) This crossing of boundaries, and recognition of the strengths of other parts of the larger area, has precedence in the original human history of the region.

The Ngarigo people have lived in, and looked after, the steepest stretches of the Snowy Mountains for millennia. The Canberra District and Tumbarumba regions overlap with lands of the Ngarigo Nation. Gundagai vineyards are on Wiradjuri Country – the flatter lands to the west. And the vineyards of Hilltops and Canberra District sit on the northern slopes of the Snowy Mountains, in Ngunnawal and Gundungurra Country. The seasonal movement of the Ngarigo took them from the heights of the mountains, to the lower-lying river plains inland (towards Wiradjuri and Jaitmatang Country), due north towards Ngunnawal

Country, and towards the coast, where the Yuin Nation lived in rhythm with the sea.

All these neighbours would be welcomed onto Ngarigo Country each summer to celebrate the arrival of the bogong moth. Thousands of people gathered among the mountains, harvesting, celebrating, feasting on and preserving the fat and nutrient-packed moths. Thousands of years of knowledge, skilful custodianship, and a strong community helped the Ngarigo and the surrounding nations thrive in the Australian Alps, especially during the end of the last ice age.

The Ngarigo and Ngunnawal Nations are growing in size and presence today. But they are still dealing with the trauma caused by the government refusing to acknowledge the title claims for their ancestral lands. The government grants land rights based on its concept of ownership and proof of first settlement. These Nations, however, embrace a different paradigm than ownership, one based on care, custodianship and connection – concepts that are harder to prove in court.

The vignerons of the region, though perhaps not always intentionally, work to embody a similar connection to land as the original custodians. With their thoughtful approach to community and farming, they are not only crafting some of Australia's most exciting wines, they are also furthering the conversation about long-term land care.

Evolution of Wine

Though there were some plantings as early as the 1840s in the township of Yass (in today's northern Canberra District region) and Young (the epicentre of wine production in today's Hilltops region), these vineyards had all but vanished by the turn of the century, due to the Australia-wide economic recession and movement away from **table wines**. It wasn't until the 1970s that viticulture re-emerged in Southern New South Wales, when cool-climate wines were beginning to experience a renaissance in Australia; Canberra and its environs presented an ideal climate.

Hilltops saw the first modern plantings in Southern New South Wales in 1969, when Peter Robertson planted vines at his later-renowned Barwang property. Robertson beat his neighbours around Canberra to the punch by two years: from 1971, three 'PhD vignerons' (as James Halliday coined them) emerged who would establish modern viticulture in Canberra District.

The first was Dr Edgar Riek, an entomologist and invertebrate zoologist, who found a second career as a viticulturist in Canberra. Riek moved to Canberra in 1945 to work for the **CSIRO** (Commonwealth Scientific and Industrial Research Organisation). In 1971 he planted some of the region's first vines at Lake George: pinot noir, chardonnay and cabernet sauvignon were his initial picks for the region. Riek also actively encouraged wine culture in Canberra, starting the

An alpine summer pond formed from melted snow at about 2000 metres above sea level, approaching the peak of Mt Kosciuszko in the Snowy Mountains.

Canberra Horticultural Society and the Canberra Wine & Food Club in the 1950s, as well as the Canberra Wine Show in 1975.

The second PhD vigneron was Dr John Kirk. Like Riek, Kirk was an accomplished scientist before he found wine. He moved to Australia from the UK in 1968 to be a research biochemist with the Australian government – naturally taking him to the nation's capital. Kirk was a wine enthusiast who had the idea to make wine in Murrumbateman, 45 kilometres north of Canberra. Kirk named his winery Clonakilla, after his family's farm in County Clare, Ireland.

Tim Kirk, John's son and the current proprietor of Clonakilla, recounts: 'A lot of people he consulted about the idea just thought it was ridiculous. It was too cold. But to his great credit he persevered.' John planted his first vines (cabernet sauvignon, riesling and chardonnay) in 1971, squarely landing a tie with Riek for first in Canberra District, though Kirk can claim the first commercial wines in the region, released in 1976.

Ken Helm, a **CSIRO** insect ecologist, completed the trifecta, planting his Nanima Creek vineyard (Helm Wines) in Murrumbateman in 1973. Helm was the driving force for establishing riesling as one of the premier grapes of Canberra District, as well as one of the region's greatest overall champions.

Indeed, 1973 was a banner year for plantings in the region. In addition to Ken Helm's plantings, Wing Commander Harvey Smith planted Doonkuna (now owned by Eden Road), Geoff and Trish Middleton planted Broughton Park (now known as Murrumbateman Wines), Captain Geoff Hood planted Westering Vineyard (now a part of Lake George Winery) and Dr Max Blake planted Shingle House (later known as Brooks Creek). All of these vineyards still produce fruit to this day.

The rest of the 1970s saw a steady trickle of new plantings, the most notable being Dr Dave and Sue Carpenter's Lark Hill, which was planted in 1978 at the southern tip of Lake George, in the township of Bungendore. The Carpenters harvested their first vintage in 1981 – tiny amounts of riesling and chardonnay. Lark Hill is one of Canberra's most important producers today, with notable milestones, such as being the first **biodynamic** winery in Canberra District and the first producer of grüner veltliner in all of Australia.

There were two additions in the 1980s that would prove to be of continued importance in Canberra District. The first was Dr Roger Harris, another **CSIRO** scientist, who planted his 3.2-hectare Brindabella Hill vineyard on the escarpment of the Murrumbidgee River, near the ACT border. Harris was a renowned biochemist and plant pathologist, and turned out to be 'an outstanding winemaker', according to Ken Helm, who also lauded Harris's work in researching suitable grape varieties and wine styles for the region.

The second important addition was Mount Majura, planted in 1988 with the help of Dr Edgar Riek. On the east-facing limestone slopes of Mt Majura, the original vineyard was

Southern New South Wales Viticultural Footprint

	CANBERRA DISTRICT	HILLTOPS	GUNDAGAI	TUMBARUMBA
Total delimited area (km²)	8610	3110	8850	2970
Total planted area (hectares)	329	595	591	214
% of delimited area planted	0.038%	0.190%	0.067%	0.072%
Total elevation range	264–1419 masl	249–716 masl	179–1168 masl	209–1290 masl
Elevation range of plantings	450–900 masl	380–600 masl	200–400 masl	300–843 masl
Number of producers	39	9	5	15

planted to pinot noir, chardonnay, cabernet franc and merlot. To this day, Mount Majura is one of the few vineyards within the ACT – as opposed to New South Wales, where most of Canberra District's vineyards lie.

So it was slow but consistent growth, fuelled by the dedication of a handful of individuals, that propelled Canberra through the 1970s, 1980s and 1990s. The way Ken Helm describes it, the beginning was maddeningly slow, due to the academic nature of the region's founders. 'We'd have meetings, and they'd say, well let's do a trial now on what sort of **trellising** we should use, then we'll do a trial on what grapes we should grow, let's do a trial on this and a bit of research on that ... And I'd say, "Let's just get on with it, grow some grapes and make some wine!".'

This resistance to action without copious investigation was not the only obstacle the academics of Canberra brought to the table; they were also poorly funded. Academics, compared to the lawyers and medical doctors that were piloting other regions across Australia, were not very well paid.

And though the energy was good in these early years – with plenty of wine show accolades and an atmosphere of collaboration – it was still a grind. As Helm says, 'The life of the Canberra small vigneron has been one of long hours and sleepless nights wondering how the bills might be paid – sustained by hope and a belief that the area can make top-notch wines.'

Meanwhile, throughout the rest of Southern New South Wales, interest began to blossom. Tumbarumba saw its first plantings in 1981 by two couples: Ian Cowell and Juliet Cullen, and Frank and Christine Minutello. They targeted cool-climate Tumbarumba as an inexpensive source for sparkling wines. The region soon attracted big corporates like Southcorp, Thomas Hardy & Sons and, later, McWilliam's – the most notable qualitative example being Penfolds' Yattarna (owned by Southcorp at the time), a premium cool-climate chardonnay that has regularly relied on Tumbarumba fruit since 1996.

In Gundagai, just north of Tumbarumba, viticulture didn't gain traction until the mid-1990s, when the sprawling, historic Borambola homestead tried its hand at wine. Southcorp

planted the large and significant Tumblong vineyard (Tumblong Hills today) in the late 90s as well. And plantings in Hilltops grew significantly in this era, with national group McWilliam's buying Robertson's Barwang property in 1988.

Through the late 1990s, though, Canberra District stayed on its trajectory, with no large-scale vineyards or mass production. Compared to the neighbouring regions of Cowra (in the Central Ranges zone) and Hilltops, quantities were diminutive. Small production would have been fine if the prices fetched could buffer them, but Canberra District was still not nationally recognised as a fine wine region and most of Canberra's wine was consumed within its borders. As local wine writer Chris Shanahan put it, the wine industry of Canberra in the mid-90s was 'fragile ... struggling for capital and almost totally reliant on the sheer hard graft of individuals and families devoting their lives and total wealth to a dream'.

But by 2000, Canberra had attracted corporate investment. The ACT government's Chief Minister at the time, Kate Carnell, along with Canberra wine merchant Jim Murphy (and support from Ken Helm), persuaded BRL Hardy Limited to make a $10 million investment in Canberra, creating the Kamberra winery. Along with the Kamberra brand came the Lyneham winemaking facility, capable of a 2200-tonne annual grape crush, and BRL Hardy's 83-hectare vineyard at Holt, 20 kilometres northwest of Canberra. BRL Hardy also identified about 300 hectares of excellent vineyard sites across Canberra District and contracted private growers to work them.

By 2006, though, BRL Hardy had pulled out of the region, leaving a glut of facilities and grapes. Though it was short-lived and, by many standards, a failure, the virtues of BRL Hardy's involvement are numerous. When the company came to Canberra District, there were less than 100 hectares planted across the region, and that number swelled to nearly 500 by the time they pulled out. Helm recounts, 'they brought professional winemakers to the district, they brought professional viticulturists to the district and they identified perfect sites in which to grow grapes. The two best things for the Canberra

Southern New South Wales

75

Lake Jindabyne has grown significantly from its original size. It is the site of one of 16 dams that make up the Snowy Mountains Scheme, generating hydropower for over 65 years.

wine industry were when Hardys came and when they left.' BRL Hardy turned the environs of Canberra from a hobby district into a serious winemaking appellation.

Before BRL Hardy, there also wasn't much of an identity across the region. With diverse soil types and disparate elevations, the region was capable of producing solid examples of riesling, chardonnay, pinot noir, cabernet sauvignon, shiraz and viognier – a great feat, no doubt, but not helpful for attracting the kind of brand recognition enjoyed by regions like the Hunter Valley and Coonawarra, who had found their signature grapes. BRL Hardy's 'relentless benchmarking', as Shanahan coined it, led to three grapes being identified as the region's calling cards: shiraz, viognier and riesling. These three – especially shiraz and riesling – would go on to help cement Canberra District's national reputation, creating more clear external branding and internal vision.

The BRL Hardy lineage also fostered winemakers and investors who would prove to be influential in the development of Canberra District. Alex McKay, the winemaker for Kamberra, was recognised for producing excellent wines in his time there. After Kamberra crumbled, McKay released his first solo wines from the 2005 vintage – naming his winery Collector, one of the most quality-minded and highly regarded wineries in Canberra District today.

BRL Hardy's facilities and vineyards were sold to local investment group Elvin in 2007. Cooper Coffman, a collaboration between winemaker Martin Cooper and investment banker Chris Coffman, entered into a long-term lease agreement with Elvin in 2008. Cooper Coffman continued to act as a contract winemaking facility, bringing on Nick Spencer as its winemaker, as well as developing its own label, Eden Road.

Eden Road, based in Murrumbateman and also made by Nick Spencer, quickly became noteworthy in Southern New South Wales, with their 2008 Hilltops Shiraz winning a **Jimmy Watson Memorial Trophy**. The legacy of BRL Hardy continues to evolve, with Nick Spencer founding his eponymous winery in Gundagai and Eden Road growing in importance in the

Canberra District under the guidance of Celine Rousseau, who became the winery's winemaker and general manager in 2017.

The 'Hardy years' – which coincided with great financial hardship around Australia and world – was the galvanising era for Canberra District. The region was finally getting the national (and international) attention it deserved. Its flagship wine, Clonakilla's Shiraz Viognier – which saw its first vintage in 1992 – was recognised on the **Langton's Classification** in 2005, hitting the top 'Exceptional' status in 2010.

The doyens of the region – including Clonakilla, Helm, Lark Hill and Mount Majura – were as strong as ever, with invigoration from newly formed wineries like Gallagher Wines (1995), Long Rail Gully (1998), Shaw Vineyard (1999), Ravensworth (2001), Collector Wines (2005), McKellar Ridge (2005), Nick O'Leary (2007) and Eden Road (2008). By the end of the decade, the fragility of the 1990s had all but vanished, replaced by a regional identity that was not only strong, but had built its strength on the backs of independent wineries and vineyards rather than corporate branding – a feat just a few premium Australian wine regions have managed.

The late 2010s saw another resurgence for Canberra District, with young winemakers building labels that embody the classic cool-climate trappings of the region, but that also push the boundaries stylistically. These wineries – like Mallaluka (2014), The Vintner's Daughter (2014), Sholto (2016), Mada (2016) and Linear (2018) – may make classic regional expressions of shiraz and riesling, but they have also experimented with alternative grapes (vermentino, gamay and aligoté, among others), **pét-nat** sparkling methods and ceramic egg fermentation.

Canberra District's development has been a slow burn over the last 50 years, but the result is an oasis of a wine region: one replete with quality-minded independent growers and wineries, a collaborative energy invigorating all four regions in the Southern New South Wales zone, and a premiumisation that is only continuing upward.

Looking northeast from the Mount Majura vineyard, about 650 metres above sea level, towards the peaks of the Great Dividing Range.

Lay of the Land

All four regions within the Southern New South Wales zone encircle and traverse the foothills of the Snowy Mountains (nicknamed 'the Snowies') – monuments of volcanic activity sitting atop granite and basalt bedrocks. The soils are largely of moderate to low fertility, and neutral to slightly acidic. Soils drain well, yet still retain moisture at depth.

The specific constitution of soils and sediments varies across regions, largely defined by their proximity to mountains. The closer a site is to either the Snowies or their northern offshoot, the Brindabellas, the more granite and basalt rock with thinner top soils.

When sites are closer to rivers and lakes, more eroded sediments mixed with sands and clays are found. These changes also correlate with changes in elevation and climate, creating unique **microclimates**. Upslope is alpine-like and cooler in climate, with resulting wines of delicacy and acid. Downslope has warmer daytime temperatures, generally creating riper fruit and bigger wines.

In Canberra District, this variety of **microclimates** allows for two rather disparate signature grapes: riesling and shiraz. (Historically, shiraz and cabernet sauvignon have been the breadwinners, but many cabernet sauvignon vines have been removed or grafted to more suited varieties, according to Collector Wines' Alex McKay.) However, all types of grapes are seen throughout the region, including riesling, chardonnay, pinot noir, grüner veltliner, tempranillo, shiraz, grenache and sangiovese.

Canberra District is a continental climate, only magnified as altitude increases within the region. Canberra District has the largest **diurnal swing** of the four GIs, with warm days and chilly nights helping wines find a balance of concentration and freshness.

Canberra District can be thought about in four distinct subregions, or clusters of plantings. The first is the ACT, and only one vineyard of significance is within this territory – Mount Majura. With plantings ranging from 660 to 700 metres above sea level, these are some of the southernmost plantings in the Canberra District. They are defined by the Ainslie volcanics that form Mt Majura itself, and by underlying limestone deposits.

The second cluster of plantings is centred between the town of Hall and the upper Murrumbidgee River. While it has not achieved the name-recognition of some other pockets of the district, notable wineries like Nick O'Leary, Brindabella Wines and Pankhurst are based here.

Southern New South Wales

HOW TO READ THIS MAP

This map includes the four unique regions of the Southern New South Wales zone, strewn across the Australian Alps. Elevation is the region's greatest influencer and is on display here.

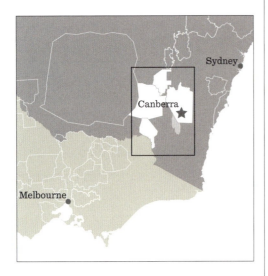

1	Allawah Park Vineyard
2	Allegiance Wines
3	Ballinaclash
4	Billinudgel
5	Borambola
6	Brindabella Hills
7	Clonakilla
8	Collector Wines
9	Coppabella of Tumbarumba
10	Courabyra
11	Cullarin Vineyard
12	The Echoes Vineyard
13	Eden Road
14	Excelsior Peak
15	Freeman Vineyards
16	Grove Estate
17	Gundog Estate
18	Helm Wines
19	Johansen Wines
20	Lake George Winery
21	Lark Hill
22	Lerida Estate
23	Locke Family Vineyards
24	Lockwood Vineyard
25	Maipenrai
26	Mallaluka Wines
27	McKellar Ridge
28	McWilliam's Barwang Vineyard
29	Moppity Vineyards
30	Mount Majura
31	Mount Tumbarumba
32	Nick O'Leary Wines
33	Nick Spencer Wines
34	Obsession Wines
35	Paterson's
36	Ravensworth
37	Shaw
38	Sholto Wines
39	Tooma Vineyard
40	Trandari
41	Tumblong Hills
42	The Vintner's Daughter
43	Wallaroo
44	Westering Vineyard
45	Wondalma Vineyard
46	Yarramundi Vineyard
47	Yarrh

Canberra District Climate Data (°C)

	1960–1990	1991–PRESENT	2020
Heat summation/GDD	● 1481	● 1553	● 1748
Annual rain/GSR	721/416	695/404	545/352
Warmest month avg. temp.	20.3	21.3	23.2

Hilltops Climate Data (°C)

	1960–1990	1991–PRESENT	2020
Heat summation/GDD	● 1880	● 1921	● 2083
Annual rain/GSR	639/355	621/350	518/331
Warmest month avg. temp.	22.6	23.5	25.4

Tumbarumba Climate Data (°C)

	1960–1990	1991–PRESENT	2020
Heat summation/GDD	● 1419	● 1601	● 1718
Annual rain/GSR	920/449	881/451	732/400
Warmest month avg. temp.	20.1	21.8	24

Gundagai Climate Data (°C)

	1960–1990	1991–PRESENT	2020
Heat summation/GDD	● 1911	● 1979	● 2110
Annual rain/GSR	704/365	675/366	524/318
Warmest month avg. temp.	22.7	23.8	24

Winkler Scale:

● 850–1111   ● 1112–1389   ● 1390–1667   ● 1668–1944   ● 1945–2222   ● 2223–2700

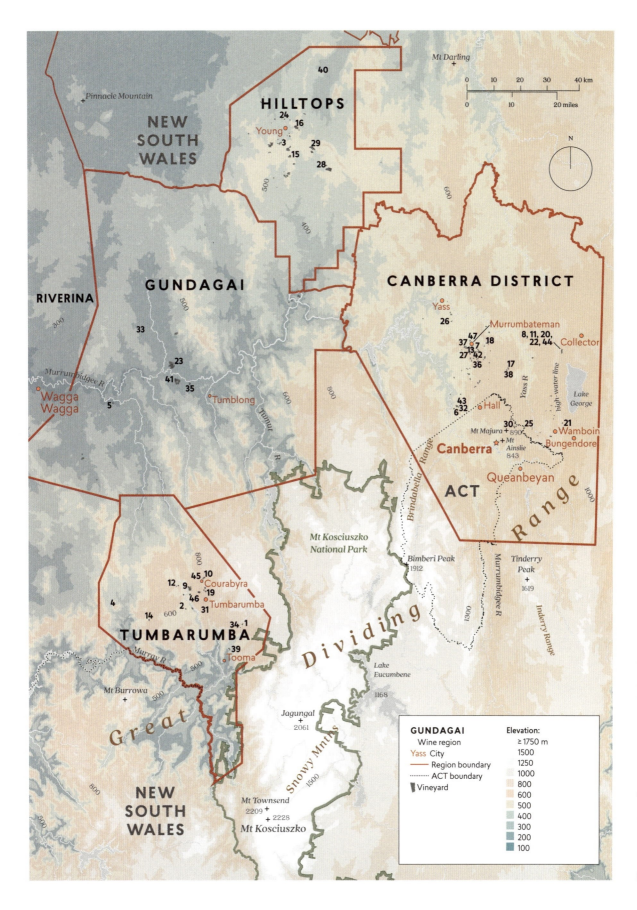

Southern New South Wales

The third cluster is defined by the towns of Yass and Murrumbateman, the latter giving its name to the informal subregion. Murrumbateman is perhaps the best-known area for premium wine, thanks to Clonakilla, but also Helm, Eden Road, Shaw and Ravensworth. Murrumbateman was one of the earlier municipalities to be designated on a label as an unofficial subregion.

The soils in Murrumbateman are 'the draw card of the area', according to Ravensworth's Bryan Martin. 'It's this very friable clay,' he continues. 'It's bright, it's really red clay, it's oxidised, and very fully draining but it absorbs water really well.' In particular, he points to a soil type that has been identified as *parna*, which came about as a result of 'intermittent high wind events during the **Quaternary**', according to the **CSIRO**. 'It's what the best wines, shiraz mainly, are planted on,' says Martin. 'In theory what drew the First Nations people into this cold climate was the quality of the land and the fauna and insect life that would have been thriving, still does. Likewise, the first colonists would have been drawn to this land for its rich, bountiful soil.'

With Murrumbateman's desirable soils, rolling hills, and mild weather, it is one of the more versatile areas in the Canberra District, producing successful examples of everything from riesling (Helm's calling card) to the shiraz-viognier combo made so famous by Clonakilla.

The fourth subregion in Canberra District surrounds Lake George. There are vineyards on three sides of Lake George – the eastern shore,

at over 900 metres above sea level, has yet to be planted (though, according to Ken Helm, the soil and climate would be suitable). Lake George Winery and the original Riek plantings sit off the very northern tip of the Lake. The township of Collector lies further north; it's the home base for Alex McKay's Collector Wines, which sources fruit from across Southern New South Wales. But despite housing the original Canberra District plantings, vineyards north of Lake George are relatively scarce today.

South and southwest of Lake George lie Bungendore and Wamboin, respectively, both climbing to around 850 metres in elevation. Bungendore, directly south of Lake George, is the coldest climate of the Canberra District vineyards. Historic Lark Hill vineyard was planted here in 1978 at 860 metres above sea level and has attracted other quality-minded producers to the region.

The climate in Bungendore, as well as in the vineyards of Wamboin to the west, approaches alpine characteristics, and is suitable for nuanced and delicate expressions of sparkling wine, riesling and grüner veltliner, as well as lighter-bodied pinot noir and chardonnay.

Outside Canberra District, the other three regions of Southern New South Wales have their own distinct landscapes. Gundagai (east of Canberra) traverses the lowest altitude levels in the zone and is the warmest region (Region 4 on the **Winkler Scale**). As a result, Gundagai can ripen grapes like nebbiolo and cabernet sauvignon that struggle in higher-altitude areas of the zone. It is the most commercially viable of the four regions, with the potential for higher yields and easy access to water from the Murrumbidgee River.

In the past, Gundagai's climate was misunderstood to be much cooler than it is, which has fed the perception that fine wine is not possible here. Of course, great pinot noir is not going to be produced in Gundagai, but neither will it be in the Barossa – that doesn't make either any less viable for fine wine. Early McWilliam's bottlings and current Nick Spencer bottlings have worked to prove this maxim.

Hilltops surrounds the town of Young – the unofficial cherry capital of Australia. As a wine region, it is uniform and compact, with vineyards

In the past, Gundagai's climate was misunderstood to be much cooler than it is, which has fed the perception that fine wine is not possible here.

largely situated at a moderate altitude level of 450 metres – higher than Gundagai, but lower than Yass in nearby Canberra District. It also sits between the two in terms of climate and average temperatures (on the margin of the **Winkler Scale's** Region 3 and Region 4).

Clonakilla put Hilltops on the map with their 'Hilltops' labelled shiraz, first made in 2000. 'We routinely pick Hilltops shiraz two to three weeks earlier than our own [Canberra District] shiraz,' says Clonakilla's Tim Kirk. 'It's on quite deep soils and has a darker set of flavours,' continues Kirk. Hilltops continues to be known for high-quality shiraz and cabernet sauvignon, and some excellent expressions of Italian grapes.

If Southern New South Wales is the Snowy Mountains zone, Tumbarumba is the snowiest. It is New South Wales' coolest region, with about 20% more rain during the year than its neighbours. Sparkling wines are thus a focus of Tumbarumba. Pinot noir and pinot meunier top the red plantings. Chardonnay is the most prominent white grape by far, with pinot gris, sauvignon blanc, a dash of riesling and a growing amount of 'prosecco' (p. 240).

Tumbarumba is no higher than the most elevated parts of Canberra District, with vineyards topping out at 800 metres above sea level. However, several vineyard areas are in the direct path of cold air from the southwest. Even the southernmost plantings near Tooma on Maragle Creek, at a relatively low 400 metres in elevation, maintain their chilliness due to cold air moving down from adjacent peaks.

The collective vineyard area in and among the foothills of the Snowies is one of the most diverse concentrations of **microclimates** within any Australian GI zone. These vineyards are further north, and therefore closer to the equator, than one might think. Tumbarumba (35.46°S) shares an identical latitude to Tangiers (35.46°N), but with about half of the **Heat Summation Index**. The sunshine is abundant, heat is both easily found and avoided, and the elevation dynamics allow for near-infinite wine expressions. As far as the land goes, the Snowy Mountains zone (as we'll continue to call it) has just about everything going for it.

Hubbub

This chapter includes the entire Southern New South Wales zone (and not just one GI region) for a reason: many producers based in one appellation of the zone (usually Canberra District) source or grow grapes, and make wine, from others. This is relatively uncommon throughout Australia – producers based in the Mornington Peninsula do not typically also make wine from Macedon Ranges.

Ravensworth's Bryan Martin articulates the spirit of Southern New South Wales simply: 'We see the whole area, the greater area, as linked.' Clonakilla, in Canberra District, still produces their Hilltops shiraz, which has garnered a great cult following. Nick Spencer produces wines made from Gundagai, Hilltops and Tumbarumba. Eden Road, in addition to their Canberra District wines, makes Tumbarumba chardonnay and pinot noir, as well as Gundagai sangiovese. The list goes on, with Collector, Nick O'Leary, Helm and Ravensworth also making wines from outside their home base in Canberra District. And the most telling part is that they're all labelled by their individual region, not relying on the strength of the Canberra name, nor defaulting to a general zone delineation.

But brand recognition is still weak for the regions other than Canberra District, according to Nick Spencer. 'What we don't have in these regions,' he says, 'particularly Gundagai, but Tumbarumba as well, and Hilltops to a lesser extent, is brands and winemakers'. And this is true: many of the well-known bottlings from these appellations, with the exception of Nick Spencer's, are made by wineries based in Canberra District or outside the zone altogether, from the likes of Hungerford Hill, Penfolds, De Bortoli and McWilliam's.

Historically, there have been few wineries within these regions who are pushing regional brand and identity, but that is beginning to change. Wineries like Freeman, Tumblong Hills, Courabyra, Johansen, Coppabella and Ballinaclash 'are developing strong voices from within their region', says Collector Wines' Alex

McKay. These appellations will be ones to watch for growth and development in the years to come.

Growth, though, as in Central Ranges, is hindered by the high cost of land and lack of access to water. Gundagai is the least affected by these constraints, and Canberra District the most, but land continues to get more expensive and water more scarce across the zone as a whole. McKay reports, 'Land prices are very, very high … the economics of growing grapes in this area aren't great because of the low yields and the scarcity of water … so it's not easy to attract new investment in growing grapes.'

Ken Helm concurs, citing the lack of water as the primary impediment to establishing and maintaining grapes. 'Best thing that could happen is another Hardys would come, stay for seven years and leave again. It would be good for the district, expand it … and they'll source the water.' Research has been done into how to solve the district's water problems. The main focus is a pipeline that brings the city of Canberra's grey water 30 kilometres north to Murrumbateman. Projected costs for a project like this top AUD $15 million, so having a corporation interested in managing its funding would be ideal.

Water shortages are of course related to climate change, which is prompting discussions about everything from fluctuations in temperature (and corresponding greater frost risk) to the orientation of vines, and grape suitability across the region. Canberra District doesn't seem poised to pivot from its stalwarts of shiraz or riesling, but it is also experimenting with heat-hardy grapes like cinsault, grenache, mourvèdre, marsanne, roussanne and tempranillo.

It's in the warmer regions of Southern New South Wales where varietal identity has not been as strong as it has for Canberra District, where vintners have found the freedom to experiment with alternative grapes on a larger scale. Hilltops is garnering attention for grapes as varied as barbera, zinfandel and montepulciano, while Gundagai is turning toward grapes like fiano, vermentino and grenache. It's an occasion not only to adapt to climate change, but also to build up regional identity and branding: 'There's a good opportunity to react to that warming by

putting in the right varieties,' says Nick Spencer, 'and bringing the consumer along for that ride as well.'

Climate change has also provoked bushfires in the zone – as with the Central Ranges, the most destructive in recent history being those of the 2019–2020 summer. Hilltops fared the best, only down about 30% on the year from smoke taint. There was no 2020 vintage for Tumbarumba – valued at more than an AUD $9 million loss. Of the 19 vineyards in Tumbarumba, five had direct fire damage, two were completely demolished and every single one was smoke-taint affected. Canberra District also didn't report much of a harvest, and what was picked went to basic rosés and whites that would have undergone a considerable amount of filtering. Bryan Martin at Ravensworth collaborated with Sydney brewery Wildflower to make beers from his smoke-tainted grapes and didn't release a single wine from the vintage. Gundagai's intake reports were a mere 10% of what was reported in 2019.

The region needs great thinking and – to Ken Helm's earlier point – great action if they are to combat the threats of rising land prices, water shortages, frosts, bushfires and climate change. But if anyone is up to the challenge, it's the minds of Canberra District and its environs.

Canberra District's academic origins, though part of its slow start, will hopefully engender a long lifespan. 'I think the region is still growing up,' says Tim Kirk. 'We're 50 years old, but that's still, in the scheme of things, youngish as wine regions go. But the quality of our wines is speaking for itself.' The Canberra District, and the larger Southern New South Wales zone, has already overcome great adversity to assert itself on the fine-wine stage, and the vintners of today are ever-motivated to continue that legacy.

A vineyard pest looking for grapes to eat in Canberra District.

PRODUCERS

CANBERRA DISTRICT

CLONAKILLA

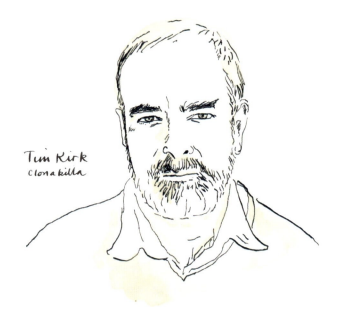

Tim Kirk
Clonakilla

Irish-born John Kirk immigrated to Australia from the UK in 1968 to work as a research scientist, going on to plant the first vines in Murrumbateman in 1971. In 1976, John produced the first commercial wines from the region; a riesling-sauvignon blanc and a cabernet-shiraz. In the 1990s John's son Tim pioneered the shiraz-viognier blend in Australia, after spending time in the Rhône Valley and being inspired by the single-vineyard wines crafted by Guigal in Côte Rôtie. Tim studied theology in school, but was drawn back to the family business, and considers himself a custodian of the noble site. Aside from their flagship Shiraz Viognier, Clonakilla's repertoire, with Tim at the helm, has expanded into a variety of other styles: a shiraz from the Hilltops region, a vibrant **nouveau** style of viognier, a razor-sharp riesling and a variety of small-batch releases including grapes such as counoise, roussanne and cabernet franc.
clonakilla.com.au

COLLECTOR WINES

Beginning a career working alongside one of the pioneers of the Canberra District is an enviable start. Alex McKay landed his first winemaking job at Lake George with Edgar Riek, but later moved on to BRL Hardy's state-of-the-art Kamberra. It was here that Alex developed the intricate knowledge of soil and vineyard that has served him well in launching Collector. His riesling is picked in Tumbarumba, fiano is from Hilltops, and there is shiraz from both Canberra District and the Pyrenees (the latter in Victoria): a collection of the best sites from Southern New South Wales (and beyond). Alex's time 'collecting' vineyard sites led

---

 What we're drinking

Clonakilla's O'Riada (pronounced o-reeda) Shiraz might be one of the greatest values in Australian wine. It's made from about 50% 'declassified' fruit from their deservedly iconic Shiraz Viognier bottling each year, as well as a few other select sites across Canberra District. It uniquely displays the Canberra style at an accessible price point: floral, lifted, gauzy, aromatic and long ... it's a brilliant wine. – **Jane Lopes**

him to a kinship with the sculptor Rosalie Gascoigne, whose evocative pieces upcycle objects found in the towns surrounding Canberra. The Collector labels pay reference to her work. *collectorwines.com.au*

EDEN ROAD

Eden Road was established in the Eden Valley (South Australia), but moved to Canberra in 2008 in the aftermath of BRL Hardy's departure. Their inaugural release, the 2008 Long Road Shiraz, made by winemakers Martin Cooper and Nick Spencer, won one of Australia's most coveted wine awards, the **Jimmy Watson Memorial Trophy**. A decade later, French-born Celine Rousseau took over winemaking and, alongside viticulturist Thomas Lefebvre, has worked to organically manage the vineyards, achieving certification in 2020. Eden Road celebrated the 50th anniversary of the Cullarin vineyard in 2021 – the original vineyard planted by Edgar Riek on Lake George in 1971. They also own the Doonkuna vineyard in Murrumbateman, where the winery is now based, and buy pinot noir and chardonnay from growers in Tumbarumba. *edenroadwines.com.au*

HELM WINES

Ken Helm grew up on vineyards near Albury and Rutherglen, established by his German viticulturist ancestors in the 1850s. He established Helm Wines in Murrumbateman with his wife Judith in 1973, and the pair began selling wine in 1980. Coming from an academic background – like a number of his fellow Canberra District pioneers, Ken also worked for the **CSIRO** – Ken became one of the driving forces in the region's commercial success. Their focus is the production of cabernet sauvignon and riesling – the latter of which, in no small part thanks to Helm, has become a signature grape of the region. Helm produces four different styles of riesling, and the estate lays claim to the oldest riesling vines in Canberra District. In 2000, Ken established the Canberra International Riesling Challenge, a competition for producers of the variety from across the world. *helmwines.com.au*

Ken Helm
Helm Wines

LAKE GEORGE WINERY

On the northwestern shores of Lake George, Dr Edgar Riek planted some of the first vines in the Canberra District. While working on a project studying potato moths, Riek would drive from Canberra to Crookwell and noticed a particularly green patch of land, where it was warm enough to thaw his windscreen. In 1971, Riek planted a vineyard there, which he

---

JR | **What we're drinking**

At **Lark Hill**, the Carpenter family's drive to farm **biodynamically** on the cold, high-altitude margins of Canberra District serves us all well. Their **traditional method** sparkling wine is certainly one of Australia's most compelling contributions to the category. Bracing and pure, like the snowy alpine hills it's born from. – *Jonathan Ross*

named Cullarin – after the nearby Cullarin Ranges. He experimented with variety and style, trying everything from age-worthy sweet semillon to cabernet blends to pinots and chardonnays. In 1998, Riek sold the estate and Lake George went through a series of different incarnations, with talents like Alex McKay (Collector) and Nick O'Leary serving as winemakers throughout its modern history. Today, Lake George is home to a restaurant, accommodation and event venue, and the harvest of the Cullarin vineyard has become part of Eden Road's production. lakegeorgewinery.com.au

Bryan Martin
Ravensworth

LARK HILL

On a chilly hillside in 1978, Sue and Dave Carpenter planted the Lark Hill vineyard, at one of the highest elevations (860 metres) in the region. Tiny amounts of riesling and chardonnay were produced for their first vintage in 1981. The couple's son, Chris, who completed wine science and viticulture degrees, joined the team in 2002, and the following year Lark Hill began the transition to **biodynamic** certification. **Traditional method** sparkling wine has long been a part of their offering, and in 2005 they planted Australia's first grüner veltliner. Due to the exceedingly cool nature of their vineyard, the Carpenters set out to find a site suitable to also grow a wide variety of reds. They found it in Murrumbateman in 2011; the now-named Dark Horse Vineyard comprises shiraz, sangiovese, teroldego, garganega, viognier, marsanne and roussanne.
larkhill.wine

MOUNT MAJURA

Mount Majura is just outside the city of Canberra at the top of the Majura Valley. Canberra District pioneer Edgar Riek saw the deposits of limestone and volcanic rock there as a call to plant grapes, and in 1988, with then owner Dinny Killen, planted a hectare of pinot noir, chardonnay and a field blend of cabernet franc and merlot. Winemaking duties moved from Dr Riek to a series of contract makers before Frank van de Loo took over managing all aspects of the estate. The turn of the century also brought new ownership, and an expansion of the original single hectare to today's 9.3 hectares. Tempranillo has since become the most planted variety, with dedicated wines made from each of the three tempranillo blocks. Mount Majura has also focused its attention on some lesser-known Iberian and alpine varieties, such as graciano, touriga nacional and mondeuse, rounding out their unique and iconic offerings.
mountmajura.com.au

NICK O'LEARY WINES

Nick O'Leary has done a bit of everything in the wine industry. Hailing from the Adelaide Hills, Nick has worked in bottle shops, spent time with his uncle David O'Leary (O'Leary Walker) in the Clare Valley, and at BRL Hardy's Kamberra winery under Alex McKay (Collector). Like Alex, Nick gleaned an excellent knowledge of growers and vineyards from his time at BRL Hardy. When Kamberra was sold in 2006, he was in good stead to start up on his own. His early wines were highly decorated; his shiraz won the New South Wales Wine of the Year in 2013 and 2014 – the only winery to win in consecutive years. His wines continue to attract attention and

favour, largely based around the production of riesling, chardonnay, shiraz, tempranillo and sangiovese.
nickolearywines.com.au

RAVENSWORTH

While studying viticulture and wine science, Bryan Martin and his wife Jocelyn bought a plot of land in Murrumbateman and started planting vines in 2000, which are now certified organic. Sourcing viognier cuttings for the vineyard, Bryan met Tim Kirk, who brought him on as assistant winemaker at Clonakilla in 2004 (*Gourmet Traveller Wine* called Bryan 'Clonakilla's secret weapon'). Perhaps thanks to a richly patchworked career as a cook, food writer and forager, Bryan's approach to winemaking steers firmly towards experimental, but with an uncompromising commitment to expressing the land. This has seen amphorae, flor-ageing and extended skin-contact all grace the winery floor, alongside some traditional bottlings of the region's stalwart riesling and shiraz. When Bryan devoted his smoke-tainted harvest to beer production in 2020, he raised about $10,000 for Firesticks (an Indigenous cultural burning organisation). As Bryan says, 'The more we talk, acknowledge and celebrate this ancient land and its original custodians, the closer we will get to making amends for all the shit that is still continuing today.'
ravensworthwines.com.au

TUMBARUMBA

COPPABELLA OF TUMBARUMBA

Bitter winters and fierce frosts almost forced the owners of this vineyard to pull out its vines – until Jason and Alecia Brown stepped in. Enamoured by the high altitude and established vines, they renamed the site Coppabella and set about grafting over with pinot noir and chardonnay. The duo produce award-winning sparkling and still wines from these grapes, and are at the forefront of Tumbarumba winemaking. The couple also own vineyards in Hilltops and Canberra District.
coppabella.com.au

HILLTOPS

FREEMAN VINEYARDS

Dr Brian Freeman would have trained many of the winemakers and viticulturists mentioned in this book during his tenure heading up wine science at Charles Sturt University. In 1999, he put his teachings into practice and established a vineyard in Hilltops. His vineyards are diverse, planted mostly to Italian grapes, including the original rondinella and corvina vines in Australia. His Secco pays tribute to the Amarone- and Ripasso-style wines of Valpolicella in Italy. Brian's daughter Xanthe has followed in his footsteps and now works with him at the winery. They are now producing more experimental styles of wine, including excellent **pét-nats**, orange wines and fruit-wine hybrids. In addition to their own wines, Freeman is also a significant source of grapes for others in the industry, and has in particular become a huge resource for avant-garde wine producers throughout Australia.
freemanvineyards.com.au

MOPPITY VINEYARDS

Initially planted in 1973, Jason and Alecia Brown (of Coppabella) bought Moppity Vineyards in 2004. They started as an important supplier to local wineries – there was Moppity fruit in Eden Road's **Jimmy Watson**-winning shiraz in 2008 – but have since moved to producing wine for their own label. They now own vineyards in what Jason believes is the 'holy trinity' of Southern New South Wales winemaking: Canberra District, Tumbarumba and Hilltops. Apart from their award-winning shiraz fruit, Moppity has feet firmly planted in both the traditional and emerging grape variety camps.
moppity.com.au

Southern New South Wales

GUNDAGAI

NICK SPENCER WINES

Nick Spencer spent the beginning of his career working for notable wineries around Australia before landing at Eden Road Wines, where he took home a **Jimmy Watson** trophy for his 2008 Shiraz. After a decade leading the team and travelling extensively across the world, Nick launched his own label, the product of his passion for the New South Wales high country. Perhaps the most notable recent influence on his style would be his use of amphora – a technique used for millennia in Georgia – implemented after spending 2014 in Kakheti making wine. He has made minuscule quantities of chardonnay, pinot noir and gamay; each aged in ceramic amphorae, with fruit coming from nearby Tumbarumba and Orange in the Central Ranges. Spencer has engaged a new generation in Gundagai, planting his own vineyard there and bringing greater attention to all the regions of Southern New South Wales.
nickspencerwines.com.au

TUMBLONG HILLS

Simon Robertson, a second-generation Southern New South Wales vigneron, heads up the Tumblong Hills team. The vineyard was originally planted by Southcorp (now Treasury Wine Estates) in the 1990s, but bought by three colleagues in 2009, who instated Robertson at the helm. Shiraz and cabernet sauvignon are the oldest vines on site, with newer plantings of nebbiolo, barbera, sangiovese, nero d'Avola and grenache.
tumblonghills.com

And don't forget ...
Ballinaclash is everyone's favourite Hilltops winery and pick-your-own-fruit orchard, producing everything from award-winning cabernet sauvignon and shiraz to cherry and plum wine ... **Brindabella Hills** is known for Roger and Faye Harris's early commitment to finding the most suitable grapes for Canberra District and its current offerings of affordable and approachable wines ... **Courabyra** is one of Tumbarumba's premier hospitality sites and makes ambitious sparkling wine, chardonnay, pinot noir, sauvignon blanc, pinot gris and shiraz to match ... **Johansen Wines** combines classic styles and more eccentric drops (the latter made by Ravensworth's Bryan Martin) in a quaint Tumbarumba setting, replete with cottage accommodation ... **Linear Wines**, a new label from Nathan Brown, is a testament to the excellent alternative varieties grown in Southern New South Wales, including fiano, gewürztraminer, sangiovese and tempranillo ... **Mada Wines**, Hamish Young's own project after working a decade at Eden Road, with eye-catching labels foreshadowing energetic wines made from fruit sourced across Southern New South Wales, including chardonnay, gewürztraminer, nebbiolo, pinot gris, riesling and syrah ... **Maipenrai**, planted by astronomers Brian Schmidt and Jennifer Gordon (Brian won the Nobel Prize in Physics in 2011, no big deal) at 760 metres in Canberra District, is turning out exceptional pinot noir ... **Mallaluka Wines**, from Clonakilla alumnus Sam Leyshon, who took over his family's vineyard in the Yass Valley to establish his own label, makes an exciting array of styles and grapes ... **Sholto Wines** was launched by Jacob Carter in 2016, with the aim of pushing the boundaries of traditional varieties in Canberra District ... **The Vintner's Daughter**, named after winemaker Stephanie Helm (daughter of Ken Helm), who bought land with husband and viticulturist Ben Osborne in Murrumbateman in 2014, has a focus on riesling (like her dad), as well as co-fermented shiraz-viognier, **fortified** shiraz and rosé.

> **What we're drinking**
>
> *If you're going to drink grüner veltliner from anywhere in Australia, **Nick Spencer Wines** is the place. Nick's in particular is taut and racy with a sprinkle of celery salt. I'm looking forward to seeing more of this variety from southern New South Wales.* — **Kavita Faiella**

Collector Wines in the northeastern reaches of Canberra District, set against the western slopes of the Great Dividing Range.

Other Regions of New South Wales

While most of New South Wales' notable fine wine regions are within the Hunter Valley, Central Ranges and Southern New South Wales zones, other regions in the state are notable for other reasons (large-scale production, tourism and high-elevation viticulture among them), and several are making a run towards more renown for the quality of their wines.

There are only two wine regions north of the Hunter Valley in New South Wales (and besides the two appellations of Queensland, the northernmost in all of Australia): Hastings River, on Biripi and Dainggati Country; and New England Australia, on the traditional lands of the Ngarabal, Bundjalung and Nganyaywana people.

Situated among the slopes of the Great Dividing Range, with its northern border touching Queensland, is New England Australia, the only region in the Northern Slopes zone. Though it is often considered an emerging wine region, with only 77 hectares under vine, it has an illustrious past.

George Wyndham (of Hunter Valley fame) formed a sizable estate here in the 1850s (though only about 4 hectares were under vine). By the end of the century the region was winning awards and international renown for its wines. Like most other Australian wine regions with early histories, though, its industry crumbled by the early 20th century due to economic recession and changing wine tastes, and it has yet to see the revival many others have enjoyed.

The climate is continental here, with elevations of 400–1300 metres above sea level. At 1306 metres above sea level, New England Australia has Australia's highest vineyard site (and highest agricultural site, in fact). The site is called Black Mountain vineyard and has been most notably produced by young vintner Jared Dixon, of Jilly Wine Co, who is single-handedly doing much to revitalise interest in New England Australia (alongside the monumental contributions of Topper's Mountain).

From cool, high-elevation sites along the spine of the Great Dividing Range, the region extends out west along the plateaus of the New England Tableland, where warmer climate viticulture is possible. Though modern exploration has been limited, many are watching this region in anticipation of good things to come.

Hastings River, also a solo region in its zone (called Northern Rivers), is south of New England Australia but north of Hunter Valley. Nestled along the coast, it is vulnerable to the same inclement climate pressures as the Hunter, without many of the latter's mitigating graces. Only 13 hectares of vines are planted in Hastings River, with mainly soft, ripe reds (including mildew-resistant hybrids such as chambourcin, p. 245) and acid-driven whites produced, picked early to avoid fungal problems and served with local seafood.

New South Wales has two other coastal wine regions. About 120 kilometres south of Sydney begins the Shoalhaven Coast GI, Yuin Country, just south of Wollongong along the water. Shoalhaven

Coast, though cooler, has some of the same moisture issues that plague Hastings River. Only 41 hectares are under vine here, and the dominant grape is chambourcin, chosen – much like Hastings River – for its ability to resist mildew. Semillon has also made a name for itself in the region, most notably from historic Coolangatta Estate, whose wines were vinified at Tyrrell's in the Hunter Valley for years.

Southern Highlands, the other remaining coastal GI, is on the traditional lands of the Gundungurra and Tharawal. It sits at a higher elevation, just west of Wollongong, with most vineyards between 500 and 700 metres above sea level. Humidity and moisture are still present, but less pernicious than in Shoalhaven Coast, and hybrid grapes are not employed. Though there are a couple of notable producers making solid wines in the region, its 140 hectares under vine has served more to satiate local tourism appetite than garner national or international attention for the quality of its wines. Pinot noir is a grape to watch, though, with quality improving significantly in recent years.

Besides Western Plains, which occupies the arid northwestern corner of New South Wales (and has zero viticultural significance besides bulk wine for distillation), the final zone in New South Wales is Big Rivers, which covers the entire southwestern quadrant of the state. The titular 'big rivers' are the Murray River – which marks the dividing line between New South Wales and Victoria below it, running all the way to its outlet at Lake Alexandrina in South Australia – and its tributaries Darling, Murrumbidgee and Lachlan. The Big Rivers zone can be generalised as hot, arid, heavily irrigated and mostly used for bulk-produced wines – but that's not the whole story.

The Big Rivers zone has four GI regions within it. Perricoota is a tiny region, tucked in an alcove of the Murray River. Though it is cooler and higher than the other regions, little production of interest currently takes place here. To the west of Perricoota, also on the Murray River, are the Murray Darling and Swan Hill regions. Both straddle the Victorian border and are discussed in more detail in the Other Victoria chapter (p. 238).

The zone's most significant region, from a commercial perspective, is Riverina. On Wiradjuri land, Riverina is responsible for 15% of Australia's total grape production, with over 17,000 hectares under vine. (Though it is Australia's most productive wine region, by comparison, the plantings amount to only about half of those in France's Champagne.)

Riverina was first planted by J.J. McWilliam in 1913. Following World War I, the vine area

Third-generation Michael Calabria, of Calabria Family Wines, scoops up the productive loamy soils of their Riverina estate, first established in 1945.

An autumn sunset across the McWilliam's Riverina estate, where viticulture in the region began over 100 years ago.

Riverina and these large companies serve an important role in the Australian wine industry: they are responsible for creating and maintaining new wine drinkers.

expanded rapidly, encouraged by the subsidised settlement on farms of ex-servicemen, particularly in the newly developed Murrumbidgee Irrigation Area of New South Wales and along the Murray River. Masses of Italian immigrants settled in the region after World War II.

Though few are arguing for Riverina's place in the annals of Australian fine wine, there are virtues that can be sung. Riverina is dry, so the need for fungicides and pesticides is nil. And though it is an arid region, there's enough healthy moisture near the rivers to produce some excellent botrytis-affected sweet wines, such as De Bortoli's iconic Noble One.

Large producers – De Bortoli, McWilliam's, Calabria and Casella – comprise the backbone of Riverina's production. These wineries, all historic and family-owned, are often ignored by the boutique trade, but have contributed significantly to the Australian wine industry: championing wine regions that were underexposed, introducing new styles to the nation (hello – Noble One!) and bolstering wine consumption among the populace.

'If we get it wrong, they won't come back,' says Emma Norbiato, chief winemaker for Calabria (a family-owned Riverina winery established in 1945). 'When you start drinking wine, you don't go straight for the $50 bottle. You start at $5, and the better the quality that $5 bottle of wine, the more likely that the consumer is going to come back to wine … if we get that right in this region, we set the tone for people to stay drinking wine.' Riverina and these large companies serve an important role in the Australian wine industry: they are responsible for creating and maintaining new wine drinkers.

Yellow Tail (and Mass Production)

Yellow Tail is one of the most famous brands of wine worldwide. In 2006 it became the most-sold wine in the United States, ousting Beringer and Kendall-Jackson, which typically held the top two spots at that time. The global correlation between Yellow Tail and Australia has given it a reputation of being a mass-producing wine country. And while there are a few Australian brands (Yellow Tail, Jacob's Creek and 19 Crimes) that are massive globally, the overall output of the country is not on this scale, and the domestic market is actually dominated by small and mid-sized producers. Australia currently sits sixth in global production, behind Italy, France, Spain, the US and Argentina; Australia makes close to five times less wine than both Italy and France, and four times less than Spain. And the Aussie regions best known for commercial production (Riverina and Riverland) are dwarfed by fine wine-associated European regions like the Rhône Valley and Bordeaux. In fact, Australia as a whole has only about 4.5 times more total vineyard surface than Champagne!

PRODUCERS

Emma Norbiato, Calabria Family Wines

RIVERINA

CALABRIA FAMILY WINES

Calabria was founded in the 1940s as a distribution business that sold barrels of wine to family and friends of its southern Italian founders. It wasn't until 1970 that the first wine was officially bottled under the Calabria name. Three generations later, the family has added three sites in the Barossa Valley (South Australia) to their expansive holdings in New South Wales. Determined to develop the Riverina brand, Calabria has been instrumental in raising the profile of drought-hardy varieties in the area. Chief winemaker Emma Norbiato describes French-native durif as 'a bit of an institution' for the estate, with significant plantings of nero d'Avola and montepulciano also of importance. In 2021, the Calabria empire expanded again, snapping up the McWilliam's Hanwood winery and other Riverina vineyards.

calabriawines.com.au

CASELLA FAMILY BRANDS

Chances are, you've seen a Casella wine on the shelf at your local supermarket, but under its most famous brand's name: Yellow Tail. Filippo and Maria Casella migrated from Sicily in 1957 and within the decade had bought a farm in the Riverina where they grew grapes for local winemakers. They continued to develop their family winery, and in 1998 the Yellow Tail brand was born. In 2001, the first Yellow Tail wines left for the US – and within the first two years, they had sold over five million cases. With the success of their consistent and affordable wines, the Casella family has turned to developing a portfolio of premium wineries. They purchased Peter Lehmann in the Barossa Valley (South Australia) in 2014 and Morris Wines of Rutherglen (Victoria) in 2016. The company has historically been a huge landholder in Australia, but in 2021 made the decision to offload 7258 hectares, with the goal to focus funds on brand building rather than land holding.

casellafamilybrands.com

DE BORTOLI

(See also Yarra Valley, p. 116)

Vittorio De Bortoli arrived from the hills of northern Italy to the exceedingly flat Riverina in 1924. A homemade shiraz from local grapes launched the De Bortoli brand, which quickly became a booming interstate business. Third-generation Darren De Bortoli became particularly interested in botrytis-affected wines during his studies. With a surplus of semillon in 1982, he created the famous Noble One Botrytis Semillon, which has won countless awards both in Australia and abroad. For

a large-scale company, De Bortoli has made great strides in environmentalism, installing a huge collection of solar panels, managing water resources and overhauling their waste management and packing, with the goal to achieve zero waste.
debortoli.com.au

MCWILLIAM'S

J.J. McWilliam planted a nursery of 50,000 cuttings in the Riverina in 1913 – the first vines in the region, prior even to irrigation. He opened Hanwood Estate in 1917 – and such was his success that McWilliam's began to export internationally in 1935. In its early days, McWilliam's was producing **fortified wines** and spirits, but thanks to the acquisition of Mount Pleasant in 1941 (see Hunter Valley, p. 48), they were able to develop their brand and release **table wines**. Today, most of their Riverina production goes to value-for-money and cask wine.
mcwilliams.com.au

NEW ENGLAND

JILLY

Jilly is curious and creative, a reflection of the personality of winemaker Jared Dixon. His wines are experimental, with a strong focus on environmental practices – the winery is off the grid, powered completely by solar panels and lithium batteries, and all waste is composted. Jilly's signature wine has been Black Mountain Pinot Noir, coming from Australia's highest vineyard at 1306 metres above sea level (though rumour has it Dixon will not be working with this site going forward). It is supplemented by white grapes like gewürztraminer, sauvignon blanc and chardonnay (often treated to skin-contact), some uncommon Italian grapes in large format, and a few unique red blends. A compelling and modern look at an underexplored wine region.
jillywines.com.au

TOPPER'S MOUNTAIN

Determined to make the most of New England's rich, volcanic, red soils, Mark Kirkby established vineyards between 1998 and 2002, planting both traditional and alternative varieties, including a 'fruit salad' block of 15 rows to experiment with grape suitability for the area. Of the original 22 grapes (plus other new trials), 18 remain to this day, with gewürztraminer, gros manseng and nebbiolo the most successful. Floods and fires are brutally regular for Topper's Mountain; the vineyard was ravaged by bushfires in 2019, just hours before harvest was meant to start. The team have begun to replant and are collaborating with winemakers Glen Roberts and Andrew Scott (Bent Road, La Petite Mort) from Granite Belt in Queensland, and Jared Dixon (Jilly) from further south in Clunes.
toppers.com.au

And don't forget ...

Centennial Vineyards, just over an hour south of Sydney, in the Southern Highlands region, produces high-elevation, **traditional method** sparkling wines, as well as cool-climate whites and reds ...
Coolangatta Estate is most known for its mature, Hunter-style semillon, also making fine-boned, medium-bodied reds from cabernet sauvignon, tannat and chambourcin in the Shoalhaven Coast region ...
Tertini Wines, the Southern Highlands' first vineyard (dating back to 1855), is a site for reliable pinot noir, chardonnay, riesling and arneis.

 What we're drinking

*Can focus and funk be found simultaneously? The answer is yes, and it's in the bottle at **Jilly** ... or box even. Check out their pecorino, grechetto and sagrantino packaged in 3 litre cask format. A win for your palate and the planet. – Kavita Faiella*

 New Guard   Environmental Hero   Rising Star   Legend   Regional Stalwart   Must Visit   Cult Following   Historic Estate

VICTORIA

Yarra Valley 104

Mornington Peninsula 122

Geelong 138

Macedon Ranges 152

Gippsland 166

Heathcote 180

Western Victoria 194

Beechworth 212

Rutherglen 226

Other Victoria 238

Victoria is the runner-up in several Australian superlatives: the most populous state after New South Wales; the smallest and coolest state after Tasmania; its capital, Melbourne, is the second largest after Sydney.

The one area where Victoria takes home the top accolade is in how much of its total area is devoted to wine regions. While most other states have just a fraction of their land covered by GIs, in Victoria you are never too far from a wine region. As a result, wine culture is pervasive in Victoria.

The other defining factor of Victorian wine culture is that it's fairly new. With Victoria being hit first and hardest by **phylloxera** in the late 19th century, the changing tastes away from cool-climate **table wine** at that time, as well as the economic depression felt across Australia, wine culture nearly ceased between 1900 and 1960. With the exception of Rutherglen and the Grampians, and a few other small pockets that saw a trickle of continued industry in this era, Victoria has largely been built (or rebuilt) since the 1960s.

But as young as Victoria is as a wine region, it is quite old in many ways. Victoria's landscape has largely been shaped by over 500 million years of volcanic activity. At the start of the Cambrian era, some 575 million years ago, Australia's east coast was drawn by the Mount Lofty and Flinders Ranges (in modern-day South Australia) – Victoria was underwater.

During the subsequent 150 million years, Victoria (and the rest of the east coast) filled in with sedimentary formations, setting the stage for giant, explosive Devonian era eruptions. These created much of the hard basalt and granodiorite formations found in the Dandenong Ranges and portions of the Victorian Alps. These igneous rocks were much harder than their surrounding sedimentary deposits that have since eroded away, revealing solid granite boulders visible across the vineyards of Tooborac (in Heathcote), Macedon Ranges and Strathbogie Ranges. Mt Macedon itself is an eroded volcano filled in by the igneous rock it once spewed.

As Australia and Antarctica continued to drift apart – and the Tasman Sea, Southern Ocean and Indian Ocean filled in – magma intrusions persisted. The most recent eruptions were late enough to be seen by Victoria's earliest inhabitants, with stories of the eruptions passed down by elders across thousands of generations.

While there is archaeological proof that people were living across all of Australia for at least 40,000 years, there is current evidence that supports a much longer history in Victoria. Archaeological findings at Moyjil, at the mouth of the Hopkins River (on Gunditjmara Country, the eastern edge of today's Henty GI) point to the possibility of human settlement as far back as 120,000 years ago.

Victoria has at least 38 First Nations, with many individual language groups and clans creating further nuance. As is seen throughout Australia, a multitude of First Nations often equates to a diversity of landscape, with geographic features acting as natural border divisions. Victoria is a wildly diverse landscape, from the flatlands of the Murray River to the southern end of the Australian Alps, with towering rainforests in the Otways and pockets east of Melbourne, and a southern coastline that was once a giant estuary and has since filled in to create Port Phillip Bay.

Victoria is celebrated as a cool-climate viticultural state, but its climate is as diverse as its landscape. Victoria successfully grows everything from warmer-climate grapes like grenache, mourvèdre and viognier to cooler-region staples like riesling, pinot noir and grapes for sparkling wine. Each region has its own story, its own specialties and its own all-star producers. Perhaps more so than any other state in Australia, Victoria makes a case for a painstaking approach to **regionality**: there is no such thing as 'Victorian wine' – each GI, region and even unofficial subregion, must be accounted for individually.

Parkside Farm in Macedon Ranges, Australia's coolest climate mainland region.

Victoria Geographical Indications

ZONE	REGION	SUBREGION
Central Victoria	Bendigo	
	Goulburn Valley	Nagambie Lakes
	Heathcote	
	Strathbogie Ranges	
	Upper Goulburn	
Gippsland		
North East Victoria	Alpine Valleys	
	Beechworth	
	Glenrowan	
	King Valley	
	Rutherglen	
North West Victoria	Murray Darling	
	Swan Hill	
Port Phillip	Geelong	
	Macedon Ranges	
	Mornington Peninsula	
	Sunbury	
	Yarra Valley	
Western Victoria	Grampians	Great Western
	Henty	
	Pyrenees	

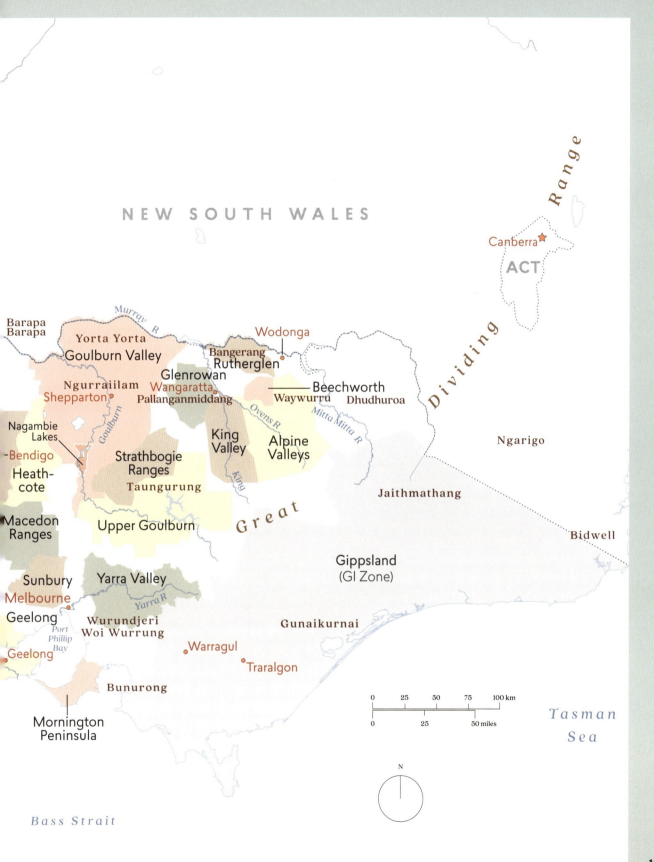

Yarra Valley

Introduction

What is commonly known today as the Yarra Valley is the traditional land of the Wurundjeri Woi Wurrung people. Their name is taken from the manna gum eucalyptus tree *wurun*, and the grub commonly found on the tree *djeri* – an identity connected by the lifeforms they looked after and their source of sustenance. Of the Woi Wurrung language groups, the Wurundjeri are the only surviving. Therefore, an acknowledgement that includes all caretakers of the land, past and present, is Wurundjeri Woi Wurrung.

Pre-colonisation, the Wurundjeri lived according to the two unique influences of the Yarra Valley: mountain and river. Winter months brought the Wurundjeri to the Upper Yarra, an area that provided shelter, where the flooding of the Yarra River posed no threat. In the summer they would become more permanent, living near the river. Fishing, hunting and gathering fruits and vegetables provided sustenance, all while burning parts of Country to create new and vibrant growth.

William Barak is recognised as the last Wurundjeri *Ngurungaeta* (the Woi Wurrung word meaning 'head man'). Barak was born in 1824 during early colonial dispossession and became the most important figure in the survival of Coranderrk Station – a site established by the Victorian government in 1863 as a 'reserve' for Aboriginal people displaced from their lands. Despite these inauspicious circumstances, Coranderrk ran successfully for years under the leadership of Barak, who forged friendships with many of the white settlers of the region, including some early grape-growers (most notably Baron Frédéric Guillaume de Pury of today's Yeringberg). Barak translated Wurundjeri culture through his art, including the depiction of the original vineyard at Yeringberg.

Yarra Valley's rich history of the vine – and its rich socio-formative history in general – is one of the points of pride among vintners today. The region spans all the way from the metropolitan eastern suburbs of Melbourne, east to the Yarra Ranges National Park. Its diverse landscape is home to some of the great wines of Australia – led by the grapes chardonnay, pinot noir, cabernet sauvignon and shiraz – but also some of the most disparate plantings, with exemplary examples of everything from gamay and sauvignon blanc to nebbiolo and marsanne. The people growing these grapes and making these wines are some of the greats of Australia. Their collective talent and personality make the Yarra Valley today not only one of Australia's most consistent wine regions, but one of its most exciting.

Evolution of Wine

Home to Victoria's first vines, the Yarra Valley also represents a significant site of economic and cultural development for the state. The Yarra River has always been a key supply of fresh water to Melbourne and its environs, and was an important feature en route to the 1850s gold-rush town of Warburton, creating an early hub of society and commerce in the Yarra Valley.

The earliest plantings date back to 1838, when the Scottish-born Ryrie brothers travelled down from New South Wales to set up their vineyard and cattle farm. They planted pinot noir, known as 'black cluster' at the time, as well as chasselas blanc, referred to as 'sweetwater'. The site was named 'Yering', which was the Wurundjeri word for the area – thought to be derived either from *yerrang*, meaning 'scrubby', or *yerring*, meaning 'beard'. Yering was a small town in the 1850s and has lent its name to several of the region's historic wineries.

The Ryrie site was sold in the 1850s to a Swiss immigrant named Paul de Castella, who significantly increased the land under vine and built an expansive mansion on the estate, now a premium hotel (and heritage landmark) called Château Yering. The vineyards changed hands several times during the 20th century, before being purchased in 1996 by the Rathbone family, assuming its current identity as the winery Yering Station, a much-loved Yarra producer to this day.

Paul's brother Hubert also established a significant vineyard in the mid-19th century named St Huberts (the name it retains today), planting it to shiraz, cabernet sauvignon and marsanne. The site grew to over 80 hectares, and was, at its peak, supplying over half a million bottles of wine each year to Melbourne (a bustling metropolis even then).

The 1860s and 1870s saw a huge expansion of the Yarra Valley, in terms of infrastructure and population as well as vineyard plantings. This campaign was led by the de Castella family, as well as Frédéric Guillaume de Pury, another Swiss-born immigrant who planted in Yering as well. De Pury's notions of viticulture went beyond cursory farming: his famed friendship with local Wurundjeri leader William Barak reinforced the ideals of caring for Country in the de Pury family, which would go on to influence them (and the region) for generations to come.

These early Swiss families exported their wines to European markets, won awards and established the Yarra Valley as a major player in **table wine** production. One of de Castella's wines was awarded the 'Grand Prix' at the

Exposition Universelle in Paris in 1889, the only Southern Hemisphere wine to ever do so.

This relative success and fame protected the Yarra Valley against one of the hardships suffered by many Victorian wineries around the turn of the 20th century: its wines had enough stature to survive the economic depression that befell the nation. The region also avoided widespread devastation by the **phylloxera** louse. The Yarra Valley, however, could not survive the overwhelming preference that cemented itself in the early 20th century for sweet, **fortified wines**, and all production ceased in 1921.

It would take a full 40 years for interest in replanting to start in the Yarra Valley. The first modern vineyard was planted by Reg and Bertina Egan. Reg was a Melbourne lawyer, who planted on the very southwestern border of the modern-day Yarra Valley appellation, creating Wantirna Estate. The original plantings were largely obscure grapes – crouchen, pedro ximénez, barbera and dolcetto – though some of the original cabernet and merlot vines planted in 1963 still bear fruit to this day.

St Huberts was revived soon after, its vineyards replanted by Tom Cester and his brother Mark in 1966. The Cesters sold the winery in 1987, and it eventually found its way into the hands of Treasury Wine Estates. The winery was known for its cabernets in the 1970s and 1980s, as well as a line of single-vineyard roussannes, though quality has become more commercially oriented in recent years.

Three figures emerged in the late 1960s and early 1970s who would become beacons of quality in the Yarra. Guill de Pury (Frédéric Guillaume's grandson) and his wife Katherine replanted the family vineyards in 1969, launching their winery Yeringberg. Dr Bailey Carrodus, who held degrees in horticulture, winemaking and plant physiology, also planted his vines in 1969 and established the winery Yarra Yering. He beat all the previous growers to the punch, releasing the Yarra Valley's first modern commercial wine in 1973. And Marli and John Middleton – inspired by the early Swiss growers of the region, as well as the wines of Bordeaux and Burgundy – established their site Mount Mary, planting it to French varieties in 1971. These three wineries were founded on quality – experimenting with low yields and minimal irrigation during a time when these practices were largely unheard of.

In the early days, cabernet was king. Wantirna, Yeringberg, Yarra Yering and Mount Mary all planted cabernet sauvignon from the start, each becoming known for the grape early on (and to this day). But through the 1980s, as Yarra Valley benefited from the rising cool-climate wine region trend, it saw a turn toward pinot noir and chardonnay, along with a significant infusion of outside interest in the region.

By the mid-1980s, when many Victorian wine regions were just beginning to see their pioneering producers take root, the Yarra Valley already had enough clout to attract several big outside investments. The first was James Halliday, who was on the lengthy upturn of his career as prolific vintner, show judge and wine writer. Halliday established Coldstream Hills with plantings of cabernet sauvignon, chardonnay and pinot noir, releasing his first vintage in 1985. Coldstream Hills enjoyed an illustrious run as a boutique producer before being purchased by Southcorp in 1996 (which would later become

Shiraz vs. Syrah, Part 2

On page 32, we describe how shiraz came to be the common name for the syrah grape in Australia. Both terms are used today in Australia, though shiraz in greater numbers. Some producers label theirs 'syrah' instead of 'shiraz' to convey something about the wine stylistically — usually that it is more savoury and less fruit-forward than the classic Barossa shiraz. However, plenty of producers making a savoury, cool-climate version of the grape still label their wines shiraz. What you don't see is wines that are big, ripe and jammy labelled syrah. So bottom line: you can't glean too much from an Australian wine being labelled syrah or shiraz, though typically you won't find the classic, bold, warm-climate style labelled as syrah.

Foster's, then Treasury Wine Estates), though the quality of wines has largely been maintained throughout the transitions.

By the time Coldstream Hills had its first vintage, Champagne conglomerate Moët Hennessy had already planted flags in the Yarra Valley. Moët had previously established outposts in Argentina, Brazil and California, and had been buzzing around Australia since 1982. In 1985, they enlisted the help of renowned oenologist Dr Tony Jordan to find the perfect site for sparkling wine, and the Yarra Valley is where he landed – not far from Halliday, in the township of Coldstream. The late 1980s also saw historic Riverina producer De Bortoli set up in the Yarra Valley, with a focus on chardonnay and pinot noir.

The Yarra Valley was clearly not immune to the 1990s trend of corporatisation (though its reach was more limited here than in other premium regions of Australia), but the trend of **Parkerisation** did not take hold in the same way. Perhaps it was the simplification of Yarra Valley as a 'cool-climate region' – which was not the favoured locale for Parker's 100-point scores, except for the occasional Grand Cru Burgundy, Loire and German sweet wine, or opulent Sonoma release – but the Yarra Valley seemed to realise early on that their optimal expression did not match the Parker mould.

The early 2000s brought a notable flock of winemakers to the region who continued a steadfast devotion to expressing the land of the Yarra (rather than trying to conform to international trends). De Bortoli's Steve Webber (the first of the bunch, arriving to the Yarra in the late 90s), Oakridge's David Bicknell, and Giant Steps' Steve Flamsteed led this pack, soon supported by a handful of upstarts, who promoted this vision in a smaller, more grassroots sort of way. Mac Forbes, Luke Lambert and Timo Mayer all started their eponymous wineries in the early to mid-2000s.

The result of these winemakers' work was a detailed pursuit to match grape variety to site and make balanced wines representative of Yarra Valley's cool-ish, yet diverse climates. Chardonnay and pinot noir excelled, but so did leaner expressions of cabernet, merlot and shiraz, and eventually all manner of grapes, from nebbiolo

The early 2000s brought a notable flock of winemakers to the region who continued a steadfast devotion to expressing the land of the Yarra.

to marsanne, sauvignon blanc to malbec, and unique blends thereof. Shiraz in particular made a splash, turning Australia's quintessential Barossa version on its head and expressing a less ripe and more savoury version of the grape.

While many Australian regions saw a lag in boutique interest after the somewhat stifling trends of the 90s, the Yarra Valley didn't miss a beat. Though this generation has released some experimental wines, the overwhelming focus has continued to be on site-conscious, balanced and approachable pinot noir, chardonnay and shiraz – a movement that continues to this day. Though a few **pét-nats**, skin-macerated whites and cloudy wines have cropped up around the region (generally done quite well), the Yarra Valley has made it cool to be classic.

Lay of the Land

The Yarra Valley is a large swath of land – just over 3100 square kilometres – spanning from the metropolitan eastern suburbs of Melbourne all the way east to the Yarra Ranges National Park. The sprawling (and somewhat arbitrary) designation of the Yarra Valley is based on the boundaries of Evelyn County drawn in 1849.

Though the Yarra Valley has more plantings than most other GIs in Victoria, with about

2800 hectares under vine, there are still vast areas of the appellation that are not planted densely (or at all) to the vine, and probably never will be – less than 1% of the total area of the Yarra Valley is under vine. Its western and eastern extremities have few plantings: the western side is succumbing to urban sprawl, while the eastern side encompasses a protected national park.

The Yarra's proximity to Melbourne has made it a tourism hotspot. Robust cellar doors, winery restaurants of all sorts, holiday rentals, farmers' markets, wedding venues and stand-alone eateries are regularly inundated with visitors, as are Yarra-specific attractions like the Healesville Sanctuary and rides on the Puffing Billy Railway. In 2019, the Yarra received more than 6.5 million visitors (domestic and foreign combined), and over AUD $870 million in visitor spend.

While Melbourne and the Yarra Ranges provide the western and eastern borders for the Yarra Valley, respectively, the region's southern border is formed by the Dandenong Ranges. When the continental folding responsible for the Great Dividing Range occurred, various intrusions of magma materialised, resulting in acidic granite formations – namely the Macedon, Cobaw and Dandenong Ranges. The Dandenongs provide gentle slopes for north-facing vineyards in the south of the region, but still allow in the oceanic influence of the Bass Strait, keeping the Yarra Valley fairly temperate.

The Yarra Valley has assumed the role of Australia's cool-climate darling. Its average January temperature in Healesville is 18.9°C, though some areas register well below or above that number. Some of the region's pockets rival Macedon Ranges for being the coldest growing areas on Australia's mainland. However, there is an over 400-metre elevation change across plantings in the GI, with complex systems of airflow, precipitation changes and an endless array of slopes and **aspects** – it's hard to generalise about the Yarra Valley.

With an area so vast, and so much diversity across it, there have naturally been attempts for further delineation. Mac Forbes, who launched his eponymous winery in 2004, commissioned a map of the Yarra Valley with seven distinct subregions outlined. Several more could easily be tagged on, with multiple townships and areas expressing a unique combination of altitude, **aspects**, moisture and soil type. Many believe, though, that such detailed subregional definition can be overbearing and confusing to the consumer. In the wake of such divided opinion, most have settled on speaking of the Yarra Valley in two general areas: Lower Yarra and Upper Yarra.

Lower Yarra, confusingly enough, is further north and west. ('Lower' refers to being lower in elevation and downstream on the Yarra River, not further south geographically.) It is largely composed of the classic valley floor townships Lilydale, Gruyere, Coldstream and Yering, and is home to a variety of western agricultural systems. Produce farms and pastures raising cattle and sheep share the landscape with vineyards and fruit orchards. This is the most historic region of the Yarra Valley – home to the early Swiss settlers in Yering, and substantial growth in Coldstream in the 1980s.

The Lower Yarra valleys are the warmest parts of the GI. They ripen cabernet sauvignon,

Yarra Valley Viticultural Footprint
(Healesville Weather Station)

Total delimited area (km²)	3120
Total planted area (hectares)	2837
% of delimited area planted	0.910%
Total elevation range	17–1338 masl
Elevation range of plantings	80–695 masl
Number of producers	84

Healesville, Yarra Valley Climate Data (°C)

	1960–1990	1991–PRESENT	2020
Heat summation/GDD	1238	1277	1242
Annual rain/GSR	1130/573	1094/549	1385/767
Warmest month avg. temp.	18.2	18.9	19

Winkler Scale:

● 850–1111   ● 1112–1389   ● 1390–1667   ● 1668–1944   ● 1945–2222   ● 2223–2700

An Upper Yarra vantage point looking northwest towards the Lower Yarra, covered in a low-lying morning fog.

nebbiolo and shiraz fully without difficulty, though they also see the cover of mist and fog each morning as it rolls in from Port Phillip Bay, avoiding overripeness and sun damage. Pinot noir and chardonnay are still ubiquitous on this side of the valley, tending to result in riper and more powerful styles of the Yarra's signature grapes.

North of this central stretch of the Lower Yarra, the areas of Dixon's Creek and Yarra Glen – some of the northernmost sites in the region – find a slight increase in elevation over those townships on the valley floor, topping out at around 150 metres above sea level. This area is still considered Lower Yarra, though it runs a bit cooler than the lowest sites.

While the Lower Yarra vineyards cap at around 150 metres in elevation (most clock in well under that), the Upper Yarra's elevation begins at that mark. The Upper Yarra is to the south and further east, rising up the foothills of the Great Dividing Range and its subsection, the Yarra Ranges. This region includes areas like Woori Yallock, Gladysdale, Wesburn, Gembrook, Hoddles Creek and Yarra Junction. The Upper Yarra tends to get colder at night and experiences a milder summer than the Lower Yarra. There is an even stronger focus on pinot noir and chardonnay in the Upper Yarra, and the secondary grapes lean cooler-climate – like chenin blanc, sauvignon blanc,

With an area so vast, and so much diversity across it, there have naturally been attempts for further delineation.

gamay, pinot meunier and shiraz (the latter of which sees its apogee of savoury flavours in the Upper townships).

A variety of **aspects** are achieved across the region; the Yarra Ranges provide suitable vineyard areas facing in all directions. While it has historically been commonplace to plant on north-facing slopes – to capture the sun – producers experiment with south, west and east-facing ones to curate an ideal **microclimate** (though east is rare given the rising elevation in that direction). Some even believe that the north-facing slopes are getting too warm to express the traditional grapes and styles of the Yarra Valley.

Rainfall varies across the GI, with the lower sections and valley floors experiencing less

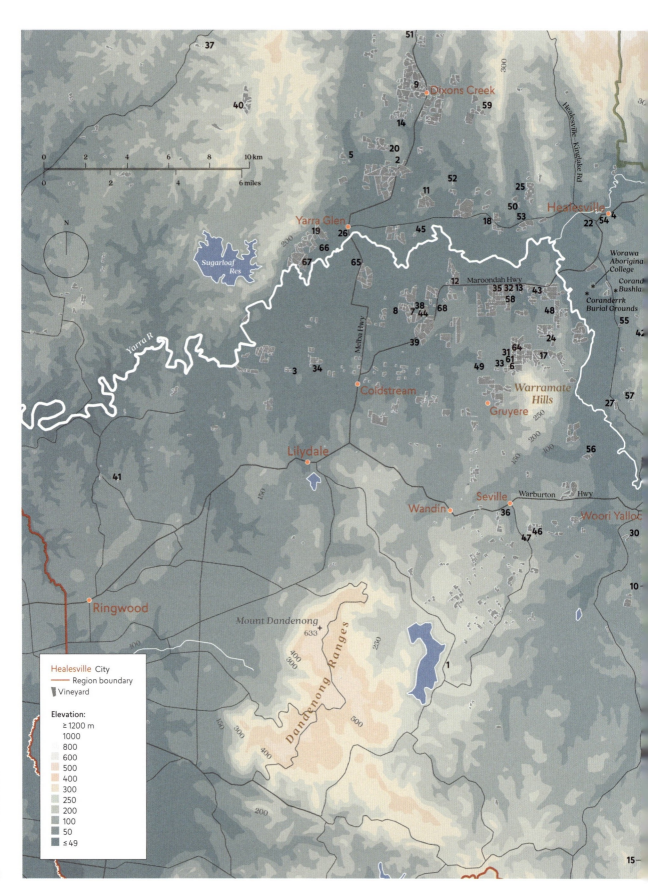

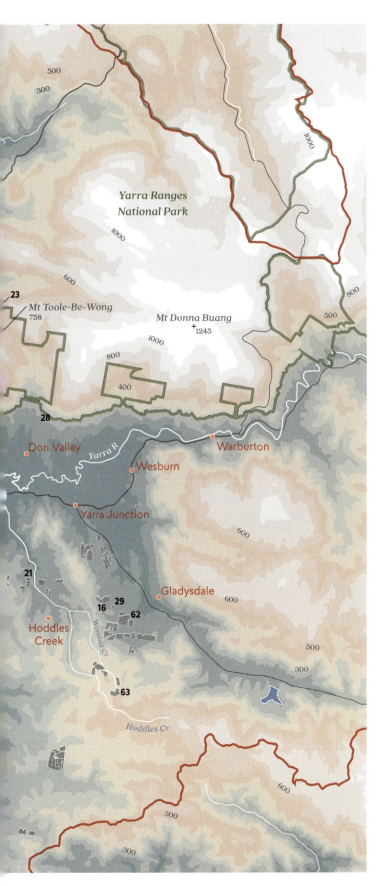

Yarra Valley

HOW TO READ THIS MAP

The Dandenong and Yarra Ranges converge to create several unique wine-growing areas. These subregions and their vineyard areas are mapped across the region's changes in elevation. Note the numerous corridors, valleys and **aspects** specific to each.

1 Alkimi
2 Balgownie Estate Yarra Vineyard
3 Bianchet Winery
4 Bird on a Wire
5 Bobar
6 Coldstream Hills
7 Coombe
8 Copperhead
9 De Bortoli
10 De Bortoli Lusatia Park Vineyard
11 Denton View Hill Vineyard
12 Chandon Australia
13 Dominique Portet
14 Fergusson
15 Gembrook Hill
16 Giant Steps Applejack Vineyard
17 Giant Steps Sexton Vineyard
18 Giant Steps Tarraford Vineyard
19 Greenstone
20 Highbow Hill Vineyard
21 Hoddles Creek
22 Jayden Ong
23 Jayden Ong Forest Garden Vineyard
24 Levantine Hill
25 Long Gully Estate
26 Luke Lambert
27 Mac Forbes
28 Mac Forbes Don Valley
29 Mac Forbes Little Yarra
30 Mac Forbes Woori Yallock
31 Maddens Rise Back Block Vineyard
32 Maddens Rise Front Block Vineyard
33 Medhurst
34 Mount Mary
35 Oakridge Wines
36 Payne's Rise
37 Punch
38 Punt Road
39 Punt Road Sovereign Hill Vineyard
40 Rising Vineyard
41 Rob Dolan Wines
42 Rob Hall
43 Rochford Wines
44 St Huberts
45 Serrat
46 Seville Estate
47 Seville Estate Ducks Lane Vineyard
48 Soumah
49 Squitchy Lane
50 Stefani Estate
51 Sutherland Estate
52 Tarrahill
53 TarraWarra Estate
54 Thick as Thieves
55 Thick as Thieves Cypress Ridge Vineyard
56 Thousand Candles
57 Timo Mayer
58 Tokar Estate
59 Toolangi
60 Wantirna Estate
61 Warramate
62 Willow Lake Vineyard
63 Wombat Creek Vineyard
64 Yarra Yering
65 Yering Station
66 Yering Station Laura Barnes Vineyard
67 Yering Station Muirs Vineyard
68 Yeringberg

than vineyards in the hills of the Upper Yarra. Precipitation rarely drops below 700 millimetres in the growing season, high enough to support a vine without the need for irrigation most years and at most sites. The flip side is that with consistent moisture, mildew-related disease management is paramount.

There are two main soil types across the Yarra Valley: ancient sedimentary soils of grey sandy clay loams that sit atop layers of mudstone and siltstone, and slightly less ancient (though still a few hundred million years old) red volcanic loam. The grey sedimentary soils have a lower **nutrient load** than the red volcanic soils and create a somewhat more stressful environment for the vine (in a good way). However, both soil types drain well and are slightly acidic in nature – good conditions for growing grapes.

Conversations around these soils often simplify their location as a uniform split, with the grey sedimentary soils in the northern Lower Yarra and the red volcanic soils in the southern Upper Yarra. But there is complex interplay of these two soil types across the region, especially with the grey soils appearing at elevation. Winemaker Mac Forbes points to the limitations of this binary division, and how rarely the nuances of soil type are taken into account: 'I'm still horrified at how little reverence or respect is given to where the vines are planted on what soils. It's still just where in the Yarra, in terms of Lower or Upper. I think it's the next big challenge for the region to recognise that.'

It's about understanding how the two major soil types interact throughout the region, but it's also about understanding that there are other soils at work too. As the area was shaped by volcanic activity, there are two outcroppings of granite that have been planted to the vine. Both see granitic sandy loams atop more solid granite boulders. One of note, the View Hill vineyard at Denton in Yarra Glen, is planted on a dome-like hill that is the result of a granite plug remnant of a 370-million-year-old volcano. It has been weathered into a sandy hill that sits just 105 metres in elevation.

The general consumer's understanding of the Yarra Valley is clearly based on generalisations. But the Yarra Valley's best producers, to their continuous credit, do not try to conform to this

understanding. 'It's a really diverse region,' Yarra Yering's Sarah Crowe attests. 'We're always trying to understand ourselves better.' The Valley's most sensitive producers, like Crowe, are constantly studying soil types, **aspects**, moisture levels and temperatures to find the perfect confluence of site and style – achieving everything from chiselled sparkling wines to robust **GSM**s.

Chardonnay and pinot noir, though, are still the calling cards of the region. Cabernet sauvignon and shiraz often play second fiddle, though both have achieved much in the Yarra. Cabernet in particular is a stalwart of the region and deserves more attention than it perhaps receives. Margaret River and Coonawarra usually take centre stage in discussions on Australian cabernet, but the Yarra Valley offers up some of the nation's greatest examples, from the likes of Dominique Portet, Mac Forbes, Mount Mary, Wantirna, Yarra Yering and Yeringberg. Ben Portet, the second-generation proprietor of Dominique Portet, says Yarra cabernet argues its distinction by being understated: 'They whisper, not shout, yet they show this lovely fine tannin profile – almost silky when young – and at the same time have this ability to age so gracefully over decades.'

Producers continue to experiment with less typical grape varieties, as well. Yarra Yering's Dry Red No. 3 is a blend of grapes native to the Duoro in Portugal. Seville Estate is well known for its tempranillo, and new plantings of grapes like mencía, grenache blanc and chenin blanc continue to crop up. These are just a few examples of the innovative efforts – always tied to research, not whimsy – that have become a hallmark of the Valley's producers.

The historic Yeringberg vineyard in the town of Coldstream, sloping gently downhill towards the lower Yarra River in the background.

Yarra Valley

Hubbub

The Yarra Valley has a lot – almost everything – going for it. Jayden Ong, a winemaker who made his entrance into the Yarra Valley in the 2010s, sums it up when he describes his reasoning for choosing the Yarra: 'There is good history here, yet it felt like there were still new sites to be discovered. And the Yarra Valley is quite diverse: from one end to the other, it's almost completely different,' says Ong. 'We felt we had the opportunity to find a marginal site in this area, and, logistically, it was ideal because of business interests in Melbourne.' That's the Yarra in a nutshell: proximity to Melbourne, proven track record, historical foundation, diversity of landscape, cool-climate pedigree, and still-untapped opportunity.

Melbourne's effect on Yarra Valley is hard to overstate. According to Steve Flamsteed, long-time Giant Steps chief winemaker, 'the Yarra wouldn't be the Yarra if we weren't as close to four-and-a-half million people … it obviously gives businesses the opportunity to have a bit of access to a critical mass, an audience. And it allows the growth of a proper industry of professionals here.'

But just as Sydney has encouraged some mediocrity in the Hunter Valley, so too has Melbourne fostered some complacency in the Yarra Valley. Mac Forbes, often the (beloved) contrarian in the region, states that 'a lot of people stopped questioning and searching for a while. Because they were selling out of the wines they were making, it didn't matter whether they were good or bad, or whether they were happy with them. Why would they tinker if it's working?' Forbes' gripe is with quality, yes, but more than that, it's with an absent spirit of experimentation.

Forbes sees a salve for this phenomenon in one of the topics causing the most strife in the Yarra Valley: **phylloxera**. The Yarra avoided **phylloxera** when it first made its rounds in the late 19th century, but has not been so lucky in recent times. The root louse was first detected in the Valley in December of 2006; fast-forward to today, and it is estimated that over 1000 hectares of the region have been affected. Even those who have not seen **phylloxera** in their own vineyards know it's just a matter of time and have established replanting programs. Forbes sees the bright side: 'So, forget about all the varieties that might come out of the replanting … I just think the fact that people are forced to re-examine what they stand for is far more interesting.'

This forced re-evaluation also allows vintners to respond to another (more distant) threat to the region: climate change. Many regions across Australia are planting anew to adapt to the shifting climate; the Yarra Valley's **phylloxera** replantings have encouraged growers in the region to consider the long-term viability of vines they are putting in the ground, perhaps earlier than they would have otherwise. 'The silver lining to all this,' says Mount Mary's Sam Middleton, referring to **phylloxera**, 'is that it has allowed us to critically assess where certain varieties have been planted around the property in the past, and assess if there are improvements that can be made here. For example, most of our pinot and chardonnay is being replanted on cooler south-facing slopes instead of the more sun-exposed north-facing **aspects**.'

For Sarah Crowe, at Yarra Yering, it's row orientation that they are shifting. Other considerations include matching grape astutely to site, planting more drought-tolerant, warm-climate varieties, **clonal selection**, **canopy management**, irrigation decisions, **planting density** and more. The thoughtfulness, and even experimentation, that had faded among some producers, has made a mandated return.

This is not to negate the challenges **phylloxera** has presented, namely that replanting is 'bloody expensive and takes a massive effort', according to Ong. Yarra Valley is an expensive region to begin with – land prices are rising, its signature grape, pinot noir, is a pricey one to farm, and yields tend to be kept low. The Yarra Valley has always had the reputation of being more of an approachable region, price-point wise, than the other Melbourne-proximate GI of Mornington Peninsula. But with the increased farming costs compounding previous expenses, the Yarra Valley seems poised to price itself out of that reputation. Flamsteed concurs: 'One of the most misunderstood things about the Yarra

Valley is that the wines are too expensive' – when, in fact, they are appropriately expensive.

As the Yarra Valley approaches its 50th anniversary of modern wine production, there is recognition among growers that the region, despite its success, is still quite young – still figuring itself out. Flamsteed relays how long true knowledge and understanding takes to acquire: 'It's quite humbling, actually, when you sort of realise that after 10, 15 years that you've just begun to understand something that's quite fundamental and basic.'

The vintners of the region are looking back, far beyond their 50 years of making wine in the region, with regular visits to the site of Coranderrk Station by Yarra Valley growers, winemakers and proprietors. The site was closed in 1924, but in 1999 the Indigenous Lands and Sea Corporation bought the land and returned it to the Wandoon Estate Aboriginal Corporation, which represents the Wurundjeri people. It is now a private residence and working cattle farm, and though the intentions are never to become a tourist destination, they are 'working towards an expanded visitor program showcasing the property and its produce, Coranderrk's story and Wurundjeri culture'.

What Mac Forbes took away from his time there included not only specific insights on land custodianship, but truths about identity and adaptation. 'There's something quite calming and magnificent about going and hearing this group of people talk about how they've lived through three climate change events over 60,000 years,' Forbes says. 'And while we're always trying to learn how to farm to help the plants adapt, they're talking about how they've survived climate change through adapting themselves – how they've survived through European colonisation here through adapting. And that they're not hanging on to the past and who they were, they're who they are by the way they respond.'

The vintners of the region are looking back, far beyond their 50 years of making wine in the region, with regular visits to the site of Coranderrk Station by Yarra Valley growers, winemakers and proprietors.

Yarra Valley

PRODUCERS

BEN HAINES

Ben Haines cut his teeth at iconic wineries Mount Langi Ghiran (Grampians) and Yering Station before focusing full time on his own wines in 2003. Now based in the Yarra Valley, he also makes McLaren Vale syrah as well as a nebbiolo from Malakoff Vineyard in the Pyrenees. Early wines were made from Nagambie Lakes fruit. His newly released Flowers Flor marsanne has been in the works since landing in barrel in 2011, aged under a veil of yeast for 10 years. **benhaines.wine**

BIRD ON A WIRE

With eight global vintages under her belt, Caroline Mooney launched Bird on a Wire in 2008. Inspired by her experiences working at Domaine J.L. Chave in the Northern Rhône, she is particularly passionate about syrah and marsanne. The fruit for these wines comes from single-vineyard sites in Yarra Glen, with chardonnay from the Willow Lake vineyard at Gladysdale. Caroline holds onto her marsanne, releasing it with bottle age when she believes it is at its best expression. **birdonawirewines.com.au**

CHANDON AUSTRALIA

Champagne house Moët & Chandon established their Australian outpost in Coldstream in 1986. Legendary oenologist Dr Tony Jordan was tasked with finding the site and stayed on as managing director until 2008. The aim here is clear: cool climate, **traditional method** sparkling wines, made from the three great Champenoise varietals. The offering has evolved in line with the empire's expansion: Chandon bought a vineyard in the Strathbogie Ranges in the 90s and a high-altitude King Valley vineyard from Brown Brothers in 2014. Winemaking director, Dan Buckle, has been with Chandon since 2012. Wines come in every style, from blanc de blancs to rosé and even a pinot noir–led take on the Aussie classic, sparkling shiraz. **chandon.com.au**

COLDSTREAM HILLS

Founded by renowned Australian wine writer James Halliday and his wife Suzanne in 1985, Coldstream Hills helped shaped the modern trajectory of the Yarra Valley. There are currently 100 hectares of vineyards across the Yarra, planted to chardonnay, pinot noir, sauvignon blanc, cabernet sauvignon and merlot. Andrew Fleming has been chief winemaker since 2001, maintaining the consistent quality that Coldstream Hills has become known for, even under the larger corporate banner of Treasury Wine Estates. **coldstreamhills.com.au**

DE BORTOLI
(See also Riverina, p. 96)

Beginning life in the Riverina, the De Bortoli family purchased a vineyard in the Yarra in 1987. Steve Webber spent years working at Lindeman's and Leo Buring before meeting his wife Leanne De Bortoli and moving to the Yarra Valley in 1990 to run De Bortoli's latest venture. It has since grown to be one of the biggest in the region. While they have chosen

---

What we're drinking

*The Yarra Valley is one of the most diverse wine-growing regions in the entire world (yes, I do mean the WHOLE world). However, few people have the confidence and skill to really show that breadth as **Bird on a Wire's** Caroline Mooney. Her marsanne is potentially the truest example of the grape outside of the Rhône Valley, with texture, weight, supreme balance and serious ageing potential. This wine is fire.* — Jonathan Ross

region. While they have chosen to rest solidly on the powerhouse grapes of the region – pinot noir and chardonnay – there is also a small amount of pinot blanc and gamay made from their estate vineyard in Dixons Creek. **debortoli.com.au**

DENTON

Denton's View Hill vineyard sits on an isolated rise in Yarra Glen, with one of the Yarra's most iconic winery buildings on its apex. Melbourne architect John Denton and his son Simon started planting in 1997, also building the View Hill House, completed in 2011, which looks like two precariously stacked shipping containers. In addition to the striking architecture, the granitic sandy soils are quite rare in the Yarra, producing high-quality pinot noir, chardonnay, and nebbiolo especially. The vineyard is an important source of nebbiolo for the Yarra; Luke Lambert is a major buyer for his eponymous label and also makes the Denton wines. **dentonwine.com**

DOMINIQUE PORTET

Dominique Portet's family winemaking heritage stretches back 10 generations – his father was régisseur (vineyard and winery manager) at Château Lafite-Rothschild. As a 'flying winemaker', Dominique travelled the globe before putting down roots in the Yarra Valley. In 2000, he found the perfect site to plant a mix of Bordeaux varieties and build a winery and cellar door. Dominique's son, Ben – the 10th generation – is continuing the family tradition and has taken over as executive winemaker. The Fontaine rosé is a pioneer of the Australian Provençal-style, wildly popular in bistro ice buckets across the country each summer, and the cabernet sauvignons are some of the region's most highly regarded. **dominiqueportet.com**

GEMBROOK HILL

Perhaps a little too cold at the time, Ian and June Marks' Upper Yarra site, planted in 1983, has rewarded them handsomely. The rise in temperature over 40 years makes their northeasterly site perfect for chardonnay, sauvignon blanc and pinot noir today. With most of their vines now over 20 years old, the resulting wines are graceful and well-constructed. Ian and June's son Andrew has taken up the mantle of chief winemaker and viticulturist at the family estate, while also working on his own projects. He started The Wanderer in 2005, focusing on minimally handled pinot noir, syrah and chardonnay, and founded The Melbourne Gin Company in 2012, which distils at Gembrook Hill. **gembrookhill.com.au**

GIANT STEPS

Phil Sexton is another soul who wandered the slopes of the valley

Steve Flamsteed
Giant Steps

in search of the perfect place to plant pinot noir and chardonnay. He planted in Warramate Hills and Gruyere in 1997, and the first vintage – the only one bottled under cork – was in 2001. Steve Flamsteed joined Giant Steps as chief winemaker in 2003, after an eclectic career as a chef, cheesemaker and a brief attempt as a circus performer. Needing cash flow to begin making the pricier single-vineyard wines, they started the Innocent Bystander label, which has been well received and profitable. Currently, they make four single-vineyard chardonnays and pinot noirs, including one from the Coal River Valley in Tasmania. Giant Steps was acquired in 2020 by US-based Jackson Family Wines, who have proven their interest in maintaining (and building) quality viticulture and winemaking in Australia. Melanie Chester, formerly of Bendigo's Sutton Grange, has been tasked as custodian for the next era of Giant Steps, taking over as head of winemaking and viticulture in late 2021. **giantstepswine.com.au**

JAYDEN ONG/ONE BLOCK

Jayden Ong got into wine as many do – working in hospitality – but few have done both with so much success. He started as a sommelier, before co-founding restaurant Cumulus Inc. with celebrated Melbourne chef Andrew McConnell, sneaking in vintages and a wine science degree in between late nights at the restaurant. In 2010 he launched his first label, One Block, with the aim of focusing on single-vineyard wines. He and his wife Morgan bought their own property in the Yarra in 2015 – Forest Garden on Mt Toolebewong, the highest vineyard in the Yarra. They release wines under three other labels: La Maison de Ong, which focuses on Yarra pinot noir and syrah; Moonlit Forest, Jayden's foray into low-intervention winemaking and experimental techniques; and Jayden Ong, from the Chestnut Hill and Forest Garden vineyards.
jaydenong.com

LUKE LAMBERT

Luke Lambert knew he wanted to be a winemaker at 14. After high school he travelled extensively through Europe's most notable wine regions, gleaning all the intel he could. His penchant for cool-climate wines drew him to the Yarra Valley, where he worked at Coldstream Hills during the day and made wine in his garage at night. Having branched out on his own, Luke buys fruit from two single vineyards: chardonnay, shiraz and nebbiolo from Denton's View Hill vineyard, and chardonnay and syrah from Tibooburra Estate. In 2020 he finished planting his estate vineyard of nebbiolo; the property was named Sparkletown by his nine-year-old daughter, with enough reflective light to warrant it. Luke's nebbiolos have been a driving force in the idea that this variety is Yarra Valley's next big thing. *lukelambertwines.com.au*

Mac Forbes

MAC FORBES

Mac Forbes grew up in the Yarra Valley, but it took running out of money backpacking in France for him to start working in a vineyard. His return home saw him study winemaking and gain practical experience (including a stint as a winemaker at renowned Yarra winery Mount Mary), before he jetted off again, working as a winemaker, marketer and educator, spreading the word on Australian wine across the world. Drawn back to the Yarra in search of good earth, Mac developed an intricate connection to the soils of the region. He launched his own winery in 2004 and strives to produce a range of wines that give the clearest snapshot of the diversity of sites across the Yarra Valley. The EB (Experimental Batch) range are the wines with licence to sit outside the box, but Mac's bread and butter is single-site chardonnay and pinot noir. He also makes riesling from the oldest vineyard in the Strathbogie Ranges, and a modern take on the

---

What we're drinking

Luke Lambert's is the benchmark in Australian nebbiolo. What is the secret? Perhaps that Luke's Slavonian oak foudre lay nestled next to his drumkit in the winery? There is no doubt far more goes into making some of the country's best expression of this variety, but they definitely don't miss a beat. – **Kavita Faiella**

cabernet sauvignon and merlot of the Yarra's formative years.
macforbes.com

MEDHURST

Ross Wilson became passionate about wine as CEO of Southcorp (now Treasury Wine Estates). When deciding where to establish a vineyard, his wife Robyn's home town of the Yarra Valley called, and Medhurst was planted in 2000 to chardonnay, pinot noir, cabernet sauvignon and shiraz. Winemaker Simon Steele was a welcome addition to the team in 2015, having just finished up as Iain Riggs's right-hand man at Brokenwood in the Hunter Valley. The Medhurst wines are some of the most consistent and best-value wines coming out of the Yarra.
medhurstwines.com.au

MOUNT MARY

Dr John Middleton got the idea in his head that Australia had yet to produce an elegant style of cabernet, and he made this his mission. John and his wife Marli came across a property called Mount Mary in 1971 and, finding it ideal for vines, they began planting. Great lovers of Bordeaux and Burgundy, the estate wines harken to these regions: a chardonnay and pinot noir (Burgundy's main grapes) and white and red Bordeaux blends, called Triolet and Quintet, respectively. Mount Mary currently has 16 hectares under vine, comprising 18 varieties. Sam Middleton is the third generation to work in the winery, taking over as head winemaker in 2011. In 2008, Sam and his father David started looking to the Southern Rhône for drought-hardy varieties, and began planting marsanne, roussanne, clairette, grenache, syrah, mourvèdre and cinsault. In 2014 they released a new range of wines from these grapes, called Marli Russell after the family's matriarch. In addition to these climate-aware plantings, Mount Mary has other plans for an environmentally conscious future, with the goal to become organic in the vineyard and a carbon-neutral business. *mountmary.com.au*

OAKRIDGE WINES

Oakridge was originally planted in the 1970s by the Zitzlaff family and has changed hands several times since then. The gamechanger for the winery was the arrival of winemaker David Bicknell in 2002, after he had spent a decade with Steve Webber at De Bortoli. David has long been an advocate for a more elegant, refined style of wine and this is especially evident in his chardonnays. Alcohol is kept at bay, oak used as a supporting player, complementary of depth, acidity and orchard fruit. The Oakridge 864 has propelled Australian chardonnay onto an international stage. David doesn't pick favourites though – his pinot noirs are just as impressive.
oakridgewines.com.au

PUNT ROAD

In 1978, as the Yarra Valley grape industry was beginning to revive, the Napoleone family purchased the old St Huberts vineyards and winery. They planted grapes in 1987 and built a modern winery in the late 90s. The first Punt Road wines were released in 2001. Today the property consists of over 60 hectares of pinot gris, chardonnay, pinot noir, gamay, shiraz and Bordeaux varieties. Tim Shand took over winemaking in 2014 and was responsible for the consistent nature of the Punt Road wines until his departure in 2021. The Airlie Bank label gives the team the opportunity to be more playful and boundary pushing – and release wines at a lower price-point. The family also make Napoleone cider, reviving their background as orchardists.
puntroadwines.com.au

> **What we're drinking**
>
> *Awesome and inspiring wines emerge from **Mount Mary**. The 1970s winery reflects a basic need to vinify with judicious but limited interference, resulting in wines of architecture and intensity, with impressive character in youth but formidable presence for very long-term cellaring. The cabernet blend Quintet is one of Australia's greatest, and sets a global high watermark for cabernet wines anywhere. – Mike Bennie*

THOUSAND CANDLES

The expansive Thousand Candles vineyard was planted between 1995 and 2000. It rolls from a couple of hundred metres above sea level all the way down to the flood plains. Scattered around a large catchment dam are sauvignon blanc, pinot noir, shiraz, malbec, merlot, cabernet sauvignon and cabernet franc. The Thousand Candles label began in 2011, with William Downie (p. 178) as winemaker and Stuart Proud as viticulturist. Biological farming (chemical free) is central to Stuart's approach in the vineyard. When Bill Downie left in 2016, Stuart took on the role of winemaker. His ultra-premium fruit is also sold to wineries across the Yarra. **thousandcandles.com.au**

TIMO MAYER

German-born Timo Mayer is one of Yarra Valley's most iconic characters. His family back in Germany have a long history of winemaking, but Timo set off to see the world, landing in Wagga Wagga, NSW, to study oenology. Timo worked with Steve Webber at De Bortoli before taking over production at Gembrook Hill. It was there that his eponymous label began. Timo and his wife Rhonda planted their vineyard on the steep slope of Mt Toolebewong and aptly named it Bloody Hill ('it's bloody steep') – a **high-density planting**, with the bulk made up of pinot noir and smaller amounts of chardonnay and shiraz. Timo's winemaking dogma is 'bring back the funk', though his wines aren't the 'funkiest' in modern winemaking. They are highly individual, but always aiming to display classical parameters of place. **timomayer.com.au**

Sarah Crowe
Yarra Yering

WANTIRNA ESTATE

Reg and Bertina Egan planted vines in 1963, setting off the second coming for the Yarra Valley wine industry. Reg was a lawyer, who found himself dashing back to the winery to check on his ferments at the end of the workday. Nowadays, his daughter Maryann holds the winemaking responsibility, after finishing up a six-year stint at Chandon Australia. Just four wines are made, named after Reg and Bertina's four granddaughters – a chardonnay, pinot noir, cabernet sauvignon-merlot blend and a cabernet franc-merlot blend – still considered some of the Yarra's most iconic wines. The labels feature cartoons drawn by Australian artist Michael Leunig. **wantirnaestate.com.au**

YARRA YERING

Dr Bailey Carrodus made the Yarra Valley's first wines of its modern era. He was a horticulturist and academic by trade, working at Melbourne University while searching for a vineyard site on the side. The 1973 release was a Bordeaux-inspired blend and a northern Rhône blend, named Dry Red No. 1 and Dry Red No. 2, respectively. Yarra Yering was quick to gain national and international acclaim, such was Dr Bailey's skill as a winemaker and innovator. After he passed away in 2008, two businessmen (and big Yarra Yering fans) bought the vineyard and heeded Bailey's wishes for any subsequent management to continue in the style he had developed over his 40-year career. In 2013, the formidable Sarah Crowe was appointed winemaker. Sarah, who had spent 12 years working in wineries in the Hunter, is also a horticulturist. She made significant changes to vineyard management during her first few vintages, but the

changes to the wines have been incremental. Yarra Yering has gone from strength to strength during her reign, buried in awards and critical (as well as consumer) acclaim.
yarrayering.com

YERINGBERG

Guill de Pury had grown up alongside his family's defunct winery. In 1969, he and his wife Katherine decided to replant right where his grandfather had once grown grapes. The first new Yeringberg wines were produced in 1974 from just over 2 hectares of vines (which has become 20 hectares over the years). Guill and Katherine's children are now custodians of the winery, with Sandra in charge of winemaking and David looking after viticulture. The wines are known for their longevity: savoury marsanne-roussanne and earthy cabernet blends that continue to evolve and deliver. The de Pury family's early friendship with Wurundjeri man William Barak has been instrumental in the Yarra Valley's evolving consciousness of its original custodians. *yeringberg.com.au*

And don't forget ...

Bicknell FC makes impressive chardonnay and pinot noir from Oakridge's head-honcho David Bicknell and viticulturist Nicky Harris ... **Dappled Wine** produces classic takes and some unusual ones (think: Jura-style 'ullaged chardonnay') from winemaker Shaun Crinion ... **Ephemera Wines** makes electric wines from grapes grown organically in in the Yarra as well as some unique styles (try the white negroamaro!) from fruit off the Chalmers Heathcote vineyard (p. 190) ... **Goodman Wines**, in addition to being a delicious drop, all profits from Kate Goodman's Nikkal Rose label goes to supporting breast cancer research ... **Hoddles Creek**, planted in 1997 by the d'Anna family, makes Yarra classics and a mean pinot blanc ... **Journey Wines**, Damian North's pitch-perfect renditions of Yarra pinot noir and chardonnay, with some Heathcote fiano and shiraz to boot ... **Levantine Hill** makes premium Bordeaux-blends, has a lavish cellar door and restaurant, and even employs a helicopter to transport guests from Melbourne ... **Proud Primary Produce**, from famed viticulturist Stuart Proud, employs biological farming practices to produce site-driven grapes with minimal intervention in the winery ... **Punch** produces estate-grown chardonnay, pinot noir and cabernet sauvignon, with a second label 'Friends of Punch' from outstanding purchased grapes ... **Salo** is the side hustle of Giant Steps' Steve Flamsteed and Kiwi Dave Mackintosh for killer chardonnay ... **Serrat** is a 2001 **close-planted** vineyard run by Tom Carson (Yabby Lake, Mornington Peninsula) and his wife Nadège Sune ... the historic **Seville Estate**, with first vines planted in 1972, has become known for its perfumed and powerful shiraz ... **Soumah** makes a compelling mix of classic French varieties and some from northern Italy, the likes of nebbiolo, barbera, brachetto and marzemino ... **TarraWarra Estate** was first planted in 1983 and still turns out impressive pinot noir and chardonnay under the watch of winemaker Clare Halloran and viticulturist Stuart Sissins ... **Thick as Thieves** has a light-hearted take on the Yarra, with joyful names and an eclectic mix of estate-grown grapes, including the stalwart pinot noir, as well as nebbiolo, gamay and mencía ... **Toolangi** was established in 1995, and revitalised under Rochford owner Helmut Konecsny and winemaker Kasper Hermann ... **Yarrabank** is a joint venture between Yering Station and Champagne house Devaux, churning out some of the Valley's best **traditional-method** sparkling wines ... **Yering Station**, one of the most historic estates in the Yarra, revived by the Rathbone family in 1996, has built their reputation on chardonnay, pinot noir and shiraz.

What we're drinking

*I'll say it: the Yarra Valley is one of the best cabernet sauvignon regions in the world, and **Yeringberg's** is the perfect example. The balance of fresh fruit and herbaceousness is propped up by a thin seam of oak, supporting but never overwhelming. Delicious young and with age.* — **Jane Lopes**

Mornington Peninsula

Introduction

No wine region embodies the concept of luxury more than Mornington Peninsula: its wines, restaurants, accommodation, architecture, art and spectacular scenery ooze a sophistication and fineness that goes unmatched in Australia. Sitting just an hour's drive south of Melbourne, Mornington (as it's often shortened to), has built itself up as easily the premier wine tourism destination in Australia.

And the wines live up to their end of the bargain, delivering world-class chardonnay and pinot noir, in particular, that satisfy the gourmet traveller, while also commanding a large following across Australia and internationally. The wines tend to echo the same elegance and polish that the region as a whole is known for – and come with a price tag to match. This is not a region where many wines retail for under AUD $30/bottle, and plenty are in the $50–100/bottle range. In Burgundy terms, it's premier cru here, not Bourgogne rouge.

Just as tourists have been attracted to the region for decades, so too were the British, who first set foot on the peninsula in 1803, at its tip in today's Sorrento. Their approach was heralded from Bass Strait, seen by the Bunurong people who had inhabited the land for over 50,000 years. The Bunurong live off and care for the complex ecosystems of the region; their diet at the time of colonisation included everything from eel to emu, yam daisy and salt bush. By 1835, the settlement of Melbourne solidified the displacement of the Bunurong people, though the changing landscape of Port Phillip Bay – from grasslands to swamplands to water – had already initiated the exodus.

The tourism of Mornington has intersected somewhat with its First Nations: there is an interest among visitors to understand the original custodianship of the land, and Elders of the region are providing this service. Though the COVID-19 pandemic shook the tourism industry, the vignerons of Mornington have everything to be optimistic about. They care for an enchanted piece of land that they've successfully cultivated to make world-class wine (namely pinot noir, with chardonnay and pinot gris in support) – and, importantly, they have created a tourism industry that cultivates a sense of belonging among visitors and locals alike.

Evolution of Wine

The Mornington Peninsula set its ambitions high from the very beginning. Wines made from some of the region's earliest plantings, at the bayside town of Dromana, won honourable mention at the 1886 Intercontinental Exhibition in London.

Growth was moderate in those early years, with a handful of registered vineyards by the turn of the century. But quality was rumoured to be excellent, supplying its local population as well as the flourishing city of Melbourne.

Like most Australian wine regions, and especially those with cooler climates, the first half of the 20th century was barren. While **phylloxera** did not hit Mornington – the sliver of water known as 'The Rip' separated it from Geelong's vicious outbreak on the other side of Port Phillip Bay – its fledgling industry could not survive the economic recession and changing tastes toward **fortified** and sweet wines. By 1920, all vineyards had been abandoned or uprooted.

The next attempt at viticulture was in the late 1930s, at a site on Mount Eliza, just north of the city of Mornington. The vineyard was called Morning Star, owned by an adjacent Franciscan monastery. The wines produced at the time never amounted to more than altar wine, though the site was purchased by pharmacy tycoon Mario Verrocchi in 2020, and will perhaps enjoy a new chapter.

In the 1940s, after the conclusion of World War II, Tuisko Turso 'TT' Seppelt, of the famous Barossa Seppelt family (p. 315), planted in Dromana at the site of an old passionfruit grove. Due to poor health (his, not the vineyard's), he sold the site to the Seabrook family, owners of an important Melbourne wine and spirits merchant, who maintained the vineyard as a hobby until it burned down in 1967.

Finally, a commercial vineyard stuck: the Myer family's 1972 plantings in Dromana, later named Elgee Park. Soon after, Nat and Rosalie White purchased a lemon orchard in Red Hill, just east of Dromana, and replanted it to grapevines in 1976. Their first commercial vintage – Mornington's first as well – was in 1980 and released in 1981 under the name Main Ridge Estate: a pinot meunier for $5.50, a pinot noir for $5.60, and a cabernet sauvignon for $6.50.

Much like the earliest plantings in Mornington, the ambition was clear immediately, with gold medals being awarded to Main Ridge at the 1983 Lilydale Wine Show. Significantly, the Whites also petitioned for a cellar liquor licence, allowing them to sell wine directly from their cellar door. It was granted in 1980, another Mornington Peninsula first, kicking off a bountiful tourism industry that defines the region to this day.

The region soon attracted others to put down vines, some even before Main Ridge's first vintage had been released. Brian Stonier planted his family's vineyard to chardonnay at Merricks in 1978, adding pinot noir vines in 1982. George

James Sexton tending to fragile, early-spring growth at the Main Ridge Estate vineyard.

Kefford planted the same two grapes in 1978 on what would become Merricks Estate.

The 1980s brought more significant vineyard plantings and winery openings to the region. Garry Crittenden (Crittenden Estate) and Dr Richard McIntyre (Moorooduc) planted in 1982 and 1983, respectively. The climate data at the time, and in particular the maritime influence, pointed to Bordeaux varieties being successful, advice the two followed. Also founded in the 1980s were Eldridge (1984), Paringa (1985) and Hickinbotham of Dromana (1988).

By the early 1990s, the quality and potential of the Mornington Peninsula was clear. Dr John Gladstones, most famous for his work in Western Australia (p. 413), addressed the region in his 1992 book *Viticulture & Environment*, stating that the Mornington Peninsula 'has arguably the best ripening climate in Victoria for light to medium bodied **table wines** ... this would appear to be one of the few regions of Australia where the precise characteristics of the great Burgundy wines (both red and white) might reasonably be aspired to.' From here on out, chardonnay and pinot noir (and especially pinot noir) became the focus for the region, and the Bordelaise varieties were relegated to only specific, warmer, pockets.

The 1990s and 2000s, with their near universal practices of external investment and corporatisation, saw lite versions of these trends enacted in Mornington. Port Phillip Estate and Kooyong were both established in the 1990s, then purchased in 2000 and 2004, respectively, by Giorgio and Dianne Gjergja, who had made their fortune in the electrical manufacturing business. Ten Minutes by Tractor was formed in 1997, then purchased by Sydney tech CEO Martin Spedding and his wife Karen in 2003. And in 1998, the Kirby family (who own 42% of the multi-billion-dollar entertainment company Village Roadshow) founded Yabby Lake.

Rather than depleting integrity or encouraging bulk production, these instances of capital infusion promoted quality and site-specificity in the Mornington Peninsula. There was no impulse to bulldoze the wines with loads of oak or extraction, nor was there an idea to mass-produce. These new faces bought into the specialty of Mornington and doubled down on cultivating it as a fine wine region. They also contributed to the already booming tourism industry in the region, with a turn toward ultra-luxury accommodation and restaurants.

Pinot gris emerged as a strong supporting grape for chardonnay and pinot noir in the 1990s as well, in a story that intersects with one of Mornington's true cases of corporate ownership (along with Accolade's acquisition of Stonier in 2016). In 1990, wife and husband team Kathleen Quealy and Kevin McCarthy founded T'Gallant, with a focus on pinot gris/grigio. Their work launched an appreciation for the grape across Australia that has yet to dwindle, and placed it firmly in third place for prominence in Mornington. Though they sold off the company to Southcorp (now Treasury) in 2003, they still produce some of the most serious pinot gris/grigio in the region under the Quealy label.

The Mornington Peninsula Vignerons Association has always played a strong role in advocating for the wines of the region, since its formation in 1982. One of its grandest

Mornington Peninsula Viticultural Footprint

Total delimited area (km²)	720
Total planted area (hectares)	976
% of delimited area planted	1.360%
Total elevation range	0–315 masl
Elevation range of plantings	15–220 masl
Number of producers	50

Mornington Peninsula Climate Data (°C)

	1960–1990	1991–PRESENT	2020
Heat summation/GDD	● 1437	● 1470	● 1452
Annual rain/GSR	798/393	735/377	842/443
Warmest month avg. temp.	18.7	19.2	19.3

Winkler Scale:

● 850–1111 ● 1112–1389 ● 1390–1667 ● 1668–1944 ● 1945–2222 ● 2223–2700

accomplishments has been the biennial Mornington Peninsula International Pinot Noir Celebration, which brings together journalists, sommeliers and winemakers from all over the world to discuss and celebrate (and of course, drink) the signature grape of the region.

As the luxury tourism and fine wine industries have grown in tandem, Mornington Peninsula has largely outpriced itself for the bootstrap and experimental winery operations. Land, labour and farming are all expensive in Mornington. A few younger upstarts have been able to infiltrate, largely working on a micro-negociant basis (purchasing fruit rather than owning vineyards), including Allies, Onannon, Mattara, Garagiste and Kerri Greens, as well as producers based outside the region who work with Mornington fruit, like A.R.C., Jane Eyre, Mada, Reed and Fleet.

These producers have brought in a bit more experimentation and novelty to the region, but many stay true to the stalwart pinot noir and chardonnay. The veterans of Mornington remain (justifiably) committed to the region's key grapes and continue to set the bar for quality. These wineries, like Elgee Park, Main Ridge, Crittenden and Moorooduc – in addition to their more contemporary counterparts – remain at the top of their game, creating world-class wines that command top dollar.

The Mornington Peninsula is now home to more than 60 wineries, with over 80% of them hosting some sort of tourist facilities, whether a cellar door, restaurant and/or accommodation. The region has become the model, Australia-wide, for finding identity, building branding, cultivating fine wine and attracting luxury tourism.

Lay of the Land

Mornington Peninsula is thought of as a fairly compact wine region, when in fact it is the size of Burgundy's Côte d'Or; it is roughly the same distance from Chambertin to Montrachet as it is from Pearcedale to Cape Schanck: about 45 kilometres. It's apt to compare the two regions for other reasons: they are both well known for pinot noir and chardonnay, they both command a hefty price tag, and they both have **microclimates** within that produce differences in the wines. Where they differ is that Mornington has about 20% of the plantings of the Côte d'Or – and it's still considered a concise and relatively densely planted wine region by Australian standards.

The Peninsula is home to 9% of Australia's pinot noir plantings, though less than 1% of the nation's vineyards. Pinot noir accounts for 52% of the plantings in the region; chardonnay clocks in at 27%; pinot gris solidly nabs the third place spot with 13% of plantings; and shiraz and sauvignon blanc combine for a total of 5% (one of shiraz's lowest planting percentages in any Australian wine region). The other 3% includes riesling, savagnin, fiano, arneis and cabernet sauvignon.

To continue the comparison, the **microclimates** of Burgundy are well codified – less so for Mornington. The Peninsula has lots of famous hamlet names – Red Hill, Balnarring, Moorooduc, Merricks, Main Ridge and Dromana, among others – but few within the appellation are wanting to define subregional boundaries quite yet. Distinctions do exist, though perhaps not in as plentiful and distinct a way as to line up with the different townships.

The Mornington Peninsula, as a whole, is a heavily maritime-influenced Mediterranean climate with copious amounts of sunlight. On the **Winkler Scale**, the Mornington ranges from Region 1a (the coldest, like Germany's Ruwer) to Region 2 (much more moderate, like Italy's Piedmont); these fluctuations are caused by altitude, **aspect** and wind. The region does often experience heat spikes in the summer, sometimes up to 40°C, though there is ample access to watershed for irrigation, which helps

Mornington Peninsula

HOW TO READ THIS MAP
The vineyards of the Peninsula are home to just a handful of grape varieties. The numerous suburbs and subtle elevation shown in this map can provide a roadmap to discovering the nuances across the wines they make.

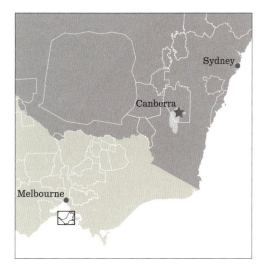

1 Avani
2 Baillieu Vineyard
3 Capella Vineyard
4 Circe Wines
5 Crittenden Estate
6 Dexter
7 Elan
8 Eldridge
9 Elgee Park
10 Hurley Vineyard
11 Kerri Greens
12 Kooyong
13 Main Ridge Estate
14 Merricks Estate
15 Merricks Grove Vineyard
16 Miceli
17 Montalto
18 Montalto Main Ridge Vineyard
19 Moorooduc Estate
20 Morning Star
21 Nazaaray
22 Ocean Eight
23 Ocean Eight Tuerong Vineyard
24 Paradigm Hill
25 Paringa Estate
26 Point Leo Road Vineyard
27 Polperro
28 Port Phillip Estate
29 Portsea Estate
30 Principia
31 Quealy Winemakers
32 Red Hill Estate
33 Red Ridge Vineyard
34 Rivendel Vineyard
35 Robinson Vineyard
36 Scorpo
37 Shippen
38 Silverwood
39 Staindl
40 Stonier Wines
41 Taturry
42 Ten Minutes by Tractor
43 Ten Minutes by Tractor Judd Vineyard
44 Ten Minutes by Tractor McCutcheon Vineyard
45 Ten Minutes by Tractor Wallis Vineyard
46 Trofeo Estate
47 Yabby Lake
48 Yabby Lake Arthurs Seat Vineyard

Victoria

126

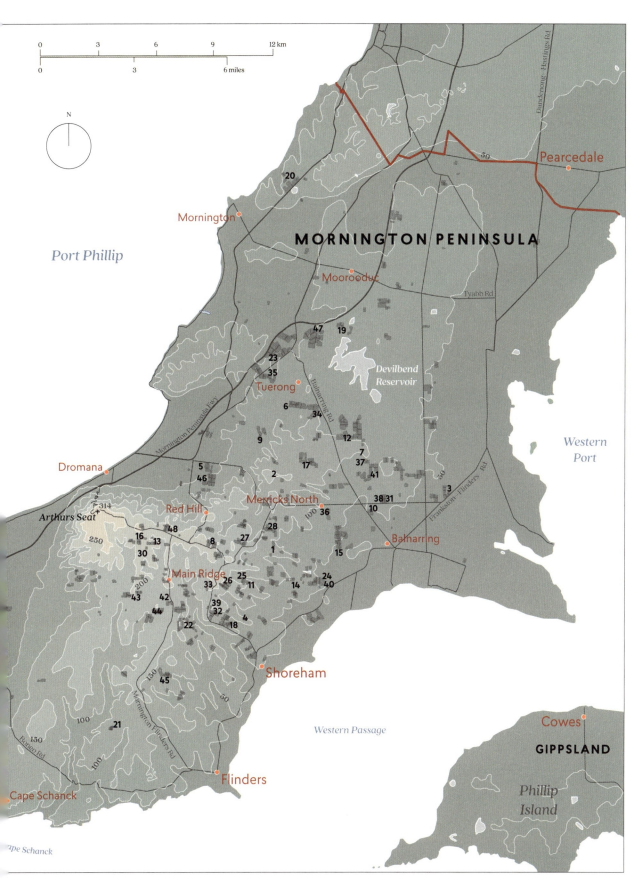

Mornington Peninsula

mitigate. Humidity is abundant. Vine stress is low, though vineyards require quite a bit of disease management. Rainfall is plentiful, and high and low temperatures throughout the year are usually moderate.

Beyond these commonalities, there are three distinct climate zones on the peninsula. The first surrounds the Main Ridge/Red Hill area. This is the least coastal of the areas of Mornington (though you're never too far from the water). This area is defined by elevation and red soils. Producers in this area can either face Port Phillip Bay (northwest) or the Bass Strait/Western Passage (southeast), so **microclimates** in the areas are quite varied. The elevation here, though only a modest 190–230 metres, provides a cooling influence.

The next zone is the southeast-facing side of the peninsula, consisting of the towns of Balnarring, Merricks and Point Leo. This area is more exposed to southeasterly winds and cold fronts. Lower-lying sections are warmer than those moving up the southeastern facing slope.

On the Port Phillip Bay-facing side of Mornington Peninsula – what can be considered the third climatic zone – the vineyards are warmer (even more so than the low-elevation vineyards on the other side), with protection from the southeasterlies. Warm fronts come out of the northwest to meet these sites. Moorooduc, Dromana and Arthurs Seat are towns in this area.

To add to the matrix, there are four main soil types in Mornington. The first is centred at Dromana: a yellow duplex soil composed of a hard, acidic sandy cement-like layer above friable, well-draining clay. Red Hills and Main Ridge have deep, red loamy volcanic soils similar to what can be found in the Upper Yarra and parts of Gippsland. Brown, clay duplex soils are common on the Bass Strait–facing shore, near Merricks and

Balnarring. The northern end of the GI, in and around Moorooduc, tends to be sandier.

The geological underpinnings of these soil types come from old marine sediments (510–405 million years ago), a magma intrusion in the Devonian era (370 million years ago), and younger extrusions of basalt (40 million years ago).

Though vintners in the area agree that these differences in soil and climate have an impact on the finished wine, most also agree that the hand of the winemaker (and viticulturist) can have an equal, or sometimes greater, effect.

Farming in general has moved to reduce chemical inputs, as in many regions across Australia. Mornington is still not a region that boasts many of its top producers as devotees of organic and **biodynamic** farming – disease pressure in many parts makes this proposition difficult. However, there is a small but devoted cadre of producers who undertake these farming practices – Avani, Prancing Horse Estate, Nazaaray, Staindl – and there is more traction in this arena among the historic estates.

Dry-farming is possible on the Peninsula, and somewhat common throughout the sandier and more volcanic-based soils. It's all about soil-viability and farming for Avani's Shashi Singh, in describing their ability to **dry-farm**: 'We get about 760 millimetres [of rain] through the year. And if we can retain all that, if our soils are good and they can penetrate and keep that, then we don't need to irrigate.' Irrigation has become not just an issue of fruit quality and minimal inputs, but a question of survival for many vineyards as climate change threatens water security. The current climatic conditions of the Mornington Peninsula are ideal for achieving the desired wine expression, but one of the questions weighing on the region is: will this change in the future?

Albariño-Savagnin Mix-up

For decades, Australian winemakers planted and made what they thought was the Iberian grape albariño. About 150 hectares of the grape were planted under the belief that it was albariño, based on a mistake in the CSIRO's plant collection. In 2009 it was revealed that those vines were in fact savagnin, a grape made famous by the Jura region of France. Now there are a number of interesting savagnins on the market in Australia, including a flor-aged version from Mornington's Crittenden Estate.

Looking southeast down to Merricks Beach and out onto the Western Passage from the top of the Stonier Wines vineyard.

Hubbub

The COVID-19 pandemic affected every corner of the wine world, but the Mornington Peninsula, as a region that relies on tourism, was hit particularly hard. Normally a boon for the region, the Peninsula's robust tourism industry was crippled throughout the pandemic and the ensuing strict (and long) lockdowns throughout Victoria and New South Wales. Many wineries were able to pivot (the dreaded word of 2020) to online sales and virtual tastings, but the properties with significant accommodation and restaurants had no means of compensating for that income. It's been a rough time for the Peninsula that, as of publishing, has yet to fully resolve itself.

Excepting the anomaly of a global pandemic, business is usually quite good for Mornington, and worries are few and far between. The region has caught a bit of flak over the years for being a rich person's playground, with many of the founders of the 1980s and 1990s earning their wealth in other industries and investing in their passion – growing pinot noir. But, perhaps in this criticism there's a tinge of jealousy or 'tall poppy syndrome' (as Australians call the desire to sabotage the successful, p. 131). As Moorooduc's Kate McIntyre notes, the combination of this financial structure and the formally trained winemakers the region has been able to attract has brought 'a level of passion and professionalism for making something really

> Excepting the anomaly of a global pandemic, business is usually quite good for the Mornington, and worries are few and far between.

top class', without the burden of needing a winery to make money quickly.

The more current flak comes from the outside (and especially the media) wanting the region to give them a bit more to work with. 'Some might say we're not exciting enough,' relates McIntyre; 'not doing enough in terms of trying new things, innovating, moving in different directions ... but I would say rather than trying to do something different (just to be newsworthy), we are working on improving on what we know we can do well, so we do it even better.'

One of the areas of forced hubbub centres around defining subregions, which doesn't seem to be pressing among the vignerons of the region. The differences across the region are recognised (though perhaps not fully excavated),

Paringa Estate in Red Hill is home to an infamous flock of Toulouse geese, which roam the property. Online reviews advise which geese are friendly and which is the grumpy goose to avoid!

but equally so is the effect of the winemaker on ultimate style. Second-generation Mornington winemaker Rollo Crittenden explains it like this: 'We're a young region. I think it's important that we let it roll out, let the subregions speak for themselves over a long period of time as to what they are, because there are so many influences that we are bringing as producers, whether it be **clonal** or site selection or viticultural process, and these variables are defining the wine styles, I would say equally.'

The two concerns that *are* top of mind, though perhaps less interesting for the onlooker, are **phylloxera** and climate change. After four years of diligent testing and government investment, Mornington Peninsula was downgraded from a **Phylloxera** Risk Zone to a **Phylloxera** Exclusion Zone in 2021. This means serious biosecurity directives and an internal vigilance demanded of producers. Avani's Shashi Singh recounts, 'I have very strict protocols for people coming in. I sit down on my knees and I brush their boots. I don't trust them. If I have a contractor, anybody, coming in. I've washed the tractors myself.' And despite caution, most recognise that the absence of **phylloxera** can't last indefinitely and are starting to replant on rootstock. Biosecurity measures also mean added expense for the wineries: contract equipment can't come in so growers must own their own.

Climate change, as for many regions, is also a persistent concern. Will the region become too warm for its signature grape, pinot noir? Will bushfires and water rights become issues? Will those who rely on irrigation be priced out of

The differences across the region are recognised (though perhaps not fully excavated), but equally so is the effect of the winemaker on ultimate style.

accessing it? These are all questions that weigh on the minds of the vignerons of Mornington, without clear answers in sight. Though some are experimenting with different grape varieties, most don't want to think about a day when Mornington Peninsula would not be synonymous with pinot noir, and instead are focusing on 'farming decisions and how to optimise them', in the words of Rohit Singh, Shashi's son. These practices include **dry-farming** where possible, redistributing **canopies**, changing the orientation of vineyards and – of course – farming more regeneratively.

The global warming conversation has led many to feel that we as humans have taken too much from the earth, and not given back. As McIntyre puts it, 'we're just thinking about how we can be a little more considerate of the bit of dirt that we're trying to live off'.

Tall Poppy Syndrome

What happens when a poppy gets too tall? You cut it down, of course. That is the logic of the 'tall poppy syndrome' – a facet of Australian social culture that all agree is real, though few are proud of. In general, Australians are humble and down-to-earth, to the extent that sometimes those who enjoy too much success (and particularly those who celebrate it too loudly) are targets for critique and contempt. This can manifest in the wine industry with derision for high prices, pooh-poohing commercially successful estates or regions, and awarding the underdog.

PRODUCERS

AVANI

Shashi and Devendra Singh operated restaurants in Mornington for decades before buying the property that became Avani. The site was an established vineyard called Wildcroft Estate, planted to pinot noir, chardonnay, merlot, cabernet sauvignon and syrah. Shashi took up studies in viticulture and oenology before landing a job at the great Bass Phillip (Gippsland) with Phillip Jones. In 2006, Shashi made the decision to graft and replant all her vines over to syrah, despite being told she would never sell the grape from Mornington Peninsula. Her connection to the vineyard and ability to read plant development has proved the naysayers wrong. Shashi farms using organic and **biodynamic** principles, techniques she learnt from her grandparents, and she has seen the benefits translated into the wine. Aside from syrah, there is a playful set of wines made from other vineyards around the Mornington, bottled under the label Amrit. Her son, Rohit, has recently joined the farm, adding to the excitement of what's to come.
avanisyrah.com.au

Shashi Singh
Avani

CRITTENDEN ESTATE

A horticulturist by trade, Garry Crittenden moved to Mornington to develop nurseries. As his interest in viticulture peaked, he and wife Margaret planted their first vines in 1982. Garry took on no formal wine education, instead working closely with fellow regional pioneer, Nat White (Main Ridge). Early wines, under the name Dromana Estate, were cabernet-centric, though chardonnay and pinot noir also made up the modest original plantings and eventually took centre stage. Garry's son Rollo took over winemaking in 2007, building on a consistently successful range of pinots and chardonnays, as well as introducing more Italian and Spanish varieties from outside Mornington. In 2009, Rollo grafted a small amount of chardonnay over to what he thought was albariño and was rather disappointed with the result. The discovery that it was actually savagnin, the pride of France's mountainous Jura, led him through a fascinating exploration of how the

---

 What we're drinking

As a region not known for its alternative varieties and experimental styles, one of the best wines from those categories is produced in Mornington. **Crittenden's** *Cri de Coeur is a flor-aged savagnin that provides all the waxy and resinous notes of its prototype (Jura Vin Jaune), but with a juiciness of fruit that offers a serious deliciousness factor.* **– Jane Lopes**

traditional techniques of the region could be applied in an Australian setting. *crittendenwines.com.au*

ELGEE PARK

Elgee Park was the first commercial vineyard in Mornington, planted by the Myer family in 1972. Purchased as a getaway house, the estate was developed with stables, a vineyard, winery, orchard and a collection of more than 45 sculptures. Elgee Park is home to some of Australia's oldest viognier plantings, with trial vines first popping up in 1979. Sitting on the hills of Merricks North, the vineyard is still warm enough to ripen cabernet sauvignon, which is blended with earlier-ripening merlot.
elgeeparkwines.com.au

GARAGISTE

After working at vineyards in the Rhône and US, Barnaby Flanders founded Allies Wines with David Chapman while they were working at Moorooduc Estate. The Garagiste label fell under this banner and, when the two parted ways, Barnaby took Garagiste with him. He makes a concise range of Mornington Peninsula classics with fruit from Merricks, Balnarring and Moorooduc. The Le Stagiaire wines are multi-site blends, whereas Côtier focuses on smaller expressions of place, even down to the half acre. *garagiste.com.au*

HURLEY VINEYARD

Kevin Bell and Tricia Byrnes come from the legal system (Victorian Supreme Court judge and barrister respectively) and have applied a learned and fastidious approach to Mornington pinot noir. They planted their Balnarring vineyard in the late 90s, expressly to create single-vineyard pinot noirs. Kevin and Tricia both share a great respect for the environment and the traditional owners of the land on which they farm; their understanding of site expression is evident in each glass.
hurleyvineyard.com.au

KERRI GREENS

Tom McCarthy and Lucas Blanck have a fair amount of wine heritage between them. They met working at Quealy Winemakers, owned and run by Tom's parents, and Lucas's family estate is Domaine Paul Blanck in his native Alsace. The duo took over managing a vineyard in Balnarring with chardonnay plantings from the early 80s, sparking an interest in sensible farming and **lo-fi** techniques. They've since brought production to their own winery space in Red Hill. Tom and Lucas focus primarily on single-vineyard pinot noir and chardonnay, with a couple of nods to Lucas' heritage in some riesling and gewürztraminer bottlings.
kerrigreens.com

KOOYONG

The Aylward family planted Kooyong in the subregion of Tuerong in 1996, at a time when growth in Mornington Peninsula was rapid. Kooyong quickly became well-respected under the reign of winemaker Sandro Mosele. The Gjergja family bought Kooyong in 2004, four years after establishing Port Phillip Estate, and have developed a state-of-the-art winery, as well as a grand cellar door and restaurant. Kooyong highlights single-site chardonnay and pinot noir from five distinct blocks on their estate, in addition to a wide range of bottlings that are produced under various labels.
portphillipestate.com.au

MAIN RIDGE ESTATE

Nat and Rosalie White produced Mornington's first commercial vintage in 1980: a pinot noir, a pinot meunier and a cabernet sauvignon. The Whites had bought their property, an old orchard, five years earlier. Since then, pinot noir and chardonnay have emerged as the enduring varieties of the estate. As his reputation and skill as a winemaker grew, Nat White became a mentor to many on the Peninsula. The Whites retired in 2015 and sold Main Ridge to a Melbourne couple; quality has been maintained through the transition. *mre.com.au*

MOOROODUC ESTATE

Dr Richard McIntyre decided that once his days as a surgeon were numbered, he wanted to make wine. It was early days for Mornington, but Richard believed the region had great potential. With the help of Garry Crittenden, he founded his property in Moorooduc, planting the first vines in 1983. Richard filled his time trialling and experimenting with grape and science, which is fortuitous, as pinot noir was originally planted 'just in case'. Richard's daughter Kate has taken over marketing for her parents' business, despite a defiant desire to steer clear early in life. It wasn't until she got a job in a wine store in her 20s that her interest in wine ignited. Completing the **Master of Wine** program (no easy feat), Kate has become an important voice on the Peninsula. The pinnacle of the Moorooduc style is pinot noir and chardonnay from their oldest home block, but their skin-macerated pinot gris has garnered much attention for the estate. *moorooducestate.com.au*

OCEAN EIGHT

After the Aylward family sold Kooyong in 2003, they began developing their property in Shoreham for son Mike Aylward to spread his winemaking wings. Mike's first wine was a pinot gris from the original 6 hectares on the property. The Aylwards bought a second site, which they planted to chardonnay and pinot noir, rounding out the trifecta of grapes that has defined Mike's wines. He champions a racier, leaner style, especially in his chardonnay, balancing tension with flavour. *oceaneight.com.au*

PARADIGM HILL

George and Ruth Mihaly left careers in medical research and food for the 'vine change' that is Paradigm Hill. They have long been passionate about climate action and were early adopters of solar energy in the 2000s, when the business was just getting started; Paradigm Hill are committed to becoming a carbon-neutral winery. Their vineyard in Merricks is planted to just over 2 hectares of pinot noir, with the rest made up of shiraz, riesling and pinot gris. Ruth looks after viticulture, while George drew on his scientific background to master the process of winemaking (with early assistance from Nat White at Main Ridge Estate). Pinot production is divided into three wines, with particular elegance and complexity coming from single vineyards Les Cinq and L'ami Sage. *paradigmhill.com.au*

PARINGA ESTATE

Lindsay McCall had his 'aha' wine moment in a restaurant in 1983 when he tasted a bottle of 1980 Seville Estate. Having not realised that Victorian wines could be so good, he bought an old north-facing orchard, planting grapes in 1984. Lindsay

---

 What we're drinking

Pinot gris is often overlooked as simple juice in a bottle. Let me assure you there is nothing one-dimensional about Mike Aylward's pinot gris from **Ocean Eight***; it is layered and textural while also being juicy and vibrant. If you are looking for a bottle to grab the next time you are headed for a Vietnamese feast, this is the one!* — **Kavita Faiella**

produced his first wine in an old fish tank in 1987, though safe to say this was not the first commercial release. He worked vintages and made wine around his schedule as a schoolteacher until he took on winemaking full time in 1996. A particularly talented winemaker, Lindsay has become well known for his shiraz and pinot noir. His son Jamie has also caught the winemaking bug and joined his dad in the winery. **paringaestate.com.au**

POLPERRO/EVEN KEEL

Sam Coverdale is stoked with his job: great wine, great surf and proximity to the great city of Melbourne, Mornington is the perfect home for him and his winery Polperro. After working his way through wineries in Australia, Spain, Italy and France, Sam launched his first label, Even Keel, in 2006. He sources Even Keel fruit from around the Peninsula, Tumbarumba and Canberra District, making bright, early-drinking wines. Polperro was born in 2008, out of a desire to focus on premium single-vineyard sites around the Mornington. Sam crafts refined pinot noir and chardonnay under this banner and has boutique accommodation and a restaurant on site. **polperrowines.com.au**

QUEALY WINEMAKERS

Kathleen Quealy and Kevin McCarthy have made pinot grigio/gris a household name. They started the incredibly successful T'Gallant in the 90s, which was bought by Foster's (now Treasury Wine Estates), before the eponymous label Quealy began in 2006. Kathleen and Kevin have always been big fans of the lesser-known Italian varieties and were among the first to plant friulano in Australia. Kevin travelled extensively in the 90s to study Italian pinot grigio, which is when he developed a fascination with skin-contact wines. The Pobblebonk field blend is an ode to the Friulian wines of Jermann, theirs a blend of pinot grigio, friulano, riesling and moscato giallo. Their son Tom joined the business in 2012 and Lucas Blanck manages their vineyards, which have been certified organic since 2019. **quealy.com.au**

> **What we're drinking**
>
> *A kaleidoscopic array of wines are released from the quixotic and yet incredibly considered **Quealy**, though it's the use of astute skin fermentation of white grapes that draws attention. As one of the first, if not arguably the first in a modern epoch, to extend skin fermentation beyond the norm, Quealy has a track record of finding inimitable complexity from white grapes distinct from chardonnay in this region.* — **Mike Bennie**

STONIER WINES

Brian Stonier was one of the early adopters in the Mornington grapevine renaissance. He planted chardonnay in 1978 in Merricks and added pinot noir in 1982. Former winemaker Mike Symons, who joined Stonier in 2008, brought philosophies of organic farming to the estate, which have been steadily

Kathleen Quealy & Kevin McCarthy
Quealy

Mornington Peninsula

employed. And current winemaker Justin Purser, formerly of Best's Great Western, has brought fresh energy to the wines. Stonier has become particularly synonymous with pinot noir over the years, in no small part due to the efforts of Brian, who has spearheaded an international pinot tasting in Mornington. Stonier is now owned by Accolade Wines.
stonier.com.au

TEN MINUTES BY TRACTOR

Ten Minutes by Tractor began in 1997, a collection of three family-owned vineyards in Main Ridge – McCutcheon, Judd and Wallis – that were all within a 10-minute drive by tractor. It was a bottle of the 2001 Reserve Pinot Noir that led Martin Spedding to purchase Ten Minutes by Tractor. A tech company CEO with dreams of winemaking, Martin had been searching for his own cool-climate vineyard. He bought the business in 2004 with his wife Karen, and the couple set the fledgling winery on the path to becoming one of the most well-known estates in the area. Four new vineyards have been added, two of which are **high-density plantings**, with the Gabrielle vineyard being certified organic. Ten Minutes by Tractor also maintains one of the most-acclaimed restaurants in the region.
tenminutesbytractor.com.au

YABBY LAKE VINEYARD

When the Kirby family started Yabby Lake in 1998, no expense was spared to find the very best spot for grapes. Every inch of soil was surveyed and the area carefully mapped before anything went in the ground. The vineyard is a north-facing slope in Tuerong that enjoys both sunshine and maritime breezes. The main focus is on single vineyards, with pinot noir, chardonnay and small amounts of pinot gris and syrah planted. Tom Carson came on as chief winemaker in 2008 and brought home the coveted **Jimmy Watson Memorial Trophy** for his 2012 Block 1 Pinot Noir – the first ever **Jimmy Watson** for pinot noir in the award's history. They also release entry-level wines under the Red Claw range, approachable and easy drinking in style. *yabbylake.com*

And don't forget ...
Allies Wines, from chef and somm-turned winemaker David Chapman, has a mission to showcase the diversity of Mornington pinot noir ... **Circe Wines**, a collab between Dan Buckle (Chandon Australia, p. 116) and Aaron Drummond, focuses on Mornington pinot noir, pinot meunier and chardonnay (and one Gippsland bottling) ... **Eldridge**, a project from scientist David Lloyd, has estate-grown pinot noir, chardonnay and gamay at its heart ... **Montalto** is one of the most striking sites of the Mornington (hello sculpture garden and olive grove!), with creative and elegant wines to match, crafted by the talented Simon Black ...

Nazaaray Estate occupies a plot in Flinders, on the southern tip of the Peninsula, where Paramdeep and Nirmal Ghumman make some of the finest values in the region ... **Onannon** is the pinot noir-focused side hustle of winemakers Sam Middleton (Mount Mary), Kasper Hermann (Rochford) and Will Byron (ex-Stonier) ... **Principia**, Darrin Gaffy's Red Hill property, is built on gravity-flow to move their estate-grown, unirrigated pinot noir and chardonnay ... **Staindl** puts out well-crafted pinot noir, chardonnay and riesling from their **biodynamically** grown home vineyard ... **Taturry** is the solo project of long-time Red Hill Estate winemaker Luke Curry, with elegant expressions of pinot noir, chardonnay and syrah ... **Willow Creek Vineyard**, planted in 1989 and now made by superstar Geraldine McFaul, is owned by the same group who built the successful luxury hotel Jackalope.

Looking east from Wallis vineyard, part of the Ten Minutes by Tractor estate, across to Phillip Island.

Geelong

Introduction

Geelong's story is one of glory lost – or perhaps taken. Victoria's second largest city, and one of Australia's oldest and most storied wine regions, Geelong is about an hour's drive west then south out of Melbourne. The city sits on Corio Bay, an enclave created by the Bellarine Peninsula in the western portion of the larger Port Phillip Bay.

The GI is one large swath of land, but the vineyard areas are non-contiguous. Separated by large distances, the three distinct areas, or unofficial subregions, encircle the city starting with the Moorabool Valley to the city's northwest, the Surf Coast to the south, and the Bellarine Peninsula to the southeast. A fourth subregion can be considered; the vineyards of the Otway hinterland are often discussed with Geelong, and will be here as well, but lie just west of the GI's borders.

The city of Geelong was established by Europeans between 1836 and 1838, about 30 years after the first non-Indigenous person landed in the area of Port Phillip in early 1802. Subsequent surveyors arrived from Sydney in and around the area. While seeking to establish the Sullivan Penal Colony, the HMS *Calcutta* sent a party to what is now known as Corio Bay; this is where the first recorded death of a member of the Kulin Nation occurred at the hands of a European.

Over the next 15 years, the Wathaurong population declined from 300 people to less than 40 due to novel influenza, loss of food sources (from the introduction of cattle and sheep) and murder. Over 140 archaeological sites have been discovered across the area known to be Wathaurong Country, speaking to the complexity and size of the First Nation. The Wathaurong people were the ones who named the area 'Djillong', which, depending on which clan Elder you speak to, means either 'Land, Cliffs, Tongue of Land', or 'Peninsula Over the Sea'.

Today, the greater Geelong region ranges from a dense city of 250,000 residents, rolling grasslands full of grazing sheep, a breathtaking coastline home to the start of the Great Ocean Road, beachside estates, plus vineyards and wineries of all shapes and sizes. There are two wineries credited for putting Geelong on the map – Bannockburn and By Farr – but its accomplishments and diversity expand much further than these.

Geelong's diversity – one could even say its fragmentation – makes it difficult to generalise about as a wine region. It's a collection of vineyards across three distinct subregions, housing all sorts of grape varieties, ambitions and personalities. Geelong is poised to reclaim the glory of its early days, beyond its two big names, but it won't be homogenised. It is a region that demands nuanced attention – but trust us, it's worth it.

Evolution of Wine

Geelong started with a bang. The first commercial grape harvest occurred in 1845 from the Neuchâtel vineyard, planted in 1842 to pinot noir and pinot meunier. By 1861 Geelong was one of the most productive and prestigious wine regions in Australia. The city and region were booming and wine exports back to Europe were common, with the equivalent of nearly 150,000 cases of Victorian wine exported to the UK annually through the mid-1860s. Geelong had grown to 226 hectares of vines by 1861 and accounted for over half of the entire Victorian vineyard surface.

In 1875, **phylloxera** was discovered in the vineyards of Geelong – the first sighting of the infamous root louse in Australia. In response, the government ordered the complete removal of every affected vineyard in the area to prevent further spread. Some believe that local officials held financial interests in competing wine regions, and the drastic response was not solely motivated by the impulse to stop **phylloxera** from spreading further. But for whatever reason, by 1883, the industry in Geelong had come to a screeching halt.

In 1892, the region was permitted to begin planting vineyard land that had laid fallow for 10 years (part of the mandated treatment). However, a massive economic depression in 1893 – combined with changing tastes toward **fortified wine** – prevented the wine industry from re-establishing itself until well into the 20th century.

It wasn't until 1966 that the region reignited its viticulture, when Darryl and Nini Sefton planted the Idyll Vineyard in the Moorabool Valley: 20 hectares of shiraz, cabernet sauvignon and gewürztraminer. In the early 1970s, a Melbourne businessman named Stuart Hooper sought out a site in Geelong for a vineyard, finding one near the township of Bannockburn in the Moorabool Valley. Thus began Bannockburn Vineyards, with a small plot of shiraz, becoming one of the icon producers in Geelong to this day.

Bannockburn's success owes significantly to the contributions of Gary Farr, the chief winemaker at Bannockburn from 1978–2004. In 1994 and 1998, Gary and his wife Robyn purchased their own vineyards adjacent to the Bannockburn site, and after the 2004 vintage, Farr left Bannockburn to focus exclusively on his own wine label, By Farr.

Stuart Hooper was a big Burgundy aficionado, a quality significant in the styling of the wines of Bannockburn, By Farr, and eventually Geelong and Australia as a whole. Gary Farr spent off-seasons with Jacques Seysses of Domaine

Looking north across Corio Bay from the top of Nurringa Park vineyard on the Bellarine Peninsula, the peaks of the You Yangs in the distance.

Dujac in Morey-Saint-Denis (with Seysses's off-seasons spent in Geelong). Gary's pinot noirs at Bannockburn were some of the first modern pinots in Australia that employed a significant proportion of whole bunches (a style Domaine Dujac was known for), and today the Bannockburn Serré vineyard is Australia's oldest **close-planted** pinot noir vineyard, which Gary planted when he returned from his first vintage in Burgundy in 1984.

These two producers – Bannockburn and By Farr – have almost single-handedly (double-handedly?) driven quality and recognition for Geelong over the years. But as viticulture, winemaking and tourism developed in Geelong, a few additional makers have made significant marks. Clyde Park, with plantings dating back to the 1970s, has been a consistent source for reliable wine in Geelong, with new ownership in 1996 creating one of the area's best restaurant and event spaces. Lethbridge was planted by two ex-scientists in 1996 and continues to be one of the region's most interesting and ambitious producers. And Shadowfax, though based outside the boundaries of Geelong (in Werribee Park, about halfway between Geelong and Melbourne), has been a long-time champion of the region.

And though the new generation of winemakers investing their talents in Geelong are few and far between, they are tenacious and quality-minded enough to be making a difference.

Sierra Reed, based in Torquay, had her first vintage in 2015, sourcing grapes from some of the top single vineyards in Geelong and across Australia for her label Reed Wines. In 2021, she began grafting over an old semillon site in Springs Creek (within Torquay on the Surf Coast) to riesling and gamay. James Thomas, formerly of Clyde Park and Bannockburn, established Heroes Vineyard in the Otway hinterland in 2016, and has been quietly churning out some excellent riesling, chardonnay, pinot noir and sparkling wine (all while converting and certifying his now-organic site). In 2017, Tash Webster launched her label, Empire of Dirt, sourcing fruit from the Moorabool Valley and Bellarine Peninsula. And in 2019, Niki Nikolovski and Tim Byrne picked their first vintage of Babche Wines – initially sourcing from organic growers on the Bellarine Peninsula, before planting their own permaculture farm west of the Otways in 2021. And producers like Attwoods and Mulline, though based outside of Geelong, are putting the region's best foot forward with their deft care of its fruit.

Though Geelong's current plantings have just exceeded where they were pre-**phylloxera**, the prestige and glory has not been restored (for all but a few). Geelong hasn't had the broad influx of new plantings and interest (like Gippsland, p. 166), nor the fellowship of many well-esteemed pioneers (like the Yarra Valley, p. 104), nor has it enjoyed the concert between tourism and serious wine-growing (like Mornington Peninsula, p. 122). The region's renaissance has been much more of a slow burn, with only a few producers of significance emerging every decade. Geelong is Victoria's best kept wine secret, but perhaps too well kept: a bit more energy, investment and cohesion of community could do the region good.

Geelong Valley Viticultural Footprint

Total delimited area (km²)	2830
Total planted area (hectares)	466
% of delimited area planted	0.16%
Total elevation range	0–396 masl
Elevation range of plantings	30–396 masl
Number of producers	52

Geelong Climate Data (°C)

	1960–1990	1991–PRESENT	2020
Heat summation/GDD	● 1402	● 1467	● 1461
Annual rain/GSR	589/318	539/297	534/341
Warmest month avg. temp.	18.8	19.5	19.7

Winkler Scale:

● 850–1111　● 1112–1389　● 1390–1667　● 1668–1944　● 1945–2222　● 2223–2700

Lay of the Land

The area, like most of Australia, is a patchwork of both ancient soils and recent formations, **microclimates** and **mesoclimates**, elevations and **aspects**. But unlike many Australian wine appellations, the boundaries of the Geelong GI have not done the region service in tying together a region with distinct commonalities. It's no one's fault: at the time of GI formation, in the 1990s, the Geelong area did not have the production to warrant further delineation. Geelong was destined, like others (Henty and Gippsland come to mind), to merely be an area tied together by geographic proximity, rather than any real similarity.

It's useful to think about GI in terms of its three distinct (though still unofficial) subregions: Moorabool Valley in the north, Bellarine Peninsula out east (on the peninsula, as the name implies), and the Surf Coast to the south. A fourth subregion can be considered; the vineyards of the Otway hinterland are often discussed with Geelong, and will be here as well, but lie just west of the GI's borders.

The subregion with the most history – both vinous and geological – is the Moorabool Valley. Much of the lower areas of western Victoria were once seabed. In the Moorabool Valley, some of this seabed remains at the surface, uncovered by volcanic activity then eroded, spread and shifted by the ever-changing path of the Moorabool River over time. Where the rare limestone deposits and marly soils aren't found, red and black volcanic loams, ironstone mixed with sandy loams (called buckshot soils), volcanic basalt and alluvial gravels appear. When he was looking to plant in the Moorabool, Lethbridge's Ray Nadeson compared the region's soils to the greatest in the world: 'Mosel, Douro, Burgundy ... all free draining, rocky, low vigour ... we were blown away by the soils here.'

The Moorabool River originates further north near Ballarat, where the Great Dividing Range fades away northwest of Melbourne. The meandering path of the Moorabool River creates a valley with highly favourable northern exposures on gentle slopes. The river valley

> # Geelong was destined, like others, to merely be an area tied together by geographic proximity, rather than any real similarity.

acts as a wind tunnel, similar to that of California's Napa Valley. However, rather than Napa's cool coastal air coming in, hot, dry winds rip down the valley and can impact flowering. This results in a stark Mediterranean rainfall pattern, with a majority of precipitation happening in winter.

Of the three subregions, Moorabool Valley is the driest. Though its rainfall patterns operate in a Mediterranean manner, its climate operates in more of a continental one (especially moving inland), with higher summer heat spikes, lower humidity and higher **diurnal swings** than the other subregions of Geelong. With its mild autumn and cool nights, Moorabool often harvests up to 3–4 weeks later than the other parts of Geelong.

While the river provides moisture for the lowest-lying farmland in the area, the lack of precipitation prevents growers from **dry-farming**. There has been no shortage of experimentation, but **dry-farming** in the Moorabool often results in imbalanced vines, under so much water stress that you can literally taste it.

Growers must collect their irrigation supply in dams from winter runoff and rain, though a full dam at budbreak is rare, often a product of **La Niña** weather patterns. Planting cover crops, mulching and reducing the tilling of soils are common techniques for retaining ground moisture and reducing water usage.

There is a good bit of elevation change as one moves downstream from the northwestern limits of the GI at Meredith (340 metres), through

Geelong

HOW TO READ THIS MAP

The interplay of Geelong's ancient marine sediments and more recent volcanic deposits are shown in this map, as well as the three unofficial subregions that are a part of the region's identity. The Otways, sometimes considered an extension of the Surf Coast beyond the borders of Geelong GI, is also featured on this map, along with some vineyards that dot the undefined expanse between Geelong and Western Victoria.

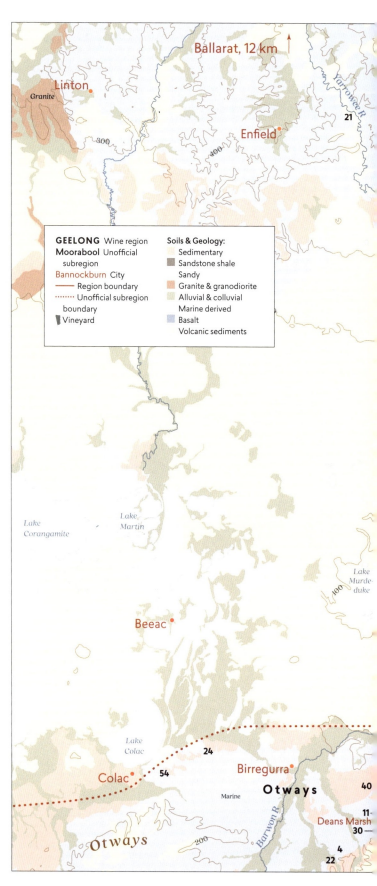

1. Amietta Vineyard
2. Attwoods Scotsburn Vineyard
3. Austin's Wines
4. Babernoek
5. Bacchus Hill
6. BAIE
7. Banks Road
8. Bannockburn Vineyards
9. Barrgowan
10. Bellbrae Estate
11. Blakes Estate
12. Brown Magpie
13. By Farr
14. Clyde Park Vineyard
15. Coastal Estate
16. Curlewis
17. Del Rios of Mt Anakie
18. Dinny Goonan
19. Eagles Rise
20. Fenwick
21. Garibaldi
22. Heroes Vineyard
23. Idyll Wine
24. Irrewarra
25. Kilgour Wines
26. Kissan Estate
27. Lethbridge Wines
28. Lethbridge Pindari Vineyard
29. Leura Park Estate
30. Maluka Estate
31. Marcus Hill Vineyard
32. Mermerus
33. The Minya
34. Moorabool Ridge
35. Moshulu Estate
36. Oakdene
37. Paradise IV
38. Pettavel
39. Ponda Estate
40. Pondalowie
41. Prince Albert Vineyard
42. Provenance Wines
43. Reed
44. Rowsley Fault Vineyard
45. Scotchmans Hill
46. Shadowfax
47. Spence
48. Spring Creek Vineyard
49. Staughton Vale Vineyard
50. Tarcoola Estate
51. Terindah Estate
52. Wayawa Estate
53. Waybourne
54. Yeowarra Hill

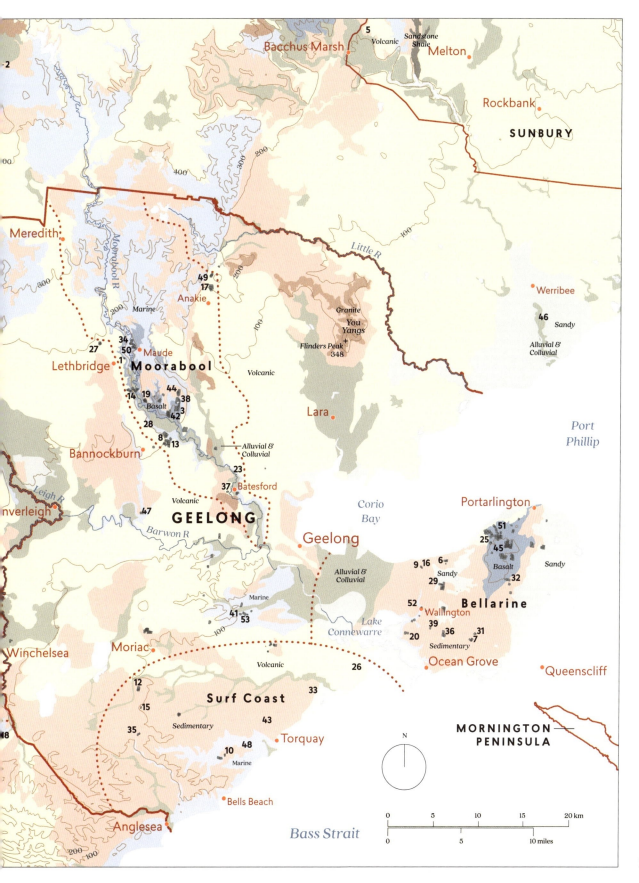

Geelong

Lethbridge (175 metres) and Bannockburn (100 metres), to the vineyards near Batesford (35 metres). Those further upstream, further from the bay at higher elevations, see regularly cooler low temperatures, but are more prone to sharp temperature spikes above 40°C, as well as random hailstorms. (In 1998, Bannockburn lost its whole crop to hail; the Australian wine community donated fruit to help keep the winery afloat.)

In the Moorabool Valley, pinot noir, shiraz and chardonnay are the most notable plantings, delivering the highest-quality wines with the most consistency. Pinot gris, sauvignon blanc, riesling, cabernet sauvignon, merlot, viognier, semillon, albariño and gamay can be found throughout the region as well. The climate is still moderate enough where, in difficult cooler vintages, late-ripening varieties like cabernet sauvignon fail to fully develop. There have been some recent explorations into a variety of grapes that are more drought-tolerant, but the Moorabool Valley's top producers continue to churn out what the region has come to be known for: powerful but finessed pinot noir and chardonnay.

Southeast of the city of Geelong, the Bellarine Peninsula forms the southwestern barrier of Port Phillip Bay and the smaller Corio Bay on its northern shores. While the peninsula's climate range is narrower than other parts of Geelong, it receives southerly cold fronts and warmer influences out of the north. Melbourne residents often complain that one can experience all four seasons within a day, and this is exacerbated on the Bellarine Peninsula.

The Bellarine, unlike the Moorabool Valley, is a picturesque peninsula home to both bayside and seaside estates, tourist destinations, bustling cellar doors, restaurants and wedding venues. The two largest producers in the region are Oakdene and Scotchmans Hill, who produce everything from pinot noir and chardonnay to sauvignon blanc, pinot gris, riesling, shiraz and cabernet sauvignon.

As sometimes accompanies tourism-minded regions, the focus here is at times more on lifestyle than on great wine. Newcomers Babche and Empire of Dirt have proven that this area is capable of producing excellent, terroir-driven wines, but the focus historically has largely been on generally pleasing ones, rather than profound ones. 'There's so much potential in vineyards of the Bellarine to make amazing wines,' Babche's Niki Nikolovski exalts. 'It produces good grapes, full stop.'

While the names are often used interchangeably, the Surf Coast and the Otways describe two distinct areas and influences as one travels west from the Bellarine. The Surf Coast describes the area near the coast, just west of the city of Geelong, including the seaside towns of Bremlea, Torquay and Bells Beach. The vineyards of the Surf Coast range from just 1.5 kilometres from the coast (some even have Great Ocean Road addresses) to 20 kilometres inland, as the crow flies.

Though geographically distinct, the vineyards of Surf Coast and Bellarine Peninsula have similar temperature and precipitation averages. The inland soils of the Surf Coast consist of older sediments, while those closer to the coast are marine-derived sands, clays, small pockets of limestone and shales. There is some alluvial wash from the Moorabool River's path and other water migration.

This part of Australia has long been a drawcard for sightseers, so it is perhaps no

The Country Pub

A 'pub' in Australia has a bit of a different vibe than the word intones for the rest of the world. The identity of the country pub is, to us, defined by distinctive character, commitment to quality and honest hospitality. The trappings are usually not elaborate or trendy, but neither is this just a place to grab a cheap beer. Even in the far reaches of the country, pub owners take great pride in creating a unique presentation of their region and hospitality. And this almost always includes great wine. There are plenty of fancy and urbane places to drink wine throughout Australia, but it is also a beverage that exists in common and everyday settings, speaking to the universality of wine culture.

surprise that, historically, the wineries of Surf Coast and Bellarine have been more constituted for tourism than for fine wine production. Mount Duneed, Bellbrae and Brown Magpie are the largest operations of the area, boasting big cellar door restaurants and event venues.

Moving west, the Otways are a low-altitude coastal mountain range comprised of 65-million-year-old tertiary marine siltstone, sandstone and mudstone deposits that formed as the sea levels sank. The range tops out at 670 metres above sea level and significantly influences the climate. Warm fronts from the north push the moisture band south until it hits the range, where over 1200 millimetres of rainfall per year has grown a lush, fern-filled temperate rainforest of towering mountain ash gum trees.

Along the inland slopes, vineyards are planted between 150 and 200 metres above sea level in well-structured, low-fertility soils well suited for premium viticulture. The mean January temperature at Deans Marsh (a town in the Otway hinterland) is 18.6°C, about a degree lower than in the Moorabool Valley, and 2 below the Bellarine. Rainfall is about 50% higher over the year in the hinterland compared to the Moorabool.

James Thomas of the Otways' Heroes Vineyard notes that the higher elevations are 'currently too cold and wet to plant', and believes that 'whilst nowhere in Australia should be considered drought-proof, the region receives consistent, and regular rainfall between 600–800 millimetres in the areas currently planted to vines', with monthly rainfall at its highest in winter and spring months.

A chilly, wet spring usually leads to a long, cool growing season in the Otways, with harvests as early as late March or as late as mid-May. Shiraz will only ripen in the warmest sites, with the Otways being more well suited to the organic, **dry-farming** of pinot noir, chardonnay, riesling and pinot gris. There can be large variation of suitable grapes, even among nearby sites, given the region's patchwork of soils, and the increase in rainfall being so pegged to altitude.

The Otway Wine Co-Op was recently formed as a place to collectively market and sell the wines of the Otways. The producers – Maluka Estate, Heroes Vineyard, Dinny Goonan, Blakes and Babenorek Estate – though little known, are a passionate group of farmers working to further define and grow their region.

Further north from the Otway hinterland towards the town of Colac, this cooler and wetter climate is still felt. The Farr family has started working with a vineyard here in the suburb of Irrewarra. Nick Farr observes: 'The site remains moist throughout the year, averaging one-third more rainfall than Bannockburn [the town By Farr is based in] … the wines show considerable **regionality** with damp earth character, when compared to the mineral and structured wines of Bannockburn.'

The Otway hinterland, and its surrounding areas, prove that not all great growing regions have been found, codified and legally defined; the prospects for exploration in the Australian wine country are virtually limitless.

Hubbub

Geelong has gone from being one of the most esteemed and productive regions of the 19th century to an underdog in the present day. Of the 136 wines on the 7th Edition of **Langton's Classification**, only two of them are from Geelong (and both produced by the same winery – By Farr). Geelong's boundaries are more geographic than anything else, and its subregions carry more distinction than the whole GI – though they could stand to carry more weight and recognition. This is a region that continues to grow and impress, with new wineries from inside and outside its boundaries interested in the quality and diversity of fruit grown.

It is a region, though, that lacks cohesion. In addition to all the geographic divides, there is division in how the spread of producers approach their craft. There is a sizeable segment of the wineries in Geelong whose focus is not solely to grow premium grapes and create fine wine, and whose ambitions for regional identity centre more on creating winery tourism than on the wines and growing practices.

One organic grower on the Bellarine Peninsula has made multiple attempts to encourage more of a farming focus in the producer-directed programming of Wine Geelong, the grower's organisation for the appellation, but with little support or traction from the group. Instead of 'only being about discussing how you're doing financially', the grower (who preferred to stay anonymous) said: 'Let's start some discussions and do some practical, engaging events that are around viticulture.'

Wine Geelong's membership does not boast the region's marquee producers By Farr and Bannockburn. These two wineries have historically preferred to focus their energies on the task at hand – creating world-class wine – rather than engaging the community at large, especially when that community is largely focused on matters outside the purview of ambitious grape-growing.

The general messaging of Wine Geelong is about tourism, in which Bannockburn and By Farr don't participate. And while many other regions have an overlap of producers who offer tourism amenities *and* 'manage to go the hardcore path of where wine comes first' (in James Thomas's words) – think Mornington Peninsula, Yarra Valley, Tasmania and McLaren Vale – in Geelong, these two traits don't coexist in many of the same wineries.

Treading this hardcore path was always difficult, and is becoming less and less feasible, especially in Geelong. 'As well as the 100% estate-grown Heroes wines, I make the Anti-Hero wines [from purchased fruit],' says Thomas, 'in order to have a business that makes *some* money. My ideal would be to only make wine from my own grapes, and I hope that this is one day where I get to ... but I have to make wine for the market as well as the "terroir".' The land that Babche has recently acquired is in Timboon, 150 kilometres due west of the Bellarine, largely because of land prices (and the potential for organic viticulture on the virgin land). And Sierra Reed long purchased grapes and rented space before being able to recently farm (not even lease or own) her own plot of land.

Evan Milne, a Torquay-based wine distributor and Sierra Reed's husband, gives an example:

'There's a property that is about to go on the market in Bellbrae [on the Surf Coast], which is what Sierra is interested in planting on – sandy soils, maritime influence – that sold in 1997 for $200,000. It's a hundred acres, and it's going to go on the market today for $3.5 million. How, as a young producer, can you have the chance of buying a bit of dirt and experimenting ... you just can't.'

Even though Geelong's list of 'hardcore terroir' producers is slim, it's a wonder that any exist given the barriers to produce that style of wine in Geelong. 'In a sense, the greatest strength of the region, low yield and great intensity, is also its biggest weakness because of the inability to attract money and the talented people that invariably follow,' says Ray Nadeson. Its illustrious history and proven track record for excellence bode well for the region – but it's evident that greater access and resources are needed for the next generation to get in and expand upon the work of Bannockburn, By Farr and Lethbridge.

'For me on the Surf Coast,' says Reed, 'the climate and soils haven't been looked at in a way that aligns with us being able to actually see what they look like in a glass.' From a fine wine perspective, the Surf Coast and Bellarine Peninsula (and parts of the Moorabool Valley and Otway hinterland) have been largely left unexplored. This is both exciting and daunting, with a high likelihood that some of the area's best sites have not yet been planted. The potential for excellence and innovation is vast in Geelong; the conditions just need to arise for those who would be capable of executing it to do so.

The Clyde Park vineyard, nestled within the windy Moorabool River Valley.

PRODUCERS

BABCHE

Niki Nikolovski and Tim Byrne met on the Bellarine Peninsula, where they have purchased and farmed organic grapes to craft their no-additive wines. Niki, a Toronto-native, drew inspiration from watching her grandparents farm in a similar way in rural Macedonia and hearing stories of a simpler time. Tim crafted his first wine well before he studied oenology, from a vineyard his family grew organically. Babche (an endearing name for grandmother in Macedonian) was formed out of these holistic ideologies. Niki and Tim have started to develop their own estate in Timboon, a couple of hours west of Geelong, planting a vineyard and a permaculture farm. *babchewines.com*

BANNOCKBURN VINEYARDS

Stuart Hooper began planting in the Moorabool Valley in 1974, with a dream to emulate the great vineyards of France. The first vines were shiraz, but with Hooper's deep love of Burgundy, plantings soon expanded to include pinot noir and chardonnay. The Serré vineyard was planted to MV6, the pinot noir **clone** that was propagated from vines in Clos Vougeot by James Busby. But it is not only the grapes that have built up the reputation of Bannockburn. Gary Farr (see By Farr) began his career here as winemaker in 1978, establishing an uncompromising and characterful style. Current winemaker Matt Holmes, alongside Bannockburn's faithful viticulturist of 30 years, Lucas Grisby, have achieved organic certification in their close-planted vineyards, with the remainder in transition. Bannockburn continues to produce the weighty chardonnays and powerful pinots for which they have become so well known. *bannockburnvineyards.com*

BY FARR

Gary Farr began his illustrious career at Bannockburn, before planting the Clyde Park vineyards and then his own in 1994. Following in his dad's footsteps, Nick Farr grew up working in the family winery. Both worked stints in Oregon, California and Burgundy, developing a voracious appetite for chardonnay and pinot noir. Nick also makes the Farr Rising label and a wine in Irrewarra, about an hour away in the rainy Otway hinterland. The By Farr chardonnays are layered and kissed by oak, and their viognier achieves a finesse rarely seen outside of the best vineyards in the Rhône. Like his dad, Nick is typically fond of utilising whole-bunch techniques in pinot, gleaned from their decades' long friendship with the father–son team at Domaine Dujac. These are currently some of the most highly sought after and well-regarded wines in all of Victoria. *byfarr.com.au*

Nick Farr, By Farr

> **JR — What we're drinking**
>
> Though **Bannockburn** is viewed as a standard-bearer for Geelong pinot noir, their SRH Chardonnay is as impressive — vinified from likely the oldest chardonnay vines in Geelong, and often released with quite some cellar age. A great classic — though somewhat under-the-radar — Victorian chardonnay. – Jonathan Ross

CLYDE PARK VINEYARD

While working his first winemaking job, Gary Farr (see By Farr) started Clyde Park in 1979. The vines were planted in an amphitheatre, sorted into varying small blocks of different **aspects**. Thanks to this foresight, Clyde Park is now home to quality mature plantings of chardonnay, pinot noir and shiraz. Since Gary sold Clyde Park in the 90s, the vineyard has been through several owners and winemakers, including the likes of James Thomas (Heroes Vineyard) and Ben Mullen (Mulline). When Ben left in late 2018, current proprietor Terry Jongebloed decided to offer the grapes to five winemakers, who made the Clyde Park single-block wines for the 2019 vintage. The resulting wines are a fascinating guide to the thumbprint of a winemaker. **clydepark.com.au**

EMPIRE OF DIRT

Named for a line in the Nine Inch Nails song 'Hurt', Empire of Dirt is the bright beginning arising from a self-proclaimed difficult period in Tash Webster's life. She settled with her family (and a handful of non-wine qualifications) in Geelong, across the road from a winemaker who offered her work while she was a stay-at-home mum. She became hooked, completing a wine science degree and working at several reputable wineries in the region before launching Empire of Dirt with the 2018 vintage. Her voluptuous Moorabool Valley reds and linear Bellarine chardonnay are Tash's ode to the great dirt of Geelong. **empireofdirtwines.com.au**

HEROES VINEYARD

British expat James Thomas has been taken with the Geelong region since moving to Australia in 2004. He made his first major foray into winemaking at Bannockburn, then after making the wines at Clyde Park for a few years he leased the Heroes vineyard in the Otway hinterland. The climate is very different from the other subregions of the Geelong GI and James was floored by the greenness and condition of the site: just a little under 4 hectares of riesling, shiraz, pinot noir, sauvignon blanc and, more recently added, chardonnay. Thanks to its well-drained sandy clays and high moisture, Heroes produces fruitful, yet structural wines that are beginning to put this little-known (and unofficial) wine region on the map. Paired with a deep belief in organics, the wines are distinctive, living snapshots of his growing year. **heroesvineyard.com**

LETHBRIDGE WINES

Ray Nadeson, Maree Collis and Adrian Thomas are all scientists who share a love of great wine. Their passion led them to spend several years searching for the ideal piece of land on which they could grow grapes. Researched down to the perfect combination of soil type, temperature and other climatic elements, they found a rundown piece of land that had all the factors – it had even been planted to grapes in the 1870s, prior to **phylloxera**. With nearly twice as much elevation, Lethbridge is noticeably cooler than the town of Bannockburn down the road. The Lethbridge range is broad – Ray made an astounding 58 wines in 2020 – and diverse as can be.

Ray Nadeson
Lethbridge

Aside from the original estate vineyard and the more southerly Rebenberg Vineyard on Mt Duneed, they make wines from the Chalmers vineyards in Heathcote, Malakoff vineyard in the Pyrenees, extraordinary sparkling from the Drumborg vineyard in Henty, and are undergoing new plantings at their estate and on the Bellarine. Experimentation is a constant in pursuit of knowledge at Lethbridge, which Ray explains 'gives clarity of where the edge is'. **lethbridgewines.com**

MULLINE

Mulline is a partnership between winemaker Ben Mullen, and wine drinker Ben Hine. Having studied oenology and worked at some legendary addresses across Australia, Mullen takes care of the tending and the making. Hine, a lawyer with an impressive stint in the hospitality industry, oversees all things business. The wines are fresh and aromatic expressions of the distinction that Geelong has to offer. The different subregions of Geelong are a focus, with numerous single sites and subregional bottlings from the Moorabool Valley and Bellarine Peninsula. Mulline places a deep importance on social and environmental justice in their business, from paperless office operations and carbon offsets to a healthy workplace and everything in between. Mulline has achieved a lot in a little time – their first vintage was 2019 – and are poised to keep on impressing. **mulline.com**

> **What we're drinking**
>
> *Newcomers to Geelong, **Mulline** (which rhymes with divine) has been well-received in the region and in Australia as a whole. I particularly like the Portarlington chardonnay from their single vineyard selection. I'm looking forward to what the future hold for the two Bens. – Kavita Faiella*

REED

It's not often you hear model, TV presenter, reality star and winemaker in the same sentence, but Sierra Reed has lived many lives in her short time on the planet. She became intrigued by grapes while filming in New Zealand and set off on a whirlwind tour of vintages in some of the world's greatest wine regions. Sierra began making her own wines in 2015, and while she is based on the Surf Coast, she is devoted to picking special plots of grapes from regions as varied as Barossa, Heathcote and the Grampians. She is a big believer in the ability to produce amazing riesling in Geelong: her White Heart riesling from the Moorabool Valley responds to the vintage, either bone dry or with a bit of sweetness, whatever the balance the year demands. She has recently grafted over a plot on the Surf Coast to gamay and riesling: after several years of successful winemaking, it marks her first foray into grape-growing. **reedwines.com**

And don't forget ...

Bellbrae Estate, with an address on the Great Ocean Road, offers elegant wines and a seaside view on the Surf Coast ... **Brown Magpie**, a Surf Coast visitor favourite, produces everything from blanc de noirs to botrytis pinot gris ... **Oakdene**, a gorgeous Bellarine estate – replete with a rental cottage, a bistro, a restaurant and a wine bar – produces a range of affordable wines and estate-grown olive oil ... **Provenance Wines**, based in Fyansford (just outside the city of Geelong) in a refurbished old paper mill, offers a huge urban winery space and arts centre, and wines from Geelong, Henty, Ballarat and Macedon ... **Scotchmans Hill** is the Bellarine's largest producer (and oldest, established in 1982), known for its charming cellar door and bistro, as well as a wide selection of wines (under several different labels), great companions for their food.

The Oakdene vineyard, just 4 kilometres from the coast on the Bellarine Peninsula.

Macedon Ranges

Introduction

An easy 45-minute drive northwest of Melbourne, and up an elevation gain of about 400 metres, lies the doorstep of mainland Australia's coldest region. After Tasmania, Macedon Ranges is on average the coolest GI in Australia (with some pockets cooler than Tasmania). With the marginal climate come common cool-climate hazards: frost, untimely rain and mildew pressure being the most pressing.

Though the risks of farming in this region are great, so are the rewards. This southern outcropping of the Great Dividing Range is unabashedly premium vineyard land. There isn't the degree of experimental winemaking present in other wine regions across Australia; most of the historic and modern winemakers alike, though they may grow a small variety of grapes, maintain a strong focus on the flagships chardonnay and pinot noir.

Macedon Ranges, as the name implies, is defined by its mountains – Mt Macedon and the Cobaw Ranges provide minor (and sometimes major) differences in **aspect** and elevation that define the various sites of the region. These mountains also defined the socio-formative development of the region. The Macedon Ranges GI sits on the Country of three different peoples within the Kulin Nation. The Wurundjeri Woi Wurrung, Taungurung and Dja Dja Wurrung peoples identify where their Country lies based on natural land formations. The Great Dividing Range, of which Mt Macedon and the Cobaw Ranges are a part, provides these natural boundaries.

Macedon Ranges may very well be the most *thoughtful* wine region in all Australia, led by the visionary and contemplative Michael Dhillon of Bindi Wines. It is not a region that falls prey to the trends of the day. It is not a reactionary region. It's a region that has confidence in the quality of its grapes and lets the wine speak for itself. The name 'Macedon Ranges' on a bottle of wine commands respect – and delivers on that reputation. With a small number of wineries and number of hectares under vine – just 200 hectares, compared to neighbour Heathcote's nearly 2000 hectares – Macedon has done a remarkable job of carving out its niche in the market: premium chardonnay and pinot noir that is only improving over time.

Evolution of Wine

Macedon Ranges has followed a similar pattern to many Victorian wine regions: some early plantings in the mid-19th century were lost due to a combination of economic downturn and **phylloxera**. Macedon fell doubly hard because of its cool climate – warmer regions found earlier and sustained investment with their ability to produce then-trendy **fortifieds** and later-trendy big, bold shiraz.

Macedon's revival started in the late 1960s, with a winery called Virgin Hills, planted in 1968 by Melbourne restaurateur Tom Lazar. The vines – a mix of red grapes, most notably cabernet sauvignon, shiraz, malbec and pinot noir – were planted high up in the hills of Lauriston, at about 600 metres above sea level. Virgin Hills developed a somewhat cult-like following, helping initiate the appreciation for both cool-climate and minimal-intervention winemaking in Australia.

The second modern plantings came from Gordon and Heather Knight in Baynton, in the northeast of today's Macedon Ranges GI. The Knights planted vines in 1970 to diversify their sheep farm, and found particular success with cabernet sauvignon, shiraz and riesling. The Knights and their winery Granite Hills, though somewhat under the radar, have been formative figures in Macedon's development, and continue to produce excellent wines under the charge of second-generation Llew Knight.

The next vineyards didn't come until the late 1970s; Macedon was still considered very much a long-shot in the fine wine sector, thought by many to be too cold to produce the robust styles of wine that Australia was becoming known for. In 1977, when Gordon Cope-Williams planted at nearly 800 metres above sea level in eastern Macedon, he wasn't sure that it would work – and it didn't. In 1982, Gordon and his wife Judy bought a site about 150 metres lower in the town

> **Macedon fell doubly hard because of its cool climate – warmer regions found earlier and sustained investment with their ability to produce then-trendy fortifieds and later-trendy big, bold shiraz.**

Early spring buds on the oldest block of pinot noir at Curly Flat in Lancefield, Macedon Ranges. The large fan above the vines is employed to move cold, moist air out of the vineyards to lessen the risk of frost.

The mid-1980s through the early 1990s was the golden era for the Macedon Ranges, seeing the formation of the wineries that would put the region on the map for fine wine production.

of Romsey, which proved to be more hospitable to growing chardonnay and pinot noir, though still just on the verge of vine suitability – having the same **heat summation** as Champagne. Cope-Williams Winery became known for sparkling wine but saw its last vintage in 2014; the vineyards continue to thrive, acting as a source for young wineries like Dilworth & Allain and Joshua Cooper.

The mid-1980s through the early 1990s was the golden era for the Macedon Ranges, seeing the formation of the wineries that would put the region on the map for fine wine production. John Ellis and his wife Ann (née Tyrrell, of Hunter Valley fame) purchased their winery in 1982, what would become Hanging Rock. Alan and Nelly Cooper planted their first vines in Pastoria East (about 15 kilometres east of Kyneton) in 1985, establishing Cobaw Ridge, a regional leader in **biodynamic** farming, producing some of the region's greatest wines to this day. And Mount Gisborne began plantings in 1986, largely significant because of Stuart Anderson (of Bendigo's Balgownie Estate) joining the winery in 1991 and becoming a force for development and mentorship in the region.

One such mentee was Dhillon, the son of Bill Dhillon (who was born Darshan Singh Dhillon in 1937 in Punjab, India). Michael was 20 years old when he and his father planted Bindi in 1988, in the rolling hills of Gisborne, south of Mt Macedon. Michael's first vintage work was with Stuart Anderson at Mount Gisborne, and the first Bindi pinot noirs were vinified there. Michael Dhillon – his father passing in 2013 – has become one of the most influential figures in Australian winemaking, the quality of his wine and thoughtfulness of his approach nearly unparalleled.

Curly Flat emerged in the early 1990s, planted in Lancefield by once husband-and-wife team Phillip Moraghan and Jenifer Kolkka. Now under the sole ownership of Kolkka, Curly Flat has steadily become a staple for Australian pinot noir and chardonnay, with the wines making a substantial jump in quality upon the arrival of current head winemaker Matt Harrop in 2017.

The region underwent somewhat of a lull in new establishments in the late 1990s and early 2000s, but has seen a number of young producers launch in the last 10 years. This generation tends to be heavily involved in the viticulture, even if leasing land or purchasing fruit, and is pushing farming practices continually toward organics and **biodynamics**. This lot includes Dilworth & Allain, Lyons Will, Joshua Cooper (son of Cobaw Ridge's Alan and Nelly Cooper), Silent Way (owned by Curly Flat's Matt Harrop and his wife, and head of auctions at **Langton's**, Tamara Grischy), Wilimee and Place of Changing Winds.

Today, Macedon Ranges is a landscape of small, independently owned wineries, completely void of any sort of corporate ownership or interest. Of the 40-plus wineries in the region, only three produce more than 100 tonnes of fruit annually, about a 6000-case production. Young growers are reinvigorating interest in early plantings, with a laser-like focus on chardonnay and pinot noir. While Macedon may not be on the cutting edge of alternative varieties and styles, the raw material and human talent to make exemplary cool-climate wines makes it one of the most classic yet thrilling wine regions in Australia.

Lay of the Land

When asked, 'why Macedon?' Joshua Cooper responds, 'Everything about the region. The climate, the soil. Especially because I'm drawn to more marginal sites … there's nowhere else like Macedon.'

Macedon is mainland Australia's coolest region, and even though some harvests are happening earlier as the climate warms, the grapes reach full ripeness well into autumn most years. 'Our fruit is veraising [starting to ripen] in February, the hottest month,' says Curly Flat and Silent Way's Matt Harrop, 'when warmer places – Yarra, Geelong, Mornington – are already harvesting. Our last four weeks of ripening have a lot cooler days and much colder nights. So pinot in particular retains freshness and ripens evenly.'

Altitude plays a key part in Macedon's climate. The Macedon Ranges are one of the final formations of the Great Dividing Range as it fades into the plains further west. The collective area of the GI covers not only Mt Macedon and its adjacent peaks and ridges, but the Cobaw Ranges, 20 kilometres to the north, and the Jim Jim, Hanging Rock and Camel's Hump peaks in between.

Even in a region so small (production-wise), there is a well-researched desire to identify the unique parcels of the region. Macedon Ranges Wine, the vignerons association for the region, has divided Macedon into five different geo-climatic zones, meant to 'demonstrate the climatic differences that lead to [their] diverse wine styles'. Though these distinctions aren't used widely in general parlance, they are useful in understanding the **microclimates** of the region.

The first identified zone is the area south of Mt Macedon, labelled as 'Southern Vineyards'. Mt Macedon and its adjacent peaks orient east to west, separating its southern hillsides from the rest of the region. These hillsides are unobstructed from Port Phillip Bay, enjoying slightly warmer temperatures moderated by the coast. Here, Mount Gisborne (641 metres) is a backdrop to the region's most iconic producer, Bindi, with other vineyards across the plateau south of the town of Gisborne.

To the north, over the peak of Mt Macedon, lies the region's coldest sites at the highest altitudes, with the upper limits near Trentham and Daylesford (on the western end of the appellation): the 'High Vineyards' geo-climatic zone. Vineyards look northeast, capturing warm morning sun to keep them on the productive side of their marginal locations.

East and downslope are the towns of Romsey and Lancefield, composing some of the most populated vineyard areas of the region. This area is referred to as the 'Central Vineyards'. Cooled by mountain air flowing down from the east and the tiny Cobaw Range on its north side, vineyards here experience the midpoint of the region's climate.

Just to the west of the Central Vineyards, and north of the High Vineyards, is an area referred to as the 'Western Vineyards'. The vineyards here sit northwest of the Great Dividing Range and generally have a milder climate: balmy summer days with cool nights and a modicum of shelter from cold, southerly winds.

The 'Northern Vineyards' of the region are exposed to some fierce winds coming from the north, which are usually warm and push the cold front south. These winds, along with this area's northerly **aspect**, keep vineyards a bit warmer than the rest of the region. Much of the cabernet sauvignon and shiraz planted in the Macedon Ranges is found here, though there are a few plots in the lowest-lying areas near Romsey. Shiraz expresses its savoury side in Macedon; only in select years can a few sites ripen the grape enough to bear resemblance to more traditional expressions of Australian shiraz. However, the marginal climate barely gets cabernet sauvignon to full maturity, and these grapes are often found in rosé, blends and even in sparkling cabernet.

Though these divisions are largely based on elevation and climate, soil type impacts the expression of grapes across the region as well. The three main soil types of the region are red basalt/volcanics, granite and Ordovician sandstone/shale. Josh Cooper describes the differences: granite 'seems to favour aromatics and some nervosity, with maybe less tannic depth'; the red basalt creates 'a sweeter fruit profile and fuller mid-palate, often with plenty

Macedon Ranges

HOW TO READ THIS MAP

The geo-climatic subregions drawn by the Macedon Ranges growers' association, and the changes in elevation that define them, provide the backdrop for this map of the GI's vineyard surface.

1. Athletes of Wine
2. Attwoods
3. Bindi
4. Botanica Estate
5. Chanters Ridge Vineyard
6. Cleveland Winery
7. Cobaw Ridge
8. Cold Acre
9. Cope-Williams
10. Curly Flat
11. Double Oaks Estate
12. Gisborne Peak
13. Glen Erin
14. Glenlyon Estate
15. Granite Hills
16. Guildford
17. Hanging Rock Winery
18. Hesket Estate
19. Hunter-Gatherer Vintners
20. Joshua Cooper Wines
21. Kilchurn
22. Kyneton Ridge
23. Lane's End Vineyard
24. Limestone Track Vineyard
25. Little Reddie
26. Lord Malmsbury
27. Lyons Will
28. Metcalfe Valley
29. Midhill Vineyard
30. Mount Charlie
31. Mt Macedon Winery
32. Mount Monument Vineyard
33. Mount Towrong Vineyard
34. Musk Lane
35. North
36. Northern Hope
37. Paramoor
38. Parkside Estate
39. Passing Clouds
40. Patrick's Vineyard
41. Pegeric Vineyard
42. Place of Changing Winds
43. Rowanston on the Track
44. Shadowfax Little Hampton Vineyard
45. Silent Way
46. Virgin Hills
47. Wilimee
48. Wombat Forest Vineyard
49. Zig Zag Road

Victoria

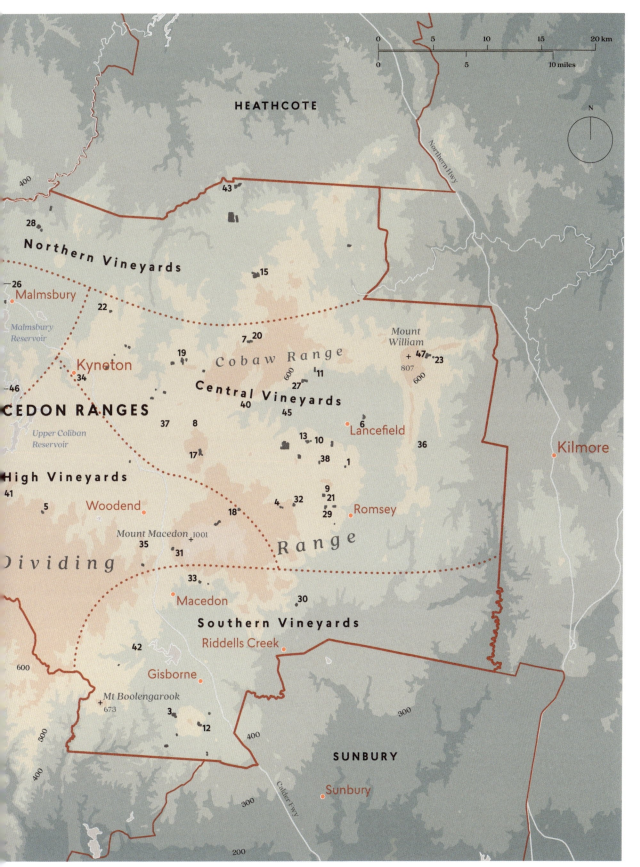

Macedon Ranges

of tannin'; and the sandstone and shale produce 'powerful and deep' wines, with lots of compact structure. The Macedon Ranges Wine website lists the soil type that each Macedon vineyard is planted on – a great resource for better understanding how soil contributes to flavour profile in the region.

Though Macedon is known for a limited number of grapes, there is plenty of play beyond pinot noir and chardonnay. While temperatures are low, the area is blessed by an abundance of sun, like most of Australia. Alsatian varieties, such as riesling (a specialty of Granite Hills), pinot gris and gewürztraminer, find success, along with sauvignon blanc, gamay, merlot, malbec and lagrein – the latter a notable planting from Alan and Nelly Cooper at Cobaw Ridge.

That said, pinot noir and chardonnay are still king, and have become synonymous with Macedon Ranges. Chardonnay styles range from riper, sun-kissed examples at low elevations, to finer, pale and ultra-delicate styles that result from the great heights of the region. For pinot noir, the grape displays a power and even ripeness when it finds a warmer pocket; at chilly highs in elevation, the pinots are more chiselled and taut – finely woven gauze hung over a robust structure.

An old wine idiom goes that pinot noir is the messenger not the message (meaning it effectively conveys the character of the land rather than imposing its own character), which is certainly true of the Macedon Ranges – and this thinking could be extended to include chardonnay too. But the message is not just about the land, it's also about how the people of the land care for it – a fitting ode to the careful and skilled vignerons of the Macedon Ranges.

Macedon Ranges Viticultural Footprint

Total delimited area (km²)	2820
Total planted area (hectares)	245
% of delimited area planted	0.087%
Total elevation range	211–1033 masl
Elevation range of plantings	300–800 masl
Number of producers	46

Macedon Ranges Climate Data (°C)

	1960–1990	1991–PRESENT	2020
Heat summation/GDD	1167	1289	1307
Annual rain/GSR	794/380	734/354	748/433
Warmest month avg. temp.	18.3	19.3	19.7

Winkler Scale:

● 850–1111 ● 1112–1389 ● 1390–1667 ● 1668–1944 ● 1945–2222 ● 2223–2700

The winery at Hanging Rock, built from corrugated iron and local eucalyptus trees.

Hubbub

Weather and climate have historically presented the Macedon Ranges with its biggest challenges: starting with Gordon Cope-Williams moving his vineyard from a too-cold 800 metres above sea level in 1982, through to today, where seasons of late frosts can wipe out vintages, and downy mildew presents unprecedented disease pressure.

Climate change has made some of the previously marginal sites more reliable – full ripening is less of a problem than it used to be. But there is no shortage of still-marginal sites in the Macedon, especially in the high elevations out by Trentham and Daylesford, and these are being explored by those seeking the coldest of the cold. 'We will always be cool enough for chardonnay and pinot noir,' says Cobaw Ridge's Alan Cooper. 'Altitude does amazing things!'

Very few growers employ strict organics in every year, but viticulture in the region is moving in that direction. There is a mindful approach toward farming in the Macedon: it's not about grasping the latest trend or using it as a marketing ploy, but about doing what's best for the land and the wines. Cobaw Ridge has easily taken the strongest stance in the region on farming practices. They were an early adopter of organics and **biodynamics**, becoming certified in 2009 and 2011, respectively. Newcomers North and Place of Changing Winds are farming their vineyards organically. And the younger generation who started out buying fruit – Joshua Cooper and Dilworth & Allain, most notably – encourage better farming practices from their growers.

The younger generation has also helped alleviate one of Macedon's other historical problems: expanding its reach. Though Macedon has long been associated with quality, 'there haven't been enough vineyards making enough wine to get traction around the place,' says Bindi's Michael Dhillon. Macedon's reputation has been an impediment in this respect, allowing producers to sell out their wines in Victoria, without needing to seek interstate or overseas distribution.

But this tide is changing too, with the influx of young talent taking new approaches. Joshua Cooper, Dilworth & Allain, Athletes of Wine, Lyons Will, Wilimee, Silent Way and Place of Changing Winds and Attwoods are all building buzz for the region. 'Those guys are active in the marketplace, telling the story. They know the journos, they know the sommeliers, they get out and about more,' says Dhillon. 'I read about Macedon Ranges now, and there are so many more to mention than Bindi and Curly Flat. It's terrific.' Alan Cooper concurs: 'More people, making more great wine, will only build the region going forward.'

Ngannelong, more commonly known as Hanging Rock, is a central place of spiritual magnitude, and once the site of corroborees, trade and ceremony for the Dja Dja Wurrung, Woi Wurrung and Taungurung nations. The vertical rock forms display how hard, dense lava forced through a narrow vent in the bedrock 6.25 million years ago.

PRODUCERS

BINDI

Michael Dhillon was studying economics at university when he helped his father, Darshan, plant a vineyard on their property in 1988. It soon became very clear to him that 'wine was much more interesting than economics' and Michael joined the family business. The Bindi vineyards are farmed using practices from both the organic and **biodynamic** schools of thought, but neither is strictly followed. Michael is of the belief that holistic sustainability, including the ability to actually produce the wine you are growing grapes for, is what matters: 'there's no story if there's no wine,' he says, echoing a sentiment of Burgundy's Frédéric Mugnier.

And the Bindi wines tell the clearest of stories. Pristine, mineral-driven chardonnay comes from their two 1988-planted sites, Quartz and Kostas Rind, and perfumed pinot noir comes from sites across 5 hectares, including the Original vineyard and more recent **high-density plantings** of Block K and Block 5. The newest chapter, the Darshan vineyard, a tribute to Michael's father, was planted in 2014 at 11,300 vines per hectare – quite dense, to promote low yields and high concentration.
bindiwines.com.au

COBAW RIDGE

Alan and Nelly Cooper began planting their vineyard in 1985. 'The land chose us,' says Alan Cooper, of his and Nelly's search to find the perfect site to set up their farm. Their vineyard sits on a natural amphitheatre that backs up to Cobaw National Park. Cobaw Ridge has become renowned across Australia for their complex chardonnays, graceful pinots and peppery syrahs. But there is an equal joy in experimentation. In 1998, they made the first commercial lagrein in Australia, an ancient grape hailing from Alto Adige in Italy. Nelly is the business manager and CFO and Alan does most of the winemaking; the two share vineyard work. Alan is increasingly using **qvevri** (Georgian underground amphorae) instead of new oak for ageing purposes, and the sole addition in the winery is a touch of **sulphur**. Cobaw Ridge is the only winery in the region that is certified organic and **biodynamic**. Their son Josh also helps out in the winery, when he is not making his own wines (see Joshua Cooper Wines, p. 164).
cobawridge.com.au

CURLY FLAT

Curly Flat was started by Phillip Moraghan and Jenifer Kolkka in 1989. Passionate drinkers of Burgundy, they identified the site as ideal for growing premium chardonnay and pinot noir. Jenifer took over sole ownership in 2017 and Matt Harrop now heads up winemaking, while also managing his own vineyard and label, Silent Way.

Michael Dhillon
Bindi

Alan, Nelly & Josh Cooper
Cobaw Ridge / Joshua Cooper Wines

Matt has wasted no time since coming on board, reinvigorating the soils and adding plots, while continuing the fascinating estate tradition of bottling trial wines for future evaluation. In 2018, two additional pinot noirs were added to the fold, to highlight key differences within the Curly Flat vineyard.
curlyflat.com

DILWORTH & ALLAIN

Chris Dilworth and Loïque Allain have made an almighty splash, despite only releasing their first wine in 2017. They won the Young Gun of Wine's top prize and its Best New Act award in 2020, the first time these gongs have been taken out by the same producer. Chris grew up in a hospitality family, before going on to study oenology and viticulture. Loïque is an artist, working mostly in linocuts, which are stunning features on their labels. With their two young kids, the pair live off the land in the Macedon: both its fruit for wine, but also a veggie garden in their backyard, with six chickens and one rooster. The Dilworth & Allain wines are made at Owen Latta's Eastern Peake winery in Ballarat, where Chris also works as a winemaker and viticulturist. They seek out distinctive sites expressing the best of Macedon chardonnay and pinot noir, as well as bottlings as diverse as Pyrenees grenache and Macedon dolcetto, with aspirations to plant their own site. *dilworthandallain.com.au*

GRANITE HILLS

Granite Hills was first planted in 1970 by Gordon and Heather Knight. Tom Lazar, an eccentric restaurateur and founder of Virgin Hills, encouraged Gordon to plant grapes on his property, saying he would buy them for his wines. The Knights' first vintage of their own wine was made in 1974 – just a few dozen bottles of cabernet-shiraz – which was filtered through a pair of Heather's pantyhose. Their son, Llew, took over winemaking in 1979, bringing a focus and purity to their shiraz and riesling, the latter grape in particular becoming a speciality of the winery. Playing to the success of their cool climate, some older plantings of cabernet sauvignon and shiraz have made way for grüner veltliner, pinot blanc and gamay. Alan Cooper of Cobaw Ridge calls Granite Hills 'some of the most underrated wines in Australia ... to thrive and survive for 50 years around here is a huge achievement.'
granitehills.com.au

> **KF** **What we're drinking**
>
> *Tension. Tightly wound acid around a core of fruit, just balancing on the precipice. Perhaps it's the rocky outcrops and peaks which stand sentinel over the vines at **Granite Hills** that make the wines feel like they are always on edge – just what I want from a great riesling.* – Kavita Faiella

Macedon Ranges

163

> **JL** **What we're drinking**
>
> Australian gamay is an underutilised category, and **Lyons Will** makes a shining example, replete with fresh fruit, stony minerality and strong lines.
> – Jane Lopes

JOSHUA COOPER WINES

Josh Cooper has an impressive résumé for a guy in his early 30s. His parents Alan and Nelly own Cobaw Ridge, and he has worked for wineries all across Australia and throughout Burgundy. Josh started his own label in 2012, highlighting single vineyards of exception in the Macedon Ranges and surrounds. His intimate knowledge of these well-established pinot noir and chardonnay sites is thanks to the home soil advantage of growing up in the Macedon Ranges. Itching to plant his own grapes, Josh and his partner Meghan Madden bought a property at the end of 2020 (and leased another), which are both destined for **close-planted** pinot and chardonnay. Following in his parents' footsteps, Josh is a hands-off winemaker who uses very few additions. *joshuacooperwines.com.au*

LYONS WILL

Oliver Rapson and Renata Morello founded their vineyard and winery, Lyons Will, in 2013. Their vineyard had 2 hectares of pinot noir and chardonnay, planted in 1996, which they doubled with gamay and riesling. All wines are made with their estate-grown fruit and bottled on site, generating a buzz among those who've have the pleasure of tasting them. *lyonswillestate.com.au*

NORTH

Etienne Mangier, the one-man show behind North, is an expat from France's Jura region, having travelled and worked in South Africa, Canada, United States and South Korea after obtaining his Masters in Oenology in Lyon. Mangier settled down in Australia in 2010 and launched North in 2013, finding 'a hidden gem of a vineyard' on a north-facing slope in Macedon Ranges. The site sits at 540 metres, planted to chardonnay, pinot noir and shiraz, all farmed organically and made with minimal intervention. The small production of North is still somewhat under-the-radar – an insider's secret of Macedon Ranges. *northwine.com.au*

PLACE OF CHANGING WINDS

The Place of Changing Winds vineyard is located between Mt Macedon and Mt Bullengarook. The name is translated from the local Wurundjeri word *warekilla*. Robert Walters, who has spent most of his career tracking down the very best wines for his importing business, Bibendum, has applied the same fastidious approach to finding and developing the vineyard. The site, planted to pinot noir and chardonnay, is managed organically (certified) and planted to an extremely **high density** of between 12,500 and 33,000 vines per hectare. The vineyard is managed by Frenchman Rémi Jacquemain, who works very closely with Rob. Aside from fine pinot and complex chardonnay from estate vines, they also make some syrah and marsanne from two vineyards further north in Heathcote and Mt Alexander. *placeofchangingwinds.com.au*

SILENT WAY

Named for Miles Davis' revolutionary 1969 record, Silent Way is the brainchild of husband-and-wife team Matt Harrop, winemaker for Curly

> **JR** **What we're drinking**
>
> The home vineyard at **Silent Way** — tended by Matt, Tamara and their children — yields a chardonnay that is both complex and brightly expressive at the same time. It is exciting to drink and share in the joy that this family clearly brings to caring for their land. – Jonathan Ross

Flat, and Tamara Grischy, head of auctions for **Langton's**. The formidable couple bought their property in 2007 and planted a pint-sized chardonnay vineyard in 2010. Pinot noir comes from the nearby Quarry Ridge vineyard in Kilmore. Small in size, but big on character, the Silent Way wines are incredible value when considering the know-how, farming, and winemaking skill behind them. *silentway.com.au*

WILIMEE

Wilimee sits at 600 metres in altitude: a perfect perch for pinot noir and chardonnay. The vineyard, planted in 1982, was originally named Portree, but was left without irrigation or care until 2013. Winemaker and viticulturist Ben Ranken has set about regenerating it, with **biodynamic** certification in his sights. His winemaking outlook is self-proclaimed as 'simple': no fining or filtration of his wines, just touches of **sulphur** additions and very little oak. A quarter of Wilimee's pinot production in 2015 was aged underwater for five years. This experiment was inspired by Ben's interest in bottles rescued from shipwrecks, often gracefully aged due to the pressure and stable temperature at the bottom of the sea. *wilimeewines.com.au*

And don't forget …
Athletes of Wine, an energising look at Macedon, produces a range of blends and unusual grapes to help the drinker flex their wine muscles …
Gisborne Peak, which dates back to 1978, has become one of the most built-out tourism outposts of Macedon, offering eco-cottages, a restaurant and a cellar door on site …
Hanging Rock Winery, one of the most historic vineyards of Macedon (founded in 1982) is known for its unique icy-cool enclave and singular sparkling wines … **Little Reddie**, Pat Underwood's ode to Central Victoria, which has recently been moved to the Macedon, produces an exciting array of grapes from chardonnay and cabernet to nebbiolo and refosco …
Virgin Hills, Macedon's most historic winery, which has seen a fall from grace, is on the verge of an exciting revitalisation under new ownership and new winemaker Pat Underwood (from Little Reddie, above).

Gippsland

Introduction

Gippsland is an anomaly in the taxonomy of Australia's GI system. It is a zone with no further regions or subregions defined within it. It is unclear why exactly this designation was adopted for Gippsland (there are no different legal requirements for a zone and a region), except the obvious fact that Gippsland is a large area, and perhaps additional regions were envisioned within it. Gippsland covers the entire southern coastline of Victoria east of Mornington Peninsula and extends northward well into the Kosciuszko National Park, covering over 40,000 square kilometres in total. Of that, fewer than 200 hectares are under vine: 0.0046% of the entire area of the GI is planted to wine grapes, one of the lowest ratios in Australia.

Despite Australia being home to over 500 First Nations, some as small as a modern-day neighbourhood, the wine regions of Gippsland are on the traditional lands of just two nations: the Gunai or Kurnai (often referred to today as the Gunaikurnai), and the Bunurong, a member of the Kulin Nation. Bunurong country runs from the Werribee River west of Melbourne to the eastern edge of Anderson Inlet (modern day Tarwin Lower/Venus Bay area) and Wilsons Promontory, which is generally thought to be disputed territory. Apparently, the two nations didn't get along very well.

The Bunurong have not yet achieved a land title claim, despite over a decade of attempts. In Victoria, a group needs to prove a continuous presence on a piece of land since colonisation in order to make a claim for it – a task made considerably harder by the very act of colonisation, which often displaces original inhabitants, as it did in the case of the Bunurong.

The Gunaikurnai's land title claim, on the other hand, was made soon after the Victorian Aboriginal Heritage Act was passed (2006), and formally codified in 2010. The recognised territory spans from the area surrounding Warragul and the foothills of Mt Baw Baw, east to the Snowy River, north to the Great Dividing Range, and south 200 metres offshore.

Five major language groups are part of the Gunaikurnai Nation, though much of the original dialects have been lost. Traditionally these groups, as well as divisions between larger nations, would be formed based on biophysical changes in the land. Though a single GI might imply that the area of Gippsland is homogenous, this fact speaks to its diversity.

Production is just now starting to approach a level that might warrant further GI delineation. Historically, Gippsland was a late bloomer and then a one-trick pony. Ten years ago, if any wine enthusiast or professional was asked to name a Gippsland winery, 'Bass Phillip' would be the answer without hesitation. Indeed, Bass Phillip has made an indelible impact on the Australian wine scene, known for their often-extraordinary (and often-pricey) pinot noirs, from a vast, largely unexplored wine region.

The scene today in Gippsland is one of the most exciting in all of Australia – perhaps the most exciting. The region has a singular combination of things going for it – proximity to a major metropolis, viticultural know-how, counter-culture buzz and proven wine excellence – that no other region is conjuring right now. The substance rarely matches the hype in the wine world, but in the case of Gippsland, having long awaited its time in the sun, it surely deserves even more fanfare than this buzzy region has already received.

Evolution of Wine

Like with most Victoria wine regions, there's evidence of grape growing in the 19th century, but the industry didn't stick. Dairy farming and coal mining proved to be much more reliable and profitable. When Phillip Jones planted his vineyard in Leongatha (South Gippsland) in 1979, he was one of the first to reintroduce viticulture to the region. His first commercial vintage of Bass Phillip was 1989, released in 1991, though neighbouring winemakers remember having wines dating back to 1984. By 2000, the wines were featured on the **Langton's Classification** (the Reserve Pinot Noir reaching the top 'Exceptional' tier in 2005).

Bass Phillip became known for its pinot noirs, given high marks by nearly every domestic wine writer (and many around the world), but it also gained notoriety for its eccentric proprietor, Phillip Jones, as well as its high prices – to this day, unrivalled by any other pinot noir produced outside of Burgundy, France.

Other wineries cropped up. McAlister and Nicholson River were two that received early acclaim – but decades went by in Gippsland with few producers catching the widespread interest of the Australian wine consumer or professional, nor doing anything to create a collective identity for the region. As described by wine writer Max Allen in a 2021 article for the *Australian Financial Review*, Gippsland, up until recently, was considered pretty 'daggy'.

With few producers proving the quality of the region, combined with overall difficult growing conditions (cool, rainy and windy to different degrees), corporate or outside interest was non-existent in the 90s and 2000s, when this type of investment was a common bolster throughout many wine regions of Australia. In 2010, when Phillip Jones started to put out feelers to sell Bass Phillip, it appeared to the outside world as though Gippsland could very well dwindle into obscurity.

But there was already a current underway, though exceedingly low profile, to prove Gippsland's veracity as a fine wine region (beyond the perimeter of a single estate in Leongatha). Neil Prentice had planted his **biodynamic** estate Moondarra in the foothills of Mt Baw Baw, in the northern extremes of West Gippsland, in 1991. Father-and-son team Pasquale and Frank Butera planted in Leongatha in 1998, establishing Bass River. Dean and Dayna Roberts, of Lithostylis and Dr Folk, started growing grapes in South Gippsland in 2005. And William Downie, who had previously worked for Bass Phillip, began making his own pinot noir from Gippsland in 2006.

It would be another decade, though, before Gippsland's renaissance truly began. While most Australian regions experienced waves of interest and influx throughout the 90s and 2000s (usually compounding previous waves of the 70s and 80s), it wasn't until the mid-2010s that Gippsland saw its first big ingress.

These are small-scale farmers and winemakers, investing their labour and personal capital in a region they believe is capable of creating world-class wines.

Marcus Satchell, a Gippsland native, launched Dirty Three in 2012, the same year Philippa Farr had her first vintage of Gippsland pinot noir. Anna and Neil Hawkins moved to Gippsland to start The Wine Farm in 2014. Patrick Sullivan bought his farm in the same year, and began planting his vineyard in 2016. Justin and Lisa Jenkins had their first vintage at Fleet in 2016. Dane Johns of Momento Mori bought a vineyard in Gippsland in 2017, the same year James and Jess Audas launched A.R.C. (adding to their vineyard land in 2020). Many other winery launches have brewed excitement for the region, including Bandicoot Run (2017), Xavier Goodridge (2017), Entropy (2018) and Vino Idda (2020).

The difference between this boom and others across Australia? For the most part, these aren't producers jumping on a bandwagon, buying a little (or a lot of) fruit, and capitalising on a name. These are small-scale farmers and winemakers, investing their labour and personal capital in a region they believe is capable of creating world-class wines. Some of the new-wave have fallen under the 'natural' banner, making **pét-nats**, skin-contact wines and more alternative styles. These wines are not to be discounted – the cool climate of Gippsland offers a good backdrop for this experimentation (pHs are low, therefore bacterial growth is slow), and the results have been largely successful. But beyond this, many producers are dedicated to proving that Gippsland is the next important *premium* wine region in Australia, especially for the likes of pinot noir and chardonnay.

Bass Phillip has become re-energised to join this pursuit, after finally being sold to a group of investors and Burgundy's esteemed Jean-Marie Fourrier in 2020. Fourrier has stated that '[becoming] the DRC of the southern hemisphere eventually is our aim', referring to the legendary Domaine de la Romanée Conti of Burgundy, whose wines command thousands (and sometimes tens of thousands) of dollars on wine lists across the world.

This time around, Bass Phillip is not alone. Instead of being the outlier for upmarket wines in Gippsland, they are now surrounded by a cadre of skilled vignerons who have similar goals and the skills to execute them. Gippsland is already one of the most exciting regions of Australia, and poised to become one of the most premium. With still over 99.9% of its land unplanted, the potential is nearly limitless.

Gippsland Viticultural Footprint

Total delimited area (km²)	41,147
Total planted area (hectares)	191
% of delimited area planted	0.005%
Total elevation range	0–1200 masl
Elevation range of plantings	25–370 masl
Number of producers	31

Gippsland Climate Data (°C)

	WEST GIPPSLAND (Warragul)	SOUTH GIPPSLAND (Leongatha)	EAST GIPPSLAND (Bairnsdale)
Heat summation/GDD	n/a	n/a	n/a
Annual rain/GSR	861/401	859/395	771/389
Warmest month avg. temp.	19.1	19.1	19.6

Lay of the Land

Bound by the Great Dividing Range to the north and the Bass Strait to the south, the only thing that ties Gippsland together are the two grapes that have become calling cards for every corner of the region: chardonnay and pinot noir. Gippsland is uniformly cool, but that's where the uniformities end. The region houses a variety of climatic conditions, creating areas that are drought-prone, areas that are temperate rainforests and everything in between.

Gippsland's most northwesterly vineyard sits nearly 150 kilometres north of the southern vineyards of Fish Creek, and both are separated by over 200 kilometres from the region's easternmost vineyards. This is a sprawling region.

On the whole, Gippsland is a landscape of rolling hills fanning out along a southern coast lined by estuaries, barrier islands and hundreds of kilometres of uninterrupted white sand beaches. Alpine forests in the north transition to cool-temperate rainforests in protected gullies between 600 and 1200 metres in elevation, and warm-temperate rainforests below that. The central and western, lower-lying areas of the region are verdant, rolling pastures that narrow as one heads east.

Alluvial fans mix sandy, gravelly loams and richer, dark loams across various formations. These deposits formed in the past 1.6 million years through to the end of the Last Glacial Period, about 11,000 years ago (young for Australia, and most of the world for that matter).

Gippsland needs to be thought of as a minimum of three areas. This is often how the region is talked about – West Gippsland, South Gippsland and East Gippsland – and it's a useful way to begin thinking about the differences across this vast region.

West Gippsland is considered the rolling hills of Warragul and the surrounding areas north of the Strzelecki Ranges. This area is adjacent to the Yarra Valley to the north. The soils here are a mix of red volcanic loams with gravel/sand alluvial fans. The producers of note in West Gippsland include Patrick Sullivan, William Downie and Moondarra (the latter in the easternmost stretches of what would be considered West Gippsland).

Sullivan and Downie, who have emerged as two of the greats in this region, think about this area in terms of the county that occupies most of it: Baw Baw Shire. While dividing this subregion on county lines would leave out some of the northwestern-most producers in Gippsland, it includes most of the others and isolates their geographic commonalities. And, as Downie says, 'it's already a line on a map' – often the true challenge when establishing appellations: deciding exactly where they start and end.

South Gippsland is, you guessed it, further south from West Gippsland, but equally far west. The two are not far apart in geographic distance, separated by the Strzelecki Ranges as they taper out to the west, which imparts a sometimes-dramatic difference in climate features and weather conditions; in a given day, one area could be rainy and cold and the other sunny and clear. South Gippsland is much more influenced by southeasterly weather, while West Gippsland is more influenced by westerly weather that crosses over Port Phillip Bay and Melbourne.

Both South and West Gippsland see vines planted in two general soil types: those of friable red clays and loams based on iron-rich volcanic basalt, and others planted to granitic sandy loams. A variety of watersheds create some saturated areas and other broad alluvial mixes that are rarely planted. South Gippsland is lower in elevation and tends to be slightly warmer, with the greatest difference between the two in their winter temperatures.

South Gippsland also has lower sunlight hours during the growing season, is more exposed to southerly winds and weather extremes, and sees less annual rainfall than the vineyards north of the Strzeleckis. Producers based in South Gippsland include Bass Phillip, Fleet, Dirty Three, The Wine Farm, Dr Folk and Lithostylis.

Dry-farming is abundant in both South and West Gippsland: an attractive feature for many young vignerons who want to employ as few additives as possible (and who don't want to have to rely on the sometimes scarce and expensive resource that is water). This is one of the very few places in Australia (and perhaps the world) where the combination of **dry-grown**, organic, **biodynamic**, **no-till farming** can occur without

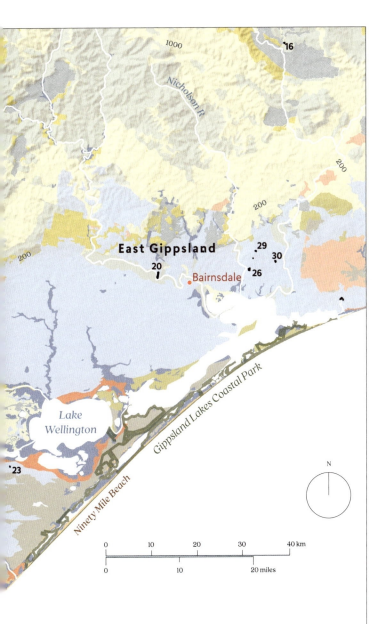

Gippsland

HOW TO READ THIS MAP

This map shows Gippsland's vineyards, which are few and very far between, covering less than 200 hectares across 41,000 km^2, planted in 10 major soil groups.

1	A.R.C.	18	Fleet
2	Ada River	19	Gippsland Wine Company
3	Allie	20	Lightfoot & Sons
4	Avon Ridge	21	Lithostylis/Dr Folk/Din
5	Bass Phillip	22	Lyre Bird
6	Bass Phillip Belrose Estate	23	McAlister Vineyards
7	Bass Phillip Crown Prince Vineyard	24	Momento Mori/Nikau Farm
8	Bass Phillip Issan Vineyard	25	Moondarra
9	Bass River	26	Nicholson River
10	Blue Gables	27	Parnassus
11	Caledonia Australis	28	Patrick Sullivan
12	Cannibal Creek	29	Sarsfield Estate
13	Clair de Lune	30	Tambo Estate
14	Dirty Three Wines	31	William Downie
15	Djinta Djinta	32	The Wine Farm
16	Ensay	33	Xavier Goodridge
17	Entropy		

GIPPSLAND Wine region
West Gippsland Unofficial subregion
Glengarry City
——— Region boundary
▌ Vineyard

Soils & Geology:
- Deforested clay/loam
- Old, weathered mixtures of sand, clay and loam
- Tertiary, red, friable basalt high in free iron oxide
- Tertiary loams over hard rock
- Granitic sandy loam over clay
- Dense, saturated, soft brown clay or sandy loams
- Loamy soils among forests, atop igneous rock
- Waterlogged flood plains and river flats
- Younger Pleistocene alluvial plains
- Thin sandy soils found on steep hills and sand dunes

sacrificing the viability of production – and does occur with some regularity.

The combination of moderate land cost and elevated farming cost (because of disease pressure) nets out to affordable, though not commercially cheap, wine. These areas, for the moment, occupy a happy medium of well-priced wines, but with enough disease pressure and associated farming costs to deter big corporates or multi-nationals from coming in.

The best sites in South and West Gippsland are about the best soils. In a variety of places, soils can be quite deep, making them less desirable for vines. Where the volcanic red loam thins out over the top of clay and mother rock, vines find a perfect balance. The best vineyards are on the transitions where the loam narrows to 1–2 metres deep. These soils are often found at mid-level elevations on the northwest and southwest-facing lower foothills of the Strzeleckis. (Too high and the topsoil is too shallow.)

These soil types are found less consistently through South Gippsland, and rarely at all in vineyards on the western extremes of the region (west of Baw Baw Shire in West Gippsland or in the Bass Coast/Phillip Island areas of South Gippsland). East Gippsland also sees a very different set of soil types. The peaks of Central-East Gippsland were at their highest during the Tertiary period, and their erosion greatly contributes to the soil makeup of the region, defined by eroded sediments of sand and loam, often with granitic origins, that tend to be more acidic than preferred.

East Gippsland sees nearly as much rainfall as West Gippsland and South Gippsland – the difference is timing. Many of the vineyards at low elevations in East Gippsland can suffer from drought as they receive their precipitation in massive, isolated rain events, and often at the worst parts of the growing season (such as flowering and fruit set). Here, irrigation can be required, though there is easy access to water, collected from the giant northernly watershed and redistributed. East Gippsland has fewer and further-between vineyards, the most notable of which are McAlister, Nicholson River and Lightfoot & Sons.

With at least three-hours' travel time from Melbourne, less ability to **dry-farm**, and the absence of the red, volcanic soils, East Gippsland has seen less of a renaissance than the regions further west. The region is responsible for some solid wines (Nicholson River was an early darling for its chardonnay), but the excitement and influx that is pervading the west and south is less palpable here.

The best sites in South and West Gippsland are about the best soils … Where the volcanic red loam thins out over the top of clay and mother rock, vines find a perfect balance.

Hubbub

Historically, Gippsland hubbub has centred around the region's personalities: many of the original producers of the region, like Ken Eckersley (Nicholson River), Phillip Jones (Bass Phillip), John Farrington (Wild Dog Winery) and Peter Edwards (McAlister), by all accounts, didn't get along. Some propose that's why Gippsland is so spread out: they wanted to get as far away from each other as possible.

Phillip Jones individually also became a character of great discussion, with everyone in the Australian wine industry having something to say about the man. Published descriptions of Jones include 'eccentric', 'erratic', 'gruff' and even 'mad', but those traits haven't deterred writers,

Necessities of a wine life, courtesy of Patrick Sullivan.

reviewers and wine professionals from heaping praise on the wines – 99-point ratings and **Langton's** top-tier classifications were common for Jones. Some argued the wines were inconsistent, others that they were overpriced, but perhaps the real squabble was that Gippsland had become associated with just one name.

Today, that's not the case, and the spotlight that Bass Phillip once occupied alone is now shared with excellent producers across the region.

With disease pressure and low average temperatures, the vineyards of Gippsland often deal with some of the more marginal growing conditions in Australia. But this is not a gripe that you hear in the mouths of the region's producers. In fact, if anything, this fact seems to be a point of pride. Sullivan states, 'When you come here, you definitely see the nuance: the site. And that's because we're right on the cusp of being able to ripen things ... it's right on the edge of what's possible, which I think is what makes great wine.'

Perhaps the biggest problem in Gippsland is there's just not enough of the pie for everyone to get a piece. When asked about the challenges facing Gippsland, Sullivan responds, 'There's just not enough grapes, that's pretty much it ... there's not enough fruit for the amount of people that want to buy it.' The solution is, of course, to plant more – which is easier said than done, but not impossible for Gippsland. Although land ownership is always an expensive proposition, it's not out of reach (yet!). Downie adds, 'Gippsland's a lot cheaper than – well not *a lot* anymore – but it's cheaper than the Yarra Valley or Mornington or parts of Geelong ... Property prices are up here a little bit. But it's still doable. There are opportunities for sure. And there's a huge number of possible vineyard sites.'

With growth in plantings and production, Gippsland should soon be at the point where further GI definition would be feasible. If any region in Australia is in need of further appellations, Gippsland seems to be the primary contender. Producers of the region are generally in favour of it, though aren't at the point of actively petitioning yet. Patience seems to be a trait in common among the producers of the region: no one came to Gippsland for a quick buck. They're in it for the long haul, and are starting to see the fruits (literally and figuratively) of their investment.

The rolling hills of the Strzelecki Ranges in the early summer sun, with the Great Dividing Range further north in the distance.

PRODUCERS

A.R.C.

James and Jessica Audas both worked in high-profile hospitality venues before moving off the grid to their permaculture farm in West Gippsland. Working vintage with Bill Downie inspired them to take the plunge with A.R.C. – aptly standing for A Random Collection. They started with fruit from Mornington, and have since planted a **high-density** site on their Gippsland farm to aligoté, gamay and chenin blanc. They also took over management of a vineyard from Bill Downie and Pat Sullivan, giving them the opportunity to work with Gippsland fruit while their vineyard matures.
arcwines.com.au

BASS PHILLIP

Phillip Jones left a career in telecommunications at 32 to pursue wine, planting his vineyard in South Gippsland in 1979. His first vineyard had only a couple of rows of pinot noir, the grape that would go on to make him famous; the bulk of it was comprised of Bordeaux varieties, with the hopes of making wine like his favourite château, Ducru Beaucaillou. He soon found the pinot and chardonnay outperformed the cabernet and friends, so those vines were replanted to the former. Jones toiled away diligently for years, not releasing his first wines until 1991. The wines have piled up scores of accolades over the years. Bass Phillip makes the most expensive pinot noir in Australia – the Reserve retails for around $800 a bottle. Small amounts of chardonnay, gamay and gewürztraminer are also made. Now in his 70s, Jones spent several years looking for a buyer for the historic estate. In 2020, Bass Phillip was purchased by two Singaporean businessmen and Jean-Marie Fourrier (of Domaine Fourrier in Gevrey-Chambertin), the latter of whom will take on the role of chief winemaker. **bassphillip.com**

Phillip Jones
Bass Phillip

ENTROPY

While Ryan Ponsford was working in Melbourne as a photographer, he was introduced to a William Downie wine one night in a restaurant. He was so taken by it, he emailed Bill and went down to the farm to meet him. Though Ryan never planned on starting a wine label, Bill gave him some pinot noir to play with in 2018, which became the first Entropy wine. Ryan farms a plot of the Wild Dog property and is organically tending a small vineyard in West Gippsland by himself. He chooses to toe a more traditional line in winemaking, trading the orange wines and **pét-nats** of the moment for peppery syrah, barrel-fermented sauvignon

blanc-semillon, and a true field blend of pinot noir and pinot gris.
entropywines.com

FLEET

When Lisa and Justin Jenkins were offered just over 2 tonnes of cabernet franc in 2016, they leapt at the opportunity and haven't looked back. They've both had long careers in hospitality, so great wine has always been a part of their work. And with Justin growing up in South Gippsland, it seemed like a natural place to set up shop. Aside from elegant Gippsland pinot noir, syrah and chardonnay, they have a short lease on a vineyard at Moorooduc Estate in the Mornington Peninsula and continue to source some fruit from the Yarra Valley. Lisa and Justin bought their own farm, Ever Reve, in Leongatha (South Gippsland) in 2019, and are establishing what will surely become an important site for the region. *fleetwines.com.au*

> **JR** | **What we're drinking**
>
> *When one thinks of beef and wine, it's usually cabernet or shiraz. But at **Moondarra** it's pinot noir that grows alongside grazing wagyu cows. Prentice's self-dubbed 'funkosité' approach to creating robustly aromatic pinot is best expressed in his Conception bottling: a nuanced, savoury pinot that is the perfect complement to his grass-fed wagyu.* — Jonathan Ross

---

LITHOSTYLIS/DR FOLK/DIN

Since 2005, Dean Roberts has been making wine in South Gippsland. He started Lithostylis with the established **close-planted** vineyard, the Red Dwarf, so-named for its deep, red volcanic soils. He has come to the conclusion, as many have today, that the best wines made in the region are from pinot noir and chardonnay. His aim is to grow pristine fruit, so there is little work to do in the winery. Dean is also the viticulturist half of Dr Folk, alongside friend and winemaker Folkert Janssen, and makes a label called Din (his nickname) exclusively from pinot noir. *lithostylis.com*

MOMENTO MORI/ NIKAU FARM

Once a barista and musician, Dane Johns has transferred his aroma-analysing and art-making skills to wine production. He and his wife Hannah tend several vineyards across Gippsland and work with growers outside of the region to produce the Momento Mori wines. They have recently begun to produce wine from two vineyards on their own property, which is bottled under the Nikau Farm label. The wines are uncompromisingly minimalist, with zero additions (save for a small amount of SO$_2$ for one Momento Mori bottling) and careful, focused winemaking.
momentomoriwines.com.au

MOONDARRA

Neil Prentice is an eccentric character, seen around the traps in Melbourne's hospitality scene and at his parent's beef farm in Gippsland. He started life as a 'wine waiter' and developed an interest in **biodynamics** through learning about his favourite Burgundian domaines.

> | **What we're drinking**
>
> **Fleet's** *Chorus is made up of 80% pinot noir, 10% chardonnay and 10% syrah from their Leongatha vineyard in South Gippsland. What might seem a strange mix-match of grapes results in a harmonious light, al dente red in bottle that will have you singing out for more. Yum.* — Kavita Faiella

 New Guard   Environmental Hero   Rising Star   Legend   Regional Stalwart   Must Visit   Cult Following   Historic Estate

WILLIAM DOWNIE

Bill, as most call him, grew up in Gippsland. A short stint in the vineyard at Bass Phillip then pushed him to the Yarra Valley, starting at De Bortoli in 2001. He spent several years between home and Burgundy, launching his own label in 2003, while working for Jean-Marie Fourrier, and then as winemaker under Hubert Lignier in 2004 and 2005. The first wines of his eponymous label were pinot noirs from the Yarra and Mornington, adding Gippsland in 2008. Bill now focuses almost solely on Gippsland pinot noir, farming the Camp Hill and Bull Swamp vineyards **biodynamically**. He and his wife Rachel also lovingly tend their own farm called Guendulain, on which they have a **close-planted**, organically certified pinot noir vineyard. No doubt about it: Bill is making some of Australia's greatest pinot noirs. **williamdownie.com.au**

When his parents were looking for land in 1991, Neil had them under instruction that it should have an appropriate northeast-facing site for growing pinot noir. He doesn't adhere to strict **biodynamics**, instead using techniques where he sees fit for his vineyard, which has never been irrigated or seen chemical fertiliser. Aside from pinot, he makes a bit of sparkling in Whitlands (King Valley) from his Holly's Garden vineyard and a range of wines from his fruit-salad home vineyard of chardonnay, pinot bianco, pinot grigio, nebbiolo, friulano and picolit. Neil's style is a little bit punk, a little bit rock and roll, and a lot of what he calls 'funkosité'. **moondarra.com.au**

starting to make his own wines. He bought a 69-hectare farm with his wife Megan in 2014 at the base of the Strzelecki Ranges, where they have planted pinot noir and chardonnay vineyards, drawn to the area for its ability to allow **dry-farming** with **biodynamic** methods. His trio of chardonnays come from Millstream, Ada River and Bull Swamp vineyards, as well as a selection labelled by the county: Baw Baw Shire. Patrick's thoughtful and nuanced approach to farming and winemaking has landed him on the 'must-have' list for top restaurants and retailers across the globe. **patricksullivan.com.au**

THE WINE FARM

Neil and Anna Hawkins moved to South Gippsland in 2011 with a deep-seated interest in making cool-climate wines. They overhauled

PATRICK SULLIVAN

Patrick Sullivan first planted vines at the age of 15, before jumping the pond to work in Europe. On his return to Australia, he began working with William Downie and viticulturist Stuart Proud at Thousand Candles (p. 120) in the Yarra Valley before

---

 What we're drinking

*Quietly spoken and incredibly considered, Neil Hawkins of **The Wine Farm** is one of those vignerons who preaches detail and takes it to the infinitesimal. The wines — white, red (and other!) — speak with a purity and effortlessness, gentle savouriness, drive and briny acidity. It's one of those wine projects where each year reveals more about the people and place, with distinct wines that reek of high quality and immense drinkability. — Mike Bennie*

Victoria

the original vineyard they purchased in 2014, converting to **biodynamic** practices and grafting over new varieties. They have also bought a plot of land next to the famed Bass Phillip in Leongatha South. The Wine Farm is planted to 1 hectare each of riesling, syrah, chardonnay and pinot noir – and they are one of only eight Demeter-certified **biodynamic** producers in Australia.
thewinefarm.com.au

And don't forget ...
Bass River, the Butera family's ode to Gippsland's unique biodiversity, has an offering that ranges from Gippsland classics (pinot noir and chardonnay) to merlot, limoncello and estate-grown olive oil ... **Bellvale**, in the Tarwin River Valley, manages an ambitious vineyard of dry-grown, densely-planted pinot noir, chardonnay, pinot grigio and nebbiolo ... **Dirty Three Wines** is from husband-and-wife team Marcus Satchwell and Lisa Sartori, a couple who have been doing the hard yards to get Gippsland the acclaim it deserves for its site-specific pinot noir ... **Gippsland Wine Company** is a viticultural endeavour at heart, with Mark Heath coaxing rundown vineyards back to life and wines made by Dirty Three's Marcus Satchwell ... **Lightfoot & Sons**, truly a family affair, with second-generation Rob and Tom Lightfoot at the helm, is based in the Gippsland Lakes district and produces a wide array of wines from their Myrtle Point vineyard, first planted in 1995 ... **McAlister Vineyards**, one of the pioneers of the region, has plantings of cabernet sauvignon, cabernet franc, merlot and petit verdot dating back to 1977 ... **Nicholson River** boasts Ken and Juliet Eckersley's 1978 plantings, some of the oldest in the region today ... **Philippa Farr Wines** is a pinot-focused label of both Gippsland and Mornington fruit, from a woman with an impressive wine lineage (By Farr in Geelong, p. 148) and an equally impressive personal résumé ... **South Gippsland Wine Company** encompasses two labels, Caledonia Australis and Mount Macleod, both made by Mark Matthews since 2008, displaying his deft hand with pinot noir, chardonnay and grüner veltliner ... **Xavier Goodridge**'s 2 hectare Gippsland plot will see its first release of chardonnay and pinot noir, made in a **lo-fi** manner, in 2022.

William Downie

Heathcote

Introduction

Heathcote – a warm, narrow region in Central Victoria – has done a commendable job of building its brand, almost unintentionally. The name Heathcote (especially when preceding 'shiraz') commands a certain recognition and prestige across Australia. With this reputation in mind, you'd be surprised to visit Heathcote and find a rather provincial town – no traffic lights, no McDonald's, 'a little bit backwards' as Jasper Hill's Emily McNally lovingly describes it. It's clear when setting sight on Heathcote that no mastermind marketing scheme has been behind its success – it was a few key people doing the right thing at the right time (and many others riding the wave).

Heathcote is Taungurung Country. There are 15 different familial groups within the Taungurung Nation, and today many members of these groups live on their Country, and work as cultural heritage advisors, land management officers, artists and educators. The land is gently undulating, with nuanced climate variations across it, which yielded more permanent early settlements without the need to rotate through high and low Country as the seasons changed. As with grapevine plantings in Heathcote today, changes in soil dictated which flora, and therefore which fauna, were present.

Heathcote has become known for its bold and rich styles of shiraz. A warm, continental climate – one of the overall warmest for premium wine in Victoria – engenders this style. To the average Australian drinker, Heathcote's outlook should be rather sunny (both literally and figuratively): the region commands good prices and sells a lot of wine. But within its borders, there is a recognition that things will have to change. The wine cognoscenti of Australia has been murmuring for a while that, despite the region's image, only a handful of producers are delivering on this reputation. Combined with a directive provided by climate change, Heathcote is clearly at a turning point – the Heathcote of tomorrow is potentially one we wouldn't recognise today.

Evolution of Wine

The first plantings in the Heathcote area date back to the 1860s, when German immigrant Henning Rathjen planted shiraz and marsanne vines on his land in Colbinabbin, on the northern stretches of the Mount Camel Range. Despite some early wine show wins, and a few other vineyards cropping up, the Heathcote wine region was destined to take a long pause. Like so many Australian wine regions, the turn of the century brought with it a downturn in the ability to grow and sell **table wine**, and nearly all viticulture ceased in Heathcote. One vineyard from the 19th century still survives today, planted by Baptista Governa in 1891 at Graytown, just on the border of Goulburn Valley in today's far eastern Heathcote.

The first modern vines were planted in 1955 by Paul Osicka, a Czech immigrant who had been a vigneron in his homeland. It would be over a decade until the next vines were planted, when an Italian immigrant named Albino Zuber planted the Pink Cliffs vineyard, just outside Heathcote's Pink Cliff Geological Reserve. The grape chosen was shiraz: a logical one, considering the growing popularity of the grape and Australia's penchant for planting it in warmer climates. Zuber made wine under his own label for a time, though the vineyard's real lustre has been found under the bottlings of non-Heathcote wineries, first Macedon's Granite Hills (p. 163) and then Shadowfax (Other Victoria, p. 249). The now-named Cavalry vineyard was also planted in the 1960s.

But it was in 1975 that a couple emerged on the scene who would set the standard in Heathcote for decades to come: Ron and Elva Laughton of Jasper Hill. From day one they had ambition for greatness: never once using a synthetic chemical on their land, **dry-farming** from the beginning, and even gluing a vintage ribbon to the neck of each bottle. Ron was a food scientist, Elva a milliner, and together they found a winning formula for world-class wines in a region no one had ever heard of. The exalted reputation of Heathcote was unquestionably formed in their cellars – and continues to be.

Even before Jasper Hill's first vintage in 1982, though, other ambitious upstarts had found their way to the region. Mount Ida Vineyard, now part of the Beringer Blass (and thus Treasury Wine Estates) holdings, was planted to shiraz in 1975. Heathcote Winery, pioneers of chardonnay in the region, established themselves in the early 1980s, as did Wild Duck Creek founders, Dave and Dianna Anderson.

Wild Duck Creek made a splash in the 1990s with their release of Duck Muck – a single barrel of 'super-ripe' (in their own words) shiraz, topped with cabernet sauvignon pressings and aged in 100% new French **barrique** for 27 months. The 1997 Duck Muck garnered 99 points from a then-commanding Robert Parker, and within weeks, bottles were going for over a thousand dollars a pop – all over the world.

Troy McInnes, viticulturist for Chalmers Heathcote vineyard, holding 550 million-year-old Cambrian basalt.

Whether this sudden notoriety was a good thing for Heathcote can be debated. Undoubtedly, it brought an influx of both new producers and new customers to the region. But the focus seemed to be about capitalising on the name Heathcote, rather than investing in the region. Very few producers were coming into Heathcote with an eye toward the long game: of planting vineyards and making world-class wine, or even of making Heathcote a tourist destination. Contrary to the cachet of the name Heathcote, the region itself, to this day, is relatively underdeveloped.

Stylistically, Duck Muck encouraged a departure as well. Up until that time, the overall style of Heathcote was to make shiraz that was moderate in body and alcohol, with structure, freshness and perfume. The one-two punch of global warming making bigger styles possible, and Robert Parker increasing the appetite for them, was seductive to the new and existing producers of Heathcote. Syrahmi's Adam Foster, a producer in the southern stretches of Heathcote, describes that era as a time when 'all the ex-teachers and doctors and retirees bought a block of land, planted these vineyards, [Duck Muck] got 99, and they're like "We can make our wine at 16.5% [alcohol]. We can do that."' And everyone just started copying each other.'

Perhaps not surprisingly then, only a few notable producers emerged in the following decade. Mario Marson planted his vineyards in 2000, establishing Vinea Marson with his wife and daughters, an ode to their Italian heritage. The Chalmers family saw the potential for Italian grape varieties in Heathcote as well, planting their vineyard in northern Heathcote, near Colbinabbin, in 2009. Foster also got his foot in Heathcote's door in the mid-2000s, after spending years working vintages in France's Northern Rhône. He identified Heathcote as having the potential for producing world-class shiraz – and not in the 16.5% style, either.

In addition to retired teachers and doctors, many companies from outside the region (mainly large conglomerates) started making wine from Heathcote fruit in those years – Beringer Blass, BRL Hardy, Brown Brothers, De Bortoli, Seppelt, Southcorp, Tyrrell's, even France's M.Chapoutier. This external interest solidified Heathcote as a region that was more about vineyards than it was vignerons. In fact, for a region that grows a significant amount of grapes (1836 hectares under vine), very few producers of note make wine within its borders.

Heathcote, in this sense, remains a region that rests (somewhat precariously) on this paradox: its name is associated with quality, due in large part to the work of the Laughtons at Jasper Hill, as well as a number of other producers who established Heathcote as a reliable region for bold shiraz. But its prospects for the future rest in the hands of a minute group (including Jasper Hill) who are truly focusing on quality farming and styles that appeal to the modern wine audience. This group has their work cut out for them: to wrest Heathcote's future from the hands of those who would just assume to make another conventionally farmed, bold shiraz – and to showcase the true potential of this obviously world-class wine region.

Heathcote Viticultural Footprint

Total delimited area (km²)	1913
Total planted area (hectares)	1836
% of delimited area planted	0.960%
Total elevation range	112–600 masl
Elevation range of plantings	160–380 masl
Number of producers	50

Heathcote Climate Data (°C)

	1960–1990	1991–PRESENT	2020
Heat summation/GDD	1642	1746	1814
Annual rain/GSR	575/279	518/267	537/352
Warmest month avg. temp.	20.9	22	22.4

Winkler Scale:

850–1111 1112–1389 1390–1667 1668–1944 1945–2222 2223–2700

Lay of the Land

Heathcote is a long, skinny appellation in Central Victoria, its southern border touching Macedon Ranges, and its northern tip extending towards the Murray River. The region lines up parallel with a series of faults in the greater Lachlan Fold Belt. Nearly all vineyards of the region are lined up along the Mt Camel Range and the corresponding Mt William Fault. Heathcote experiences a true, continental **diurnal shift** – with night-time temperatures dropping significantly compared to the warm daytimes.

Most vineyards along Mt Camel Ridge, north of Heathcote, face east, receiving morning sun and consistent easterly winds. At the north, where the mountains fade into undulating hillsides, the **aspects** become more varied. Only a few vineyards sit in these far-northern stretches, Brown Brothers and Seppelt among them. In the far south, **aspects** are varied as well, with some cooler sites seeking out north-facing slopes.

The northern part of Heathcote is home to the soil type the region is most famous for: red, Cambrian-era soil formed approximately 540 million years ago. This soil is the result of lava extruding through marine-based sediments and the basalt mother rock weathering over time. The soil today is an iron-rich mixture of gravel, sand and clay with fragments of basalt, heavy silicified shale (chert), ironstone and mudstone. This soil runs deep, with a marked water retention capability, though drains freely thanks to the green-coloured sandstone mixed throughout.

This soil type has become synonymous with the region; the northern boundaries of Heathcote were largely drawn because of it. Mark Walpole (p. 223), renowned Australian viticulturist (who co-authored the Heathcote GI application), relates that 'they originally wanted to cap [the Heathcote borders] south of Colbinabbin based on the temperature, but the region needed to go as far as the red soils ... that was the most important part of it'.

This is somewhat ironic (or perhaps just inconsistent) when the whole southern portion is not privy to these soils. The southern portion has as much (if not more) in common with the bordering Macedon Ranges as it does with the northern portion of Heathcote. The Cambrian ridge line fades away at the town of Heathcote and further south; younger Ordovician, Silurian and Devonian formations reside. At Tooborac, the undulating hills hold up giant granite boulders – a striking visual for the soil lying below.

The south is not a lower quality area, but the reputation of the Cambrian soils has overshadowed the special character of the granite in the south. In fact, Foster, who has become the torchbearer for the south, jokingly boasts the superiority of his soil type: 'I want to call this Tooborac,' he says of his wine. 'I don't want to call it Heathcote because, you know, the shitty red soils of the north, who cares?'

Certainly no one (including Foster) thinks Heathcote's Cambrian red soils are lousy – or even more that no one cares about them – but there's something to be said for recognising the quality of the south, even though it doesn't happen to be the soil type historically associated with the region's best wines. (Nor does it happen to be over half a billion years old, which is a good soundbite.) Heathcote has two great soil types, not just one.

Climate also varies from one end of Heathcote to the other. The south is cooler. While clocking an average of only one degree colder than the north, growers say the southeast looks a lot more like the Macedon Ranges (mainland Australia's coldest wine region) than the rest of Heathcote. **Diurnal swing** is greater in the north, which accounts for why this temperature disparity is more significant than it registers on paper. At any given moment, it can be a good 5–7°C cooler in the south, with often double the rainfall and significant frost risk.

The **diurnal swing** has historically been a point of differentiation for the shiraz of Heathcote; most Australian warm-climate shiraz-producing regions (think Barossa and McLaren Vale) are Mediterranean in climate, not continental, and thus don't experience the same degree of **diurnal shift**. This shift is becoming less meaningful in the warmest sites, though, as even a large downturn at night is not compensating for accelerating daytime temperatures (and resulting potential alcohols pushing 17%).

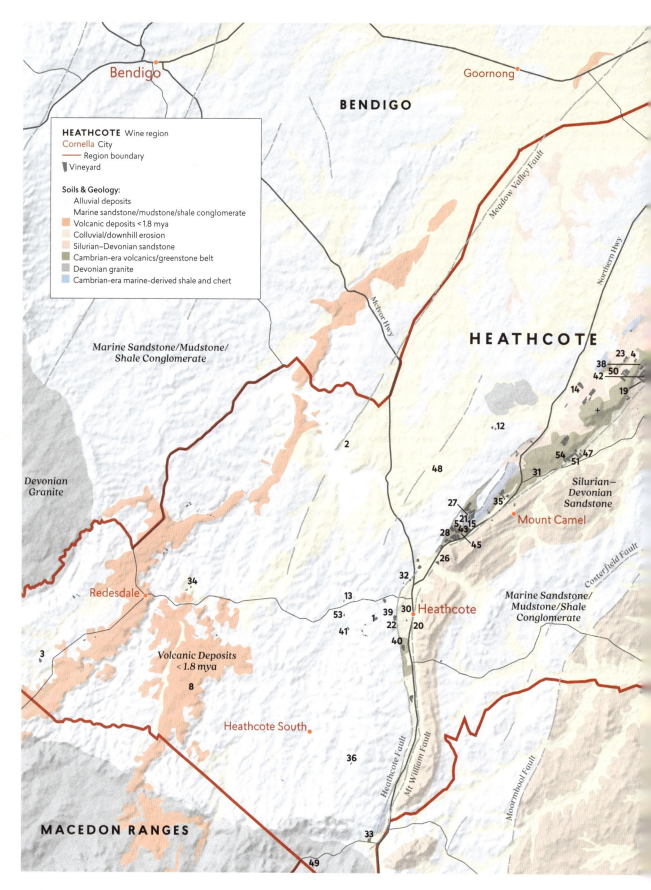

Heathcote

HOW TO READ THIS MAP

Home to Victoria's oldest soils dedicated to the vine, Heathcote changes drastically from south to north. This map shows how those changes are defined by the region's soils and topography, with many of the region's vineyards clinging to the central Mt Camel ridge.

1. Argyle Forest Estate
2. Armstead Estate
3. Barfold Estate
4. Barnadown Run
5. The Bridge Vineyard
6. Brown Brothers
7. Buckshot Vineyard
8. Burke & Wills
9. Chalmers
10. Colbinabbin Estate
11. Coliban Valley
12. Condie
13. Condie Van Cordinaire Vineyard
14. Domaine Asmara
15. Downing Estate
16. Ellis
17. Farmer & The Scientist
18. Greenstone Vineyard
19. Hanging Rock
20. Heathcote Estate
21. Heathcote Estate Brecon Vineyard
22. Heathcote Estate Golden Gully Vineyard
23. Heathcote II
24. Hennings View Vineyard
25. Humis Vineyard
26. Idavue Estate
27. Jasper Hill (Emily's Paddock)
28. Jasper Hill (Georgia's Paddock)
29. Kennedy Vintners
30. M.Chapoutier
31. M.Chapoutier Lady's Pass Vineyard
32. Meehan Vineyard
33. Merindoc
34. Mia Valley
35. Munari
36. Mundy Gully
37. Paul Osicka
38. Peregrine Ridge
39. Red Edge
40. Red Edge Jacksons Lane Vineyard
41. Rogues Lane Vineyard
42. St Michael's Vineyard
43. Sanguine Estate
44. Seppelt (Treasury)
45. She-Oak Hill Vineyard
46. Shiraz Republic
47. Silver Spoon Estate
48. Sutherland
49. Syrahmi
50. Tellurian
51. Vinea Marson
52. Whistling Eagle
53. Wild Duck Creek
54. Wren Estate

185

A bird's eye view of the Pink Cliffs Geological Reserve just outside the town of Heathcote — another facet in the dynamic geology across the region. The limestone ridges, coloured pink by the presence of ironstone, were uncovered in the 1880s as a result of gold mining. These are fragile canyons carved through the earth, not ridges that rise above, and visits are for looking not hiking!

Hubbub

Across Victoria (and to a lesser extent, the rest of Australia), Heathcote shiraz dots wine lists and populates retail shelves. It is a brand that people know and trust. Very few regions in Australia (or really, anywhere outside of Europe), have been able to supersede the cache of individual producers, but Heathcote has done just that. Consumers will ask for a Heathcote shiraz, not minding which one is recommended, and expect a full-bodied, inky style to be delivered. And they're willing to pay for it.

Sure enough, there's a flood of quite serviceable, though rarely exciting, versions of this style coming out of Heathcote. But glance at the wine lists of the best restaurants of Australia, and very few Heathcote producers make the cut: Jasper Hill, Adam Foster's Syrahmi and Garden of Earthly Delights labels, Chalmers, Whistling Eagle, Vinea Marson, Chapoutier, Osicka and Tellurian – and that's about the extent of it. Of the 50-plus wineries based in the region, not to mention the dozens of other Heathcote-labelled brands made outside its borders, this is a scant showing.

Foster describes the problem plainly: 'We need to make better wine.' Marketing is not the problem – the region has actually proven to achieve that quite well – but making wine that is nuanced, site-specific and complex rather than a caricature of the 1990s Parker-bait wines. There is an energy within the region to do this, largely fuelled by a generational change. Paul Osicka's son Simon is running his family's eponymous winery, Emily McNally has now joined her dad at the helm of Jasper Hill, and Liam Anderson has taken over from his father at Wild Duck Creek. Already, a stylistic change is palpable, with new farming techniques to mitigate climate change, less new oak, and a greater attention to site-specificity.

Many members of the community are coming together with quality in mind. Through a government grant, over a dozen weather stations have been placed throughout the vineyards of Heathcote, with the goal of better understanding the intricacies of the land. A group of about 15 producers in the region has started to meet annually to benchmark wines – internationally, across Australia, and within the different stretches of Heathcote. And global warming, which has pushed harvest forward about four weeks over the last 40 years, is being seriously addressed.

The warmth of Heathcote – in the context of largely cool-climate Victoria – was a prideful point of distinction in the early days. Today it threatens to debilitate the vineyards of the region – and offers few stylistic alternatives to those who want them. Emily McNally of Jasper Hill recounts how their wines, during the 1980s, 'could be 11, 11.5, 12, 12.5% alcohol and they're consistently 15.5% now. And we have to really work at keeping them at 15.5, because they would like to go higher.'

To address climate change, producers are looking at a combination of vineyard management and new grapes. For Jasper Hill, they're changing the **canopy** shade in their vineyard and converting some portions from north–south to east–west **trellising**. They're picking earlier. And they've put in a large dam – a big step for the family who crafted the Jasper Hill style based on the small berries created by **dry-farming**. 'We're not wanting to irrigate our vineyard,' Emily notes, 'but we might have to irrigate it once or twice if we have a summer like 2019–2020 again, just for survival.' The summer in reference is one that produced one of the lowest yields on record for Jasper Hill, and prevented them from making any Emily's Paddock (one of their single-vineyard shiraz sites), nebbiolo, riesling or semillon.

Drier conditions, of course, also call into question water security. Heathcote has one natural water source: the Waranga Channel, which runs west from the Goulburn River via the Waranga Basin to the base of the Mt Camel Range at Colbinabbin, then turns north following the edge of the Cambrian soils. A private pipeline has been set up to take the water south, along the eastern edge of the ridge. 'The channel is like a small river, supplying a permanent and guaranteed water source of high quality for viticulture,' says Mark Walpole. The channel supplies many vineyards across the north and east sides of Heathcote. 'That's the reason we

The winery and cellar at Jasper Hill seen through the vines of Emily's Paddock, named after Ron and Elva Laughton's daughter who now runs the estate. Her sister Georgia also works at the estate, and has her own Georgia's Paddock.

[Brown Brothers and Greenstone] chose the northern part of the range,' he continues, 'and why all the big players are on the eastern side of the range ... all the small players are at the whim of the gods, which haven't been kind.'

Those who don't have access to that water source and wish to irrigate are left with the option to create a dam (as Jasper Hill has done), and rely on rainwater in other parts of the year to be sufficient, or to truck water in – which is expensive and rather frowned upon in the environmental conversation. Biosecurity is also an issue for some, with **phylloxera** in nearby Nagambie Lakes (p. 239) threatening to breach the borders of Heathcote – though many do not register this as a top concern. (Kim Chalmers, of Chalmers Wine, contends that 'there is a bit of apathy in the wine industry towards biosecurity issues'.) Heathcote is especially vulnerable in this respect, as so much of its fruit is processed outside the region – equipment and material go in and out of its borders all the time.

The other front being fought for climate change is in the grape varieties planted in Heathcote. Shiraz has historically been the grape of the region, but it's far less well-suited to hot, dry climates than many others. Producers like Brown Brothers, Chalmers, Greenstone and Vinea Marson have long seen the potential for Italian grapes in the region – grapes that tend to be drought-hardy and respond well to the heat – and have based most or all their production around these varieties. Grenache and mourvèdre are being looked to more and more, as well as Iberian varieties, which have increasingly been recognised as champion grapes across the dry, warm regions of Australia. In the future of Heathcote, shiraz will perhaps see more plantings in the cooler southeast near Macedon, off the Cambrian soils and on the granitic ones.

Clearly Heathcote is at a turning point, with distinct challenges ahead. But the region has the raw materials – the history, the people, the soils and the reputable name – to evolve and meet these challenges. The emergent Heathcote might just be one that isn't tied so closely to the rich shiraz of its past, and that might just be a very good thing.

PRODUCERS

CHALMERS

The Chalmers family has been instrumental in shaping the face of viticulture in Australia. Bruce and Jenni Chalmers started growing grapes in the Murray Darling in the early 80s and their research into grape suitability led to establishing a nursery in 1989. By the late 90s, Chalmers had imported almost 70 different **clones** and varieties from Italy. Bruce approached some large-scale companies in the early 2000s, thinking they'd jump at the opportunity to work with these new varieties that were so well-suited to many Australian climates. When he was knocked back, the family took it upon themselves to find the right premium spot for them.

On the advice of Mark Walpole (p. 223), Chalmers found the right combination of heat, rainfall and soil in the Mt Camel Ranges, with the first Heathcote vines planted in 2009. The Chalmers daughters, Kim and Tennille, have taken what their parents built and amplified it tenfold. The Chalmers wines have gone from strength to strength and the team is leading the charge in increasing diversity of grapes available in Australia. *chalmers.com.au*

JASPER HILL

Jasper Hill has always been a small family business at heart, even with the highly sought-after nature of their wines. Ron and Elva Laughton planted first in 1975, and quickly brought attention to themselves and the region with their concentrated and expressive shiraz. Georgia's Paddock and Emily's Paddock are named after the Laughton's two daughters. Both vineyards are planted with shiraz, along with a little cabernet franc on Emily's. Emily returned to Heathcote after doing the rounds in hospitality and completing a teaching degree, today sharing the title of vigneron with her father. As if taking on Jasper Hill wasn't enough, Emily also works on a couple of other Heathcote-based projects. Lo Stesso is a fiano produced with friend Georgia Roberts from a blend of Jasper Hill and Chalmers grapes. And Emily and her husband Nick have their own label Occam's Razor, named for a 14th century theologian's philosophy that 'less is more'. The first and constant icon of the region. *jasperhill.com.au*

PAUL OSICKA

Simon Osicka is the third generation to tend the vines at his family's Graytown vineyard. His grandfather, Paul Osicka Sr, made wine in Czechoslovakia before heading to Australia and planting vines in 1955. Paul Jr, Simon's father, steered the business away from bulk wine production to wholly estate-bottled fruit. Simon joined the business in 2010, having completed vintages

Kim & Tennille Chalmers
Chalmers

Emily McNally
Jasper Hill

both locally and overseas, including at the domaine of Rhône syrah master, J.L. Chave. He has continued to redevelop the vineyards and is highly focused on combatting the warming climate's effects. Simon has developed a **bush-vine** block of the heat-hardy grenache, and has breathed new life into the 65-year-old vineyard. *paulosickawines.com.au*

SYRAHMI

A vintage at Barossa's shiraz giant Torbreck enticed Adam Foster to the world of winemaking after years working as a chef in both Australia and London. He undertook no formal training, instead opting for back-to-back vintages, switching between hemispheres every season, with the likes of Stéphane Ogier, Mitchelton, Pierre Gaillard, Jasper Hill and Chapoutier. In 2004, he bought some grapes and launched his own label, Syrahmi, derived from *syrah* and the French *ami* ('friend'). Adam is striving to make the refined, mid-weight shiraz that first drew him to the Heathcote region, but also inspired by the syrahs of his time in the Northern Rhône. A grenache and mourvèdre also fall under the Syrahmi banner, and Heathcote sangiovese and pinot noir from Macedon are staples in his Garden of Earthly Delights label. In 2017, Adam planted his own **high-density** shiraz vineyard among striking granite boulders in the southeastern corner of Heathcote at Tooborac, continuing to buy grapes from trusted growers to complete his offerings. *syrahmi.com.au*

TELLURIAN

Tellurian was born out of Ian Hopkins's love for Heathcote shiraz, planting his vineyard on the western side of Mt Camel in 2002. Alongside winemaker Tobias Ansted, viticulturist Tim Brown, and his son Daniel, Ian bottled the first Tellurian shiraz in 2008. Plantings were expanded in 2011 to include more Rhône Valley varieties, plus nero d'Avola and fiano. The vineyards are certified organic. *tellurianwines.com.au*

VINEA MARSON

Mario Marson spent many years working as a winemaker, including 15 with John Middleton at Mount Mary (Yarra Valley, p. 119), before settling on a place for his own vineyard. He chose nebbiolo, barbera and sangiovese for the Cambrian soils of Mt Camel, where they have thrived for over 20 years, alongside

> **What we're drinking**
>
> It feels twee to call the **Osicka** site the 'Wendouree of Heathcote', but this is a singular place with unique vines and distinct terroir-driven character. Reds are heartier than the current vogue of Australian winemaking, but they feel overlaid with this unique 'Aussie bush' character that could be described as local **garrigue**. These are remarkable wines for their individuality, complexity and abundance of character. — Mike Bennie

> **What we're drinking**
>
> **Vinea Marson** makes a range of Italian-inspired wines that blend Australian and Mediterranean sensibilities. The Grazia is a favourite: a blend of pinot bianco, malvasia, friulano and picolit that combines stone fruit and smoky **reduction** on the nose with a fleshy yet fresh body. The perfect prosciutto wine. – **Jane Lopes**

the more traditional shiraz and viognier. The Vinea Marson Heritage wines link Mario to his upbringing, growing Friulian varietals pinot bianco, malvasia d'Istria, friulano and picolit. Mario has been joined in the winery by his daughter Madeleine as assistant winemaker.
vineamarson.com

WHISTLING EAGLE

Henning Rathjen planted the first vines in the Colbinabbin district in the 1860s. Though the original plantings no longer exist, Ian Rathjen is the fourth generation to care for the same land. Ian decided to try his hand at winemaking in 1997, making just 11 bottles of shiraz. He increased his production two years later to share with family and friends, before a retailer encouraged him to sell the wines in 2001. His daughter Trish and nephew Guy have joined him in the winery and vineyard, crafting traditional and balanced Heathcote bottlings. *whistlingeagle.com*

WILD DUCK CREEK

A forgotten and late-picked block of shiraz threw Wild Duck Creek onto a global stage, when the resulting wine, labelled Duck Muck, was blessed by Robert Parker. The wines are made as big and flavourful as possible by founder David Anderson (nicknamed 'Duck'), with shiraz and cabernet sauvignon being the heroes. His vineyards are meticulously managed and are in the process of transitioning to **biodynamic**. David's son Liam, also a winemaker, now works alongside him at Wild Duck Creek and the duo own and operate eight vineyards across Heathcote. For every annually made wine in their portfolio, there are just as many under the 'rare' banner (like Duck Muck), made only in the best years.
wildduckcreekestate.com.au

And don't forget ...
Farmer & the Scientist is named for Brian and Jess Dwyer, respectively, who've combined their valuable skills to craft several different shiraz, a tempranillo and a handful of Italian-inspired whites ... **Heathcote Estate**, planted by the Kirby Family (see Mornington's Yabby Lake, p. 136), has the sole intention of producing single-vineyard and single-block shiraz (though a small crop of grenache also makes an appearance) ... **Heathcote Winery**, established in 1978, was one of the first commercial wineries of the region, with a current focus on shiraz and viognier, as well as a charming cellar door ... **Merindoc**, the home property of the Shelmerdine family, has been an important figure in the Heathcote region, with Stephen Shelmerdine writing the GI with Ron Laughton and Mark Walpole ... **Wanted Man** is the product of an all-star team, assembled by restaurateur Peter Bartholomew, including Mark Walpole, Callan Randall and Allistair Timms (Shadowfax), with help from Simon Osicka and Adrian Rodda.

Adam Foster
Syrahmi

The granite boulders that define the landscape of Tooborac, in the southeastern corner of Heathcote, set the stage for the estate vineyard of Syrahmi.

Western Victoria

Introduction

The zone of Western Victoria contains three regional GIs – the Pyrenees, the Grampians and Henty – that cascade down the southwest remnants of the Great Dividing Range, in that order, toward the ocean and the western border of Victoria.

The Grampians, the central appellation, is named after the Grampians National Park, one of Australia's most striking natural settings: a 1000-plus square kilometre park replete with natural sandstone mountain ranges, waterfalls, hiking trails, look-out spots, climbing rocks, echidnas, wallabies and wildflowers.

The area has long been known to the Jardwadjali and Djab Wurrung (a member of the Kulin nation) peoples as Gariwerd, and it is central to the cultural identity of both these nations, who share a border at the eastern edge of what is now Grampians GI. Alliance and partnership formed between the two prior to colonisation, merging culture, trade and society.

The Budja Budja Aboriginal Corporation is a modern-day organisation founded by members of the Djab Wurrung and Jardwadjali Nations. 'Budja Budja' is their name for Halls Gap, one of the gateways to Gariwerd, and place of spiritual connectivity for these nations. Budja Budja, without official land title claims, has maintained their connection in other ways. Their health clinic, for one, has successfully integrated support from established medicare systems and infused them with Indigenous traditions of the area.

The Pyrenees GI, just east and slightly north of the Grampians, sits at the intersection of numerous First Nations, circling the traditional lands of the Jardwadjali and Djab Wurrung, as well as the Taungurung people.

The Grampians and the Pyrenees have more in common with each other than either do with Henty. Both are shiraz-dominated regions in the last foothills of the Great Dividing Range, their reputations hinged to the backs of a handful of historic producers (though 'historic' in the Grampians dates back much further than it does in the Pyrenees). Moving into Henty, the Great Dividing Range disappears completely, and is replaced by chilly flatlands barrelling towards the blustery coast, where pinot noir and riesling find preference over shiraz.

Henty is Gunditjmara and Eastern Maar Country; the two nations' traditional custodianship overlaps for a slim slice of land, beginning just east of the modern-day township of Portland, extending from the coast up nearly to the Grampians National Park. This is land of shared custodianship, with the Eastern Maar Nation extending to the east and Gunditjmara Country to the west.

The area of Western Victoria is one of spectacular natural beauty and rich agricultural heritage, clouded by few areas of society and commerce. The wine-growing areas of today are known for this beauty and isolation, but also for the ability to create truly fine wine. While it might not currently be the wine region that is most targeted for investment and enthusiasm, the torchbearers of Western Victoria's wine industry understand the precious natural resource they are handling.

Evolution of Wine

The Henty brothers arrived in Portland Bay in 1834, establishing Victoria's first permanent European colony in the modern-day wine region that takes their name. According to their manifest, they also brought with them Victoria's first grapevines. As a gold rush took hold throughout the hills of Western Victoria, the area became well populated in the mid-19th century, and vine cultivation followed soon after.

Though both the Pyrenees and Henty had early plantings, it was the region between them – what would become known as the Grampians GI – that was able to stake early viticultural strongholds with lasting effects. In 1866, Henry Best purchased 12 hectares of land, from a property known as Concongella in Great Western, and started planting vines two years later. His winery, with its first vintage in 1872, was called Best's Great Western, and from that year on, it would produce wine continuously for the next 150 years (and counting).

Twenty years later, a man named Hans Irvine entered the wine industry, leaving his own indelible mark. Hans became wealthy early in life through investing in land and mining, and in 1888 purchased Joseph Best's Great Western vineyard (Henry Best's brother and neighbour). Hans came to work with a man named Charles Pierlot, a French national who had previously worked with the Champagne house Pommery. In 1890, the two laid down 2000 bottles of sparkling wine to age and planted 21 hectares of vines for sparkling production. This 'Australian Champagne' was the first domestic sparkling wine widely consumed domestically, gaining much renown for the region.

By the early 1890s, Hans was purchasing about two-thirds of the fruit grown in the Grampians area each year, producing a substantial amount of brandy, but also 'Claret', 'Hock', 'Chablis', 'Burgundy' and 'Hermitage'. His wines were exported to London, where they won top awards at various international shows.

Western Victoria avoided **phylloxera**, and Grampians in particular had a strong and diverse enough industry (brandy, sparkling wine, **fortified wines**) to survive the economic depression that hit at the turn of the century. The region wasn't thriving, per se, but there was enough commerce to keep vines in health and businesses afloat – most notably those of Hans Irvine and Henry Best.

Both of these early Grampians businesses sold within a few years of each other in the early 20th century. In 1918, in his 60s and without an heir, Hans Irvine sold his Great Western vineyard to Benno Seppelt (p. 315). And in 1920, after the

Dusty bottles of 1969 Malbec in the original 1866 cellar at Best's Great Western.

death of Henry Best, his son sold Best's Great Western to local vigneron Frederick P. Thomson. Both Seppelt Wines Great Western and Best's Great Western, under their respective new owners, continued to be trailblazers for the region. The duo is responsible for the continuous viticulture in the region for the first half of the 20th century, a time when most other Victorian wine regions (including neighbours Pyrenees and Henty) lay dormant.

In particular, Seppelt Wines Great Western winemaker Colin Preece, who joined the team in 1932, navigated the winery (and the region) out of a still-precarious time. In the early 1950s he released four wines that many attribute, alongside Maurice O'Shea's Hunter Valley wines at Mount Pleasant (p. 48), as the harbingers of the modern winemaking era. They were called 'Moyston Claret', 'Chalambar Burgundy', 'Arawatta Riesling' and 'Rhymney Chablis'. Intentional or not, they seemed to harken back to the great wines of Hans Irvine.

The duo – Best's Great Western and Seppelt Wines Great Western – weren't great bedfellows though, and by the mid-1920s found themselves in court over the name 'Great Western'. 'Seppelt back then wanted to have sole use of the name Great Western,' relates Ben Thomson, fifth-generation proprietor of Best's Great Western, 'and we went to court to be able to use the name Great Western … because we're very parochial. We like to say, it's fruit from Great Western or Grampians – it's got to have that on there.' In the end, Best's won, and the precedent was set that Great Western was a region, not a brand.

By the 1960s, when Australia's interest in **table wines** was piqued again, all three areas of Western Victoria began to flourish. The next producer of import to launch in the Grampians was Mount Langi Ghiran. The Fratin brothers, Italian immigrants, replanted a site in 1969 in the township of Bayindeen that had been under vine in the late 19th century. In 1980, the Fratins hired a consultant who went on to purchase the winery, a man named Trevor Mast. Trevor, along with Viv Thomson at Best's Great Western and Ian McKenzie at Seppelt Great Western, led the charge in establishing Grampians' identity for the next generation. That identity largely centred around shiraz – the grape that had been identified as the Grampians' modern calling card – but in a more chiselled savoury style than was seen from the Barossa Valley.

Meanwhile, further northeast, the first modern plantings in the Pyrenees were from Brandy house Rémy Martin in 1963. Rémy Martin's investment in brandy grapes was a few years too late, as the taste for **fortified wines** and spirits was giving way to a re-found appreciation for **table wine**.

The Drives of Seppelt Great Western — an underground wine cellar dug out of granite bedrock by local gold miners commissioned by Joseph Best in 1868. The space has grown to over 3 kilometres of tunnels, making it the largest underground cellar in Australia, with the capacity to store 3 million bottles of wine.

Château Rémy didn't survive, but it became Blue Pyrenees, one of the most important commercial wineries of the region today. Other early Pyrenees wineries include Dalwhinnie Vineyard, Mount Avoca Vineyard, Mountain Creek, Summerfield Vineyards, Redbank Winery (now known as Sally's Paddock), Taltarni Vineyards and Warrenmang Vineyard. Of this early bunch, Dalwhinnie is the most qualitatively significant today, making excellent shiraz, cabernet sauvignon and chardonnay, often released with bottle age, out of their Moonambel township estate. Blue Pyrenees and Taltarni are the most commercially significant producers of the Pyrenees, of any era, accounting for about a third of the region's hectares under vine between the two.

The Pyrenees enjoyed some further excitement at the hands of a superstar from the Rhône Valley – Michel Chapoutier – who created a brand based in the Pyrenees with his American importer called Terlato & Chapoutier, planting Malakoff Estate in 2004, and then going on to create another brand called Domaine Tournon. Today, Chapoutier's future in the Pyrenees is unsure; the company has formally announced a willingness to sell both the Pyrenees vineyards and the brand Tournon, with focus turning to their operations in Heathcote if an appropriate offer were to be made.

Confusingly, there are two Malakoff vineyards in the Pyrenees. The non-Chapoutier one is owned by father-and-son team Robert and Cameron John, who sell fruit to notables, such as Brown Brothers, Fletcher, Ben Haines, Owen Latta, Lethbridge and Shadowfax. The headlining grapes in the Johns' Malakoff are nebbiolo and shiraz; the vineyard has become a premier Victorian source for the two.

Meanwhile, further south, Henty saw its first modern plantings at the hands of the Seppelt family, who took a risk planting 200 kilometres south of their Great Western vineyards, in a region so cold, windy and rainy that no one else had yet ventured to undertake viticulture there. The 100-hectare parcel, planted in 1964 in the locality of Drumborg, took the region's name and became known as the Seppelt Drumborg vineyard. With the focus on sparkling wine at Seppelt Great Western, chardonnay and pinot

By the 1960s, when Australia's interest in table wines was piqued again, all three areas of Western Victoria began to flourish.

noir were natural grapes to plant at their new cool-climate site. Riesling, though, became the hero variety of the vineyard, and created a precedent for Henty to be known for the grape.

Catherine and John Thomson (unrelated to the Thomsons of Best's Great Western) were responsible for the next Henty plantings in 1975. After researching the great wine regions of the world, the couple settled on cool-climate Henty to set down vines (largely riesling and cabernet sauvignon) and create their winery: Crawford River. Their success paved the way for other small, boutique wineries to get started in Henty, most notably Jennifer and John Nagorcka's Hochkirch in the early 1990s.

The modern landscape of Henty isn't all that different from 30 years ago. There are 145 hectares under vine in Henty. That statistic makes it one of the smallest wine regions in Australia, but when you take out Seppelt Drumborg's nearly 100 hectares, it is, as Crawford River states on their website, just 'a blot on the canvas'. Despite the credibility that the name garners in wine circles, Henty is a largely unexplored wine terrain.

Further north, the 1990s brought another Great Western dispute between its two major players. In 1992, the Grampians GI was formed and use of the name 'Great Western' came to bear again. 'We went through the same thing again,' Ben Thomson relates. '[Seppelt] wanted to have the sole use of the name Great Western. And we argued against that, because we felt that at that stage, to have Great Western on the label, the wine should have to be Great Western fruit.

197

They wanted to use the name Great Western as a brand, but it could have fruit from anywhere.' Best's triumphed again, and the Great Western subregion of the Grampians was formed, to legally protect its usage.

Treasury Wine Estates (who now own Seppelt Wines) still maintains the Seppelt cellar door and vineyards in Great Western, though all grapes are shipped off to South Australia to be processed. No wines are branded 'Seppelt Great Western' anymore, though a few do carry the Great Western GI, most notably the Show Sparkling Shiraz. Seppelt refers to this as its 'rarest and most iconic wine', a style first made by Hans Irvine in 1894. This wine is only made in select vintages and usually aged for around 10 years before release; 1994, 2004 and 2008 have been the only releases of the last 25 years.

Today, while many wine regions across Victoria are being hailed for their modern renaissance, Western Victoria has not seen much of an experimental next generation. There are a few: Rory Lane's The Story has offered a more modern take on wines of the Grampians (as well as a handful of other wine regions across Victoria). Adam Louder and Nancy Panter's SubRosa traffics in elegant takes on shiraz, nebbiolo and viognier from the Grampians and Pyrenees. Black & Ginger is a newcomer in Grampians, with a focus on the proven shiraz, as well as wines like skin-contact white blends and **nouveau**-style reds. And Pyren Vineyard in the Pyrenees, planted in 1999 and run today by second-generation Leighton Joy, has found a balance of traditional styles and ones that are more avant-garde.

But Western Victoria largely remains a region defined by its most long-standing producers making more traditional styles: Best's Great Western, Seppelt and Mount Langi Ghiran in the Grampians; Crawford River, Seppelt Drumborg and Hochkirch in Henty; and Dalwhinnie and Pyren in the Pyrenees (the latter, as mentioned, straddling the innovative and traditional camps with gumption). Though the regions are not hubs of experimentation, there is not a sense that anything is lacking either. The quality among these producers has been consistent and high for decades; the only real question is: why haven't more producers flocked to these regions?

Lay of the Land

Terroir-wise, what the three GIs of Western Victoria have in common is the Great Dividing Range. Victoria's most significant mountain range, by the time it reaches its western stretches, provides a unique landscape for each of the three appellations. In the Pyrenees, weathered mountains form several non-contiguous valleys where the vineyards reside. For Grampians, the last formations of the Great Dividing Range sit west of the growing regions, placing them on gentle hillsides. And for Henty, the ranges peter out almost completely, creating mainly flatlands and gentle undulations, though with a few escarpments that impact weather patterns.

Henty, of the three appellations, is the furthest south and coolest, with intense influence from the Indian Ocean. Henty is at times quite rainy, cloudy and cold, with air from the sea drawing inland. The region is enormous, with only 145 hectares in total plantings on over 14,700 square kilometres of delineated area: about 0.010% of the region is planted. Beyond its few plantings, Henty is also known for its minute population and geographic isolation (a four-hour drive from Melbourne and 5½-hour drive from Adelaide).

Proximity to the ocean is a defining factor for the regions of Henty, which imparts 'serious **microclimate** changes', according to Crawford River's Belinda Thomson. 'Even macroclimate, frankly', she adds.

Closest to the coast is the most maritime climate, separated from the rest of Henty by the

Western Victoria Viticultural Footprint

	PYRENEES	GRAMPIANS	HENTY
Total delimited area (km²)	2720	9450	14,760
Total planted area (hectares)	887	651	145
% of delimited area planted	0.320%	0.070%	0.010%
Total elevation range	171–788 masl	142–1161 masl	0–458 masl
Elevation range of plantings	280–495 masl	220–375 masl	30–220 masl
Number of producers	22	19	13

Mount Clay (alternatively called, Heywood) Escarpment, which runs south-east to north-west from the coast up to the Drumborg area.

The Seppelt Drumborg vineyard, at nearly 100 hectares under vine, occupies about two-thirds of the planted land of Henty. It sits about 30 kilometres from the coast, facing south, a target for all the intense weather off the Indian Ocean. Drumborg receives some of the highest rainfall in Henty, 'way more than anyone else in the region by a country mile', says Thomson. Probably due to insurance-minded corporates, Seppelt Drumborg does sport irrigation gear, despite its 750 millimetres of annual rainfall (though shouldn't have to use it in our lifetime). Soils on the Drumborg site range from rich, black loamy clay to redder, loamy clay, with some ironstone buckshot and gravels – planted to riesling, chardonnay, pinot noir and pinot meunier.

Pyrenees Climate Data (°C)

	1960–1990	1991–PRESENT	2020
Heat summation/GDD	● 1536	● 1590	● 1602
Annual rain/GSR	570/261	516/242	433/229
Warmest month avg. temp.	20.3	21	21.1

Grampians Climate Data (°C)

	1960–1990	1991–PRESENT	2020
Heat summation/GDD	● 1395	● 1440	● 1429
Annual rain/GSR	609/281	572/260	529/247
Warmest month avg. temp.	19.4	20	20.1

Henty Climate Data (°C)

	1960–1990	1991–PRESENT	2020
Heat summation/GDD	● 1295	● 1347	● 1323
Annual rain/GSR	702/305	679/288	658/264
Warmest month avg. temp.	18.4	18.9	18.9

Winkler Scale:

● 850–1111 ● 1112–1389 ● 1390–1667 ● 1668–1944 ● 1945–2222 ● 2223–2700

Crawford River is about 20 kilometres further inland/north from Drumborg, composed of a north-northwest facing amphitheatre. It sits on the other side of the Mount Clay Escarpment from Drumborg and sees much less rainfall. This area is neither coastal nor continental; Thomson calls it 'coastal influence'. At her family's site, they get a cooling coastal breeze every summer afternoon and mild night-time temperatures, thanks to the proximity to the water. The vineyard is planted on the slope of a hill that flows down to a river system, allowing for the coastal breezes to flow in and for good soil drainage. Soils here are red, volcanic buckshot, with a duplex of clay-loam over pure limestone at the base of the hill from an ancient, risen seabed.

The third climate striation occurs another 50-odd-kilometres inland, where the conditions reach a truly continental status near the town of Hamilton. It's on average about 5°C warmer here than where Crawford River is situated, with a more significant **diurnal swing** (much cooler nights). Notable **biodynamic** estate Hochkirch is based just west of Hamilton, with high-nutrient rich black loamy soil, intermixed with stony gravels and basalt buckshot.

Thomson summarises the unique **microclimates** of Henty like so: 'You've got coastal, you've got coastal-influence, and then you've got continental, all in the same region, which isn't particularly common.'

This northern stretch of Henty is the gateway to the Grampians GI and its subregion Great Western. Looking at a map, Great Western is a tiny blip in the overall area of Grampians – 155 square kilometres out of Grampians' nearly 9500. But the plantings ratio is nearly inverted, with 473 of Grampians' total 651 hectares found in Great Western. If you think about Grampians as a doughnut (with Great Western as the hole), almost all the plantings are in that hole, with most of the remaining vineyards in the stretch just east of it. The peaks of the Grampians themselves (and the Grampians National Park) are to the west, on the other side of Great Western, and largely unplanted.

The winds coming from the west – more specifically, the southwest, around the Grampians National Park – play an important role in the

Western Victoria

HOW TO READ THIS MAP

The Great Dividing Range fades away across the Pyrenees, Grampians and Henty regions, giving way to desert land in the north and the cooler coastline to the south. These sparsely planted regions host a broad change in precipitation and temperatures (warmer to the north, cooler to the south). This map shows the change in precipitation moving inland and how isolated mountains influence that change across the vineyard areas.

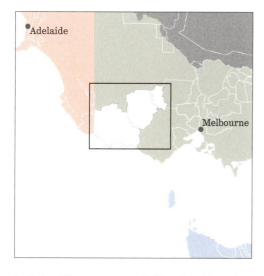

1 Amherst Winery
2 A.T.R.
3 Basalt Vineyard
4 Best's Great Western
5 Best's Salvation Hills Vineyard
6 Bigibila
7 Black & Ginger
8 Blue Pyrenees
9 Bochara
10 Clayfield
11 Crawford River Wines
12 Dalwhinnie
13 Dalwhinnie Forest Hut Vineyard
14 DogRock
15 Eastern Peake/Latta
16 Equus
17 Fallen Giants
18 Forest Gate Estate
19 Glenlofty Wines
20 Grampians Estate
21 Grape Farm Wines
22 Gwynnyth Vineyard
23 Henty Estate
24 Herrmann
25 Hochkirch Wines
26 John Family's Malakoff
27 Kara Kara Vineyard
28 Kimbarra
29 Lamplough Estate
30 M.Chapoutier Malakoff Vineyard
31 Miners Ridge Vineyard
32 Montara
33 Mount Avoca
34 Mount Langi Ghiran
35 Mount Langi Ghiran Warrak Rd Vineyard
36 Mt Napier Vineyard
37 Mountainside
38 Moyston Hills Organic Vineyard
39 Nappa Merri
40 Peerick Vineyard
41 Pomonal Estate
42 Pyren Vineyard
43 Quartz Hill Vineyard
44 Quoin Hill Vineyard
45 Rowans Lane Wines
46 Sally's Paddock & Redbank Winery
47 Seppelt Arrawatta Vineyards
48 Seppelt Drumborg Vineyard
49 Seppelt Great Western
50 Seppelt St Peters Vineyard
51 Stonefield Estate
52 Suffoir Winery
53 Summerfield
54 Taltarni
55 Warrenmang
56 Westgate Vineyard
57 Wimmera Hills

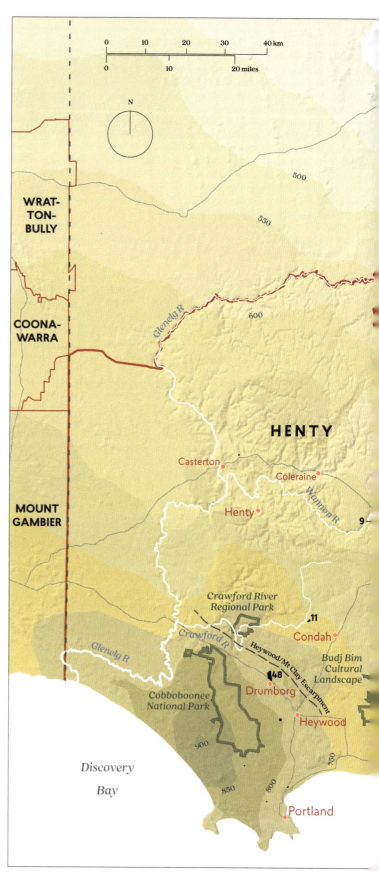

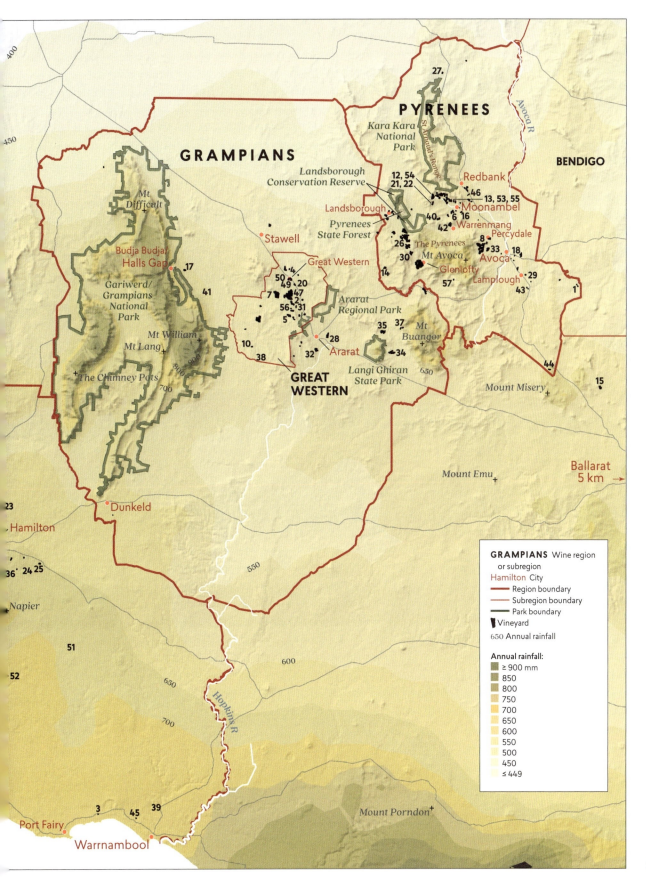

weather systems of the Grampians. The westerly winds are often quite cold ('bloody freezing', as Best's Ben Thomson puts it), whereas the occasional northeasterly wind brings with it a warmer front – and often, powerful rain. The more acute effects from the wind and rain are felt in eastern Grampians, rather than Great Western, as the Grampians National Park offers a shield against the intensity of these conditions.

Ten kilometres east of Great Western lies Ararat, with a handful of vineyards surrounding the town. Ararat, on average, sees its summer high temperatures at least 2°C cooler than Great Western, with about 15% more rainfall. The vineyards outside of Great Western are also slightly more frost prone and experience four times more high wind days (defined by winds over 25 knots). Great Western sees more clear, cloud-free days, equating to more sunshine hours.

In general, eastern Grampians sees colder, windier and rainier conditions than Great Western, though a few smaller peaks (like those found in Langi Ghiran State Park) offer protection from the elements. The vineyards of Mount Langi Ghiran sit within the valley east of the Langi Ghiran State Park, another 30 kilometres east of Ararat. This is the coldest climate of the entire Grampians GI, often one of the last in the nation to pick shiraz.

Soils in Great Western and the larger Grampians area are identified as three series: Concongella, Great Western and Stawell. All are essentially sandy loams that transition into heavier clays before reaching bedrock at about 1 metre deep. Topsoils are based on siliceous sands that have weathered down and are dispersed across the region from the Grampians. Some are sandstone dominant, others have fragments of shale and mudstone and all are free draining.

As one moves further east from the Grampians mountains, through Great Western and to the other plantings of the Grampians, the granite influence and granitic sand within the loamy topsoil starts to disappear. The intermixing of the weathered granitic sandy loam topsoil from the Grampians, and the Paleozoic sandstone, shale, mudstone basin below, creates unique soil profiles across the Grampians. Most vineyards in the Grampians are close enough to Great Western and the Grampians mountains to maintain this granitic profile, and not lose the interplay of both soil types.

No vineyards occupy the part of the Grampians between the northeastern border of Great Western and the Pyrenees. Large farms and agricultural businesses are based here, including

The westerly winds are often quite cold ('bloody freezing', as Best's Ben Thomson puts it).

Ben Thomson, proprietor of Best's Great Western, crushing a handful of the region's signature shiraz.

a wind farm – testament to how truly windy it can be in this area.

Continuing east and slightly north from the Grampians, the Pyrenees GI is situated among two adjacent weathered mountains: the Pyrenees and St Arnaud range. These are the second-to-last of the formations along the Great Dividing Range (the Grampians being the last). Broadly, the Pyrenees GI is drier and warmer than nearby Grampians GI, which is warmer and drier than Henty GI.

The Pyrenees is a Palaeozoic form of folded sandstone, shale and mudstone. Much of the once-deposited soil has been mined away, resulting in newly deposited soils from surrounding areas, of the same origin. Weathered clays and loams mix with sandstone, shale and mudstone, sitting below loamy topsoils. These rocks are present in much of the lower areas west of Melbourne, notably in Geelong's Moorabool Valley.

The vineyard areas of the Pyrenees can be looked at in three distinct areas, corresponding with non-contiguous valleys or pockets created by the mountain ranges. The Pyrenees Range State Forest, with mountain peaks topping out at 788 metres above sea level, curves from a northwest–southeast path to something more horizonal, drawing a crooked line from Glenlofty in the west to Avoca in the east. The south-southwest side of the range is home to a good portion of the region's plantings, centred around the town of Landsborough.

Though some climate data sources vary, the southwestern side of the Pyrenees is the coolest section, seeing a bit more rain and slightly lower mean January temperatures. This area has a variety of different **aspects** though the major elevation climb is to the northeast. Vineyards are off the immediate slopes, meaning vineyard **aspect** is not uniformly southeast facing – in fact, the two most famous vineyards of the region face northeast.

The Johns' Malakoff vineyard – certainly the most important and well known of the area – has a northeasterly **aspect** (which serves the increasingly notable plantings of nebbiolo, as well as their shiraz and viognier). The Chapoutier Malakoff site also faces northeast, situated about 5.5 kilometres south of the Johns' Malakoff, and is planted exclusively to shiraz. Vineyards here are planted on a mix of red clays mixed with quartz gravel and ironstone. The area is quite free draining too.

About 7 kilometres north of the Pyrenees foothills (the end of the park) rises the lower elevation St Arnaud Range and its surrounding Kara Kara Park. The St Arnaud Ranges are oriented north–south, and aside from a few sizeable vineyards on the eastern-facing slopes near Redbank, the area further north is generally considered too warm. Sally's Paddock is the northernmost winery of note in the Pyrenees, sitting at 260–290 metres in the cradle of the Kara Kara Park. Just south, though, between the Pyrenees and the St Arnaud Ranges, lie the valley

Vineyard plantings across the Western Victoria Zone are the standard Australian fruit salad driven by English francophilia.

towns of Moonambel and Warrenmang, home to the second sizeable portion of vineyards. There is a slightly warmer and drier climate here than south of the Pyrenees range, with rainfall sitting around 520 millimetres on the year and the mean January temperature about a degree warmer.

Vineyards occupy the benchland sitting above 300 metres in elevation, running up to about 400 metres on the Moonambel side and 360 metres on the Warrenmang side. There is a variety of **aspects**; the area is not just one slope falling from the mountains, but rather an undulating area with smaller rock outcrops and ridges among the hills. Producers in this valley include Camfield, Dalwhinnie, Gwynnyth, Peerick, Pyren, Summerfield and Taltarni.

The third area, though with fewer plantings than in the valleys north or south of the Pyrenees ridge, is centred further east around the townships of Percydale and Avoca. This area sees a touch more rainfall than Warrenmang and Moonambel, more similar to that of the southside at Landsborough (proving that there is something of a rain shadow effect operating, even with the low altitude of the Pyrenees). Peaks are low and flat, with vineyards lying between 260 and 290 metres above sea level. Blue Pyrenees and Mount Avoca are the two most prominent producers in this area.

Vineyard plantings across the Western Victoria Zone are the standard Australian fruit salad driven by English francophilia. The two northernmost regions – Pyrenees and Grampians – share a similar profile when it comes to plantings, with shiraz leading the way. Shiraz comprises 50% of the Pyrenees plantings and over two-thirds of the plantings across Grampians. Chardonnay is the most popular white-wine grape, followed by cabernet sauvignon, sauvignon blanc, merlot and other more Mediterranean grapes, found in good proportion.

Stylistically, shiraz traverses a spectrum as it moves from Heathcote to Bendigo to the Pyrenees to the Grampians – from Central Victoria down the slopes of Western Victoria, moving northeast to southwest (and mainly east to west). Heathcote shiraz is the biggest of the bunch, with many styles easily reaching 16% alcohol if left to their own devices these days. Moving west, the vineyards become incrementally cooler and wetter, and the styles reflect that. Pyrenees typically showcases a bit more brawn and fruit than the Grampians, but achieves structure and peppery notes as well. The Grampians is well known for its savoury, more delicately drawn styles.

Henty is the outlier of the three regions; of the 612 tonnes harvested in Henty for the 2021 vintage, only eight were shiraz (according to Wine Australia's voluntary reporting). Pinot noir accounted for 50% of the pick, with chardonnay, pinot gris, riesling and grüner veltliner being the most popular white grapes. Only 5 tonnes of cabernet sauvignon and 2 tonnes of sauvignon blanc were reported, though Crawford River has made a name for both these grapes in Henty. Their premier grape, though, and thus the recognised premier grape of the region, is riesling, typically made in dry, powerful and age-worthy styles.

The sprawling Blue Pyrenees estate in Avoca, whose production has become a house wine for many in the area.

The Mount Langi Ghiran estate, tucked behind the mountain it is named for.

Hubbub

The Pyrenees, the Grampians and Henty are all isolated, to some extent. Though the Pyrenees is only a two-hour drive from Melbourne (the closest of the three), it's proven to be enough distance to discourage would-be growers, wineries and consumers, alike. When you get to Henty, the situation is even more dire. Getting labour and equipment out to Henty, combined with the lifestyle deterrents associated with living so far removed from urban centres, has been crippling to growth. And these things are not poised to change: 'I'd like to see Henty grow, but I think it's unlikely in the near future because of our tyranny of distance,' says Belinda Thomson. 'The most pressing concern for our region,' she continues, 'is really a question around labour shortage.'

The comparative upper hand in proximity has allowed the Pyrenees and Grampians to not suffer this tyranny quite so dramatically. There are also many more plantings – 887 and 651 hectares, respectively, compared to Henty's 145 hectares – in the northern regions of Western Victoria. Henty is truly a region with only a handful of growers and producers (and thus a minuscule number with reach outside of the appellation). With the substantial increase in fruit coming out of Pyrenees and Grampians, there is more of an economic impact – though still very few producers of note. As Ben Thomson says of Great Western: 'We're one of the oldest wine regions in Australia, but we're probably one of the least known … We have to work really hard to be known – it's only half a dozen wineries in the region.'

To be exact, there are seven wineries based in Great Western, where a majority of the greater region's plantings are. Many of these wineries grow for themselves, but also sell fruit to producers outside the region. In the Grampians areas outside Great Western, Mount Langi's vineyards account for nearly half the remaining plantings, with a few other growers making up the balance.

The names 'Grampians' and 'Great Western' carry a good amount of weight – largely thanks to the efforts of Best's, Seppelt and Mount Langi Ghiran – enticing a handful of exciting producers (Sierra Reed, Ben Haines and Circe, among others) to proudly label their purchased shiraz with these appellation names.

Pyrenees experiences a similar phenomenon to an even greater extreme: 'A lot of the more interesting stuff,' Pyren's Leighton Joy notes, 'is coming from external winemakers purchasing fruit.' While the Grampians has its giants of commerce (and quality) in Best's Great Western and Mount Langi Ghiran, the producers based in the Pyrenees who most often show up on the great wine lists of Australia are Dalwhinnie, Pyren, and to a lesser extent, M.Chapoutier – end of list.

But the Pyrenees' reach extends beyond these two because of those purchasing fruit from the region. In particular, the 23-hectare Malakoff vineyard owned by Robert and Cameron John has been a great attraction to star winemakers from outside the region, who not only label 'Pyrenees' prominently, but 'Malakoff vineyard' as well.

There are some climatic concerns for each region: climate change-related yield concerns for Pyrenees, frost and water scarcity for Grampians, and blustering conditions for the coastal vineyards in Henty. But the true challenge for these regions, even though each has their unique set of circumstances, is attracting more people (proprietors and workers) who want to invest in growing premium grapes and making fine wine.

There are several Western Victorian wines that sit on the **Langton's Classification** (demonstrating each region's ability to make fine wine that commands high prices), but these regions are missing the investment, curiosity and community that's created by a critical mass of strong producers. It's incredible what has already been created by the small group who has invested; the potential seems infinite if others were to follow suit.

PRODUCERS

PYRENEES

DALWHINNIE

Architect Ewan Jones planted vineyards and founded Dalwhinnie in 1976, his oldest son David taking over management in 1983. Plantings of chardonnay, shiraz and cabernet sauvignon are **dry-farmed** and organically tended, leading to low-yields and remarkable depth of flavour. The vines form an amphitheatre in the ranges, sheltered by the highest peaks. This formation funnels cool air away from the grapes, leaving the vineyards free of frost and enabling cabernet sauvignon to reach full ripeness and develop the complexity for which Dalwhinnie has become known. Dalwhinnie was purchased by the Fogarty Wine Group in 1994, doubling down on the estate's quality and dedication to release wines with considerable bottle age. *dalwhinnie.wine*

M.CHAPOUTIER

Michel Chapoutier joined forces with international wine importer Terlato Wines in 2000 to make Australian shiraz under the label Domaine Terlato & Chapoutier. The estate established a shiraz vineyard named Malakoff, which is (confusingly) separate to the high-quality grower Malakoff vineyard, just down the road. In 2009, M.Chapoutier bought two neighbouring vineyards, Shay's Flat and Landsborough Valley, to set up the label Domaine Tournon. M.Chapoutier recently announced plans to sell off its Pyrenees vineyards and the Tournon label itself, in which case, production would focus on the company's Heathcote vineyards. *mchapoutier.com.au*

PYREN VINEYARD

Brothers Brian and Kevyn Joy founded Pyren in 1999, with plantings over the years of sauvignon blanc, shiraz, cabernet sauvignon, cabernet franc, malbec and petit verdot. Brian's son Leighton manages the winery, overseeing their organically farmed, unirrigated vineyard (with viticulturist Graeme Miles) and their four wine ranges. The Earthscape wines are varietal expressions, with each label illustrating a time of day. The Little Ra Ra wines are more experimental and modern blends, and the Pentagon and Reserve wines come from the best-performing spots on the vineyard. Pyren marries modern and traditional styles to great effect, showcasing the broad spectrum of what the Pyrenees is capable of. *pyrenvineyard.com*

SALLY'S PADDOCK

Sally's Paddock was started by Neill Robb in 1973, named Redbank at the time. Neill inherited his father's passion for the region, who had established the first modern winery in the Pyrenees, Château Rémy (now Blue Pyrenees). The Redbank brand was bought by the Hill-Smith family (of Yalumba, p. 317), but the winery and estate vineyards were retained by the Robb family, who continue to produce wine under the Sally's Paddock name. Third-generation Sasha Fair (née Robb) has now joined the team to carry on her family's lineage. *sallyspaddock.com.au*

 What we're drinking

One of the most exciting things about **Dalwhinnie** *is their commitment to release their wines with age: both their cabernet sauvignon and shiraz, readily available with 5–8 years of age, express heady secondaries in addition to powerful fruit.* – Jane Lopes

Ben & Viv Thomson
Best's Great Western

GRAMPIANS

BEST'S GREAT WESTERN

Best's is home to some of the rarest pre-**phylloxera** plantings in the world. Pinot meunier was first planted in their vineyards in 1868, making theirs the world's oldest vines of the grape. The Nursery Block inside the original Concongella vineyard is home to almost 40 varieties, some of which still haven't been identified. The Thomson family has been custodians of these astounding historical vineyards since 1925. Fourth-generation Viv Thomson completed a mighty 60 consecutive vintages at Best's. Viv's son Ben took over running Best's in 2008, with Justin Purser making the wine from 2011-2022, and ex-Montara winemaker Simon Fennell currently at the helm. Alongside the old-vine pinot meunier, the winery releases two shiraz in the Icon Range, limited to only the best vintages. Bin No. 0 Shiraz dates back to the late 1800s, with fruit selected from low-yielding vines on the original Concongella vineyard. And the Thomson Family Shiraz was created to celebrate the centenary of the family settling in Great Western and is produced from just 15 rows of 1868 vines.
bestswines.com

MOUNT LANGI GHIRAN

Founders of Mount Langi Ghiran, the Fratin brothers, hired Trevor Mast as a winemaking consultant in 1981. He ended up buying the estate six years later. Trevor had become fond of the peppery shiraz of the area when working as assistant winemaker at Seppelt, long before it was ever fashionable to utter the words 'cool climate'. Trevor worked tirelessly in the vineyard and forged boldly forward with the new wave, cool-climate Australian style. The reputation of Grampians shiraz today is in no small part thanks to Trevor. The Rathbone Wine Group purchased the estate in 2002, with no signs of quality letting up.
langi.com.au

SEPPELT WINES GREAT WESTERN

The beginnings of Seppelt were not actually in Great Western, but instead in the Barossa (see Seppeltsfield, p. 315). But in 1918, Benno Seppelt bought the Great Western winery for his family's holdings and proceeded to enact a litany of achievements: in 1890, Seppelt became the first Australian winery to produce **traditional method** sparkling wines; Colin Preece took over as chief winemaker in 1932 and stayed on for three decades; Karl Seppelt planted the nearly 100-hectare Drumborg vineyard in 1964, which today consists of riesling, chardonnay, pinot noir and pinot meunier; and Seppelt Great Western made one of the earliest sparkling shiraz in the country, a style that has become quintessentially Australian. Today Seppelt is owned by Treasury Wine Estates. Winemaking no longer takes place at the Great Western estate, though the vineyards are thriving, and the cellar door is still active.
seppelt.com.au

Western Victoria

Belinda Thomson, Crawford River

THE STORY WINES

Rory Lane's degree specialising in ancient Greek tragedy probably doesn't come up much in the winery, but certainly makes for an interesting guy. In a shiraz dominant region, Rory is homing in hard on Grampians grenache as a varietal wine and as a source for his **GSM** blend. He also plays with a range of fruit from regions as diverse as Nagambie, the Whitlands Plateau and Henty. The uber-fancy stuff gets labelled as R.Lane Vintners, and his native botanical gin is bottled both with oak aging and without. *thestory.com.au*

HENTY

CRAWFORD RIVER WINES

In far southwest Victoria, Crawford River took root in 1975. John and Catherine Thomson's meticulous research helped them arrive at the most well-suited grapes for the region. By 1977, the vineyard consisted of riesling, semillon, sauvignon blanc, cabernet sauvignon and cabernet franc, and by 2000, with a few additions, they reached their current footprint of 11.5 hectares. Belinda, John and Catherine's oldest daughter, studied arts and teaching and worked as a journalist in Sydney before deciding to go to wine science school in New Zealand. She spent several years jumping between Crawford River and wine jobs in Germany, Italy, New Zealand and Spain, before returning home to take over full-time from her father in 2012. The wines are consistently fabulous; the Young Vines Riesling is one of Australia's best value wines and the Reserve Riesling is one of the country's most profound expressions of the grape. The vineyard is managed only with organic materials, and with a focus on increasing the natural biodiversity of the farm – something their flock of sheep helps with! Belinda continues to push the estate forward in all aspects of environmentalism, land care and experimentation.
crawfordriverwines.com

HOCHKIRCH WINES

Just to the southwest of the Grampians, Hochkirch sits on nearly 300 hectares of certified **biodynamic** farmland. The first vines were planted in 1990 by founders John and Jennifer Nagorcka, and trials soon indicated that **high-density plantings** of riesling, chardonnay and pinot noir would perform best in the climate, so long as the vines were trained low to the ground for greater warmth. Semillon, sauvignon blanc and syrah have been added to the now 8 hectares of vineyard, all Demeter-certified **biodynamic**. The wines, with a focus on pinot noir, are some of Victoria's best.
hochkirchwines.com.au

KF **What we're drinking**

*I'm not usually one to judge a book by its cover, or a wine by its label, but bloody hell these bottles from **The Story Wines** are beautifully packaged. They make me want to try every single one. Good thing is, the juice inside is equally impressive. I like the lot, but in particular the Super G **GSM** blend. Super yum! – Kavita Faiella*

What we're drinking

*The purity and brightness of **Hochkirch's** pinot noir reverberates in the glass the moment it's poured. Wine is often described as a living thing, and these wines are brimming with life. – Jonathan Ross*

And don't forget …

Amherst Winery, run by second-generation Luke Jones, has shiraz plantings dating back to 1989, as well as the Pyrenees stalwarts of cabernet sauvignon and chardonnay coming on line soon after … **Black & Ginger**, launched in 2015 by high school mates Hadyn Black and Darcy 'Ginger' Naughton, the duo make small batches of wine from their estate vineyard in Great Western, as well as purchased fruit from other sites in Grampians, Henty and Pyrenees … **Bochara** releases sauvignon blanc, pinot noir and gewürztraminer from Martin Slocombe and Kylie McIntyre's estate vineyard in Henty, planted in 1998 … **DogRock**, a Pyrenees staple dating back to 1998, has the first Australian plantings of the Portuguese variety Azal …
Mount Avoca, the Pyrenees' only certified organic vineyard, is managed by second-generation Matthew Barry … **SubRosa** is an impressive new venture from Mount Langi alum Adam Louder and his wife Nancy Panter, with a focus on shiraz and nebbiolo from Grampians and Pyrenees … **Summerfield**, which began from a small plot in the 1970s planted by Ian Summerfield, is now a full-fledged winery, with boutique accommodation and a wood-fired pizza restaurant on site …
Warrenmang was an early staple of the Pyrenees, with first vines planted by Wally Henning in the 1970s, and a successful restaurant and resort owned by Luigi and Athalie Bazzani up until its sale in 2017.

 New Guard   Environmental Hero   Rising Star   Legend   Regional Stalwart   Must Visit   Cult Following Historic Estate

Beechworth

Introduction

When Major Thomas Mitchell returned to Sydney from an expedition traversing Victoria in 1836, word spread about the spectacular pasture and open woodlands that his party had observed soon after crossing the Murray River. By 1838, pastoralists had spread across the Stanley and Beechworth plateaus, invading the traditional lands of the Waywurru (potentially a Kulin exonym for the Pallanganmiddang). In 1852, gold was discovered in Spring Creek, and within months the diggings became a busy settlement: Beechworth was born. The Victorian gold rushes created such wealth that local merchants soon stocked wines from all over Europe. In Beechworth, celebratory gold diggers played skittles – a type of bowling – with bottles of Champagne instead of pins.

Beechworth's viticultural bounty garners a similarly enthusiastic reaction today: it is a small and premium wine region, its bottles gracing the shelves of the best wine stores and restaurant lists around Australia. Beechworth is one of five GIs in the North East Victoria Zone, alongside Rutherglen, Glenrowan, Alpine Valleys and King Valley. With vineyards breaching heights of 800 metres above sea level, it stands out as an anomaly against its neighbours in largely fertile, lower-lying valleys.

Beechworth's minute existence between larger GIs somewhat echoes the Waywurru as a small, isolated pocket 'surrounded by the vastly larger language areas of Yorta Yorta to the west, Wiradjuri to the north, Snowy Mountains Language (including the nearly extinct Ngarigu) to the north and east, and Taungurung (and more generally Kulin languages) to the south', according to local historian Jacqui Durrant. She goes on to ask: 'Were they gradually being crushed by outside influences?'

And indeed, the people and reach of the Waywurru are almost non-existent today. But that doesn't mean that the vignerons of the region don't think about their influence and grapple with what it means to live on land they once cared for. 'You know, I'm still sitting with the dichotomy of colonialism and how do we own land when it was never ceded and things like that,' says Tessa Brown, of Vignerons Schmölzer and Brown. 'And that's not a great feeling. But if you just keep the dichotomy close to hand in the cupboard and you can pull it out and refresh yourself with it every now and then, hopefully you don't get too big for your boots.'

The name Beechworth, today, carries a weight of prestige and quality to those in the know, but its diminutive size ensures that this knowledgeable group remains somewhat small. The exposure and education around Beechworth wines has historically been focused on a tiny group of pioneering producers, but this seems poised to change. With the outstanding quality achieved by the pioneers and up-and-comers alike, Beechworth is coming into its own as one of Australia's foremost wine regions.

Evolution of Wine

Beechworth's first vines are thought to have been planted by 1856 off Havelock Road, one of the main thoroughfares leading east out of the town of Beechworth. The vine material was most likely sourced from the Adelaide Botanic gardens, and thus from the original James Busby cuttings. The Beechworthians (as they may or may not be known) made haste getting the vines productive: the Melbourne Intercolonial Exhibition of 1866–1867 awarded an honourable mention to both an 1863 'Hermitage' and 1864 Chasselas from Beechworth.

This growth was a direct result of Beechworth's gold rush. Gold was first discovered by Europeans at Spring Creek in 1852, just northwest of today's city centre. As the community ballooned, so did the interest in vine cultivation and urban development. In this time, Beechworth also had a brush with infamous outlaw Ned Kelly, who was imprisoned and tried in the township in the 1870s. To this day, Beechworth is recognised as Victoria's best-preserved gold-mining town, with 32 of its buildings listed by the National Trust.

Through the early 1890s, Beechworth amassed around 30 growers, and 70 hectares of grapevines, but by 1916 only 2 hectares remained. Though there are no detailed accounts of why this decline occurred, it is most likely a cocktail similar to what many cool-climate Victorian wine regions in the late 19th and early 20th centuries were dealing with: economic depression and changing tastes toward **fortified wine**.

Though a vineyard was planted in Everton Hills (the western side of Beechworth) in the 1940s, it wasn't until the late 1970s that a proper revival of the region was staged. Di and Pete Smith are credited with this feat, planting chardonnay and cabernet sauvignon on a 2-hectare plot just west of the township of Beechworth. Smith's Vineyard is prized to this day, sourced by such notable producers as A. Rodda and Fighting Gully Road.

The Everton Hills plantings were significant in *who* they introduced to the region. Brown Brothers, a historic producer based in Milawa, just west of the modern-day GI of Beechworth in King Valley, came to own this site in the 1950s. Though the site saw its last vintage for Brown Brothers in 1978, its custodianship in their portfolio was enough to introduce several key Brown Brothers vignerons to the region: Rick Kinzbrunner, Barry Morey and later Mark Walpole. All did time with the company, and got their first taste of Beechworth through these plantings.

Rick Kinzbrunner founded Giaconda in 1981, on the north side of Wangaratta Road, near Everton Hills. What started as a humble plot of chardonnay and cabernet sauvignon would eventually become one of the most acclaimed Australian wineries, putting the name Beechworth on the fine wine map. Giaconda Chardonnay was lauded with an 'Exceptional'

Harvest at the Fighting Gully Road estate vineyard at 550 metres above sea level, overlooking the cloud-covered Ovens River Valley below.

The Giaconda Amphitheatre Block, planted to shiraz, faces north to catch the sun's warm rays. Off to the left, and under netting, is the south-facing Chardonnay block, which avoids direct sunlight.

status in the 2005 edition of **Langton's Classification**, one of the few white wines (and the only wine from Beechworth) to ever receive such an accolade.

Other early wineries include Elizabeth and Stephen Morris's Pennyweight, planted in 1982 just south of the Beechworth township, and Barry and Jan Morey's Sorrenberg (from another Brown Brothers veteran), planted in 1985 just east of the town's borders. These three wineries, still leaders in the region, built the foundation for many more to thrive.

The 1990s brought a new wave of important viticulturists and winemakers: Mark Walpole planted Fighting Gully Road while still with Brown Brothers, Keppell Smith started Savaterre on the south side of Wangaratta Road, and Julian Castagna founded his eponymous winery Castagna. All three helped build the prestige that the 1980s wineries had started.

Among these early pioneers, there was a huge focus on environmental practices, before the larger industry really knew what that meant. Castagna launched as a **biodynamic** winery in 1997, with Pennyweight and Sorrenberg following soon after, both starting to work with **biodynamics** in the early 2000s – a position that saw them labelled at the time as 'mad hippies', as Castagna puts it. Rick Kinzbrunner's Giaconda very quickly eschewed any chemical inputs, converting to organics and focusing on regenerative agriculture by the early 1990s.

The 2000s brought a younger generation eager to continue Beechworth's legacy of excellence, and the old guard has been largely welcoming. An interesting function of Beechworth being such a young region is that the founding wineries are still first generation (with the second just beginning to come in and assist). No one inherited an established vineyard, winery or region: they've all felt the crunch building it themselves and are eager to welcome newbies who are invested in the region. As Jeremy Schmölzer, who planted in Beechworth with his wife Tessa Brown in 2014, puts it: 'They were the pioneers themselves. And you get a sense [from them], "How great, other people are taking this on".'

Lay of the Land

The focus of Beechworth is often minimised to three grapes: chardonnay, shiraz and pinot noir. These three are monumental grapes and Beechworth grows them monumentally well (though many believe that the climate is increasingly too warm for pinot noir). However, it would be a mistake to ignore all the other interesting plantings and winemaking in Beechworth. From Giaconda's amphora roussanne to Pennyweight's palomino-based **fortified wines**, Sorrenberg's famous gamay to Schmölzer & Brown's off-dry rieslings, Fighting Gully Road's sangiovese (with Brunello **clones**) and tempranillo to Castagna's viognier, myriad grapes and styles are made with near-universal success in Beechworth.

Beechworth Viticultural Footprint

Total delimited area (km²)	400
Total planted area (hectares)	134
% of delimited area planted	0.330%
Total elevation range	204–1045 masl
Elevation range of plantings	240–830 masl
Number of producers	33

Beechworth Climate Data (°C)

	1960–1990	1991–PRESENT	2020
Heat summation/GDD	● 1468	● 1624	● 1699
Annual rain/GSR	1002/445	879/429	784/474
Warmest month avg. temp.	20.4	21.9	22.4

Winkler Scale:

● 850–1111 ● 1112–1389 ● 1390–1667 ● 1668–1944 ● 1945–2222 ● 2223–2700

It seems bizarre that the same tiny region (about the same area under vine as the Rhône Valley's famed Hermitage) can grow a cool-climate variety like riesling as well as it can a warmer-climate grape like viognier. But Beechworth has a large climate range due to its variety of elevations, with plantings around Everton Hills starting at 250 metres, moving up to as high as 830 metres near Stanley.

Beechworth's lofty plateau sits uniquely among a series of low-lying river valleys within the Victorian Alps. The Ovens, Buckland, King, Buffalo and Kiewa rivers all cascade away from alpine peaks that rise to around 1900 metres above sea level. These gently sloping valleys are verdant and fertile, and get warmer as they approach the Murray River downstream; quite the contrast to the pedestal of Beechworth that sits above them.

The powers-that-be did not originally place import on these differences. Walpole and Castagna both note how close Beechworth came to being swallowed up by the overarching Alpine Valleys GI, even though Beechworth is the literal opposite of a valley. Circa 1999, Beechworth's own wine industry wasn't large enough to meet Wine Australia's minimum standards for a GI (five producers farming at least five hectares each, with a total area harvest of at least 500 tonnes), so it was set to be lumped into the nearby Alpine Valleys GI. They 'fought like hell', as Castagna notes, to ensure Beechworth's singularity was codified into law. And it was, in 2000.

Walpole, the author of the GI, likens the area to that of Montalcino, Italy, home to the famed Brunello di Montalcino wines. Just as the vineyards of Montalcino drape around a small mountain, so do the vineyards of Beechworth drape around Mt Stanley. Montalcino, however, is limited by the need for agreeable sites for sangiovese (the only grape permitted in the region); the edges of elevation are better explored in Beechworth. Mean daily temperatures will decline as elevation moves higher, thus most cool-climate grapes are planted at higher elevations, while Rhône, Italian, and other warmer-climate varieties are seen at mid to lower elevations.

The vineyards near the town of Stanley (situated at 700–830 metres in elevation) have a **heat summation** of 1240°C degree days, comparable to Oregon's Willamette Valley. The township of Beechworth (550 metres) has 1420°C degree days, akin to Rias Baixas in Galicia, Spain. Wooragee, on the eastern edge of the region (300 metres), sees 1687°C degree days, which puts it within a few degrees of Friuli, Italy. And the Golden Ball area (280 metres) experiences about 1725°C degree days, much like Italy's Umbria. With these numbers, it's easy to see why everything from pinot noir to aglianico can find a home in the region.

Temperature is not the only factor to fluctuate with elevation; rainfall also becomes more prevalent at higher altitudes, with plantings near Stanley seeing as much as 1200 millimetres per year, while lower elevation outcroppings can see less than 500 millimetres. Irrigation in some cases is necessary, as in most regions in Australia, but it is not universally practised. The site at Pennyweight, planted in 1982 and situated southwest of the township of Beechworth, was chosen specifically because the Morris family wanted to farm without irrigation. When irrigation is practised by the vintners of Beechworth, it's made possible through catchment wells dug into the friable soils, and the region's unique positioning at the convergence of the alpine watershed.

There are two main types of soil bases seen throughout the region: Ordovician greywacke, sandstone, mudstone and shales (of marine origin, 460–440 million years ago) and younger Devonian granites and granodiorite (of igneous origin, 380–360 million years ago).

Though these two major geological formations are not dictated by elevation, Beechworth's elevation rose from this geology! Stay with us: the distinct elevation of the Beechworth region is a direct result of three volcanic intrusions resulting in harder granite cradling the more friable mudstones and shales; the latter would have eroded much more dramatically were it not for the igneous rocks keeping them in place. This phenomenon has resulted in the distinct soil types and steep rise in elevation that make Beechworth so unique.

Numerous quartz reefs appear on the mudstones between Beechworth and Stanley. Moving out toward Everton Hills, west of the

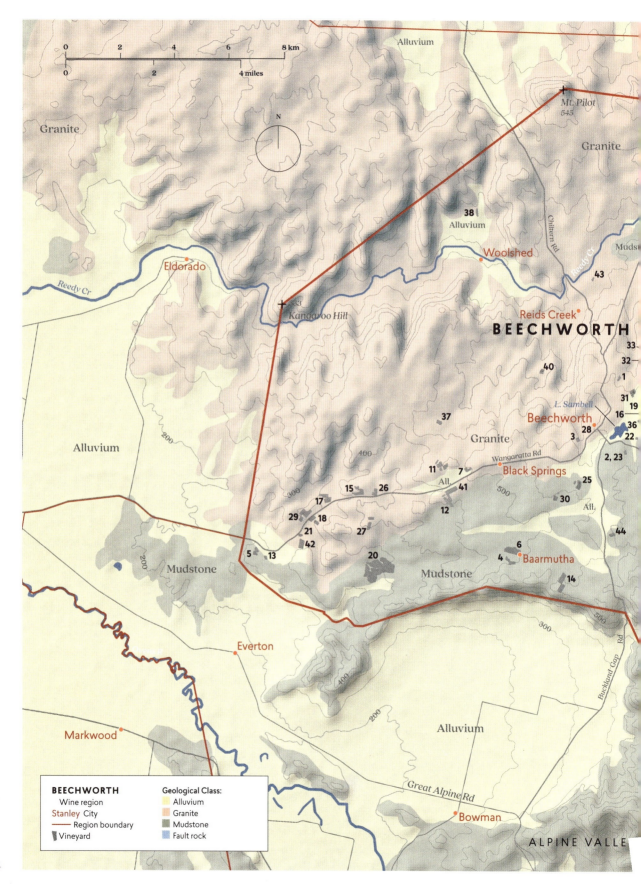

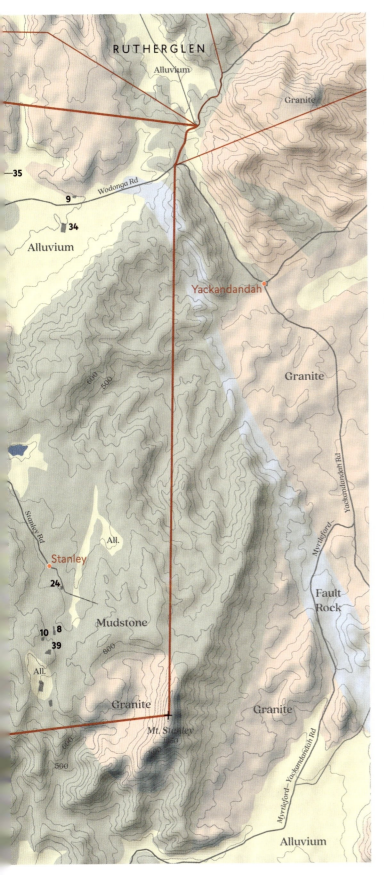

Beechworth

HOW TO READ THIS MAP

The intersection of elevation, **aspect** and geology contribute to great diversity across the vineyards of Beechworth. This map shows the region's dramatic change in elevation set against its major geological formations.

1. 700 Vines
2. A. Rodda Wines
3. Arcadia
4. Baarmutha
5. Battely
6. Beechworth Wine Estates
7. Black Springs Vineyard
8. Blackwood Vineyard
9. Bowmans Run
10. Brunnen Vineyard
11. Castagna
12. Domenica Wines
13. Everton Hills Estate
14. Fighting Gully Road
15. Giaconda
16. Giaconda Red Hill
17. Glenbosch Wine Estate
18. Golden Ball
19. Haldon Estate
20. Indigo Vineyard
21. Indigo Vineyard 2
22. Madman's Gully
23. The Ninth Mile Mayday Hills Vineyard
24. The Ninth Mile Stanley Vineyard
25. Pennyweight
26. Piano Piano
27. Savaterre
28. Sentio
29. Serengale
30. Smith's Vineyard
31. Sorrenberg
32. Sorrenberg Bindarra Vineyard
33. Sorrenberg Rhino Vineyard
34. Star Lane
35. Star Lane 2
36. Traviarti
37. Two Dogs Vineyard
38. Van Malsem
39. Vignerons Schmölzer & Brown
40. Vinelea
41. Warner Vineyard
42. Weathercraft
43. Weeping Grass Creek
44. Willem Kurt

Beechworth township, granite becomes more common, with three types unique to the region: Golden Ball adamelite, Everton Porphyritic granodiorite and Golden Ball silicified quartz (say those three times fast!). Some red-coloured Permian (300–250 million years ago) glacial deposits peppered with ground white quartz appear in a small area northeast of the city of Beechworth, out toward Wooragee. They've yet to be extensively planted but have sparked some curiosity among the region's top growers.

The soil and geology even vary significantly from one side of a road to another, as both Julian Castagna and Rick Kinzbrunner have noted about the differences from the north side to the south side of Wangaratta Road, the main thoroughfare heading west out of Beechworth township. Both Kinzbrunner and Castagna use the words 'grand cru' to talk about this area of Beechworth: not as a dig at other areas, but as a means of illuminating the minute changes from one piece of land to the next. This complexity has been noted for centuries in the vineyards of Burgundy (whose 'grand cru' system is alluded to), yet very rarely proffered toward any non-European wine regions. It is these minute differences in geology and elevation – and the growers' confidence in their exceptionalism – that make Beechworth one of the most nuanced and exciting stretches of land in Australia.

Hubbub

Despite the petite size of the GI, the varying elevation and geology make a strong argument for additional subregions to be defined – a sentiment echoed by several winemakers in the region. In particular, the high-altitude area around Stanley and the glacial sites east of the Beechworth township are cited as capable of creating unique wines to the rest of the region. Further official GI subregions are unlikely though, at least in the imminent future, and some worry that further delineation would dilute an already understated brand.

Despite the universal quality of the wines being produced in Beechworth, the small production has equated to a lack of widespread exposure. Regions like the Yarra Valley and Heathcote produce enough wine, and much at a moderate price-point, to populate the shelves of large retailers around Australia, and even around the world. Beechworth, on the other hand, doesn't have the output quantities to compete and hasn't developed the international renown that it perhaps deserves.

These concerns aren't pressing for most vignerons in the region, though. Beechworth enjoys an elite stature in the top retailers and restaurants of Australia. Producers are able to sell all their wines. There isn't much disease or pest pressure. And most vintages are conducive to making excellent wine. The main concerns cited by winemakers would probably be minor or distant concerns in other regions: global warming is on the minds of many with regards to new and current plantings; urban sprawl has the potential to infringe on future vineyard land; government bureaucracy can be an annoyance; and due to its positioning on the northern Victorian stretches of the Great Dividing Range, it is highly susceptible to smoke taint when bushfires ravage nearby (very little wine was made in the 2020 vintage from Beechworth).

Though these concerns aren't to be minimised, the overall outlook for Beechworth is overwhelmingly positive. A unique set of geological and climate circumstances forged this singular wine region, capable of producing a wide range of grapes and styles with one commonality: an almost universal premium nature. And a small but special set of vignerons have chosen Beechworth because of its potential for excellence, innovating in their time there. As Julian Castagna notes: 'I don't believe there are many other places in the world that produce the variety of products that we produce of a very high quality. Where else in the world can you grow cabernet, shiraz, chardonnay, sangiovese, nebbiolo, chenin, viognier, where else? And I think that makes Beechworth unique.'

The **biodynamic** Sorrenberg vineyard, sporting ripe fruit that's almost ready to be picked — and therefore also sporting bird nets to make sure there are grapes to harvest!

PRODUCERS

A. RODDA WINES

Adrian Rodda's first instinct pointed him in the right direction when the opportunity to lease the oldest vineyard in Beechworth (Smith's), alongside legendary viticulturist Mark Walpole, became a reality. Adrian, his wife Christie and their young family committed to the region, moving in 2010. Prior to that he had spent more than a decade at Oakridge Wines in the Yarra Valley (p. 119) where his appreciation of the Willow Lake Vineyard encouraged him to start the 'Chardonnay Project', whereby he continues to source a small parcel from this vineyard in the Yarra Valley, as well as the Baxendale vineyard on the Whitlands Plateau (King Valley), and vinifies them in parallel with the Smith's Vineyard Chardonnay. Adrian has a deft touch with the variety that he has honed over two decades, making wines today which, at their best, can be considered in the very top echelon of Australian chardonnay. **aroddawines.com.au**

CASTAGNA

Julian Castagna grew up in Australia, but his early work as a film director took him to London, where he became besotted with fine wine. Julian and wife Carolann returned to Australia in the mid-80s and ran Enigma, one of Sydney's most successful film production houses. In the 90s, they decided to sell their apartment in the city and move into a caravan on the land. They built the winery and house out of straw-bale, learning everything on the job as they went along. The vineyard was planted in 1997 on what was previously grazing land. Their 4 hectares have been farmed **biodynamically** from the beginning and it is this farming method that, Julian believes, allows the minerality of the ancient granitic soils of Beechworth to show through in the wine. They now produce three distinct ranges of wines, his son Adam responsible for the Adam's Rib wines, a white and red blend that complement the long-running Castagna range, which continues to focus on single varieties. **castagna.com.au**

Mark Walpole
Fighting Gully Road

DOMENICA WINES

Launched in 2012 by Peter Graham, Domenica materialised when he purchased a 4-hectare hand-tended, organic farm that was established by a bygone M.Chapoutier/Giaconda joint venture. It sits 460 metres above sea level atop the granite ridge sweeping away to the southwest of Beechworth, adjacent to the renowned Warner vineyard. Having spent 13 years as assistant winemaker to his uncle, Rick Kinzbrunner of Giaconda, it's understandable that the Domenica chardonnay is highly sought after. However, it is shiraz,

---

 What we're drinking

*It's rare to encounter a wine that is wholly unique, yet qualitatively holds its own against the finest wines in the world. Enter: **Castagna's** Sparkling Genesis. A sparkling shiraz that ages on **lees** for around eight years and emerges as a sort of über-syrah. This wine blows my mind.*
– Jane Lopes

roussanne and marsanne that Graham believes to have a natural affinity with the warm summers, granitic soils, slopes and altitude provided by Beechworth. His nebbiolo is also not to miss!
domenicawines.com.au

FIGHTING GULLY ROAD

In 1995, while working his decades-long stint as the viticulturist for Brown Brothers, Mark Walpole and his wife Carolyn De Poi purchased a north-facing farm at an elevation of 530–580 metres above sea level in Beechworth. The breeze-blown slopes were 'covered in scrub, stumps and thousands of rabbits', but the potential was palpable. A long-time champion of alternative varieties, the cool site to Beechworth's south is today planted to a significant amount of sangiovese and tempranillo, alongside cabernet sauvignon, shiraz and pinot noir. In 2009, Walpole, alongside long-time friend Adrian Rodda, leased Smith's vineyard, the region's oldest, planted in 1978 to chardonnay and cabernet sauvignon. The pair also share a winery space, Mayday Hills, a decommissioned mental asylum dating back to 1867. Mark is universally regarded as one of the finest viticulturists in Australia, and the person who knows the land of Beechworth (and most of the regions of Victoria) better than anyone.
fightinggullyroadwines.com.au

GIACONDA

Giaconda, one of Australia's most revered producers, was the first winery to establish itself in modern Beechworth, when owner and winemaker Rick Kinzbrunner released his first wines in 1987, made from the 1985 vintage. Giaconda has become dedicated to regenerative agriculture and minimal-intervention winemaking, though it is known first and foremost as the home of one of the country's best chardonnays. Planted at an altitude of 400 metres on granitic loam over decomposed gravel and clay, the chardonnay can be found on a relatively cool south-facing slope of the vineyard, sheltered from the direct impact of the sun, resulting in a much slower ripening period, greater flavour complexity and natural acid levels. Unlike any other in the country, it uniquely harnesses both power and finesse in equal parts – it's a true benchmark for the heights that can be achieved with the variety in Australia. This single wine has resulted in the region now being synonymous with the variety, though the estate's shiraz and amphora-aged roussanne are also exemplary.
giaconda.com.au

PENNYWEIGHT

Pennyweight is a small traditional winery, owned and operated by the fourth and fifth generation of Rutherglen's Morris family, Elizabeth and Stephen Morris and their three sons. It is comprised of two certified organic and **biodynamic**, **dry-grown** vineyards situated in both the Beechworth and Rutherglen wine regions, producing a range of solely estate-grown **table wines** and **fortified wines**, and especially known for their apera (sherry-styled) wines.
pennyweight.com.au

Rick Kinzbrunner
Giaconda

Beechworth

 New Guard   Environmental Hero   Rising Star   Legend   Regional Stalwart   Must Visit   Cult Following   Historic Estate

> **What we're drinking**
>
> Any wine produced under a **Sorrenberg** label is a true treasure to behold. Its facets uniquely capture not only Beechworth, but the spirit of Jan and Barry and the pride they have for the very small parcel they call home. Their gamay should be found in every cellar. – *Kavita Faiella*

SAVATERRE

The Savaterre vineyard was established by Keppell Smith in 1996. Kep (as most call him), influenced by his time working under Phillip Jones at Bass Phillip, committed to **close-planting** chardonnay and pinot noir at 7500 vines per hectare on the thin soils of granitic buckshot over decomposed clay at his 40-hectare property. Shiraz and sagrantino have since been planted at similar densities, all farmed using organic and some **biodynamic** practices. Kep believes 'that if we are to truly represent our wines' origins', then winemaking influences must be reduced to the very minimum. Wines are hence vinified with a hands-off approach that prioritises patience, with the ultimate aim of producing intense, complex and textural wines that speak clearly of this unique site in northern Victoria. *savaterre.com*

SENTIO

A Beechworth native, Chris Catlow has been working with wine in the region since he was a teenager. After being employed by Barry Morey of Sorrenberg, who inspired him to study winemaking, he found tutelage under Sandro Mosele in the Mornington Peninsula, where his passion for chardonnay crystallised. Several vintages with Benjamin Leroux in Burgundy also encouraged him to champion site expression when establishing the Sentio label, where he now makes noteworthy chardonnay from Beechworth, Macedon, Tumbarumba, Yarra Valley and the Alpine Valleys. *sentiowines.com.au*

SORRENBERG

Sorrenberg is a 2.5-hectare vineyard owned by Barry and Jan Morey. Planted in 1985, they were one of the first to produce wine in Beechworth with the 1989 vintage. The family has a tradition of winemaking that goes back over 500 years to Germany; the name Sorrenberg comes from a small vineyard owned by Barry's grandfather's family in the lower Mosel River valley. The estate is home to a garden of varieties: chardonnay, sauvignon blanc, cabernet sauvignon and gamay, with smaller quantities of cabernet franc, merlot, semillon and pinot noir. Using non-conventional farming methods in the vineyard from early on, they have been Demeter-certified **biodynamic** since 2008. *sorrenberg.com*

TRAVIARTI

Traviarti's name, Italian for 'those led astray', is a potential lead to understanding how Simon Grant and Helen Murray found themselves in Beechworth after several years, looking for the perfect place to plant nebbiolo. Grounded, however – not astray – is where they have been since planting their vineyard in 2011, dubbed Red Hill and planted exclusively to nebbiolo with multiple **clones** on a combination of different rootstocks and own-root material. In 2018 they planted a second vineyard called the Rosso Block adding another source for nebbiolo, along with barbera and the region's most renowned variety, chardonnay. *traviarti.com*

> **What we're drinking**
>
> **Vignerons Schmölzer & Brown** are a rising star and very much marching to their own beat. This is a project of incredible thought and detail, yielding an array of compelling wines from further flung places to augment their more focused-vineyard derived projects. In essence, they produce bloody amazing wines in a variety of styles, particularly those that reflect touchstones of their own drinking and global winemaking interests. – *Mike Bennie*

Tessa Brown
Vignerons Schmölzer & Brown

VIGNERONS SCHMÖLZER & BROWN

Relatively recent arrivals to Beechworth, Tessa Brown and Jeremy Schmölzer are vignerons in every sense of the word. They manage each aspect of the vineyard and grape-growing, making the wines from their small 2-hectare parcel planted in 2014 and 2015. Their farm is located on the southeast outskirts of the region, a whole 200 metres higher than Beechworth township, sitting on mudstone soils where they have unearthed a lighter and leaner expression of the region. The pair have a delicate touch in both the footprint they intend to leave on the earth and the wines they make, which have an ethereal signature to them. In addition to their estate vineyard, they also source fruit from the neighbouring Brunnen vineyard, and both the Alpine and King Valleys, with a special focus on exemplary riesling. *vsandb.com.au*

And don't forget ...

Arcadia, a new project from Peter Bartholomew, Melbourne restaurateur (MoVida, Lee Ho Fook) and vigneron (Wanted Man, Heathcote, p. 192), involving the restoration of a vineyard originally planted in the 1860s and replanted in 2016 ... **Eldorado Road** combines the talents of vintners Paul Dahlenburg and Lauretta Schulz, who tend their estate vineyard alongside a historic Glenrowan one, with a focus on chardonnay, syrah, durif and nero d'Avola ... **Eminence Wines**, run by Clare Burder and Pete Allen, has taken a particular stake in serious bubbly, bringing on Australian sparkling wine royalty Tony Jordan to help craft long-aged, **traditional method** fizz, in addition to elegant still takes on Champagne grapes chardonnay, pinot noir, and pinot meunier ... **Indigo Vineyard**, the largest single vineyard in Beechworth, made famous by the Hunter Valley's Brokenwood, have built renown for the site with their Indigo Shiraz ...**Piano Piano**, Italian for 'slowly slowly', represents Marc Scalzo and Lisa Hernan's measured approach to making Beechworth chardonnay, shiraz and merlot, as well as a few unique offerings from King Valley ... **Vinelea**, a small vineyard and winery owned and managed by Stuart Smith and Rhonda Parish, takes an academic approach leading to peak expressiveness of pinot noir, shiraz, chardonnay and a roussanne-marsanne blend ... **Warner Vineyard**, long-time Wangaratta Road grower turned winery in 2012, has a focus on the Rhône varieties shiraz, marsanne and roussanne ... **Weathercraft**, a relative newbie on the scene, the Jones family relocated to Beechworth in 2014 and had their first vintage in 2017 (from a site planted in 1998), making everything from shiraz and chardonnay to tempranillo and amphora-albariño.

Rutherglen

Introduction

Rutherglen has achieved wide recognition across Australia and the world, tied largely to the **fortified** muscats the region has produced for over a century. It would be easy to think that perhaps that name and history has inflated Rutherglen beyond its capabilities, but this evolution is not the story of Rutherglen – quite the opposite in fact.

Rutherglen is nestled south of the Murray River in northeastern Victoria, and has 781 hectares under vine – compare that to another famous **fortified**-producing region, Portugal's Douro Valley, which has a staggering 43,000 hectares under vine. Rutherglen has a few spots of corporate ownership across the region – historic estate Morris is owned by Casella, and Rutherglen Estate is owned by De Bortoli (both family-owned, though large, Australian wine companies) – but the region is largely defined by small, independent owner-operators.

It would also be easy to think that the region is a somewhat staid appellation, which would not be wholly incorrect. Rutherglen has crafted a phenomenal **fortified wine** industry, and continuously delivers aged masterpieces in this genre. **Table wine** production has focused on robust reds and simple whites, pleasing local tourism, but with only rare wines from this category hitting the top wine lists or capturing media attention across Australia. A few younger producers have played with alternative expressions for the region, often with great success, but this story is still a minority one. The larger story is one of history, tradition and community – a narrative that, though some might say lacks in novelty and diversity, delivers on quality and the excitement that comes from making one of the world's benchmark wine styles.

Of course, the story of human development in Rutherglen starts tens of thousands of years ago. Modern-day Rutherglen sits on what is formally recognised as Yorta Yorta Country. The Yorta Yorta are the traditional caretakers of a portion of the Murray River and the lands surrounding it. Their land title claim covers an expansive area, and within it there are numerous smaller language and familial groups; Rutherglen is Bangerang Country. The erasure of Aboriginal culture since the arrival of Europeans has made it impossible for the Bangerang people of today to make a land title claim that is acknowledged by the Victorian government.

The Murray River, called *Dunggula* by the Bangerang people, is where they constructed complex fish races and firestick-farmed in the adjacent flatlands. You can still find numerous 'canoe trees' in Rutherglen's waterside vineyards – river red gums from which bark was used for constructing canoes. It is also a river that has defined the climate, history and output of Rutherglen's rich vinous exploration.

Evolution of Wine

Though Hovell and Hume certainly passed through Rutherglen on their voyage south across the Murray River, most historical texts of the region give Major Thomas Mitchell the nod as the first European explorer to champion Rutherglen. Of his 1836 expedition, Mitchell spoke favourably in his reports of the 'lofty ... trees and the low verdant alluvial flats of the Murray', spawning an ongoing season of squatter's runs for the next decade. By 1846, the entire area of modern-day Rutherglen was occupied by squatters, down from Sydney or up from Melbourne.

Lindsay Brown was one of the squatters who made the Rutherglen area home in the 1840s, and in 1851 he planted a 1.6-hectare vineyard just west of the township – recognised as the area's first vines. With the gold rush sweeping Rutherglen and the surrounding Murray-Darling basin townships, the local wine industry grew exponentially between these first plantings and the end of the century.

Many of the top names of Rutherglen were established in this time: Chambers Rosewood (1858), Morris (1859), Jones (1860), All Saints (1864), Campbells (1870) and Stanton & Killeen (1875), among others. Any one of these wineries' founders – with their early and continued prominence in the region – could be singled out for stewarding viticulture in Rutherglen. By virtue of there being so many dominant producers (with continued relevance), this group is often treated collectively. The brief and communal history shouldn't neutralise the significance of each of these producers; if anything, it points to how extraordinary Rutherglen is and the talent and grit of so many founding vintners.

By the 1880s, Rutherglen had nearly 1200 hectares under vine spread over more than 50 vineyards, generating a third of Australia's entire wine production. Fairfield (owned by the Morris family), with 300 hectares under vine, was the Southern Hemisphere's largest vineyard at the time. And it wasn't just quantity; Rutherglen's wines were celebrated at domestic and international wine shows, and made up a sizeable portion of the Australian exports to England. In 1873, All Saints was the first Australian winery to win an international gold medal at the London Exhibition, followed by two Rutherglen gold medals at the 1878 Paris Exhibition.

Two events in this time period fostered additional growth. In 1879 a railway was built connecting Wahgunyah, Rutherglen, Lilliput and Springhurst, towns spanning about 25 kilometres in and around the current borders of Rutherglen GI. Though this seems like a provincially minute distance to modern sensibilities, it was enough to allow a substantially larger audience for the wines of Rutherglen. And in 1889, the Australian government offered a cash incentive of £2 per acre (0.41 hectares) to plant vines in the region.

Expansion during this time can also be credited to the Chinese immigrants of

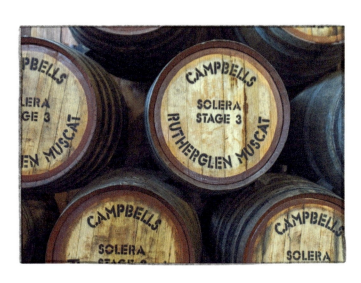

The third of five stages in the solera-aged journey of Campbells Muscat: a system of old hogsheads (300-litre barrels) assembled in the 1960s.

Rutherglen, many of whom came to Australia for the gold rush. When the gold rush abated in the late 1860s and 1870s, Chinese men and women were hired as vineyard and cellar hands, allowing the wine industry to prosper and grow during a time when labour was scarce.

In the early days the grapes of choice were a kaleidoscope: shiraz, malbec, cabernet sauvignon, muscat blanc à petits grains, muscat rouge à petits grains and pedro ximénez. The styles, equally diverse, reflected a general exploration of the popular wines of the world at the time, including 'hock', 'roussillon', 'sherry', 'sauternes', 'constantia', 'burgundy', 'chablis' and 'claret', without much heed paid to matching the style with its traditional grape.

Rutherglen's heyday was slowed by the infamous **phylloxera** pest, hitting the region in 1899. The root aphid didn't sound the death knell for the region, though, in the way it did for many other regions. As **phylloxera** had hit southern Victoria in the 1870s, there was already knowledge about how to mitigate the pest by grafting on American rootstock.

But times were tough for a while. Many vineyards were ripped up and not replanted. Many of the region's wineries – reaching beyond 100 in number at Rutherglen's peak – shut their doors for good. The farms that did endure diversified heavily to survive the recession. But what Rutherglen did have going for it, that many other regions did not, was the shifting taste for sweet and **fortified wines**.

By 1925, Rutherglen had reached its pre-**phylloxera** planting levels. That year, Australia sent 750,000 gallons (2.8 million litres) of wine to England – and much of it was **fortified wine** from Rutherglen. In 1930, Rutherglen began selling **fortified wine** in bulk to the rest of Australia. While most cool- and moderate-climate Australian wine regions were at near or total dormancy in these decades, Rutherglen was thriving.

There isn't much scholarship available on the exact evolution of Rutherglen Muscat – the region's signature style. What is known is that as **fortified wines** gained in popularity, the vignerons of Rutherglen began to pay special attention to muscat rouge à petits grains and how well suited the grape was to the region. With the warm and dry climate of Rutherglen, the grapes could hang on the vine for extended periods of time without fear of rot or damage. When picked, the sugar-rich ferments were arrested with the addition of neutral grape spirits and laid away in various format barrels for years, sometimes decades. The muscadelle grape was also vinified in this way – to a lighter and drier effect – and historically referred to as Tokay, though known today as Topaque.

These styles buoyed Rutherglen through the first half of the 20th century. In 1950, **fortified wines** accounted for 86% of Australia's wine production, but preferences began shifting soon after and **fortified** production waned. Rutherglen began planting vines for **table wines** in the 1960s, though – miraculously – the vision for its Muscat and 'Tokay' wines was maintained, with old stocks continuing to age in the region's cellars.

Durif had been planted in 1908 in the region, stepping into a starring role as **table wines** became the vogue. Durif is a grape that

Durif: A Classic Aussie Red

Durif is a spontaneous crossing of syrah and the obscure grape peloursin that occurred in the nursery of French botanist François Durif, released in 1880. The TTB (Alcohol and Tobacco Tax Trade Bureau, the US's regulatory body for wine) considers durif and petite sirah to be synonymous, and indeed, according to famed grape geneticist Dr Carole Meredith, 90% of what is thought to be petite sirah in the US is in fact durif. (The other 10% are old vineyards that also have plantings of peloursin, syrah and a crossing of peloursin x durif.) Durif was first planted in Rutherglen at the beginning of the 20th century; it is still the region that the grape is most associated with, making robust, highly pigmented, black-fruited, tannic red wines.

originated in southern France, most likely a cross between syrah and the obscure peloursin. Durif is often considered synonymous to America's petite sirah, though technically the latter can be a field blend of durif, syrah, peloursin and a durif x peloursin cross. Though durif was used in some of the **fortified wines** of Rutherglen, it has forged its identity mainly through its use to make dry, full-bodied and highly pigmented dry reds.

The **table wine** scene continued to progress for the second half of the 20th century, with myriad grapes finding success in the region, including marsanne, chardonnay, tempranillo, shiraz and cabernet sauvignon. In particular, durif, shiraz and cabernet sauvignon have been the heroes of the region for **table wines**, able to withstand the occasional extremes of temperature and drought. To this day, **table wine** sales far exceed those of **fortifieds**: 'We talk about the **fortifieds**, but sell the **table wines**,' says Fred Morris, a descendant of the original Morris family and the current viticulturist at Campbells.

Rutherglen did well encouraging tourism in this time as well, with the launch of the Rutherglen Wine Festival in 1967 and the Rutherglen Winery Walkabout in 1974, the latter attracting an astounding 10,000 people to the region for the festival weekend.

Rutherglen Muscat continued to gain renown, but with very little organisational structure to its production or transparency in its labelling, the region's producers formed the Rutherglen Muscat Classification in 1995. The classification splits the muscats of the region into four categories: Rutherglen Muscat, Classic Rutherglen Muscat, Grand Rutherglen Muscat and Rare Rutherglen Muscat. The wines are classified based on a tasting panel, much in the way that Portugal's Tawnies are given age statements, but there are loose residual sugar and ageing requirements.

Rutherglen Muscat, the first tier, is designed to be the freshest and most youthful of the four, focusing on forward fruit flavours and subtle raisination. The average age expression is three to five years, with 180–240 grams per litre residual sugar (yep, it's serious! – often double the average sugar in a port).

Classic Rutherglen Muscat is aimed at expressing more wood-aged and **oxidative**

'We talk about the fortifieds, but sell the table wines,' says Fred Morris.

characteristics, with an average age of 6–10 years and 200–280 grams per litre of residual sugar.

Grand Rutherglen Muscat expands on the aged characteristics of the Classic tier, with even more complexity and concentration. The average age is 11–19 years and residual sugar falls between 270–400 grams per litre.

The final tier, Rare Rutherglen Muscat, is the apogee of the style's expression. Often displaying a nearly motor-oil colour, the wines are indeed designed to be rare: a selection and careful blending of a cellar's most mature and fine barrels. The residual sugar is also 270-400 grams per litre, like Grand expressions, but the minimum age is 20 years.

Important to note, all this sugar is accumulated on the vine – grapes for Rutherglen Muscat are not dried or concentrated post-harvest, so the climate and viticulture is paramount to get the best quality possible.

As always seems to be the case with Rutherglen, there was a spirit of collaboration in the creation and adherence to the Classification, and no dissenters have emerged. The Classification has created much needed structure in the region, and allows easy consumer comprehension of the region's styles, and various levels of quality. While it may subsume individual wines to a more collective identity, the region's vintners don't seem to mind. (And indeed, the great wines of the world are often more about a style or a site than any one producer.)

Modern-day Rutherglen is a monument to its past. Many of the historic 19th-century buildings still dot the landscape, and the roll call of names that pioneered the region are still the beacons of quality, with fourth-, fifth- and sixth-generation vintners at the helm. And the style that made it all possible, Rutherglen Muscat, is still king.

A spirit of experimentation, though deferential to the spirit of tradition, is not absent. The general tone of innovation is one that embraces history, and only offers small tweaks of modernisation. As they say, *if it ain't broke, don't fix it*, and what has always worked for Rutherglen still does: a focus on some of the most profound **fortified wines** in the world, with enough **table wine** diversity to keep the lights on and maintain momentum.

Lay of the Land

Rutherglen has often been defined by its heat and proximity to the river: two qualities that made it an attractive bet in the early years, and continue to ensure its success. The climate here is hot, sunny and dry; Rutherglen firmly sits in the Region 4 category on the **Winkler Scale** (Region 5 being the hottest defined), with sunshine hours similar to Queensland's Gold Coast. We're talking subtropical sunshine – about 300 days a year of it! The evenings cool down a bit for Rutherglen (unlike its subtropical analogues), a blessing that helps retain acidity and freshness in the grapes. Also, unlike any subtropical region, Rutherglen is defined by its dryness; the region sees very little humidity, which a degree of windiness helps further mitigate, and rain is concentrated in the winter months.

The Murray River is the other defining attribute of Rutherglen's landscape (and early success). A constant supply of water was a necessary amenity for a fledgling community in the early 19th century, and today, it still contributes significantly to the viticultural success of the region. With growing-season rain rarely surpassing 375 millimetres, irrigation is necessary for all but the oldest sites in the region (those planted before 1930). Landowners have water rights to access overflow from the Murray River: based on amount of farmland, the season, and the flow of the river, producers are prescribed a percentage of their water rights that they can access each year. (Most Australian wine regions are not afforded this luxury: they must either truck in water, an expensive proposition, or maintain their own catchment systems for rainwater.)

The majority of Rutherglen's vineyards are within 10 kilometres of the river, and often much closer. The proximity to the river is not just about water usage, but also influences soil type. The overarching summary of Rutherglen soils is that they are clay subsoils with alluvial deposits, sand and red loams dispersed throughout. The famous 'Black Dog' soils of the region are sand with sandy clay below. These soils are focused west of the town of Rutherglen, closer to the Murray itself. They have less **nutrient load** and are more alkaline or neutral than the red soils of the region. They are named for Black Dog Creek, which originates from the watershed of Chiltern-Mt Pilot and meets the Murray River just downstream of the GI limits. Producers on this soil include All Saints and Pfeiffer.

The second major soil type of the region is the red volcanic loam. These soils are more prevalent, centred at the town of Rutherglen and through the east. The best sites have a higher concentration of quartz in the soils. It is recognised that as one moves north or south

Rutherglen Viticultural Footprint

Total delimited area (km²)	980
Total planted area (hectares)	781
% of delimited area planted	0.800%
Total elevation range	122–592 masl
Elevation range of plantings	134–398 masl
Number of producers	19

Rutherglen Climate Data (°C)

	1960–1990	1991–PRESENT	2020
Heat summation/GDD	● 1912	● 1967	● 2025
Annual rain/GSR	624/301	615/326	527/348
Warmest month avg. temp.	22.8	23.7	24

Winkler Scale:

● 850–1111 ● 1112–1389 ● 1390–1667 ● 1668–1944 ● 1945–2222 ● 2223–2700

The muscat rouge à petits grains grapevines at Morris not far from the river Murray.

off the band of red loam, where levels of quartz decrease and soils become heavier, the wines are less age-worthy. Producers on the red volcanic loams include Campbells, Chambers, Stanton & Killeen and Morris.

The sandy Black Dog soils result in wines with high-toned aromatics and higher acidity/lower pH (relatively speaking, with wines of 3.8–4 pH rather than 4–4.2, which is more common of the red loams). Red loamy soils also create denser, darker, more brooding and powerful wines. Both are very skilled at ageing.

As far as topography goes, Rutherglen is quite flat. The southeastern portion of the GI gains elevation towards the Chiltern-Mt Pilot National Park, which creates the southeast border of the appellation and separates the GI from Beechworth. The highest plantings are at Indigo Jack on north-facing slopes below the mountain, scraping 330 metres above sea level. More olives are planted here than grapes, though. Many great sites are planted on 'lumps' (as Scion's Rowly Milhinch calls them, 'because they're not quite hills') of 140–190 metres in elevation. These sites tend to contain quartz and shale; the vines work hard on these sites, which can produce great intensity of flavour.

Rutherglen was formerly a region with conventional farming practices and very little biodiversity. The vineyards of the 1980s had little life besides grapevines: chemicals were common, only dirt resided between the vines, and overhead or flood irrigation was employed. Though this sounds bleak by today's standards, Rutherglen was always a region that was on top of whatever the best practice of the day was. It was one of the first regions to move away from ploughing and undervine weeding in the 1960s, and when drip irrigation and synthetic fertilisers became de rigueur in the 1980s, Rutherglen adopted those practices as well.

So, it's no surprise that the region has progressed from those days, and continues to adopt the best practices. Today, cover crops, mulch and grasses keep soils full of life and moist. No heavy tractors are employed in the vineyards. And drip irrigation is used only when needed – wineries have an incentive to minimise water usage, as overirrigation just feeds **canopy** growth and creates large, dilute berries.

To make things official, Rutherglen has engaged Sustainable Winegrowing Australia, and is seeking to be the first region to have every producer certified by the organisation. Already, over 60% of producers have signed up for its enrichment program.

The vintners of Rutherglen have also adopted a more holistic approach toward land care.

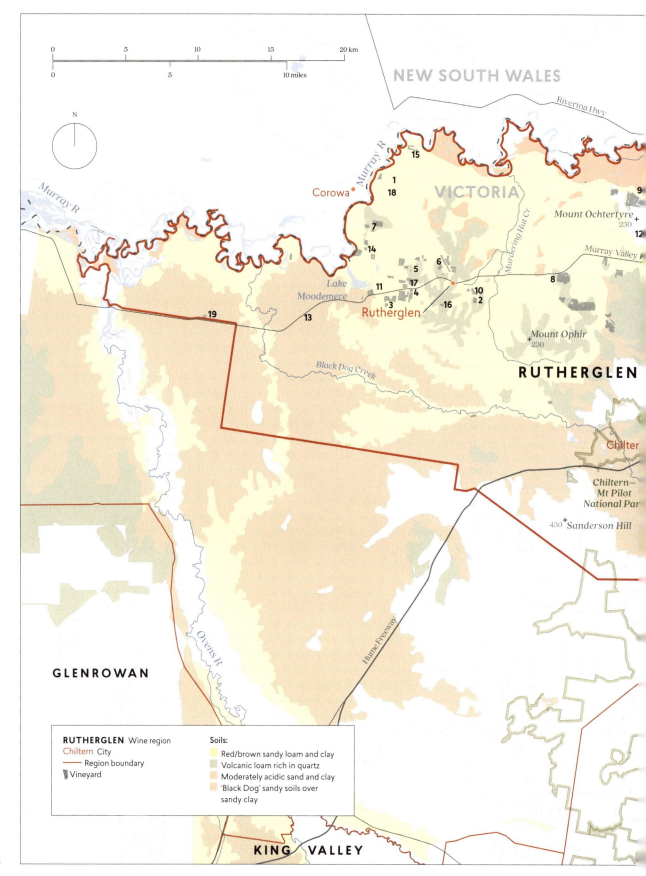

Rutherglen

HOW TO READ THIS MAP

The soils of Rutherglen have been transformed and placed by the nearby Murray River. Both soils and river are mapped here, with each vineyard of the region.

1. All Saints Estate
2. Anderson
3. Buller Wines
4. Campbells
5. Cannobie
6. Chambers Rosewood
7. Cofield
8. De Bortoli
9. John Gehrig
10. Jones
11. Lake Moodemere Estate
12. Morris
13. Olive Hills Estate
14. Pfeiffer
15. St Leonards
16. Scion
17. Stanton & Killeen Wines
18. Valhalla
19. Warrabilla

The collective community recognises that they are at the Upper Murray, and there is a conscious attempt to ensure the quality, cleanliness and life of the river is intact and thriving as it reaches communities further downstream. The notions of social and environmental responsibility in the region are predicated on an understanding of how, literally, what they do has a downstream impact. 'There's a custodianship mentality,' Morris says. 'What we do today has a far-reaching effect on tomorrow.'

Hubbub

Ask the vignerons: Rutherglen has two problems. The first is marketing its wines. It's a small region with an illustrious history, but that doesn't always translate into proper recognition and sales. With a new generation of Eurocentric sommeliers and wine writers who are infatuated by novelty, Rutherglen's traditional personality doesn't ignite fire in their eyes. Rowly Milhinch, a descendant of the Morris family, who planted vines for his label Scion in 2002, tells it like this: 'That's a challenge because we've had history, family lineage, sweet wines – they've been our bread and butter for over one hundred years. I think one of the strengths of the region is that it doesn't bend to vogue. But I think while you might not change your vision for what you're producing, keeping that in line with how a market needs to see it is one of the challenges.' Jen Pfeiffer of Pfeiffer Wines agrees, saying, 'the biggest challenge is how do we encourage the wine consumer, the new wine consumer, to try these wines, to be excited about these wines, and teach them how and when do we drink these wines?'

Pfeiffer and Scion come from different stylistic bents – the former a producer of more traditionally styled Rutherglen wines, and the latter on the more progressive end of the spectrum – but both see this as a common challenge: telling the story of the region in a way that gets the industry and consumers excited about Rutherglen.

The second problem the region faces is climate change. Pfeiffer recounts how the climate has shifted in her 20 years making wine: 'When I first came home, we used to start harvest in the middle of March, and now we start in the middle of February. It's climate warming, extreme heat events, bushfires, heatwaves, but then wet summers and frost as well.' Fred Morris acknowledges the effects of climate change, but says that the 'net result of climate change is not as noticeable [in Rutherglen] as in a more temperate climate'. And that, by comparison, Rutherglen has been quite manageable in the face of climate change.

Morris's outlook reflects a general optimism in the region, founded in its deep history. Rutherglen has survived **phylloxera**, economic recession and changing trends without losing sight of what it does best. It is a region that has sought to improve and expand upon the present, building toward the future without abandoning the past. 'If you think about it,' Pfeiffer says, 'we've successfully grown grapes in the region for over 150 years. And what it tells me is that wine grapes are pretty adaptable, but also, wine growers and good viticulturists learn how to manage their vineyards in changing climate.'

Rutherglen has weathered the storm so far, and there is no sign it is letting up.

With a new generation of sommeliers and wine writers who are infatuated by novelty, Rutherglen's traditional personality doesn't ignite fire in their eyes.

Winter in Rutherglen brings an eerie morning fog into vineyards like Scion's, thanks to surrounding creeks, lakes and the Murray River.

PRODUCERS

ALL SAINTS ESTATE

The All Saints castle was built by Scottish settlers in 1864. Today the property is owned and run by the fourth generation of the Brown family (see Brown Brothers, p. 247), siblings Eliza, Angela and Nick. The Browns took over All Saints and St Leonard's Vineyard in 2005 and purchased Mount Ophir, another Rutherglen estate, in 2016. Aside from the four traditional muscat and muscadelle classifications in Rutherglen, All Saints makes a Museum Release of each variety with base wine dating back to 1920. These treacle-coloured wines represent 100 years of multi-generational winemaking history. With Nick in charge of winemaking, All Saints is also producing a large amount of reputable still wines, from varieties like marsanne and durif.
allsaintswine.com.au

CAMPBELLS

The Campbells family has prevailed through difficult times: world wars, the Depression, **phylloxera** and early deaths in the family. John Campbell founded the vineyard in 1870 and the tradition has been passed down through five generations. Julie Campbell is the presiding winemaker, having taken over after her father's passing in 2019. Julie and her sisters, who also work in the business, are firmly carrying on the family legacy, while keeping an eye to the future. Campbells Merchant Prince Rare Muscat gained international attention in 2003 when Robert Parker rated the wine 99 points, calling it 'pure nectar'. *campbellswines.com.au*

CHAMBERS ROSEWOOD

The epitome of old-school Rutherglen, Chambers Rosewood was founded in 1858. Stephen Chambers is at the helm today, with his father Bill keeping a close eye. The Chambers family solera has been going for over 60 years, resulting in dense, luxurious muscats and muscadelles that are consistently decorated across the world. Stephen and his dad also make a number of still and sparkling wines, including from the rare ancient variety gouais – parent to notable grapes like chardonnay and gamay and grown for over 100 years in the region. *chambersrosewood.com.au*

MORRIS

Thanks to his success on the goldfields, George Francis Morris planted vines in Rutherglen in 1859. Post-**phylloxera**, George's son, Charles Hughes Morris planted a new vineyard a couple of kilometres away in Mia Mia. David Morris is the fifth generation of the family to work for the business and remained as chief winemaker and custodian when the winery was bought by Casella in 2016. The Morris **fortifieds** are still seen as a benchmark of the Rutherglen style. *morriswines.com*

PFEIFFER

Chris and Robyn Pfeiffer bought their property in 1984. Originally an old distillery for the Rutherglen arm of Seppelt, the property had just under

---

What we're drinking

Few things in the world take the foresight, patience and dedication that the creation of great **fortified wines** *require. The museum release from* **All Saints Estate** *is the culmination of over a century's work, and results in an other-worldly wine experience.* – Jonathan Ross

Jen Pfeiffer
Pfeiffer

5 hectares of old-vine pinot noir, gamay, chardonnay and Portuguese varieties, the latter of which are still in use today. Chris had worked as chief **fortified** winemaker for Lindeman's and was welcomed by the multi-generational Rutherglen winemakers with open arms. In 2000, Chris and Robyn's youngest daughter, Jen, returned home from study and was coaxed by her dad to make the Pfeiffer shiraz that year. She caught the bug and today is a self-confessed 'winemaking addict'. Jen's time working in Portugal's Douro Valley led to her creating Australia's first rosé **fortified**.
pfeifferwinesrutherglen.com.au

SCION

Rowly Milhinch is one of the true new-wave winemakers in a wonderfully tradition-steeped region. A descendant of George Francis Morris (see Morris), Rowly was working as a graphic designer in Melbourne before he was persuaded to return home by his mum, who had planted a vineyard in her retirement. Milhinch learned the winemaking ropes from friends and eventually began making everything on site, focusing on traditional grapes (like durif and muscat) and massaging them into modern styles.
scionwine.com.au

STANTON & KILLEEN WINES

Stanton & Killeen represents seven generations of family winemaking, with the first vintages made in 1875. Dubbed Australia's 'Prince of Port', sixth-generation Chris Killeen planted several Portuguese varieties in the 1990s with visions of creating a Rutherglen vintage 'port'. Veering away from the cloyingly sweet styles that were traditionally produced in Australia, Killeen blended the Portuguese grapes with shiraz and durif, creating a more savoury expression of vintage **fortified**. Stanton & Killeen's The Prince blend was created in honour of Killeen, who passed away in 2007. Sixth and seventh generations, Wendy and Natasha Killeen, have taken up custodianship of the winery, putting significant research into drought-hardy grapes to combat the changing climate. *stantonandkilleen.com.au*

And don't forget ...
Buller Wines, established in 1921 by the Buller family and purchased by the Judds in 2013, has a range of impressive **fortifieds** and still wines ... **Jones**, with roots back to the 19th century in Rutherglen, is today run by fifth-generation siblings Mandy and Arthur Jones, who look after plantings dating back to 1905 ... **Simão & Co**, an important Rutherglen winery that is on pause as of publishing; Simon Killeen embraced his lineage (of Stanton & Killeen) to put his own mark on tradition, working with grapes from all over North East Victoria, in both dry and **fortified** styles.

Rowly Milhinch
Scion

JL | **What we're drinking**

The **fortified** wines at **Stanton & Killeen Wines** need no endorsement, having been recognised as some of the region's finest for over a century. It's the **table wines** that took me by surprise, especially the Portuguese grapes: arinto, alvarinho and tinta roriz that combine freshness with grit and complexity. — Jane Lopes

Rutherglen

Other Regions of Victoria

The wine regions of Victoria can be thought of as starting at the water – at the capital city of Melbourne and the adjacent Port Phillip Bay – and expanding outward. The Bay gives its name to the Port Phillip Bay zone, which comprises five wine regions that wrap around the bay itself (none more than a 90-minute drive from Melbourne): Yarra Valley (p. 104), Mornington Peninsula (p. 122), Geelong (p. 138), Macedon Ranges (p. 152) and Sunbury.

Sunbury, on the traditional lands of the Wurundjeri, is one of the more historic wine regions of Victoria, with viticulture dating to 1860. Its modern wine resurgence, though, has been late and understated, with only a handful of producers commanding attention outside the region (and only a humble 100 hectares under vine). Craiglee is one such producer – the marquee producer of Sunbury – with a history dating to 1863, and a resurrection starting in 1976 (by Pat Carmody, who has become a Victorian wine legend). Craiglee is well known and respected to this day, especially for its age-worthy cabernet sauvignon and shiraz, but the chardonnay and viognier are equally compelling.

A few members of Australia's young guard of winemakers have started to look to Sunbury for a reliable source for moderately priced fruit: Vino Intrepido's pinot grigio, Born & Raised's shiraz and skinsy sauvignon blanc, and Konpira Maru's syrah are all sourced from this region. No large wineries or modern champions for the region have yet emerged, though, and the region's identity has largely been formed around Craiglee.

Sunbury's amorphous identity is also tied to the fact that its geographic situation is an amalgam of its neighbours: it enjoys the moderating influence of Port Phillip Bay (though not quite as strongly as Geelong and Mornington Peninsula) and the chilly winds off Mt Macedon (though not quite as strongly as Macedon Ranges). Its soils and elevation vary across the region, providing yet another factor that has made branding a difficult proposition. And, there's always the risk with Sunbury that it will be swallowed up by the growing footprint of Melbourne.

But while Sunbury hasn't quite been able to establish its identity for any one thing, perhaps its identity should be centred in the very fact that it can do many things well (and affordably). There is no qualitative reason why Sunbury shouldn't enjoy the renaissance now emerging in many GIs across Australia: it just needs the right set of vintners to invest in it.

Due northwest of Sunbury (through the Macedon Ranges), Bendigo GI is the western outpost of the Central Victoria zone, sandwiched between Western Victoria's Pyrenees (p. 194) to the west and Heathcote (p. 180) to the east. Bendigo is on the traditional lands of the Dja Dja Wurrung and Taungurung peoples of the Kulin Nation. The wine region is centred around the township of Bendigo, with much to offer the wine tourist in terms of cafe culture, art galleries, antique shops, historic gardens, and, of course, cellar doors.

Bendigo had a sizeable gold rush boom in the 1850s and grapevines went in the ground soon after. Bendigo found early success in Australia and abroad, with a judge at the 1878 Vienna Exhibition exclaiming of a Bendigo 'Hermitage' (aka shiraz), that 'no colonial wine can be that good'. But Bendigo fell to **phylloxera** in 1893, crippling the region's wine industry for over half a century. Balgownie Estate, Connor Park and Byronsvale are credited as the first of Bendigo's revival, in the late 1960s.

Bendigo's identity as a region is tied to the friendliness of the area for tourism. In fact, Bendigo refers to itself as a 'winemaker's region' because visitors are bound to encounter the winemakers themselves when they visit. Few of the region's wineries have made much of an impact beyond the boundaries of the GI, with the exception of Sutton Grange.

Sutton Grange was planted in southern Bendigo in 1998. Between Sutton Grange and the more 'approachable, fresh and fruit driven' Fairbank label, the winery has become recognised for its reliable, affordable and expressive iterations of syrah, cabernet sauvignon/merlot, fiano, viognier, aglianico and sangiovese.

The plantings at Sutton Grange represent a microcosm of the larger Bendigo GI, which produces standard-bearers like shiraz, cabernet and chardonnay, but increasingly explores alternative grapes like sangiovese, nebbiolo, roussanne and mourvèdre. The region is defined by its Mediterranean climate – warm, dry summers and mild, wet winters – as well as its gravel, sand, clay and volcanic soils.

East of Heathcote is the massive Goulburn Valley GI, extending clear up to the Murray River and the New South Wales border, and straddling the traditional lands of the Yorta Yorta and Ngurai Illum Wurrung. (The Taungurung Land and Waters Council was granted a substantial Recognition and Settlement Agreement by Victoria in 2018, but many contest the Taungurung claim to ancestry in this specific area.) The most quality-minded (and commercially minded) producers of the Goulburn Valley are clustered in the Nagambie Lakes GI, one of two official subregional GIs in Victoria (along with Grampians' Great Western). This is where the historic Tahbilk winery is based, whose 1860 vines were the first plantings in the entire Goulburn Valley.

Today, Tahbilk is a sizeable producer, with over 200 hectares under vine. Tahbilk has become a model of environmentalism and regenerative farming, establishing a local wildlife walk with the Taungurung Land and Waters Council and achieving carbon-neutral status in

Vineyards of the King Valley, nestled among the foothills of the Great Dividing Range.

2013. Tahbilk makes dozens of different wines – with grapes including shiraz, cabernet sauvignon, chardonnay, pinot gris, verdelho and riesling – but has become most famous for their marsanne. With vines dating back to 1927, commonly accepted as the oldest marsanne vines in the world, Tahbilk releases several different marsanne bottlings each year. The most famous is the (appropriately named) 1927 Vines, which is made in a 'Hunter semillon style' – early picked, cold-fermented, released with bottle age, and often clocking in near 11% alcohol.

Nagambie Lakes is most known geographically for its waterways: lakes, rivers and billabongs that keep the surrounding areas cool. The sub-GI is on the southern border of the Goulburn Valley GI, a stone's throw from its neighbour, the Strathbogie Ranges. The northern stretches of the Goulburn Valley GI are warmer, drier and highly irrigated (thanks to the adjacent Murray River) – and not known for quality wine production, nor much in the way of quantity.

On the southeast border of Goulburn Valley is Strathbogie Ranges GI: Taungurung Country. Strathbogie Ranges was a granite peninsula 360 million years ago, pushed up by the ocean, now sitting at 600 metres in elevation. The northwestern parts of the region are lower and warmer, tending to be more suitable for higher-production, machine-harvested red wines. The higher altitude southeastern portion has become known for its ability to produce premium wine. Fowles is a notable producer in the region, making shiraz, chardonnay, riesling, pinot noir, sauvignon blanc and others off their two estate vineyards. Yarra Valley-based Mac Forbes has also brought interest to the region with his with his beloved rieslings all made from Strathbogie Ranges fruit.

Continuing southeast, the last GI in the Central Victoria zone, is the (rather confusingly named) Upper Goulburn region, so dubbed because it occupies most of the upper catchment of the Goulburn River (but is situated south of Goulburn Valley and Strathbogie Ranges). Also on Taungurung land, the region was formerly called 'Central Victorian High Country', with vineyards between 250 and 800 metres above sea level. With its elevation, the Upper Goulburn is quite cool-climate, and most known for grapes like riesling, gewürztraminer, chardonnay, sauvignon blanc and pinot noir. Mount Buller, Victoria's premier skiing destination, is within the GI's borders.

Upper Goulburn has made little imprint on the Australian wine scene: with few producers accelerating into the premium sector and not enough volume to make an impression commercially, the region occupies a sort of wine limbo. But with increasing interest in cool-climate wines (coupled with global warming making them harder to come by), Upper Goulburn is poised for renewed interest.

Situated northeast of Central Victoria is the North East Victoria zone. The two southernmost GIs in the zone, hugging Upper Goulburn's eastern shoulder, are the King Valley GI and Alpine Valleys GI (from west to east). Often mentioned in the same breath, these two regions occupy low-lying river valleys west of the Great Dividing Range, on the northern edge of the Victorian Alps.

These two GIs cover a vast amount of land and varying terrain. The King Valley is formally

Prosecco

Up until 2009, Prosecco referred both to the style of wine being made (bubbly from the Veneto in Italy, typically made in the **charmat method**) and the grape used to make said-style. In 2009, several Italian DOCGs were reformed, which codified Prosecco as part of the appellation name and nominated another name for the-grape-previously-known-as-prosecco: glera. Glera is an ancient name for the grape that the Italians dredged up in order to protect the word Prosecco. They want it to be like Champagne: it can only come from one place in the world. But Australia, with a booming 'prosecco' industry, has fought back: Italy presented legal challenges in both 2013 and 2018 that were struck down, and Australian producers continue to use the grape name prosecco, arguing that its fame as a grape well-outdates Italy's attempt to make it specific to place.

North East Valleys

HOW TO READ THIS MAP

The vineyards that dot the foothills of the Victorian Alps are the sources for a number of emerging grape varieties and styles. The highlighted Whitlands Plateau has emerged as a notable subregion.

KING VALLEY Wine region
Whitlands Plateau Unofficial subregion
Bright City
— Region boundary
······ Unofficial subregion boundary
▮ Vineyard

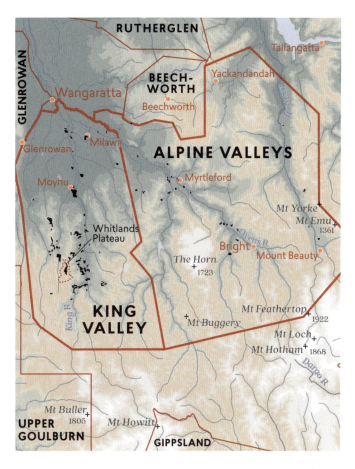

recognised as Taungurung Country, while much of the Alpine Valleys serves as a painful reminder of the missing right to self-determination. Dhudhuroa, Waywurru, Pallanganmiddang, Jaithmathang and Gunaikurnai people, past and present, all have traditional connections to these lands.

The plural Alpine Valleys refers to the Ovens, Buffalo, Buckland and Kiewa River basins that occupy the GI, while the King Valley straddles the King River. Both regions are defined by their elevation, which can be minimal on valley floors and the northern mouths of the river basins (about 150 metres above sea level), working up to nearly 900 metres on the upper slopes and southern peaks.

The Whitlands Plateau, in southern King Valley, has become known for its high altitude and cool climate, ranging from 750–900 metres in elevation. Since the inception of negotiations over the King Valley GI, producers in the Whitlands Plateau have argued for a separate identity, based on unique elevation and soil type. Their pleas and appeals were finally quashed in 2007, when the Federal Court of Australia upheld an earlier Administrative Appeals Tribunal decision to keep the Whitlands Plateau as part of the King Valley GI.

But the Whitlands Plateau is still celebrated as a unique part of the larger GI. The region is most known for its pinot noir and chardonnay destined for sparkling wine, but some notable riesling and pinot gris are coming off the plateau as well. In 2013, the Yarra Valley's Chandon Australia purchased a sparkling vineyard from Brown Brothers, planted in 1958 at 800–850 metres above sea level. Chandon has since released a Whitlands Plateau labelled bottling, which has raised consumer awareness of the region.

Summer in the Victorian Alps.

King Valley and Alpine Valleys are also particularly known for their widespread plantings of Italian grape varieties. John Francis Brown (who would go on to establish Brown Brothers) planted 4 hectares of land in Milawa, modern-day northern King Valley, in 1885. The original grapes planted were shiraz, riesling and muscat, but Brown Brothers has championed alternative varieties over the years, everything from prosecco to tempranillo, graciano, fiano and malbec. Brown Brothers is one of the most significant producers in Victoria – from a historical and commercial perspective – and its influence can be seen across the state's vineyards and winemakers.

Pizzini and Dal Zotto, both founded by Italian families in the 1970s and 1980s, have cemented the King Valley's status as the Australian wine scene's 'Italian spirit' (per the Wines of the King Valley website). Though these wineries both produce a significant quantity of wine, the quality is consistent, and the ownership has remained in the family. Plus, their dedication to Italian grapes clearly expands beyond the tried-and-true commercial hits (like pinot grigio and prosecco); the two producers between them produce such grapes as verduzzo, arneis, garganega, sangiovese, nebbiolo, barbera, canaiolo and brachetto.

Pizzini, Dal Zotto and Brown Brothers (along with the Chalmers family in Murray Darling and Heathcote) are responsible for making Italian grapes as commonplace as they are in Australia. After Italy, Australia has the most hectares planted to Italian grapes of any nation in the world, as well as the greatest diversity of Italian grape varieties produced. Most good restaurants and wine shops in Australia stock domestic wine made from Italian grapes. They're not only sought after by consumers, the quality and value is astoundingly high.

The quality to price ratio tends to be exemplary in the King and Alpine Valleys in general, which has attracted outside interest. These regions are now significant producers of bulk wine, often sold to large producers based outside the region.

An interesting facet of these negociant relationships is that, because of the high risk of **phylloxera** in these zones, unfermented grape solids are not allowed to leave the region. This has led to the formation of several contract wine processing companies in the region, most notably the Victorian Alps Wine Company (and its most prominent brand, Gapsted) and Michelini Wines. While this structure keeps the processing money inside the region, it can have a detrimental impact on quality. Single vineyards or small lots aren't kept separate, as transactions are in bulk, and fermentation options are limited, as solids can't leave the region. Red wines are fermented at contract facilities and most whites are transported out as clarified juice. 'I think this is what has held the region back,' says Billy Button's Jo Marsh.

Billy Button is one of the few boutique producers in these valleys that has captured the attention of the Australian wine industry; Mayford Wines, Cavedon Wines and Konpira Maru would be the others at top of the list, as well as smaller producers outside the region, working with its fruit, like Vignerons Schmölzer & Brown, Terrason, The Story Wines, Sentio and Thick as Thieves.

And though they share many qualities, Alpine and King valleys are distinct as well. King Valley production dwarfs that of Alpine Valleys, with six times the land under vine. With the exception of King Valley's Whitlands Plateau, the Alpine Valleys tend to be higher in elevation, cooler and wetter. King Valley's name has become more established because of the bigger companies working out of the region, but Jo Marsh, whose Billy Button wines have made the biggest modern impact for Alpine Valleys, hopes that 'in the next 20 years there are more small wineries in the region, making high-quality labelled, appellated wine, driving demand for fruit and comparable fruit pricing to other regions of similar high quality. It would be great to have Alpine Valleys held in the same esteem as regions like Beechworth [right next door], Yarra Valley and Mornington Peninsula.'

After Beechworth (p. 212), nestled in the lofty peaks north of Alpine Valleys, the final two GIs in the North East Victoria zone are Rutherglen (p. 226) and Glenrowan, the latter on the traditional lands of the Pallangmiddang and Bangerang people. These two GIs are often partnered when discussing Victorian wine, though Rutherglen's fame and volume has far exceeded its western neighbour. Both regions are known for their full-bodied red wines of shiraz and durif, their long-aged **fortified wines** made from brown muscat and muscadelle, and their shared Ned Kelly-era lore.

The classically enumerated geographic differences between the two regions are minute: Rutherglen is slightly warmer in the summer, though has a lower total **heat summation** than Glenrowan. It is wetter during the growing season, yet drier year round, and Rutherglen is situated on the Murray River, which has provided both a constant irrigation supply as well as deposits contributing to Rutherglen's unique 'Black Dog' soils.

Rutherglen's proximity to the Murray River is a boon for the above reasons, but also for the population it attracted. Glenrowan had its one founding family (Baileys); Rutherglen had a trove of early settlers who made significant viticultural inroads (most of whom are still of importance to this day). Glenrowan is also dominated by this one producer, Baileys of Glenrowan, whose plantings account for 70% of the total in the GI – hardly a recipe for promoting growth and branding for Glenrowan as a region, rather than just a single producer.

The final zone in Victoria is one that has had, until now, little significance to the fine wine conversation: the North West Victoria zone. This zone includes the GIs Murray Darling and Swan Hill (both shared with New South Wales, straddling the Murray River). These GIs are cut from the same cloth as New South Wales' Riverina and South Australia's Riverland: hot, dry, flat, highly irrigated, and most well-suited for bulk production.

Or at least that's been the classic reputation. Like the renaissance in South Australia's Riverland is proving: these regions are capable of more than has historically been allotted to them. Though Riverland is a few years ahead in terms of generating buzz, a similar spark of interest is just now igniting in Murray Darling, which is Nari Nari and Latji Latji Country. A 2021 *Gourmet Traveller* article about the region led with the headline 'a taste of Italy is growing on the banks of the Murray River' and went on to name the 'one family at the forefront': the Chalmers family.

Jenni and Bruce Chalmers founded their eponymous estate in Merbein, a suburb of Mildura, in the 1980s. Along with their daughters Kim and Tennille, who now run the enterprise, they have imported over 70 grape varieties to Australia over the years; it is estimated that an astounding 20% of the vines planted across Australia came from their Murray Darling nursery. Though a large focus of their wine production is their Heathcote site, acquired in 2000, the Merbein vineyard is the 'mother block' and is planted to many of the vines that they have imported and distributed throughout Australia. Though these vines have historically been used to collect cuttings for propagation, in recent years, they have started making small amounts of wine from them (under the label Mother Block), displaying remarkable quality and value. These appellations, Murray Darling and Swan Hill, are ones to watch for alternative grapes and maximum value in the years to come.

Red Grape Crosses

For a time, red grape hybrids and crossings seemed like they'd be the next big thing in Australia. Chambourcin is a French hybrid that began to crop up with some frequency around coastal New South Wales in the 1980s, valued for its ability to thrive in moist climates. But the grape had its detractors: Tim White wrote in a 2001 article for the *Australian Financial Review* that 'chambourcin lacks distinction. Its only virtue seems to be its extreme hardiness and its ability to withstand mildew and rot like no other variety on the planet. This is why I refer to it as the cockroach: my bet is that chambourcin would be the one variety to emerge unscathed from a nuclear winter.' And indeed, its potential popularity in Australian wine was overstated. In a similar vein, the red grape crosses that the CSIRO developed for Australian climates — tarrango, tyrian, cienna and rubienne — have not had the market presence and longevity that some expected. Tarrango did the best: the grape was developed for Brown Brothers (a crossing of sultana x touriga nacional) and marketed as a light, chillable red wine. It had a heyday in the 80s and 90s, before disappearing for decades, only to be reintroduced in 2022.

PRODUCERS

BENDIGO

SUTTON GRANGE

The Sutton Grange vineyards were planted on a horse-training property in 1998 to shiraz, cabernet sauvignon, merlot and viognier. Taking cues from the nearby Heathcote region, and its propensity for Italian varieties, fiano, sangiovese and aglianico were added soon after. Their Fairbank label is a more modern and approachable introduction to the winery, blending their Bendigo vineyard fruit with sources from around central Victoria. Sutton Grange has had a string of notable winemakers: Gilles Lapalus came on in 2001, introducing **biodynamic** and organic farming practices. Melanie Chester took over from 2015 to 2021, starting at age 26 with a string of accolades trailing behind her, bringing a renewed attention to the winery. *suttongrange.com.au*

STRATHBOGIE RANGES

FOWLES WINE

Matt Fowles left his law career and headed to his parents' farm to start Fowles Wine. He bought an out-of-use winery and planted extensive vineyards across two sites. Matt is a big believer in food provenance – knowing where or how your food was produced – and has structured his wines around this concept, with different ranges designed to complement either farm-raised or wild-game meats. *fowleswine.com*

ALPINE VALLEYS

BILLY BUTTON WINES

Jo Marsh led the team at Seppelt Great Western and Feathertop in the Alpine Valleys before branching out on her own in 2014. She attributes time with Kevin McCarthy at T'Gallant (Mornington Peninsula) as having heavily influenced the way she makes wine today. Named for the bright yellow daisies that grow in the Alpine Valleys, Billy Button works with a long list of grapes, many of them rare in Australia and indigenous to Italy, including friulano, verduzzo, malvasia, refosco, saperavi and schioppettino. The wines are setting the bar high for each style, and Jo remains a continuous advocate for Alpine Valleys.
billybuttonwines.com.au

Jo Marsh, Billy Button

GLENROWAN

BAILEYS OF GLENROWAN

Richard Bailey planted one of the area's first vineyards in 1870, though it was destroyed by **phylloxera** in the 1890s. Undeterred, Richard's son Varley replanted with American rootstock in 1904, including a shiraz vineyard that still produces fruit today. Baileys has made a name for itself with wines similar to those made in nearby Rutherglen: rich, full-bodied shiraz and luscious **fortified** muscat and muscadelle. Baileys' vineyards (comprising about 70% of the total plantings in Glenrowan) have been undergoing conversion to organics since 2011, with the first certified range released in 2019. Baileys of Glenrowan has passed through several hands during its time and is now owned by the Casella family (see Riverina, p. 96).
baileysofglenrowan.com

KING VALLEY

BROWN BROTHERS

Four generations of the Brown family have helped craft wine over their 130-year history. The latest to take up the mantle is Katherine Brown. She is also the family's first female winemaker (and the only one ever to not be named John!). The management of the wine group is currently heavily dominated by powerhouse Brown family women: Eliza and Cynthia are board members and Caroline and Emma have taken up various roles in the business. Brown Brothers celebrated 100 years of winemaking with a 'Kindergarten Winery': a mini winery for trialling and experimenting on a small scale. They have also worked closely with the **CSIRO** on the establishment of unique Australian varieties – notably a grape called cienna, a cross between cabernet sauvignon and the Spanish variety sumoll, and tarrango, a crossing of sultana and touriga nacional. Aside from its extensive vineyard holdings, the wider Brown Family Wine Group bought Innocent Bystander from Giant Steps (Yarra Valley) in 2016 and owns three wineries in Tasmania.
brownbrothers.com.au

DAL ZOTTO WINES

Otto Dal Zotto was born in Valdobbiadene, Italy – the home of prosecco. He arrived in Australia in 1967 and bought land that had been used for tobacco farming. As Australia began to gain awareness around the dangers of smoking, and tobacco looked less profitable, Otto looked to the nearby King Valley vineyards for inspiration. Otto and his wife Elena began with the grapes of their heritage, planting barbera, sangiovese, pinot grigio, arneis and (of course) prosecco. When the latter went in the ground in 1999, it was the first serious planting of the grape in Australia, which continues to be called by its more historic name rather than the newly donned glera. Otto and Elena's sons Michael and Christian now work in the winery, continuing the family legacy.
dalzotto.com.au

KONPIRA MARU

A collaboration between Sam Cook and Dr Alastair Reed – who met while Sam was studying viticulture and winemaking and Dr Reed was his lecturer – formed around the goal 'to produce wines [they] wanted to drink and to inject a little fun into [the] industry'. The first vintage was 2014. Fruit, over the years, has been sourced from the Granite Belt and South Burnett regions in Queensland, as well as Kilmore, just outside Macedon Ranges in Victoria. In 2016, the pair took on their own vineyard in the Whitlands Plateau area of King Valley, where pinot noir, chardonnay, pinot meunier and pinot gris are farmed organically.
konpiramaruwinecompany.com

PIZZINI

The Pizzini family started life as grape growers, selling mostly riesling, chardonnay and cabernet sauvignon. In the mid-80s, Alfredo Pizzini began to experiment in the vineyard with nebbiolo and sangiovese and then began to diversify, working with verduzzo, picolit and arneis. Though Pizzini's first wine was a chardonnay, they soon became known for Italian varieties, putting themselves and King Valley on the map for them.
pizzini.com.au

MURRAY DARLING

CHALMERS
(See Heathcote, p. 190)

SUNBURY

CRAIGLEE

Melbourne businessman James Stewart Johnson planted the first vines at Craiglee in 1863. The winemaking tradition continued at Craiglee until the 1920s when the vineyards were turned to paddocks for lamb production. Fifty years down the track, a bottle of Craiglee 1872 'Hermitage' (shiraz) was opened at a dinner party, which had won several awards overseas in its day. John Brown Sr of Brown Brothers was so taken by the 100-year-old wine that he travelled to Sunbury to see if the site still existed. It was here that he met a young Patrick Carmody, who was working on the farm while studying agricultural science. John suggested he plant grapes. Pat decided to return shiraz to the land and also planted chardonnay, a bold move before the white wine boom of the 80s. Pat continues to make wine at Craiglee today and, like the original vigneron of the site, his wines are extremely age-worthy.
craigleevineyard.com

BALLARAT & WERRIBEE

ATTWOODS

Splashed across the Attwoods website is the phrase: 'Old sommeliers don't die, they become winemakers.' Troy Walsh did 12 years as a sommelier in London, before joining the 'flying winemaker' fold. Walsh worked for Domaine de l'Arlot and Domaine David Duband in Burgundy before settling in Scotsburn, up the Moorabool River from Geelong, to create the wines he loves, primarily with pinot noir, chardonnay and shiraz. In addition to his 1-hectare, **close-planted** home vineyard, Walsh also manages a vineyard at Garibaldi, near Scotsburn, owns a vineyard in Glenlyon (Macedon Ranges), where he also manages a cellar door, and still buys a little fruit from Bannockburn in Geelong.
attwoodswines.com.au

 What we're drinking

*Take your pick of **Attwoods'** wines: the chardonnays and pinot noirs are all stunning, combining savoury flavours, filigreed structure and fruit expression to great effect. Winemaker Troy Walsh's eye for fruit and vision for winemaking has resulted in some of the most impressive (and under-the-radar) wines in Australia. — Jane Lopes*

GRAPE BY GRAPE, REGION BY REGION

WHERE THE ACTION IS

> **What we're drinking**
>
> From some of Victoria's finest, more classically styled chardonnay and pinot noir (**Eastern Peake**) through to the innovative wines of **Latta Vino**, this is one of Australia's great tearaway producers, showcasing the topflight skills of winemaker Owen Latta. Arguably, at the apex of Australia's avant-garde wineries. – Mike Bennie

LATTA VINO/EASTERN PEAKE

Owen Latta was thrown into winemaking at the age of 15, when an accident mid-harvest meant his dad, Norm, couldn't complete vintage. He worked in the winery in every spare moment, before and after school, with guidance from his dad. Eastern Peake had been established by his parents in 1983 (with the help of legendary Mount Langi Ghiran – p. 209 – winemaker Trevor Mast), focusing firmly on chardonnay, pinot noir and syrah. Owen has been working full time in the family winery since 2007, elevating the quality and renown of the wines. He also makes wine under his own label, Latta Vino, which features a more creative bent. Zero-**sulphur** viognier, experimental rolling ferments, pinot gris-pinot noir **pét-nat** and **nouveau**-style sangiovese are just a few of the gems you can expect. **lattavino.com.au easternpeake.com.au**

SHADOWFAX

About halfway between Melbourne and Geelong is the town of Werribee, where Shadowfax is based. Started in 1998, there are 10 hectares of vineyard in Werribee, plus another two sites in Macedon. Current winemaker Alister Timms began as assistant winemaker to Matt Harrop (Curly Flat, p. 162 and Silent Way, p. 164, Macedon Ranges), who oversaw the establishment of Shadowfax. Their focus is on pinot noir, with their best sources being Macedon Ranges vineyards. Shiraz follows, with the odd (and exciting) mondeuse and nebbiolo making appearances. **shadowfax.com.au**

NAGAMBIE LAKES

MITCHELTON

Mitchelton was the Shelmerdine family's first vineyard (established 1969), before subsequently expanding into Heathcote and the Yarra Valley. Mitchelton focuses on riesling, shiraz and Rhône blends, though their offerings are vast. They have invested considerably in minimising their environmental impact, including innovative wastewater recycling, minimal use of synthetic pesticides in the vineyard, and composting winery waste. Mitchelton also offers a chock-full sleekly designed tourism campus in Nagambie, with a restaurant, hotel (and second Airstream hotel!), day spa, art gallery and cellar door. **mitchelton.com.au**

TAHBILK

The first vines in the Goulburn Valley were planted in 1860, before being purchased by the Purbrick family in 1925. Tahbilk specialises in the Rhône Valley varieties of marsanne, roussanne, viognier, shiraz, grenache and mourvèdre, but other grapes are also planted. Tahbilk's marsanne holdings are the largest and oldest in the world. They make four different wines from the grape, all picked early to retain high natural acid and lower alcohol. There is also still half a hectare of **ungrafted**, pre-**phylloxera** shiraz, and the winery buildings have been classified by the National Trust. Tahbilk has become a leader in environmentally responsible viticulture and wine production, rehabilitating 160 hectares of wetland and wildlife reserve around the property. The wines feel traditionally Australian in style, but the farming and altruistic practices of Tahbilk are ever evolving to meet modern concerns. **tahbilk.com.au**

What we're drinking

*Gary Mills's offering at **Jamsheed** is a tour of some of Victoria's most notable regions and vineyards. His roussanne from the Warner vineyard in Beechworth and syrah from the Garden Gully vineyard in Great Western are the 'must see' stops along that tour. – Jonathan Ross*

OTHER

JAMSHEED

Gary Mills worked vintages in California, Oregon and across Australia before starting his label Jamsheed in 2003. He was an early adopter of using whole-bunch fermentation in his shiraz, and celebrated the little-known sites and subregions by putting them in clear view on his labels. He sources fruit from the Yarra Valley, Grampians, Beechworth and the Pyrenees. He bottles under several different series, each with their own range of striking labels. A trio of **pét-nats** – a **piquette**, rosé and light syrah – make up the ultimate park pack. The single-vineyard wines are way more serious, but all carry the classic Gazza (an Australian nickname for Gary) charm. In 2020, he launched his urban winery on the edge of Melbourne, which acts as a cellar door, bar, bistro and barrel room. *jamsheed.com.au*

And don't forget ...

Balgownie Estate, one of the oldest vineyards of Bendigo, offers museum stock of shiraz and cabernet sauvignon back to 2005 ... **Bush Track Wines**, overlooking the Beechworth plateau in Alpine Valleys, features smart wines made by Jo Marsh (Billy Button) and Eleana Anderson (Mayford) ... **Cavedon Wines**, a boutique King Valley winery by third-generation grape growers, is committed to showcasing prosecco in a modern and high-quality light ... **Dhiaga** is the side-project of Best's Great Western winemaker Justin Purser, with unique drops from all over Victoria, including a hop-infused moscato, nebbiolo rosé and gewürztraminer **pét-nat** ... **Eminence Wines**, run by Clare Burder and Pete Allen, has taken a particular stake in serious bubbly, bringing on Australian sparkling wine royalty Tony Jordan to help craft long-aged, **traditional method** fizz from the Whitlands Plateau, in addition to elegant still takes on Champagne grapes chardonnay, pinot noir and pinot meunier ... **Maison Lapalus/Bertrand Bespoke**, two labels that are the brainchild of Gilles Lapalus, produce a selection of **lo-fi** wines from across Central Victoria, as well as the beloved Maidenii vermouths ... **Mayford Wines**, Eleana Anderson and Bryan Nicholson's estate-grown winery in the Alpine Valleys, specialises in shiraz, tempranillo and chardonnay, with plantings back to 1995 ... **Minimum Wines**, in the Goulburn Valley, stands on one of the more impressive sustainability manifestos in Australia, with B-corp status, organic certification, and 5% of revenue donated to positive social and environmental impact (plus, delicious wines like a sangiovese-syrah blend and chardonnay with a kiss of sauvignon blanc) ... **Pipan Steel**, in Mudgegonga (just southeast of Beechworth), is a nebbiolo specialist, isolating 10 different **clones** in their vineyards and releasing them individually or as blends.

Tahbilk's famed 1927 plantings of marsanne within the Nagambie Lakes GI: the oldest marsanne vines in the world.

TASMANIA

The island state of Tasmania is not only home to some of Australia's top cool-climate wines, but is considered to have one of the nation's brightest viticultural futures in terms of climate and financial investment. With roughly 2000 hectares under vine (about the size of Italy's Barolo), Tasmania is a small growing region largely dedicated to premium wine.

A 45-minute flight (or a nine-hour ferry ride) from Melbourne, the main island of Tasmania is home to just over half a million people and accounts for 94% of the state, with the remaining land mass spread across over 300 small islands (which do not support any commercial viticulture). The main island squarely sits on the 42nd parallel and, coincidentally, 42% of its lands are protected as national parks or UNESCO World Heritage Sites.

Northeastern Tasmania was once connected to Wilson's Promontory in Southern Victoria by a land bridge, and archaeological findings show that there was a human settlement along the banks of the Jordan River near Hobart at least 42,000 years ago. The collection of fertile and safe estuaries, lagoons and bays along the southeastern corner drew the peninsula's first European settlers south, and this area remains the most densely populated today.

Fluctuations in temperature as the world neared the end of its last ice age resulted in the land bridge to Victoria becoming temporarily flooded around 36,000 years ago, giving Tasmania a preview of the island fate that would lie ahead. The climate cooled, and when the land bridge reappeared about 6000 years later, more people travelled further south to Tasmania. By 12,000 years ago, the ice age came to an end, permanently (for now) turning Tasmania into the island it is today.

Much of the original history of Tasmania has been lost or rewritten. In other parts of Australia, the languages of some of the First Nations have been preserved, but this is not the case for Tasmania. The western coast of the island was home to the Peerapper and Toogee Nations. Along the north, the Tommeginne, Tyerrernotepanner and Pyemmairrener Nations; the east coast was Paredarerme Country, and the coast south of today's Hobart is the Nuenonne Country. The Lairmairrener Nation were the only people to not occupy any coastland. Historians believe there were between 3000 and 15,000 people living across these eight Tasmanian nations at the time of European colonisation.

The terminal fluent speaker of any of these first languages, Fanny Cochrane Smith, died in 1905 and took with her much of the history of previous human life in Tasmania. Today, only about 40 words remain, most of them describing notable places. The Tasmanian Aboriginal Centre (established 1970) preserved these words, and, with the help of remaining members of the First Nations, established the palawa kani (intentionally lower case), an attempted reconstruction of Tasmanian Aboriginal languages. The palawa name for Tasmania is lutruwita; it is taken from language spoken by the Bruny Tribe, whose traditional lands were the islands that were part of the Nuenonne Nation, off the southeastern coast of Tasmania.

Lutruwita was first sighted by Europeans in 1642 when Abel Tasman, sailing on behalf of the Dutch East India Company, spotted the fires of the Peerapper and Toogee Nations along the west coast. He dubbed Tasmania 'Van Diemen's Land' for his governor, before sailing on to the South Island of New

Fog-covered tree tops of the Snug Tiers Nature Recreation Area, a popular hiking destination just east of the Huon Valley town of Cygnet.

Zealand, without ever setting foot on the island. Upon his return to the Dutch outpost of Jakarta, word of the land south spread, spawning numerous European exploratory visits to Tasmania.

The relations between European colonisers and the First Nations of Tasmania are some of the bloodiest and most horrific, the recounting of which would only serve to re-inflict the trauma. The state government of Tasmania clearly agreed they had – and still have – much to answer for, and starting in 1985, began the process of making reparations.

It was in that year, after much petitioning from First Nations, that the government legislated the return of all Aboriginal remains sitting in museums to their proper communities. In 1995, 3800 hectares of land, including Risdon Cove (where one of the most brutal massacres occurred), was returned to the Aboriginal community. And in 1997, Tasmania became the first state to formally apologise for the forced removal of children. Today, numerous culturally rich lands have been returned to the Aboriginal community, and in 2006, Tasmania became the first state to legislate compensation to the 'Stolen Generations' and their families.

There is still much healing to be done. The vintners of Tasmania are part of that conversation and, like most of what they do on the island, are approaching it in a methodical and thoughtful way. 'The history here is so fraught,' says Stargazer's Samantha Connew. 'The lies and the distortions of truth here have been perpetuated for so long that trying to get through to what the actual truth is, is very hard.'

But getting to that truth systematically is what the official growers' organisation, Wine Tasmania, is seeking to do. Connew sits on the board, where the focus is very much on this topic. 'We're trying to find out more about geographical naming conventions, but then also doing some more educational elements associated with that. So we're hoping to organise some courses in association with the Tasmanian Aboriginal Centre about how we should be approaching these topics ... doing it with respect and acknowledgement of what's happened previously.'

King Island

titima/Trefoil Island
pennemuker
manegin
tayapalaka/Green Point
nungu/West Point
laraturunawn/Sundown Point

takayana/Tarkine

Southern Ocean

Pipers River Unofficial subregion
Hobart City
panninher First Nations group
pinmatik/Rocky Cape Place name in palawa kani/English

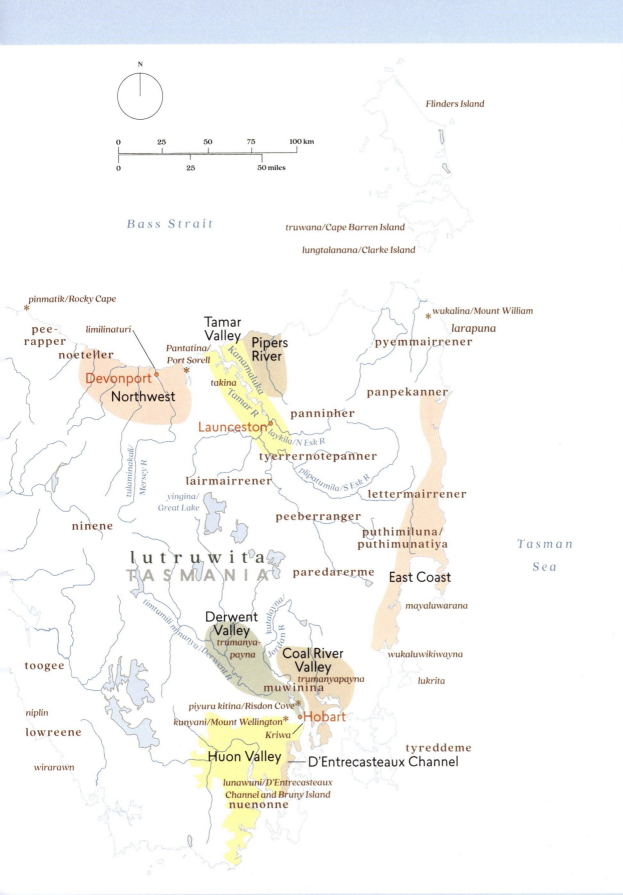

Evolution of Wine

Bartholomew Broughton, an Englishman who served in the Royal Navy during the War of 1812 (and then arrived in Tasmania as a convict), is responsible for planting Tasmania's first commercial vineyard (and its only one for over a century). His 1823 plantings in New Town, just north of today's Hobart city centre, produced wine from the 1826 harvest, sold in 1827 – some of the first commercially sold wine in Australia.

While Tasmania had over 40 different grape varieties planted by the mid-1860s – thanks in large part to a Captain Swanson, who bought the New Town vineyard when Broughton abruptly died in 1828 – the island's wine industry came to a halt in the latter portion of the 19th century. Several reasons are discussed for this: as the gold rush on mainland Australia took form, interest in Tasmania dwindled; there was not a big enough local market to sustain production; skilled labour was non-existent; and Tasmania presented (as it does today) a marginal growing climate for grapevines.

The modern age of Tasmanian wine starts in the 1950s with the establishment of two vineyards. Jean Miguet had arrived from Provence to work on a large hydroelectric plant through a government commission. He originally leased, and later purchased, his property just outside the city of Launceston near the Tamar River. Known today as Providence Vineyards, the estate has changed hands numerous times over the years, though still celebrates its origin story today.

The second vineyard was planted by Italian textile merchant Claudio Alcorso in 1958. The vineyard sits on what is known as Frying Pan Island, on the Derwent River, just northwest of the Hobart city centre, and was planted with the assistance of **CSIRO** officer Dr Don Martin. Alcorso named the estate Moorilla – one of the most important names in Tasmanian wine production to this day.

In the decades to come – slowly but consistently – other vineyards were established in Tasmania. Graham Wiltshire established his Legana vineyard in 1966, just north of Launceston on the west bank of the Tamar River. This vineyard would go on to become the pilot vineyard of Heemskerk, a collaboration between Wiltshire, Sydney wine merchant Bill Fesq, and Colin Haselgrove from Reynella Wines in McLaren Vale. They released their first wine, a cabernet sauvignon, from the 1975 vintage. Also in northern Tasmania, Andrew Pirie and his brother David established Pipers Brook vineyard

Sauvignon blanc vines within the Coal River Valley's Stoney vineyard, which make their way into Domaine A's Lady A — a wine that is perhaps Australia's greatest expression of barrel-aged sauvignon blanc.

in 1974; riesling and chardonnay were the most successful early plantings.

Meanwhile, on the south side of the island, George and Priscilla Park planted Stoney vineyard in the Coal River Valley in 1973 (as for Alcorso, with the help of the **CSIRO**'s Dr Martin). The original plantings consisted of riesling, pinot noir, cabernet sauvignon, shiraz and zinfandel, but cabernet sauvignon quickly rose to the top of the pack as a specialty of the vineyard. GlenAyr and Morningside vineyards were established in the Coal River soon after, in 1975 and 1980, respectively. Nearby in the Derwent Valley, Gerard Ellis began planting Meadowbank in 1976. And the east coast saw its first foray into viticulture in 1980 as well, with the establishment of Freycinet vineyard.

In 1984, The Mews vineyard was planted by the Holyman family, a 0.6-hectare plot of pinot noir and chardonnay at the Mount Pleasant estate in Launceston (which would eventually be bought by Pipers Brook/Kreglinger). The Pooley family planted in 1985 – seven rows of pinot noir and 10 rows of riesling in the heart of the Coal River Valley. And Jansz was established in 1987, a joint venture between Heemskerk and Champagne house Louis Roederer – today one of the most famous and internationally distributed Tasmanian wine producers.

Though a few others emerged in the 1980s (notably Bream Creek, Delamere and Lake Barrington Estate), it was in the 1990s that a generation of winemakers emerged who would be instrumental in the development and expansion of Tasmania's wine industry. Peter and Ruth Althaus acquired Stoney vineyard in 1989, establishing Domaine A; Stefano Lubiana founded his eponymous estate on the Derwent River in 1990; Alain Rousseau arrived from France in that same year, working with Domaine A and Moorilla before taking the helm at Frogmore Creek; and in 1995, self-described 'Tasmanian gambler' David Walsh, a brilliant finance guy with a penchant for art and wine, purchased Moorilla, building onsite his art gallery complex MONA (Museum of Old and New Art).

The 1990s were also when Tasmania became an official Geographical Indication. Tasmania felt the pressure early on to legally protect its name:

in the 1970s, a vineyard called Chateau Lorraine cropped up in the Huon Valley that was known to ship in barrels of South Australian shiraz and grenache and bottle it as Tasmanian wine. The state of Tasmania outlawed this practice, eventually stripping Chateau Lorraine of its licences, and forming their own 'wine appellation of origin scheme' in 1985 before becoming an official GI in the national system in 1994.

As the 1990s wore on, thanks in large part to Heemskerk and Pipers Brook, sparkling wine was already a clear part of the Tasmanian narrative. Ed Carr, the chief sparkling winemaker for BRL Hardy (later Accolade), was also scouting Tasmania as a source for grapes by the mid-1990s. So impressed by the potential of the region for sparkling wine, Carr and BRL Hardy established House of Arras in 1995. The 1998 vintage, released in 2002, was their first wine made from 100% Tasmanian fruit.

Tasmania had just 47 hectares under vine in 1986, and by 2003 that figure had increased to 801 hectares. Just as BRL Hardy has found potential in Tasmania, so too had other multi-regional (and multinational) corporations: in 1998, the Hill-Smith family of Yalumba purchased Jansz; Foster's (now Treasury Wine Estates) bought Heemskerk in 1997; in 2000, a majority ownership of Pipers Brook vineyard (and its second label Ninth Island) was acquired by Kreglinger, a wine company with Belgian origins; and in 2003, Constellation merged with BRL Hardy (who had started their second Tasmanian winery, Bay of Fires, in 2002), and was later purchased by Accolade in 2011. Other corporate machinations would come later, with Brown Brothers purchasing Tamar Ridge and Devil's Corner in 2010 and, most recently, Fogarty Wine Group acquiring Winemaking Tasmania in 2019 (renamed Tasmanian Vintners), where it has increased landholdings significantly.

But Tasmania is not, nor will it ever be, defined by corporations. There is an independent spirit to the island, supported by local consumption as well as a fascination from sommeliers and collectors across Australia (and, increasingly, the world). And as much as the 1990s and early 2000s brought expansion to Tasmania, the producers who have emerged from the mid-2000s onwards have further

Today Tasmania is a complex mix of big business vineyard ownership and small family-run estates, scattered across many unique growing areas that sit under the single GI of Tasmania.

defined Tasmania – as a premium wine–producing region, with regionally specific chardonnay, pinot noir, riesling and sparkling wine (among other expressions) that rival the greatest wines in the world.

The names that emerge in this conversation about the soul of Tasmania are plentiful. Joe Holyman made the jump from South Australia's Limestone Coast to Tasmania, acquiring a vineyard near the Tamar River in 2004. With the help of Graham Wiltshire, the two would foster some of the most diverse **clonal** trials for pinot noir in all of Australia. The late Vaughn Dell and his wife Linda Morice bought their Pipers Brook vineyard in 2005, naming it Sinapius. And Shane Holloway took over the 1981-established Delamere site in 2007, and along with wife Fran Austin (formerly of Bay of Fires), restored it to glory.

The list goes on, and multiplies, into the second decade of the 21st century – 2010

brought Barossa royalty Nick Glaetzer to the scene, championing Tasmanian shiraz, riesling and pinot noir. In 2011, Michael Hill Smith and Martin Shaw, who had started their Shaw+Smith label in 1989 in the Adelaide Hills, bought into Tasmania with their Tolpuddle vineyard in Coal River Valley. Also in 2011, Jonny and Matthew Hughes planted Mewstone on the banks of the D'Entrecasteaux Channel. Jim Chatto, after establishing his reputation in New South Wales' Hunter Valley and northern Tassie's Tamar Valley, produced the first vintage of his eponymous Huon Valley pinot noir label in 2012. Gilli and Paul Lipscombe made the first wines from their own vineyard in 2013, under the label Sailor Seeks Horse. Also in 2013, on the other side of the island, a former Bay of Fires winemaker named Ricky Evans made his first vintage from two tonnes of pinot noir – calling the winery Two Tonne Tasmania. Again in 2013, Samantha

Tasmania Viticultural Footprint

Total delimited area (km²)	68,582
Total planted area (hectares)	2084
% of delimited area planted	0.030%
Total elevation range	0–1617 masl
Elevation range of plantings	3–500 masl
Number of producers	131

Tasmania Climate Data Average Numbers (°C)

	1960–1990	1991–PRESENT	2020
Heat summation/GDD	● 669	● 797	● 768
Annual rain/GSR	983/524	921/459	970/483
Warmest month avg. temp.	14.7	15.7	16.7

Winkler Scale:
● < 850 ● 850–1111 ● 1112–1389 ● 1390–1667 ● 1668–1944 ● 1945–2222
● 2223–2700

The view from East Coast winery Devil's Corner, looking out over Moulting Lagoon (an important breeding area for black swans) to the Freycinet Peninsula in the distance.

Connew released her first vintage of Stargazer, becoming known for her deft treatment of Alsatian grapes (riesling, pinot gris and gewürztraminer) in addition to pinot noir and chardonnay. Peter Dredge, an alum of Bay of Fires, started his semi-eponymous label Dr. Edge (get it?) in 2015, simultaneously becoming the winemaker for historic Meadowbank, and starting a label called Brian for a more alternative approach to winemaking – a joint project with Joe Holyman and renowned wine writer/retailer (and collaborator on this book), Mike Bennie.

This may read like a bit of a laundry list, but it's hard to leave out any of these names when speaking of the ascendency of Tasmanian wine. This generation of producers, as well as several of their forebears, are heavily involved in the environmental conversation as well. VinØ is a sustainability initiative developed by Wine Tasmania, which seeks to measure, improve and report upon vineyard management practices across Tasmania. VinØ goes beyond organics and defines key areas of sustainability in soil health, responsible pest and disease management, biodiversity, water usage, waste management, labour rights, biosecurity, economic sustainability and carbon emissions mitigation.

Wines falling under the natural wine label often go hand in hand with environmentalism, but Tasmania has largely stuck to a traditional aesthetic. Part of this is clearly because fruit is so expensive: it's hard to make a **pét-nat** that will retail for $25 with fruit that costs $3000/tonne (compared to the mainland average of $700). It's easier to command high prices for traditionally made sparkling wine, pinot noir and chardonnay than it is for more alternative styles of wine.

A few producers have been successful in pushing some experimentation – Mewstone's Hughes & Hughes Living Wines range, Domaine Simha's self-described 'avant-garde fine wine', the aforementioned Brian, and some newer arrivals on the scene like Anim, Sonnen, R. D'Meure and Made by Monks – but these wines represent a fraction of the Tasmanian landscape.

Today Tasmania is a complex mix of big business vineyard ownership and small family-run estates, scattered across many unique growing areas that sit under the single GI of Tasmania. With vineyard establishment and management being so expensive, the model of micro-negociant, or hybrid negociant-grower, is quite prevalent among newcomers, though many young winemakers are taking it upon themselves to plant and grow, as well as make.

As climate change becomes more drastic and volatile, Tasmania is experiencing its own 'gold rush'; this cool-climate growing region with access to water is highly attractive in the world of viticultural speculation. Tensions exist – between big producers and small, between the desire for innovation and the cost of land, between environmentally minded individuals and a marginal climate – but, for the moment at least, the result is nothing short of a phenomenal, world-class wine region.

Lay of the Land

There's no shortage of celebration around Tasmania's cool climate. Considering mainland Australia is nearly 35% desert and only a small slice of the southern section is considered temperate, there's reason to embrace Tasmania. And though it is cool, Tasmanian viticultural areas enjoy a lot of sunshine. In the northeast, near the Tamar River Valley, vineyards get an average of 2550 sunshine hours annually. By comparison, Champagne sees about 1650 sunshine hours annually, but is a touch warmer than the Tamar, on average.

Tasmania has a singular geological history, with drastically different origins from the rest of Australia. Its oldest history dates from over 1.2 billion years ago, found in the form of metamorphic quartzite in the western portion of the island. This part of the island is now varied, with multiple formations of basalt, schist and quartzite created between 400 million and 1 billion years ago.

The eastern half of the island is much more uniform: the world's largest formation of dolerite, a volcanic basalt that formed when molten magma from the Earth's mantle forced its way to the surface. Nearly all of Tasmania's agricultural areas sit upon this bedrock, aside from the northeastern corner. This formation began during glacial conditions and created what stands today as the Tasmanian Basin. Volcanic activity during the Jurassic period brought a massive magma intrusion, creating a mountainous landscape and the dolerite bedrock upon which Tasmania's vineyards grow. Sandstone and quartzite weave through beds of Devonian granite at Pipers River in the north and cap the northeastern corner of the island, stopping just before Wineglass Bay on the east coast.

Tasmania's western coast is a temperate rainforest, firmly isolated by a series of elevations, mountains and highland plateaus that define the central portion of the island. Notables like Mt Ossa (1600 metres), Mt Field (1400 metres), Cradle Mountain (1500 metres), Mt Pelion (1560 metres), the Du Cane Range (1520 metres), and kunanyi/Mount Wellington (1260 metres), along with 50 others, were all formed during the Jurassic intrusion – creating a temperate rainforest in the west (inhospitable to most types of farming) and a stark rain shadow effect in the east, where all types of agriculture are possible. In the northeast, river valleys enjoy gentle rainfall that creeps south from the Bass Strait. But much of the southeast is drier still (excepting the Huon Valley), with many sites demanding irrigation.

Though there is plenty of elevation throughout the island, most agriculture and viticulture takes place in lower-lying river valleys. Despite the heights of the aforementioned peaks (important in the rain shadow they create), all vineyards are planted below 500 metres, with most along river valley floors less than 200 metres above sea level.

Central North (Launceston) Climate Data (°C)

	1960–1990	1991–PRESENT	2020
Heat summation/GDD	● 896	● 940	● 888
Annual rain/GSR	854/394	816/365	783/448
Warmest month avg. temp.	16.4	17	17.4

Northeast Climate Data (°C)

	1960–1990	1991–PRESENT	2020
Heat summation/GDD	● 816	● 848	● 856
Annual rain/GSR	1035/492	961/4433	938/504
Warmest month avg. temp.	15.8	16.5	17

Northwest (Devonport) Climate Data (°C)

	1960–1990	1991–PRESENT	2020
Heat summation/GDD	● 741	● 817	● 736
Annual rain/GSR	1309/576	1246/525	1217/599
Warmest month avg. temp.	15.2	15.9	16.1

Winkler Scale:

● < 850   ● 850–1111   ● 1112–1389   ● 1390–1667   ● 1668–1944   ● 1945–2222
● 2223–2700

Although Tasmania carries just a single official Geographical Indication, many recognise (and commonly label) a variety of subregions. The agreed-upon major areas, starting on the north coast, are (west to east) the Northwest, Tamar Valley, Pipers River and the Northeast; the long stretch of the East Coast, which extends 150 kilometres south from Freycinet to Boomer Bay; and the Southeast where the Huon, Derwent and Coal River valleys surround the greater Hobart area.

The Northwest subregion extends 45 kilometres west along the coast from Port Sorell and Devonport to Burnie, and spreads inland in its eastern portion for about 30 kilometres from Devonport to Sheffield. The coastal and inland areas are quite different, with the inland area receiving 20% more rain than the coastal areas during the peak rainfall months, as well as being drier in dry months. The inland area also experiences greater temperature fluctuations, with warmer highs and colder lows.

The Northwest has not achieved the critical acclaim or commercial success of many other Tasmanian regions, but is nonetheless the source of some reliable wines. Production varies here, with colder sites being well suited for the production of sparkling wines, and still wines produced from sauvignon blanc, riesling, chardonnay, pinot gris and pinot noir. Grapes from the Northwest are often blended with other sources as well – it's a subregion that rarely makes its way onto wine labels.

Moving east, the Tamar Valley is Tasmania's most planted and productive wine-growing region. Nearly 40% of Tasmania's 2084 hectares of vineyards are in the Tamar Valley, though more producers are based in the neighbouring Pipers River.

The Tamar River itself is Australia's longest tidal river (where flow and level are affected by changes in ocean tides). Its head is at the city of Launceston, 65 kilometres south of where it empties into the Bass Strait, surrounded by wide, sandy beaches. The valley's inland borders are defined by the Tamar's tributaries – the North and South Esk Rivers. Receiving gentle westerly rains, the land is rich and fertile, supporting a variety of agriculture beyond grapevines.

A diverse set of fruit sources allows a producer to avoid being fully exposed to the potential loss of a vintage if one area is devastated by smoke, hail, late rains, frost or any other hazard.

Elevation is consistent across the Tamar Valley, and therefore less climate variation occurs as one moves inland. Vineyards along the interior, upper reaches of the Tamar rarely sit above 60 metres in elevation, and the tidal nature of the Tamar River speaks to the small elevation gains. The valley is framed by a few mountains, namely the Briggs Reserve in the lower western portion of the valley. Three mountains – Mt Barrow, Mt Arthur and Ben Lomond – cradle the eastern interior, retaining moisture that travels up the river valley from the coast.

The Tamar Valley sits on the 41.5th parallel, and the growing region enjoys a climate similar to Chablis. Pinot noir is the most planted grape in Tasmania, and that holds true in the Tamar, with chardonnay and riesling also in abundance, as well as plantings of other varieties like gewürztraminer, grüner veltliner, gamay, pinot gris and sauvignon blanc. Sparkling wine has long been associated with the Tamar, though today that honour is shared with Pipers River to its east.

The Tamar and Pipers River Valleys are often grouped together, with producers sourcing from both. This is a tactic to mitigate risk and hazards. Tasmania is so marginal that a diverse set of fruit sources allows a producer to avoid being fully exposed to the potential loss of a vintage if one area is devastated by smoke, hail, late rains, frost or any other hazard.

The Pipers River is narrower than the Tamar River, and coupled with more elevation (vineyards up to 270 metres), there is greater frost risk. Pipers River is also at greater risk of damage due to autumn rains, as harvest is one to two weeks later here than in the Tamar. Both regions deal with a strong amount of disease pressure from moisture; selecting north- and east-facing slopes for vineyards is the first and most important step in managing both disease and frost.

Generally, the Tamar is warmer (thus the earlier picking date). Where the Tamar skilfully crafts pure still wines, Pipers River is as focused as ever on sparkling wines. Larger producers like Jansz, Pipers Brook, Bay of Fires, Arras and Ninth Island all bolster the Pipers River banner, but also source grapes for their sparkling and their still wines from the Tamar, and sometimes beyond. Moorilla's St Matthias vineyard, in the Tamar, provides grapes for their still and sparkling wines. And producers like Stoney Rise, Sinapius and Two Tonne have shown how bright the future is for Tamar Valley and Pipers River still wines.

East of the Pipers River Valley lies more of Tasmania's cool temperate rainforest. When speaking of wine regions, this area is sometimes referred to as the Northeast, but often just skipped over altogether in viticulture conversations. Viticulture has been tested here, but the high moisture brings with it serious disease issues.

The vineyards of the East Coast have historically been sparse, but it is now one of the focal points for rapid planting and industry growth. The current vineyards and estates don't have much in the way of market share or critical acclaim, but that seems poised to change. The East Coast is the warmest wine-growing region of Tasmania, often a couple of degrees warmer than Hobart. It also receives about 12% more rain annually. Freycinet Peninsula, which began as a sealing and whaling outpost (cues taken from Aboriginal groups who lived there), is a huge tourist draw, and much wine produced in the region is consumed locally. Pinot noir is the most abundant grape here, and the East Coast produces the fullest and ripest examples in Tasmania.

The southeastern coastline of Tasmania is made up of a variety of rivers, lagoons, bays,

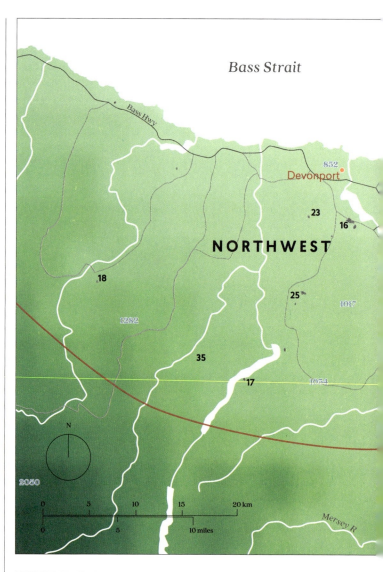

NORTHWEST Unofficial subregion
Launceston City
—— Unofficial subregion boundary
Vineyard
Annual rainfall:
2400 mm
440

HOW TO READ THIS MAP

Tasmania's vineyards bask in a rain shadow. Moving from west to east across the three (unofficial) subregions of the north coast shows how quickly rainfall disappears, and the changing levels of precipitation across the region.

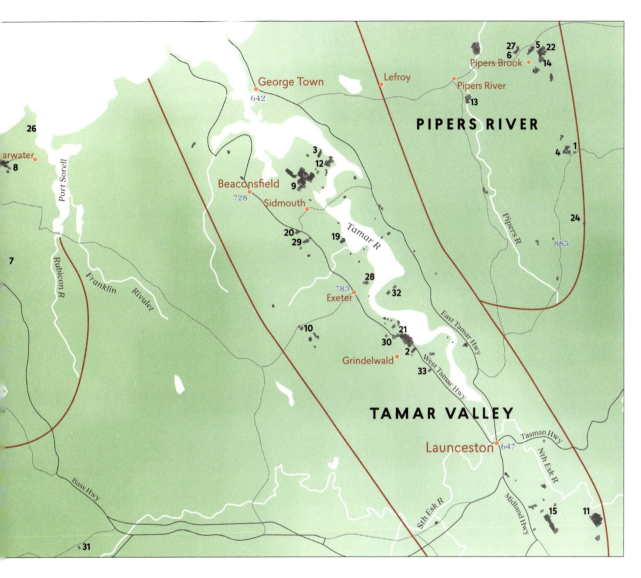

North Tasmania

1 Apogee
2 Beautiful Isle
3 Chartley Estate
4 Clover Hill
5 Dalrymple Vineyards
6 Delamere Vineyards
7 Eastford Creek Vineyard
8 Ghost Rock
9 Goaty Hill
10 Grey Sands
11 Heemskerk
12 Holm Oak
13 House of Arras/ Bay of Fires
14 Jansz Tasmania
15 Josef Chromy Wines
16 La Villa
17 Lake Barrington Estate
18 Leven Valley
19 Marion's Vineyard
20 Moores Hill
21 Moorilla St Matthias Vineyard
22 Pipers Brook Vineyard
23 Prickly Mo
24 The Ridge
25 Roland View Vineyard
26 Rubicon
27 Sinapius
28 Stoney Rise
29 Swinging Gate
30 Tamar Ridge
31 Three Willows Vineyard (Deloraine)
32 Two Tonne Tasmania
33 Velo Wines
34 White Rock Vineyard
35 Wilmot Hills

265

small islands, estuaries and peninsulas. It is home to the Coal River Valley, Derwent Valley, Huon Valley, and the more newly established growing area around the D'Entrecasteaux Channel. These growing areas all surround the city of Hobart with vineyards ranging from a 15-minute drive out of the city to about an hour. These are the most visited wine regions in Tasmania and support the most diverse grape varieties and expressions of wine produced in the GI.

The Coal River Valley begins just a 20-minute drive northeast of Hobart, extending north through the Coal River Catchment. Vineyards mainly sit to the west of the Coal River, between it and the Derwent. The valley is one of Tasmania's driest areas (and becoming drier), with a 10-year rainfall average of just under 500 millimetres per year – a decrease of nearly 10% from the previous 10-year average – and some years dipping down as low as 360 millimetres. Rainfall was previously spread evenly throughout the year, but in recent years it has become quite erratic, with some years getting over 50% of annual precipitation in winter alone.

Three areas can be carved out of the Coal River Valley: Lower, Upper and Tea Tree, though climatically they don't differ greatly. Tea Tree, slightly further from the river itself, sees a touch more rainfall and a bit more of a temperature swing – a slightly more continental climate – though there is only about 25 kilometres from one end of the Coal River Valley to the other.

Vineyard plantings throughout the Coal River Valley are diverse and range from the red and white Bordeaux varieties first planted at Stoney Vineyard, to chardonnay and pinot noir; a range of **microclimates** exist across the valley. Riesling finds a home as well, and is reared to produce everything from lean and mean Clare Valley-styled expressions, rich dessert wine, and – in between the two – harmoniously dry wines that find superb balance between acid, weight and small amounts of residual sugar.

The Derwent Valley extends inland and east from the city of Hobart, which sits at the mouth of the Derwent River. The neighbouring (and parallel) Derwent and Coal River valleys experience similar climates; however the Derwent River – the larger of the two, and often referred to as the 'River

Derwent' – has a greater effect on its region. The Derwent Valley also receives slightly more rainfall, which varies as one travels inland from the Derwent Estuary to the Upper Derwent River. Hobart, Australia's second-driest capital city, sees about 570 millimetres of rain annually, while the innermost areas of the region near Meadowbank see about 460 millimetres.

Late-winter frost is the most concerning viticultural hazard in the Derwent, especially as you move further from the estuary's maritime influence. The plentiful natural water sources throughout Tasmania – and in particular the southeast – make access to water for irrigation abundant. Like much of Tasmania, the focus here is on cool- to moderate-climate grape varieties, including pinot noir, chardonnay, riesling, sauvignon blanc, shiraz and pinot gris, as

East Coast Climate Data (°C)

	1960–1990	1991–PRESENT	2020
Heat summation/GDD	746	848	842
Annual rain/GSR	758/421	671/382	694/403
Warmest month avg. temp.	15.4	16.3	17.2

Southeast (Hobart) Climate Data (°C)

	1960–1990	1991–PRESENT	2020
Heat summation/GDD	669	797	768
Annual rain/GSR	983/524	921/459	970/480
Warmest month avg. temp.	14.7	15.7	16.7

Upper Derwent River Valley Climate Data (°C)

	1960–1990	1991–PRESENT	2020
Heat summation/GDD	632	671	609
Annual rain/GSR	803/436	777/383	876/420
Warmest month avg. temp.	14.8	15.4	15.8

Winkler Scale:

● < 850 ● 850–1111 ● 1112–1389 ● 1390–1667 ● 1668–1944 ● 1945–2222
● 2223–2700

Black truffles from Deloraine, just north of Tasmania's Central Plateau, which marks the transition point from temperate rainforest to verdant farmlands. It was here in 1999 that Australia's black truffle industry started, which has since grown into a $40 million industry, the fourth largest in the world.

well as some unusual grapes like gamay, blaufränkisch and malvasia.

The Huon Valley is yet further southwest, reaching below the 43rd parallel. The Huon River originates in the mountains to the west, meanders through Lake Pedder, then is joined by a series of other tributaries, meeting the Sunken Rock Bay before emptying into the D'Entrecasteaux Channel and then the Tasman Sea. The Huon is considerably colder and wetter than the Derwent and Coal River valleys, with **dry-farming** often possible here. In any given year, the Huon Valley might see double the rainfall of the Coal River Valley, even though a mere 60 kilometres separate the two. This increase in precipitation is largely due to kunyani/Mt Wellington keeping the southwesterly weather concentrated over the valley.

Pinot noir and chardonnay, as in many parts of Tasmania, are king here, and the region is known for its chiselled, aromatic expressions. The Huon Valley is also home to Tasmania's most vibrant apple orchards, with numerous cideries including the historic Willie Smith's, a commercially relevant farm since 1888 and an acclaimed cidery since the 1990s.

About 20 kilometres east of Huon's town of Cygnet, looking out onto the D'Entrecasteaux Channel and across from Bruny Island, lies a strip of planted vineyard land becoming known itself as the D'Entrecasteaux Channel. The eastern coast of the Channel houses the southernmost extension of the kunanyi ranges, which leave only one to two kilometres between the mountains and the water for planting.

The plantings on the D'Entrecasteaux Channel have often been lumped into the Huon Valley, though its producers are championing a separate identity. 'The Channel,' says Mewstone's Jonny Hughes, 'is strongly influenced by

Sunshine in a Bottle

While this phrase has typically been used to market Australian wine overseas as cheap and cheerful, there is a climatic legitimacy to it. Australia is a high-UV country (lots of sunlight). Take Tasmania: it's a bit colder than Champagne in terms of **heat summation**, but sees nearly 1000 more sunlight hours in an average year than its European counterpart – 1000! Although sun can bring its own problems, requiring consideration for planting and **canopy** decisions, when correctly managed, the increased sun without a corresponding increase in temperature can result in an enhancement of **phenolic ripeness** (without a corresponding increase in sugar ripeness, which results in higher alcohol). A bit jargony, but here's the bottom line: Australia's sunny disposition, when grapes are matched to their appropriate climates, results in wines that have extreme depth of flavour coupled with extreme freshness. A winning and unique combination.

The plantings on the D'Entrecasteaux Channel have often been lumped into the Huon Valley, though its producers are championing a separate identity.

water, be it from the sky or ocean.' Just shy of 1000 millimetres in rainfall each year, 'in a great pattern for growing,' says Hughes. 'Regular winter rains charge the soil, but very few harvest periods are compromised by rains.' The proximity to the water also nearly eliminates frost risk, and the air circulation reduces disease pressure.

The main challenges in the D'Entrecasteaux Channel area include compromised flowering from inclement easterly weather (causing low yields), as well as the expensiveness of land making expansion difficult. Mewstone is the champion for the Channel (though Anim has also emerged as a strong proponent of the area), producing a variety of expressions, most notably generously fruited pinot noir and powerful, nearly-dry riesling.

South Tasmania

HOW TO READ THIS MAP

Just a couple of hairs warmer than the north coast, the wine regions centred around the city of Hobart become warmer and drier as one moves clockwise from the Huon Valley. The degree of rain shadow cast across the south coast's four unofficial subregions is mapped here.

1 Altaness
2 Back Paddock Vineyard
3 Bangor
4 Bream Creek
5 Brinktop
6 Bruny Island Premium Wines
7 Cambridge Valley
8 Cathedral Rock Winery
9 Chatto
10 Clover Hill Tea Tree Vineyard
11 Darlington
12 Derwent Estate
13 Domain Simha
14 Domaine A/Stoney Vineyard
15 Elsewhere Vineyard
16 Ese Vineyard
17 Every Man & His Dog
18 Fluted Cape Vineyard
19 Frogmore Creek
20 Glaetzer-Dixon Family Winemakers
21 GlenAyr
22 Hartzview
23 Henskens Rankin
24 Heriots Point
25 Home Hill
26 Invercarron
27 Kate Hill
28 Kinvarra Estate
29 Laurel Bank
30 Mac Forbes Huon Valley Vineyard
31 Mapleton Vineyard
32 Meadowbank Estate
33 Merriworth
34 Mewstone Wines
35 Moorilla
36 Nandroya
37 Pooley Wines
38 Pooley Butcher's Hill Vineyard
39 Pressing Matters
40 Puddleduck
41 R. D'Meure
42 Resolution Vineyard
43 Ryelands
44 Sailor Seeks Horse
45 Southwood
46 Stargazer
47 Stefano Lubiana
48 Tasmanian Vintners
49 Tertini
50 Tinderbox Vineyard
51 Tolpuddle Vineyard
52 Trial Bay Estate
53 Two Bud Spur
54 Uplands
55 Winstead
56 Wobbly Boot Vineyard

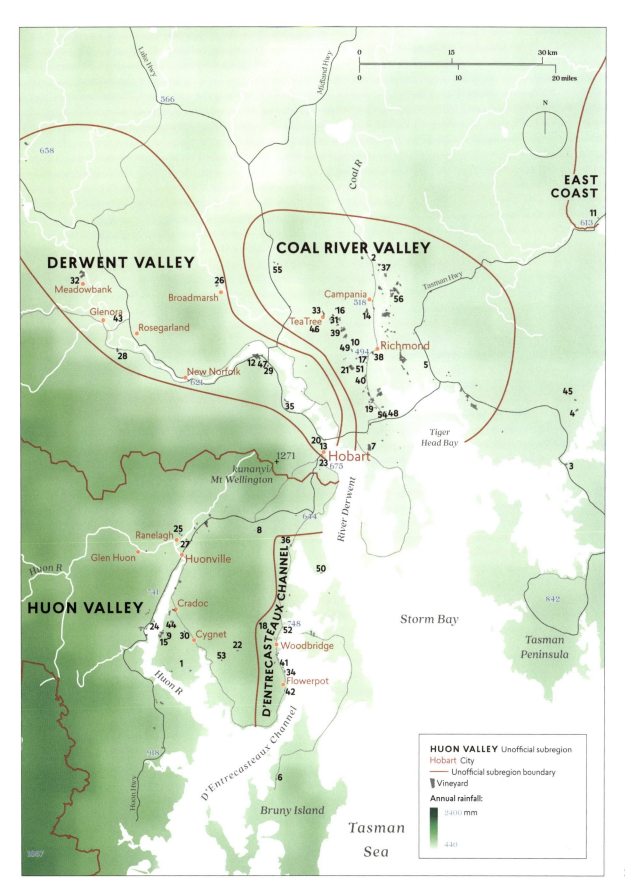

The Iron House estate vineyard sits adjacent to the Tasman Sea, along the northern end of Tasmania's east coast.

Hubbub

Tasmania is an island with a reputation. Before even thinking about wine, Tasmania has a mythology, a lore, around it. There's the Tasmanian devil: an animal that has been glorified in cartoon, with an even more interesting true story behind it. There's MONA: one of the world's most eccentric and spectacular modern art museums. There's Cape Grim: site of the cleanest air on Earth, in Tasmania's northwest corner. There's renewable energy: the island is 100% powered by it, achieving this goal in 2020, two years ahead of schedule. It's an island rich in protected natural resources, spectacular national parks and awe-inducing coastal and mountain scenery.

'The Tasmanian wine industry has been able to benefit from brand Tasmania,' says Stargazer's Samantha Connew, 'but it's also a potential liability.' The Tasmanian wine industry is hinged to this pure and premium image – rightfully so – but any blemishes to that image could threaten the stature of the wines, and its ability to fetch the prices needed to sustain itself.

Tasmania's entire production sits under one appellation: Tasmania GI. There are reasons argued for and against further delineation. An argument against more than one GI is that fruit is expensive and hard to come by, making it necessary for many Tasmanian wineries to blend from multiple subregions. Marginal growing conditions also encourage diversification to mitigate risk. The wide breadth of quality sparkling wines produced here is thanks to the assemblage of various sites across the island. A single GI allows for these producers to contribute to, and benefit from, brand Tasmania.

Others in favour of a single GI cite the global lack of understanding about Australian wine, and the desire to keep its appellations simple, and not risk diminishing brand Tasmania. Yet others argue that Tasmania does not present enough geographic differentiation from subregion to subregion to warrant multiple appellations (though this is a minority argument; most recognise the diversity).

Those in favour of further delineation – whether official or not – cite that the single GI mentality mutes the uniqueness of the different growing areas across Tasmania, keeping professional and consumer knowledge at the surface. As in any other wine region of Australia, producers are allowed to label by subregion (and many do); the names are just not officially designated or legally protected. Though some crave the legitimacy of an official appellation, most are happy to continue to label unofficially, and keep the focus on the larger brand Tasmania. (And most subregions of Tasmania couldn't even be officially delineated under law, as Wine Australia requires an annual output of 500 tonnes, which few would hit.)

With its dramatic growth and reputable brand, the concerns of Tasmania largely centre on maintenance. 'How do we maintain the prestige and the iconic nature of Tasmania,' asks Connew, 'knowing that there's going to be a lot more fruit coming on board in the next few years?' That's why some argue that moving away from brand Tasmania is the right move, as the region becomes more saturated. 'There's more and more hectarage being put into Tassie, more big companies coming down here,' Sailor Seeks Horse's Paul Lipscombe says, 'so the thought is that Tasmania as a brand could become less and less valuable ... and that fine tuning, and coming down to the Huon and the [D'Entrecasteaux] Channel, or whatever it is, becomes much more important.'

But beyond the brand recognition aspects of labelling by subregion, embracing specific locality is paramount to making the best wine: a work in progress for a relatively young region. 'Sites and varieties are more suited to some areas than others', says Dr. Edge's Peter Dredge. 'It takes decades of work to come to some pretty simple conclusions regarding suitability, which is taken for granted at times.' Jim Chatto of Chatto Wines concurs: 'If you embrace the locale, the broader climate of where you are, you have to embrace your **microclimate** as well, then a lot of the hurdles are out of your way to make the best wine.'

And making the best possible wine is certainly the focus in Tasmania – a focus not without its legitimate climatic challenges. Depending on where they're based in Tasmania, producers cite all types of woes: water access, droughts, irrigation, **dry-farming**, inconsistent flowering, frost, hail, rain, steep **aspects**, erosion, low yields, too much vigour, too little vigour ... the list goes on. But all agree that despite being the coolest state in Australia, climate change presents a huge threat.

While Australia attracted international attention in 2020 for its bushfires, the summer of 2018–2019 was the one that wreaked havoc in Tasmania. That year was the second-largest bushfire season on record for the state, with over 205,000 hectares burnt on the southern side of the island. While no vineyards were directly hit, the smoke that settled on the grapes made a vintage unfeasible for many producers. Because of Tasmania's aridity (in agriculture regions, on the east side), when there are heat spikes, the island is vulnerable to bushfires running their course. And with climate change, heat spikes and dryness are becoming more common and more extreme.

While climate change might cause some of the most marginal parts of Tasmania to just have more reliable vintages, it threatens to change the identity of the warmer parts of the island. 'Most of the rest of Tassie,' says Lipscombe, 'is probably not going to be pinot [noir] country, if some of it even is these days.' This changing landscape presents a challenge, but also a source of excitement: 'Arguably, the future best sites and subregions are yet to be discovered,' says Chatto. 'Climate change will be a significant driver of this.'

The combined challenges of dramatic growth and changing climate stand to rattle Tasmania's identity. But it has also galvanised a generation of talented, experienced and ambitious wine professionals to keep pushing for excellence. Sure, there are some tourism-focused producers, hobby vineyards and yield-pushers on the island, but the overwhelming focus in Tasmania is this question: *How can we get better?* Tasmania is still a young wine region that is evolving rapidly and settling into its position as one of the spots for premium cool-climate Australian varieties. Its current generation is not only skilled, but also increasingly collegiate, cooperative and inquisitive – focused on maintaining momentum and upward trajectory, as well as fortifying their identity against the unknowns of the future.

The combined challenges of dramatic growth and changing climate stand to rattle Tasmania's identity. But it has also galvanised a generation to keep pushing for excellence.

PRODUCERS

APOGEE

Apogee brought Andrew Pirie back to his roots, after having established the wildly successful Pipers Brook and Pirie brands. He has no desire for large-scale winemaking, focusing instead on a tiny 2-hectare site named Apogee, meaning 'highest point'. The vineyard is planted to pinot noir, pinot gris, chardonnay and pinot meunier, dedicated almost exclusively to **traditional method** sparkling wines. After a 50+ year career, Andrew is still playing the long game: his Deluxe Vintage Brut spends a mighty 45 months ageing on **lees**. *apogeetasmania.com*

BAY OF FIRES

A pursuit led by Ed Carr (see House of Arras), the mammoth BRL Hardy came to Tasmania in search of the perfect spot to make great sparkling wine. Bay of Fires weathered some years of corporate consolidation, expansion and deflation, but had a lineage of great winemakers seeing them through: Fran Austin (now at Delamere), Peter Dredge (of Dr. Edge and Meadowbank) and today, Penny Jones. Bay of Fires has always made classic wines showcasing the potential of the region, from **traditional method** sparkling wines to still wines of pinot gris, riesling, sauvignon blanc, chardonnay and pinot noir. *bayoffireswines.com.au*

BELLEBONNE

Natalie Fryer ('Nat' to most) has been repeatedly dubbed 'Australia's sparkling queen', a moniker earned by her long stint at Jansz, and confirmed by her solo project Bellebonne. Under the Bellebonne label, Natalie exclusively makes sparkling wine, classically styled to emphasise the purity of fruit coming out of Tasmania. There's a vintage chardonnay/pinot blend, a vintage rosé from 100% pinot noir, a longer-aged vintage blanc de blancs, and an affordable non-vintage rosé. Each wine represents some of the finest of its category coming out of Australia. *bellebonne.wine*

CHATTO

Jim Chatto fell in love with Tasmanian pinot noir in 1998, when he moved to the Tamar Valley to become Rosevears Estate's first winemaker. The fascination continued after relocating to the Hunter, so he and his wife Daisy began looking for their own vineyard site in Tassie. Planting began in 2007 and their first wine was released in 2013, the year Jim became chief winemaker for McWilliam's (p. 97). He produces just two pinots from their vineyard in the Huon Valley, which sell out very fast.

Jim's expert palate and trust in vineyard expression results in wines of elegance and exceptional character, quickly becoming some of Australia's favourite pinot noirs. *chattowines.com*

CLOVER HILL

Chardonnay was first planted at Clover Hill in 1986, with visions of creating Australian sparkling to rival Champagne. After the success of the inaugural vintage in 1991, pinot noir and pinot meunier were added to the vineyard. Clover Hill expanded outside of Pipers River in 2008, planting another vineyard destined for sparkling wine in the Coal River Valley. *cloverhillwines.com.au*

DALRYMPLE VINEYARDS

Bertel and Anne Sundstrup travelled to France for inspiration before planting Dalrymple in 1987. The wines are made by vigneron Peter Caldwell, who makes pinot noir from four sites across Tasmania, including their own home vineyard in Pipers River, which is also planted to sauvignon blanc. Dalrymple was purchased by the Hill Smith family (of Yalumba) in 2007. *dalrymplevineyards.com.au*

DELAMERE VINEYARDS

Delamere was one of the first vineyards to appear in the Pipers Brook area. Today it is owned and run by husband-and-wife team Shane Holloway and Fran Austin. The vineyards are densely planted, exclusively to pinot noir and chardonnay. Due to their steep slopes, everything is managed by hand. Frosty temperatures make it perfect for sparkling wine production, as well as finely woven and linear still expressions. *delamerevineyards.com.au*

DOMAINE A

George and Priscilla Park pioneered the rebirth of the Coal River Valley wine industry, planting Stoney vineyard in 1973. However, it wasn't until 1989 that Domaine A came to be, when Peter and Ruth Althaus purchased the vineyard and founded the domain with a focus on great cabernet and sauvignon blanc–based blends, echoing the wines of Bordeaux. Domaine A's are some of Australia's most age-worthy wines: spritely acid interwoven with savoury notes, structure and robust fruit are a testament to the long sunshine hours that warm their chilly slopes. On Peter's retirement in 2018, David Walsh (see Moorilla, p. 277) bought Domaine A, with winemaking taken over by Moorilla's Conor van der Reest. *domaine-a.com.au*

DR. EDGE

Peter Dredge began his foray into wine in a lab at Petaluma (Adelaide Hills, p. 355). Originally a gap-year position to make a bit of cash, Peter was bitten by the winemaking bug and switched his degree to agricultural science. During his 12 years at Petaluma, Peter was able to make wine in the Mosel and Oregon, two regions that later informed the Dr. Edge style. A position at Bay of Fires brought Peter to Tasmania, giving him a unique understanding of the breadth of fruit available across the regions. Central to the Dr. Edge stable is his range of 'compass point' pinot noirs, chardonnays and rieslings: he sources single-site expressions from the north, east and south of Tasmania from varying soil types, though the **clones** and treatment in the winery remains the same. He also uses connections made in Oregon to produce Willamette Valley pinot noir and gamay. *dr-edge.com*

 What we're drinking

*Peter Dredge of **Dr. Edge** is one of the best in the business. He makes excellent chardonnay, pinot noir — and most recently riesling — from across the island for Dr. Edge, labelled North, South and East. I feel confident in prescribing anything Dr. Edge puts into bottle. Warning: side effects are most likely to leave you with a mouth salivating for more, a happy heart and a big fat smile on your face.* – Kavita Faiella

What we're drinking

*There's no misstep when picking up a bottle of **Henskens Rankin** sparkling wine: each cuvée delivers on the promise of complexity, profundity, deliciousness and — though they're not inexpensive — absolutely on value as well. To compare with sparkling wine's mothership, a Champagne of this quality, age and small production would garner a much steeper price tag.*
– Jane Lopes

FREYCINET

Geoff and Susan Bull established the first commercial winery on the east coast of Tasmania, planting vines in 1979. Daughter Lindy and her partner Claudio Radenti have since taken the reins. Production is largely focused on pinot noir, though chardonnay, riesling and sparkling are also made. Lindy and Claudio are important personalities on the East Coast, known for their hospitality and know-how, as well as their thoughtfulness and humility.
freycinetvineyard.com.au

GLAETZER-DIXON FAMILY WINEMAKERS

Though Nick Glaetzer's family has been making wine in the Barossa for generations, he decided to try his hand at a cooler climate. Two years after starting Glaetzer-Dixon, his 2010 Mon Père shiraz won the coveted **Jimmy Watson Memorial Trophy**, the first Tasmanian wine to do so. Grapes are sourced from premium vineyards of riesling, pinot noir and shiraz, with Nick and wife Sally's own vineyard in the Tea Tree area of Coal Valley seeing its first harvest in 2022. *gdfwinemakers.com*

HEEMSKERK

The Heemskerk vineyard was planted by George Wiltshire in 1975 and has seen several changes in the intervening years, such as acquisition by Treasury Wine Estates, a collaboration with the luxury Danish designer Georg Jensen, and the launch of the Abel's Tempest label. Fruit is no longer estate grown (those original vineyards are under the Jansz banner), but sourced from top plots across the Tamar Valley, Coal River Valley, Derwent Valley and other southern sites. *heemskerk.com.au*

HENSKENS RANKIN

Henskens Rankin began in 2010 with just 2 tonnes of fruit and a determination to create excellent Tasmanian sparkling. This focus has not changed, with production remaining deliberately small and the style 'unashamedly luxury'. Frieda and David see luxury as ethical, choosing to work with regenerative growers and sourcing product and packaging in the most environmentally sound way possible. They have only released a handful of wines, including a blanc de blancs, a brut rosé and a vintage sparkling: all pinot noir and chardonnay-based, vintage-dated, hand-numbered, and all spending extended periods ageing on **lees**, often up to six years.
henskensrankin.com

HOUSE OF ARRAS

Ed Carr came to Tasmania while working for BRL Hardy in the 90s. He had started working at a winery lab in McLaren Vale and found his way into winemaking due to his studies in chemistry and microbiology. In the 1980s, Ed was a sparkling specialist for Penfolds, a time when cooler climate regions in Australia were starting to emerge. House of Arras began in 1995, with an eye on raising the quality of Australian sparkling wine. House of Arras has switched the narrative of Australian sparkling wine from being consumed young and unaged, to releasing thoroughly aged and developed styles. All House of Arras wines are matured for a minimum of

 ## What we're drinking

***House of Arras** is one of the world's great sparkling wine practitioners. Late-disgorged releases are extraordinarily complex, intense and precise, while vintage wines and judiciously blended staples under the Arras label speak fluently of cool vineyards and building detail through careful winemaking. – Mike Bennie*

Tasmania

two years and up to 14 years of **lees** ageing for the magnificent E.J. Carr Late Disgorged, the winery's flagship bottling. *houseofarras.com.au*

JANSZ TASMANIA

In 1986, Champagne house Louis Roederer collaborated with Heemskerk to plant pinot noir and chardonnay, culminating in Tasmania's first vintage sparkling wine. The tradition has continued, and Jansz is now one of the region's most recognised labels. The vineyard composition is almost the exact same as the varietal blend of the Jansz wines: chardonnay-dominant, with strong representation in pinot noir and a splash of pinot meunier. Various styles of sparkling are produced, including late-disgorged and single vineyards. Jansz is owned by South Australia's Hill-Smith family, of Yalumba fame. *jansz.com.au*

MARCO LUBIANA

Marco Lubiana is the second generation in his family to fall in love with the Tasmanian terroir (see Stefano Lubiana, p. 279). Having finished his winemaking studies in 2018, he is already making waves with high-quality pinot noir and chardonnay made from his family's Lucille vineyard in the Huon Valley. Following in his father's footsteps, Marco focuses closely on **biodynamic** practices, with certification for the vineyard expected in the next few years. *marcolubiana.com.au*

MEADOWBANK ESTATE

Gerald Ellis was ahead of his time. He was told that grapes couldn't grow in Tasmania, but he planted them anyway: vines replaced sheep in 1976 and Meadowbank was born. The estate has grown to 52 hectares of vineyard, much of it mature vines. Plantings are dominated by pinot noir, with the balance made up of riesling, sauvignon blanc, chardonnay, pinot gris, pinot meunier, shiraz and a quarter of a hectare of gamay. Meadowbank supplies grapes to some glittering names across Tasmania, as well as being crafted into benchmark wines by the excellent Peter Dredge. The wines have seen significant improvement (and success) under the stewardship of Dredge, who also uses Meadowbank fruit for his own label, Dr. Edge (p. 275). *meadowbank.com.au*

MEWSTONE WINES

Jonny and Matthew Hughes established Mewstone on a former cherry orchard in 2011, after Jonny had spent seven years as the assistant winemaker at Moorilla. Their vineyard in Flowerpot, along the D'Entrecasteaux Channel, consists mainly of pinot noir, some chardonnay and riesling, and a tiny amount of syrah. They also make a second label, Hughes and Hughes, where they focus on fruit purchased from across Tasmania. This label is also Jonny's opportunity to employ the more experimental techniques he picked up as a flying winemaker. The Mewstone wines are some of Tasmania's most precise and filigreed (especially those rieslings), making a name for the little-known D'Entrecasteaux Channel. *mewstonewines.com.au*

MOORILLA

Established in 1958, Moorilla is the second-oldest winery in Tasmania. Claudio Alcorso had purchased the 19 hectares of land on the Derwent River a decade earlier, which was home to a neglected apple and pear orchard. Alcorso set out to plant vineyards, despite being advised against it by the government, and started with 90 cuttings of riesling from South Australia. The first harvest in 1962 was wild-fermented after being foot-stomped by the entire Alcorso family. The anomalous businessman David Walsh, who lived across the river from Moorilla, bought the winery on a whim in 1995, two years after it had gone into receivership. Walsh invited winemaker Conor van der Reest to overhaul the wine program in 2007. Australia's largest private museum, MONA, was opened on site at Moorilla in 2011. The gallery acts as a magnificent setting to consume Moorilla's offering, which oscillates between traditional and unusual wine styles with great skill. *moorilla.com.au*

Anna Pooley — Pooley

well as Italy and Austria, before returning to Tasmania to redevelop Heemskerk for Treasury. The vineyards are planted to pinot noir, chardonnay, riesling, pinot grigio and syrah, with conditions at Cooinda Vale producing more delicate wines, and the long sunlight hours at Butcher's Hill yielding more robust flavours. The Pooley family is a staple of Tasmania in the strong quality of the wines as well as their communal spirit. *pooleywines.com.au*

PIPERS BROOK VINEYARD

With true determination and belief in chilly Tasmania's suitability for grapes, Andrew Pirie became Australia's first PhD in viticulture. He and his brother David planted Pipers Brook in 1974, a small vineyard that has grown into a big one with a vast impact. Now owned by Kreglinger, a Belgian company founded in 1797, the 200-hectare vineyard fuels the wines of the Pipers Brook, Ninth Island and Kreglinger brands. *kreglingerwineestates.com*

POOLEY WINES

Denis and Margaret Pooley planted 17 rows of vines on their property Cooinda Vale in 1985, a retirement project that has grown into a thriving family business. Denis and Margaret's son John and his wife Libby later purchased a property just outside Richmond, allowing the family to establish a second vineyard, Butcher's Hill. With a third generation now working at the winery, Pooley wines are entirely made by the family, from vineyard to bottle. John's son Matthew is the viticulturist, and his daughter Anna took over winemaking in 2013 with husband Justin Bubb (who together have started a separate label called Bubb & Pooley). Anna started her career working in the Barossa Valley as

SAILOR SEEKS HORSE

Gilli and Paul Lipscombe met in London, both looking for a career change. They set their sights on making wine, and with vintages in France, the US, New Zealand and Margaret River, their goal became clear: to make sensational Aussie chardonnay and pinot noir. Paul and Gilli settled on the Huon Valley and soon found a vineyard that had been planted in 2005, then abandoned.

Gilli & Paul Lipscombe — Sailor Seeks Horse

It was a hard slog to the present day, but the benefits are clear in their wines, which are scintillatingly bright, sewn through with fresh natural acid and the lightest touches of oak. *sailorseekshorse.com.au*

SINAPIUS

Purchased by Linda Morice and Vaughn Dell in 2005, the original 2 hectares of vines were planted in 1994. Dell, who planted an additional 30,000 vines by hand, passed away suddenly in 2020, leaving Linda, an occupational therapist by trade, to take over winemaking and vineyard management. The vineyard is modelled on Burgundian **high-density planting**, with multiple **clones** of pinot noir and chardonnay. While focus naturally falls on these two varieties, grüner veltliner, gamay, pinot blanc, pinot gris, gewürztraminer, riesling and new plantings of ribolla gialla are also grown. The loss of Vaughn Dell was a hard blow to Sinapius (and to the Australian wine industry as a whole), but Linda is ensuring the wines live on as a fitting tribute. *sinapius.com.au*

STARGAZER

Samantha Connew, originally from the South Island of New Zealand, was a career Aussie winemaker (with stints in the Hunter and McLaren Vale), before launching her one-woman-show Stargazer in 2013. Her vineyard, in the Tea Tree area of Coal River Valley, was originally planted in 2004, half to pinot noir and half to riesling, but she has since added more of each plus four **clones** of chardonnay. Riesling has become a star performer for Sam, finding plush expression with a finely whittled balance of residual sugar and taut acid lines. Biodiversity and revegetation are near and dear to Stargazer, with 700 bee- and bird-friendly natives planted in recent years, beekeeping on site, the regeneration of 200 olive trees, the planting of a dozen nut and mulberry trees (and a feijoa hedge) as a wind/shelterbelt, and a small flock of sheep in the vineyard for weed control. *stargazerwine.com.au*

Sam Connew, Stargazer

STEFANO LUBIANA

The Lubiana family have been making wine since the late 1800s, first in Italy, then South Australia and, beginning with Steve Lubiana, in Tasmania. Steve and his wife Monique moved to the region in 1990 to pursue their passion for sparkling wine, beginning with plantings of chardonnay and pinot noir, and later adding riesling, pinot gris, sauvignon blanc, syrah and lesser known malvasia and blaufränkisch, which are treated to their own cuvées. Stefano Lubiana is the first and only

---

JR | **What we're drinking**

Tasmania garners a ton of excitement, and Joe Holyman's suite of Tamar Valley wines proves why. His **Stoney Rise** *wines are aromatic and bright, but it's his eponymous label,* **Holyman***, that sets the bar for excellence in Tassie. His chardonnay is fine and pure, and the Project X Pinot Noir builds power and structure on top of the same purity.* — *Jonathan Ross*

biodynamically certified vineyard in Tasmania and one of the leading vineyards of the region. **slw.com.au**

STONEY RISE/HOLYMAN

The Stoney Rise label began in 2000, when Joe and Lou Holyman bottled their first wines in South Australia. In 2004, the couple landed in Tasmania and bought a 20-year-old vineyard in the Tamar Valley. Having grown up around the vineyards in the area, Joe set about pulling out cabernet sauvignon, adding pinot noir and small amounts of grüner veltliner and trousseau, and experimenting with **high-density plantings**. Aside from the Stoney Rise wines, Joe is making a **sulphur**-free pinot gris and pinot noir under his No Clothes range, with all stops pulled out for the Holyman label. The Holyman Project X Pinot Noir is made with 1 tonne of hand-selected bunches from a single block, treated to 100% new oak and 100% whole bunch. **stoneyrise.com**

TAMAR RIDGE

Tamar Ridge has seen many iterations in its nearly 30-year history. Planted in 1994, Tamar Ridge was purchased in 2003 by Gunns Limited, a timber and forestry company, which grew to own about 20% of Tasmania's vines at its peak. Brown Brothers purchased Tamar Ridge in 2010, including the labels Pirie (founded by the legendary Andrew Pirie when he was managing Tamar Ridge) and the value-brand Devil's Corner. Pirie stayed on as a consultant for a time after the Brown Brothers purchase, but is no longer associated with the brands, including his namesake one. The premium wines rely on fruit from the prized estate Kayena and Rosevears vineyards, while the Devil's Corner wines are turned out from large plots on the East Coast. **tamarridge.com.au**

TOLPUDDLE VINEYARD

The 'Tolpuddle Martyrs' were a small group of agricultural labourers sent to Australia as prisoners in the 1830s for the offence of forming a secret agrarian union. The leader of the union, George Loveless, served some of his sentence working on a property near Richmond, part of which is now Tolpuddle Vineyard. Vines were established here in 1988 by viticultural royalty Tony Jordan (Chandon Australia, p. 116) and Garry Crittenden (Crittenden Estate, p. 132) before being purchased by further wine nobility, Michael Hill Smith **MW** and Martin Shaw (Shaw+Smith, Adelaide Hills). The climate is cold and dry and the **aspect** a long, northeast-facing slope of 20 hectares planted to chardonnay and pinot noir, which go into two single-vineyard wines. While many have compared the Tolpuddle wines to some of the best out of Burgundy, Michael says what he really wants to hear is, 'this is quintessential Southern Tasmania': flinty chardonnay and savoury spiced pinot, with a balanced backbone of freshness.
tolpuddlevineyard.com

TWO TONNE TASMANIA

Ricky Evans found it difficult at first to acquire fruit to make his wines. In 2013, he was offered 2 tonnes of pinot noir, giving him both his first wine and the name of his winery. His operation is naturally bigger these days, but his approach hasn't changed: 'small parcels, big love'. Ricky's wines are pure, flavourful, juicy, modern takes on riesling, chardonnay and pinot noir, with a desire to point out the **regionality** of Tasmania. There's the EST, STH and TMV bottlings, which showcase the east coast, southern bits and Tamar Valley, respectively. And then there's The Wolf, an occasionally made whole-bunch pinot noir from the best of the Three Wishes vineyard in the Tamar Valley. **tttwine.com.au**

And don't forget ...

Anim, an advocate for creative thinking and a champion of the emerging D'Entrecasteaux Channel region, releases everything from a cider/**pét-nat** hybrid to pinot noir aged on white grape skins ... **Apsley Gorge Vineyard** is an east coast vineyard and winery where proprietor Brian Franklin draws inspiration from his annual sojourns to Burgundy ... **Brian** is the eccentric collab between Tassie institutions Joe Holyman and Peter Dredge, along with wine writer (and contributor to this book) Mike Bennie ... **Dawson James**, a collaboration between Peter Dawson and Tim James, who met while working in South Australia in the 70s, produces chardonnay and pinot noir sourced from the Derwent's Meadowbank vineyard ... **Derwent Estate** is a long-respected grower in the Derwent, whose more recent foray into winemaking has commanded attention ... **Domaine Simha** is the project of Nav Singh and Louise Radman, employing alternative vessel ageing, whole bunch and skin maceration, to put an avant-garde spin on high-end pinot noir, chardonnay, sauvignon blanc and riesling ... **Elsewhere Vineyard**, originally planted in 1984 and revived by Owen and Eve Knight, is a 10-hectare Huon Valley vineyard of pinot noir, chardonnay and Alsatian grapes ... **Frogmore Creek**, originally established in 1997 under organic principles, has expanded greatly, the star in the crown now their cellar door, restaurant and events venue in Coal River Valley ... **Ghost Rock** is one of the handful of wineries in northwest Tasmania, with plantings of pinot noir, chardonnay, pinot gris, riesling and sauvignon blanc back to 1989 ... **Grey Sands Vineyard** was planted in the Tamar Valley in the late 1980s by Bob and Rita Richter, known for their merlot, malbec and pinot noir, as well as their historical bent, with wine names like 'Byzantine' and 'Romanesque' ... **Haddow & Dineen** is a collab between Bruny Island cheesemaker Nick Haddow and ex-Josef Chromy winemaker Jeremy Dineen, releasing 'intensely Tasmanian wines' from a small vineyard on the Tamar River ... **Holm Oak** is Bec and Tim Duffy's Tamar Valley vineyard and winery, with classic Tassie plantings as well as 35-year-old cabernet franc and the only arneis in the state ... **Home Hill** is a Huon Valley staple, with pinot noir, chardonnay, pinot gris and sylvaner (!) from the Bennett family ... **Josef Chromy Wines**, just outside of Launceston, tells the story of a Czech-immigrant, who had a successful career in the Australian meat industry before opening his eponymous winery at the age of 76, and is known for its reliable wines and beautiful estate ... **Lowestoft** is an old farm, but a new brand (now part of the Fogarty Wine Group), launching premium offerings and taking out big trophies in their few years of production ... **Made by Monks**, the pint-sized label from Glaetzer-Dixon winemaker Luke Monks, was designed to add a bit of levity and eclecticism into the Tasmanian wine scene ... **Ossa Wines**, a two-vintage-deep project on the East Coast from Rod and Cecile Roberts, crafts high-end pinot noir, chardonnay, grüner and sparkling from their sprawling 600-hectare estate ... **Pirie** is the sparkling wine label founded by Andrew Pirie, of Pipers Brook and Apogee fame, turning out pristine bubbles from pinot noir and chardonnay ... **Pressing Matters** is well known for making superbly balanced Coal River riesling, with the amount of residual sugar called out on the label ... **R. D'Meure**, one of the earliest plantings on the emerging D'Entrecasteaux Channel, is a collab between Rory Duggan and Dirk Meure, with site-specific pinot noir at its heart (and a little bit of riesling and **oxidative** chardonnay) ... **Spring Vale Vineyards** is based on a Freycinet coast site that has been in the Lyne family since the 1870s, producing textured chardonnay, pinot noir, pinot gris and sauvignon blanc ... **Sonnen**, from Mewstone viticulturist Luke Andree, is a **lo-fi** label specialising in weighty riesling and pinot-syrah blends ... **Utzinger** is the union of a Tassie woman and a Swiss man (Lauren and Matthias Utzinger), who fell in love with the west side of the Tamar Valley, showing their immense potential in just a few years of production.

SOUTH AUSTRALIA

Barossa 288

Clare Valley 320

Adelaide Hills 336

McLaren Vale 356

**Coonawarra
& Wrattonbully** 380

**Other South
Australia** 398

The wine regions of South Australia occupy a small sliver of the state's total area, which is nearly 80% desert. Most of that desert is hot (naturally), with a transition to cooler semi-arid areas before meeting the influence of the coast at the southern end. South Australia's wine-growing regions include warm or hot Mediterranean climates, as well as cooler climates moderated by altitude, more southerly latitudes and coastal influences.

The Flinders and Mount Lofty ranges are the two major mountain formations in the state. They were deposited between 870 and 500 million years ago. Limestone, shale, sandstone and younger volcanics created a ridge over 1000 kilometres long, stretching from Kangaroo Island through to the top of the Flinders Ranges and, in some places, several hundred kilometres wide. These deposits, in their infancy, reached up to 14 kilometres in elevation.

So, while the Barossa and Clare valleys reach metaphoric heights as wine regions today, they once reached literal heights – up to 15,000 metres above sea level. This ridge was, at the time, the east coast of the Australian continent. The area further east was then the ocean floor. The only watery remains today are the Darling and Murray rivers, scratched across hot, red earth.

The growing areas of South Australia are starkly influenced by the climatic ebbs and flows of the **El Niño** and **La Niña** weather patterns. In the longer-lasting, fiercer **El Niño**, South Australia is dry and hot, often suffering from blazing bushfires. During **La Niña**, an increasingly shorter pattern, precipitation is at its peak and growing, though more concentrated in winter and very early spring.

Life in South Australia has historically not just endured, but thrived, in all its climates. First Nations people flourished in climates that non-Indigenous Australians might call uninhabitable. In the north, the Kokatha, Barngarla, Adnyamathanha, Kuyani and Dieri people are just a few of the many that looked after desert lands.

South Australia was the first English outpost to be established as a free colony and not a penal colony. The coastline of South Australia was visited by European whalers and sealers in the early 1800s; the coastal lands, waters and peoples of the Kaurna and Ngarrindjeri nations were the first victims of kidnapping, dispossession and murder. Approaching South Australia from the other side, Charles Sturt travelled the Murray River in a whale boat with seven other men exploring what they thought was a pathway to an inland northern sea. When they finally reached the Coorong Estuary and Lagoon – and saw the bounty of it – they immediately sought to capitalise, creating a commercial fishing industry that is still alive today.

These points of contact started the spread of viruses throughout South Australia, and by the time it was formally deemed an English colony in 1836, the Indigenous population had already decreased significantly from disease. The Murray waterway was drained and rerouted to establish the usual systems of western agriculture. Cattle and sheep pastures, wheat and other crops covered the land, drawing water and life away from Country along the river.

Though wine exports to Europe weren't massive for Australia at that time, they were an important part of South Australia's expansion in the 19th century. Before the Australian Federation was created in 1901, there were hefty tariffs applied to interstate wine sales; South Australia's blossoming wine industry didn't have access to the more populous Victorian market, which stunted growth and encouraged the

state to look to overseas markets. Exports to Britain increased four-fold by 1860 and doubled again by the mid-1870s.

South Australia's economic situation in the mid- to late 19th century was also formative in another way: because South Australia didn't have the built-in market for premium wines, the state's wineries had to focus on ways to keep their prices down. Economies of scale and mass production were built in these early days in South Australia.

While Victoria enjoyed its robust local markets in this period, South Australia would have the last laugh (or at least the next laugh). The end of the century brought **phylloxera** for Victoria and the creation of the Federation in 1901 meant the dissolution of interstate wine tariffs that favoured Victorian wine. Within five years of the Federation of Australia in 1901, South Australia's wine production per capita more than doubled (to five times the national average), while every other state's production remained stagnant or dropped.

Today, South Australia's reputation is sometimes reduced to its more famous regions, and the bold red wines they produce. But the state is home to a diverse array of wine production, traversing everything from the most filigreed sparkling wines to, yes, the brawniest of reds. It's home to some of Australia's most traditional wine-producing regions as well as some of its most avant-garde and groundbreaking. With nearly 200 years of winemaking in their blood, South Australians are preparing for the next 200 with verve and tenacity.

South Australia Geographical Indications

ZONE	REGION	SUBREGION
Barossa	Barossa Valley	
	Eden Valley	High Eden
Far North	Southern Flinders Ranges	
Fleurieu	Currency Creek	
	Kangaroo Island	
	Langhorne Creek	
	McLaren Vale	
	Southern Fleurieu	
Limestone Coast	Coonawarra	
	Mount Benson	
	Mount Gambier	
	Padthaway	
	Robe	
	Wrattonbully	
Lower Murray	Riverland	
Mount Lofty Ranges	Adelaide Hills	Lenswood
		Piccadilly Valley
	Adelaide Plains	
	Clare Valley	
The Peninsulas		

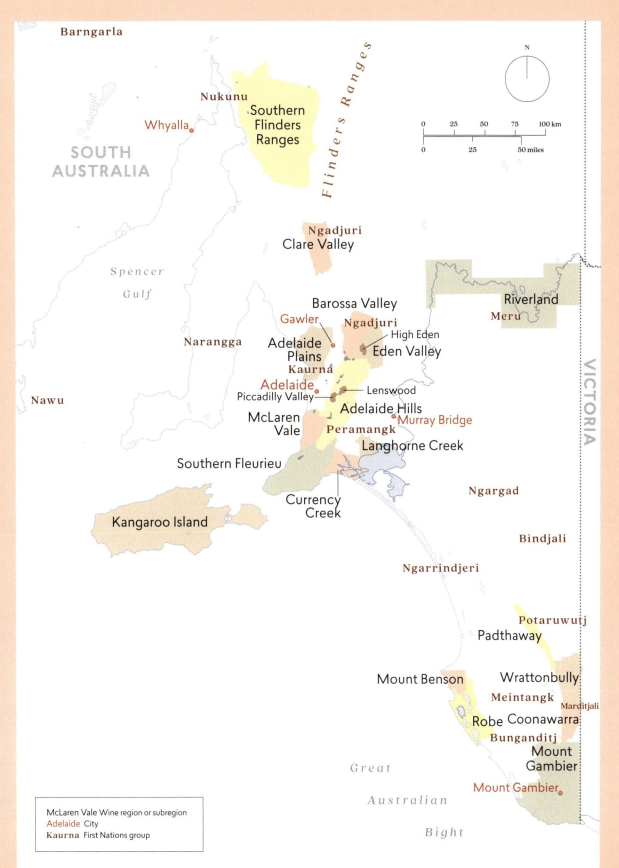

Barossa

Introduction

The Barossa. Australia's most famous and iconic wine region. A region that has become nearly synonymous with Australia's signature grape. Shiraz accounts for 60% of the plantings across the Barossa zone, which is comprised of the regional GIs of Eden Valley and Barossa Valley together, plus other small plantings outside these two. The Barossa shiraz style has been canonised as rich (sometimes containing residual sugar), alcoholic, eucalyptus-laden and American-oaked – altogether bombastic and over the top.

This style is actually a minority in the Barossa. Though big, bold reds are still the region's primary offering, there is more structure and freshness than sappiness and jamminess. American oak and strong eucalyptus are both, largely, sensations of the past. And grapes beyond shiraz are getting some attention, everything from the stalwart riesling in Eden Valley, to grenache and mourvèdre (often called mataro in parts of Australia, see p. 358) in both rich and lithe styles, to modern renditions (with ancient plantings) of grapes like muscat, semillon, carignan, graciano and cinsault.

The vineyards of the Barossa GI sit on the traditional lands of the Peramangk, Ngadjuri and Kaurna nations. The Eden Valley is Peramangk Country. The Barossa Valley, on the other side of the Barossa Range, is both Kaurna Country and Ngadjuri Country. The Peramangk people are few, and the assertion over their title claim has been slim to none. The Barossa Wine Growers' Association has an acknowledgement that speaks to all three nations, and references that most of modern-day Barossa is Kaurna Country.

All three nations have central lore – Dreamtime stories – that recognises the unique soils, lands and animals of the (now-called) Barossa region. Though, in many ways, we talk about the geography of the Barossa in similar terms to all other wine regions today – described with terms like soil type, elevation, **aspect**, temperature, slope – the geographic features of the Barossa are undoubtedly unique. These facets, and their interconnected existence, inspired the Kaurna word *pangkarra*, which describes the culmination of all that makes a place unique and informs the responsibility of land care. The Peramangk, Ngadjuri and Kaurna nations knew the singularity of this land, and the early European colonisers clearly knew it as well: of all the places to set down some of Australia's first vines, this was the one chosen.

And it is the one that has stood the test of time. Many of the oldest vines in the world are in the Barossa; it is believed to house the longest continually productive shiraz, grenache, mourvèdre, semillon and cabernet sauvignon vines. It is a region that has survived great growth and great loss, and has emerged with a vision for the future: one that centres on its great, powerful reds, but leaves room for plenty of exploration and imagination, without forgetting the solid foundation of the region's past.

Evolution of Wine

Shortly after South Australia was colonised by the British in 1836, the Barossa was 'established' by wealthy English merchant George Fife Angas. The first Surveyor General of the Barossa named the region after Andalusia's Barrosa Ridge (a clerical error yielded the spelling difference).

The story goes that Angas – who owned 11,300 hectares across the Barossa – needed help farming his land. Angas struck a deal to bring out hundreds of Silesian Lutherans, who were escaping religious persecution in their homeland. The first boat arrived in 1842. This group of immigrants have had an indelible impact on the region's food, culture and – of course – wine.

But the first noted vineyard comes not from a Silesian immigrant, but rather, an English one. Dorset brewer Samuel Smith moved his wife and five children to the Barossa in 1847 and started working for Angas. Noticing the region's beneficial grape-growing climate (in contrast to his chilly and wet homeland), he bought 30 hectares from Angas and made quick work of planting his first vineyard in 1849: a vineyard that would come to be known as Yalumba.

Johann Gramp was another early vintner. Gramp was a Bavarian farmer who settled in the Barossa Valley in 1847, right on the banks of a small tributary creek of the North Para River: Jacob's Creek. He, like Smith, noticed the region's suitability for the vine. Gramp sent a message back to Germany, asking for riesling cuttings to be sent over, and soon had his own vineyards planted, which continued to expand over the rest of the century. The Gramp family founded Orlando Wines in 1874 (the Orlando brand Jacob's Creek would not debut until the 1973 vintage).

The year 1847 was a big one for the region. Joseph Gilbert, who arrived from England in 1839, planted a 0.4-hectare vineyard high up in the Barossa Range (today's Eden Valley). He named the property Pewsey Vale after his home in the Vale of Pewsey in Wiltshire. This was the Eden Valley's first established vineyard, and one of Australia's first high-altitude, cool-climate sites. The initial plantings were shiraz, cabernet sauvignon, verdelho, gouais and riesling – the last of which would go on to become famous for the site and region.

Meanwhile, back on the west side of the Barossa Range, Joseph and Johanna Seppelt were two of the Silesian immigrants who found their way to the Barossa Valley, and by 1851, had formed Seppeltsfield Estate. Joseph purchased 77 hectares of land outside of Tanunda, in a

Yalumba cooper Corey Roehr burns the bung hole of a new French oak **barrique**. The Yalumba Cooperage has been continually operating since 1890 and is the only working winery cooperage in Australia.

township that has come to bear the Seppeltsfield name. The family originally planned to farm tobacco and wheat, but by 1867, the grape-growing and winemaking vision was clear. This was the year that the beginnings of the Seppeltsfield estate and cellars were constructed.

Joseph's son Benno took the helm of the estate the next year, and made several important decisions in the coming decade: he expanded the winery's cellar in 1875, he erected a distillery in 1877, and in 1878 he laid down two barrels of **fortified wine** with the intention of aging them for 100 years. (The estate debuted their first 100 Year Vintage Para Tawny in 1978 and has released the wine every vintage since – perhaps Australia's greatest and most famous vinous feat.)

Johann Christian Henschke was also an early Silesian immigrant, buying land in Krondorf (Barossa Valley) and Keyneton (Eden Valley). By the early 1860s, Henschke had planted vineyards, and his first commercial release of wine was in 1868: a riesling and a shiraz. Also in 1860, the first vines were planted at the Hill of Grace site, which would come under Henschke ownership in the 1890s, and prove to be one of Australia's most significant vineyards.

By the 1890s, dozens of wineries had been established, including several more of importance: William and son Edward Salter's Saltram, which helped further the success of **fortified wines** in the Barossa (and also employed a travelling salesman, Alfred Birks, who would become famous in the Clare Valley); Château Tanunda was born in 1890,

quickly becoming one of the most productive estates in the area. And the original names continued to expand production and plantings as well, with Pewsey Vale, Orlando, Yalumba, Seppelt and Henschke all growing and thriving.

The end of the 19th century required some ingenuity for the Barossa, though. Without built-in domestic markets – Adelaide was (and is) still small compared to Sydney and Melbourne – the wineries of the Barossa embraced exports, marketing and the industrial revolution. South Australia learned early that it wasn't just about the quality of the wine, but if you could sell it – an idea that the Barossa in particular picked up and ran with. By the turn of the century, Barossa was the biggest-producing area in South Australia, with Seppelt, Orlando, Château Tanunda and Yalumba all turning out considerable amounts of wine.

In 1901, the conditions that had demanded ingenuity of South Australians shifted. This was the year that the Federation of Australia was formed, uniting the colonies of New South Wales, Victoria, South Australia, Western Australia, Tasmania and Queensland. This meant the dissolution of the steep interstate tariffs that had been so punitive on South Australia – a state that had lots of wine but fewer people to sell it to.

By the turn of the century, **phylloxera** had also taken its toll on parts of Victoria and New South Wales. South Australia had the luxury of distance, protecting itself via appropriate quarantines before the root louse could reach its borders. To this day the state remains famously

The red clay soils of Torbreck's Hillside vineyard in Lyndoch, at the southern end of the Barossa Valley.

fastidious, maintaining strict biological quarantine laws that have prevented **phylloxera** from ever taking root in its vineyards.

With these newfound advantages, South Australia was able to flourish, both domestically and through exports. And with its warm climates to produce **fortified wines**, which were becoming increasingly popular, South Australia was poised to become the most important player in Australian wine. Within a couple of years, this prophecy was proven: by 1905, Thomas Hardy & Sons (in McLaren Vale, p. 374), Penfolds and Seppelt had all established offices in cities as far and wide as Sydney, Melbourne, Fremantle and Brisbane.

With these names, the first national wine brands were born. Purchasing across regions became common, with Penfolds in particular flexing in this respect. The Magill Estate, now often referred to as the spiritual home of Penfolds, sits in the eastern foothills of Adelaide, but Penfolds quickly became a figurehead for the Barossa Valley when they built a winery and distillery in Nuriootpa in 1911. In 1912, Penfolds purchased Minchinbury, a vineyard on the outskirts of Sydney, which had been producing renowned sparkling wines under the guidance of Leo Buring.

South Australia, and the Barossa Valley in particular, was experiencing a boom. World War I brought some hiccups: the loss of exports to Europe during the war, a short-lived anti-German sentiment in Australia (that saw some place names in the Barossa changed), and a quirky 'patriotic prohibitionist movement' that contended Australia's drinking culture had somehow interfered with Britain's ability to fully perform in the war. But the Barossa endured, and even grew.

Post-war, incentives were offered both at home and in Britain: in Australia, a generous bounty for domestic winemakers to export **fortified wine** was instated; and abroad, the UK's Imperial Preference favoured Australian wine. Plantings soared. Barossa, by 1927, accounted for 60% of Australia's wine. Oversaturation was the word of the day, with both a surplus of wine hitting Europe, and a surplus of vines in the Australian ground.

It was only a matter of time before oversupply got the better of the Barossa – the first of many seasons of expand and contract for the region. Soon the Australian Wine Board issued the warning: 'Owing to a dangerous position arising from overproduction, growers are warned against any further planting of wine grapes.' Combined with the government beginning to fix prices for grapes to avoid deflation, and the concurrent reduction of **fortified** export bounties, growers and winemakers were put in a perilous position.

Time is often the only healer for ailments such as these, and in the case of Barossa's recovery, it indeed took until the late 1930s – and formal or informal unionisation on the part of both growers and winemakers – for a state of balance to be recovered.

Tragedy soon struck though: in October 1938, the federal government in Canberra called a meeting for prominent members of the wine industry. Tom Mayfield Hardy, Sidney Hill-Smith and Hugo Gramp – the third-generation leaders of Thomas Hardy & Sons, Yalumba and Orlando, respectively – flew together on the *Kyeema*, a plane whose name would not have been remembered had it not crashed en route to the meeting. In one fell swoop, much of South Australia's wine leadership was gone.

World War II triggered a similar slump in exports to Europe as the first, but a huge increase in domestic drinking. Australians consumed 14.5 million litres of wine in 1939, and by 1944 that number had risen to 37 million litres. Tastes were changing as well, both at home and abroad. The sweet **fortified wines** of the past were beginning to plateau, and interest in **table wine** (i.e. dry, non-**fortified wines**) started to remerge. Post-war European immigration compounded this, bringing cultures to Australia who viewed wine as an important part of the meal, and dining as an important part of life.

At the end of the 1940s and into the 1950s, the Barossa started to look to the great dry reds of Europe for inspiration, in search of an ageable fine wine that would be unique to the region. Max Schubert, the chief winemaker for Penfolds, travelled to Europe in 1950 to study winemaking in France and Portugal, and emerged with the idea of 'producing an Australian red wine capable of staying alive for a minimum of 20 years and comparable with those of Bordeaux', according to Penfolds' book *Rewards of Patience*.

Schubert returned to South Australia, confident in the region's ability to produce such a wine: 'I elected to use Hermitage or Shiraz only (which was in plentiful supply) – knowing full well that if I was careful enough in the choice of area and vineyard and coupled that with the correct production procedure I would be able to make the type and style of wine I wanted.'

The choice of 'area and vineyard' for the first experimental 1951 Grange (called Grange Hermitage at the time), was the Magill Estate in the outskirts of Adelaide and a private vineyard 'some distance south' of the city. The 'correct production procedure' Schubert mentioned involved harvesting grapes between exactly 11.5° and 12° baumé and 6.5 and 7 grams per litre total acidity, temperature-controlled and yeast-inoculated fermentation, submersive cap-management, and – perhaps most importantly – the use of five new, untreated, American oak hogsheads. In his words: 'The objective was to produce a big full-bodied wine containing maximum extraction of all components in the grape material used.'

Schubert produced Grange each year after, meticulously tucking the wines away to age in cask for 18 months, then years in bottle. By 1956, the powers-that-be at Penfolds started to get antsy to sample (and sell) this investment. A tasting was arranged that year of the vintages 1951 through 1956, first for a select group of tastemakers in Sydney, followed by a group of professionals back home in Adelaide. The results were effusive, but not in the way Schubert had hoped: everyone hated the wines.

The Penfolds board instructed Schubert to stop making the wine before the 1957 vintage. Schubert described it as 'Grange's darkest hour', but he maintained his conviction in the wine. Though he couldn't buy new oak barrels without raising alarm bells, he continued to make small amounts of Grange throughout the end of the 1950s, unbeknown to Penfolds, and ageing it in used oak from previous vintages.

Why did everyone hate the wines?

European immigration compounded this emergence of table wines, bringing cultures to Australia who viewed wine as an important part of the meal, and dining as an important part of life.

The grenache vine is one of the few that, with age, can support itself without any **trellising**. Lovingly referred to as a **bush vine**, this plant's roots dig deep into the red clay of Seppeltsfield's Great Terraced vineyard, which was first planted in 1855 in the western flank of the Barossa Valley.

According to Peter Gago, Penfolds' chief winemaker since 2002: 'Upon release, most commented that the Grange style was alien to that of the day ... a quite different, full-bodied wine matured in 100% new American oak 300-litre hogsheads ... certainly not befitting that of the "Claret" or "Burgundy" red-wine monikers of 1950s Australia ... wines that were invariably matured in large, seasoned oak.'

The style that did capture national attention at the time was Orlando's Barossa Pearl. Colin Gramp wagered on the success of a new style of wine, based on Germany's Perlwein: a lightly sweet, low-alcohol sparkling wine that debuted at the Melbourne Olympics in 1956. The style became wildly popular and inspired other similar expressions to emerge across the nation; perhaps its charm was in the contrast to the thick, rich styles of **fortified wine** that had been popular (while still cushioning the transition with a bit of sweetness). The Barossa Pearl style became so popular, specifically among young people, that the Barossa Grape & Wine Association cites it as the real reason for the 1950s baby boom.

Back in the Penfolds cellars, though, the tide was not out on Schubert for too long: prior to the 1960 vintage, the board at Penfolds reinstated the production of Grange. 'My theory has always been,' says Gago, 'that Max showed his new Grange blend(s) too early – usually not long-bottled, without the necessary bottle maturation that Grange mandates.' Gago details how the 1955 Grange wowed at the 1962 Sydney Wine Show, changing perceptions, liberating earlier 'hidden Granges' and 'inducing adequate bottle maturation pre-release.' Grange was back in action, and Schubert's dogged and defiant refusal to ever cease its production created an unbroken lineage of the wine dating back to 1951.

And the folks at Penfolds weren't the only ones in the area crafting ageable red wines. In the 1950s, Henschke began making their two premium single-vineyard shiraz: Mount Edelstone (first vintage 1952) and Hill of Grace (first vintage 1958), which have gone on to become two of the most acclaimed Australian wines. These were also the wines that put the idea of single-vineyard bottlings on the map – a concept that had previously carried little significance.

These early pioneers of red **table wine** created a huge boom for the style in the 1960s. When prime minister Robert Menzies declared the 1961 Yalumba Galway Claret the greatest wine he'd ever had, it set off a national craze for the style, which eventually led to Yalumba naming a Coonawarra vineyard and wine 'The Menzies'. Lindeman's, the dominant Hunter Valley producer, arrived in the Barossa in the

1960s, purchasing Leo Buring, and making riesling as well as shiraz. Peter Lehmann was the winemaker at Saltram in the 1960s, helping to further develop the Barossa red. And Wolf Blass started his eponymous label in the 1960s, fashioning red wine blended from multiple regions and aged in new French oak, contributing to the infatuation with the style.

The 1970s saw this red wine fever turn toward white, with technological innovations like fine filtration, stainless steel tanks, centrifuge filters, carbon dioxide blanketing and better refrigeration supporting the latter. The red wine style that the Barossa had worked so hard to cultivate was in commercial peril, with a fervent rush toward white grape plantings. While some of this energy was misplaced (think: chardonnay, which is not the best fit for Barossa's climate), some of it was well founded. Eden Valley riesling flourished in this time, especially those produced by the likes of Leo Buring, Orlando and Pewsey Vale (which had been reinvigorated in the 1960s by the Hill-Smith family of Yalumba after lying dormant for over 30 years).

Domestic and multinational consolidation hit the Barossa in these years, with such producers as Orlando, Lindeman's, Saltram and Penfolds selling off to larger wine companies. The result was a greater focus on mass production, and far less loyalty to Barossa growers – without the label integrity laws of today, purchased grapes from less expensive regions were still labelled as Barossa.

With the upswing of white wine, and in particular chardonnay, new vines were hurriedly planted during the 1970s and early 1980s. A glut of wine grapes was loosed upon South Australia, and in 1985, the government reacted.

The infamous Vine Pull Scheme subsidised the removal of vines throughout South Australia, with the idea to encourage unsuccessful growers to grub up vines and leave the industry entirely. But the result was considerably more sinister, with some of the Barossa's oldest shiraz and grenache vines pulled out of the ground.

This was a bleak time for the Barossa, but it encouraged what the rest of Australia had seen in the 1970s: a real movement toward boutique wineries that focused on local fruit. Peter Lehmann had started this trend even before the Vine Pull Scheme, leaving Saltram to start his eponymous winery in 1980. It bore the name Masterson for two years – so named for Sky Masterson from *Guys and Dolls*, a compulsive gambler, reflecting the gamble Lehmann believed he was taking. Lehmann has been called 'the man who saved the Barossa Valley', and indeed, Lehmann's willingness to pay growers, not supplant local grapes with cheaper fruit from other regions, and to stake his success on the name Barossa was, in a word, monumental.

Others followed this approach: The Ashmead family purchased a derelict vineyard in 1980 and made the first Elderton wines in 1982; Robert O'Callaghan planted vines in the 1970s and made his first vintage of Rockford Wines in 1984; Charles Melton launched in 1984 as well, with his founding principles grounded in old-vine Barossa; also in 1984, Greenock Creek was founded; and Grant Burge set up his eponymous winery in 1988.

Corporate machinations continued through the 1980s and 1990s, but a new energy had emerged, one that was once again heavily invested in brand Barossa, and the styles of wine that best suited the region. To cap off this period

Eucalyptus-flavoured Wine

Australian wine is often thought of as having a strong eucalyptus flavour, due to the abundance of eucalypt trees and shrubs throughout the landscape. Their oils are airborne and can influence the taste of a finished wine, such as in the Barossa and Coonawarra regions. In small amounts, this flavour can be seen as an element of the Australian terroir, as **garrigue** vegetation is to southern France. But if a single leaf or piece of eucalyptus bark physically makes its way into a ferment, the flavour can become overwhelming. This is somewhat rare today: most wineries agree that a strong eucalyptus flavour is undesirable and take measures to preclude it, including hand harvesting when a vineyard is close to eucalyptus trees (mechanical harvesters can grab more than is desired), careful sorting of grapes, and less **stem inclusion** when oils are present.

of growth and regional pride: the Barossa GI zone was established in 1997, with its two GI regions Barossa Valley and Eden Valley. This was a unifying moment for the Barossa, as Yalumba chief winemaker Louisa Rose recounts: 'The drawing of the Barossa GI boundary, when that happened, was incredibly motivating for the Barossa grape and wine community. It was a very inclusive process, and it drew people together. All the work that went into it made people incredibly proud of what the Barossa was.'

Exports also rebounded in the 1990s: by the end of the decade, the surplus was a thing of the past and no longer were vines pulled out with abandon. (Except, perhaps, for chardonnay, as growers realised its unsuitability for the Barossa Valley. Semillon, though more by reputation than volume, became the favoured white grape for the region.) With the increase in prices fetched for grapes, growers were able to focus on quality and concentration rather than yields. Barossa settled into the style it's become famous for: the full-bodied shiraz, often aged in American oak.

The old guard was leading the luxury wine charge, with Penfolds Grange (as well as a number of other Penfolds wines, particularly Bin 707 Cabernet Sauvignon) and Henschke's Mount Edelston and Hill of Grace continuing to garner praise and command high prices. Grange and Hill of Grace topped the **Langton's Classification** from its inception in 1990, and have consistently held their spots since. *Wine Spectator* named Grange its Wine of the Year in 1995 (for the 1990 vintage), the first time a wine from outside California or France had achieved the honour.

But the 1990s also introduced to the Barossa several new wineries that would propel the region – in terms of prices, scores and international renown. Chris Ringland, while working at Rockford, had his first vintage of Three Rivers Shiraz in 1989. In 1997, the first Torbreck wine was released: the 1995 vintage RunRig Shiraz. David Powell had started Torbreck, named after a Scottish forest where he was once a lumberjack, by share-cropping old-vine vineyards across the Barossa to gain experience and capital (also while working for Robert O'Callaghan at Rockford).

Barossa became a darling of Robert Parker's *Wine Advocate*, with high scores and effusive verbiage for the likes of Penfolds, Henschke, Greenock Creek, Torbreck, Chris Ringland and The Standish Wine Company (founded in 1999 by Dan Standish, who had been a winemaker at Torbreck). Prices soared, with the top releases from the aforementioned producers retailing for hundreds of dollars per bottle. By the early 2000s, at home as well as abroad, the Barossa had ascended as the headliner of Australian wine regions. Especially in the United States, the richest, heaviest, oakiest (and most expensive) Barossa shiraz wines were in high demand.

Another crash was in store for the Barossa though. With the global financial crisis of 2007–2008, eager buyers stopped stocking their cellars, investors ceased speculation, and the bottom fell out of grape prices in the region (which, at their peak, had reached over AUD $10,000/tonne). A similar impulse, though, took hold in the region as had in the dark days of the mid-1980s. The Barossa, once again, looked inward to the integrity and quality of the grapes to stabilise the region. Artifact was toned down: French oak replaced American, ripeness was subdued (slightly), and the overt eucalyptus quality, which had hitherto defined the wines of the Barossa, was more actively avoided. Commercial styles – that had become caricatures of themselves – were eschewed in favour of a more subtle and authentic representation of place.

This period also prompted a focus on preserving and promoting the old vines of the region. In 2009, the Barossa Old Vine Charter was developed to classify vines by their age. An 'old vine' was anything over 35 years in age, 'survivor vines' must be at least 70, 'centenarian vines' are (you guessed it) over 100 years old, and if a vine reaches 125 years in age, it is considered an 'ancestor'. This classification has become a great marketing tool to describe an otherwise nebulous concept, often used on Barossa wine labels or in tasting notes to give credit to the ancient vines of the region.

Today, the Barossa is as diverse and exciting a region as any. The stalwart shiraz that made the region famous is still king. The styles are diverse; the syrupy and intensely alcoholic versions of the past are increasingly rare. The classic wines are still bold, and oftentimes laced with ample

French oak, but there is a less bombastic character in general. Other producers – Eperosa, Sami-Odi, Sigurd and Spinifex come to mind – don't totally eschew ripeness, but are interested in presenting a more savoury and structured edge to shiraz, often without the contribution of new oak. Still others, Tom Shobbrook being the most notable, are framing Barossa shiraz in a nearly-**nouveau** style – early picked, **carbonic** and turbid.

A focus on grenache is an exciting development for the Barossa, where the grape has often played second fiddle to the favoured shiraz. Cirillo, in possession of the oldest grenache vines in the world, makes their 1850 bottling from these vines (actually planted in 1848), as well as an entry level grenache called Vincent, made from its 'younger' vines – which are still 100 years old. Yalumba has long been a champion of grenache, with excellent bottlings ranging from their humble **Bush Vine** Grenache up to their Tri-Centenary (from vines planted in 1889). Seppeltsfield has joined the grenache game too, with a powerful debut in 2019 from their Great Terraced vineyard, originally planted in 1855.

Stylistically, grenache has enjoyed a favourable change over recent years. In Barossa's heyday of overripe and oaky styles of shiraz, grenache was often mangled to resemble these wines: bombastic, late-picked (and super alcoholic), overextracted and purple, with copious oak. In the last 10–15 years there has been a definitive paradigm shift, with vintners using a lighter hand toward the production of grenache. The resulting wines are red-fruited and transparent, delicate and savoury; the trope of the 'pinosity' of grenache in the Barossa is alive and well.

Riesling, over in the Eden Valley, is still the signature grape of the region. Pewsey Vale vineyard, under the care of the Hill-Smith family, continues to release powerful, dry styles of riesling (such as its famed The Contours), but is also experimenting with lighter, off-dry versions to great success. Rieslings from Leo Buring and Orlando are still on the market, but a younger generation has taken up the torch too: wineries such as Rieslingfreak, Worlds Apart and Edenflo are making Eden Valley riesling, often with

In the last 10–15 years there has been a definitive paradigm shift, with vintners using a lighter hand toward the production of grenache.

unique takes on the style, such as barrel ferments, skin-contact and residual sugar.

This younger generation has offered a fresh take on the Barossa, but it embraces the unique character of the region instead of obscuring it. Take Abel Gibson at Ruggabellus, working with old-vine semillon, muscat and riesling to create skin-contact whites of precision and power; or Andy Cummins of Rasa, embracing the Barossa's warm climate to craft a rich rosé of old-vine cinsault, grenache, mourvédre and riesling; or Wayne Ahrens of Smallfry, the custodian of a sandy plot of **biodynamic** grenache and cinsault, among others, which is beloved across the region.

The Barossa is a region defined by a magical mix of history and innovation, with a common commitment to express the unique character of the land. There are different approaches to how this expression is best achieved, but this just adds to the dynamism of the region. The Barossa continues to fire on its classic cylinders – but at the same time, it may just be one of the more exciting and novel regions in Australia.

Lay of the Land

Today, there are many sophisticated tools used to map the precise qualities of a wine-growing region: soil qualities (**nutrient load, water-holding capacity**), **aspect**, slope, elevation, **heat summation** and so on. But in the first half of the 19th century, when the Barossa was first planted, the metrics were much more rudimentary: sites were planted by creeks, on sandy loam over clay, where the red gumtrees lived.

This equation for early vineyard success is noted by both Prue Henschke and Dylan Grigg, viticulturists from both sides of the region. The Barossa zone is bisected by the Barossa Range, a small section of the Southern Mount Lofty Ranges, with the Barossa Valley GI on their west side and the Eden Valley GI to the east. The two are often thought about as being distinct entities – and, indeed, their differences are notable – but both regions' early plantings were undertaken based on this logic: find a spot where other perennial plants set down roots and where water is available, and the vines will thrive. This logic proved sound, with some of these original Barossa plantings still producing fruit to this day.

There are some useful generalisations to be made about the differences between the Barossa and Eden valleys. West of the Barossa Range lies the Barossa Valley, where 85% of the delimited area sits below 350 metres in elevation, with 60% of the GIs plantings below 280 metres, and only 2% sitting at or above 350 metres. Conversely, on the eastern side of the range, over 95% of the plantings sit at or above 350 metres in the Eden Valley. Nothing is planted below 280 metres.

In both the Barossa and Eden valleys, where a vineyard sits in relation to the Barossa Range (and the resulting elevation), plays a major role in the resulting climate, soils and therefore wines.

The variation of climate across the entire zone ranges from a Region 1b on the **Winkler Scale** in the highest elevation areas of the Eden Valley (specifically at Pewsey Vale in High Eden) to a Region 4 in the Valley's south and western extremes of the Barossa, in towns like Rosedale and Gomersal, and the southwestern end of Seppeltsfield and Lyndoch.

Generally, the elevated Eden Valley GI, is noticeably cooler than the Barossa Valley: days and nights in the Eden Valley are much cooler, with average daytime temperatures 2–3°C lower in the Eden and night-time temperatures 5–7°C lower.

The Eden is more humid (44% to Barossa Valley's 39%), which relates to greater soil moisture retention and slower groundwater evaporation. And while the average growing season humidity is higher in the Eden Valley, precipitation is less predictable. The Eden Valley typically sees more annual rainfall than the Barossa Valley, with both seeing about 60% of it in the winter due to their Mediterranean climate patterns. However, in drought years like the 2020 vintage, the Eden Valley received only 386 millimetres of annual rainfall compared to the Barossa's 420 millimetres, due to its greater distance from the moderating coast. But the average growing season rainfall is 50% higher in the Eden Valley, 240 millimetres compared to 160 millimetres.

Barossa Valley Viticultural Footprint

Total delimited area (km²)	590
Total planted area (hectares)	11,609
% of delimited area planted	19.680%
Total elevation range	112–596 masl
Elevation range of plantings	120–450 masl
Number of producers (Barossa total)	174

Barossa Valley Climate Data (°C)

	1960–1990	1991–PRESENT	2020
Heat summation/GDD	● 1775	● 1855	● 1862
Annual rain/GSR	533/206	539/215	420/167
Warmest month avg. temp.	21.4	22	21.6

Winkler Scale:

● 850–1111 ● 1112–1389 ● 1390–1667 ● 1668–1944 ● 1945–2222 ● 2223–2700

The Eden Valley has 20% of the plantings of the Barossa Valley – 2169 hectares compared to 11,609 – though the total delimited area is very similar. The Barossa Valley is Australia's second-most densely planted GI, with 20% of its total area under vine. White grapes account for almost half the harvest in the Eden Valley (4300 of 9700 tonnes in 2021), with about only 7% (4000 of 60,000 tonnes in 2021) of the harvest in the Barossa Valley.

In 2008, the Barossa Grape & Wine Association, South Australia's state government, and leading soil scientists, viticulturists and wine critics launched the Barossa Grounds initiative, to better understand the unique **microclimates** of the Barossa – both Eden and Barossa Valleys. Today, more than 80 sites have been analysed in terms of soil types (and corresponding **water-holding capacity**), surface geology, slope, **aspect**, temperature, rainfall and elevation. This analysis has coincided with numerous blind tastings of shiraz to combine geographic factors with more subjective (but equally, if not more, important) sensory data collection.

The conclusion the project came to was that the Barossa zone can be split into four parts, based on this sensory analysis, which are not only distinct in their elevation, climate and soils, but also result in demonstrable differences in the taste of shiraz. One of these four areas is the Eden Valley GI; the other three are portions of the Barossa Valley GI labelled 'Southern Grounds', 'Central Grounds' and 'Northern Grounds'. This framework gives us a lens to explore the regions in more detail, beyond the generalisations of Barossa Valley versus Eden Valley.

The Eden Valley's altitude is noted as being between 219–632 metres above sea level, though vineyards do not exceed the 600-metre threshold. The Barossa Grounds tasting profile for the shiraz of Eden Valley is described as 'more elegant, perfumed, linear-shaped wine', as well as noting the red-fruited character, savoury notes and 'dusty, powdery' tannins.

Despite its unique expression, Eden Valley shiraz has historically not been labelled as such; it's more common to see the wines being labelled as the Barossa (zone), probably to capitalise on the more famous region name for shiraz. Eden Valley Shiraz, aside from the efforts of Henschke, Peter Lehmann and Poonawatta, has had less commercial presence, historically. The bottling of Eden Valley-specific shiraz is a newer trend, with producers like Sons of Eden, Powell and Sons, Eperosa, Massena, Thistledown, Yalumba, Spinifex, Dandelion and Heirloom participating in this movement.

The Eden Valley is often spoken about as having thinner, poorer soils. Prue Henschke, the viticulturist for her family's important and historic estate, says this is not exactly true. 'Eden Valley's got lighter soils,' she says. 'From Kaiserstuhl down, you go into granitic sand – so that would be the low-nutrient, low-water-holding type soil – but that stops at a certain point.' After that, the soils move into a variety of sandy loams, prismatic clays and sandstone rocks, all moderately deep and with better water supply than up on the peak.

The Eden Valley is not explored in a more detailed fashion in the Barossa Grounds conclusions, as the focus is on shiraz, and much

Eden Valley Viticultural Footprint

Total delimited area (km²)	600
Total planted area (hectares)	2169
% of delimited area planted	3.62%
Total elevation range	219–632 masl
Elevation range of plantings	280–545 masl
Number of producers (Barossa total)	174

Eden Valley Climate Data (°C)

	1960–1990	1991–PRESENT	2020
Heat summation/GDD	● 1531	● 1730	● 1744
Annual rain/GSR	606/230	541/210	386/144
Warmest month avg. temp.	20.1	21.4	21.1

Winkler Scale:

● 850–1111 ● 1112–1389 ● 1390–1667 ● 1668–1944 ● 1945–2222 ● 2223–2700

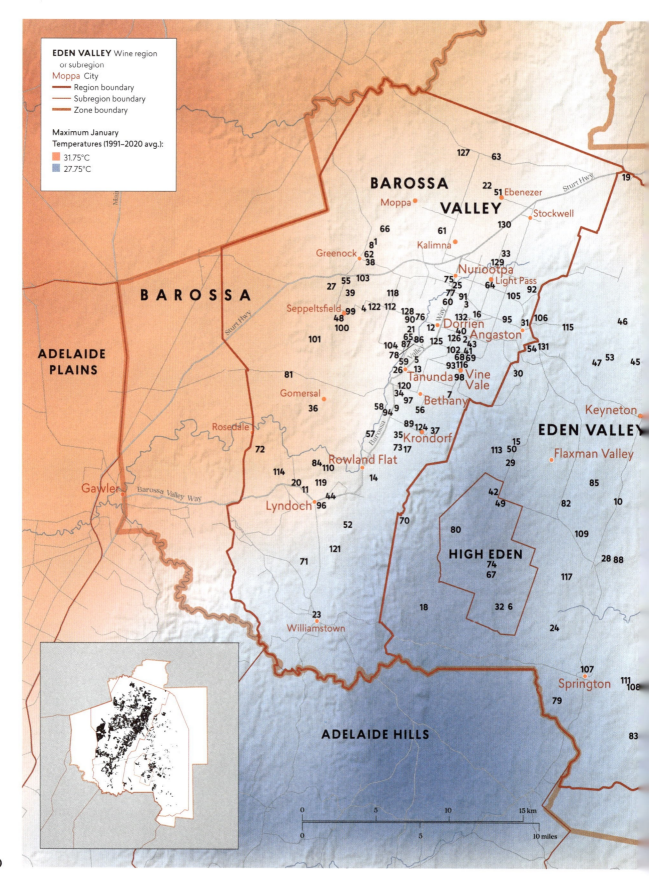

Barossa

HOW TO READ THIS MAP

Spanning both the Eden and Barossa valleys, this Barossa Zone map shows the variation in temperature across the GI. The coolest areas sit at the highest elevation points, with the Barossa Range drawing the boundary between both valleys and signifying a broad change in elevation and temperatures. The density of vineyards in the Barossa is highlighted in the small map at bottom left.

1. Alkina
2. An Approach to Relaxation
3. Atze's Corner
4. Barossa Valley Estate
5. Basedow of Barossa
6. Berton Vineyard
7. Bethany Wines
8. Binder-Mitchell
9. Biscay Wines
10. Blackets Vineyard
11. Burge Family Winemakers
12. Chateau Dorrien
13. Château Tanunda
14. Chateau Yaldara
15. Chris Ringland
16. Cirillo
17. Clancy Fuller
18. Corryton Park Vineyard
19. Craneford
20. Creed of Barossa
21. David Franz
22. Dimchurch Vineyard
23. Domain Day
24. Eden Hall
25. Elderton
26. Eperosa
27. Epsilon
28. Fernfield
29. Flaxman Wines
30. Forbes & Forbes
31. Frederick Stevenson
32. Gatt
33. Gibson Wines
34. Glaetzer Wines
35. Glen Eldon
36. Gomersal
37. Grant Burge Wines
38. Greenock Creek
39. Greenock Creek Roennfeldt Road
40. Haan
41. Hart of the Barossa
42. Heggies
43. Heidenreich Estate
44. Hemera Estate
45. Henschke
46. Henschke Hill of Grace Vineyard
47. Henschke Mount Edelstone Vineyard
48. Hentley Farm Wines
49. Hill-Smith Estate
50. Hobbs of Barossa
51. Hoffmann's Dalwitz Block
52. Hoffnungsthal Vineyard
53. Hutton Vale
54. Irvine
55. Izway
56. JB Wines
57. Jacob's Creek Visitor Centre
58. Jacob's Creek Nursery
59. John Duval Wines
60. Kaesler Wines
61. Kalimna Vineyard
62. Kalleske
63. Koonunga Hill
64. Kurtz
65. Langmeil/Freedom Vineyard
66. Laughing Jack
67. Leo Buring
68. Mardia
69. Maverick
70. Maverick's Trial Hill Vineyard
71. Miamba Vineyard
72. Moolanda Vineyard
73. Moorooroo Park
74. Mountadam
75. Outlaw
76. Paulmara
77. Penfolds Cellar Door
78. Peter Lehmann
79. Peter Seppelt
80. Pewsey Vale Vineyard
81. Pindarie
82. Poonawatta
83. Poverty Hill
84. Powell & Son/ Neldner Road
85. Radford Dale
86. Richmond Grove
87. Rieslingfreak
88. Rileys
89. Rockford
90. Rolf Binder
91. Rosenvale
92. Ruggabellus
93. Rusden
94. St Hallett
95. Saltram/Pepperjack
96. Schild Estate
97. Schwarz
98. Seabrook
99. Seppeltsfield
100. Shobbrook Wines
101. Sieber
102. Smallfry
103. Small Gully
104. Smyth Road
105. Sons of Eden
106. Spinifex
107. Springton Cellars
108. Springton Hills
109. The Standish Wine Company
110. Standish/Massena/ JC's Own
111. Stonegarten Vineyard
112. Stonewell Vineyard
113. Summer's Vineyard
114. Tait
115. Thorn-Clarke
116. Tim Smith
117. Tollana
118. Torbreck Vintners
119. Torbreck Hillside Vineyard
120. Turkey Flat
121. Twin Valley Estate
122. Two Hands
123. Uleybury
124. Villa Tinto
125. Vinecrest & Simpatico
126. Vinya Vella
127. Westlake
128. Whistler
129. The Willows Vineyard
130. Wolf Blass
131. Yalumba
132. Yalumba Nursery

of Eden Valley's diversity is expressed through different grapes. The Eden Valley's variability is also harder to group into specific areas, as it fluctuates greatly throughout the region. 'Eden Valley is rounded hills,' says Henschke, 'so you've got lots of different **aspects** and you've got lots of different soil types.'

High Eden is the pocket of Eden Valley that expresses enough commonalities to isolate – as has officially been done, when it became a legal subregion of the Eden Valley in 2001, four years after the larger region was codified. As its name implies, High Eden is a high elevation subclimate of the Eden Valley, with slopes starting at 400 metres above sea level, and 75% of plantings between 450 and 600 metres.

Vineyard **aspects** in High Eden face primarily to the east, with north and south variants. The region is always the last to harvest, in the whole Barossa, being the coldest and wettest part of the zone. The High Eden GI ranges from Pewsey Vale Vineyard at the region's highest points to Flaxman Valley at its lowest points. Notable vineyards in High Eden include The Contours vineyard (of Pewsey Vale), Mountadam and Berton.

Flaxman Valley is a notable pocket and has become an epicentre for premium shiraz in the Eden Valley. Created by a 36-million-year-old meteorite impact, the land is a unique mix of dark quartzite and granite subsoils, beneath a thin layer of loam. A number of premium shiraz are made from this region, including a former Rockford bottling, the **bush-vine** Barr-Eden vineyard of the late Bob McLean, the Powell & Son (now Noldner Road) Steinert vineyard, Chris Ringland's Stone Creek vineyard, and a new entry from Agricola (made by Callum Powell, the 'son' in Powell & Son). Tom Shobbrook and Ruggabellus are also based here.

Besides Flaxman Valley, High Eden is generally known for its riesling, but so are many other places in the region; with its overall cool climate, the Eden Valley doesn't need extreme elevation to grow the grape. Riesling accounted for 22% of the crush in the Eden Valley in 2021, over double the next most planted white grape (chardonnay), but behind shiraz, which accounted for almost 35%.

The Clare and Eden valleys are often put toe-to-toe as the classic riesling regions of Australia, both known for their bone-dry and high-acid styles. Though Clare is, on average, warmer and slightly lower than the Eden, riesling is often planted in the higher and cooler sites of both (negating these averages a bit). Clare riesling is often described as limey and stony, and sometimes fuller and more acidic, than the floral and talcy rieslings of the Eden (but ask ten people and get ten different opinions). In reality, most people would be hard pressed to reliably distinguish the two regions in a glass – site and producer being more the determining factors than overall region.

After shiraz and riesling, cabernet sauvignon is the third-most planted grape in the Eden Valley. Prue Henschke notes that cabernet can struggle to ripen in certain years in the Eden Valley, but the resulting style tends to be more savoury and filigreed than its counterparts from across the Barossa Range.

Though Pewsey Vale Vineyard has made a name for itself, the two most famous vineyards of the Eden are planted to shiraz and are part of the Henschke stable: Hill of Grace and Mount Edelstone. Hill of Grace sits at 400 metres in elevation and was first planted in 1860. The soils are alluvial, sandy loam over clay, with a variety of westerly **aspects** running from north to south, a full 180 degrees of warm afternoon sun. Mount Edelstone sits just south of Hill of Grace, also at 400 metres in elevation: red-brown clay-loam soils that face east, catch cooler morning sun, and receive more rainfall than Hill of Grace. Both vineyards are **dry-farmed** organically and **biodynamically**, on **ungrafted vines**. Not only did these two vineyards start the trend for single-vineyard bottlings in Australia, they are two of the most revered Australian wines to this day, and showcase the Eden shiraz style noted by Barossa Grounds: red-fruited, perfumed and savoury, with finely chiselled tannins.

On the other side of the Range, the 'Northern Grounds' of the Barossa largely include the townships of Ebenezer, Moppa, Kalimna, Seppeltsfield and Greenock. As Yalumba's chief winemaker Louisa Rose points out, in regard to drawing boundaries between subregions, 'what we know about the different grounds is that they're really more overlapping – with fuzzy edges'. And indeed, the Barossa Grounds' map shows more of a transparent brushstroke separating the Northern from the Central Grounds, with Seppeltsfield and Greenock right on that border.

The other problem that the Barossa has found with nominating even unofficial subregions is that many of its township names are brand names: Kalimna is a brand of Penfolds, Seppeltsfield is a historic winery (which the town was named after, not the other way around), and Bethany, Château Tanunda and Greenock Creek are wineries named after their townships. As such, the directions on a compass were the most neutral, and legally safest, labels to claim.

The study found that the Northern Grounds is home to 'the most powerful expressions of Barossa Valley shiraz, structured for aging with black fruits wrapped in fine muscular tannins'. This is the highest elevation area of the Barossa Valley, with vineyards running 280–450 metres above sea level.

Shallow soils of shattered ironstone over rock sit among the steeper slopes of the Barossa Range's western ridge (on the east side of the Barossa Valley GI). Below, further west, sand over clay is mixed alongside the Barossa Valley's most dominant soil: duplex soils of hard, red-brown clay over an alkaline base. Kalimna is known for its yellow and white sands, and can almost be thought of as a northern extension of the eastern section of the Central Grounds (noted below).

Moving west, sand becomes less of a dominant fixture in the Northern Grounds: more clay resides at the surface, ranging from red to brown clay loams to harder clays that sit atop limestone. Often, the soils' higher **water-holding capacity** is referenced here, with the clay at the surface being the major contributor.

The most eastern vineyards of the Northern Grounds, hugging the ridge, are some of the coolest and wettest in the Barossa Valley. Moving southwest, the elevated sections of Moppa and Greenock have similar rainfall and temperatures to these eastern vineyards, while lower-lying sites are warmer and drier. Ebenezer, warmer and drier still, sits at the confluence of the sands of the eastern vineyards and the harder clays of the west. And Seppeltsfield is a gateway to the lowest, warmest and driest areas that continue further south and west.

The Central Grounds presents the most diversity of any cross-section of the region. The flats that sit below the Barossa Range in the east are a vast departure from the western reaches of this central zone.

East of the Barossa Valley Way (B19) is the most densely planted area, the flattest area, and one of the most historic areas of the Barossa Valley, including the towns of Nuriootpa, Rowland Flat, Krondorf, Bethany, Vine Vale and the east side of Tanunda. It is a uniform, contiguous patch of sandy vineyard area that sits below the Barossa Range. There is a slight warming and drying of the climate as one moves north from Krondorf through to Nuriootpa, though it is minor and seems to have less of an impact on the finished wines. Hugging the Barossa Range, Krondorf and Bethany are the coolest and wettest of the towns, followed closely by Vine Vale.

These vineyards are impacted by the Vine Vale Nurse, a regular cold wind that pours out of the Eden Valley down the Barossa Range and into the Barossa Valley, similar to the cool easterly winds that flow into McLaren Vale from the adjacent Adelaide Hills vineyards. Pockets of lower-lying warmer air to the west draw down cold air from higher elevations. Viticulturist Dylan Grigg comments on the wind: 'It can be freezing there in the morning. And it also adds a stress, even the wind just blowing past the shoots and the leaves … that shapes the wines on that [eastern] side as well.'

Here, soils have much more sand, as what has eroded from the hills doesn't cross the town of Nuriootpa – the low point as one moves from the eastern to the western side of the northern half of the Barossa Valley. Sandy topsoils have lower **water-holding capacity**, but have a mulching quality that helps the clay below retain water. Vine Vale in particular has been lauded for its sandy soils that produce ethereal wines, most notably from grenache.

One of the significant changes when moving west in the Central Grounds is the transition to harder alkaline subsoils, often limestone-based soils that offer little root permeability and even

Dry-grown, own-rooted, and literal living monuments, these vineyards are a testament to the suitability of the Barossa to produce some of the world's great wines.

less **water-holding capacity** (akin to soils in the northwest). It's not a difference in quality, just style. The western side is known for more structured and denser wines than the east. Soils and warmth are often said to be the points of of differentiation in these wines.

The Southern Grounds centres around the township of Lyndoch, with parts of Gomersal, Rosedale and Rowland Flat falling under this area as well. Rowland Flat is known for its unique patches of deep sand deposits mixed throughout sandy soils that sit on top of clay. Vines don't thrive on the deep sand deposits alone, and plantings tend to be on soils of sand and clay together.

Lyndoch is the most densely planted area of the southern part of the valley and sees the sandy soils of the east fade to the clay-based soils of the west. Vineyards are largely planted on the clay soils rather than the sandier soils that drew the original growers in – the advent of irrigation caused the **water-holding capacity** at the surface of clay to become more attractive. As one continues to move west and south, the climate becomes hotter and drier, with the vineyards on the southwestern end of Gomersal and Rosedale being the hottest and driest of the region.

While the south and western areas of the valley tend to have a younger average vine age and see more irrigation, there are many exceptions to this rule. Torbreck's Hillside vineyard, on a west-facing slope just north of Lyndoch township, just turned 70 and is **dry-farmed** (though the fact that it's planted to

grenache is probably one of the reasons it sees success in this area).

Barossa Grounds' description of the resulting shiraz from the Central and Southern regions are variations on a theme: both 'medium to full-bodied', but with greater 'vibrancy' and firmer structure coming from the Central and more 'lushness' and 'gentle tannins' in the South.

The Barossa Grounds Project, up until this point at least, has been solely focused on shiraz. So although the geographic particularities they identify are obviously true of whichever grapes are planted across a region, the sensory analysis has not extended to other grapes. Grenache, though, is a planting that clearly responds to the nuances of its environment, showing distinction across the region.

From the sandy flats of Yalumba's Vine Vale plots, to those from the hillsides of Torbreck's vineyard in Lyndoch, and the hotter, darker-soiled vineyards in Moppa and Greenock bottled by Greenock Creek, the variation in colour, fruit flavour, density and tannin is palpable across these areas for grenache – maybe even more so than shiraz. In general, the lightest styles (both in colour and body) are from Vine Vale in the centre, then Lyndoch in the south, while Moppa and Greenock produce the Valley's darkest and fullest expressions of grenache.

The directional distinctions of the Barossa Grounds project have started to show up on bottlings in the region. Seppeltsfield introduced their Grounds range in 2018, which labels

The team at Cirillo are custodians of the world's oldest grenache vineyard, planted in 1848. Here's to another 175 years!

single-site shiraz bottlings as Northing, Southing, Easting and Westing to showcase the different expressions of Barossa's compass. Bethany Wines, based in the village of Bethany, has bottled their East Grounds shiraz since 2013 (which refers to eastern Barossa Valley, not eastern Barossa, which would be the Eden Valley). An Australia-wide negociant called Epic Negociants bottles a Northern Grounds shiraz. Though these terms have started to make appearances, they haven't caught on widely.

But that's not really the point of the Barossa Grounds Project. The aim of the project, and the study of the physical differences of the Barossa in general, is not to draw official boundaries or point to the superiority of any part or subregion.

Fiona Donald, chief winemaker at Seppeltsfield comments: 'The Barossa Grounds Project was not meant to put lines on the ground and create subregions. It is a project in collecting information that further helps us understand our region, our land, and how to grow and produce better wine.'

Louisa Rose elaborates on this idea, noting: 'Once you start drawing boundaries, you also start competing – "Which one's better?" – and that's not what we want to do either. We want to really be celebrating the differences, loving the differences, and comparing them.'

And indeed, no one pocket in the Barossa has emerged as better than any other – just different. Some of the most notable (and oldest) vineyards of the Barossa are spread across its surface: Eden Valley has The Contours riesling block in High Eden, as well as Hill of Grace and Mount Edelstone in the region's northwest. Cirillo is home to the world's oldest active grenache vines, planted in the Light Pass region of east-central Barossa. Langmeil's Freedom vineyard, planted in 1843 – the world's oldest shiraz vines – sits just west of the B19 in the Central Grounds. Further south, in Rowland Flat, is Hewittson's Old Garden vineyard, home to the world's oldest mourvèdre vines, planted in 1853. Block 42 at Penfolds' Kalimna vineyard, in the Northern Grounds, is believed to have the world's oldest cabernet sauvignon vines, planted in 1888.

Dry-grown, own-rooted and literal living monuments, these vineyards are a testament to the suitability of the Barossa to produce some of the world's great wines. Whether the compass leads there based on a well-researched matrix of factors, or the mere presence of creeks and gumtrees, all roads point to the Barossa – then and now.

Hubbub

Preserving the Barossa's historic vineyards is one of the region's great concerns. **Phylloxera** is unlikely given the region's isolation, though that same isolation has bred a somewhat cavalier attitude toward the aphid: biosecurity measures are not uniformly nor vigilantly enforced across the Barossa.

But even more so than **phylloxera**, the old vines are at risk of being pulled out because the demand has not been communicated to growers – or rather, it doesn't exist. Many of these old vineyards are not under the care of a winery, but rather, independent growers who are at the whims of what the market will pay for fruit. With the feeble yields of old vines, those vineyards must command top dollar to make them a sustainable prospect for growers.

Shiraz can easily make an argument for itself, but the less fashionable old vines of the region are at risk of uprooting – these include grenache (though it has seen a recent resurgence), muscat blanc à petits grains, cinsault, palomino and semillon. To wine geeks, 'old vine' seems like an imperative enough to keep the vines in the ground, but that's not a given to farmers. 'It's getting that communication out there that there is a value,' says viticulturist Dylan Grigg.

The other way that old vines prove their worth, beyond the historic value and quality factor, is their ability to be **dry-grown**. In a region, and nation, that is somewhat water-insecure, this is a valuable attribute. Old vines have roots that reach deep, accessing underground water. But most vines in the Barossa are not able to be unirrigated. 'There's not a lot of new land being planted,' says Louisa Rose, 'and one of the reasons for that is the availability of water.'

Barossa Infrastructure is a private company that supplies supplemental irrigation water to the Barossa Valley. They've been instrumental in the survival of the region and the quality of the groundwater, which had become increasingly saline with water mining. Their water mainly comes from the Warren Reservoir, just south of the Barossa zone, which is supplemented with Murray River water, as well as a small amount of treated municipal wastewater from the Barossa area.

Another such water diversion project is Bunyip Water, formerly known as the Gawler River Water Re-Use Scheme, which has been operational in the Barossa since 2016. A 42-kilometre pipeline was built to divert surplus winter stormwater from the Gawler River and pump it north to the Barossa, providing a sustainable source of water that does not rely on the 'ailing Murray River', according to Seppeltsfield, who purchased Bunyip from the Light Regional Council in 2022 – an example of a successful public to private partnership.

Though these strides are critical, water supply is not infinite, and Barossa Valley still feels the crunch of its limited water resources. And the Eden Valley is even worse off. Though it is a wetter region than its western neighbour, there are no water pipelines going into the region. Producers must rely on what falls out of the sky – either directly or collected in dams – and that, increasingly, is not enough.

Climate change is the culprit for water insecurity. But unlike in other regions, where climate change is forcing hard conversations about grape suitability in the future, the on-the-ground concerns of Barossa climate change largely centre on water. In a 2016 paper on Barossa climate change, Mark Pygott **MW** summarises his findings: 'The key findings are that the BV [Barossa Valley] has become warmer with a greater incidence of heatwaves and increase in maximum temperatures. It is also experiencing depletion in winter and spring rainfall, a pattern more marked in the north of the valley than the south. Adaptation specifically related to a changing climate is being practised, with the focus on securing access to water and improving its use and speed of delivery to the vineyard. Adaptation incurs both financial costs as well as potential costs to wine quality, however the resilience of the BV, its growers and the principal variety shiraz, suggests the BV's reputation is, at present, not under serious threat.'

And while plantings are slowing due to water access, many Barossa wineries are also acclimating to changing export demands. China, up until recently, accounted for about 40% of Australia's

Henschke winemaker Andy Cummins (also of Rasa) digs shiraz skins and pulp out of their open-top concrete fermentation tanks. These were built by second-generation caretaker Paul Gotthard Henschke when he expanded the winery and vineyard holdings at the end of the 19th century.

exports by value (and was a major market for the Barossa in particular). The average price of wines being sent to China was AUD $11.59 per litre, the highest such number for Australian exports (compare that to the US' AUD $4.22/litre average).

In March 2021, China announced that it would levy tariffs against Australian wine for five years, ranging from a staggering 116% to an even more staggering 218%. Australia, and the Barossa in particular, has been left with a glut of wine that will be hard to be sell elsewhere for the prices garnered in China. Reuters reported that Australian exports to China fell by 96% in the quarter following the tariff implementation.

The tariffs only apply to still **table wines** in containers of 2 litres or less. So bulk wine, **fortified wine**, sparkling wine and jeroboams and larger are unimpacted. The tariffs hurt smaller producers and growers the most, who contribute to exported bottled wines rather than bulk-packed ones. And the move instilled a general insecurity in the region. 'We're struggling at the moment because of what's taken place in China,' says Rasa's Andy Cummins, 'there's a lot of growers getting dropped, a lot of vineyards getting pulled out ... there's a lack of confidence.'

But the current timidity has not been all bad. With some of the big company interest and speculation more cautiously approaching the

The other way that old vines prove their worth, beyond the historic value and quality factor, is their ability to be dry-grown.

region, the younger generation has stepped in to claim and preserve some of the heritage vines of the region. 'For people of my ilk,' Cummins continues, 'this is a green light. We can take a little bit of power back.'

Barossa – with its corporate interest, powerful brand, and hearty production – seems to be destined for continued cycles of expansion and contraction, as it has experienced in the past. But the region has survived many other peaks and troughs, proving itself to be a region of considerable ingenuity and resilience. Its roots dig deep, figuratively and literally, and it will undoubtedly continue to assert itself on the world stage for decades to come.

PRODUCERS

ALKINA

Alkina is an ambitious new addition to the Barossa Valley, established in 2015 when Argentinian wine entrepreneur Alejandro Bulgheroni bought land near Greenock. The estate now has 43 hectares of vines, with 6 hectares dating back to the 1950s (planted by Lee Kalleske), including semillon, semillon gris, grenache, shiraz and mataro. The property also had old heritage buildings dating back to the 1850s, which Alkina has revived as a boutique accommodation and cellar door. But the investment in luxury tourism is surpassed by the investment in the land and the wines: the team brought in legendary soil and geology specialist Pedro Parra to analyse the estate, all vines are being farmed organically and **biodynamically** (NASAA certified), and the famed Alberto Antonini (long-time Antinori winemaker) is consulting on the vinification. Alkina, named after an Indigenous girl's name meaning moon or moonlight, seeks to give respect to the Ngadjuri people, who were the original inhabitants of their land, by promoting land guardianship rather than ownership. *alkinawine.com*

CHARLES MELTON

Charles Melton was established in 1984, one of the small cadre of wineries (most famously, Peter Lehmann, Rockford and Elderton) who invested in the threatened viticultural heritage of the Barossa in the early 80s. Charlie himself had worked as an apprentice to Peter Lehmann before starting his eponymous winery. He has gone on to pioneer several iconic styles: the Nine Popes is recognised as the premier Barossa **GSM** (grenache/shiraz/mataro), and the Rosé of Virginia (named after Charlie's wife) was one of the original Aussie dry rosés, almost a light red in its deep, vivid colour. Charlie and Virginia still run the day-to-day operations of the winery almost 40 years later, accompanied by their adored dalmatians. *charlesmeltonwines.com.au*

CHÂTEAU TANUNDA

The 'château' is not just a stately name; when it was first built in 1890, the building was one of the largest in South Australia and maintained an illustrious early winemaking history. After being passed into corporate ownership and later abandoned, Château Tanunda was in a bleak state by the mid-1990s. In 1998, South African John Gerber bought the property and restored it to glory. The Gerber family still owns and runs the estate, not only revitalising the château, but the winery and vineyards as well, with recent acclaim touting the wines – a wide range of Barossa classics – as outstanding. *chateautanunda.com*

CHRIS RINGLAND

Chris Ringland's name has become synonymous with rich and powerful Barossa shiraz, though the winemaker's reach surpasses this style. Ringland was born in New Zealand and attended the famed Australian oenology program at Roseworthy, graduating in 1982. He went to California before returning to work in the Barossa, eventually

---

 What we're drinking

*The Kin Semillon from **Alkina** is a modern take on the heritage Barossa variety, which showcases savouriness and texture first and foremost. With its evolving approach to skin contact, it is a long way from classic incarnations the region has produced of this grape, but one I welcome with open arms and will drink with gusto.* – **Kavita Faiella**

> **What we're drinking**
>
> *My jaw dropped when I first compared the age of **Cirillo's** vines with the price of their wines: few values like this exist in the world of wine. You can sample wine made from the oldest grenache vines in the world for a modest sum, offering perfumed red fruit and the perfect combination of lift and concentration. – Jane Lopes*

landing at Rockford Wines, where he stayed for 18 vintages. While at Rockford, Ringland started acquiring land and making wine, releasing the first Three Rivers Shiraz from the 1989 vintage. Following some enthusiastic media, largely from Robert Parker's *Wine Advocate*, Ringland developed a cult following for his wines. Ringland's original flagship wine, Three Rivers, was renamed to Chris Ringland Shiraz in 1998, and a second label called Randall's Hill was developed. Today, the Barossa Range bottling is Ringland's top tier, coming from the over 100-year-old vines on his Stone Chimney Creek property, one of the mere 22 wines on the top tier of **Langton's** Australia-wide classification. Ringland doesn't rest on his achievements though, and is constantly adding projects to his résumé, including the launch of two Spanish wineries in 2002, a new vineyard site in 2006, and a label called Solita focusing on nebbiolo. *chrisringland.com*

CIRILLO

The Cirillo family are custodians of the oldest-known grenache and semillon vines in the world, both planted in 1848 in the Barossa Valley town Light Pass. Since 1970, Vincent Cirillo and his son Marco have been the only people to **prune** these historic vineyards, and for over three decades, sold off their fruit to luminaries of the Barossa: Rockford, Peter Lehmann, St Hallett and Torbreck. Marco took an interest in winemaking, and after completing his studies, the family released their first estate-bottled wine in 2006, from the 2003 vintage. The 1850 series includes a semillon, grenache and grenache rosé – all from those original vines and at a surprisingly affordable price for the provenance. Cirillo also makes malbec, shiraz, mataro, Eden Valley riesling and the quaffable Vincent, which is perhaps Australia's best vinous value, a grenache coming from two plots of over 100-year-old vines. *cirilloestatewines.com.au*

ELDERTON

The Elderton vineyard was first planted in 1894 in Nuriootpa, and later acquired by Samuel Elderton Tolley, who gave it its name and grew the site into a successful homestead and fruit source for his family's winery (Tolley Wines). The Vine Pull era was not kind to the Elderton site, and it fell into disrepair in the 1970s. The vineyard had become so devalued that when Lorraine and Neil Ashmead came along in 1980, they were offered the 30-hectare vineyard for free with the purchase of the house. Elderton had its first vintage in 1982, and counts a **Jimmy Watson** and a place on the **Langton's Classification** among its achievements. Production is largely devoted to shiraz and cabernet sauvignon, with the flagship Command Shiraz coming from those 1894 vines and seeing 30 months in new American and French puncheons. *eldertonwines.com.au*

EPEROSA

Brett Grocke is a sixth-generation Barossa vigneron, his ancestors having tended vines and made wine in the region since the 1840s. The first vintage of Eperosa – a name combining two of Grocke's wine-related loves, Epernay and terra rossa – was in 2005. Grocke has two estate vineyards, one called Magnolia in Vine Vale, first planted in the 1890s, and one in Krondorf, first planted in 1903. The varieties planted include shiraz, grenache, mataro, semillon and grenache blanc. The style is unique: Grocke doesn't shy away from the ripeness inherent to the Barossa, but his wines are always savory, nimble and elegant, and never see new oak. *eperosa.com.au*

GEYER WINE CO

Coming from a family of Barossa grape growers, David Geyer started

Barossa

his career at Torbreck before spending several years working with Pete Schell at Spinifex. It was here that he began to develop his own set of wines, releasing the first one in 2015, a blend of montepulciano, petit verdot, mataro and shiraz. David's winemaking ethos errs towards the minimal, staying connected at every step of the process, but allowing the fruit to shine through. The Geyer reds are light and juicy, and the whites toy with varying levels of texture; his semillon is fermented on skins with partial **carbonic maceration**. *geyerwines.com.au*

Prue Henschke
Henschke

GLAETZER WINES

The Glaetzer family can trace its lineage in the Barossa back to 1888 – some of the region's earliest recorded viticulturists. Over a century later, in 1995, Colin and Judith Glaetzer established the family's winery, with son Ben continuing the family tradition. All fruit is sourced from the northern Barossa subsection of Ebenezer, which imparts, according to the winery, a 'softness, elegance and approachability' to the Glaetzer wines. Shiraz is the firm backbone of the estate, with small amounts of grenache and cabernet sauvignon contributing to blends. Its Amon-Ra Shiraz is the most iconic Glaetzer wine, establishing a worldwide name for the brand and landing it on each **Langton's Classification** since 2014. *glaetzer.com*

GRANT BURGE WINES

Fifth-generation Barossa vigneron Grant Burge and his wife Helen established Grant Burge Wines in 1988, and it quickly grew into one of the largest family-owned wineries in the Barossa. Accolade purchased Grant Burge in 2015, expanding the footprint even wider. The portfolio includes everything from $19 sparkling moscato to the $230 Meshach Shiraz, the winery's flagship shiraz, named after Grant Burge's great-grandfather; the wine is full-bodied but has moderate new oak by Barossa flagship standards (the 2016 saw 18% new oak), and has had a spot on the **Langton's Classification** since 2005. *grantburgewines.com.au*

GREENOCK CREEK

Greenock Creek was established by stonemason Michael Waugh in 1984, on the banks of an actual creek called Greenock, in the township of Seppeltsfield. The 1990s brought the Marananga Roennfeldt Road property into the estate's holdings, where 130-year-old cabernet sauvignon and shiraz is grown for their Roennfeldt Road bottlings. These are some of the most Robert Parker–awarded Australian wines, receiving numerous 100-point scores in the 1990s and 2000s, as well as placement on the **Langton's Classification** since 2005. *greenockcreekwines.com.au*

HENSCHKE

Henschke is one of the most important names in Australian wine, with continuous family ownership and wine production since 1868. Over six generations, the Henschkes have been at the forefront of stewardship in the Barossa (and later Adelaide Hills). The Eden Valley, specifically Keyneton in the northwest, is where first-generation Johann Christian Henschke bought 32 hectares in 1862, and where the family has called home ever since. Henschke pioneered single-vineyard bottlings in the 1950s, with their Mount Edelstone and Hill of Grace shiraz, still two of the most prized Australian wines in production.

Fifth-generation Stephen Henschke and his wife Prue are the formidable pair leading the estate now, Stephen as winemaker and Prue as viticulturist. Gwyn Olsen, previously of Pepper Tree Wines (p. 50) is senior winemaker. The sixth generation is in the wings, with Johann, Justine and Andreas all involved in the family business. In Prue's words, the future of Henschke is about 'better not bigger': pursuing quality viticulture (organic and **biodynamic**), crafting expressive, site-specific wines, and continuing their leadership in the Barossa and Australia as a whole. *henschke.com.au*

HENTLEY FARM WINES

Keith and Alison Hentschke established Hentley Farm in 1997, with a vision 'to craft exceptional single estate wines from the Barossa Valley'. The site they found, using an old soil map from the 1950s (in the pre-Barossa Grounds days), is on the banks of Greenock Creek in Seppeltsfield, in Barossa's northwest. Keith, with a degree from Roseworthy and an MBA, had the education and know-how to establish one of the modern luxury estates of the Barossa, with their icon Clos Otto Shiraz (a new entry on **Langton's Classification** in 2020) and their Atrium restaurant, both highly acclaimed. Hentley Farm also won the **Jimmy Watson** in 2022 for their 2021 Old Legend Grenache, only the second time ever a grenache has taken out this gong. *hentleyfarm.com.au*

LANGMEIL

Langmeil's claim to fame is the custodianship of the world's oldest-known shiraz vines. Planted in 1843, the Freedom vineyard sits in northern Tanunda, on **dry-grown**, own-rooted vines that penetrate through loam and red clay to reach limestone, ironstone, quarry sand and gravel. The resulting wine (debuting with the 1997 vintage) is firmly in the traditional Barossa style, with layers of rich fruit, oak-influenced spice and vanilla notes, as well as serious length and power. *langmeilwinery.com.au*

LEO BURING

Leo Buring the man lived between 1876 and 1961, born to a wine family in the Clare Valley. He studied in Germany and France before returning to Australia, working across the country and eventually becoming the governing director of Lindeman's. In 1931 he established Leo Buring Pty Ltd while still in New South Wales, but Leo Buring as a brand found its identity with the development of Château Léonay in Barossa's Tanunda, starting in the mid-1940s, and even more so with the arrival of John Vickery in 1955, who proved himself to be one of Australia's great riesling winemakers. The brand today is owned by Treasury Wine Estates and produces exclusively larger-scale riesling, from Clare Valley, Eden Valley and Tasmania. *tweglobal.com/brands/leo-buring*

ORLANDO/JACOB'S CREEK

Fuelled by the Gramp family, Orlando wines was one of the most influential wineries in Australia for over a century, with vines first planted on the banks of Jacob's Creek in 1847. Orlando became one of Australia's largest wine companies, in particular pioneering sparkling wine technology in the 1950s (for their famous Orlando Pearl). Orlando launched the Jacob's Creek brand in 1973, which has become one of the largest global wine labels. Pernod Ricard acquired Orlando in 1989, helping to propel Jacob's Creek into the stratosphere, today selling about 6.5 million cases around the world annually. Orlando has continued separately from Jacob's Creek, with a rebranding in 2020 to focus on premium wines and classic styles, most notably the Eden Valley Steingarten riesling. *orlandowines.com, jacobscreek.com*

PENFOLDS

Christopher and Mary Penfold arrived in Australia from the UK in 1844 and founded Magill Estate with the support of family members back home. Christopher was a doctor who believed in the medicinal properties of wine (hear hear!) and planted several French varieties on his property to make a 'wine tonic' for his patients. Initial wines were made in port and sherry styles and Christopher's practice was so popular that Mary took over production in the winery, eventually running it after her husband's death. At the turn of the century, Penfolds was the largest winery in the Adelaide region and had begun buying up vineyard sites in McLaren Vale and New South Wales. When Max Schubert began as chief winemaker, he travelled to Europe with the intention of studying **fortified** production, but instead spent most of his time in Bordeaux, leading to the development of Penfolds Grange – Australia's most iconic wine, which saw its first vintage in 1951. Peter Gago, a former science teacher, joined the Penfolds winemaking team in 1989, initially to look after sparkling wine production, but soon moved on to reds. In 2002, he became the fourth chief winemaker of Penfolds since the debut of Grange. Despite producing riesling, chardonnay and **fortifieds**, Penfolds remains a giant in the red wine arena, making shiraz and cabernet sauvignon from vineyards across southeast Australia, China, France and California. *penfolds.com*

PETER LEHMANN

Peter Lehmann took out a loan and built his winery in 1979 to support Barossa growers. He had been working as a winemaker at Saltram when he was instructed not to buy grapes from local growers due to the surplus. His first estate wine was called The Futures: a promise to pay the growers once it had sold. The incredibly popular Stonewell Shiraz was first produced in 1987. Peter Lehmann was purchased by Casella in 2016, and continues to put out consistent wines at both the premium and commercial ends of the spectrum. *peterlehmannwines.com*

PEWSEY VALE VINEYARD

English immigrant Joseph Gilbert established the first winery in the Eden Valley in 1847, though operation of Pewsey Vale has not been continuous. George Angas Parsons discovered in 1961 he owned the original site of the region's first vineyard and brought the idea of its restoration to his friend Wyndham Hill-Smith. The pair began to replant the vineyard to riesling and cabernet sauvignon, though focus is now firmly on riesling. Pewsey Vale was ahead of its time when, in 1977, the winery began sealing its wines under screw cap, a decision that was not received well by consumers. They reverted to cork in the 80s, but reintroduced screw caps to their museum-release rieslings in 1995 to demonstrate the ageing capability of the closure. The Contours block, made up of the oldest vines in the vineyard, was certified organic in 2013 and continues to be a benchmark for Australian riesling. *pewseyvale.com.au*

POWELL & SON/NELDNER ROAD

Dave Powell, founder of Torbreck, and his son Callum started Powell & Son in 2014, a tribute to the wines of the Rhône Valley and the versatility of the Barossa and Eden valleys. There's a heavy focus on shiraz in their range, picked from sites as diverse as Flaxman Valley in Eden and the ironstone-rich Marananga in the Barossa Valley. Callum has a particular passion for their whites however, creating elegant riesling and a rich, barrel-fermented marsanne-roussanne. The wines have quickly become modern classics; no surprise with such a formidable figure as Dave Powell at the helm. There is never any shortage of drama and intrigue around Powell: two newsworthy recent happenings include changing the name of the winery to Neldner Road after his son 'wanted to take it in a different direction' (according to the *Australian Financial Review*) and the offering of barrels of his 2021 single-vineyard wines via NFT. *powellandson.com*

RASA

Rasa is the joint project of Andy Cummins and Emma Welling, who are making wines that preserve history and promote evolution at the same time. Rasa is in the micro-negociant mould, buying grapes from small plots of old vines in an effort to keep them in the ground: the likes of muscat, semillon, riesling, grenache, mourvèdre and cinsault. They exclusively work with farmers whose practices align with their own values (organic farming at a minimum) and aim to express a sense of place in an approachable yet complex way. *rasawines.com.au*

RIESLINGFREAK

The name of the winery leaves little ambiguity of the focus here. Established in 2009 by John Hughes, a self-proclaimed 'freak for all things riesling', the project straddles several regions with the goal to tell a story of South Australian riesling, with sites across the Clare and Eden valleys.

The styles are diverse, everything from the classic bone-dry rendition to off-dry styles, fully sweet ones, and even a sekt (sparkling under its traditional German name). rieslingfreak.com

ROCKFORD

Rockford, though only established in 1984 (in its infancy by Barossa standards), has become one of the most important names in the region. Robert O'Callaghan is the man behind Rockford, who quietly persevered in his vision: preserving old vines, harkening back to traditional winemaking techniques, and encouraging new talent in the region (both Chris Ringland and Torbreck's Dave Powell cite their time at Rockford, and the support of O'Callaghan, as influential in their careers). Rockford's flagship wine, the Basket Press Shiraz, is made with traditional methods, including the use of a 19th-century wooden Bagshaw crusher, open-vat fermentation with native yeasts, and – of course – use of an old, manual, wooden basket press. It is a constant in Aussie collectors' cellars and sits in the top tier of **Langton's classification**. Ben Radford, a fifth-generation Barossa farmer, is the current winemaker and managing director. rockfordwines.com.au

RUGGABELLUS

With their first vintage in 2009, Abel and Emma Gibson have made an undeniable impact on the modern expression of the Barossa. Based in the Eden Valley, the Gibsons have been buying and growing small parcels of grenache, mataro, cinsault, syrah, riesling, semillon and muscat, making their wines in a way that seems modern, but is really just about honouring rare, ancient vineyards and expressing a sense of place: the whites are typically fermented with extended skin-contact and the reds made with a light touch to remain nuanced and savoury. ruggabellus.com.au

> **JR What we're drinking**
>
> **Sami-Odi's** *Fraser McKinley is old-school, but in a new-school package. The Hoffmann family's Dallwitz vineyard finds its fruit in the hands of John Duval, Torbreck, Chris Ringland and many other A-list producers across the Barossa Valley — but for those completely taken by the savoury aromatics of syrah, this is the apogee. — Jonathan Ross*

SAMI-ODI

Sami-Odi is the syrah-only label of Fraser and Andrea McKinley, which has redefined what was previously thought possible of the grape in the Barossa. Fraser comes from an art and design background (evident in his uniquely styled bottles and labels) and spent years working at Torbreck and Standish before venturing out on his own. He farms portions of the famed Ebenezer Dallwitz vineyard (owned by the historic Hoffmann family), the base for his flagship Hoffmann-Dallwitz Syrah, as well as his 'Little Wine', a multi-vintage blend spanning four to six years. The wines marry concentration with nuance and airiness, redefining the genre of Barossa shiraz. sami-odi.com

SEPPELTSFIELD

Seppeltsfield is one of Australia's most important historic estates, founded in 1851. It is home to the

> **MB What we're drinking**
>
> **Ruggabellus's** *wines are produced without fear or favour. They are made with a cool intelligence married to expressive winemaking approaches, with a view to produce styles that sit outside the norm, while being evocative of the place they come from. The skin-fermented whites are exercises in patience, resolved and complex, utilising old-vine and distinct sites. Reds are ethereal, delicate and beautiful. The wines soar for their originality and vivacity. — Mike Bennie*

world's longest unbroken lineage of single-vintage wine – named the Centennial Collection – and is the only winery to release a 100-year-old vintage wine every year. In the Centennial Cellar, barrels of tawny-style **fortified wines** line the walls dating back to 1878: a liquid catalogue of Australian wine history. The Seppelt family empire grew rapidly in the 1800s, after the decision to plant grapes led to the production of wine and spirits for the export market, plus brandy for Australian hospitals (it was a different time). The turn of the century saw the expansion of vineyards across various regions, plus the addition of other spirits, cordials and vinegars to the fold. Winemaker and viticulturist Warren Randall, a former Seppelt winemaker, raised funds to purchase the original Seppeltsfield estate from Seppelt (now owned by Treasury Wine Estates) in 2007. Chief winemaker Fiona Donald, who joined the estate in 2009, recently oversaw the restoration of the 1888-built gravity cellar. She has also spearheaded Seppeltsfield's still wine offering, which though only a few years on the market, has attracted critical acclaim. *seppeltsfield.com.au*

SHOBBROOK WINES

Tom Shobbrook has been a leading voice in the natural wine movement in the Barossa, helping define modern Australian wine culture. After 12 years growing grapes in the Seppeltsfield area of Barossa Valley at his family's farm, Shobbrook moved his operations to Eden's Flaxman Valley, though still sources from well-farmed vineyards in Barossa and Adelaide Hills. A few of his wines have become icons: Giallo, a skin-contact muscat-riesling blend, and Poolside, a quick-pressed and fresh style of syrah. Tom employs a 'zero-zero' ideology, taking nothing away from the wines (no fining or filtration), nor adding anything (including the near-ubiquitous **sulphur**). *shobbrookwines.com.au*

SMALLFRY

Smallfry is a partnership 'in business and life' between Suzi Hilder and Wayne Ahrens, who are the custodians of two extraordinary vineyards in the Barossa (both certified organic and **biodynamic**). Schlieb's Family Farm, in the Vine Vale area of the Barossa Valley, has attracted copious attention from winemakers across Australia, with plantings as diverse as trousseau, cinsault, grenache, graciano, semillon and pedro ximénez dating back over a hundred years. Wineries like Ochota Barrels, Rasa, Reed, Shobbrook and Frederick Stevenson all buy fruit from Suzi and Wayne. The pair established their second vineyard just on the outskirts of the High Eden subregion in 1994. For their own wines, Smallfry is firmly **lo-fi**, known for everything from fizzy marsanne to **nouveau** trousseau and skin-contact semillon-pedro ximénez, all with minimal or zero **sulphur** additions. *smallfrywines.com.au*

SPINIFEX

Peter Schell and Magali Gely have made their home in the Barossa for 20 years, though always with an eye toward France, where both of them have spent much time (and where Magali's family calls home). The result is a focus on Mediterranean varieties (shiraz, mataro, grenache, cinsault, carignan, ugni blanc, grenache gris, marsanne and semillon) grounded in Barossa old-vine terroir. *spinifexwines.com.au*

THE STANDISH WINE COMPANY

A modern cult classic of the Barossa, Dan Standish started his eponymous winery in 1999, after cutting his teeth at Torbreck (and a family lineage in the region back six generations). Dan has also picked up experience in California, Rioja and the Rhône Valley. Standish makes four wines, all 100% shiraz (except for a small percentage of viognier in The Relic). Each features a different single-vineyard old-vine site across the Barossa, made in a traditional way: native yeast, open-fermented, then basket-pressed and aged in French oak. The wines have a loyal following and are made in somewhat minuscule quantities. *standishwineco.com*

TORBRECK VINTNERS

Dave Powell was working at Rockford when he discovered some vineyards of abandoned old vines. He set about restoring the **dry-grown** vineyards, which were considered too low yielding and high maintenance by their previous growers, founding Torbreck in 1994. His first wine was the 1995 RunRig, a shiraz-viognier blend, which garnered significant international attention, cementing an interest in Torbreck on a world stage. Dave's wines were driven by a love of the Rhône Valley and he continued to seek out and work with growers of old-vine shiraz, grenache and mataro across the Barossa. Despite his obvious success and association with the brand, Dave moved on from Torbreck after falling out with the current owner, Peter Kight, who purchased the estate outright in 2008. Torbreck continues to produce a wide range of mostly red Rhône-style wines, and their semillon is one of the Barossa's finest. No expense is spared, including the acquisition and farming of both historic and newly established vineyards. Barossa Valley-grown Ian Hongell has only pushed the standard-setting estate further as chief winemaker and general manager. *torbreck.com*

TURKEY FLAT

Shiraz was first planted in 1847 at Turkey Flat, the site so-named because the Prussian settlers commented on how often a turkey-like bird (actually *Ardeotis australis*, or the Australian bustard) frequented its flats. The Schulz family have been the custodians of Turkey Flat since the 1860s, and today, fourth-generation Christie Schulz oversees the winery. Christie and her team have put a strong focus on environmentalism in this generation, moving away from monoculture, collecting rainwater for use and relying on solar power. The wines focus on grenache, shiraz and mataro, with a pedro ximénez **fortified** and marsanne-based vermouth rounding out the offerings. *turkeyflat.com.au*

VANGUARDIST

Vanguardist may be based in the Barossa, but winemaker Michael John Corbett sources stunning fruit for his wines from across South Australia and his home region of Hawke's Bay, New Zealand. Michael searches for the very best combinations of soil and climate, making riesling from 70-year-old vines in Watervale (Clare Valley), **GSM** from an organically farmed vineyard in Seppeltsfield (Barossa Valley), **dry-grown** grenache and mourvèdre from Blewitt Springs, McLaren Vale, with chardonnay from the Adelaide Hills thrown in for good measure. *vanguardistwines.com*

WOLF BLASS

Established in 1966 by German immigrant Wolfgang Blass, the eponymous winery blossomed from a boutique affair to one of the largest (and most awarded) Australian wine brands, now under the Treasury Wine Estates umbrella. The Wolf Blass Black Label has won the **Jimmy Watson** trophy four times since 1973, a feat no other Australian wine has accomplished. Blass himself, still kicking at nearly 90 years old, has been a beloved character of the Barossa. The winery today makes a wide range of wines, nearly every grape at every price-point, under their signature colour labels: red, platinum, brown, gold, grey, white, yellow and black. *wolfblass.com*

YALUMBA

Yalumba was founded in 1849 by the same family who remain its custodians today. The Hill-Smiths have taken on this task with aplomb, never resting on their laurels, but instead constantly evolving and striving towards new goals and visions. This has manifested in several ways: from a cooperage and industry-leading nursery (managed for 10-plus years by the influential Nick Dry), to having the most extensive solar energy system of any Australian winery, to being one of the world's largest producers of vegan wines (before anyone knew what that meant), to pioneering the cabernet-shiraz blend, to expanding into both sides of the Barossa, Coonawarra and beyond ... Yalumba really does seek to do it all. One of the most reliable producers on both the commercial and the premium end, the flagships The Caley (cab-shiraz), The Octavius (shiraz) and Tri-Centenary (grenache) are regarded with respect by critics and collectors alike. Chief winemaker Louisa Rose, who celebrated her 30th vintage with Yalumba in 2022, has become an ambassador for the estate and for her wine regions, a constant voice in championing Yalumba and Australian wine. Regarding what's next for the winery, she says: 'We're really curious people here. We do a lot thinking. We don't follow every fashion ... I suppose we've always had this idea of creating the future here.' *yalumba.com*

Louisa Rose
Yalumba

And don't forget …

Agricola is the winery of Callum Powell, who went out on his own after the dissolution of Powell & Son, and is now approaching serious vineyard sites in a **lo-fi** and expressive way … **An Approach to Relaxation** is a wonderfully executed project from American somm duo Carla and Richard Rza Betts, and offers elegant grenache and textural semillon from top Barossa sites … **Barossa Valley Estate**, a reliable producer largely on the commercial spectrum, whose famous E&E Black Pepper shiraz has not been released since 2016 … **Edenflo** is Andrew Wardlaw's project to showcase the best of Eden Valley, using minimal intervention winemaking and little to no **sulphur** … **Flaxman Wines**, custodians of riesling, shiraz and semillon dating back to 1929, is one of the most visible voices in the Eden's Flaxman Valley … **Frederick Stevenson** is the alias of winemaker/owner Steve Crawford, whose wines display a balance of modern freshness and openness, without any dogged commitment to being experimental or avant-garde … **Gibson Wines**, a family-affair with Rob Gibson, his wife and son working together, is based around a 2-hectare plot of merlot, cabernet sauvignon and fiano in the Light Pass region of northern Barossa … **Head Wines** is Alex Head's eponymous ode to the great syrahs of the Northern Rhône, going as far as labelling his two flagship wines The Blonde and The Brunette after the two main soil types of Côte-Rôtie … **Irvine**, established in 1983, has made a name for their Grand Merlot, in addition to the numerous ranges and styles they produce today … **John Duval Wines**, a Barossa staple, has built its brand on the high-quality mid-range Plexus, an old-vine **GSM** that overdelivers … **Kaesler Wines**, now under management of only its third owners since 1893, has reinvented itself through sustainability and regenerative farming, while still delivering Barossa classics like the Old Bastard Shiraz … The **Kalleske** family has been growing grapes in the Barossa since 1853 but didn't release wine under their eponymous label until 2004, feeling like instant classics … **Mountadam** is one of the Eden Valley icons (planted in 1972), who, in addition to other offerings, proudly waves the flag for Eden chardonnay … **Saltram**, dating back to 1859, is most famous today for their Pepperjack label, the most-sold shiraz in Australia … **Sigurd** is Dan Graham's small-batch project of modern Barossa drops, including semillon-vermentino and early picked syrah … **Tim Smith** has held down winemaking gigs with some of the world's top wineries while also making his own wines, equally inspired by the Rhône and Barossa valleys … **Vinya Vella** is the name of a 6-hectare old-vine grenache vineyard in Vine Vale and the new project from rockstar viticulturist Dylan Grigg.

The famous contoured rows of Pewsey Vale Vineyard in the High Eden subregion of the Eden Valley. The vine rows follow the contours of the slope to help draw a favourable breeze in between the vines as well as capture the right amount of sunshine.

Clare Valley

Introduction

The Clare Valley is riesling country. It is not by the numbers the most planted grape (that honour goes to shiraz), but it is the grape the region is most associated with. Or, perhaps more importantly, the Clare Valley is the one Australian region most associated with riesling. The Clare (as it is often called, dropping the 'valley' for brevity) has become known for its distinctive style of riesling that has come to define the Australian approach to the grape: acid-driven, bone-dry, and aged for a short time in stainless steel.

And though this style is pervasive, the Clare has much more to offer. From ripe and forward cabernet sauvignon and shiraz, to structured and savoury old-vine reds (including the aforementioned grapes), to experimental approaches to grapes like vermentino and sangiovese, and even unique treatments of riesling (barrel fermentation and residual sugar, among them) – the Clare Valley is a diverse playing field. And with a handful of big names leading the charge – Jim Barry, Jeffrey Grosset and Wendouree most famously – the Clare has proven itself capable of making some of the great wines of Australia (and the world).

The vineyards of the Clare Valley sit along ridgelines and valleys that run north to south as part of the Mount Lofty Ranges. Such large natural formations often create inherent boundaries that define the locale of Australia's First Nations. The Clare Valley's western ridgeline in the Mount Lofty Ranges, which runs south through the Barossa Valley as well, marks the transition between the Kaurna and Ngadjuri Nations.

The Kaurna People are the original custodians of the western slopes of the entirety of the Mount Lofty Ranges, from the tip of the Fleurieu Peninsula to the northern end of the Loftys, where the green grass turns to ancient red earth and the Flinders Ranges begin to rise in the north. The Kaurna Nation is much more active today, and tends to be more present in First Nations conversations in the region, but the majority of the Clare Valley is actually on Ngadjuri land. Ngadjuri Country extends north to the Flinders Ranges and east to Manna Hill, running along the ridgeline that defines both the Clare and Barossa valleys.

Conversations around Indigenous rights and relations haven't yet taken hold among a critical mass of Clare Valley vintners, but there is an increasing attention to land care, which is sure to serve and define the (already stellar) wine production going forward. Adelina's Colin McBryde recalls, 'As Tony Brady [of Wendouree] always said, "we've got the oldest soils on planet earth" … and we have to be exceptionally respectful and thoughtful about how to keep them going.'

Evolution of Wine

The first vines in Clare Valley were planted by English immigrant John Horrocks in 1840: grenache vines in the township of Penwortham. Edward Burton Gleeson, the 'founder' of Clare (who named it after his home of County Clare, Ireland), also put a reputed 800 vines in the ground that decade at his property called Inchiquin.

The next viticultural deployment came at the hands of a Jesuit priest. Like the Silesian Lutherans who helped establish the Barossa Valley, the Jesuits were also experiencing religious persecution in Europe in the early 19th century and found relief in Australia. Father Kranewitter made the trek northward, settling about 130 kilometres outside Adelaide. He named his property Sevenhill, after the seven hills of Rome, and put grapevines in the ground in 1851. Five years later, Sevenhill produced its inaugural wine and Clare Valley's first winery was born.

By 1850, the Clare was also enjoying a small gold mining boom, which brought farmers and settlers to the area. With this new influx, the wine industry of the Clare continued to develop hardily over the rest of the century, in tandem with wheat paddocks, sheep pastures and fruit orchards. By 1870, there were 130 hectares of vines in the ground – more than quadruple the number of the previous decade.

In 1889, Carl Sobels and Hermann Buring took ownership of the Springvale vineyard, soon renaming it Quelltaler (the German translation of 'spring valley'). Since 1868 Sobels had been a winemaker for the property, which was originally planted in 1853 by Englishman Francis Treloar, coming to be dominated by cultivars of cabernet, shiraz, malbec and riesling. Soon after the acquisition, the next-generation Sobels and Burings became active in the winery: giving a young Leo Buring (see Barossa, p. 313) an early taste for riesling.

In 1892 a vineyard was planted by Alfred Percy Birks that would go on to become one of the Clare's (and Australia's) most significant. It started as a 0.2-hectare cabernet sauvignon block that grew to 12 hectares over the years, with additions of shiraz, malbec, mataro and muscat of Alexandria, among other grapes. Most vines were planted in the 1890s and early 1900s. The name of the winery? A.P. Birks Wendouree, often just referred to as Wendouree.

The Clare continued to grow exponentially. The 130 hectares under vine in 1870 turned into 580 hectares by the turn of the century. The region was capitalising on exports back to England, and was poised to take advantage of

The original cellar of Sevenhill, dug out and built of local stone by Jesuit monks when the winery was founded in 1851.

the open state borders as Federation was formed in 1901. But wineries were not cropping up with the same multiplicity as vineyards in the Clare, and the question arose: who is going to make all this wine? The Stanley Wine Company formed in 1894 as an answer to that question, promising to take any fruit that it was offered. By 1901, their biggest year yet, they were vinifying over 350,000 litres per vintage.

Stanley – which by 1911 was solely in the hands of J.H. Knappstein – and Quelltaler continued to grow into the beginning of the 20th century. By the century's second decade, the two producers were responsible for 75% of the Clare Valley's wine production. The Clare was not immune, though, to the economic depression of early 20th-century Australia, and experienced a slew of setbacks and closures, including trustee ownership of Stanley upon Knappstein's death, driving the company £45,000 in debt. By 1930, the region had turned to **fortifieds**, the export lifeblood sustaining the Australian wine industry at the time. (Quelltaler had a sherry-style bottling called Granfiesta that became popular in those decades.)

But the Clare continued to develop its industry and regain its focus on **table wine** production, rather than **fortified**: in 1937, Quelltaler Hock (riesling) became the first Australian wine served at the Lord Mayor's Banquet in London; in 1938, the Knappstein family came back into ownership of the Stanley Wine Company, doubling down on riesling as one of the signature grapes of the region, preserving old vines as well as planting new; and in 1947, a young Jim Barry earned the 17th ever degree from prestigious Roseworthy Agricultural College, applying himself immediately to the production of Clare Valley wine, and becoming the region's first degreed winemaker.

Barry went to work for Clarevale Cooperative, where he was for 22 years, before helping to launch Taylor's (formerly known as Château Clare). But as Barry was working for others, he began acquiring his own land: first in 1959, with a site that was part of Edward Burton Gleeson's original property, and then another 28 hectares in 1964, in the Armagh area of the region. He started making trial batches of wine in the 1960s

at Wendouree. He made his first wine under his eponymous label in 1974, creating a new benchmark for quality in the region and pushing forward its two-pronged identity: for steely, high-acid riesling and for bold, structured shiraz and cabernet sauvignon.

Also in 1974, Tony and Lita Brady came into ownership of A.P. Birks Wendouree. Tony was a retired academic, whose father-in-law somewhat strong-armed him and Lita into running the estate, which had been left in severe neglect by previous owners. Lita took up wine science, and Roly Birks– a descendent of Alfred Percy – stayed on for seven years to help the Bradys acclimate (until he was 88 years old!). Wendouree has become one of the most legendary and enigmatic estates of Australia: small production and a cult following, with famously luddite practices (both in production and distribution), and wines of notorious reticence, needing years to open up. Along with Jim Barry's efforts, Wendouree continued to establish the Clare's reputation as a serious red wine-producing region.

In 1981, at the age of 26, another major player of the Clare Valley made his entrance: Jeffrey Grosset. Though Grosset works with a handful of grape varieties, riesling is the one that made him decide to be a winemaker, and it's the grape that has been the overwhelming focus of the winery. As a result of his work, areas like Watervale, Springvale and Polish Hill River have become famous for the different characteristics they impart on riesling. So great is his impact, it's hard to imagine that Clare Valley would be celebrated for riesling the way it is without the work of Jeffrey Grosset, who continues to be an active champion for the region to this day.

Rather than looking at Clare Valley as having discrete eras of development, the region experienced a more consistent flow of small- to medium-sized producers in the last five decades, the likes of Taylor's (1969), Skillogalee (1970), Mount Horrocks (1982), Pikes (1985), Tim Adams (1986), Kilikanoon (1997), O'Leary Walker (2000), Adelina (2002), Wines by KT (2006) and Koerner (2014) in addition to those mentioned previously. The valley was not without its corporate manoeuvrings, as well, with the likes of Stanley, Tim Knappstein Wines and Quelltaler all passing

You may not get glitzy cellar doors and cutting-edge wine bars, but what you will get is wine that is solid, reliable and – with some frequency – exceptional.

into the hands of various multiregionals and multinationals, as well as the common practice of Clare land and fruit being purchased by external companies.

The overarching culture, though, of the important wineries of the Clare Valley has historically been somewhat similar. Styles and grapes may vary amongst these producers – from a traditional riesling and shiraz-based producer like Skillogalee to Koerner's play with grapes like mammolo, pigato and nielluccio – but they have historically occupied a single model that prioritises honest farming, small production, a terroir-forward approach, independent ownership, and moderate-intervention winemaking (think yes to **sulphur**, no to **reverse osmosis**). Provincial and traditional, in the best possible way. Not big and glam, nor edgy and experimental.

These margins have widened in the last five years, on both sides of the spectrum. While there have been the aforementioned few corporate-owned wineries in the Clare, more interest has materialised in recent years, especially from China. The Yinmore Group purchased Knappstein Wines in 2019 (previously owned by Accolade); the year before, Yantai Changyu Pioneer Wine Co, China's largest wine producer, bought Kilikanoon. It's too soon to say (especially with the COVID-19 pandemic in the intervening years), if these new investments will impact the overall structure and culture of the Clare.

On the other side of the spectrum, there is a handful of wineries (most of them based outside the region) that have looked to the Clare in recent years to produce some off-kilter wines. Some Young Punks (Clare-based, with Adelina's Colin McBryde as a founder), Frederick Stevenson (p. 318), Travis Tausend (p. 355) and Bink have been some of the producers representing the new guard working with Clare Valley fruit and playing with alternative styles: no **sulphur**, skin-contact, chillable reds, turbidity, et al.

But these new developments remain marginal. Overall, the Clare Valley is a region that feels surprisingly rustic given its exalted reputation; a region that sticks to what it is good at, with 80% of plantings dedicated to riesling, shiraz and cabernet sauvignon; and a region that is comfortable in its identity. You may not get glitzy cellar doors and cutting-edge wine bars, but what you will get is wine that is solid, reliable and – with some frequency – exceptional.

Lay of the Land

Clare Valley is Australia's most famous region for riesling. Though it is the third-most planted grape in the region (after shiraz and barely after cabernet sauvignon), its production can sometimes outperform its red counterparts, usually in drought vintages (such as in 2019 and 2020, where it accounted for the largest portion of the Clare Valley crush). And its reputation in Australia is nearly synonymous with the Clare Valley. What makes the Clare such a good region for riesling? The answer to this question normally focuses on two facets: elevation and soil.

But climate, and certainly its interplay with elevation, is as important a factor as any. The Clare is a top agent for undermining the **heat summation index** when applied to a whole region. The Clare Valley is a high Region 3 on the **Winkler Scale**, with 1895 growing degree days (Celsius) – which is more akin to appellations like Rioja and the Rhône Valley than classic riesling-growing regions like Germany, Alsace and Tasmania (who all fall under Region 1a – the coolest). But at the highest elevations, the temperature summation is closer to Region 1: a good argument for paying attention to **subregionality** in the Clare.

The Clare defies conventional climate classifications, with critics often oscillating between labelling it as a Mediterranean or Continental climate. And indeed, it has qualities of both. It receives 80% of its rainfall outside the growing season and enjoys cooling sea breezes coming off the Gulf of St Vincent (very Mediterranean). However, it also has a large **diurnal shift**, and at times can experience both heat spikes in the summer, and late spring frosts after bud break (more continental).

Elevation and **aspect** play a key role in how a vineyard experiences the unique Clare Valley climate. The higher up, the larger the **diurnal shift**. This also lessens the frost risk posed by frigid, moist air at the valley floor. Riesling is typically found at the region's highest elevations, though the highest vineyard in the region is Jeff Grosset's Gaia vineyard (570 metres), planted to cabernet sauvignon and cabernet franc, and on a southeasterly **aspect**, no less (another example of the Clare's counterintuitive climate!).

The southern end of the region is slightly higher in elevation, more noticeably along the eastern side of the valley. As the western end is a more undulating and varied surface, altitude fluctuates with little rhyme or reason. According to Jeff Grosset, it's 'altitude first', when

The Clare defies conventional climate classifications, with critics often oscillating between labelling the region as a Mediterranean or Continental climate.

Clare Valley Viticultural Footprint

Total delimited area (km²)	690
Total planted area (hectares)	5093
% of delimited area planted	7.380%
Total elevation range	190–609 masl
Elevation range of plantings	300–570 masl
Number of producers	55

Clare Valley Climate Data (°C)

	1960–1990	1991–PRESENT	2020
Heat summation/GDD	● 1778	● 1895	● 1875
Annual rain/GSR	568/218	532/224	401/203
Warmest month avg. temp.	21.6	22.4	21.6

Winkler Scale:

● 850–1111 ● 1112–1389 ● 1390–1667 ● 1668–1944 ● 1945–2222 ● 2223–2700

South Australia

Koerner's estate vineyard located in the Watervale subregion. Damon and Jono Koerner have become champions of Mediterranean grapes in the Clare, with Corsican varieties sciaccarellu, vermentinu and nielluccio leading the charge.

referencing the unique growing conditions that impact the Clare, 'but in combination with geology. The geological variance across the region is enormous. Over 40 variants that I am aware of.'

Nearly all the rocks found today in the region are a result of silt, sand and carbonate sediments from the marine basin – a basin that at one time extended as far south as Antarctica, when the two continents were connected. At the beginning of the Cambrian era, the accumulation of sediments ceased, and the volcanic intrusions and continental folding of the Delamerian Orogeny began. Today, the valleys of the Clare are among the weathered peaks of mountains that were once over 10 kilometres tall.

More recent geological activity and gentle uplifting carved a series of north–south oriented valleys through softer silts and dolomite rocks in between the Rhynie Sandstone Ridge to the west and the Gilbert Range Quartzite ridges to the east. Numerous formations and deposits appear at the surface among these valleys, creating a complex patchwork of soils across a fairly concise wine appellation. Riesling is thought to most classically pair with slate soils (thanks, Germany), but it is planted across all types of different settings in the Clare: red terra rossa, sandstone, dolerite, shale and, indeed, slate.

Most vineyards sit between the two ridges with a few new plantings exploring the outer foothills. Vineyards across the region generally face north, with some east-to-west variability. The afternoon sun collected by west-facing vineyards is verging on becoming too intense today, but it was favoured in the Clare's early years. On the eastern end of the region, vineyards are more exposed to (sometimes harsh) winds. While wind can limit yields, it also keeps some diseases and pests at bay.

The Clare's topography has created five unique (though unofficial) subregions: Polish Hill River, Watervale, Sevenhill, Clare and Auburn. When looking at the highest spots in each, this order corresponds to their relative warmth, with Polish Hill River being the coolest site and Auburn the warmest.

Polish Hill River sits in the foothills of the eastern ridge. Most vineyards face west to get

Clare Valley

HOW TO READ THIS MAP

The Clare Valley's kaleidoscopic spread of geological formations creates elevation changes that provide the valley with five identifiable unofficial subregions. Those subregions, along with changes in elevation across the region, are shown here.

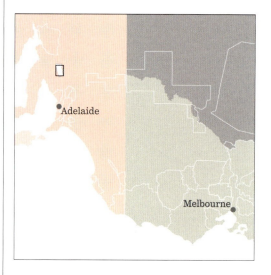

1 Adelina
2 A.P. Birks Wendouree
3 Byrne
4 Cardinham Home Block
5 Churinga Vineyard
6 Claymore Wines
7 Claymore Wines Leasingham Road Vineyard
8 Clos Clare
9 Crabtree
10 Eldredge
11 Farrell
12 Florita Vineyard
13 Grosset
14 Grosset Gaia Vineyard
15 Grosset Polish Hill Vineyard
16 Grosset Rockwood Vineyard
17 Grosset Springvale Vineyard
18 Hill River Clare Estate
19 Jim Barry Wines
20 Jim Barry Lodge Hill Vineyard
21 Kilikanoon
22 Kirrihill
23 Knappstein
24 Koerner
25 Little Brampton
26 Mintaro Wines
27 Mitchell
28 Mount Horrocks
29 Pauletts
30 Penna Lane
31 Petaluma Hanlin Hill Vineyard
32 Pikes
33 Pycnantha Hill Estate
34 Quelltaler Estate
35 Ruddenklau
36 Sevenhill
37 Skillogalee
38 Stringy Brae
39 Taylors
40 Tim Adams
41 Tim Gramp
42 Waninga Vineyard
43 Wilson
44 Wines by KT
45 Wykari

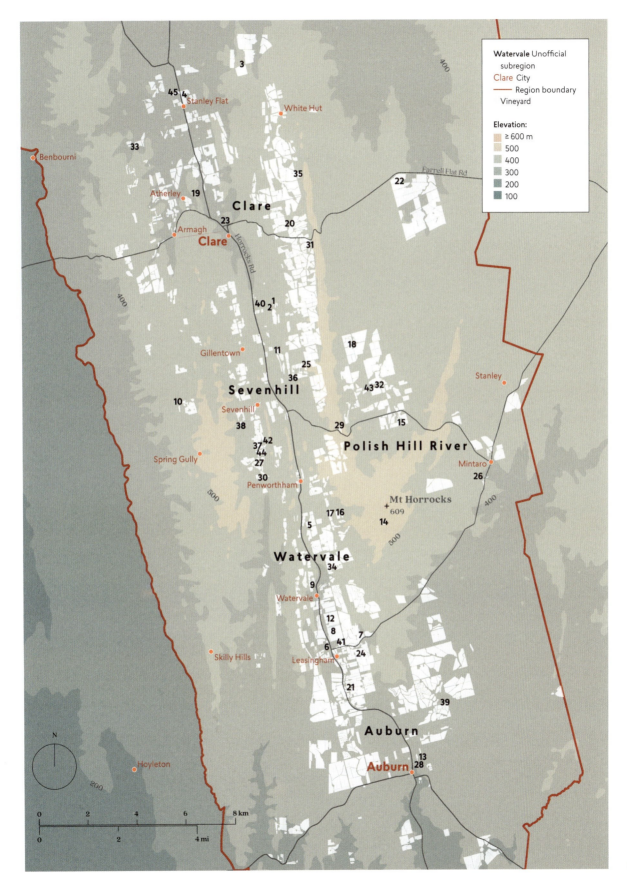

Clare Valley

This terra rossa is red volcanic loam over limestone, nearly identical to the storied soils of Coonawarra and parts of the Barossa.

afternoon sun, as well as protection from the region's strong winds. The area is extremely windy, with gales coming from the north (Grosset's Gaia was planted on a southeast **aspect** near Polish Hill River because the northern sites were so eroded by wind.)

Polish Hill River's vineyards run from 440 metres above sea level to Gaia's lofty 570. Polish Hill River is where some of the 'youngest' geological formations can be found. Here, the Gilbert Ridge Quartzite, which was deposited in shallow seas about 700 million years ago, is mixed through marly shales and siltstones and, in some areas, overlays blue slate. This area's soils are the most varied, in some cases changing drastically across one vineyard. Just south of Polish Hill River is Mount Horrocks, which helps

provide protection to the downwind vineyards in Watervale and Auburn, and gives its name to one of the Clare's top producers.

Watervale is further south from Polish Hill River, and more central in the appellation. It has flatter slopes, though still at 350–460 metres in elevation. Watervale's soils are primarily shale and quartzite – inward valley formations adjacent to terra rossa on the edges. This terra rossa is red volcanic loam over limestone, nearly identical to the storied soils of Coonawarra and parts of the Barossa. Grosset's Springvale vineyard sits on these terra rossa soils. The Florita vineyard also sits on red loamy clay over limestone in Watervale. Made famous by John Vickery's Leo Buring rieslings in the 1960s and 70s, Florita is now a famed single vineyard of Jim Barry.

Sevenhill is north of Watervale and due west of Polish Hill River, consisting of a narrow band of vineyard area between more distinct ridges. There's less airflow here, but some cooler **aspects** when wanted. And the ridges create points of shadow that can limit sunshine hours at the beginning and end of the day. Skillogalee dolomite encircles the exterior of the whole Clare, but appears in the Sevenhill subregion in particular. The wineries Skillogalee, Mitchell and Kilikanoon are based on the outskirts of Sevenhill.

The township of Clare has a population of just 3400. It houses a few local cellar doors and is home to the wineries Tim Adams and Wendouree, just south of the township itself (between it and Sevenhill).

Springtime brings bud burst and cover-crop blossoms to these gnarly old malbec vines in the original block of the Wendouree vineyard, planted between 1890 and 1900.

Wendouree is one of the only notable Clare Valley producers (perhaps the only) that doesn't focus on riesling (although there have been a few bottlings of the grape in the past). Wendouree's focus is its old-vine shiraz, malbec, cabernet sauvignon, mataro and muscat of Alexandria, all **dry-grown** on red loam over limestone soils at 450 metres above sea level. Shiraz vines dating back to 1893 and malbec vines from 1898 are still in production. Many plantings are from the 1920s. The latest are from the early 1980s.

Jim Barry Wines is based on the western outskirts of the town of Clare – the famed Lodge Hill and Armagh vineyards are within a five-minute drive. Lodge Hill is east of the town of Clare and sits at 480 metres above sea level – one of the higher sites in all of Clare. A northern-facing patch houses the vineyard's shiraz plantings, and the rest is dedicated to riesling. Both vineyards are on loam and clay, with a slate bedrock under the riesling section. The Armagh was planted by Jim Barry in 1968, on a north-facing slope of sandy gravel at 400 metres above sea level (Clare's western ridge is known for its 'Rhynie Sandstone'). Since 1985, Barry has released a single-vineyard The Armagh Shiraz, one of the Clare wines to hit **Langton's** Exceptional status (along with Grosset's Polish Hill Riesling and Wendouree's Shiraz).

Auburn is the southernmost township of the Clare, and its warmest. Elevations range from 300–340 metres above sea level. Mount Horrocks' Cordon Cut vineyard is in Auburn – a site and a wine that has become one of the most cherished in the region. For this vineyard, the fruiting canes are cut late in each season, with berries still on the vine, to allow the riesling grapes to partially dehydrate, concentrating the fruit. The resulting wine is different every year, but tends to have over 100 grams per litre of residual sugar – one of Australia's finest sweet wines.

In addition to the Clare's staples of shiraz, cabernet sauvignon and riesling, which account for a whopping 80% of production, other plantings include merlot (5%), chardonnay, pinot gris, malbec, semillon, grenache, sangiovese, mourvèdre, tempranillo and gewürztraminer. These grapes – as well as experimental others like aglianico, fiano, tourigal nacional, barbera, nebbiolo and even assyrtiko – are a vast minority in the Clare's footprint, but the energy around their production is one of excitement.

The Jim Barry-mobile, referred to by the family as 'Old Merc', is an iconic sight around the Clare Valley.

Hubbub

Water is an issue in many Australian wine regions, and acutely so in the Clare Valley. Sunshine hours are high in the Clare, and rainfall is low. The region only receives 500–600 millimetres per year in precipitation, so some type of irrigation is needed for most vineyards, with healthy old vines on deep soils being the last to be challenged.

'Access to water is essential for us to mitigate climate change impacts,' says Jeff Grosset. 'It's that simple. We never work the soil and we use a lot of certified organic mulch, topped up every three years. However, it depends completely on the season. We have sensors throughout the vineyards to tell us how much moisture is at 30, 60 and 90 centimetres at any time. We can therefore use minimal water to just avoid excessive vine stress.'

'Minimal' water is not just utilised from a quality perspective, but also out of necessity. The region is limited by law in the water that can be accessed – a maximum of one megalitre of water per hectare of vines annually (which includes what a winery requires at the production facility, most notably for cleaning). Additionally, because there is virtually no underground water in the Clare, water is accessed from the mains, just like it would be for domestic usage. It is thus charged at a retail-level cost, adding great expense to farming a vineyard. These factors, according to Grosset, 'force great diligence by [water] users'.

Currently, most of the Clare's water is sourced from the Murray River. A proposal is currently underway to replace this source with high-quality recycled water – granting greater water access at a more affordable cost, without tapping a natural resource. 'It is my belief,' Grosset says, 'that recycled water to offset [climate] changes here, just as is occurring everywhere to varying degrees, is ultimately the only rational environmental option.' As climate changes, and the Clare gets hotter and drier, access to water is paramount to preserve the integrity of the region's vineyards.

And the climate is changing. Grosset has mapped the first day of picking across his 41 harvests in the region, and found, firstly, that it's now about 35 days earlier than it once was, and, secondly, the starting date is becoming more erratic. Grosset hasn't found a negative impact on the wines, though. On the contrary, he counts the wines they've made in the last five or six years to be the winery's best ever.

But concerns about climate change are certainly alive and well in the Clare, and prompting a more serious conversation about land care. Grosset already belongs to the select few in the Clare who are farming under organic or **biodynamic** guidelines, with Mount Horrocks' Stephanie Toole leading the charge in that respect. McBryde, who buys fruit in addition to farming his own vineyards organically, says 'when we can, we buy fruit that's organic, but in Clare, that's very hard. The certified organic vineyards in Clare are: two in Polish Hill River, another one just up the road from us in Spring Farm, and then Jeffrey and Stephanie [of Grosset and Mount Horrocks, respectively], and that's it.'

Both McBryde and Grosset agree that organic viticulture should not be difficult in the Clare Valley, it just hasn't been a priority among growers so far. McBryde also reminds, despite the rather serious 5000 hectares under vine, 'we don't have that many wineries and winemakers in the Clare'. There are about 50 in total, but of those, several are large, commercial-level producers, and quite a few are small, mum-and-dad type operations that don't see their wines leave the GI boundaries. And neither of these types of producers is leading the conversation on responsible farming and fine wine.

But there is a current underway. The influx of new talent is reaching a critical point, combined with the knowledge and reputation of the old-guard, and a small handful of wineries at the forefront of responsible farming and fruit quality. As McBryde says, 'We need the stalwarts – we need the Wendourees – for a kind of resilience. And grounding. But we also need young people to be about and excited. There's a lot to offer here. That for me is where the prosperity is.'

PRODUCERS

ADELINA

Neighbouring the iconic Wendouree, in the small district of Springfarm, halfway between Sevenhill and Clare proper, is the estate vineyard of Adelina. Winemakers and scientists Col McBryde and Jennie Gardner launched their own label in 2002 when they took over management of Jennie's parents' vineyard, and have since certified it organic. Made up of mature plantings, some dating back to 1910, the vineyard features shiraz, grenache, mataro, ugni blanc, roussanne and carignan, including a mixed block of all six, which goes into their estate field blend. They make long-macerated, age-worthy reds from their home vineyard and source a range of other varieties from across South Australia. The couple also work with friend Nic Bourke on the brightly labelled Some Young Punks, drink now wines that span from off-dry Clare riesling to single-vineyard McLaren Vale mataro and cabernet sauvignon. *adelina.com.au*

Tony & Lita Brady
Wendouree

A.P. BIRKS WENDOUREE

Should you be driving through the Clare Valley and happen across the sign for Wendouree, you will notice it says 'closed' – and always does. A winery of true cult status, there is no cellar door, website or email address. Wines are sold via mail order and allocations are decided by current custodian and winemaker Tony Brady (who has never owned a mobile phone). Tony's father-in-law Max purchased Wendouree in 1974, a goldmine of old-vine shiraz, mataro, malbec and cabernet sauvignon. Max asked Tony to run it, despite him having just retired from an academic career. The 100-year-old winery has remained virtually the same since Tony and his wife Lita arrived, but the wines certainly have not. Once considered undrinkable in their youth, the wines have softened, with less focus on tannin and extraction, though ageability is still a priority. If you're not on the mailing list, check out top Australian auction sites and restaurants lists for a chance to try some. A magical experience to taste from such a historic and rarefied estate.

 What we're drinking

Adelina is one of the most exciting projects in South Australia with quality wine at the forefront but an eye on regenerative farming and custodianship of land writ large as an underpinning. Alongside Koerner, it is reinventing some of the idioms of Clare wine, with reds of finesse, tension, fine tannin and structure set alongside evocative white wines that celebrate texture and savouriness. – Mike Bennie

GROSSET

Jeffrey Grosset tasted his first riesling at the age of 15 and was so blown away that he enrolled to study winemaking on his next birthday. He worked his way up to a senior winemaker position in Germany but returned to Australia to start Grosset in 1981. Jeff has been an avid advocate for riesling for decades, being hooked since that first taste. He campaigned for only true riesling to be labelled as such in the 80s and has poured private funds into researching screw cap closure and wine maturation. Grosset has become synonymous with Clare Valley riesling – with Springvale, Watervale and the ever-popular Polish Hill sites being the sources of Jeffrey's iconic whites. Not a one-hit wonder, Jeffrey also makes a Bordeaux-style blend from his lofty Gaia vineyard, dabbles in the Italian varieties fiano and nero d'Avola, and sources pinot noir and chardonnay from the Piccadilly Valley in the Adelaide Hills. He is also a constant champion for high-quality farming and environmentalism in the region, pushing forward the agenda on everything from organics and **biodynamics** to revegetation and solar power. A true legend. *grosset.com.au*

Jeff Grosset
Grosset

JIM BARRY WINES

Jim and Nancy Barry bought their first property in the Clare Valley in 1959, beginning what today amounts to one of the most significant Australian brands. They continued buying up land, along with their sons, culminating in a whopping 345 hectares across the region and a further 35 in Coonawarra. This certainly hasn't diluted the importance of their vineyards, with each site playing its part in the Barry family's offerings. In fact, few single-vineyard bottlings have implanted themselves so concretely on the Australian consciousness as Armagh, Florita and Lodge Hill. Shiraz, riesling and, more recently, assyrtiko, are the calling cards of the winery, ranging from the value to the icon end of the spectrum. Jim Barry is now run by Jim's son Peter and the third generation is also involved in the business. *jimbarry.com*

KOERNER

Damon and Jono Koerner have gone from strength to strength in recent years, making off-the-beaten-track wines from their family vineyard, Gullyview. Their parents have been looking after Gullyview for over 40 years, which is planted mostly to riesling from the 70s and 80s and

> **JR** **What we're drinking**
>
> *Just when you thought you've learned about Australia's diversity of grapes, OG Clare Valley producer **Jim Barry** puts forth a killer example of assyrtiko — Australia's first. Bright, intense and citrusy with loads of structure. – Jonathan Ross*

> **JL** **What we're drinking**
>
> *Damon and Jono from **Koerner** have a deft touch with their reds, reminiscent of the wines of Corsica and Sardegna (yet entirely original to the Clare at the same time). In their hands, sciacarello, grenache and sangiovese are savoury, textural, food-friendly and just plain delicious. — Jane Lopes*

features some 90-year-old grenache vines. Damon and Jono readily use skin contact in their whites and early picking for their reds to craft textural and vibrant wines. The wines are often labelled with a grape's Mediterranean synonym, such as pigato or rolle for vermentino (sourced from the nearby Vivian vineyard), nielluccio for sangiovese and cannonau for grenache. They also make wine under the labels LEKO and Brothers Koerner, sourcing fruit from the Adelaide Hills. *koernerwine.com.au*

MOUNT HORROCKS

When Stephanie Toole purchased Mount Horrocks in 1993, she was looking for a hobby project. She is now one of the most respected winemakers and grape-growers in the Clare Valley. Since buying the property, she has developed three vineyard sites that are now all certified organic. Stephanie has a solid line-up of seven wines, all made from estate-grown fruit. She was an early adopter of the Sicilian grape nero d'Avola, first planting the variety in 2007. Stephanie's wines are elegant and skilfully crafted, something that is recognised both in Australia and abroad; her dessert wine, the Cordon Cut Riesling, was served to Queen Elizabeth II for her 80th birthday. Stephanie is also the leading voice in sustainable viticulture in the region, farming organically and **biodynamically** since day one. *mounthorrocks.com*

PIKES

The establishment of Pikes in 1985 was the second coming of beverage companies for the Pike family. Earlier generations had made beer, soft drinks and cordials, before economic hardship led to the business being sold. With this go-around, Neil Pike took on winemaking, while his brother Andrew, a viticulturist, managed 100 hectares of vineyard planted to 20 different grapes, including riesling, shiraz and cabernet sauvignon. When Neil finished up after 35 years at the helm, he began his retirement project Limefinger, which focuses on riesling from Polish Hill River and Watervale. *pikeswines.com.au*

SKILLOGALEE

Spencer and Margaret George purchased their property in 1969 and spent the next couple of years planting grapes. Early plantings were riesling, grenache, shiraz and crouchen, a variety formerly known as 'Clare Riesling'. Grenache and crouchen were soon grafted over with cabernet sauvignon and traminer. Diana and David Palmer began Skillogalee when they bought the vineyards in 1989, bringing the wines to new heights with the development of an onsite winery and expansion of land holdings. With their retirement in 2021, the Clausen family have taken over management, with the wines to be made by Kerri Thompson (see Wines by KT). *skillogalee.com.au*

WINES BY KT

Kerri Thompson spent eight years managing Leasingham before going out on her own. Having lived in the Clare since 1998, her love for riesling is deep. Kerri makes five different bottlings of the variety using fruit from trusted growers, but she is particularly passionate about the way it is expressed in Watervale. Her reds are quaffable and earthy, made

> **KF** **What we're drinking**
>
> *Wines by KT's Kerri Thompson is a gun and she does not muck around when it comes to riesling in particular. Melva, named after her grandma, is a wild-fermented, off-dry expression that is seriously smashable. Just as well it comes bottled in magnums, too. You'll need them! — Kavita Faiella*

mostly from Rhône and Iberian varieties. *winesbykt.com*

And don't forget …
Clos Clare is a side-project of Tom and Sam Barry (third generation at Jim Barry), whose production largely centres around Watervale riesling and single-vineyard shiraz … **Kilikanoon** makes a wide range of wines from father-and-son Mort and Kevin Mitchell, with a focus on classic Clare styles … **Knappstein** is an important historical name in the Clare Valley and now the producer of Clare staples like riesling, shiraz, cabernet sauvignon and even malbec … **Mitchell** is second-generation Andrew Mitchell and his wife Jane, who have built their eponymous winery into a thriving piece of the Clare Valley tapestry, with a focus on chemical-free and **dry-grown** farming practices, resulting in classic Clare riesling and cabernet … **O'Leary Walker** was established in 2000 by winemakers David O'Leary and Nick Walker, crafting elegant Clare riesling and shiraz, as well as a number of favourites from Adelaide Hills … **Pauletts** proudly boasts 'the world's best riesling and Clare Valley's most spectacular views' from their Polish Hill River winery and restaurant, established in 1983 … **Sevenhill** is the region's very first winery, today producing a wide range of wines, sparkling riesling all the way through to **fortified** styles, all from estate-grown fruit, much of which dates back to the 70s and earlier … **Shut the Gate** runs oft-awarded tasting rooms in both Clare Valley and the Snowy Mountains (NSW), incorporating alternative grapes into their offering, like barbera, negroamaro and fiano … **Taylor's**, one of the eleven 'Australia's First Families of Wine', is a third-generation estate with a great love and dedication to the Clare, producing a wide range of wines, largely classic and affordable.

Clare Valley

 New Guard  Environmental Hero Rising Star Legend Regional Stalwart Must Visit  Cult Following Historic Estate

335

Adelaide Hills

Introduction

The Adelaide Hills GI is 70 kilometres long and 30 kilometres wide, running parallel to Adelaide, on the city's eastern side. The closest vineyard to the city is about a 15-minute drive up the hills, due east. Driving south from the flat, sandy plains of the Barossa, or north from the hot, red earth of McLaren Vale, the Adelaide Hills feels like a different world: one defined by lush greenery, steep slopes and foggy dampness.

The Adelaide Hills is Peramangk Country. The Peramangk people's traditional lands are the hillsides and tablelands of the Adelaide Hills, up on today's Mount Lofty Ranges. The northern limits of the lands they cared for were drawn by the now-faint South Para River, which bisects the Barossa Valley. The Ngadjuri lived to the north.

Peramangk is an exonym – without any continuity of settlement in the area, we're left with the Kaurna word for them. The Kaurna are the traditional custodians of the land now known as Adelaide, Adelaide Plains and McLaren Vale, and their name for their neighbouring nation is thought to reference the red hue of the Peramangk skin when males were covered with ochre during times of initiation and conflict. Anthropologist Norman Tindale traced eight family names within the Peramangk nation, living as far north as today's Eden Valley, through to Mount Barker and south to Myponga.

Records (though sometimes unreliable) show that the relations between the Lutherans at Hahndorf and the Peramangk were first peaceful, with the Peramangk teaching colonists how to catch game and explaining which vegetation should be eaten. But, by the 1840s, as their lands became overcrowded with sheep and other constructs of European agriculture, conflict arose. The Peramangk population moved to places untouched by colonisers to achieve food security and safety. Though death from conflict and disease did occur, the Peramangk's disappearance resulted from the choice to migrate (and lose their national identity), rather than allow themselves to be decimated.

Today, descendants of the families that Tindale identified carry the Peramangk story forward, though it is not a nation that has recovered the way other larger neighbouring nations have.

Viticulture was one of the early systems of European agriculture introduced by the colonists in Adelaide Hills, but the area's modern wine industry did not develop until the late 1970s. In its under 50 years of wine-growing, one thing is clear: its raw material rivals any of the great wine regions of the world. Some of the finest chardonnay, pinot noir, sauvignon blanc and shiraz in Australia is grown within the borders of the Adelaide Hills. The region has had its bouts of shoddy winemaking and ambivalent grape growing, but even those chapters – which seem to be coming to a close – could not obscure the nearly unparalleled natural bounty that the Adelaide Hills offers.

Evolution of Wine

Adelaide Hills claims some illustrious early wine history. One of South Australia's first vineyards was planted by John Barton Hack in North Adelaide, but as urban sprawl encroached, he transplanted his vines to the Adelaide Hills in 1840, at a site in Echunga Springs near Mount Barker. In 1843, Hack sent wine from his vineyard to Queen Victoria, marking the first vinous Australian gift sent to English royalty.

Other vineyards cropped up in subsequent years. The Adelaide Hills regional organisation catalogues the following sites: 'Auldana in 1842 and Dr Christopher Rawson Penfold's "The Grange" at Magill in 1844 as well as plantings by Arthur Hardy at Mount Lofty; John Baker's Morialta Vineyard at Norton Summit; EJ Peake at Clarendon, Glen Ewin Wines at Houghton (today Willabrand Fig Orchards) and Harry Dove Young's Holmesdale at Kanmantoo.'

Adelaide Hills was growing in renown, but had yet to find its signature style, mainly growing the same shiraz, grenache and riesling vines that were dominant in their northern neighbour, the Barossa. Enter: French-trained Edmund Mazure, who started working in the Adelaide Hills in 1884, first at the historic Beaumont house, then at the Auldana and Holmesdale vineyards. Mazure pioneered sparkling wine in the Adelaide Hills, both classic **traditional method**, as well as a unique style of bubbly red wine, dubbed 'sparkling burgundy' (though made from shiraz). To this day, pinot noir, chardonnay, pinot meunier and shiraz remain important grapes to the Adelaide Hills.

By 1900, over 200 grape growers had established themselves in the region, with an identity forming around cool-climate viticulture and sparkling wine. But the turn of the century hit the region hard – the national palate gravitating toward sweet wine and severe economic depression meant that by 1930, all vineyards had been grubbed up. For the next half century, the land was dedicated to other industries, namely dairy, cattle, sheep, fruit orchards and vegetable fields.

The resurgence in Adelaide Hills started in 1979, with the planting of The Tiers Vineyard by Brian and Ann Croser. Brian had received his masters in viticulture and oenology at California's UC Davis, where he had become enamoured with the chardonnay grape in the hands of such wineries as Freemark Abbey, Chalone, Robert Mondavi, Mayacamas, Hanzell and Spring Mountain.

Returning to Australia, Brian and Ann moved to the Adelaide Hills to establish Petaluma Wines (named after the California town in Sonoma County). They found a dilapidated apple orchard in Adelaide Hills' high-altitude Piccadilly Valley and **close-planted** the 7-hectare vineyard to chardonnay. Petaluma's premise from the beginning was to match grape to place: in addition to Adelaide Hills chardonnay, they

also sourced fruit to make signature expressions from other regions, such as Clare Valley riesling and Coonawarra cabernet sauvignon.

Stephen George was soon attracted to the region, as well, but instead of a focus on chardonnay, George aimed to produce Australia's best pinot noir under his Ashton Hills label. He planted 3 hectares of vines in 1982: south-facing at 570 metres above sea level, in the Piccadilly Valley as well. Ashton Hills remains one of Adelaide Hills' most important pinot noir producers to this day.

Mark Whisson, the vineyard manager for Petaluma at the time, also planted his own vines in Piccadilly in the mid-1980s, making pinot noir for his Whisson Lake label that continues to be some of Adelaide Hills' best (and most underrated).

The early 1980s brought others, with a focus on the next major subregion of the Adelaide Hills: Lenswood. Tim and Annie Knappstein came from the Clare Valley and bought their Lenswood property in 1981, with the intention of exploring chardonnay, sauvignon blanc and pinot noir. Geoff Weaver, a Hardys (p. 374) winemaker, put down chardonnay, sauvignon blanc, riesling, pinot noir and cabernet sauvignon vines with his father in Lenswood in 1982, forming his eponymous estate. And Eden Valley's famed Prue and Stephen Henschke made their Adelaide Hills debut, converting a Lenswood apple orchard to vines in 1981.

The next significant investment in the Adelaide Hills came in 1989, when cousins Michael Hill Smith **MW** and Martin Shaw formed Shaw+Smith. In the early days, Shaw+Smith made its wine at Petaluma and Wirra Wirra (p. 377), before buying their Balhannah property and building a winery on the site in 1999. They've since acquired properties at both Lenswood and Piccadilly (and outside Adelaide Hills), becoming leaders of cool-climate viticulture in the Australian wine community.

The Adelaide Hills continued its steady growth, with Mt Lofty Ranges Vineyard, The Lane, Pike & Joyce, Longview and Golding established from the early 1990s to the early 2000s, helping bring profile and awareness to the Adelaide Hills. Up until this point, Adelaide Hills had seen little corporate involvement – Petaluma being the main exception. Brian Croser grew

Petaluma to become a group, acquiring Knappstein Wines (Clare Valley), Mitchelton (Nagambie Lakes) and Stonier (Mornington Peninsula). But Petaluma Ltd – a publicly traded company – was itself bought out in 2001 by Australian beverage company Lion Nathan (now Lion, in turn owned by Kirin) in a takeover alternatively labelled 'dramatic' and 'hostile'.

Beyond this aberration, Adelaide Hills has largely been the region of the boutique, family-owned winery, as it is the region of the renegade vintner. The definition of this rebellion has changed over the years (so much so that many of these practices are seen as classic now). In the early days, Brian Croser, Stephen George and the others were renegades for investing in an unproven region, planting grapes, such as chardonnay and pinot noir, that had yet to gain traction in Australia, and experimenting with different **clones** and **high-density plantings**.

In the early 2000s, Erinn and Janet Klein were seen as outliers for investing heavily in **biodynamics** and regenerative viticulture at their farm Ngeringa. 'Back then,' says Gareth Belton of Gentle Folk, 'organics were laughed at a little bit. I think Erinn Klein got a lot of flak back in the day, when he was going to plant an organic vineyard from day one … he's proven them all wrong.' It took a long time in the Adelaide Hills, but eventually others have started to follow suit, with Brackenwood, Shaw+Smith, CRFT, Murdoch Hill, Hahndorf Hill and Gareth himself at Gentle Folk all adding to the environmentalism conversation today.

The next set of renegades – perhaps Adelaide Hills' most famous – took hold in the early 2000s and helped define Australia's natural wine movement. This movement started in an enclave in the western hills of the region, just north of Piccadilly, called Basket Range. It started as far back as 1980, when Phillip Broderick planted Bordeaux varieties on his property, calling his winery Basket Range Wine. Over the years, particularly with his sons Louis and Sholto taking the helm more recently, the style has become firmly rooted in the natural wine aesthetic: all grapes are estate grown and organically farmed, wines tend to be low alcohol, and **sulphur** usage ranges from none to a low

25 ppm, depending on the needs of the particular wine. The Button family also planted in Basket Range in the 1990s, and would go on to become an important producer for the region when the second generation started making wine in 2014.

More doctrinaire producers would emerge, in particular, Anton van Klopper. Van Klopper bought 6 hectares in the Basket Range in 2002, establishing his winery Lucy Margaux (now known as Lucy M, rumoured to be due to pressure from Bordeaux's Château Margaux). He has gone on to be one of the most controversial figures in Australian wine: some hailing his staunchly anti-additive credo and novel wines, others finding dogmatism and flaws. James Erskine of Jauma, though perhaps less controversial, also emerged as a strictly no-**sulphur** producer, not adding the naturally occurring preservative since the 2015 vintage, and defining natural wine by its absence.

Erskine and van Klopper, along with Barossa wine-grower Tom Shobbrook (p. 316) and Sydney artist Sam Hughes, formed a group known as Natural Selection Theory, whose original website stands today (naturalselectiontheory.com) and is worth a browse. The group made and released wines together (like the 2010 Project Egg Runway 3, 'the first of its kind – "Real" Hunter Semillon'), but also created a culture around wine that veered toward performance art: releasing 'Sounds of Birth' albums with their wines, throwing Batman-themed release parties, and hosting a 'hot pants tour' (where they would just wear, yep, hot pants).

Natural Selection Theory officially disbanded by 2013, though it did much to 'shake up the system' (Erskine's stated goal in a 2019 article). The late Taras Ochota and his wife Amber helped usher in the next phase of the movement, launching Ochota Barrels in 2008. The wines straddled the line between natural and traditional in a way that almost everyone found thrilling, and Taras and Amber quickly became influential figures in the Australian wine scene. 'Taras was the glue who brought everyone together,' says Murdoch Hill's Michael Downer. 'Not divisive, no matter what, he would bring everyone together with positive energy and the sole focus of making the best, most delicious wine possible.'

Adelaide Hills remains, perhaps now more than ever, a hotbed for creativity and innovation.

Other Basket Range wineries emerged, as well as wineries based elsewhere in the Adelaide Hills, who participated in the natural wine conversation: BK Wines (2007), Jauma (2010), The Other Right (2012), Gentle Folk (2013), Commune of Buttons (2014), Charlotte Dalton (2015), Borachio (2016), Manon (2016), Travis Tausend (2016), Château Comme Ci Comme Ça (2017), Scintilla (2017), Worlds Apart (2017), Jean Bouteille (2019), Les Fruits (2019) and Parley Wine (2021) among others.

Adelaide Hills remains, perhaps now more than ever, a hotbed for creativity and innovation. This can mean unusual styles, **pét-nats**, cloudy wine, skin-contact whites, crown seals, clear glass and colourful labels: some of the hallmarks of the natural wine movement that aren't going anywhere. But it also means a creative approach to farming and winemaking among the region's best producers, that has little to do with aesthetics, and everything to do with a greater attention to land care and producing delectable wines that showcase the unique attributes of the Adelaide Hills.

Lay of the Land

Of Shaw+Smith's 30-odd year tenure in the Adelaide Hills, Michael Hill Smith says: 'We've understood, and somewhat to our cost, that you *can* plant the wrong variety in the wrong site.' While some appellations of Australia provide a ubiquitous backdrop to their marquee grapes, the Adelaide Hills is a bit more fickle.

Those marquee grapes are chardonnay, pinot noir, sauvignon blanc and shiraz, though interest is being conjured with everything from nebbiolo and sangiovese to cabernet sauvignon and merlot and even riesling. Chardonnay, in particular, has emerged as the star of the region. 'If you had to pick one variety to bet the house on in the Adelaide Hills, it's chardonnay,' says Hill Smith, who plants the grape at Shaw+Smith's Lenswood and Piccadilly vineyards. Ngeringa's Erinn Klein and Murdoch Hill's Michael Downer also cite chardonnay as the grape to beat in the Adelaide Hills, both in its current expressions, and in its resilience to climate change.

The Adelaide Hills GI sits within the slopes of the Mount Lofty Ranges, only covering vineyard sites of at least 300 metres above sea level. The peaks and valleys are a result of the Delamerian Orogeny that folded this portion of Australia when it was the continent's east coast, 870 million years ago.

The highest elevation site within the Adelaide Hills is the Mount Lofty Summit, which sits at 720 metres above sea level, only a 20-minute drive southeast of Adelaide's city centre. While no vineyards sit this high (the highest is just over 600 metres), the Mount Lofty Summit is a defining point for the region. Michael Downer, conveying a common axiom of Brian Croser, says that the Adelaide Hills can be thought about in rings that radiate from Mount Lofty Summit, with corresponding changes in moisture and temperature as one moves away from the peak.

Elevations vary throughout the Hills, with the highest plantings generally hugging the western side of the appellation in Piccadilly Valley, Summertown, Ashton and Basket Range, though a few high-elevation outposts are found further east at Lenswood and Mount Torrens. Most of these sites sit between 470 and 585 metres above sea level. Down in the Onkaparinga Valley, framed by Mount Bold and Mount Barker, vineyards sit between 320 and 400 metres in elevation.

By the numbers, there is an approximate half-degree (Celsius) drop in temperature for every 100 metres gained in elevation. For example, in the town of Mount Barker (at 350 metres elevation), the mean January temperature is 20.1°C, while in Lenswood (at 500 metres elevation), it's 18.3°C.

Soils throughout the region aren't as defining as they are in many other Australian wine regions (such as the neighbouring Barossa and McLaren Vale). Soils range from sandy loams to loams to clay loams, containing shale, ironstone and quartz at various points. The thinner soils upslope have a stonier composition compared to the thicker, deep clays at the lower elevations.

The Adelaide Hills is notable in that it has two officially designated subregions; it's a rare feat among Australian GIs to even have one. Lenswood was designated in October 1998, eight months after the larger Adelaide Hills was officially registered. Lenswood sits 30 kilometres due east

Adelaide Hills Viticultural Footprint

Total delimited area (km²)	1470
Total planted area (hectares)	3957
% of delimited area planted	2.700%
Total elevation range	149–714 masl
Elevation range of plantings	275–625 masl
Number of producers	90

Adelaide Hills Climate Data (°C)

	1960–1990	1991–PRESENT	2020
Heat summation/GDD	● 1475	● 1641	● 1653
Annual rain/GSR	801/285	749/258	688/256
Warmest month avg. temp.	19.6	20.6	20.4

Winkler Scale:

● 850–1111 ● 1112–1389 ● 1390–1667 ● 1668–1944 ● 1945–2222 ● 2223–2700

of Adelaide's city centre, the Mount Lofty Summit about equidistant between the two.

Elevations reach up to 600 metres here, with a sizable variation of rainfall across the subregion. At Stringybark, right where the Pike & Joyce winery sits in the northeastern end of the Lenswood GI, rainfall averages 785 millimetres annually, though at the southwestern end of the subregion, rainfall mirrors the Piccadilly Valley with a metre of rain each year.

Lenswood is most known for chardonnay, pinot noir and sauvignon blanc, though Eden Valley's Henschke has made a notable go of riesling in the region. Knappstein and Geoff Weaver (along with Henschke) put this subregion on the map early and were most responsible for it becoming an official GI. In 2012, Shaw+Smith bought in Lenswood, as did Murdoch Hill in 2021, both adding further credibility to the cool-climate, high-elevation potential of the region.

Lenswood's southwestern corner touches the northeastern end of Piccadilly Valley, Adelaide Hills' second official subregion, which was codified in 2000. Piccadilly, like Lenswood, reaches up to 600 metres in elevation, but with over a metre of rain annually (25% more than the drier parts of Lenswood). Michael Downer calls it a 'misty, foggy, drizzly climate', which morphs from the sunshine of Adelaide as one drives up and over the Mount Lofty Summit. Rather than being behind the rain shadow, this area is in it, often within the path of the rain's deluge. Piccadilly Valley is the coolest and wettest growing area in South Australia.

It is also the region where Brian Croser chose to plant his historic vineyards in Adelaide Hills: chardonnay on northeastern-facing slopes for

Petaluma (The Tiers vineyard), and chardonnay and pinot noir on southern-facing slopes for his eponymous sparkling label. Per Croser, the valley is uniquely formed by the 1.6 billion-year-old basement rocks of the Barossa complex, rather than the younger 800–700 million-year-old formations in the surrounding areas of the Hills and Mount Lofty Ranges. Recently Shaw+Smith planted 5.6 hectares to chardonnay and pinot noir in Piccadilly at a **planting density** of 10,666 vines per hectare.

Ashton and Summertown are two northern townships in the Piccadilly Valley – often singled out as their own unique areas, but technically within the boundaries of the Piccadilly Valley. Ashton is where Stephen George planted in 1982 to stake a name for Adelaide Hills pinot noir at his Ashton Hills vineyard. Both Summertown and Ashton clock similar rainfall averages to the more southern outposts of Piccadilly Valley, but with greater variation. Record highs reach a sopping 1790 millimetres per year, and record lows a still-moist 561 millimetres per year.

Ashton and Summertown have far fewer plantings than southern Piccadilly, though Petaluma (and Croser's subsequent project Tapanappa) has long been a champion of the latter, and Ashton Hills of the former – each proving that the area is capable of greatness, if people are willing to deal with the variable rainfall conditions.

After these two official subregions of the Adelaide Hills, there are many other areas that are recognised for their unique features. While the region is in no hurry to officially designate more GIs, many producers do label by unofficial subregions.

A Holistic View Towards Sustainability

Australian winemakers are not just thinking about the here and now; they are particularly interested in protecting their land for the next 5, 50 and 500 years. This thought is not new and builds on over 50,000 years of First Nations caring for the lands and waterways of the continent. From in-depth research on climate change and farming methods, to a national sustainability program with nearly 1000 members, to just under 50% of the world's certified organic farmland, great strides are being made. There is always more work to be done, and the most environmentally minded Australian vintners tend to be critical of where the country is at. But in our observation, Australia is further along than many grape-growing countries in its approach to sustaining and regenerating its precious natural resources.

Adelaide Hills

HOW TO READ THIS MAP

This map shows changes in elevation across the Adelaide Hills, with Mt Lofty's peak being the highest, and therefore the coolest and wettest. **Microclimates** warm as elevation decreases. Rainfall diminishes moving further away from Mt Lofty, though some eastern areas benefit from smaller rises in elevation and cold, southerly weather.

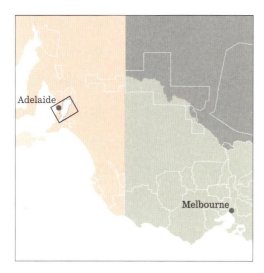

1 Anderson Hill
2 Anvers
3 Artwine
4 Ashton Hills
5 Atkins Farm
6 Barratt Wines
7 Barristers Block/ Cel a d'or
8 Basket Range Wine
9 Bird in Hand
10 Birdwood Estate
11 Birdwood High School Vineyard
12 Bowyer Ridge Vineyard
13 By Jingo Vineyard
14 Casa Freschi
15 Chain of Ponds
16 CRFT
17 Commune of Buttons
18 Deviation Road
19 Fox Gordon
20 Gentle Folk
21 Golding
22 Greenhill
23 Hahndorf Hill
24 Haselgrove Vignerons
25 Henschke Lenswood Vineyard
26 Honey Moon Vineyard
27 Howard Vineyard
28 Ilya
29 Jauma
30 K1 Wines by Geoff Hardy
31 Karrawatta
32 La Prova
33 The Lane Vineyard
34 Lansdowne
35 Lloyd Brothers
36 Lobethal Road
37 Lofty Valley
38 Longview Vineyard
39 Lucy Margaux
40 Magpie Springs Vineyard
41 Malcolm Creek Vineyard
42 Manyara Vineyard
43 Marble Hill
44 Mike Press & Top Drop
45 Mt Bera Estate
46 Mount Lofty Ranges Vineyard
47 Murdoch Hill
48 Nepenthe Charleston Vineyards
49 Nepenthe Hahndorf Vineyard
50 Nepenthe Lenswood Vineyard
51 New Era
52 Ngeringa
53 Nine Fingers
54 O'Leary Walker
55 Ochota Barrels
56 Paracombe
57 Penfolds Magill Estate
58 Petaluma
59 Pike & Joyce
60 Protero
61 Riposte
62 Romney Park
63 Saint & Scholar
64 Shaw+Smith Lenswood Vineyard
65 Shaw+Smith Piccadilly Vineyard
66 Shaw+Smith Balhannah Vineyard
67 Shining Rock
68 Sidewood Estate
69 Simon Tolley
70 Sinclair's Gully
71 Somerled
72 Tapanappa Tiers Vineyard
73 Teakles Hill
74 Ten Miles East
75 Thistledown
76 Tilbrook Estate
77 Tomich Hill
78 Top Note
79 Unico Zelo/ Applewood
80 Verdun Park
81 Vinteloper
82 Watkins
83 Whisson Lake
84 Wicks Estate

South Australia

342

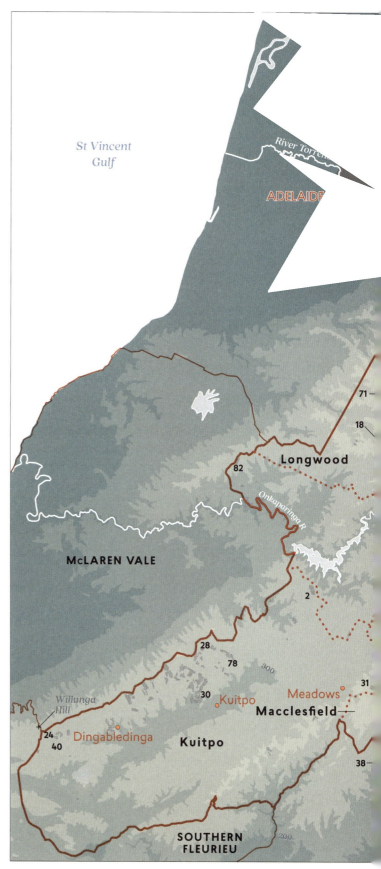

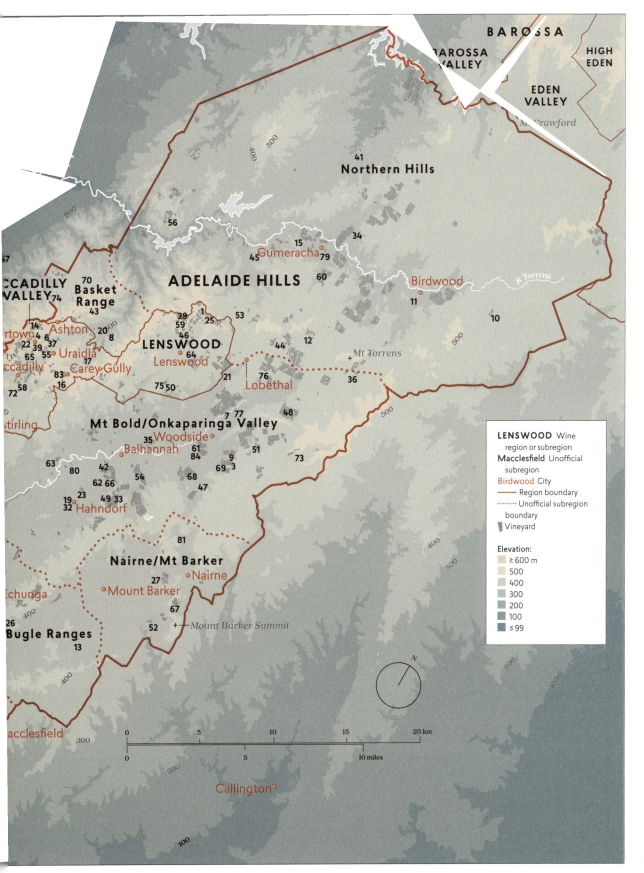

Adelaide Hills

Basket Range sits in the nook created by Piccadilly Valley's northern border and Lenswood's western one. (In fact, the boundaries of the Piccadilly Valley GI overlap with the township of Basket Range, though most who have a Basket Range address – take Commune of Buttons for example – align with the latter rather than the former.) Despite it having received much attention in recent years – mainly due to the cluster of producers forming Australia's most significant natural wine movement – it has few plantings and very little data on its conditions. As there is no an isolated weather station for the Basket Range, the closest readings for rainfall and temperatures are either those of Ashton or Uraidla (both to the south).

Uniquely, though, the Basket Range area is heavily traversed by wooded slopes, and is largely planted to fruit orchards, rather than vineyards. Basket Range Wine's estate vineyard sits at 450 metres in elevation. It has both north- and south-facing **aspects** on loamy red and blue clay over sandstone, with schist, ironstone and shale. Commune of Buttons has estate vineyards in the Basket Range at 350 metres above sea level on clay, sandstone and quartz. These two sites show the diversity across Basket Range's small plantings, with the grapes across these vineyards ranging from chardonnay and pinot noir to saperavi and nebbiolo.

The central valley of the Adelaide Hills, the Onkaparinga Valley, is a continuation of the basin that winds through McLaren Vale, following the Onkaparinga River from its northeast origin. Altitude and rainfall are in general much lower here than in many parts of the Adelaide Hills, with elevations topping out at 400 metres and rainfall usually not exceeding 700 millimetres per year.

It's in the flatter parts of the valley where the soft, sandy loams are home to grapes like the cabernets, merlot, shiraz, sauvignon blanc and cab franc. Hill Smith details planting pinot noir on Shaw+Smith's Balhannah site before realising it was 'just too warm' for the pinot that they wanted. 'So we pulled it out and planted shiraz in its place,' he says. There are certainly successful examples of pinot noir in the central valleys of the region, but they tend to be softer and less chiselled than the high-elevation plantings of the western ridges.

Shiraz and sauvignon blanc are the heroes of this central region, with Shaw+Smith in Balhannah and Murdoch Hill in Oakbank being the most notable producers. But examples of everything from pinot noir and chardonnay to grüner veltliner and cabernet sauvignon have found success in the area.

At its northeastern-most extension, the valley reaches Mount Torrens, which has become a hub of notable shiraz plantings, as well as some viognier, nebbiolo and sangiovese at mid-elevations for the Hills, sitting around 440–480 metres above sea level. Architects of Wine, Borachio, Lobethal Road, Commune of Buttons and Michael Hall all label Mount Torrens on their bottlings from the region. Other

The Tiers vineyard, the original crown jewel of Petaluma in the Piccadilly Valley.

northern Adelaide Hills locales, like Gumeracha and Kenton Valley, share a similar warmer and drier climate, and are of increasing interest for shiraz, sangiovese and nebbiolo as well. Unico Zelo's winery and their Applewood Distillery are based in Gumeracha and have brought a palpable buzz to the region.

On the other side of the Onkaparinga Valley, nestled between it and the eastern boundary of the appellation, is an area known as Mount Barker. Mount Barker itself is a lone peak of 534 metres above sea level. The vineyards of Mount Barker Summit, however, don't reach those heights, and tend to tap out at 420 metres above sea level.

What makes this area unique is the clear path that southerly winds have from the ocean, across Lake Alexandrina, and up into the vineyards. Disease pressure is quite low thanks to this airflow. Adelaide Hills' first organic and **biodynamic** vineyard, Ngeringa, is based here (still one of the few certified **biodynamic** vineyards in the region today). Ngeringa makes profound estate-wide and single-vineyard bottlings of chardonnay, pinot noir and syrah in this unique enclave.

The Mount Barker area has perhaps the most diverse **microclimates** suitable for a variety of grapes. Higher-elevation southern **aspects** can produce leaner chardonnay and pinot noir expressions that rival those of Lenswood and Piccadilly Valley, while vineyards with northerly **aspects** produce savoury expressions of shiraz. Growers in the local area are also singing the praises of sangiovese.

South of Mount Barker, vineyards sit mainly along the Adelaide Hills/McLaren Vale border, in the lower-lying hilltops of the Loftys, in the towns of Kuitpo (pronounced KY-Po) and, wait for it, Dingabledinga (a Kaurna exonym meaning 'water everywhere'). There is a dense cluster near Macclesfield, on the eastern side of the Adelaide Hills, as well as some vineyards further south, bordering Southern Fleurieu.

Rainfall here is similar to Mount Barker, ranging from low-700s to mid-800 millimetres per year. Temperature averages can be a touch cooler here, with vineyards being closer to the coast, and likely feeling even more of that southerly ocean breeze. The area has a diverse topography with vineyards planted to a number of different **aspects** and ranging from 350–400 metres in elevation.

Of these areas, Kuitpo is the most known and planted area. Geoff Hardy (fifth generation of McLaren Vale's Hardys, p. 374) first planted here in 1986. Today, Kuitpo is home to the likes of former Alpha Box & Dice owner/winemaker Justin Lane's Freddy Nerks label, Golden Child, Coates Wines and Travis Tausend. Grapes include the usual suspects of chardonnay, pinot noir, sauvignon blanc, shiraz and cabernet sauvignon, as well as some dolcetto, mourvèdre, tempranillo and verdelho. Kuitpo is still figuring out its identity, but combines some of the best of the Adelaide Hills and McLaren Vale: a beachy vibe with cooler, elevated sites.

Hubbub

The hubbub of the Adelaide Hills largely centres around the natural wine movement – though it's not exactly what you might think. When the Adelaide Hills emerged as the epicentre of the natural wine movement in the early 2000s, it caused some strife: both infighting within the movement itself, and tension between members of the movement and other Adelaide Hills producers. Up until that point, Adelaide Hills was largely defined as a conventional cool-climate growing region: a region with a proven track record for excellent wines, but with little in the way of organic or **biodynamic** farming and little in the way of winemaking that deviated from the norms of technical proficiency.

But by 2010, the region was becoming known for its 'natural wines', largely led by the noise around the seismic Natural Selection Theory. These wines, mostly from the group of winemakers clustered in the Basket Range, were some of the most radical that Australia had seen. 'Zero-zero' was the name of the game, meaning that 'zero' inputs were added (**sulphur**, enzymes, yeasts, acid, tannins) and 'zero' was taken away from the wine, alluding to an absence of fining and filtration. The results were an entirely new aesthetic to Australia: wines of cloudiness and turbidity, unusual colours of deep pinks and oranges, and occasionally a light **pétillance** – either intentional or unintentional.

The addition of **sulphur** – a naturally occurring organic compound that is often used to protect wines from oxidation and bacterial spoilage – became a pressure point for the conversation, with the rules (at the extreme non-intervention end of the spectrum) clearly stated on the website of Lucy M: 'To adulterate nature's work by filtering, fining, or any addition, including small amounts of **sulphur**, is not natural.' The 'to sulphur or not to sulphur' controversy seemed to begin in Australia with van Klopper. Ochota Barrels, another pilot in the Basket Range wine space, employs small amounts of **sulphur**. In contrast to Lucy M's creed, Taras said in a 2016 *The Real Review* interview, 'sulphur dioxide is not an enemy'.

Today, some producers of the category are firmly additive-free, while others employ small to normal amounts of **sulphur**, but most agree that the conversation needs to move beyond SO_2. 'We have a pursuit of making sans-**sulphur** wines, but we make pinot noir in the Adelaide Hills,' says Commune of Buttons' Sophie Button, with a laugh, 'so it's a challenge.' Alicia Basa from Borachio, a no-**sulphur** estate, agrees that it shouldn't be dogmatic: 'Everyone's circumstances are different and you can't have a blanket stance on it. You have to look at the context.'

Gareth Belton is also of the opinion that wine shouldn't be about **sulphur** usage – 'the final touch' – but rather about looking at the whole timeline of what goes into a bottle. (Though according to him, this final touch, adding **sulphur**, 'might at times make it more pleasurable for the consumer—and don't we all hate faulty wines'.)

While it's clear from tasting the wines of the region that some producers still accept faulty wines, the conversation is much more inclusive and thoughtful than it had once been. And its effects can be seen across Adelaide Hills (and Australian) winemaking. The success of the natural wine movement in the Adelaide Hills has led to other forays into these kinds of winemaking throughout the country, and has encouraged the more classic producers to question higher alcohol levels, limit new oak usage, peel back high-intervention winemaking, and to consider playing with some avant-garde styles.

'I definitely had a strong influence from that movement,' says Murdoch Hill's Michael Downer. 'The whole movement has made people think a bit more about what they are actually putting into the wine and trying to be a bit more conscious in that way.'

Michael Hill Smith agrees, praising the movement as an immense source of excitement in the region. 'It's important that the wine industry has diversity,' he explains. 'A bit like punk in the 80s, you need a youth movement that is challenging the status quo.' He cites the movement as helping two important concepts gain wide acceptance, both non-interventionism and quality farming. 'Without those guys, pushing and challenging, it doesn't become mainstream.'

Though there's no denying that the natural wine movement created buzz about no-synthetic farming, the ironic part is that Basket Range is 'a community of winemakers, not so much of wine-growers,' says Belton, who began leasing his first vineyard in Basket Range in 2014. While a few do predominantly own or farm their own vineyards – including Basket Range Wine, Commune of Buttons and Gentle Folk – most of the natural-identifying Basket Range producers are not farming their own land. 'The scene in Australia with natural wine is definitely a wine*making*-focused thing,' says Belton.

But most of the winemakers of the Basket Range do make an effort to source organically grown grapes. Combined with the efforts of early pioneers like Ngeringa, and more recent converts like Shaw+Smith, the Hills are looking a lot greener than they once did, though wholesale adoption of organic and **biodynamic** practices is still rare.

'The region as a whole is relatively slow in heading towards sustainable farming,' says Erinn Klein, citing neighbouring McLaren Vale as having a much wider uptake of organics and **biodynamics**. The conversion to organics by Shaw+Smith has been a turning point in the region ('everyone's like, "oh, it might actually work",' says Belton), and many are hopeful that within the next five years, there will be even more widespread investment in environmentalism.

So while the natural wine movement has advanced the low-intervention and responsible farming conversations, this positive cross-pollination (to use Erinn Klein's words) can be seen on the flip-side as well: the success of more classically styled wines of the Adelaide Hills has demanded soundness, integrity and value of the natural wine producers.

It's no secret that some flawed and sub-par wines have come out of the natural wine movement. (Hill Smith, channelling D.H. Lawrence, once described a **pét-nat** as resembling 'the aged urination of a sick horse'.) Belton also feared that the Adelaide Hills would become known just for **mousiness** (one of the more insidious wine flaws) and **piquettes** (a simple, fizzy wine made from water and grape pomace), but he points to 'an immense

The success of the natural wine movement in the Adelaide Hills has encouraged the more classic producers to peel back high-intervention winemaking and to consider playing with some avant-garde styles.

improvement in wine quality' over the last few years as well as 'the dogmas slowly moving away'.

Though the tensions within the various factions of the Adelaide Hills have not totally resolved, the resultant landscape is no longer suffering: the land is being farmed better (with continued momentum for future change) and the wines, on both ends of the stylistic spectrum, are better than ever too.

It feels like the Adelaide Hills, despite the ongoing hype surrounding the region, is just now starting to have its moment. Though climate change threatens to make conditions more variable and extreme, the region's headliner, chardonnay, is still thriving. The 2021 vintage gifted the vignerons of the area with copious quantities and excellent quality. This, combined with the general upturn in farming practices and sound winemaking, means the Adelaide Hills is poised to transcend its reputation as a natural wine region, and claim its deserved reputation as one of the world's great fine wine regions.

PRODUCERS

ASHTON HILLS

Ashton Hills has been setting the bar for Adelaide Hills pinot noir for well over three decades. Stephen George founded the estate in 1982 when there was very little else happening in the region. His vineyard sits in the Piccadilly Valley subregion, at one of the highest points in the Adelaide Hills. Pinot noir plantings are made up of five different **clones**, which were whittled down during experiments with a list of 26, resulting in all but eight rows of riesling dedicated to the grape. Ashton Hills also produces Piccadilly Valley chardonnay and an extraordinary sparkling shiraz made from fruit grown at the Wendouree vineyards (p. 332) in the Clare Valley. Stephen retired in 2015, selling Ashton Hills to Wirra Wirra, for whom he still consults. **ashtonhills.com.au**

BASKET RANGE WINE

The Broderick family pioneered winemaking and grape-growing in a region that would go on to start a movement. And though their wines have undergone stylistic changes over the years, they have always been grounded in good farming and sound winemaking, with the goal of expressing their special plot of land. Phillip Broderick planted Bordeaux varieties in 1980, expanding in 2000 to a larger neighbouring plot, and adding pinot noir, chardonnay and a small amount of saperavi. All vines are farmed organically. Phillip and Mary's two sons now run the family estate. **basketrangewine.com.au**

BK WINES

One of the early pioneers of the Basket Range, Brendon and Kirstyn Keys established BK Wines in 2007. Their goal is to create art with their wines: 'beautiful, unique, sensuous,

Charlotte Hardy

deceptively minimalist, envelope-pushing art'. Everything is minimally made, with some wines representing more familiar styles (single-site chardonnay with some new oak and bâttonage) and some wines, as they would say, pushing the envelope (like a **piquette** so explosive that they suggest you open it over a sink). **bkwines.com.au**

CHARLOTTE DALTON

Charlotte Hardy cut her teeth at wineries around the globe before settling in South Australia in 2007. She made her first wines under her own label in the shed on her Basket Range property in 2015, from just a couple of tonnes of fruit. Her focus is first and foremost on the growers, working with places and fruit that she

---

 What we're drinking

*The purity of pinot noir fruit is evident in any wine you taste from **Ashton Hills**. From one of the single-vineyard pinots to the sparkling rosé, few vineyards across Australia are achieving this fragrance, delicacy and texture.* – Jane Lopes

What we're drinking

*Fred Fiano was born when Charlotte Hardy (of **Charlotte Dalton**) was chosen to participate in the inaugural Project 5255 initiative, which aims to shine a light on the Langhorne Creek region by providing fruit from the area for a winemaker from another locale to make a limited-edition wine under their own label. Fred was so popular he will now be a permanent fixture among Charlotte Dalton's line-up of other delicious wines. — Kavita Faiella*

loves, and producing wines that are distinct and lively. Charlotte moved out of the Adelaide Hills in 2019, wanting her wines to speak for themselves, rather than getting lumped in with the narrative of the Basket Range. She settled instead in the Fleurieu Peninsula, and though she still considers herself an Adelaide Hills producer, mainly sourcing fruit from there, she has also made fiano from Langhorne Creek and syrah from Kangaroo Island, as well as begun farming a plot of pinot noir with her husband, just up the road from their cellar door on the Peninsula.
charlottedaltonwines.com.au

COMMUNE OF BUTTONS

Jasper and Sophie Button are the custodians of nearly 30 hectares of bush paddocks and vineyards in the Basket Range of Adelaide Hills, called Fernglen. The siblings have undertaken organic conversion since 2012 and make a range of vibrant low-**sulphur** wines – everything from single-block pinot noir and chardonnay to **pét-nats** and, in 2021, a field blend of all grapes on the property (white and red) called Goodlife. *communeofbuttons.com.au*

GENTLE FOLK

Gentle Folk is the winery of Gareth and Rainbo Belton, both marine scientists, who found themselves drawn to the Adelaide Hills to start making wine. With the help of viticulturist Dr Dylan Grigg, they began acquiring small plots of vines and growing their own grapes – a necessary step, in Gareth's mind, to establishing a true connection with the land. Since their first three-barrel ferment in 2013, Gentle Folk has made an impact on the Adelaide Hills wine scene, bridging the natural and traditional wine aesthetics in an honest (and delicious) way. The wines range from Rainbow Juice – a salmon-coloured drop blending pinot gris, gewürztraminer, syrah, chardonnay and sauvignon blanc – to single-site chardonnays and pinot noirs of classical proportions.
gentlefolk.com.au

JAUMA

James Erskine is one of the pioneers of Australia's natural wine movement. After a career as a sommelier, he crafted his first wine (a McLaren Vale grenache) in 2010, and quickly set about changing wine culture across the country. James focused on McLaren Vale and Adelaide Hills fruit before purchasing his own farm (an old organic cherry orchard) in Lenswood in 2018. Grenache and chenin blanc have been touchstones for James, but the offerings have spanned everything from shiraz to cab franc to muscat blanc à petits grains to arneis: the whites often fermented with skin-contact, and the reds early picked and employing **carbonic maceration**, creating a rainbow of offerings. James has eschewed any use of **sulphur** since the 2015 vintage. The marriage of experimentation and quality farming are the hallmarks of Jauma, and, with

 What we're drinking

*There's something additionally concerted, serious and grown up about Gareth Belton's wines. **Gentle Folk's** first releases were kaleidoscopic in colour, style and personality, and though early experimentation was valuable, a finesse, purity and refinement is now the norm. Indeed, it's easy to argue these are some of South Australia's finest cool-climate wine releases, ongoing. — Mike Bennie*

What we're drinking

Murdoch Hill's Rocket Chardonnay: buy all that you can of this wine on release, as it sells out fast. And no wonder — what this wine delivers for the price tag makes it one of the best-value wines in Australia. With acid for days, it's worth attempting to cellar it, but I personally have never been able to stop myself from guzzling it all as soon as it's delivered. — Kavita Faiella

new plantings on the Lenswood farm, show no sign of letting up.
jauma.com

LUCY M

Lucy M, the label formerly known as Lucy Margaux, is Anton van Klopper's (in)famous Basket Range project. Starting with a 6-hectare farm purchased in 2002, van Klopper has been a leading figure in the natural wine movement in the Adelaide Hills. He represents an extreme side of the movement, eschewing even small amounts of added **sulphur** (and decrying those who do partake in those additions as 'not natural'). The grapes employed in his wines are largely purchased from local organic farms – everything from sangiovese to pinot noir, gamay to sauvignon blanc – and made into wines that have been described alternatively as wild, sauvage, funky and flawed. More estate-grown fruit is in the pipeline, with 6000 vines going in the ground since 2019. Van Klopper co-owns natural-wine eatery The Summertown Aristologist with Commune of Buttons' Jasper Button and Château Comme Ci Comme Ça's Aaron Fenwick. *lucymwines.com*

MURDOCH HILL

The Downer family has been farming in the Onkaparinga Valley since the 1930s, but it wasn't until the 21st century that Michael Downer turned the family farm from a hobby winery to a significant estate-grown-and-made enterprise. Most grapes vinified are from their estate vineyards, though Murdoch Hill does purchase grapes from sites they find exceptional to add to their Artisan Series (each bottling named after different horse-drawn carriages, an ode to grandpa Downer, who collected them). In 2021, Murdoch Hill added a new vineyard to their estate holdings, a site in Lenswood at 500 metres above sea level. It's Murdoch Hill's goal to showcase the breadth and quality of the Adelaide Hills. Sometimes this looks like flinty chardonnay, cracking with energy, and sometimes it looks like an unusual blend of pinot gris, pinot noir and pinot meunier. It's all part of the vibe at Murdoch Hill, who in a short time estate-bottling wine, has already become one of the Hills' most celebrated producers.
murdochhill.com.au

NGERINGA

There were many naysayers when Erinn and Janet Klein planted their **biodynamic** vineyard on Mount Barker in the early 2000s. Organics (and certainly **biodynamics**) had rarely been attempted in the region, and many didn't think it was possible. But the Kleins proved them all wrong, Erinn as winemaker and Janet as viticulturist, and have set off a movement toward better farming practices in the region. Their regenerative farm today remains

Taras & Amber Ochota
Ochota Barrels

South Australia

a pinnacle for the region and beyond, not only growing top-notch grapes, but also being one of the most vital produce farms in the environs of Adelaide, providing raw materials for many of the region's top restaurants. A few uncommon wines kick off the range – a pale salmon **pét-nat**, a pithy pink semillon, and tempranillo, sangiovese and nebbiolo – but, largely, Ngeringa crafts crystalline and site-driven examples of chardonnay, pinot noir and syrah. *ngeringa.com*

OCHOTA BARRELS

It's hard to overstate the importance of Taras and Amber Ochota in the Australian wine scene. The pair rallied against the staid and overly manufactured conventional wine scene, but also didn't subscribe to the dogmatism and new rules of the natural wine movement: they created their own genre, based on love, kindness and enthusiasm. Ochota Barrels is based on a 4-hectare property in the Basket Range, though most grapes are purchased from exceptional sites around Adelaide Hills and McLaren Vale. The wines toe the line between more traditional expressions and truly avant-garde styles, always with vitality and deliciousness at the forefront. Taras passed away in 2020 at the age of 49, a devastating blow to his family and to the Australian wine industry. Amber has continued the winery in his absence, and the wines remain a testament to the couple's energy and spirit. *ochotabarrels.com*

SHAW+SMITH

The idea for Shaw+Smith was drummed up over a long lunch between cousins Michael Hill Smith **MW** and Martin Shaw in 1989. Michael was looking for a project to establish his independence from his Barossa-based family (the Hill-Smiths of Yalumba) and Martin had seen the potential of the Adelaide Hills firsthand while working for Petaluma. They had their first vintage the next year, and with a decade of success in the 90s, planted their Balhannah vineyard and built a winery and cellar door on site in 2000. The two have since established a benevolent empire, purchasing the Tolpuddle vineyard in Tasmania in 2011, adding a vineyard at Lenswood to the Shaw+Smith holdings in 2012 (and one in Piccadilly in 2020), launching the Other Wine Co. in 2015, and recently acquiring an old-vine McLaren Vale site in 2021. The McLaren Vale site has been christened MMAD, named after the four men driving Shaw+Smith's future: Michael, Martin, Adam Wadewitz, who joined the team as winemaker in 2012, and David LeMire **MW**, who joined in 2010 in sales and marketing. The latter two were appointed joint CEOs in 2021. Shaw+Smith has helped define not only the Adelaide Hills for the past three decades, but Australian wine as a whole: where their eyes go, so too should ours. *shawandsmith.com*

TAPANAPPA

When Brian Croser sold Petaluma, he retained its famous Tiers vineyard, and started Tapanappa. The Crosers see Tapanappa as the continued vision that was conceived at Petaluma, of family-owned fine wine and laser-focused site expression. Today, the company is managed by

What we're drinking

While the team at **Unico Zelo** *wows the masses with plenty of fun, fresh wines, it's their Applewood project that competes for best-in-class. The gins focus on native, locally sourced botanicals, and a reverence for honouring and acknowledging Aboriginal culture. Applewood leads the Australian gin world in its quality and its practices.* — Jonathan Ross

Brian's daughter Lucy and her husband Xavier Bizot (see Terre à Terre, p. 396), while another Croser son-in-law, Sam Barlow, looks after the winery. The three sites that form the backbone of Tapanappa are The Tiers vineyard, planted to chardonnay in Piccadilly Valley, the Foggy Hill vineyard, planted to pinot noir on the Fleurieu Peninsula, and the Whalebone vineyard, planted to Bordeaux varieties and shiraz in Wrattonbully. *tapanappa.com.au*

THE OTHER RIGHT

The Other Right is Alex Schulkin and Galit Shachaf's small-scale, minimal-intervention endeavour. The name comes from their aim to look at best practices in a new light and offer up an alternative way of operating. They source from organic vineyards in the Adelaide Hills (including a plot of wild-grown shiraz in Sellicks Hill), and make wines with no **sulphur** additions, including fizzy reds, summery rosé and skinsy whites. *theotherrightwines.com*

THISTLEDOWN

Giles Cooke and Fergal Tynan, both **Masters of Wine**, started Thistledown in 2010. Though they are based in Lenswood, they work with three South Australian regions, showcasing a signature grape from each: Adelaide Hills chardonnay, Barossa shiraz and McLaren Vale grenache. McLaren Vale grenache, in particular, has become a speciality of theirs, with a focus on spotlighting individual regions (like Blewitt Springs and Clarendon), old vines and single vineyards. The wines are full of verve and complexity: great studies of grape and place.

UNICO ZELO

Brendan and Laura Carter met at the University of Adelaide – him studying oenology and her studying agricultural science – and launched Unico Zelo right after graduation. They based themselves in Gumeracha and began crafting pinot noir, chardonnay and syrah from the Adelaide Hills. They also built their distillery onsite, Applewood, which has been a source for some of Australia's best gins, many infused with native botanicals and fruits like karkalla, saltbush and lemon aspen. The Carters have always been on the forefront of what's next in Australia, whether its alternative styles like **piquette** and skin-contact whites, championing less-regarded regions and grapes, like Riverland fiano and zibibbo, or leading the social and environmental charge, becoming one of the few Certified B-Corporation wineries in the world. *unicozelo.com.au*

WHISSON LAKE

Whisson Lake might be under the radar, but according to their loyal following and several critics, the small vineyard is producing some of the best pinot noir in the Hills. Five hectares of pinot noir were planted in 1985 on Mount Carey by Mark Whisson and Bruce Lake, at 600 metres altitude in Piccadilly. Andrie Whisson, Mark's wife and a trained nurse, began helping out in 2010, and today is Whisson Lake's winemaker, with Mark serving as the viticulturist. Organic practices are followed, and wines are made to a specific recipe, including small, warm ferments, minimal **sulphur** additions, and no filtration and fining. *whissonlake.com*

WORLDS APART

Louis Schofield worked for over a decade in high-end retail and fine dining before making the jump to production. He trained at Ochota Barrels and took inspiration from cult Australian and European favourites before launching Worlds Apart in 2017, with the goal to 'make wine thoughtfully that is also delicious'. Fruit comes from Adelaide Hills, Eden Valley and McLaren Vale to make brightly labelled (and bright-tasting) riesling, syrah and grenache. *worldsapartwines.com*

And don't forget ...

Bird in Hand is Andrew and Susie Nugent's ode to artistic expression, whether it be through the diverse spectrum of wines or the stunning sculpture garden and gallery on site … **Borachio**, Mark Warner and Alicia Bass's additive-free label, makes diverse and lively styles like a **carbonic** merlot-pinot grigio blend and a savagnin from the Fleurieu Peninsula … **Château Comme Ci Comme Ça**, the winery of Aaron Fenwick, co-owner of staple Adelaide Hills' restaurant and hangout The Summertown Aristologist, produces lithe and light no-**sulphur** wines from purchased organic fruit … **Deviation Road** turns out some of the best Australian sparkling wine, from husband-and-wife duo Hamish and Kate Laurie … **Freddy Nerks** is a new project from Alpha Box & Dice-founding winemaker Justin Lane, based in the southern Kuitpo region, with a focus on shiraz, mataro and Italian varieties … **Geoff Weaver**, the historic estate first planted in 1982, turns out classic examples of chardonnay, sauvignon blanc, riesling, pinot noir and cabernet … **Hahndorf Hill** specialises in Austrian varieties, becoming especially noted for their grüner veltliner, as well as blaufränkisch and zweigelt … **Howard Vineyard** is a hospitality staple of the Hills, offering great cellar door, restaurant and events facilities in addition to a wide range of delicious wines … **Lauren Langfield** launched her eponymous label in 2021, after working across Australia and New Zealand for years, honing her organic and **biodynamic** viticultural approach and low-intervention winemaking skills … **Longview** is the Saturno family's ode to their northern Italian heritage, crafting complex nebbiolo and barbera in addition to more standard Hills fare … **Petaluma**, Brian Croser's historic winery, is now an Accolade brand, turning out vast quantities of reliable Adelaide Hills, Clare Valley and Coonawarra wines … **Riposte** is Tim Knappstein's outpost in the Adelaide Hills, leaving his family lineage in the Clare to focus on Lenswood pinot noir, shiraz, chardonnay, riesling, sauvignon blanc and pinot gris … **Travis Tausend**, based in a southern enclave of the Adelaide Hills called Hope Forest, crafts wines firmly on the natural spectrum, with a focus on creating (and giving back to the) community … **Turon**, a young project in Lenswood from husband-and-wife Turon and Alex, is promising excitement with fresh styles and new high-elevation plantings.

McLaren Vale

Introduction

The vineyard area of McLaren Vale is Kaurna Country. The Nation's eastern boundary is marked by the rise of the Mount Lofty Ranges, its other borders extending to the coastline through the city of Adelaide, north across the Adelaide Plains region, and down the Fleurieu Peninsula. The coastline and the waters always were and always will be Kaurna Country.

In winter, grey and red kangaroo provided sustenance, and in the summer months the Kaurna miyurna (Kaurna people) fished the bounty of the sea at Witawali (today's Sellicks Beach). The adjacent washpool traditionally known as Wangkuntilla (loosely, 'opossum place'), is a coastal lagoon that is home to numerous species of birds that migrate from the Northern Hemisphere. The Kaurna miyurna would use the waterways as a place to prepare and cure animal hides. It became a communal centre for trade and a place of immense natural, spiritual and societal importance.

Just as Adelaide is South Australia's capital, the city and parklands were once the centre of the Kaurna nation, called Tarndanya ('male red kangaroo rock'). But under Kaurna care, the area was an open grassy plain with patches of trees and tended bushlands. Under colonial rule, the city became a fortress of buildings and housing, encroaching on agriculture on all its land-bound sides.

McLaren Vale would probably be Australia's most densely planted GI if it weren't for its northern third, which has largely become suburbs of Adelaide. The rest of the appellation, unlike most in Australia, is heavily blanketed with vineyard sites; there is no doubt, when visiting, that McLaren Vale is wine country.

McLaren Vale shares some of its historical development with the rest of the GIs in proximity to the city of Adelaide – most notably Barossa Valley, the northern neighbour to which it is often compared. Both have warm, Mediterranean climates; both are dominated by the red grapes shiraz, cabernet sauvignon and grenache (in reputation and/or in plantings); and both have been the settings for the establishment of some of Australia's larger wine brands.

But McLaren Vale – 'Southern Vales' as it was known in the early days – has doggedly worked to carve out its own identity. Today, that identity is crystalline if you're paying attention: based around old-vine grenache, alternative grape varieties, environmental initiatives and rigorous research.

And, of course, shiraz – the region's primary grape – is not to be intimidated by the more famous Barossa versions. Corrina Wright, who farms one of the few patches of McLaren Vale shiraz that go into Penfolds' Grange, asked the folks at Penfolds what her parcel contributes to the overall style of the wine. They replied, 'the light and the shade' – a beautiful ode to the nuanced and gauzy layers of the wines of McLaren Vale.

Evolution of Wine

The first vines in McLaren Vale were planted by John Reynell, an English immigrant who came to Australia in 1838. Reynell settled south of Adelaide, in a township that now bears his name: Reynella. He got to work tending his 32 hectares of land, and grapevines went in the ground soon after, including (according to an 1862 article on the farm) 'Verdeilho, Carbonet, Malbec, Pineau Gris, and Gouais', and later, pedro ximénez and palomino.

Reynell produced his first vintage in 1842 and built his underground cellar in 1845 (many heritage buildings remain on site). But perhaps his most significant contribution to Australian wine came in 1850, when he hired a man named Thomas Hardy to be his cellar hand. Hardy also came from England (Devon, to Reynell's Bristol), arriving in 1850 at the age of 20. In 1854, he was able to afford some of his own land, and established his first vineyard and cellars at Bankside, within the modern-day boundaries of the city of Adelaide.

By 1863, Hardy had amassed 35 hectares at the Bankside vineyard – grenache, mataro, muscat, 'roussillon' (perhaps carignan) and shiraz vines – as well as a collection of other vineyards in and around the city of Adelaide. It was in 1876 that Hardy planted his flag in McLaren Vale, with the purchase of the Tintara Vineyards Company, which had been established by Dr A.C. Kelly in 1861 and had gone bankrupt just when Hardy was looking to expand.

Hardy found early success with wine exports. He sent two hogsheads to Britain in 1857, which according to some, were the first South Australian wines to be exported (though, according to others, this milestone belongs to the Echunga Springs vineyard in Adelaide Hills, p. 337). Following the trends of the day, these early exports were largely full-bodied, dry red wines.

Without access to the populous cities of Victoria and New South Wales, due to the pre-Federation interstate tariffs, Hardy focused considerably on exports and maintaining ties to Adelaide's blossoming drinking population. By 1900, Thomas Hardy & Sons (renamed in 1887 with the addition of the next generation) was the largest wine producer in South Australia. Other 19th-century producers of importance in the Southern Vales were Kay Brothers, Wirra Wirra and Oxenberry Farm.

The turn of the century promoted a wine boom in South Australia at the expense of Victoria's bust. Though economic depression hit both equally, South Australia's lack of **phylloxera**, combined with its newfound post-Federation

Port Willunga Beach has been known as Wirruwarrungga by the Kaurna nation for thousands of years. Just inland from the shoreline is a spring that has provided fresh water for as many millennia. In the Kaurna Dreaming, the spring was created by tears from Tjilbruke, the Creator being.

ability to sell to other Australian states profitably, promoted growth in early McLaren Vale wineries.

Dry red wines maintained their dominance into the second decade of the 20th century, but **fortified wines** soon took their position at the forefront of production. Throughout the first decades of the 20th century, the national palate was shifting toward **fortified wines**. The result: high-yielding, high-sugar grapes like doradillo were planted in droves. Luckily, shiraz, grenache and cabernet sauvignon were also well suited for **fortified** production, and so stayed in the ground. In particular, grenache was well regarded for its ability to produce sugar-rich grapes and for not needing any sort of **trellising** system. (An early critic put it best, citing grenache as being 'especially valuable for its erect, self-supporting habit, its fecundity, and the richness of its must'.)

By the early 1920s, there was a huge glut of doradillo grapes, and the price had dropped by nearly two-thirds. The government tried to counter this with the Wine Export Bounty Act of 1924, which specifically subsidised exported **fortified wines**, to the tune of 8.8 cents per litre. This may sound insignificant, but the average export value of wine at the time was only 10 cents per litre: this bounty nearly doubled revenue.

Hardys invested heavily in **fortified** exports as did Emu Wines, based in Morphett Vale since 1930 (a northern township of modern-day McLaren Vale), which became Australia's largest exporter of wine in that decade. A new producer got in on the export action too: the Osborn family, with plantings back to 1912, bottled their first wine from the 1928 vintage, explicitly for export, labelled 'Bundarra Vineyards by F. E. Osborn & Sons'.

Though more **fortified wine** was being produced than ever before, the subsidies drove domestic prices up, weakening the national appetite. And just as McLaren Vale remained an epicentre of mass-produced **fortified wines** for export, it was soon ground-zero for the shift back to **table wine** that would occur in the decades following World War II.

By 1947, Australia's **fortified wine** export subsidies were revoked. At the same time, a wave of European immigrants brought a renewed food and wine culture to the area south of Adelaide. There was a quiet resurgence of plantings in this period. And wine technology was upgraded throughout the major players of McLaren Vale, predicating a successful **table wine** industry.

Emu Wines and Hardys saw growth and development in this period, but few smaller wineries had survived the first half of the 20th century. The notable exception was the Osborn family, who continued to grow grapes and innovate through the 20th century, being early adopters of technology like tractors and electric generators.

It wasn't until the late 1950s that a boutique wine industry emerged in McLaren Vale, and even then, it was a slow roll-out. In 1959 d'Arry Osborn created his own wine label. D'Arenberg became a trailblazer in the region, in terms of technological advances, promotion of tourism and quality wine production, winning the seventh

Mataro

Australians in a handful of regions (most notably Barossa Valley, Clare Valley and McLaren Vale) have taken to using the word 'mataro' to describe a grape most commonly referred to as mourvèdre. Mourvèdre is the French name for the grape, although most accept that it originated in Spain, where it is known as monastrell. The Aussie and French names are taken from Spanish towns — Mataró, near Barcelona, and Murviedro, in Valencia (and now known as Sagunto). The grape came over to Australia from Roussillon in southern France, as part of James Busby's 1831 haul. It made its way to South Australia, where the warm climate was more suitable to the late-ripening, mildew-sensitive and cold-weary grape. Mataro is known for representing the 'M' in the country's iconic 'GSM' blends, and for its ancient vines: the 1853 plantings in Barossa's Old Garden vineyard are the world's oldest of the grape. Because most in Australia still refer to the grape as mourvèdre, we've used that as our universal descriptor in this book, but divert to mataro when we are describing a producer's plantings or bottlings that use that name instead.

South Australia

ever **Jimmy Watson** trophy for their 1968 Cabernet Sauvignon. (Hardys Tintara was the first McLaren Vale winery to be awarded a **Jimmy Watson**, for its 1962 Cabernet Sauvignon.)

Other wineries emerged in the following decades: Coriole was founded by Hugh and Molly Lloyd in 1967, Wirra Wirra was rebuilt in 1969, and David Noon established his family wine business in 1976 – three producers with continued significance to this day. The stylistic leanings up until this point were fairly moderate: McLaren Vale was certainly capable of producing ripe, full-bodied red wines, but most early adopters saw the grace of the region in its ability to craft more structured and modest styles.

The 80s and 90s brought with them creeping oak usage, often American, as well as more ripeness. In these days, white and red varieties shared the acreage nearly evenly – with shiraz, cabernet sauvignon and grenache leading the red plantings, and chardonnay, sauvignon blanc and viognier dominating the white.

In 1990, biochemist Roman Bratasiuk founded Clarendon Hills on the premise of featuring McLaren Vale old vines in single-vineyard cuvées. Bratasiuk claimed that his wines were a foil to the dominant Australian red wine of the time. 'My syrahs are not typical Australian; they are not over-laden with American oak and aren't jammy,' he said.

Though they may not have been jammy, they were 'formidable' (as James Halliday described them), and though they may not have been over-laden with *American* oak, they were often aged in 100% new French **barriques**. Clarendon Hills garnered cult wine status after several superlative reviews from Robert Parker, setting a new bar for the price-point and prestige that a wine from McLaren Vale could claim. Their impact was not seen in Australia, though. The wines had little effect on influencing production or sales in the domestic market, as 98% of production was sold internationally in the early years.

By the mid-1990s, another set of winemakers emerged in McLaren Vale, who would become, as Bratasiuk had, more relevant outside Australia. Sarah and Sparky Marquis, just married and freshly degreed in oenology, worked

> # The stylistic leanings up until this point were fairly moderate: McLaren Vale was certainly capable of producing ripe, full-bodied red wines, but most early adopters saw the grace of the region in its ability to craft more structured and modest styles.

at Sarah's parents' Fox Creek Wines in McLaren Vale before starting their own bulk wine business. In 1998, they launched a joint venture with US wine importer Dan Philips. Marquis Philips was a runaway success in the United States, with the influential Robert Parker offering up for the wines such superlatives as 'the greatest red wine values in existence.'

Sarah and Sparky had a nasty and litigious breakup with Dan in 2005, and by early the next year, the duo had announced their next project: Mollydooker. Mollydooker released its first wines to enthusiastic reception, particularly among the US-based media, who bestowed scores in the high 90s immediately. The wines were ripe, lush and pleasing (usually with high alcohol levels and sugar additions); the packaging was colourful, ornate and playful.

Mollydooker became a household name in the US, but back in McLaren Vale their narrative was not central to the strong regional revitalisation in the first years of the new millennium. Instead, this was driven by

Yangarra's estate vineyard in Blewitt Springs — certified biodynamic since 2008, and recognised the world over as one of the greatest grenache vineyards.

South Australia

McLaren Vale

A focus on the environment and site specificity can often go hand-in-hand with a spirit of experimentation, and McLaren Vale is no different.

names such as Gemtree (2000), Yangarra (2000), Mitolo (2000), Samuel's Gorge (2003), Inkwell (2003), S.C. Pannell (2004) and Angove (2008). Along with d'Arenberg, Wirra Wirra, Noon and Coriole – who were all going strong – this set of wineries ushered in a new era for McLaren Vale.

The focus on red wines became much heavier than it had been in the past; the 50/50 split between reds and whites in the 90s became 80/20 by 2010. And though chardonnay remains the most-planted white grape in the region, the more sensitive winemakers put a greater focus on Mediterranean varieties (that do indeed seem better suited to the climate); today the region successfully produces fiano, vermentino, roussanne, marsanne and viognier. And though it is still out-planted by both shiraz and cabernet sauvignon (by a significant factor), old-vine grenache became a signature offering of the Vale, occupying the stylistic space on the lighter and more structured side of the classic Barossa rendition.

Environmental sustainability and site specificity also became a hallmark of McLaren Vale in the 2000s. In 2004, the Scarce Earth project (originally called Rare Earth) was conceived to identify the great shiraz sites of the Vale and create a forum whereby winemakers could submit McLaren Vale shiraz to be released as Scarce Earth bottlings. Basically, it's as wine writer Andrew Graham affectionately described it, 'a McLaren Vale Shiraz-fest', but with the goal of identifying and mapping the great shiraz sites of the region.

Starting in 2011, Dr Irina Santiago-Brown (a co-owner of Inkwell, with now-husband Dudley Brown) developed the system SAW – Sustainable Australian Winegrowing – which began in McLaren Vale, but by 2014 had been opened up to all Australian wine regions. SAW was the first Australian 'triple bottom line' sustainability system, meaning that it addressed environmental health, social responsibility and economic viability. SAW became SWA (Sustainable Winegrowing Australia) in 2019 after years of further development, and is one of the most important vehicles in Australia to this day for furthering tenets of sustainability. Over a hundred producers and vineyards from McLaren Vale are members, with many of them maintaining organic and **biodynamic** certifications as well.

A focus on the environment and site specificity can often go hand-in-hand with a spirit of experimentation, and McLaren Vale is no different. This innovative approach was adopted early by the likes of Peter Fraser of Yangarra and Steve Pannell of S.C. Pannell, who played with alternative vessel ageing and investment in uncommon varieties. A new generation has taken these values and run with them: the likes of Brash Higgins (2011), Bondar (2012), Ministry of Clouds (2012), Somos (2013), Aphelion (2014), Riley Harrison (2015) and Paralian (2018) as well as producers outside the region working with McLaren Vale fruit, like Ochota Barrels (p. 353) and Jauma (p. 351).

So where does this all leave McLaren Vale today? It's one of the more diverse and eclectic regions in Australia, truly offering something for everyone. Its proximity to Adelaide has naturally encouraged tourism; the region has accepted this challenge, with over 80 cellar doors, and myriad luxury dining and accommodation options. The focus on overarching sustainability and site-specificity is embraced near-universally. And the ambitious producers are making wine that ranks among the best in Australia, with styles ranging from classic and robust to experimental and piquant – and everything in between.

Lay of the Land

McLaren Vale is a 45-minute drive from the centre of Adelaide. The GI is framed by 30 kilometres of coastline on its western border, Adelaide's urban sprawl on its north, and the foothills of the Mount Lofty Ranges on its east side. Of the delineated area of McLaren Vale, 16.9% is under vine, making it already one of the most densely planted GIs in Australia. But if you take out its urban-sprawled northern stretches, McLaren Vale is blanketed with vineyards in its bottom two-thirds, south of the Onkaparinga River.

The Onkaparinga River Gorge acts as a high elevation point for the vineyards immediately surrounding it. To the north, only one vineyard remains: the historic Chateau Reynella. The rest of the vineyards of this area, once densely planted, have been consumed by the spreading development of the city of Adelaide.

South of the Onkaparinga River (and its corresponding National Park), vineyards gently tumble with west, south and east-facing **aspects**. Elevation climbs as one moves inland from the coast along the river gorge's edge, but then falls to the valley below. Approaching the eastern side of the region, the vineyards rise again in the foothills of the Mount Lofty Ranges.

The climate in the Vale is Mediterranean: summers are dry and winters wet, with two-thirds of annual rain occurring outside the growing season. In discordance with general trends of climate change, temperatures in McLaren Vale have been relatively stable over a long period: the mean January temperature over the past 60 years has only risen 0.5°C, with even very warm years, like 2020, staying within the average.

It is warmer and drier in the southwest corner of the appellation, on the coast, with the town of Sellicks Beach receiving 493 millimetres of rain each year and the town of Clarendon, in the northeast corner of the appellation, seeing 809 millimetres. Clarendon's average annual temperatures are cooler and its record heat spikes (slightly) less drastic (44°C as compared to 46°C). Harvest follows this path as well, with the vineyards closest to the coast in Aldinga and Willunga the first to pick, and sequentially moving up through Blewitt Springs and Clarendon in the end of harvest. The Vale as a whole is actively picking from February through to the end of April.

Wind patterns are important in McLaren Vale, providing cooling influences to help mitigate the heat. Cool breezes come inward, out of the south across the gulf, as well as from the east, drawn down from the hills above by warm sea air. Both impact the southern and coastal vineyards more than those further inland, though all vineyards feel the effects.

McLaren Vale is often described by its complex matrix of geology and soil types. Drew Noon, **MW** and long-time McLaren Vale vintner, explains the complexity of the land: 'There isn't any other way to do it other than embrace the diversity, the story of McLaren Vale is the complexity of soil … We're in a valley and there's a fault line on the southeast side against the hill there that dropped a long, long time ago. And there's a lot of infill over millions of years. And then it's moved around. And so you

McLaren Vale Viticultural Footprint

Total delimited area (km²)	440
Total planted area (hectares)	7438
% of delimited area planted	16.900%
Total elevation range	0–417 masl
Elevation range of plantings	15–350 masl
Number of producers	90

McLaren Vale Climate Data (°C)

	1960–1990	1991–PRESENT	2020
Heat summation/GDD	● 1748	● 1825	● 1827
Annual rain/GSR	631/229	624/217	637/225
Warmest month avg. temp.	20.7	21.2	21

Winkler Scale:
● 850–1111   ● 1112–1389   ● 1390–1667   ● 1668–1944   ● 1945–2222   ● 2223–2700

McLaren Vale

HOW TO READ THIS MAP

Today, only one vineyard remains north of the Onkaparinga-Clarendon fault. This map of McLaren Vale excludes the urban sprawl to the north and is informed by the 19 districts of McLaren Vale first published by the **MVGWTA** in 2010. While most maps in this book show the overlapping vineyard scan, McLaren Vale's vineyard footprint is so dense, it needed a separate presentation.

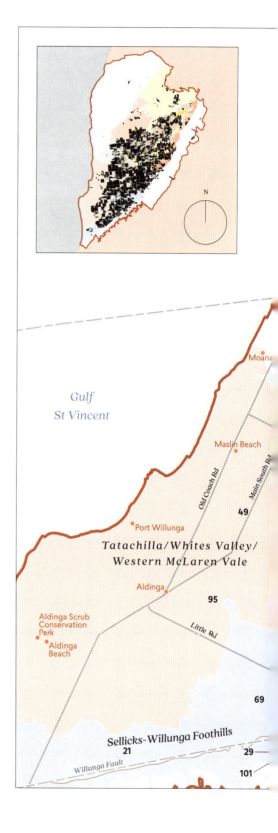

1 Alpha Box & Dice
2 Angel Gully Vineyard
3 Angove
4 Angove Warboys Vineyard
5 Anvers Park Vineyard
6 Aphelion
7 Ballast Stone Vineyard
8 Battle of Bosworth
9 Beach Road Wines
10 Bekkers
11 Bekkers Clarendon Vineyard
12 Bethany Wines Seaview Vineyard
13 Blewitt Springs Wine Co.
14 Bondar
15 Bondar Rayner Vineyard
16 Brash Higgins
17 Breakneck Creek Vineyard
18 Brini Vineyard
19 Brookman Wines
20 Cape Barren
21 Cascabel
22 Chalk Hill
23 Chapel Hill
24 Chateau Reynella
25 Clarendon Hills
26 Coriole
27 d'Arenberg
28 De Lisio
29 Delabole Heights Vineyard
30 Delabole Hill Vineyard
31 Dowie Doole Wines
32 Duck Chase Vineyard
33 Fox Creek Wines
34 Geddes Wines
35 Gemtree
36 Geoff Hardy
37 Geoff Merrill
38 Graham Stevens
39 Halifax
40 Hardys Tintara
41 Haselgrove
42 Hastwell & Lightfoot
43 Heirloom
44 Hickinbotham Vineyard
45 Hither & Yon
46 Hugh Hamilton
47 Hugo
48 Inkwell
49 Ivybrook Farm
50 Jelka
51 Kangarilla Road
52 Kay Bros Amery
53 Koltz Vineyard
54 Koomilya
55 Leconfield
56 Lino Ramble
57 Lloyd Brothers
58 Longwood Winery
59 Malpas Road Vineyard
60 Marienberg Vineyard
61 Maxwell
62 Ministry of Clouds
63 Miracle Hill Vineyard
64 Mr. Riggs Wine Co.
65 Mitolo
66 MMAD Vineyard
67 Mollydooker
68 Mongrel Hill
69 Nine Gums
70 Noon
71 Oliver's Taranga
72 Oliverhill Winery
73 Paxton
74 Paxton 19th Vineyard
75 Paxton Jones Block
76 Paxton Landcross Farm
77 Paxton Quandong Farm
78 Paxton Thomas Block
79 Penny Vineyard
80 Penny's Hill
81 Pirramimma
82 Primo Estate
83 Sabella
84 Samuel's Gorge
85 S.C. Pannell
86 S.C. Pannell Blewitt Springs Vineyard
87 Scarpantoni Estate
00 Serafino
89 Sherrah
90 Shottesbrooke
91 Smart Vineyard
92 Springs Hill Vineyard
93 Stump Hill Vineyard
94 Tatachilla
95 Thomas Vineyard
96 The Tiers Wine Company
97 Tintookie Vineyard
98 Trott Vineyard
99 Ulithorne
100 Willunga 100
101 Willunga Creek
102 Winterfold Vineyard
103 Wirra Wirra
104 Yangarra Estate Vineyard

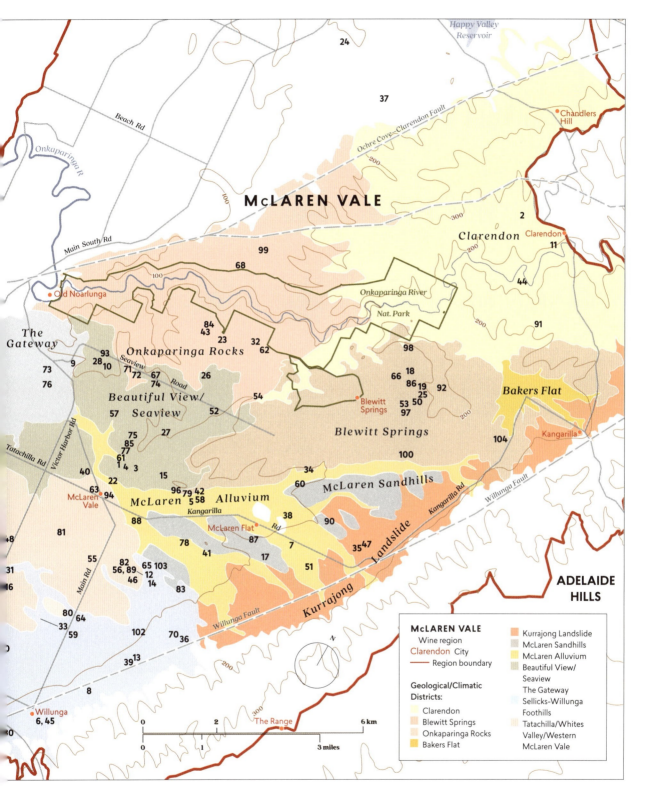

McLaren Vale

365

'McLaren Vale's simple thing is it's complex ... And if you want to dive into it further, then you've got to do just that.'

have different, quite distinctly different, soils in discrete patches throughout the valley ... And I do say (jokingly), I wish in some way, I wish there was one soil you see, because Coonawarra has its terra rossa soils and it's a great story, because it's true, but it's also easy. And McLaren Vale's simple thing is it's complex ... And if you want to dive into it further, then you've got to just do that.'

So let's dive in.

Two parallel faults frame 99.9% of vineyard land of McLaren Vale, the Ochre Cove-Clarendon fault to the northwest (which runs underneath the Onkaparinga Gorge), and the Willunga fault to the southeast. The soils and geological formations of McLaren Vale range from 11,500 years old – our current geological epoch, which started at the end of the Last Glacial Period – to over 750 million years old (quite the span!).

The Willunga and Ochre Cove-Clarendon faults, and the many smaller ones that run parallel to them, are the result of the Delamerian Orogeny folding the Adelaide Geosyncline. This caused numerous breaking points or faults in the earth's crust, which have allowed over 40 different distinct geological classifications to arise in McLaren Vale – universally recognised as one of the most geologically diverse regions in the world.

In 2008, the project of creating a McLaren Vale geology map was undertaken, with different editions released in the early 2010s. One such edition was released in 2013, which outlined 19 'districts' atop the geological map, defined by geology, soil, climate and topography. These districts are often non-contiguous,

with zig-zagged borders to truly follow the nuance of the land.

The discussion of these districts (aka subregions) hasn't been perpetuated by the GI today – the current map in circulation doesn't have this overlay – but some of the names have stuck. No one is pushing for legally defined subregions in the region, which is perhaps why they haven't been reinforced in current GI literature, but they do offer a useful educational resource to better understand the **regionality** of McLaren Vale.

The northeastern-most area of significance is referred to as Clarendon. The oldest geology in the region is here, dating to about 750 million years ago: old siltstones and shale with veins of quartz, as well as some old sandstones. Topsoils are thin, with sandy silty clays transitioning to bedrock. There are some small areas of younger sandstones mixed through, though most of those are on the north side of the Ochre Cove-Clarendon Fault, and not planted on.

A few vineyards lie in close proximity to the town of Clarendon, with many just south along the Onkaparinga River. Here, the river has yet to fall into the gorge, and the topography is more varied, with vineyard **aspects** facing all 360 degrees. Clarendon has the highest-elevation vineyard sites in McLaren Vale, planted at 220–310 metres above sea level.

Roman Bratasiuk's Clarendon Hills, though based in Blewitt Springs, has garnered the region name recognition abroad. He works with vineyards in Clarendon, planted to shiraz, grenache, merlot and cabernet sauvignon. Hickinbotham vineyard is in Clarendon, a northwestern-facing amphitheatre planted at 250 metres above sea level to cabernet sauvignon, cabernet franc, shiraz and merlot. And Angove's newly acquired (as of 2019) Angel Gully vineyard ranges from 280–310 metres above sea level, planted mainly to shiraz. Clarendon's unique mix of elevation and weather results in a relatively cooler climate, which slows down the ripening period and tends to create, according to winemaker Riley Harrison, wines of 'lots of flavour ... but an air of openness, light and restraint'.

Clarendon's most famous grenache vineyard is the Smart vineyard. It was planted by Frederick

Smart in 1922 exclusively to **bush-vine** grenache, sitting at 220–230 metres in elevation with a south-southeast **aspect**. Thistledown and S.C. Pannell have both made excellent single-vineyard bottlings of Smart vineyard grenache, noted for their floral and herbaceous qualities, with superb balance and concentration.

South of Clarendon lies Bakers Flat, which has only one vineyard, planted on a younger alluvium of silty clay, sand and gravel. The next township south is Kangarilla, where the vineyards sit on the lower slopes of the Willunga Fault, as it makes its northeastern ascent through the region.

Kangarilla was not recognised as a separate district in 2013, but sits at the confluence of Bakers Flat, Blewitt Springs, and a rarely (perhaps never) referred-to district called Kurrajong Landslide, which includes several non-contiguous areas spread along the eastern ridge of the Willunga Fault and defined by angular rock fragments, clay and silt. Kangarilla consists of only a small cluster of vineyards, but has been bolstered by Clarendon Hills, who recognises it as one of the three 'sub-districts' that they source from, citing the lower-lying vineyards of the region (in contrast to the higher sites of Clarendon and Blewitt Springs) as a unifying factor.

Blewitt Springs runs primarily southwest of Kangarilla, where the valley created by the two faults opens up a bit, giving way to more significant plantings. Blewitt Springs was originally dubbed 'Blewitt Sands' as a district, though is just referred to by its township name today. But sandy it is. The official district soil description is 'sand over sandy clay, deep sand and ironstone'.

As the valley and plantings fan out from the Willunga Fault in the east, they move from coarser sands to finer Holocene sands – the Vale's youngest formation. Coarse sands over sandy red clays with ironstone at depth define most of Blewitt Springs, as seen in Yangarra's estate vineyard.

In general, Blewitt Springs is considered one of the lighter-handed expressions of McLaren Vale. For this reason, it has historically been associated with grenache, though its softer shiraz styles are starting to be embraced. Yangarra's Pete Fraser remembers: 'Ten years ago, people kind of scoffed at shiraz in [Blewitt Springs]

because it was too light. And now it's in its glory because of that finesse that it has.'

Wines from the stonier soils of Blewitt Springs tend to be darker in colour and a bit more structured in their youth, while those from the finer sands are more ethereal and garneted in colour, with powdery tannins. Blewitt Springs producers include Yangarra, Clarendon Hills and Steve Pannell's Koomilya.

The southwestern tail of Blewitt Springs feeds into a region that has historically been known as 'Seaview' but can't use that moniker because of a Treasury Wine Estates-owned sparkling brand of the same name. 'Beautiful View' is the 2013 district name, which (not surprisingly) didn't catch on. 'So we're just "#10",' laughs Corrina Wright, whose family has farmed land in that area for six generations at Oliver's Taranga. Unofficially, 'Seaview' is still commonly used though, to describe this compact and unique area.

'The Seaview area,' says Fraser, 'is a very distinct area that produces quite early-ripening, powerful, concentrated wines.' The area surrounds Seaview Road, which runs west from Blewitt Springs for a mere 3.5 kilometres before it snakes south to meet Victor Harbor Road near the southwestern reaches of the Onkaparinga National Park. The area considered Seaview (err, '#10'), extends about 3 kilometres from north to south, incorporating a few vineyards north of Seaview Road, but mainly those south of it. Wineries in this concise area include Oliver's Taranga, Coriole, Mollydooker, d'Arenberg, S.C. Pannell, Maxwell, Alpha Box & Dice, Angove and Bekkers.

Seaview (we're just going for it) is under 100 metres above sea level, with a combination of marine and non-marine sands and loam over limestone and clay bedrock. It occupies a moderate climate in the Vale: not as rainy or elevated as its eastern neighbours, but with greater **diurnal shift** than the west, and still receiving some sea breezes.

'The Gateway' is recognised as a more coastal-proximate extension of Seaview. Both contain similar soil types, but the area further west is more influenced by the Gulf of St Vincent: temperatures are higher, on average, but with cooling sea breezes that come in mid-afternoon, providing relief.

The area just north of Seaview is often referred to as 'the Seaview Ridge', though in the 2013 district division, it was considered the 'Onkaparinga Rocks' – this name combining the Onkaparinga Gorge, which it sits on the ridge of, and the rocky soils that characterise the region. This area is planted to vineyards ranging from 150–190 metres above sea level. The soil type is similar to Seaview proper, but with more patchy gravel and rocks combined with the loam over limestone and clay. Producers here include Samuel's Gorge, Chapel Hill and Ministry of Clouds (which makes a shiraz bottling called Onkaparinga Rocks).

Most agree that Clarendon, Blewitt Springs and Seaview (and its ridge) are the most useful and homogenous boundary lines to draw in McLaren Vale. Heading south, into the areas known as McLaren Vale and McLaren Flat, there is a greater 'blurring' (as Fraser describes it) – less clear distinctions based on soil, topography, climate and geology without any sort of geographic continuity.

That's not to say that there aren't some excellent sites in these regions, there's just a lot more variety from one site to the next. The area considered McLaren Vale is southwest of the area considered McLaren Flat, both occupying central valley floor spots as the basin travels up from the southwest.

The area of McLaren Flat, wedged between Blewitt Springs and the eastern ridges of the appellation, is a combination of three main formations. The 'Kurrajong' in the east, the same as found near Kangarilla, with large rocks of quartzite and siltstone cascading down west-facing hills; sand and sandstone ridges that rise throughout, reaching up to 160 metres above sea level; and the alluvial flats below both these rises in elevation. It is generally warmer with higher heat spikes in McLaren Flat than northern neighbour Blewitt Springs, but elevation and south-facing **aspects** can help mitigate.

The area generally known as McLaren Vale lies due south of Seaview and is a natural progression southwest from McLaren Flat. The formations change here: on the northern side there's a combination of 'heavy black cracking clay' (considered difficult for vine growing) with some loam and red-brown clays (considered easier), ranging from 40–80 metres above sea level. To the south, hugging the Willunga fault, are westerly-facing alluvial fans of red-brown clay, loam and gravel, incorporating the town of Willunga in this area's southwestern corner. These sites can range from 60 metres in the west to 150 metres in the east.

The Willunga Foothills have been identified as a unique region, 'which produces bright red fruit and a ripe profile without noticeable tannin structure', according to Drew Noon, who has been conducting taste-tests of the different subdistricts for a decade. Noon himself is based in this district, as well as Willunga 100, Aphelion and Fox Creek. Willunga 100 has been important in the Vale's grenache conversation, taking a site-specific approach to old-vine grenache long before it was in style.

The valley floor (and its ridges) from McLaren Flat to McLaren Vale is well planted and houses a number of important producers, including Gemtree, Mitolo, Wirra Wirra, Bondar, Inkwell and Brash Higgins. In general, a bit more ripeness and a bit less structure can be assumed of the wines in this area, but it is hard to make generalisations about these valley floor vineyards – someone will prove them wrong. The lesser areas of these flats, though, are home to the some of the mass-produced wines of the region: big crops of shiraz, cabernet sauvignon and chardonnay.

Very few vineyards are planted within 2 kilometres of the coast – in general, despite the cooling breezes, it's too warm, too dry, and generally consists of less desirable soils.

Across this great diversity and complexity of sites (Drew Noon was not kidding), many commonalities have tied the vintners of McLaren Vale. Not the least of which is their commitment to pioneering sustainability solutions. Yes, the dry and warm climates of McLaren Vale make **biodynamic** and organic certifications more attainable than in many regions across Australia – but that shouldn't undermine the great achievements that the region has made in this area. No matter how suitable one's climate is for those practices, there is effort, expense and daily commitment to achieve and maintain them, which is still not the norm, anywhere in the world. While we have refrained from using the

The Cube at d'Arenberg is one of the world's most iconic cellar doors.

word 'sustainability' too frequently in the book, as it often is vaguely defined, with the specific definition provided by SAW (incorporating environmental practices, economic sustainability and social responsibility), it feels appropriate here.

McLaren Vale is also the first region in Australia, and likely the world, to identify and deliberately manage its water usage to ensure that its underground resource – aquifers within what is known as the Willunga Basin – remains self-replenishing. While there has yet to be any government limitation or metering on bore water irrigation, many in the region are making a comprehensive effort to end its use.

Other irrigation sources come from either catchment dams or a giant recycled water scheme. This redirects the core draw of irrigation away from the aquifers. Many producers employ moisture monitors at varying depths in the vineyard to further inform irrigation decisions – to ensure they are precise and never water more than needed. Overhead sprinkler irrigation has been out of practice for 30 years.

Irrigation is a natural part of modern life in Australia – finding a sustainable method to achieve it is paramount. McLaren Vale is the frontrunner in driving sustainable solutions across the country, making effort to ensure that they remain in concert with the natural ecosystem.

And water *is* the natural ecosystem of McLaren Vale. The region's proximity to the coast has shaped its identity and culture. Corrina Wright explains how the seaside nature of the Vale drove a lot of the experimentation with alternative white grapes and lighter styles of reds: 'There was an element of some of us just getting sick of living on the coast, eating out of the seas, and only being able to choose a shiraz to go with it,' she says.

For Charlie Seppelt of Paralian, it's the harvest ritual of going down to the beach for a swim after a long day during vintage.

And Riley Harrison points to the seaside nature of McLaren Vale defining the culture of the region and even shaping the personality of the wines: 'Coastal towns just have a different vibe to inland areas. So that influences community and therefore culture … And then that comes through in the wines.'

The Port Willunga Sea Caves are a frequently visited tourist attraction. They are what remain from an old harbour master's cottage, hewn from limestone in the 1880s.

Hubbub

The grape varieties under vine in McLaren Vale are a source of concern, but also excitement, for the wineries of McLaren Vale. Today, 54% of the plantings in the Vale are shiraz. Though grenache is a grape that is meaningful to the region, its actual footprint is shockingly low – a mere 6.15% of grapes planted in the McLaren Vale are grenache.

This is due in large part to the Australian government's Vine Pull Scheme of the 1980s. When tasked with which vines to rip out, growers chose the ones that commanded the least money and demanded the most time. And, sadly, that was grenache – 310 hectares were pulled out, and very few replanted over the years, leaving a mere 450 hectares in production today (out of McLaren Vale's total 7400 hectares).

Grenache was also never destined to be a workhorse grape, with high yields pushing productivity. 'Grenache doesn't stand abuse,' says Drew Noon. 'Shiraz, if you grow to productivity, it still makes fairly dark, pretty decent-tasting wine. If you grow grenache to productivity, it's very possible it will be pretty ordinary.' So the growers of the 1980s put their money on shiraz, which of course, has not turned out to be a bad bet.

A few growers refused to pull out their old grenache vines, though – an act probably decried as foolish at the time, but looked upon today (with gratitude) as prescient. Pete Fraser tells of one such grower – the Smart family – who had planted both Clarendon's Smart vineyard and the vineyard that would become Yangarra's High Sands vineyard in Blewitt Springs. In the 80s and 90s, '90% of the grenache got sold to Italian and Greek families who would drive up and fill up their 4x6 trailer and make wine in the garage.' These growers knew they had something special. And they did what they had to do to preserve it.

Today, grenache is finally getting its due. For the first time ever, in the 2020 vintage, grenache in McLaren Vale fetched a higher price per tonne than shiraz did. As demand for the grape rises across all of Australia, McLaren Vale is now wishing it had a few more grenache vines in the ground. Steve Pannell has predicted that there would be a 'battle for vineyards', especially the old **bush vines** of Blewitt Springs and Clarendon, and sure enough, that is already proving to be true. S.C. Pannell purchased a Blewitt Springs old-vine grenache vineyard in 2021, Bekkers purchased the Peake/Gillard Clarendon vineyard the year before (first planted in 1842), and in 2021 the team behind Adelaide Hills' Shaw+Smith made their entry into McLaren Vale with the purchase of 20 hectares of old-vine grenache, shiraz and chenin blanc (planted in the 1930s and 1960s) in Blewitt Springs – called MMAD, an acronym of the first names of their four partners.

But grenache is not the only grape causing excitement across the region. McLaren Vale has long been a supporter of 'alternative' grape varieties, which can probably be better expressed as 'more appropriate' grape varieties (to borrow a quote from Coonawarra's Sue Bell, p. 394). Long gone is the fallacy that the 'noble grapes' (i.e., chardonnay, riesling, sauvignon blanc, pinot noir, cabernet sauvignon and merlot) are the only ones that can properly transmit their place. In fact, it's the opposite belief that many vintners across Australia hold, instead looking to find and plant the exact grape (however obscure) that best suits a site.

Steve Pannell has been a leader of this movement. 'A future with more grape varieties is a path toward better expressing a proper sense of place,' he says, and his plantings back it up: everything from tinta cão to fiano, tempranillo to montepulciano. Many across the region have followed suit, with Yangarra planting every one of the 13 grapes of Châteauneuf-du-Pape (clairette, anyone?), Oliver's Taranga championing sagrantino, vermentino and mencía, and Brash Higgins making McLaren Vale semillon, nero d'Avola, mataro, chenin blanc and cinsault – among others.

'It's probably the region with the most experimental varieties in the entire country,' Corrina Wright says proudly – and certainly the one with such an established (and profitable) brand already. Many regions across Australia that fetch good money for their signature grapes don't stray, but in McLaren Vale, straying has become the signature.

There are other worries on the minds of McLaren Vale's vintners, besides what grapes

Many regions across Australia that fetch good money for their signature grapes don't stray, but in McLaren Vale, straying has become the signature.

are in the ground (tourism, branding, climate change, water access and the trunk disease Eutypa dieback among them), but no one seems too concerned. As Pete Fraser puts it: 'Ultimately, the exciting part, is it's a beautiful region. It offers so much and I think it will continue to prosper while it keeps a focus on its history and tries to continue on ... and we'll always have this beauty, this rarity of old-vine grenache.'

PRODUCERS

ALPHA BOX & DICE

Alpha Box & Dice has a wine (or multiple) for every letter of the alphabet, each an individual winemaking project that seeks to showcase the great diversity of South Australian wine. (Though based in the Vale, Alpha Box & Dice sources grapes from Adelaide Hills and Barossa Valley as well.) 'G' is for Golden Mullet Fury, a semillon-muscat-riesling blend that employs skin contact and botrytis fruit to great effect. 'L' is for Lazarus, a 'reverse ripasso' that sees every wine in their arsenal blended and passed over the skins of freshly pressed grapes. Head winemaker since 2015, Sam Berketa has maintained the true dedication to experimentation that this winery is known for, but never at the expense of quality. *alphaboxdice.com*

ANGOVE
(See Riverland, p. 404)

APHELION

Lou and Rob Mack started Aphelion in 2014 after leaving budding careers in the business sector to chase their dreams of making great wine. Grenache has been the focus of the winery, with a single tonne of Blewitt Springs grenache kicking off the whole endeavour. Since then, Aphelion has taken out several top awards across Australia and added other grapes to the mix, including mataro, sagrantino, grenache blanc, shiraz, chenin blanc, nero d'Avola and clairette (all purchased fruit, working closely with Vale growers). Though Aphelion means 'from the sun', the wines combine the best of sun and shade, displaying a cool-toned and transparent fruit quality that is as refreshing as it is complex.
aphelionwine.com.au

BEKKERS

Bekkers is the last name of Emmanuelle and Toby, a wife-and-husband team who have chosen McLaren Vale as their home. Toby has McLaren Vale wine in his blood, with ancestors from Clarendon and his grandfather working for Reynella back in the day. Emmanuelle, on the other hand, was born in Toulon, France and underwent her winemaking studies there before moving to Australia to work for BRL Hardy, where she met Toby. The two worked tirelessly for years in both hemispheres before setting up their own winery, Bekkers, buying high-quality fruit and working out of Yangarra's winemaking facilities. Their focus is admirably tapered, making three wines from McLaren Vale (a syrah, a grenache and a syrah-grenache) and, with Emmanuelle's French connections, a premier cru Vaillons Chablis every year. In 2020, the Bekkers purchased the seven-year abandoned Clarendon Vineyard Estate, originally planted in 1842, but converted to orchards in the 1930s, and back to vineyards in the 1990s. 'We are eager to see what this celebrated old hill can provide,' says Toby, 'given some love and attention.' They are making some of McLaren's most ambitious and elegant wines, which can be sampled in their picturesque tasting room.
bekkerswine.com

BONDAR

Bondar began with a couple of tonnes of McLaren Vale shiraz in the 2012 vintage, purchased and made by Andre and Selina Bondar. The next year, they acquired the historic Rayner vineyard, with grenache and shiraz vines dating back to the 1950s. Rayner sits on the border of Seaview and Blewitt Springs, and yields a lighter style, with perfume and savouriness. Beyond shiraz and grenache, Bondar has branched out to such regionally appropriate grapes as touriga, monastrell (the Spanish word for mataro/mourvèdre) and fiano, as well as the occasional Adelaide Hills wine. Bondar acknowledges the Kaurna people on their website, and 'that their cultural and heritage beliefs are still as important' to this day.
bondarwines.com.au

BRASH HIGGINS

Brad Hickey is a Chicago native, who became a top sommelier in New York City before leaving to work a harvest in McLaren Vale in 2007. A single harvest turned into a lifetime migration when he met Nicole Thorpe, who had planted grapes in the Vale in the late 1990s. The vineyard was called Omensetter and was planted to cabernet sauvignon and shiraz, which were hit hard by the recent droughts. Brad and Nicole investigated more drought-tolerant grape varieties, which led them to graft over 0.5 hectares of shiraz to nero d'Avola. They released their first wine from the 2011 vintage – an estate-grown, amphora-fermented nero d'Avola – under the label Brash Higgins (a nickname Brad had been given by the local pruners). The rest, as they say, is history, with Brash Higgins becoming synonymous with alternative grape varieties and experimentation – all in the name of creating better wine and greater long-term sustainability.
brashhiggins.com

CLARENDON HILLS

Clarendon Hills has been one of the most controversial wineries of McLaren Vale. Outspoken about the perceived shortcomings of Australian wine, biochemist Roman Bratasiuk long sold most of his wines in the United States – neither fact making him popular back home. But it's hard to deny Bratasiuk's achievements or the quality of his wines. Established in 1990, his winery was one of the first to champion subregional and single-vineyard bottlings, making wines from Blewitt Springs (where he is based), Kangarilla and Clarendon. His '1er Grand Cru' top bottling is called Astralis, the vineyard source for which is classified, and has been garnering lavish point scores since its inception in 1994. The Domaine Clarendon label comes from Bratasiuk's 2005 plantings in Clarendon, using cuttings from the Astralis vineyard source and sitting at 350 metres above sea level – McLaren Vale's highest vineyard site. His persona has softened, or maybe Australia has softened to him, but whichever way it happened, he has become more accepted (and even celebrated) of late in his home country. *clarendonhills.com.au*

CORIOLE

Coriole celebrated its 50th anniversary in 2017, with Hugh and Molly Lloyd founding the iconic McLaren winery in 1967. Second and third-generation Lloyds now run the estate, who count among their assets farmhouses built in 1860, vineyards originally planted in 1919, as well as a garden, cellar door and restaurant. Though the McLaren Vale stalwarts shiraz, cabernet and grenache have always been a part of the winery's stable, Coriole was one of the first wineries to embrace Italian varieties in McLaren Vale, introducing such grapes as sangiovese (now a signature of theirs), fiano and negroamaro as early as 1985. Third-generation Duncan Lloyd has been the senior winemaker since 2017. *coriole.com*

D'ARENBERG

D'Arenberg is a rare bird, being one of the most historically important wineries of the region – with family in the McLaren Vale wine business dating back to 1881 – but also a producer of enduring significance to this day. Chester Osborn has been the chief winemaker at his family estate since 1984, and has alternatively been referred to in the media as a 'colourful character', 'an eccentric if there ever was one' and 'Australia's Willy Wonka of wine'. Osborn is noted for his flashy attire and extravagant demeanour, but also for the out-of-the-box way he

---

JR — What we're drinking

We often think of grenache as a style choice: hefty or light, ripe or tart. The best ones seem to do both, swinging back and forth on the palate at once. At **Bondar**, *sundrenched and sea breeze-swept, Andre and Selina's Rayner vineyard captures the tension between those two poles in a generous manner. Fragrant, finessed and fruitful.* – Jonathan Ross

approaches wine. In 2003, the idea came to him to build the d'Arenberg Cube, a testament to 'the complexities and puzzles of winemaking'. The Cube is one of the most visually striking wine buildings the world over, and certainly one of the most experimental, with five floors of features, such as the Alternate Realities Museum, a wine sensory room, a virtual fermenter, a 360-degree video room, and 'many other tactile experiences'. Their wine line-up includes the icon Dead Arm Shiraz (named after the vine disease Eutypa dieback that severely decreases yields, creating super-concentrated wines), as well as affordable Stump Jump offerings, and a smattering of everything from classics like cabernet and grenache to roussanne, fiano, mencía and cinsault. Though the production is immense, so is the creativity and quality. *darenberg.com.au*

GEMTREE

Gemtree began with the 1980 purchase of a plot of land in McLaren Flat by Paul and Jill Buttery. The project took on a whole new energy when their daughter Melissa joined the team in 1994, investing herself deeply in organic and **biodynamic** farming, with all blocks achieving organic certification by 2011. In a quest to further protect and regenerate for the next generation, the winery also uses recycled water in their vineyards and has solar panels to power their irrigation pumps, winery and cellar door. Melissa's husband Mike Brown is Gemtree's chief winemaker and managing director, crafting wines of freshness and flavour. The range is large and runs from affordable tempranillo and **piquette** to their icon Subterra Shiraz, aged in a barrel buried in their vineyards. *gemtreewines.com*

HARDYS

Hardys and McLaren Vale history are one: Thomas Hardy's ascent is chronicled in this book and his devotion to the region, along with further Hardy generations to come, would indelibly shape McLaren Vale. Hardys was a leader in production and exports in the early days of the wine region, and begun to dip its toe into corporate acquisitions in the 1970s, with the purchase of Emu Wine Company, which included Swan Valley's Houghton and McLaren Vale's Morphett Vale and, soon after, Chateau Reynella, where Thomas Hardy had his start in the wine industry back in 1850. In 1992, Thomas Hardy & Sons (as it was known at the time) merged with Berri Renmano Limited to form BRL Hardy Limited, and in 2003 merged with Constellation to become the Hardy Wine Company, later Constellation Wines Australia, and later still, Accolade Wines. Today, Accolade is the largest wine company in Australia (by volume) and the fifth-largest wine company in the world, with sales of approximately 35 million cases each year. Though many of Hardys' current wines are on the commercial scale, the Eileen Hardy Shiraz is a wine that is still much sought after, having a well-worn spot on the **Langton's Classification**. The wine is named after the widow of third-generation Tom Mayfield Hardy, killed in the tragic *Kyeema* plane crash of 1938 (see p. 292); she went on to be a great brand ambassador and champion for the Hardys company and McLaren Vale. *hardyswines.com*

HARRISON WINES

Riley Harrison trained as a viticulturist, but soon found a passion for crafting wines as well as farming the vines. He worked in California, Germany and Portugal before returning home to Australia and settling down on the coast in McLaren Vale. He is currently the co-winemaker at Samuel's Gorge with owner Justin McNamee, and in 2015 started his own label: Harrison Wines. Riley sources small parcels of fruit from top vineyards in South Australia, and his arsenal includes a McLaren Vale roussanne/grenache blanc, Barossa grenache, McLaren Vale cabernet franc and Adelaide Hills syrah. His style involves meticulous care and attention, leaving the wines feeling delightfully unmade, aromatically exciting and texturally pleasing. **harrison.wine**

INKWELL

Inkwell is helmed by husband-and-wife team Dudley Brown and Dr Irina Santiago-Brown who have both, in their own right, contributed greatly to the wine-growing scene in McLaren Vale. Dudley was the Chairman of the McLaren Vale Grape Wine and Tourism Association from 2007–2010 (and a board member for a subsequent five years), where he helped launch the Scarce Earth project (originally called Rare Earth) as well as the Sustainable Australian Winegrowing (SAW) system. In fact, he met Irina when interviewing her for the position of heading up SAW.

There has been some controversy in recent years, as Dudley has been outspoken about how Irina's work was plagiarised by the **AWRI** (Australian Wine Research Institute) to create its national sustainability program, renamed Sustainable Winegrowing Australia (SWA), without her work ever being credited. While no fault has been acknowledged by the **AWRI**, the Browns continue to tread their course: farming grapes organically, tending to their cellar door and luxury accommodation (built from upcycled shipping containers), and making a diverse spread of wines – everything from classic shiraz to preservative-free bubbly in a can to obscure grapes like bela and arinto. **inkwellwines.com**

MINISTRY OF CLOUDS

Ministry of Clouds is the brainchild of Julian Forwood and Bernice Ong, a duo with decades of combined experience in the McLaren Vale wine industry. Though both came from the marketing and sales side of the industry, their interest ran deeper, and they use Ministry of Clouds to showcase specific sites and styles from across the region. When the wines first hit the market in 2013, they were met with critical acclaim and commercial reception. In 2016, the pair bought a vineyard of their own on the ridge above Seaview. They work with a collection of Mediterranean and Iberian grapes in McLaren Vale, including shiraz, grenache, mataro, carignan, tempranillo and mencía, as well as Tasmanian chardonnay and Clare Valley riesling. Their Kintsugi is a unique offering, eschewing typical varietal labelling in favour of creating 'the best Southern Rhône-inspired red' they can make in a year – patterned off the Japanese art of *kintsugi*, piecing together broken pottery fragments with gold-laced liqueur to create a sum that is greater than its parts.
ministryofclouds.com.au

MOLLYDOOKER

Mollydooker's meteoric rise to fame, after it launched with the 2005 vintage, propelled it to become one of the top names for Australian wine in the United States. Back at home,

---

 What we're drinking

A number of Iberian varieties have found a happy home in the Mediterranean climes of McLaren Vale. Garnacha (grenache) and tempranillo are regulars on the sorting table. Mencía, however, is a relative newcomer to the region. **Ministry of Clouds'** *version gives me all the Bierzo feels with delicious bright red fruits and the all-important hint of meaty chorizo. Australia loves a barbecue wine and this one is a winner.* — Kavita Faiella

Corrina Wright
Oliver's Taranga

the wines are not quite as ubiquitous, as export has long been a focus of the brand. But Sarah Marquis, owner and chief winemaker, said in a 2017 interview with *Wine Spectator* that she wants to become more involved in the McLaren Vale wine community: 'We were kind of in a bubble of our own,' she said. The year 2017 was when Sarah and her ex-husband and long-time business partner Sparky finalised their divorce arrangements that left Sarah with the controlling share of the company. The plan is to stay the course. Mollydooker has successfully marketed wines from affordable to luxury, with their marquee Velvet Glove bottling selling for AUD $195 on their website. Mollydooker has also created a language and culture around their brand: from its colourful labels and catchy names to the 'Mollydooker shake', designed to release the nitrogen used in the winemaking process, and the 'Marquis Fruit Weight' that measures what percentage of your tongue is covered by the velvety sensation of the wine. These are big wines, often with high alcohol and perceptible sugar levels. By all accounts,

Mollydooker is also a good company, creating its 'Sip it Forward' campaign to give back to communities in need, as well as being a beloved employer for its long-time staff.
mollydookerwines.com.au

NOON

Drew Noon is one of the best people in Australian wine, period. Though his wines have made a splash with some high ratings and awards, for Drew and his wife Raegan, wine is about the land and the handmade process; yields and production are kept low, and they stay true to their style. Though the pair acknowledge that lighter styles of wine have become en vogue in the media today, they stand by their production of generous, full-bodied wines. 'We produce our wines from old, low yielding vines growing in a warm climate, so we are bound to make full-bodied reds.' The Noons have been making that style of wine since Drew's father David established the family's winery in 1976. They sell all wine direct from their cellar door – and for almost criminally low prices. In a 2021 interview with Max Allen, Drew said that 'at that price, our customers are happy, we're happy, and we can make a living. It's a small living, but it's enough.' Drew Noon is also one of Australia's first **MW**s, passing the difficult exam in 1998, and one of the foremost experts on the varied terroir of McLaren Vale. **noonwinery.com.au**

OLIVER'S TARANGA

In 1994, Oliver's Taranga released its first estate-bottled and branded wine after six generations of grape growing in McLaren Vale. Their 100-hectare, 180-year-old estate sits in the middle of McLaren Vale's Seaview region, with plantings of everything from shiraz, grenache and cabernet sauvignon to mencía, white frontignac and fiano. Oliver's Taranga still sells grapes – to the likes of such luminaries as d'Arenberg, Penfolds, Wirra Wirra and Seppeltsfield – and only makes wine from their own estate grapes. Corrina Wright is the winemaker and director of her family's winery, navigating the terrain as new makers but old growers to great success. The winery offers tastings and extensive vineyard tours out of their cellar door.
oliverstaranga.com

PARALIAN WINES

Paralian means 'someone who lives by the sea' and is the project of Charlie Seppelt and Skye Salter, who do indeed live by the sea, in Port Willunga. The seaside nature of their location affects the wines and the lifestyle, with a focus on lifted and ethereal styles of grenache and shiraz from Blewitt Springs, often picked before an end-of-the-day dip in the ocean. They also make an Adelaide Hills chardonnay. Charlie is a sixth-generation Seppelt who is also on the winemaking team for Seppeltsfield (p. 315), the winery his family started in 1851. Skye was the longtime winemaker at Willunga 100, but is now devoted to Paralian full

time. The pair met while working together at Hardys Tintara in 2008. *paralian.com.au*

S.C. PANNELL

Steve Pannell is one of Australia's great wine minds and has been hugely influential in the trajectory of not only McLaren Vale wine, but Australian wine in general, especially in his adoption of alternative varieties. Steve had wine in his blood: his parents Bill and Sandra Pannell founded Margaret River's Moss Wood in 1969. But instead of going into the family business, Steve ventured out on his own, travelling to work in Burgundy, Bordeaux and Barolo before arriving at BRL Hardy, where he was the senior red winemaker for nearly a decade from the mid-1990s to 2003. It was in that year that BRL Hardy merged with Constellation, and the resultant restructuring allowed Steve to consider his next move. He and his wife Fiona Lindquist started S.C. Pannell in 2004 and haven't looked back. From a food-friendliness and sustainability perspective, Pannell champions all sorts of Mediterranean grapes, everything from touriga nacional to montepulciano, fiano and tempranillo. The label also sources riesling, pinot gris, chardonnay, syrah and barbera from the Adelaide Hills. Steve and Fiona have acquired several vineyard sites over the years, with an eye toward continued creativity and evolution.
pannell.com.au

SOMOS

Somos means 'we are' in Spanish, and is the collaboration of Bend Caldwell and Mauricio Ruiz Cantú. The two met while studying oenology at the University of Adelaide, and upon graduating, hatched a plan to make wines to send back to Ruiz Cantú's home country, Mexico. After success with that label – called Juguette – they launched Somos, whose mission is to work with responsibly farmed fruit, handled in a low-intervention way, using lesser-known grape varieties. The wines include Naranjito, a McLaren Vale verdelho skin-contact wine; Tintito, a multiregional blend changing from vintage to vintage, most recently with grenache, uva di troia, pinot meunier and mencía; and Espumito, a **pét-nat** of barbera, cortese and chardonnay.
somoswines.com

WIRRA WIRRA

Wirra Wirra was originally built in 1894, though its early tenure was short lived. The winery was rebuilt

What we're drinking

*While the bio reads like corporate winemaker turned gentle experimentalist, **S.C. Pannell** is a driving force in the diversification of wine styles from the region (if not further afield!). Fresh, thirst-slaking and minerally whites, bright, chillable reds fit for warm weather drinking, 'tomato Europe'-leaning blends, varieties and styles apt for the Mediterranean climate on hand - all of this fits neatly into a new cultural vernacular of Australian drinking. – Mike Bennie*

McLaren Vale

in the 1960s by Greg Trott, who erected not only a successful winery at Wirra Wirra, but a culture that has defined the winery to this day. Visitors and staff alike pass by a slate block upon entering the winery, which is inscribed with Trott's philosophy: 'Never give misery an even break, nor bad wine a second sip. You must be serious about quality, dedicated to your task in life, especially winemaking, but this should all be fun.' Wirra Wirra has been certified **biodynamic** since 2014. Production centres on traditional styles of shiraz, cabernet sauvignon, merlot and grenache, but with a few whites thrown in (largely sourced from Adelaide Hills), as well as some Iberian grapes like tempranillo and touriga nacional.
wirrawirra.com

YANGARRA

Pete Fraser has become one of the great legends of Australian wine. After a chance meeting with Warren Randall (see Seppeltsfield, p. 315), he plunged headfirst into the wine industry and worked his way up the ranks at Norman's in McLaren Vale. Norman's had a huge asset in its arsenal (in addition to Fraser): a vineyard called Eringa Park in Blewitt Springs, with grenache vines dating back to 1923. American-owned Jackson Family Wines purchased this site in 2000, where they met Fraser, who put his hand up for a position with the newly named Yangarra Estate. Under Fraser, Yangarra started honing its vision, which centres around old-vine grenache. An unirrigated **bush-vine** plot planted in 1946 by the Smart family would become known as High Sands under Yangarra, and contribute its grapes to their prestige wine of the same name. The High Sands grenache has redefined what Australians think the grape is capable of, with enduring structure and power that is not tied to extraction, jamminess or oak. The **biodynamic** vineyards at Yangarra also harbour many other grapes native to France's Southern Rhône Valley, including shiraz, roussanne, clairette, bourboulenc, picpoul noir and counoise. The wines have been widely accepted as some of McLaren Vale's greatest. As for the future, 'I think we just continue to finesse that finesse,' says Fraser, with a laugh. 'Having a vision that is stubborn in some ways, but open-minded in seeing the rest of the world.'
yangarra.com

And don't forget ...
Dune is a side project of the third-generation Coriole brothers from a single vineyard in Blewitt Springs called Desert Sands ... **Fox Creek Wines** was one of the wineries of the 90s that drove renown for McLaren Vale under the ownership of Jim and Helen Watts, who have sold the winery to three long-time friends and industry colleagues as of 2021 ... **Hickinbotham Vineyard** was planted in 1971 by Alan David Hickinbotham, an 85-hectare vineyard of **dry-grown** cabernet sauvignon, shiraz and merlot that has been owned by the Jackson Family since 2012, with wines made by Yangarra's Pete Fraser and American Chris Carpenter ... **Kay Brothers Amery Vineyard**, founded in 1890, was directly managed by the Kay family until third-generation Colin Kay retired in 2014, still offering regional classics including their flagship Block 6 Shiraz ... **Koomilya**, Steve Pannell's vineyard in Blewitt Springs, puts out shiraz, cabernet sauvignon, a touriga-graciano-mataro blend and tempranillo-touriga blend with a light touch ... **Marius Wines** is an exemplary, culty producer of the Vale, immortalised in text by the DBC Pierre novel *Lights Out in Wonderland*, which speaks of the 'decadent' proprietor Roger Pike, 'who is without top or bottom limits' ... **Mitolo**, a collaboration between Frank Mitolo and Ben Glaetzer, works closely with the Lopresti family vineyards to release larger-scale shiraz, cabernet, grenache, vermentino, sangiovese and sagrantino ... **Orbis** is the custodian of a high, cool shiraz plot originally planted in the 60s and 70s, which they are regenerating back to health, with gun winemaker Lauren Langfield at the helm ... **Poppelvej**, from Danish winemaker Uffe Deichmann, is making waves in the avant-garde scene, sourcing a wide range of grapes from well-farmed vineyards to make raw and vibrant styles ... **Samuel's Gorge** was established in 2003 by Justin McNamee on the ridge above Seaview, with grenache, shiraz, mourvèdre, graciano, and tempranillo as the five key varieties ... **Willunga 100** led the charge to get grenache back in the good graces of Australians, crafting elegant single-site expressions of the grape from Willunga, Blewitt Springs and Clarendon.

Coonawarra & Wrattonbully

Introduction

In South Australia, just 20 kilometres west of the Victorian border, and no more than 120 kilometres from the Indian Ocean to the west or the south, lies one of the most compelling national parks: the Naracoorte Caves. They comprise South Australia's only World Heritage site, and one of two sites in all of Australia recognised for its significance in preserving Australia's singular animal heritage.

'Megafauna' is not a word you get to use every day, describing the giant creatures that roamed the earth (many of which are extinct, including the Australian ones); typical weight thresholds include a minimum of 45 kilograms, all the way up to and exceeding 1000 kilograms. For at least 500,000 years, the Naracoorte caves acted as owl nesting sites and pitfall traps, collecting small animals as well as big.

In 1857, a reverend named Julian Tenison-Woods happened upon this site, unknowingly discovering a goldmine of animal bones, preserved in time by layers of sand, crystal and limestone. Some of the megafauna later uncovered include *Zygomaturus trilobus*, a toothy wombat-like marsupial, the size of horse, *Procoptodon goliah*, the largest known kangaroo species, standing 2 metres tall and weighing 200–240 kilograms, *Wonambi naracoortensis*, a 5 to 6-metre-long constrictor snake, and *Thylacoleo carnifex*, a marsupial lion that is thought to have had the strongest bite of any animal species, extant or extinct.

The caves also preserve evidence of human arrival in the area, dating to about 10,000 years after these megafauna fell to extinction 60,000 years ago. Unfortunately, little more exists on the original inhabitants of the region, though the caves of Naracoorte would have most certainly been an important place both spiritually and culturally for early inhabitants, as well as providing shelter. The word 'naracoorte' comes from an Aboriginal word meaning large water hole.

This area, within the boundaries of the wine region Wrattonbully today, seems to have been 'a meeting place for numerous nations with evidence of trading and gathering at the caves,' says local winemaker Sue Bell. 'The jury is still out but I feel we are getting closer to uncovering the history. Potentially the delay has not been helped by the possibility that the majority of people were possibly killed or moved on to the Portland area.' Indeed, large massacres occurred in the region. While it's unclear if just a single nation covered Wrattonbully at any one time, Bell concludes that the nation of 'Meintangk might be the best assumption at the moment'.

Coonawarra, just south of Wrattonbully, is also not clear-cut when it comes to acknowledging the First Nations of the area. Broadly, the area is thought to be of the Boandik people, but potentially Coonawarra is more specifically Pinchunga Country. When Bell acknowledges Country at her winery

Bellwether, she usually mentions Boandik and Pinchuga, but she has not listed First Nations names on her wine labels yet, as she wants to uncover the clearest and most accurate approach first. 'The conversation and layers of knowledge unfolding is accelerating,' she says, 'which really excites me.'

While unfolding knowledge of the region's First Nations, as well as limestone caves of prehistoric megafauna, brews excitement for the region, 'exciting' is a word that has rarely been applied to the wine regions of Coonawarra and Wrattonbully in the last several decades. The words 'conservative' and 'staid' are the more usual descriptors – unfair monikers in many ways.

But with 90% of Coonawarra's plantings comprised of cabernet sauvignon, shiraz and merlot (and a similar, though not quite as extreme, dominance in Wrattonbully), it's easy to see how these regions have often been viewed as one-trick ponies that are stuck in the past. As a result, the vignerons of today are working harder than ever to dispel this myth and showcase the quality of the region.

The raw material, viticultural practices and talent in these regions are undeniable. Both regions are in the process of rebuilding (or just building, in the case of Wrattonbully) their reputations and identities. But there's a clear comfort and ease: the vignerons of both regions know their part of the world is special – and how little actually needs to be done to solidify their place among the annals of Australian fine wine.

Evolution of Wine

Coonawarra's flat plains and fertile soils attracted early colonial settlers in the mid-1800s. John Riddoch, a Scottish sheep farmer, had great ambitions for the region. In 1890, he set aside 800 hectares to sell off to other colonists, establishing the Coonawarra Fruit Colony. Alongside 26 other farmers, Riddoch began planting vines the next year; 95,000 vines went in the ground in 1896, and by 1897 there were 140 hectares planted to grapevines, primarily cabernet sauvignon and shiraz, with small amounts of pinot noir, malbec and pedro ximénez.

Coonawarra's first vintage (and the first vintage of the Limestone Coast) was produced in 1895. This vintage is often described as a modest affair, though 8000 litres of wine is not insignificant. The second vintage, described in much more illustrious terms, took place in Riddoch's woolshed. The chairman of the local agricultural bureau stated of these early wines: 'I have it on the authority of various experts that the wine produced so far is of the description most desired and saleable to meet the most fastidious palate.'

John Riddoch would only live to see a handful of vintages, dying in 1901 at the age of 73. Despite its promising start (and the burgeoning reputation of the 'Coonawarra Claret'), the Coonawarra wine industry saw little success in

The Katnook Woolshed is the most iconic building in Coonawarra: the site of the region's first major vinous ferment. It is kept in impeccable shape by today's custodians.

the first half of the 20th century. This was largely due to its distance from major markets and nationwide economic depression. Though some grapevines remained in the ground, production was low, and primarily went toward brandy and **fortified wine**.

The modern era of Coonawarra began in 1951, when Melbourne-based winemakers Samuel Wynn and his son David bought the old Riddoch estate. This purchase included the historic vineyard land, as well as the famed triple-gable winery, which John Riddoch had built after growing out of the woolshed. Wynns Coonawarra Estate was formed, the first winery in the region, and the first winery in all of Australia to use the word 'estate' in its name.

Wynns had its first vintage in 1953, just in time to embrace (or perhaps help inspire) the national palate turning back toward dry wine. Another winery emerged right around the same time, who had been quietly producing bulk wine in Coonawarra for decades. Bill Redman had worked for the John Riddoch winery from 1901, before purchasing his own land in 1908. In 1952, Bill and his son Owen released their first estate-bottled wine under the Rouge Homme label, a blend of cabernet sauvignon and shiraz (just like Riddoch's first wines).

The Rouge Homme label was sold in 1965, but Owen and his wife Edna launched Redman wines the next year. Other wineries soon cropped up in the region, many of which remain important to this day. In 1968, the original vines at Majella went into the ground. Katnook, who claim John Riddoch's old woolshed as part of their property, was planted in 1971. Joy and Doug Bowen planted their first vineyards in the early 1970s, and Balnaves of Coonawarra was established in 1975.

In these early days, shiraz and cabernet sauvignon were king, either bottled varietally or blended and labelled 'claret'. Alcohols tended to be low, oak expression moderate, and sometimes malolactic fermentation was even blocked: the wines of these early days were lean, structured and savoury.

And just north of Coonawarra proper, the area that would come to be known as Wrattonbully (but often referred to as Koppamurra before its GI registration), was getting its start. The first plantings in Wrattonbully date back to 1969, when 11 hectares of shiraz, cabernet sauvignon and chardonnay were planted by the Pender family (a vineyard which would come to be an important site for Petaluma). These plantings were followed by John Greenshields' Koppamurra vineyard in 1974, planted to 4 hectares of cabernet sauvignon. This site was later purchased by Tapanappa and renamed the Whalebone vineyard.

As early as 1972, Coonawarra and its environs were already attracting corporate investment. In this year, Allied Vintners, a division of a large UK distiller, bought Wynns. In 1985, Penfolds bought Allied, which would become Southcorp, then Foster's, and eventually Treasury Wine Estates. Coonawarra and neighbouring Wrattonbully also became targets for corporations to buy fruit for multiregional blends, even if they weren't buying the wineries themselves. Plantings in Wrattonbully topped out at about 20 hectares in the 1970s and 1980s, until larger, multiregional companies scouted land in the 1990s, establishing over 1800 hectares of vineyards.

But that's not to say that quality went down. In fact, Coonawarra saw its heyday for sales and accolades in the late 1970s through to the early 2000s. Coonawarra took home the **Jimmy Watson** trophy – an apt barometer for national taste – 11 times in the years 1977–2011, more than any other wine region, dwarfing its next competitor (the Barossa Valley), which claimed the award just three times in those decades.

Except for a few shiraz, nearly every trophy winner was a cabernet sauvignon or cab-based blend. The grape had become synonymous with the region, and its expression was unique. It's been said that the famous terra rossa soils of the region produce a high amount of flavonoids in the cabernet sauvignon grape, resulting in, among other flavours, a specific 'chocolate mint' quality. 'Choco mint' became the descriptor of the day for Coonawarra.

As the 80s and 90s wore on, in contrast to the early cabernets of the 60s and 70s, the styles were ripe, often laden with American oak, and appealed to the consumer and the critic with equal fervour. The name 'Coonawarra', even though it was yet to be legally defined, became hugely influential in marketing and sales across Australia. Flocks of prospective growers flooded the region and plantings multiplied, often with a focus on yields rather than quality.

It came time to establish the Coonawarra GI in the mid-1990s, and by 1997 an interim determination had been issued by the GI Committee (GIC). Most GIs sail easily from interim to final determinations with little consternation, but the boundaries of the Coonawarra GI became one of the most hotly disputed conflicts in Australian wine. After the 1997 determination, 33 objections were lodged. The main complaints were from wineries that had historically used the Coonawarra name and were to be left out of the GI borders. The extent of the terra rossa soil was the main physical feature in question when determining the boundaries of Coonawarra.

After an appeals process with the GIC and a subsequent elevations to the Australian Appeals Tribunal and the Federal Court of Australia, a final determination was reached in 2003 for Coonawarra borders and 2005 for Wrattonbully.

The ultimate GI borders pacified some, but still left opponents on both sides of the spectrum: those who thought the GI was overreaching and those who thought it should have been more inclusive. And those it left out on the outskirts of Penola, who didn't fit into either the Coonawarra or Wrattonbully GIs, were left with no choice but to label their wines 'Limestone Coast', immediately losing the renown (and livelihood) associated with Coonawarra.

Many eyes were on Coonawarra at this time. It was the first region to attempt to draw boundaries that were anything less than 100% inclusive: attempting to follow the extent of the famed terra rossa soils to establish boundaries rather than casting a wider net that allowed all who had previously used the name Coonawarra to participate in the GI.

Whether coincidental or causal, some of Coonawarra's prestige began to deflate in the years following the GI determination. Some do believe that the GI formation, and the ill-will that

surrounded it, contributed to Coonawarra's decline. Brian Croser, the founder of Adelaide Hills' Petaluma and Tapanappa, who long worked with Coonawarra fruit, said in a 2020 interview: 'A much bigger GI inclusive of all participants ... could have enhanced the dimension, diversity and appeal of the region to international markets. Coonawarra's small dimensions and the lack of diversity have led to it being strongly eclipsed by Margaret River as Australia's premier cabernet region despite the obvious terroir advantages of Coonawarra.'

Others, many still making wine in the region, blame the planting boom of the 1990s. These negative sensations compounded each other and were picked up by some wine writers and journalists of the day, who were not kind to the region in the early 2000s.

But even though the trendiness of Coonawarra subsided, the money didn't go away. The **Langton's Classification**, which measures which Australian wines are performing best at auction, has seen a largely steady growth for Coonawarra. Three of the region's wines were on the 1990 classification, blossoming to nine in 1995, 12 in 2000, a slight abatement to 11 in 2005, 14 in 2010, 15 in 2015, and 13 in 2020. And the best wineries were still delivering on the promise of the region, producing well-balanced and structured reds capable of long ageing.

The only **Jimmy Watson** winner, though, to come from the larger region after 2001 (when Coonawarra won it for the last time) was a small batch, 1800-case cabernet sauvignon from Wrattonbully, made by the ascending monolith Yellow Tail in 2003. Though Yellow Tail's win put the region on the map with some, Wrattonbully has still had a long, and fairly unsung, modern history.

Today, Wrattonbully has less than two dozen growers, but about 50 different producers work with Wrattonbully fruit. Large, multi-brand wine companies – like Treasury Wines Estates, Accolade, Pernod Ricard, Casella Family Brands and Taylors – came to realise the allure of Wrattonbully: a region offering very similar characteristics to Coonawarra at a fraction of the price. A vineyard in the Joanna section of Wrattonbully was selected to be in the 2014

Penfolds Grange – cementing the little-known region's potential to produce ultra-premium fruit.

Despite this reputation, only a handful of producers are proudly waving the Wrattonbully flag and putting the GI's name on labels: largely Bellwether, Eight at the Gate, Land of Tomorrow, Malone, Mérite, Smith & Hooper (owned by Yalumba's Hill-Smith family), Terre á Terre, Tapanappa and Yalumba. And it's only Eight at the Gate, Land of Tomorrow, Malone and Mérite who work with exclusively estate-grown Wrattonbully fruit.

Without a single winemaking facility in the region, all these wines are vinified in either Coonawarra or further north in South Australia. And though Wrattonbully has a similarly narrow planting scope as Coonawarra – 85% of the region's vines are cabernet sauvignon, shiraz and merlot – cabernet franc, malbec, tempranillo and barbera are varieties that are becoming of interest for the region.

The 21st century has meant, for many Australian wine regions, a resurgence: an ingress of young and eager winemakers, the establishment of new icons, an embraced spirit of experimentation, and a revitalisation in interest. This hasn't been the case for Wrattonbully or Coonawarra. 'The remoteness of Coonawarra from capital cities makes it hard to lure young winemakers and all the fresh energy and ideas and dynamism that they bring,' says David LeMire, a South Australian **Master of Wine**.

But these regions are forward thinking and innovative, perhaps just not in the way we

These regions are forward thinking and innovative, perhaps just not in the way we traditionally think about those ideas.

traditionally think about those ideas. Some of Australia's most talented winemakers and viticulturists are at work today in the region – all consistently honing their craft, building community and refining the vineyards and wines of the region, without forgetting about their illustrious history. Many of the original players who shaped the region – Wynns, Redman, Majella, Highbank and Balnaves of Coonawarra – continue to produce excellent wines. And though most of the wineries are still focused on traditional renderings of cabernet sauvignon and shiraz, the style they produce is one that is constantly being fine-tuned and perfected. And it's a style that is in demand today: moderate in body and age-worthy, with balanced oak expression. Though it might not look like it from the outside, this remote corner of southeastern South Australia has quietly regained its power and is building toward the future with tenacity.

Screwcaps

Also known as a Stelvins, screwcap closures are more common in Australia than many other wine-producing countries. Though the Stelvin closure was invented in France, it was at the behest of Peter Wall, the former director of Yalumba in South Australia. Wall, like many Australians, was fed up with the rate of failure he was experiencing with natural cork, which can sometimes lead to oxidation or cause cork taint. He wanted an alternative. Though the screwcap was a reliable closure from the beginning, the general perception among consumers was that a screwcap designated a lower-quality wine. While this perception is all but gone in Australia, other parts of the world have been slower to adopt the screwcap. Some argue that it's a closure that can easily be damaged (it's not); some argue that it's a closure that makes wine **reductive** (it doesn't); and some argue that it's a closure that doesn't allow wine to age properly (it does). It's time the world came around to screwcaps in the way that Australia has: they're a super-reliable, adaptable closure that ensures the wine in the bottle is as it should be, much more consistently than natural cork does.

Lay of the Land

The Limestone Coast is one of the more useful zone names in Australia, encapsulating the GIs of Coonawarra and Wrattonbully, as well as Padthaway to Wrattonbully's north, Mount Gambier to Coonawarra's immediate south, and the coastal GIs of Mount Benson and Robe, due west of that strip.

This limestone-laden landscape was first formed by the breakaway separation of Antarctica and Australia 130 million years ago, and the infilling of both the Southern and Indian oceans between them. The generally agreed upon timing of this separation was 158–130 million years ago. According to the Limestone Coast Grape and Wine Council, this moment and process is generally referred to as the 'rifting, lifting and drying of the Australian continent'.

The Gambier Limestone is the defining geological formation of the Limestone Coast. It was deposited 38–15 million years ago and is highly fossiliferous – riddled with calcium carbonate in the form of coral and shellfish fossils.

The Kanawinka Fault, and the resulting Naracoorte Range above it, draws the line between the much older Otway Basin to the northeast – formed from Cambrian and Silurian-era volcanic basalt and granite – and the younger Gambier Basin's limestone formations to the southwest.

Numerous ridgelines, or low-lying ranges, all less than 75 metres above sea level, run parallel to the Kanawinka Fault and the Naracoorte Range, west toward the current coastline. These are stranded, calcareous beach dunes that were left behind as the sea continued to recede: a result of the onset of the last ice age.

More recently, within the last ice age and sooner (2 million to 4000 years ago), volcanics in the Otway/Gambier Basins resulted in some gentle uplifting, as well as various extrusions – Mount Gambier last erupted only 5000 years ago. These formations resulted in acidic igneous rock piercing through calcareous formations. Much of the topsoil across the region is windblown sediment eroded from those formations: various sands and ironstone, along with marine-derived clays, resulting in a variety of sandy, loamy and clay-based topsoils across the zone.

Despite there being a variety of red clay and limestone soils in the region, Coonawarra's famed terra rossa soils are structurally unique. These soils are 30% clay, though they do not stick or bind together the way that most clay does. The balancing loam provides excellent structure: there is good air content in the soil, and it is easy for vines to dig through. The clay content means that the terra rossa is quite good at retaining water, successfully setting up vines for their spring push. As the season proceeds, the soils become harder and drier, resulting in positive vine stress, and ensuring the focus is on fruit ripening rather than continued foliage growth. Terra rossa top soil ranges 5–100 centimetres in depth, and gives way to soft limestone followed by harder limestone rock.

The red strip of terra rossa soil is often referred to as the 'cigar' of Coonawarra. On the Coonawarra website, it is referenced as being

Coonawarra Viticultural Footprint

Total delimited area (km²)	400
Total planted area (hectares)	5784
% of delimited area planted	14.500%
Total elevation range	51–127 masl
Elevation range of plantings	55–66 masl
Number of producers	34

Coonawarra Climate Data (°C)

	1960–1990	1991–PRESENT	2020
Heat summation/GDD	● 1442	● 1492	● 1466
Annual rain/GSR	628/248	605/235	598/220
Warmest month avg. temp.	19.4	19.8	19.7

Winkler Scale:

● 850–1111 ● 1112–1389 ● 1390–1667 ● 1668–1944 ● 1945–2222 ● 2223–2700

Coonawarra & Wrattonbully

HOW TO READ THIS MAP
The contested establishment of these two GIs has resulted in national, if not international, viticultural fame for the singular terra rossa soil type. Here, the vineyard surfaces of both regions are mapped across the numerous soil types.

1. Balnaves of Coonawarra
2. Balnaves Punters Corner Vineyard
3. Banks Thargo
4. Bellwether
5. The Blok
6. Bowen Estate
7. Brand and Sons
8. Brands Laira
9. Bundalong Coonawarra
10. DiGiorgio Family Wines
11. Eight at the Gate
12. Highbank
13. Hollick
14. Hynam Park
15. Katnook Estate
16. Koonara
17. Ladbroke Grove
18. Leconfield
19. Majella
20. Malone
21. Mérite
22. Ottelia
23. Parker Coonawarra Estate
24. Patrick of Coonawarra
25. Pavy
26. Penley Estate
27. Pepper Tree Coonawarra Vineyard
28. Pepper Tree Wrattonbully Vineyard
29. Petaluma
30. Raïdis
31. Redden Bridge
32. Redman
33. Rymill
34. St Hugo
35. Smith & Hooper
36. Tapanappa Whalebone Vineyard
37. Tidswell
38. Wongary
39. Wynns Coonawarra Estate
40. Yalumba The Menzies
41. Yalumba Wrattonbully
42. Yelloch Creek
43. Zema Estate
44. Zema Estate Cluny Vineyard

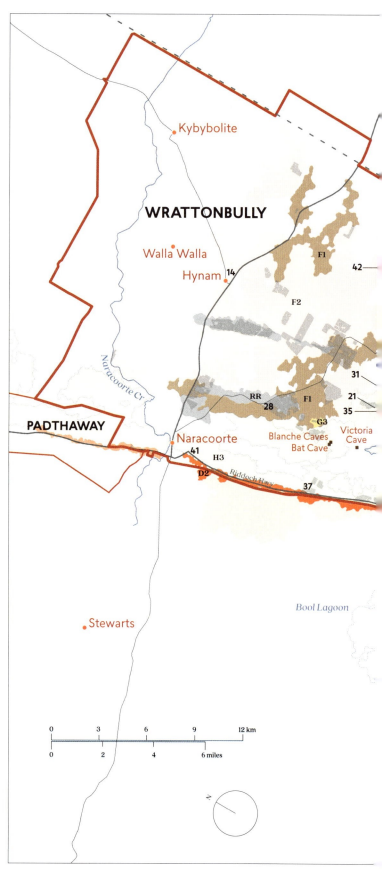

South Australia

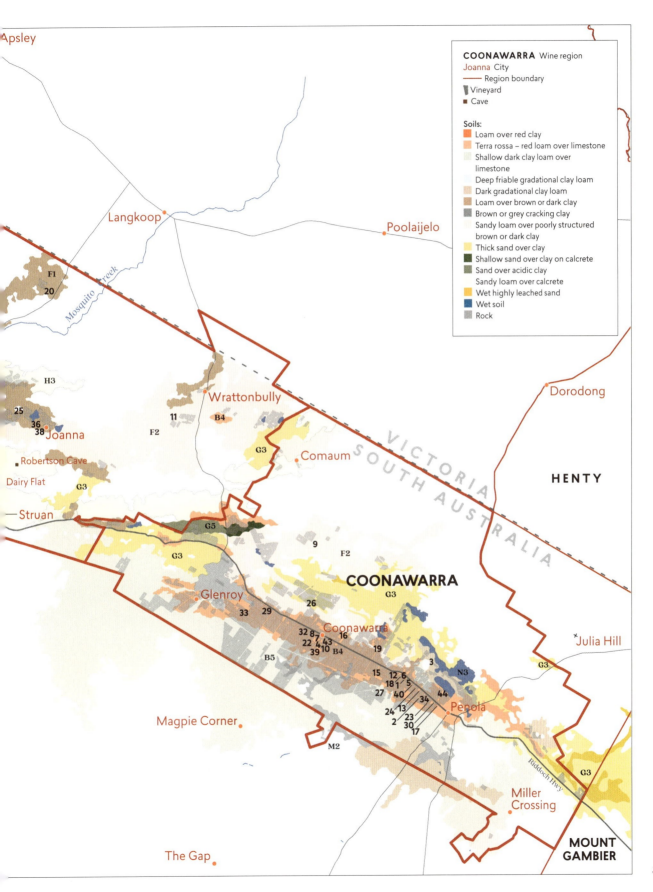

Coonawarra & Wrattonbully

27 kilometres long and 2 kilometres wide. The Coonawarra GI extends over 20 kilometres in its width, though vineyards are largely confined to the western 5 kilometres centred along the Riddoch Highway (and the terra rossa soils).

The 'cigar' is home to 47% of the region's plantings. According to a 2011 report from the Limestone Coast Grape and Wine Council, 1004 hectares of vines are planted to the soil specifically classified as terra rossa, comprising about 17% of the total plantings of the GI. The 'cigar' includes a few adjacent red to brown sandy loams, very similar to terra rossa, but not the exact same structure.

The remaining vineyards of Coonawarra are either planted to well-draining sandy soils, or heavier dark loamy clays that can suffer waterlogging in wetter vintages (this soil accounts for just under 30% of the region's vineyards). Vineyards on this soil are generally confined to small rises along the undulating topography – a change that only amounts to a 10–15 metre difference in elevation – in order to mitigate the waterlogging potential. The eastern half of the GI is almost completely unplanted.

Wrattonbully, directly north of Coonawarra, sits straddling the Naracoorte Escarpment and the Kanawinka fault, with vineyards fragmented across the GI. Significant to the region's identity is the Naracoorte Caves, which have a more specific geological timeline, forming towards the end of when the Gambier limestone was being deposited, around 18 million years ago. This specific deposit of limestone is about 6 metres thick, and creates a separate, more shallow aquifer at the caves and below the vineyards that surround it. This mitigates frost

likelihood in the area, making the risk considerably lower than in Coonawarra.

Wrattonbully's limestone is confined to the western and southern portions of the appellation with the northern and western portion sitting atop the much older Otway Basin formations of granite and basalt. The iron-red rich clay loams that define Coonawarra make a rare appearance in this area. The specific terra rossa soil, according to the same 2011 report, makes up 4% of Wrattonbully's plantings, though many very similar (some even argue identical) loam-over-limestone soils are found throughout the region.

As a west-facing coast, with few elevation gains to prevent the penetration of coastal weather, the Limestone Coast is considered a heavily maritime-influenced climate. The moderating effects of the sea are amplified due to a cold southern upwelling. This is more specifically known as the Bonney Upwelling, or the Upwelling along the Bonney Coast – a 275-kilometre stretch from Cape Jaffa in South Australia to Portland, Victoria (in the Henty GI, p. 198) – one of only two known feeding grounds in Australia for blue whales.

The summer in southern South Australia brings with it high pressure systems that increase southeasterly winds. When they hit the coast, they run parallel to it, and influence the upwelling. Cold water is brought to the surface, increasing air moisture and creating a marine fog at the coast. Temperatures across the region are moderated by the strengthened, cool sea breezes created by the upwelling.

The entire coast receives most of its rain in winter, and experiences a relative drought in the summer months. The inland regions of

Wrattonbully Viticultural Footprint

Total delimited area (km²)	760
Total planted area (hectares)	2727
% of delimited area planted	3.600%
Total elevation range	41–145 masl
Elevation range of plantings	68–105 masl
Number of producers	20

Wrattonbully Climate Data (°C)

	1960–1990	1991–PRESENT	2020
Heat summation/GDD	● 1481	● 1581	● 1555
Annual rain/GSR	588/237	533/212	472/179
Warmest month avg. temp.	19.7	20.4	20

Winkler Scale:

● 850–1111　● 1112–1389　● 1390–1667　● 1668–1944　● 1945–2222　● 2223–2700

Coonawarra and Wrattonbully receive a small (welcomed) bump in precipitation in December, whereas those on the coast show a more consistent decline in monthly rainfall as the seasons transition from winter through to summer.

Both Coonawarra and Wrattonbully have slightly warmer average temperatures than Bordeaux, though cooler than Margaret River. In general, Coonawarra and Wrattonbully enjoy a long growing season, with a slow awakening of the vine, and prolonged (but not too long) flowering phase, which transitions into a dry, sunny and warm summer. An extended autumn allows for lots of hang time – good for cabernet sauvignon. Heat spikes do occur. The warmest on record is 44.5°C, the same as that of Clarendon (in McLaren Vale) and 4°C higher than Margaret River's. However, the influence of the Bonney Upwelling means that overnight temperatures often dip below 14°C in Coonawarra and Wrattonbully, while other South Australian wine regions further north do not get as dramatic a swing – preserving freshness, acidity and structure in the wines.

Unlike Coonawarra, with many plantings dating back 30–70 years, 65% of the vines in Wrattonbully were planted in the last 20 years. With the youth of the vines, understanding how Wrattonbully differs from Coonawarra may be premature. Furthermore, few examples of Wrattonbully wines exist in the market, even less with bottle age. The differences in soils, geology and climate are far from being palpable in the bottle, though the quality of both regions is evident.

While their differences may not be fully comprehensible at this point, their similarities are – and both regions offer many benefits going into the second decade of the 21st century. The proximity to the coast has buffered against climate change, allowing the same grapes that have been successful for 70 years to continue their reign. Water is ample – both in terms of seasonal rainfall and availability of high-quality underground supply. And the overall cool climate, especially the chilliness of the nights, makes medium-bodied red wines of firm structure, finessed tannins and rich colour, which respond to the intricacies of vintage.

The proximity to the coast has buffered against climate change, allowing the same grapes that have been successful for 70 years to continue their reign.

Rich red terra rossa loam sitting on a shelf of white limestone beneath the vines at Wynns Coonawarra Estate.

Hubbub

The timeline of the 1990s and 2000s positioned Coonawarra for a fall from grace. With prestige and popularity built over decades, plantings multiplied, often with yields prized over quality. Oak, ripeness and additives trended across Australia, and Coonawarra was not immune. And the border dispute, while indicative of a region with strong stakes in its land, left a sour taste in the mouths of many. The region continued to evolve, just like everyone else, but was pigeon-holed as making a style that was overblown, overplanted, and just somewhat uncool.

Sue Bell has heard these sentiments echoed time and time again. 'I have gone through numerous experiences at wine show dinners or tastings confronting that idea of "What is wrong with Coonawarra?" – but often followed by a "BUT these wines are delicious!"' Parts of Coonawarra may have lost their way for a beat, but the region as a whole was punished for far longer, with few of the wine cognoscenti re-evaluating their opinions.

With a combination of a reputation to rebuild, yet still being a highly visible region on the world's stage, Coonawarra needs to be on its game today – and it is. 'I don't think there's anyone that could afford to not be pushing,' says Wynns viticulturist Cath Kidman. 'Coonawarra is misrepresented in terms of its innovation. I think it is probably one of the most highly innovating regions. We've undergone, and continue to undergo, a lot of rejuvenation of our vineyards and methods for both viticulture and winemaking.'

This innovation does not present in the way it does for many Australian regions, where innovation is thought of in terms of novelty of styles and grapes. While those methods may suit other regions, for Coonawarra, it's all about rigorous research and fine-tuning to continue to produce some of Australia's best classically styled red wines, most notably, cabernet sauvignon (which accounts for 63% of the plantings in the region). Practically, this philosophy has led to the examination of everything from **clonal selection** to **canopy management**, irrigation application to increasing biodiversity.

Thanks to their coastal proximity, the regions haven't been as hard hit by climate change as some, and are positioned to continue working with their stalwarts of cabernet sauvignon, shiraz and merlot for some time to come. 'We know that climate trumps pretty much everything,' says Kidman, 'so really an ongoing focus is around developing a better understanding of how our grapevines respond to climate and how we can better adapt our vines here in Coonawarra to cope with a dynamic environment.'

The current wines occupy a new paradigm that harkens back to some of the great Coonawarra 'clarets' of the 60s, 70s and 80s – all about balance, structure, aromatics and – importantly for cabernet sauvignon, in Bell's words – 'those silky, supple tannins'.

Fossils of megafauna marsupial lion *Thylacoleo carnifex*, the largest mammalian predator to have ever lived on the continent of Australia, decorate the limestone walls of the Naracoorte Caves.

Wrattonbully is evolving towards a similar style, and a similar forward-thinking philosophy, but from a different historical situation. Wrattonbully has long been a region of vineyards, but not wineries, and thus few who are interested in building up the brand and identity of the region. In fact, with so many companies buying the region's fruit for multiregional wines, the name Wrattonbully hasn't made inroads in imprinting itself on the national (let alone international) consciousness.

Treasury Wine Estates, in particular, has invested in the region. 'And with good reason,' says Wrattonbully's Colleen Miller. 'Certain varieties and sites in Wrattonbully are now proven performers, and comparable to top sites in Coonawarra.' Penfolds' chief winemaker Peter Gago agrees, saying that they've 'been very pleased with Wrattonbully fruit for a while now. As with any region, it's all about site and soil, and Wrattonbully is endowed with some wonderful vineyards. Cabernet sauvignon has intermittently made it into our flagship cabernet, Bin 707, across a number of vintages now. In 2014 Wrattonbully shiraz made it into Grange! No easy feat.'

Miller, co-founder of Mérite, one of the few producers working with exclusively estate-grown Wrattonbully fruit (and labelling it proudly), says the vineyards of Wrattonbully are 'suited to producing right-bank and left-bank varieties at their best. It's a region of vineyards,' she continues. 'That's the stage it's at but it's ripe to break out.'

Parts of Coonawarra may have lost their way for a beat, but the region as a whole was punished for far longer, with few of the wine cognoscenti re-evaluating their opinions.

Coonawarra and Wrattonbully are on a mission to show the wine industry that they deserve to be held as some of the greatest regions for red wines (and specifically Bordeaux varieties) in the world. Though this narrative lost its way in the past, it comes sharper and sharper into focus every day.

PRODUCERS

BALNAVES OF COONAWARRA

The Balnaves family settled in Coonawarra in the 1850s. In the 1970s Doug Balnaves, a farmer and viticulturist, planted 2.5 hectares each of cabernet sauvignon and shiraz, vines which are still producing fruit today. Doug had made his first wine a year prior, with the help of Bill Redman (see Redman, p. 396), the grapes for which had been driven in a children's swimming pool in the back of a ute. Winemaker Pete Bissel came on in 1995 and encouraged the family to create a reserve cabernet sauvignon, which would be named The Tally. This wine has been rated 'Outstanding' three times in the Langton's Classification and has become one of the quintessential Coonawarra cabernets. Pete retired in 2020, and Jacinta Jenkins has taken over the post, a winemaker with vast experience locally and abroad. **balnaves.com.au**

BELLWETHER

Sue Bell was working for Hardys in the early 2000s when she drove past an old woolshed that caught her eye. Though she soon resigned from Hardys (and was offered another winemaking job), she decided instead to develop the property into her own business, Bellwether. Years of hard work and dedication led to a fully functioning winery opening in that shed in 2014. Sue works in small batches, never fermenting more than 1 tonne at a time. Sue has a great commitment to community and believes that wine is a vehicle for that togetherness, rather than the endgame. She makes savoury cabernet sauvignon from Coonawarra, bright and spicy shiraz from Wrattonbully, and works with a wide range of less traditional varieties from as far afoot as Tasmania, Heathcote and the Riverland. **bellwetherwines.com.au**

BOWEN ESTATE

Doug and Joy Bowen were on their honeymoon in the 1970s when they happened across an old dairy farm they thought could be converted to vineyards. Over 40 years later, their powerful wines are part of the fabric of Coonawarra. Doug has handed over the winemaking reins to his daughter Emma, staying on as viticulturist. Their benchmark shiraz and cabernet sauvignon are consistent year in, year out. **bowenestate.com.au**

HIGHBANK

Dennis and Bonnie Vice are Americans who moved to Coonawarra in the mid-80s and planted two small vineyards to

Sue Bell, Bellwether

What we're drinking

*One of the unsung and often unseen heroes of Coonawarra, **Highbank** produces stoically old school (good school!) wines with a strong currency of organic growing underpinning things. The wines have power and presence but find superb balance, resonate with a sense of elegance and have a finesse of fine tannin. They are heart and soul stuff but often find an effortlessness despite the heft. A true Aussie gem.* — Mike Bennie

cabernet sauvignon, merlot and cabernet franc. Their vineyards are farmed according to **biodynamic** principles, without the use of any sort of chemical herbicides, insecticides or fertilisers. Highbank is one of the best-kept secrets of Coonawarra: while the wines can show up on some of Australia's best wine lists, they largely enjoy (or perhaps don't enjoy) a low profile. With Dennis and Bonnie both in their 70s, and no heir apparent for the winery and vineyards, the future of Highbank is unclear. Now is the time to snatch up and relish these important wines, easily some of Australia's best cabernet. **highbank.wine**

KATNOOK ESTATE

The second ever vintage for Coonawarra, in 1896, was conducted in Katnook's woolshed, though the winery wouldn't be born until 1971. Today Katnook is spread across 155 hectares and is planted predominantly to cabernet sauvignon, with lesser amounts of shiraz, chardonnay and others. Newer vineyards of tempranillo and malbec have been planted to make the most of the rich Coonawarra soils. The wines are Coonawarra classics, winning **Jimmy Watsons** and featuring on **Langton's Classification**. Katnook was purchased by Accolade in 2021, though appears to be operating with the same team and philosophy as before.
katnookestate.com.au

MAJELLA

The Lynn family has lived in Penola for five generations. Brian and Anthony Lynn began planting grapes in 1968, converting their lamb farm to vineyards. Majella now has 60 hectares under vine, with just over half cabernet sauvignon and the balance made up of shiraz, merlot and riesling. Majella sold off most of their grapes until 1991, when they decided to produce a single 10-tonne run of shiraz, catching a taste for winemaking. Wines were made at Brand's Laira by Bruce Gregory, the winemaker there, until a winery was developed on site at Majella in 1998. Bruce then joined the Majella team and has made every wine the estate has released. **majellawines.com.au**

MÉRITE

In a region that is already known for premium cabernet sauvignon, Colleen Miller and Mike Kloak have decided instead to focus on its traditional blending partner, merlot. The oft-avoided Bordeaux variety is here celebrated, with Colleen stating that the overuse of the United States **clone** DV314 is to blame for the unexciting examples seen in Australia. Colleen and Mike have extensively plotted their vineyards in the Joanna area of Wrattonbully and matched specific sites to four new French **clones**, planted in 2006. Just as some Australian winemakers are doing with pinot noir and chardonnay **clonal** experiments, Mérite are not only bottling single-merlot sites, but expressions of single **clones**. Cabernet sauvignon, shiraz and malbec are also grown at the vineyard, and all wines (except the merlot rosé) are released with several years of bottle age. **meritewines.com**

PENLEY ESTATE

Siblings Kym, Ang and Bec Tolley began Penley in 1988; the estate name is a portmanteau of their father's surname and mother's maiden name. Penley was initially only planted to cabernet sauvignon, with shiraz added in 1995. When Kym retired in 2015, the sisters relaunched Penley, a tribute to the strength of the matriarchal line that came before them. Kate Goodman took over winemaking in 2016, and with

> **What we're drinking**
>
> *The appointment in 2016 of Kate Goodman as winemaker marked a change not only for **Penley Estate**, from staid and traditional to one of the wunderkind producers of the region. Among the stately, premium wines of Penley, all now produced with a lighter touch, shaped with fine tannin and more pure-as expressions, fresher, youthful wines also join the ranks. Following on are lesser-sung blends, textural white wines and a general derring-do with wines that feel anarchic in a region so invested in status quo. — Mike Bennie*

Lauren Hansen joining the winemaking team, the two have propelled forward a Penley narrative that is at once contemporary and still pays respect to the traditions of the region. **penley.com.au**

REDMAN

The Redman family has been producing wine in Coonawarra for four generations and over 110 years. Bill Redman purchased a vineyard property in 1908 and began making bulk wine for other wineries. He was joined by his son Owen in 1937 and the popularity of their wines increased until the duo released their own wine – a cabernet sauvignon-shiraz under the label Rouge Homme in 1952. After they sold Rouge Homme in 1965, Bill retired, but Owen and his wife Edna purchased their own property and founded Redman. Even to this day, the focus sits firmly on long-lived reds made from cabernet sauvignon, shiraz and a small amount of merlot. Owen and Edna's sons and grandsons are now carrying on the family winemaking tradition. **redman.com.au**

TERRE À TERRE

Terre à Terre is a **close-planted** vineyard of Bordeaux varieties, just next door to Tapanappa's Wrattonbully site, the Whalebone vineyard (see Adelaide Hills). Xavier Bizot and Lucy Croser come from winemaking stock: Christian Bizot was the fifth generation to run the Bollinger Champagne house and Brian Croser pioneered the Adelaide Hills wine region. The couple planted their own vineyard in 2004 and draw on both their French and Australian heritages to inform their winemaking. After the first vintage from their Crayères vineyard, Xavier and Lucy added shiraz and cabernet franc to their plantings of sauvignon blanc and cabernet sauvignon. The rocky soils means all weed and yield management must be done by hand. Xavier and Lucy also produce sparkling wine from Piccadilly Valley, Adelaide Hills under the label Daosa. *terreaterre.com.au*

WYNNS COONAWARRA

Samuel Wynn and his son David bought Coonawarra pioneer John Riddoch's winery in 1951, with David heading up winery operations. The father-son duo weren't expecting to turn a profit, but set out to make dry red **table wines** all the same. The Wynns were undoubtedly part of turning the national tide back toward **table wine** (which had long been focused on **fortified wine**) and became figureheads for the region. Such was their success that plantings in Coonawarra had grown from almost nothing to 440 hectares by 1981. The following year, Wynns released a tribute to the man who started it all, a cabernet sauvignon labelled John Riddoch, their flagship wine that is still made today. Sue Hodder came on as senior winemaker in 1998, a set of fresh eyes who ushered in a lightness of touch not previously seen at the estate. She, along with winemaker Sarah Pidgeon, introduced single-vineyard wines to the Wynns portfolio and have overseen revitalisation of over two-thirds of the vineyard area. Dr Cath Kidman and Dr Kerry DeGaris are leading innovation at

> **What we're drinking**
>
> *One of the original champions of Wrattonbully, **Terre à Terre** not only proudly features their GI on their labels, but also their single vineyard Crayères. Crayères, which owes its name to the limestone soils and caves of the region, produces everything from botrytis sauvignon blanc to a cabernet franc-shiraz blend with brightness and finesse. — Jane Lopes*

Cath Kidman
Wynns

Wynns on the viticultural front, with a strong focus on developing sustainable vineyard techniques for the changing climate. Wynns is today under the Treasury Wine Estates umbrella. **wynns.com.au**

And don't forget ...
Eight at the Gate, owned by two sisters (with four kids each, thus the eight) who purchased Lanacoona Estate in Wrattonbully in 2002, turns out regional classics ... **Leconfield** is a Coonawarra cabernet icon (75% of their vineyards are planted to the grape) owned by the Hamilton family, who have been making wine in South Australia since the early 1800s ... **Ottelia**, based in Coonawarra, is a tribute to the whole Limestone Coast, with value-packed offerings of everything from Mount Gambier riesling to Padthaway graciano run by second-generation Matilda Innes ... **Parker Coonawarra Estate** is a staple for regional classics, known in particular for their flagship First Growth, a Bordeaux-style blend ... **Patrick of Coonawarra**, the second-generation estate of Patrick and Luke Tocaciu, crafts both classic and experimental wines (their new Méthode range, including a skinsy riesling and an intentionally eucalypt-heavy, **nouveau**-style cabernet, has been all the rage) ... **Raïdis**, from Chris Raïdis and son Steven (and his wife Emma), is known for the classic reds of the region but has a greater focus on whites than many, offering delicious and accessible riesling, pinot gris, sauvignon blanc and bubbly ... **Smith & Hooper**, the Hill-Smith family's (see Yalumba, p. 317) foray into Wrattonbully with a particular focus on cabernet and merlot.

Other Regions of South Australia

The most productive wine region of South Australia is correlated to the state's largest water source and the name says it all: Riverland. This is the sole GI region of the Lower Murray zone, spanning an area of 330 kilometres on the banks of the Murray River. The Victorian border forms the eastern boundary of Riverland, with its westernmost outpost just about 50 kilometres due east of the northern tip of the Barossa.

The lower Murray River, as it approaches the ocean, has always been a focal life source for many creatures, including humans. All along the river's path, from its origin in the Snowy Mountains to the Indian Ocean, Aboriginal communities cared for the waterway and the land it traversed. It was their sole responsibility: why they belonged to that land. It flowed through them like blood through arteries.

After colonisation, most who had cared for the Murray River for thousands of years either died of novel diseases and famine or were dispossessed by colonisers. Of the nations and people that lived along the Murray, only the Ngarrindjeri are thought to have survived. Many other nations – their cultures, knowledge and bloodline – are believed to be gone forever.

European immigrants saw the river as an opportunity, though. South Australia was having a moment for wine at the turn of the 20th century. The major players were looking for another place to grow grapes and the Riverland offered reliable climate and water. Thomas Hardy & Sons, Penfolds, Berri and Angove had all set up outposts there by 1922. By 1927, production in Riverland exceeded that of the Barossa, a region with history dating back nearly a hundred years at that point. This was the same year that the Riverland was first linked via rail to the more populous parts of South Australia, which had been its most significant limitation up until that point.

Thomas Angove went on to pioneer 'bag-in-box' technology in Riverland in the 1960s, the bag portion of which came to be colloquially called a 'goon sack'. Though Angove could never have predicted it, his invention spawned one of the most infamous Australian drinking games – Goon of Fortune – which involves spinning a goon bag on a 'Hills Hoist' rotating clothes hanger. Angove's egalitarian invention also spawned a huge uptake in wine drinking, and by the 1980s, two out of every three glasses of Australian wine consumed came from a bag-in-box.

Today, Riverland is not only South Australia's largest region, but the country's frontrunner for volume of crush, hectares under vine, and wine grape varieties, with 22,032 hectares planted – 15% of the nation's vineyards and 31% of Australia's annual crush. These are flatlands, dry and hot, with the ability to produce massive quantities thanks to irrigation off the Murray River.

Though Riverland's production is by all metrics massive, there have been growing efforts to manage it in a way that is both responsible to the land and transmits a sense of place. Vineyards in Riverland mainly sit atop ancient red soils and sandy loams, with the distance from the river often dictating the differences between sites, from river valley to cliff-top plateau.

Several of Riverland's historic wineries (notably, Berri Estates and Angove) are still prominent in the region, but the wineries that are gaining the most current acclaim are younger folks adopting alternative grape varieties. Ashley and Holly Ratcliff are two of the most notable, purchasing their Ricca Terra vineyard in Barmera in 2003. The goal of Ricca Terra, and this younger generation in general, is to find grapes that are most suited to the land: producing the best wine possible and allowing sites to be farmed more sustainably.

The Ratcliffs pulled out their cabernet sauvignon, merlot and chardonnay, and replanted with nero d'Avola, montepulciano, tinta barroca, fiano and vermentino. Delinquente and Unico Zelo are two others that have followed in a similar mould, creating of-the-moment styles of wine that have spelled a rebranding for the Riverland, which was once viewed as a bulk-producing monolith.

The lower Murray River continues south past the borders of the Riverland appellation, finding its eventual outlet into Lake Alexandrina and the Gulf of St Vincent. The appellations that border the lake and its neighbouring peninsula are part of the Fleurieu zone.

The other regions within the Fleurieu zone, besides McLaren Vale (p. 356), include Currency Creek, Kangaroo Island, Langhorne Creek and Southern Fleurieu. Among these, Langhorne Creek is the one with the most commercial importance. In fact, it is the most densely planted region in all of Australia, with its 6069 hectares under vine making up 25% of the region's delineated area.

Langhorne Creek sits on the north shore of Lake Alexandrina, a lake formed by the waters of the Murray River feeding into its eastern shore, and then bordered by the Coorong coastal lagoon system. This is Ngarrindjeri Country.

Lake Alexandrina, at 600 square kilometres, is a body of water over three times the size of Sydney Harbour. That's the size of the Eden Valley, and over one-third larger than the area of McLaren Vale – massive. The vineyards of Langhorne Creek are influenced by the 'Lake Doctor', a cooling wind that blows off Lake Alexandrina north into the vineyard area.

Langhorne Creek has a mild climate. It is Region 2 on the **Winkler Scale** and a dry-Mediterranean climate, with less than 400 millimetres of rain each year, and only 192 millimetres across the growing season.

This aridity may imply mass irrigation, and that is true of some of the appellation, but because of the flood plains of the region, many vineyards are able to **dry-farm**. The Angas and Bremer rivers deliver Adelaide Hills rain to the region's flatlands, creating flood plains that hold sufficient water in their deep clays for the vines during growing season.

This is not enough water for massive plantings though, supporting about 440 hectares

Other South Australia

399

The lower Murray River, the defining geographic feature of the Riverland GI.

up until the early 1990s. In the early 2000s, water licences to pull from Lake Alexandrina were made available and plantings sky-rocketed, reaching nearly the current volume by 2005. Recent efforts have been made to scale back how much water is tapped from the lake.

The Langhorne Creek Grape and Wine Corp lists 24 different producers as making wine from Langhorne Creek – some based there, others not – including some of the biggest commercial producers like Treasury Wine Estates, Pepperjack, Wolf Blass, Jacob's Creek, Bob Dolan, McGuigan and Geoff Hardy. Langhorne Creek, for these producers, offers a reliable source for inexpensive grapes today, though Wolf Blass put the region on the map in the 1970s when it won a **Jimmy Watson** three years running for a Langhorne Creek-based shiraz-cabernet sauvignon.

Bleasdale is the historic producer of the region, established in 1850 by the Potts family. Though in 2013 the winery acquired shareholders, it is still owned and run by the Potts family to this day. Bleasdale makes everything from a $20 cab-merlot blend to $80 shiraz and cabernet sauvignon bottlings, plus a neat selection of **fortified wines**, including a 16-year-old non-vintage verdelho. Though the winery has some commercial-scale offerings, it's amassed some serious accolades in recent years for its quality, including James Halliday Winemaker of the Year in 2017 (for the important Paul Hotker), and the **Jimmy Watson** trophy for its 2018 Wild Fig S.G.M. (which retails for AUD $22).

Lake Breeze also deserves a mention for the region, winning the James Halliday Best Value Winery for 2022, and counting grape-growing history back to the 1850s as well.

Another name that has put Langhorne Creek on the radar for premium wines is Drew Noon (p. 376). Noon is a notable McLaren Vale producer who sources shiraz and cabernet sauvignon from two vineyards in Langhorne Creek owned by the Borrett Family. Adelaide Hills' Vinteloper has also stirred up some excitement for the region, with touriga nacional and dolcetto bottlings from its vineyards.

Langhorne Creek is red wine territory, with over two-thirds of its vineyard area planted to cabernet sauvignon and shiraz. Only 15% of plantings are white grapes, with chardonnay making up the bulk of that number. The Langhorne Creek Grape and Wine Corp website recognises cabernet sauvignon as its 'varietal hero'. While some Australian wine regions (think Yarra Valley, Coonawarra, Margaret River) make cabernet sauvignon that's structured and age-worthy, Langhorne Creek advertises its cabernet as 'warm, soft, generous and immediately drinkable'. Bleasdale calls Langhorne Creek 'the middle palate of red wines in Australia', situating it somewhere between the premium wine regions of the country, and the largest bulk-producing regions along the Murray River.

Currency Creek sits to the west of Langhorne Creek, spanning the space between the northern end of the Coorong and Lake Alexandrina. Currency Creek has about one-sixth of the plantings of Langhorne Creek, in twice the delimited area. The region is historically a bit wetter and cooler than its eastern neighbour. The grape variety mix is similar to Langhorne Creek, though few producers or bottlings of significance have so far come out of the region.

Further west still is the Southern Fleurieu GI, extending from Currency Creek to the tip of the peninsula. The area is often prized more for its beaches than its wines, though over 500 hectares of vineyards are planted, mainly to the commercially successful shiraz, cabernet sauvignon and sauvignon blanc. Brian Croser's Foggy Hill vineyard, produced under the Tapanappa label, is the highest point in the GI, and has made a name for pinot noir in the region.

Kangaroo Island sits in the waters of the Indian Ocean, just a 45-minute ferry ride from the tip of the Fleurieu peninsula or a 30-minute flight from Adelaide. The island is a limestone formation with clay loams over the top. A true Mediterranean climate pervades the island, with blinding sunlight and high UV radiation (a tourism tip on their regional website recommends wearing at least SPF 50).

In December 2019, the island caught fire from lightning strikes, fuelled by commercial pine tree plantings. More storms sparked fires on the other end of the island in early January 2020, and by the end of summer, 210,000 hectares of land across the island was razed – 46% of the entire island. In the wake of the fires, locals and mainlanders alike have rallied around Kangaroo Island. There is excitement around the island's ability to bounce back even stronger, and continue to produce what's becoming its signature style: perfumed and well-structured cabernet franc.

A new beacon for the wine regions of the Fleurieu Peninsula is Charlotte Hardy. In 2019

Hardy moved her operation from Adelaide Hills' Basket Range to the coastal town of Port Elliot, which straddles the border of Currency Creek and Southern Fleurieu. Hardy, not wanting to conjure the monolithic Hardys of Australian wine (and perhaps run into copyright issues) called her winery Charlotte Dalton, using her grandfather's middle name instead.

Though still mainly working with Adelaide Hills fruit, Hardy has become a champion for the Fleurieu Peninsula, making and labelling wines from the GIs of Langhorne Creek, Southern Fleurieu and Kangaroo Island. She even has started managing a pinot noir vineyard near her winery in Southern Fleurieu with her husband Ben Cooke (who makes his family label, Cooke Brothers Wines, out of their Port Elliot winery as well).

'The people don't work any less hard,' Hardy says, of the oft-ignored regions of the Fleurieu Peninsula. 'And just because someone hasn't flown the flag for them doesn't mean they're any less deserving of recognition. But they need someone to advocate the new styles. And the people out there who are growing these amazing varieties are not flying the flag, because they're humble growers, and they're just happy doing that. It's good to have a spotlight on it.'

About 300 kilometres south of Fleurieu and the wine regions in proximity to Adelaide, is the Limestone Coast zone. Limestone Coast is one of the few Australian zone names that is used with some frequency, on wine labels as well as to describe the general area. The area has become a tourist destination, both for its natural attractions and its wine.

Rainfall across the entire coast varies from just 460 millimetres per year at the northern end of Padthaway, to just over 700 millimetres per year in Mount Gambier on the coast. All growing regions except Mount Gambier are experiencing a drying, where their last 20 years of rainfall averages are less than the long-term average. Mount Gambier shows a slight increase.

The entire coast receives most of its rain in the winter months and experiences a relative drought in the summer months. The inland regions of Coonawarra, Wrattonbully (p. 380) and Padthaway all receive a small (welcome) bump in precipitation in December, whereas those on the coast show a more consistent decline in monthly rainfall as the seasons transition from winter through to summer. All except Mount Gambier (which is cooler) have a degree day index that is greater than Bordeaux, though less than Margaret River – relevant comparisons due to cabernet sauvignon being a key grape of the region.

The Padthaway GI, north of the boundaries of Wrattonbully, saw its first vineyards established by Seppelt in 1964; the area attracted the attention of Lindeman's, Hardys and Wynns soon after. Padthaway enjoys its own Coonawarra-style terra rossa soils over limestone in various pockets, housing about 11% of the region's plantings. Its long, skinny footprint extends north from Wrattonbully along the Naracoorte Escarpment. It is the warmest GI in the Limestone Coast, with a generous production size to match: 3884 hectares are under vine in Padthaway, including shiraz, cabernet sauvignon and chardonnay (in that order) making up 80% of plantings, rounded out by merlot, pinot gris, riesling and pinot noir.

Padthaway, like Wrattonbully, has historically been a region of grape growers, less so wineries and winemaking facilities. While there are some Padthaway branded wines, very few have commanded critical attention or widespread consumer uptake.

While Padthaway saw an earlier start, the true coastal GIs in the Limestone Coast: Mount Gambier (south of Coonawarra), and Mount Benson and Robe (on the west rather than southern coast) wouldn't see their starts until the 1980s and 1990s.

Mount Gambier, directly south of Coonawarra, is the coolest climate of the Limestone Coast – and, overall, the coolest climate of South Australia (though some parts of Adelaide Hills, if they could be isolated out, would compete for that honour). Mount Gambier is centred around a volcano that last erupted just 5000 years ago. The area is filled with sink holes, lava tubes, and the bright 'Blue Lake' in its crater. The area is composed of young volcanic loams and supports a variety of agriculture.

Though this area, planted to less than 400 hectares (conflicting reports put it somewhere between 274 and 400), hasn't gained much traction across Australia, or internationally, there are a few young estates that are championing it. Good Intentions, Shapeshifter and Limus are three labels that are attempting a more modern, site-specific and low-intervention approach to Mount Gambier fruit, and beginning to conjure up some excitement for the region. Pinot noir and chardonnay are the most planted grapes, along with sauvignon blanc, semillon, riesling, pinot gris and shiraz.

While Mount Gambier sits on the southern coast of Australia, as it begins to taper north up to Adelaide, Limestone Coast's other 'Mount' has water on its western border, looking out on the Indian Ocean.

Mount Benson has its benchmark producer in Cape Jaffa, a **biodynamic** estate founded in 1993. Anna and Derek Hooper have been champions of Mount Benson through Cape Jaffa's wines, but have also sourced grapes from other areas of the Limestone Coast. France's M.Chapoutier had a soon-aborted attempt at setting down roots in Mount Benson in the late 1990s and early 2000s, bottling shiraz and cabernet sauvignon under its Tournon label (later confined to Victoria's Pyrenees and Heathcote, and now up for sale).

Wangolina, founded in 1999, has also helped Mount Benson find its identity. Both Wangolina and Cape Jaffa embrace a spirit of innovation – between them producing everything from beer to spirits, skin-contact whites to uncommon grapes like lagrein and grüner veltliner – that may become a hallmark of the region.

Robe, just south of Mount Benson, has yet to see a benchmark producer, and very few bottles labelled Robe make it outside the region. The vineyards are planted primarily to cabernet sauvignon, shiraz and chardonnay and much of the wine is sold locally, or shipped off for multiregional blends.

Heading back up north, the city of Adelaide houses a number of wine regions on its borders. The Mount Lofty Ranges zone includes the two appellations on the north and east sides of the city of Adelaide (Adelaide Plains and Adelaide Hills, p. 336, respectively), as well as the northern extension of the Mount

Mediterranean grape varieties often have robust canopies in the Riverland, like these of Delinquente, which protect the fruit zone from harsh sunlight.

Lofty Ranges, Clare Valley GI (p. 320), about 140 kilometres north of Adelaide.

The Adelaide Plains is the least significant of the three: a site for early plantings and later urban sprawl. There are still about 600 hectares under vine in Adelaide Plains, though few wines have made waves beyond their immediate surroundings. Dom Torzi deserves a mention for being the region's staunchest advocate, releasing wines from the region under his Longhop and Old Plains labels. The Adelaide Plains is one of Australia's driest wine regions, receiving an average of 180 millimetres in its growing season. With its dry, warm and flat setting, it is easy to ripen a large crop here, and that's typically what is done.

A lone wolf of a wine region sits a 90-minute drive north of the Clare Valley, in the aptly named Far North zone: Southern Flinders Ranges. The region hugs the inland northwest coast of Spencer Gulf, signifying the transition from the Mount Lofty Ranges to the Flinders Ranges, the latter continuing some 430 kilometres north into the hot desert that makes up the northern half of South Australia.

In Southern Flinders Ranges, 171 hectares cover about 0.03% of its delineated area – and are planted to a whopping 92% shiraz. The region sees approximately 420 millimetres of rain annually and is squarely a **Winkler Scale** Region 4 – warm and dry. By the numbers, it's 30% wetter and slightly cooler than the nearby Riverland (and Murray Darling, further afoot). And though shiraz is overwhelmingly dominant now, more climate-suitable grapes seem like they could find success here, just as they have in those two regions.

Access to irrigation is tough and expensive though (compared to the Murray River GIs), with the nearest inland bodies of water being salt lakes. If grape choice and water access can get sorted, this oft-forgotten region could come into relevance in the future of the modern Australian wine conversation.

The last GI of South Australia is the Adelaide 'super zone', which can be applied to blends from anywhere in the Mount Lofty Ranges, Fleurieu and Barossa zones, but is rarely used on labels.

PRODUCERS

LANGHORNE CREEK

BLEASDALE

If there was one winery responsible for creating the Langhorne Creek GI, it would be Bleasdale, which saw the region's first vines go into the ground in 1850 at the hands of Frank Potts. The estate has worn the peaks and troughs of 20th century winemaking in Australia, and has emerged stronger than ever, with several big wine-show wins in the last decade and senior winemaker Paul Hotker being named James Halliday Winemaker of the Year for 2018. The wines range in style and price-point, everything from entry-level verdelho and merlot to high-end cabernet, shiraz and **fortifieds**. *bleasdale.com.au*

LAKE BREEZE

Lake Breeze is the familiar story of a long-established grower converting to winemaker, with the resulting philosophy that the grapes and farming come first. The vineyard was established in the 1880s, but winemaking didn't begin for over a hundred years, in 1987. Lake Breeze reserves the best 40% of their fruit for their estate production, making several labels and grapes ranging from the stalwart cabernet, shiraz and chardonnay to grenache, frontignac and nero d'Avola. *lakebreeze.com.au*

FLEURIEU PENINSULA

CHARLOTTE DALTON
(See Adelaide Hills, p. 336)

RIVERLAND

ANGOVE

William Thomas Angove made his first wines in 1886, tonics for patients at his medical practice just outside Adelaide. By 1903, the Angove vineyards had expanded to 40 hectares, a fifth of the state's plantings at the time. William's son Carl opened Riverland's first winery and distillery in 1910, and began exporting wines to England in the following decade. Angove was one of the largest and most influential producers of the 20th century, laying the groundwork for Riverland to become the commercially important wine region it is today. Angove moved into McLaren Vale in 2008, acquiring a historic shiraz and grenache vineyard and renaming it Warboys, converting it immediately to organic and **biodynamic** practices. Angove has several brands under its umbrella today, sourcing from their 500 hectares of vines, which are all organically certified or under conversion. The fifth generation is at the helm. *angove.com.au*

DELINQUENTE

Con-Greg Grigoriou grew up in the Riverland, but never thought the region was capable of making the wines he wanted to drink (let alone make). But he eventually came back home to make wines that would 'represent the sun, the red dirt and uniquely Australian terroir of the Riverland'. Con-Greg is at the forefront of working with grapes that are suitable to the hot, dry climate of Riverland, largely southern Italian varieties. The resulting wines are fresh, bright and modern – everything from **pét-nats** to **piquettes** to bitter aperitivo. *delinquentewineco.com*

RICCA TERRA

After years working with some of the big names in Australian wine, including Orlando and Yalumba, Ashley Ratcliff was ready to go out on his own. Seeing the potential for more than a bulk wine region, Ashley and his wife Holly founded Ricca Terra in the Riverland in 2003. The couple are at the forefront of climate-appropriate varietals, choosing to plant drought-hardy vines like nero d'Avola, montepulciano, fiano, vermentino and a whole host of Portuguese red grapes, which have become a major source of fruit for a young and forward-thinking generation of winemakers. Ashley uses viticultural practices much the same as in a premium region, with a focus on fruit health and concentration of flavour. Despite the heat, the wines are surprisingly light on their feet – fresh whites, chillable reds and robust blends. *riccaterra.com.au*

KANGAROO ISLAND

ISLANDER ESTATE WINES

Jacques Lurton, whose family is Bordeaux winemaking royalty, was drawn to Kangaroo Island after being a 'flying winemaker' for years, and working in Australia under Brian Croser (Petaluma), Martin Shaw (Shaw+Smith) and James Halliday (Coldstream Hills). With the help of McLaren Vale's Toby Bekkers, Lurton planted his own vineyard on KI (as the island is often abbreviated to) in 2000, including cabernet franc, malbec, sangiovese, shiraz, grenache, viognier and semillon vines. He produced his first vintage in 2004 off the 12-hectare estate vineyard, under the banner of Islander Estate Wines.

The estate lost all its vineyards in the bushfires of 2019, and is in the process of rebuilding. *iev.com.au*

THE STOKE/GUROO

The Stoke/Guroo is Bec and Nick Dugmore's dual-pronged project, making wines from both Kangaroo Island and the Adelaide Hills (the latter under the Kin label). Bec is from Scotland and Nick a South Australian native, who both travelled and worked extensively before landing on KI together. The wines range from a merlot and skin-contact pinot gris **pét-nat** to fresh and vibrant renditions of sauvignon blanc, shiraz, tempranillo and cabernet sauvignon. The duo has also launched the Guroo label, with the aim of showcasing KI's ability to grow premium fruit by having a rotating head winemaker: Charlotte Hardy (Charlotte Dalton, Adelaide Hills), Stephen George (Ashton Hills, Adelaide Hills) and Sue Bell (Bellwether, Coonawarra) are the powerhouse first three choices. *thestokewines.com*

MOUNT BENSON

CAPE JAFFA

Cape Jaffa is Anna and Derek Cooper's project to showcase Mount Benson and its environs, an example of a single winery staking a monumental claim in building up the success of a region. Established in 1993, the Coopers and their team farm over 20 hectares of **biodynamic** vineyards, also working with other select growers who share their ethos. In 2017, they launched their own brewery and have started to make blends of beer and wine, as well as beginning trials with distillation. Along with pockets of experimentation, there are also several ranges that showcase grape and place in a classic way. *capejaffawines.com.au*

And don't forget ...
Bassham Wines is most famous for its certified organic vineyard that bears the same name, which has become an important source of Riverland fruit for a new generation – everything from saperavi to montepulciano is harvested from the carefully tended and family-owned vines ... **Bremerton Wines** has been a stalwart in Langhorne Creek since the 1980s, producing reliably delicious wines and offering a fun cellar door experience, now run by second-generation sisters Rebecca and Lucy Willson ... **Good Intentions**, Andrew and Louise Burchell's Mount Gambier winery, is centred on farming well, building community and creating honest, modern wines ... **Limus**, a young project from Kyatt Dixon, showcases Mount Gambier terroir with organic viticulture and additive free wines ... **Metala** vineyard was planted in 1891 and has been maintained since then by the Adams family, who recently purchased the brand Metala back from Treasury, reinvigorating a label that had become discounted and mass produced.

WESTERN AUSTRALIA

Margaret River 412
Great Southern 432
Other Western
Australia 446

Western Australia is a vast expanse, occupying the western third of the land mass of Australia. If WA was its own nation, it would be among the top ten largest globally. Much of the state is comprised of grassland and red deserts, ranging from 640 metres in elevation to 15 metres below sea level, with a largely Mediterranean (and in the northwest, tropical) 12,500 kilometres of coastline. The wine industry inhabits a small fraction of the state's southwestern corner, around the capital city of Perth, and a band approximately 400 kilometres south and east of it.

The southwestern terrain is largely defined by the Darling Fault, which originates near Shark Bay and descends 1500 kilometres to the south coast. It formed when Australia and India broke apart 130 million years ago. The fault is where Australia, India and Antarctica were formerly joined as the pre-Pangaea supercontinent, Gondwanaland, 150 kilometres west of Australia's most seismically active area. While no major earthquakes have occurred, the faint tremors felt in Perth once every year and a half (on average) are a reminder that the Darling Fault could wreak havoc. The Indian Ocean is the major climatic influence in Western Australia; its presence is felt to some extent in a vast majority of the state's vineyards, with the exception of the most inland. The Leeuwin Current brings warm water south from the tropics, while cooling afternoon sea breezes, known as the Fremantle Doctor ('Freo Doctor' or 'The Doctor' for short), come from the southwestern reaches of the Indian Ocean. The south coast sees a cooler Indian Ocean, and therefore slightly colder minimum temperatures, as it becomes influenced by the Southern Ocean surrounding Antarctica.

The amount of rain a vineyard area receives in a year fluctuates in relation to coastal proximity. Those closest to the coast, specifically within 25 kilometres, receive 15–25% more annual rainfall than those further inland. However, the Mediterranean pattern, where a large majority of rainfall occurs in the winter months, is consistent throughout Western Australia's entire vineyard area – a beneficial attribute!

Humans have been enjoying this temperate climate and majestic landscape in southwestern Australia for at least 45,000 years. In that time, the area first known as Noongar Boodjar (Noongar Country) grew to be a nation that includes 14 dialect groups (the preferred term to 'language groups' for the Noongar Nation). The Noongar followed the six seasons of the southwest to care for their Country, a responsibility that is upheld through traditional rituals and ceremonies today.

The British first arrived at Noongar Boodjar in 1806, nearly four centuries after an aborted Chinese landing in Perth. They travelled through what they later named the King George Sound, as the Dutch and French also charted the coast, and established the first British settlement of Western Australia at Albany in 1826. As in South Australia, Albany was established as a free colony (like Swan River in 1829); and the early coexistence of Europeans and Nyungah (Noongar people) was mainly peaceful, according to today's Noongar descendants.

Conflict and violence escalated quickly, though. By the time British arrived in Western Australia, the forceful removal of people from their lands, the spread of novel diseases, and various genocidal campaigns were already underway throughout the rest of the continent. Mass loss of life and Country for the Noongar Nation ensued.

Today, over 30,000 people with Noongar ancestry live within the traditional lands of the Noongar Nation. The Noongar Nation itself, along with several regional advocacy groups, actively campaigns to share Noongar history, culture, traditions, lore, language, food and land management with the current generations, to ensure their society is preserved and its descendants thrive.

The South West Aboriginal Land and Sea Council serves as the title to which the Noongar Nation lays claim as the traditional owners of the southwest of Australia. It is comprised of six regions that correspond with various dialect groups within the Noongar Nation. The wine-growing regions of Western Australia are fully within the Noongar Boodjar, and most of the six regions have some vineyards planted to them, with the exception of the inland Ballardong.

A local aphorism, mostly around Perth, has it that Western Australia's small population is one of the most isolated communities on the most isolated continent in the world. Low tourism, modest economic investment in the wine sector, and chronic worker shortages are embedded obstacles for those making wine in the vast and remote landscape of Western Australia. With some of the less-developed regions, it's unclear whether they are less suited for premium viticulture, or they just haven't been given the chance yet. The proven excellence of other sites, however, indicates that with its kind climate and good soil conditions spread over a large expanse, Western Australia has the potential to become the nation's top wine producer. But perhaps the charm of Western Australia is in not tapping this potential and remaining a region defined by its wide open spaces.

With its kind climate and good soil conditions spread over a large expanse, Western Australia has the potential to become the nation's top wine producer.

Western Australia Geographical Indications

ZONE	REGION	SUBREGION
Central Western Australia		
Eastern Plains – Inland and North of Western Australia		
Greater Perth	Peel Perth Hills Swan District	Swan Valley
South West Australia	Blackwood Valley Geographe Great Southern	Albany Denmark Frankland River Mount Barker Porongurup
	Manjimup Margaret River Pemberton	
West Australian South East Coastal		

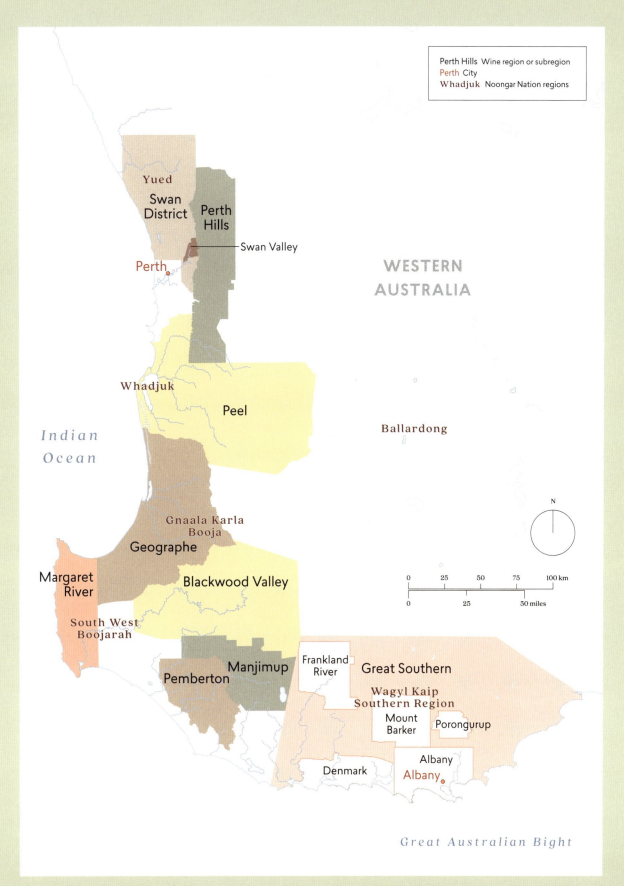

Margaret River

Introduction

Margaret River's colonial history is speckled with names that have become landmarks in its viticultural orientation: the Dutch vessel *Leeuwin* first spotted this land in 1620, though it wasn't until 1800 that the French ships *Naturaliste* and *Geographe* undertook another expedition (and lost the sailor Vasse, whose name and lore would continue to inhabit the region). In the 1830s, England's John Bussell settled there, giving his name to the nearest city of Busselton, as well as naming Margaret River after a woman alternately remembered as a friend he was trying to woo, or his step-second cousin.

But the history of Margaret River started well before it received this moniker – over 48,000 years before. This is Wardandi Boodjar, a language group of the Noongar Nation, who referred to the Margaret River as Wooditchup. The relationship between water, land, song, story, spirituality and culture has always been strong here – and understandably so. Margaret River is a region of spectacular physical beauty: the pink sky, the blue surf, the red land and the green bush create a cornucopia of raw wonder, which has entranced its inhabitants for this vast time period.

Grape growing in Margaret River is one of the greatest examples of modern-day land custodianship. Many of today's producers approach this responsibility with gravity, though the subject of land care – how to farm it, protect it and promote it – is not without its controversies.

This gravitas is only heightened by the physical remoteness of the region, a three-hour drive from Western Australia's capital, Perth (which itself is over 2000 kilometres from the next major city). While many wine regions have a nearby metropolis acting as an outlet, all of the energy, ambition and occasional vitriol of Margaret River is confined within its borders.

An early draft of this book called Margaret River 'a firecracker waiting to ignite' – and ignite it did, though not in the expected figurative manner. In December of 2021, the region experienced some of its worst ever bushfires. The Calgardup fire burnt over 6000 hectares within the Leeuwin Naturaliste National Park, though (thankfully) there was no loss of human lives, homes, vineyards or wineries.

And, if anything, the literal flames in the region have done work toward easing the metaphoric combustibility. The community rallied together, with a huge response from emergency teams and volunteers, to protect this idyllic piece of land. In a 9 December 2021 post on social media, the Wilyabrup winery L.A.S. Vino wrote: 'Until yesterday I never realised how special, beautiful and close the Margaret River community actually is. It feels good to be part of it.'

Evolution of Wine

If one person had to be named as the instigator of premium viticulture in Western Australia, it would be Dr Harold Olmo. An American viticulturist and professor at University of California Davis, he was recruited by the Western Australian Vine Fruits Research Trust to carry out research in Swan Valley in 1955. When he released his report in 1956, he named the regions further south in Western Australia as being excellent for cool-climate **table wine** viticulture (in contrast to the warm climate of Swan Valley, p. 446, which had proven itself more suited for **fortifieds** at the time).

Olmo's report spurred another professor of viticulture to take an interest in these southern regions. Dr John Gladstones, an agronomist at the University of Western Australia, made several trips to the Margaret River and Great Southern (p. 432) regions in the late 1950s and early 1960s, releasing reports in the mid-1960s espousing the potential of both. Gladstones took a particularly strong stance on Margaret River, and within 10 years of his report, nearly a dozen wineries were established in the region.

While there is evidence of a spattering of vineyard plantings in the area in the 19th century, it wasn't until Olmo and Gladstones' reports were published that a serious interest in viticulture emerged in Margaret River. The first wave of plantings was orchestrated not by professional viticulturists or winemakers though – it was doctors and lawyers, down from Perth, wanting to put in the work (and money) to make something of this undiscovered region.

Dr Thomas Cullity, a Perth cardiologist, is widely recognised as the first. He had been trial-planting vines in southwest Australia since 1965, and when he read Dr Gladstones's 1966 report about Margaret River, he set out to find the perfect site of 'red gravel in redgum country, with clay about 18 inches below the surface' (qualities recommended by Gladstones). When he finally found that site in 1967, he planted cabernet sauvignon, shiraz, malbec and riesling – Margaret River's oldest vines. His estate Vasse

The first wave of plantings was orchestrated not by professional viticulturists or winemakers – it was doctors and lawyers, down from Perth.

A vineyard row marker for cabernet sauvignon at Vasse Felix, home of the first commercial plantings in Margaret River.

Felix, named for the missing early explorer, is still considered one of Margaret River's finest.

The other founding wineries officially established soon after, though many were trialling as early as Vasse Felix. Moss Wood (1969), Cape Mentelle (1970), Cullen (1971), Sandalford (1972), Leeuwin Estate, Woodlands and Wrights (1973) were all established in a five-year period. All of these vineyards are still producing to this day (Wrights now as Juniper Estate), though it was really Vasse Felix, Moss Wood, Cape Mentelle, Cullen and Leeuwin who put the remote and sparsely populated Margaret River on the fine wine map.

The 1980s saw an influx in population across Margaret River, nearly doubling its size over the course of the decade. Producers established in the late 1970s and 1980s include Gralyn, Xanadu, Voyager, Pierro, Lenton Brae, Howard Park, Deep Woods and many others. Margaret River surf culture also took off in these years, with the region holding its first professional surf competition in 1985.

With all that the pioneering producers had done to establish the quality and brand of Margaret River wine, it's no wonder corporate interest emerged in the 1990s and 2000s. Veuve Clicquot (now part of Louis Vuitton-Moët Hennessy) bought a controlling portion of Cape Mentelle in 1990. Devil's Lair was purchased in 1996 by the Southcorp conglomerate (which came under the control of Foster's and eventually Treasury Wine Estates). BRL Hardy purchased 50% of Brookland Valley in 1997, gaining full ownership

in 2004 and finally coming under the Accolade umbrella later that decade (and now sold back to family ownership of the Swinneys). The Fogarty Wine Group acquired Deep Woods in 2005, the same year that Rathbone bought Xanadu. Everyone wanted to engage in the premium wine region that Margaret River was becoming.

This does not necessarily equate to a depreciation in quality – many of these producers remain bastions of the region, and the percentage of corporate ownership remains small – though it is perhaps not a coincidence that this era saw an escalation in alcohol, extraction and oak in the wines of Margaret River.

Parkerisation more than likely had an influence too. A similar phenomenon struck many wine regions across the world in the 1990s and 2000s, as Robert Parker's *Wine Advocate* awarded 100-point scores to robust and lush, accessible-on-release, lavishly oaked wines. 'The **Parkerisation** phenomenon definitely happened here,' says Corymbia's Rob Mann. 'Some cabernets went from 13% alcohol in the 80s to close to 15% in the early 2000s. We have seen a correction over the last 10 to 15 years to improved balance.' (Climate change is not to blame here, either, as the average January temperature has only risen 0.2°C in the region since the 1960s.)

At this same moment in Australia, and in tandem with corporate ownership, technology in the winery and chemicals in the vineyard became widespread, and Margaret River was not immune. While the pioneers of the region largely remained

A Moreish Fair Dinkum Ripper That's Ripe As

When you say to an American a wine is 'moreish' they assume you're referring to the Moors – you know, that slightly confusing Medieval term coined by European Christians to describe North African Muslims. But what could it possibly mean to describe a wine as 'Moorish'!? This British English edition, popular in Australian wine talk, is just the word 'more' (as in, 'I'd like some more') with the suffix 'ish' on the end. It describes, well, a wine that makes you want more! Other wine descriptors that seem to have originated in Australia include: 'a bit arms and legs' (a wine that's disjointed and lacks a centre), 'all lips and arseholes' (the less polite version of 'arms and legs'), 'fair dinkum' (a wine that is genuine and speaks to its place), 'a ripper' (an excellent drink!), 'plonk' (garbage) and adding 'as' after any descriptor to emphasise it ('That wine is ripe as!'). Australians sometimes colloquially refer to alcohol as 'piss' too, as in 'Let's go sink some piss', 'they're absolutely pissed', and 'I drank a heap of piss on the weekend'. And, of course, every grape and region has its own nickname: it's not a riesling from Tasmania, it's a rizza from Tassie.

Western Australia

true to their handcrafted and minimally styled roots, a flashier, overworked style emerged – a trend that enhanced Margaret River's global reputation for cabernet sauvignon and chardonnay, but didn't sit well with many locals.

A younger generation emerged that looked outside of the region for inspiration, travelling to other parts of Australia and the world at large to gain exposure to wine. People like Dormilona's Josephine Perry, Blind Corner's Ben Gould, Corymbia's Rob and Genevieve Mann, L.A.S. Vino's Nic Peterkin and Si Vintners' Sarah Morris and Iwo Jakimowicz, mostly all Western Australian natives, travelled and worked extensively abroad before coming back to Margaret River in the 2010s to incubate a new generation of winemaking. 'I think we were looking to make our own way, set our own path,' says Peterkin. 'Create wines for drinkers who didn't want to drink what their parents were drinking.'

This generation focuses on minimal intervention in the winery, and maximum sustainability in the vineyards, building on the organic and **biodynamic** practices of earlier producers like the Cullen family and Settlers Ridge. Grapes and styles outside the traditional paradigm became more common with this generation. They have also, along with some of the pioneers of the region (most notably Vanya Cullen), heightened the idea of custodianship as it relates to First Nations, and are working to care for the land in concert with the Wardandi people.

Today, the wine scene of Margaret River is world-class in nearly every way imaginable. The landscape of producers has remained relatively boutique: 65% of them make less than 4000 cases of wine each year and 25% make less than 1000 cases each year. Founding estates Cape Mentelle, Cullen, Leeuwin, Moss Wood and Vasse Felix continue to set the standard for balanced, expressive and age-worthy cabernet and chardonnay, while also incorporating less common grapes into their repertoire. Farming has become paramount, with more and more vineyards converting to organics and **biodynamics**, and incorporating responsible practices. And the younger generation is bringing a palpable energy to the region – one that seems at once traditional and cutting edge.

This generation focuses on minimal intervention in the winery, and maximum sustainability in the vineyards.

Lay of the Land

While the colonial sprawl of livestock and dairy farms dot the landscape in Margaret River, much of the autochthonous flora and fauna remains. Native bushland covers 40% of the southwestern peninsula, and the state's copious biodiversity is especially prevalent in Margaret River. The coastline is one of the region's top attractions, and its 80-plus surf breaks along a nearly unbroken string of white sand beaches stock the water full of shark bait (and, of course, sharks).

Margaret River as a wine appellation is most significantly understood (and drawn) by its climate. The region is bound by the ocean on three sides – it looks almost like a pig's snout, jutting out from the rest of the Western Australian coast. This maritime situation creates a consistent climate, with little fluctuation in growing season temperature from year to year. This dependable temperature is also elevated beyond the norm for maritime climates, thanks to the warming Leeuwin current that flows southward across the length of the region. It's often a joke among the Australian wine industry that Margaret River is immune to the vintage vagaries that plague the rest of Australia. This is largely true, though the region does see some unfavourable variations in years of **La Niña** weather patterns, where the stormy waters along the tropical coastline to the north disrupt this reliable climate.

The eastern border of Margaret River (the only one not formed by an ocean) is called Gladstones Line, named after Dr John Gladstones, who laid out this boundary in his 1966 research paper. The line (Longitude 115 18E) is the point at which the land stops enjoying the ocean's influence.

The maritime climate isn't just about consistency of temperature, though – it also helps regulate the rainfall pattern. Approximately 75% of the region's rainfall comes in the winter and spring, and less than 10% occurs during harvest. This rainfall pattern is a function of the maritime climate and creates an ideal situation that supports green growth in the spring and a dry ripening season into harvest. The marine influence also keeps frost risks quite low. And cool afternoon breezes, like the Fremantle Doctor, flow through vines to mitigate the intense Australian sun.

For all its virtues, the Indian Ocean is also the cause of the region's greatest viticultural challenge. Warm summer breezes bring sea moisture that makes vineyards prone to unfavourable botrytis, bunch rot and mildew. Management of this moisture, along with the pests that it promotes, ranges from **biodynamic** practices and organic farming to more conventional methods. Ensuring that vineyards are planted in well-draining soils is key.

This is not a given with the soil types of Margaret River. A vast majority of the region's plantings sit on the Leeuwin Complex, a geological mass of deformed granite and gneiss ranging from 1.6–1.1 billion years old. The Leeuwin Complex lies west of the Dunsborough Fault – a significant geological fault with serious implications for changes in geology, soil and topography from one side to the other.

Margaret River Viticultural Footprint

Total delimited area (km²)	2640
Total planted area (hectares)	5725
% of delimited area planted	2.170%
Total elevation range	0–234 masl
Elevation range of plantings	40–227 masl
Number of producers	131

Margaret River Climate Data (°C)

	1960–1990	1991–PRESENT	2020
Heat summation/GDD	●1809	●1852	●2021
Annual rain/GSR	1035/241	947/205	775/223
Warmest month avg. temp.	20.5	20.7	20.3

Winkler Scale:
● 850–1111 ● 1112–1389 ● 1390–1667 ● 1668–1944 ● 1945–2222 ● 2223–2700

The most concentrated vineyard area in Margaret River is between the Dunsborough Fault and Caves Road (a road that spans the length of the Margaret River top to bottom, ranging from 2–7 kilometres away from the coast). This area is largely characterised by Forest Grove soils – ironstone gravels with loamy topsoils – and the varying presence of calcareous sandy duplexes. The proportion of sandy duplexes to Forest Grove soils accounts for the main difference in soil types across the region's vineyard land.

The area west of Caves Road, hugging the coast, is where calcareous sand begins to dominate. There are some notable vineyards west of Caves Road, but as the land inches closer to the coast, it becomes more and more uninhabitable for the vine. And there are several areas of Margaret River – most of the northeast and southeast corners – that are largely waterlogged and unsuitable for viticulture, sitting close to sea level. Beyond these areas, Margaret River as a whole can still be tough for drainage, and the areas sitting within 10 kilometres of the coast, near west-draining creeks, tend to be the best situated.

Bordeaux is often referenced as a cognate for Margaret River: two swampy maritime regions with gravel soils, producing world-class cabernet sauvignon. In the Médoc of Bordeaux (the area on the left bank of the Gironde Estuary that includes Pauillac, Saint-Estèphe, Saint-Julien and Margaux), the vineyard area is nearly identical in size to Margaret River. The Médoc is somewhat cooler, being about 10 degrees latitude further from the equator. The Médoc also sees less elevation than Margaret River, though both are pretty flat wine regions. In general, a fairly good comparison, and a good lens to start talking about **subregionality** in Margaret River. The Médoc is covered by eight different legally defined appellations. Margaret River? Only one.

Dr Gladstones re-emerges yet again for this conversation. In 1999, he penned a paper calling for the subdivision of Margaret River into six regions based largely on soil and climate differences: Karridale, Wallcliffe, Treeton, Wilyabrup, Yallingup and Carbunup. These six, though still unofficial, have been well accepted by Margaret River and greater-Australian wine communities – though how they should be updated, codified and promoted is very much up for discussion.

Cullen, Moss Wood, Vasse Felix, Lenton Brae, Woodlands, Fraser Gallop, Gralyn Estate and numerous other producers are located in the area of Wilyabrup, named for the Wilyabrup Brook, in northwestern Margaret River. This is the most concentrated area of premium producers in the region and the epicentre of discussions regarding the formation of official subregions. Many view Wilyabrup as a perfect confluence of proximity to the ocean, beneficial ironstone gravels mixed with sandy duplexes, low rainfall (especially during growing season), and warm temperatures with cool nights to preserve acidity.

North of Wilyabrup is the unofficial subregion of Yallingup. This is the second most concentrated area, with vineyards mostly situated inland and south of Caves Road. Yallingup is warmer and drier than Wilyabrup and the Forest Grove gravels include more red-brown loams known as Keenan soils. Early vineyards and newcomers alike populate Yallingup, like Deep Woods, Cape Naturaliste and Windows Estate.

Moving east, the unofficial subregion Carbunup occupies the northeastern corner of Margaret River. Plantings are sparse here, due to an abundance of waterlogged and semi-wet soils. The southern section of Carbunup sits somewhat above the rest of the region (75 metres above sea level, versus less than 20 metres) and has calcareous sandy loam over gravel soils, capable of drainage in a way the rest of Carbunup is not. Annual precipitation and warmth in this southern sector – referred to as the Yelverton Shelf – is similar to Wilyabrup, though it does not benefit from the **diurnal shift** or cooling sea breezes provided by Wilyabrup's proximity to the coast.

South of Carbunup (and due east of Wilyabrup) is the unofficial subregion Treeton, named for the landscape system known as the Treeton Hills. This area generally has red-brown sandy loams interspersed with waterlogged wet or semi-wet soils unsuitable for viticulture. A variety of rivers that flow north originate here,

Margaret River

HOW TO READ THIS MAP

This map displays the Soil–Landscape Systems mapped in the 2018 report published by the Western Australian Regional Development Office, and overlays the six districts Dr Gladstones identified in 1999. Note the proximity to the coast and the soil systems that are home to the most densely planted areas.

MARGARET RIVER Wine region
Carbunup Unofficial subregion
Gracetown Town
—— Region boundary
········ Unofficial subregion boundary
WARDANDI Native language group
Treeton Hills Soil system
▌ Vineyard
■ Cave

Soil–Landscape Systems:
- **Abba:** Coastal swamp
- **Bassendean:** Coastal plain of sand dunes over wet soil
- **Blackwood Plateau:** Sand, gravel and loam; some deep sand
- **Cowaramup Uplands:** Sandy loam and gravel duplex
- **D'Entrecasteaux Dunes:** Calcareous sand dunes
- **Goodwood Valleys:** Sandy/loamy gravels and deep sand
- **Gracetown Ridge:** Limestone ridge. Deep sands and coastal scrub
- **Nillup Plain:** Poorly draining, wet sand gravel and loam
- **Quindalup South:** Calcaerous sands, scrub-covered coastal dunes
- **Scott River Plain:** Deep, poorly draining sands
- **Spearwood:** Yellow and brown sand dunes and plains
- **Treeton Hills:** Sand, loam and gravel
- **Whicher Scarp:** Deep sands with gravel and loam
- **Wilyabrup Valleys:** Granitic sand and gravel
- **Vasse System:** Tidal flat plain of saline wet sandy soils

1 Abbey Vale Estate
2 Amelia Park
3 Ashbrook Estate
4 Blind Corner
5 Brookland Valley
6 Cape Mentelle
7 Cape Mentelle Chapman Brook Vineyard
8 Cape Mentelle Crossroads Vineyard
9 Cape Mentelle Trinders Vineyard
10 Cape Mentelle
11 Corymbia
12 Cullen Wines
13 Cullen Mangan Vineyard
14 Deep Woods
15 Domaine Naturaliste
16 Dormilona
17 Evans & Tate
18 Fermoy
19 Flametree
20 Fraser Gallop Estate
21 Glenarty Road
22 Gralyn Estate
23 Howard Park
24 Juniper Estate
25 Larry Cherubino (Cherubino Wines)
26 L.A.S. Vino
27 Leeuwin Estate
28 Lenton Brae
29 McHenry Hohnen
30 McHenry Hohnen Burnside Vineyard
31 McHenry Hohnen Calgardup Brook Vineyard
32 McHenry Hohnen Hazel's Vineyard
33 Moss Wood
34 Moss Wood Ribbon Vale
35 Nocturne
36 Pierro
37 Sam Vinciullo
38 Sandalford
39 Si Vintners
40 Stella Bella
41 Stella Bella Suckfizzle Vineyard
42 Stormflower
43 Vasse Felix
44 Vasse Felix Boodjidup Vineyard
45 Vasse Felix Karridale Vineyard
46 Vasse Velix Adams Road Vineyard
47 Voyager Estate
48 Willespie
49 Windows Estate
50 Woodlands
51 Woody Nook
52 Xanadu Wines

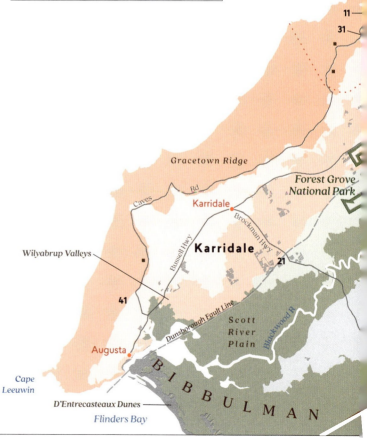

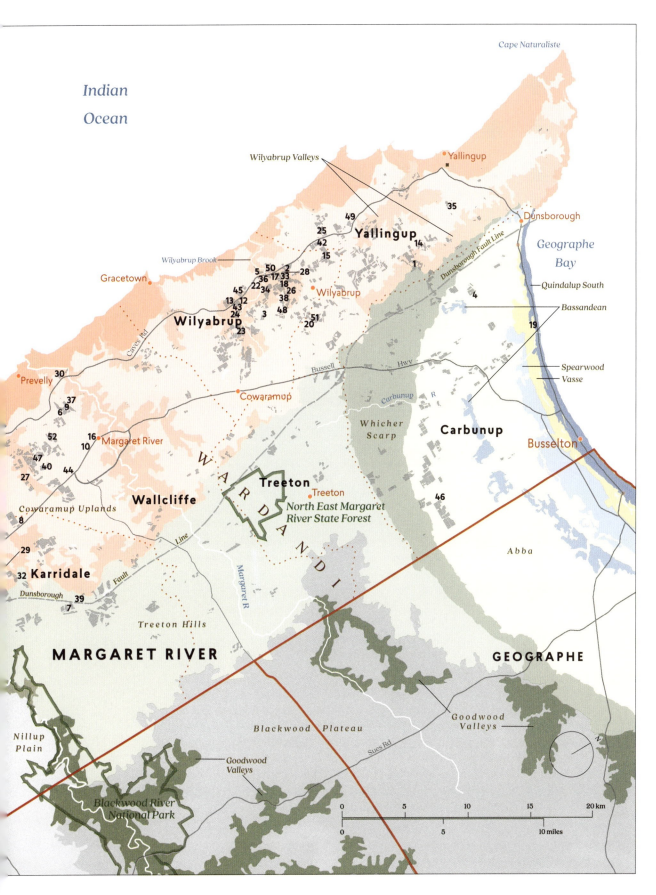
Margaret River

and much of the area is devoted to state forests and national parks.

These four regions – Wilyabrup, Yallingup, Carbunup and Treeton – form a matrix in the northern third of Margaret River. Directly below these four is Wallcliffe. Unlike its northern neighbours, the boundaries for Wallcliffe suggested by Dr Gladstones extend all the way from the coast to the eastern border of the GI. The town of Margaret River sits within the confines of this unofficial subregion, as does the Margaret River itself, a main catchment that empties into the Indian Ocean at the small township of Prevelly.

After Wilyabrup, Wallcliffe was one of the earliest planted areas of Margaret River, with Leeuwin Estate and Cape Mentelle setting up shop here in the 1970s. It is overall cooler and wetter than the areas further north. Virginia Willcock, long-time Wilyabrup winemaker at Vasse Felix, suggests that while Wilyabrup might be the epicentre for cabernet sauvignon, Wallcliffe 'could be the heart of chardonnay'.

Karridale is the southernmost of Gladstones's regions, and also runs from the coast all the way inland to Gladstones Line. This is the largest subregion geographically, but sparsely planted to vineyards. Its low-lying southeastern corner is waterlogged and its sandy coastal plain is wide, infringing on suitable vineyard land. The coolest and rainiest area of Margaret River is in Karridale, centred just south of the town of Witchcliffe.

Despite the variation in temperature, rainfall and soils across Margaret River, there are two grapes that are universally planted: cabernet sauvignon and chardonnay. These two grapes have become the calling cards for Margaret River, with wines made from both grapes commanding top dollar across Australia. Sauvignon blanc and semillon round out the top plantings – the 'SBS' blend has become something Margaret River is known for (often referred to as the 'Classic Dry White' of the region, an offshoot of Vasse Felix's wine of that name, made since 1987). These four grapes (cabernet sauvignon, chardonnay, sauvignon blanc and semillon) account for over 70% of the region's crop. The other 30% is composed of shiraz, merlot, malbec, chenin blanc, and a plethora of more niche varieties like tempranillo, fiano and sangiovese.

For cabernet sauvignon, there is a lot to live up to. It's the region's champion, and the approaches to growing and vinifying it are varied. Producer styles are often driven by their place: those with vineyards cooled by the coast will work to craft wines that show freshness and lightness, usually untethered by heavy influences of oak. Inland expressions tend to be blockier and more robust. Oak and extraction are not uncommon, though many producers are working with other variables to move in the opposite direction, like concrete fermentation vessels, **carbonic maceration**, **stem inclusion**, and co-fermenting with other supporting grapes beyond the traditional merlot.

Chardonnay gets the remainder of the spotlight. Ripeness levels and oak treatment are of course varied, and fruit handling and vinification techniques range from **oxidative** approaches to highly **reductive**. Around the world, chardonnay is a grape whose **clones** are often discussed. In Margaret River, a **clone** unique to the world of chardonnay is found: the Gingin **clone**. It was originally considered to be synonymous with the UC Davis Old Fountain Block and Mendoza **clones**, as all three were traced back to the same origin. The Gingin **clone** is the most prevalent in Margaret River: its looser berry structure and signature varied grape size helps vineyards close to the coast deal with moist air that can spawn mildew and rot.

Clones, fermentation vessels and oak application aside, great wine is predicated on the idea that the end product will communicate a sense of place. The complexity and quality of the land, especially for the cultivation of cabernet sauvignon and chardonnay grapes, is undeniable in Margaret River – and the finished product often unparalleled, with the resulting wines being some of the finest and most age-worthy in Australia.

The **biodynamic, carbon-positive** Cullen estate vineyard.

Hubbub

Ask Australians, particularly Western Australians, what regions make the best cabernet sauvignon and chardonnay in the world – you'll get a short list and Margaret River will be on it. But if you travel to the finest restaurants in New York, London, Tokyo and Paris and look at their wine lists, they'll be noticeably void of any wines from Margaret River (and most likely, anywhere in Australia). So, while international recognition for excellence is not a unique problem to Margaret River in Australia, there is greater consternation about it within this region. Margaret River is an appellation full of strong-willed and ambitious individuals and groups, who all agree that Margaret River makes world-class wine and deserves to be recognised more widely for it. (For the record, we don't think they're wrong.)

One topic that has arisen in the conversation about Margaret River's future, and how to promote its wine to the world, is **subregionality**. Since Dr Gladstones's 1999 report, the question of how to best employ the suggested six unofficial subregions has been vigorously discussed, and more recently, hotly contested.

Several producers in the historic western subregion of Wilyabrup have petitioned heavily for Wine Australia to adopt it as an official subregion of Margaret River. They are the first and only subregion so far to initiate such a petition. Wilyabrup is forging its case based on mapped differences in soil and climate, taste-tests dating back 20 years, as well as the desire to protect the sanctity of the name Wilyabrup; without legal protection, anyone can put the name Wilyabrup on their label, without the wine actually coming from that region.

The wineries Cullen, Fraser Gallop, Moss Wood and Woodlands are behind this entreaty, notably without the support of several major producers in Wilyabrup (Vasse Felix, Pierro, Howard Park) and without the support of the Margaret River Wine Association (MRWA).

In a seemingly complicated process, Wine Australia issued an 'interim determination' in December 2019 that Wilyabrup would in fact be granted GI status but, in July 2020, issued a statement saying they would not be making a final determination at that time. Opponents of the petition (like the MRWA) celebrated this decision as evidence that this conversation would be shelved indefinitely, or at least until new evidence was presented, while the authors of the application claim that this was merely a delay while all the details of the

new GI were sorted out. As time goes on, it seems the opponents are more likely correct.

The MRWA's rationale for opposing the application was that not enough research had been done to truly ascertain which regions deserve to be singled out: 'The MRWA Board holds a unified belief that the region is not yet in a position to scientifically validate where, or to what extent, uniqueness or uniformity occurs within the Margaret River GI'. Virginia Willcock concurs, pointing to the youth of the region and its need for more study: 'We all believe there are general subregional distinctions. We're just super young ... we don't believe that there's enough technical research to define them now.'

The MRWA has undertaken the 'Margaret River Region Project' to tackle this task, mapping out the **microclimates**, soils, landscapes and resulting style variations within the Margaret River GI, particularly in relation to cabernet sauvignon and chardonnay. And though she doesn't believe it's the right time to define subregions, Willcock recognises the utility of the Wilyabrup GI application in propelling this research process: 'We needed that bit of tension to drive forward,' she says.

There is additional scholarship to support this idea that the original 'Gladstones Six' does not provide sufficient evidence to warrant official subdivision. In 2019, an influential paper was published by French geologist Mathieu Lacorde, in which he argued for the region be split into a whopping 12 unique subregions based on factors including soil, topography, climate, geology and landscape.

Worth noting about both Gladstones's and Lacorde's delineation is that every inch of Margaret River is classified into a subregion – a paradigm that implies a desire to establish *unique* regions, not *superior* ones. This is clearly a very different model from the Médoc prototype, which seeks to establish the handful of areas that have the capability to create exceptional *and* singular wines (like Paulliac, Margaux, Saint-Estèphe and Saint-Julien), leaving the rest of the land to fall under more generic appellations (like Médoc, Haut-Médoc and Bas-Médoc).

The logical fear here is that some subregions rising above others will do harm to protecting and elevating Margaret River as a whole. While proponents of subregions argue that they promote the idea of complexity and nuance across the region – like, one could argue, it's done for the Médoc – others contend that it just muddies the waters, especially abroad, where wine professionals and consumers alike are still having trouble rallying behind the broader Margaret River banner.

And if winemakers are craving a greater attention to the minutiae of the land, why not champion individual vineyards? The hope for many is that a greater focus on mapping the land will result in a greater appreciation for single-vineyard sites, something that has been missing in the history of Margaret River. While many producers do confine themselves to

Cow horns ready to be filled with manure and be buried next to Si Vintners' farm, to start preparing next year's **biodynamic** inputs.

estate-grown fruit (with no vineyard names labelled), there are several notable vineyards that are sourced by multiple producers that should be amassing attention. 'We tend to say *that producer* makes really great chardonnay, or *that producer* makes really great cabernet,' says Genevieve Mann, who owns Corymbia with her husband Rob, 'but we don't say well, okay, here's an amazing *vineyard*.'

All Margaret River winemakers and growers – as well as writers, sommeliers and enthusiasts from across Australia – can agree that the region is exemplary, a near-paradise for food, surf, wine, wilderness and hospitality. And with their tiny yields and high cost of farming, all winemakers in the region are united on the path to producing world-class chardonnay and cabernet sauvignon: 'We have no choice but to be exceptional,' says Willcock. 'It's too expensive not to be.'

What can't be agreed upon in the wine industry is where the focus should lie in promoting Margaret River as one of the finest wine regions in the world. Will it be paramount to champion Margaret River as a whole, first and foremost? Or will it be key to establish official subregions, as a way of explicating the complexity and excellence of the region? Should single vineyards be identified and labelled, or does this practice leech off brand Margaret River, diminish the importance of the producer and confuse the consumer? Should the multitude of grapes and styles being produced be put on display, or does everyone need to rally behind chardonnay and cabernet – especially internationally – as the calling cards of the region?

These arguments have been alive for over 20 years in the region, and consensus looks unlikely. But perhaps it's not necessary. For Vanya Cullen, the multitude of stories and perspectives is what makes Margaret River authentic: 'For Margaret River to have dignity, it has to have many stories and not just one story ... one story is branding, and becomes a corporate way of being. And I think what people love about wine is those many stories and those many truths ... that dignity comes from the many stories of people's lives and that needs to be able to play out.'

PRODUCERS

BLIND CORNER

Like many other winemakers in the region, Ben and Naomi Gould spent time travelling through Europe, working in other people's vineyards and developing their own winemaking styles. They are the first in Western Australia to be organic and **biodynamically** certified across their winery, bottling line and vineyard. Blind Corner makes vibrant wines from a range of traditional and lesser-known varieties, including some six-year-old aligoté vines, believed to be the only plantings in Margaret River. They are also a champion of alternative styles like **pét-nats**, skin-contact whites and **nouveau** reds, making some of the best entries in these categories in all of Australia. *blindcorner.com.au*

CAPE MENTELLE

One of the founding wineries of Margaret River, Cape Mentelle was established in 1970 by industry pioneer David Hohnen and his brothers Mark and Giles. The winery takes its name from a nearby cape, named by French cartographers in the early 1800s who mapped the coastline of Western Australia. The original vineyard (now called Wallcliffe vineyard) makes up one of four holdings, which are planted to cabernet sauvignon, shiraz, chardonnay, semillon, sauvignon blanc and others (including a plot of old-vine zinfandel planted in the mid-70s). By the early 2000s, LVMH group had acquired 100% ownership of the estate, enabling development of the winery and expansion into the global market, with quality wine production still at the forefront. *capementelle.com.au*

CHERUBINO WINES

Larry Cherubino began his career as a horticulturist, before moving into winemaking. His illustrious career has included prominent positions at Hardys Tintara and Houghton and taken him across the world as a consultant. Larry and his wife bought their first piece of land in Frankland River in 2004, a parcel that was originally part of a historic holding called Riversdale. Their business began out of their spare room a year later, with the release of just one wine. Cherubino has grown exponentially since then, with the accumulation of 120 hectares of vineyards across Great Southern, Margaret River and Pemberton. Larry has since brought on additional winemakers to assist with the eight labels now made under his banner. Despite the rapid growth of his empire, Larry's philosophy still has his green beginnings at its centre: 'Good wine is relatively hands-off. You should have done all the work in the field.' *larrycherubino.com*

CLOUDBURST

From a tiny block in Wilyabrup, nestled among some of the region's heavy hitters – the exact location unknown, due to the owner's secrecy – comes a unique story. American Will Berliner moved to Margaret River in the early 2000s with no interest in winemaking, but by 2005 he had begun planting a vineyard, employing **biodynamic** practices, and studying winemaking. An avid gardener, Will **close-planted** his vines, made up of 0.2 hectares each of cabernet sauvignon and chardonnay, and 0.1 hectares of malbec. In 2010, his cabernet won three trophies at the Margaret River

Rob & Genevieve Mann
Corymbia

Wine Show, before he'd even sold a single bottle in Australia (sales were focused overseas at first). The retail price? $270 AUD – much higher than most of the Margaret River icons – but a number of his loyal international (and growing domestic) following are willing to pay for the immense quality and tiny production. cloudburstwine.com

CORYMBIA

Rob Mann comes from winemaking stock. His grandfather, Jack Mann, created the famous Houghton's White Burgundy and worked 51 consecutive vintages at Houghton (p. 450). His uncle, Dorham Mann, helped establish the vineyards that launched both the Margaret River and Great Southern wine industries. Rob worked at Cape Mentelle before being headhunted for Newton in the Napa Valley. He returned to his family vineyard in Upper Swan and launched Corymbia in 2013 with his wife, Genevieve, who made wine in her native South Africa, France, California and South Australia before taking on winemaking at Howard Park (p.428). Rob and Genevieve spent 10 years searching for the perfect piece of dirt to grow cabernet sauvignon in Margaret River, leading to their Calgardup vineyard, just 2 kilometres inland from the coast. The pair release three wines: a complex, concentrated cabernet sauvignon from Calgardup, a chenin blanc, and a tempranillo-malbec blend, the latter two from Rocket's vineyard in the Swan Valley, planted in the 80s by Rob and his father, Tony. corymbiawine.com.au

Vanya Cullen
Cullen Wines

CULLEN WINES

Had it not been for their relationship with Dr John Gladstones, Kevin and Diana Cullen might never have planted vines. The couple purchased 40.5 hectares that they thought might be appropriate for growing lupins. After visiting the property, Dr Gladstones, who had been researching the suitability of Margaret River for vine growth, suggested they plant grapes. Kevin and Diana travelled extensively to see how others made wine, then returned to Margaret River and planted 6.8 hectares of cabernet, riesling and gewürztraminer in 1971. Diana studied winemaking and took up the mantle of chief winemaker in 1981, before handing the reins to her youngest daughter Vanya in 1989. Kevin and Diana were early believers in Bordeaux varieties in Margaret River and today, the Diana Madeline

> **JR** What we're drinking
>
> My first experience with **Cloudburst** chardonnay was before my time in Australia, when Will Berliner would take his wine around to various export markets, pouring it blind next to A-list Burgundy producers. This wine's power, intensity, brightness and all-out flavour intensity is showstopping.
> – Jonathan Ross

Cabernet Merlot (along with the Kevin John Chardonnay) are benchmarks in their categories across the globe. Minimal chemical intervention and maximum care for the land has always been of utmost importance to the family. The estate is certified **biodynamic**, carbon positive, and continues to strengthen its link to the traditional custodians of the land, the local Wardandi community. Vanya is a passionate advocate for honouring the earth on which her grapes grow and says, 'the land will give back if you give it a chance'. *cullenwines.com.au*

DEEP WOODS

Based in the Yallingup Hills, the Deep Woods estate looks down on an unpopulated valley and dense woodland – from their beginnings in 1987 to this day, 'deep woods' has been a good moniker. The winery was bought by Fogarty Wine Group in 2005, and subsequently undertook some renovation and modernisation. At the helm today is general manager and chief winemaker Julian Langworthy, known and beloved across the region, who has brought home many accolades for the estate, including the **Jimmy Watson** for their 2014 Reserve Cabernet Sauvignon. *deepwoods.wine*

DORMILONA

She may be a self-confessed 'lazybones' and minimal interventionist, but Josephine Perry is anything but hands off. Experimenting from a young age, her grandfather, a brewer at Swan Brewery, had her fermenting fruit in the family home and encouraged her to participate in her first vintage at Cape Mentelle when she was 14. While studying her winemaking degree via correspondence, Jo travelled extensively, working for wineries in Spain, the Canary Islands, France, New Zealand and the US. Back in Australia, Jo and her husband Jimmy source fruit from well-farmed sites across the region, making everything from a hemp-infused semillon to seriously stylish amphora-aged cabernet and chardonnay in their Clayface label.
dormilona.com.au

FLAMETREE

Despite being a relatively young label by regional standards (established 2007), Flametree Wines have proven themselves to be a consistent and quality producer. Flametree sits on the northern shoreline of the region, along Geographe Bay, and sources fruit from a variety of Margaret River locales. The team are firm believers in the subregions of Margaret River, singling out and labelling wines by their respective area to display the differences. Their smoky, flinty chardonnays and savoury medium-bodied syrahs are of the moment and have attracted many accolades. *flametreewines.com*

HOWARD PARK

John Wade was working at Wynns in Coonawarra when he began to recognise the potential in the Great Southern region. He started Howard Park while working at Plantagenet (p. 442) in 1986, beginning with riesling and cabernet sauvignon. However, it wasn't until John partnered with the Burch family, who owned a property in Wilyabrup, that he released his first Howard Park wine, a chardonnay that was a blend of Great Southern and Margaret River fruit. When John left the estate in the late 90s, the Burch family took over full ownership. Howard Park has grown tremendously in the decades that followed, with the opening of a winery and cellar door in Margaret River, as well as acquisition of 200 hectares of land in Margaret River, and 100 hectares in Mount Barker (including the major contributing source of that first 1986 cabernet). They now have the largest holdings of pinot noir in WA thanks to a partnership with the juggernaut Pascal Marchand.
howardparkwines.com.au

What we're drinking

Dormilona's *Clayface bottlings are some of Margaret River's most exciting. 'Clayface' alludes to the amphora Jo employs to age the chardonnay and cabernet sauvignon in this series. The result is super articulate varietal expression, gauzy structure, and no influence of oak or fruit heft. Stunning.*
– *Jane Lopes*

Nic Peterkin, L.A.S. Vino

JUNIPER ESTATE

The Juniper Estate vineyard was planted in 1973 by Henry and Maureen Wright, among the pioneer plantings in Wilyabrup. Juniper was established in 1998 by the late Roger Hill and his wife Gillian Anderson, and is now run by their sons Nick and Tom. Production is focused on three vineyard sites: the original Wilyabrup estate vineyard of chardonnay and cabernet sauvignon; a plot in Karridale that includes small parcels of tempranillo and fiano; and new (2008) Wilyabrup plantings at the Metricup Road vineyard.
juniperestate.com

L.A.S. VINO

The grandson of the founding Cullens, and son of Pierro's Mike Peterkin, Nic Peterkin was originally uninterested in following in their footsteps. But with a little bit of luck, art and science (which would inspire his winery's name), the widely travelled Nic launched L.A.S. Vino, forging his own unique path in the Margaret River wine industry. From a skin-contactless (white) blend of pinot noir and chardonnay, to the Chenin Blanc Dynamic Blend from the first Demeter-certified **biodynamic** vineyard in the region, and even a 'pirate blend' of Portuguese native varieties, L.A.S. Vino is making some of Margaret River's most exciting wine.
lasvino.com

LEEUWIN ESTATE

In 1973, a chartered accountant named Denis Horgan received a phone call from his lawyer: a man named Robert Mondavi wanted to meet him. Unbeknown to Denis, the most influential man in the world's wine industry was scouting vineyards and had identified Denis's newly acquired cattle farm as ideal for the growth of premium wine grapes; Mondavi became an advisor to Denis and his wife Tricia in the early years of Leeuwin Estate. From the outset, the couple wanted the estate to be a celebration of fine wine, food, music and art. Today among the vines, Leeuwin is home to a restaurant, art gallery, amphitheatre and airstrip. After Bob Cartwright became winemaker in 1978, 89 hectares of vineyard land were developed in five years. Leeuwin Estate's flagship Art Series (chardonnay, cabernet, shiraz and riesling) have a new painting on the label each vintage, commissioned from an Australian artist. *leeuwinestate.com.au*

MOSS WOOD

While doing his medical residency in Perth in 1969, Dr Bill Pannell purchased a plot of land and planted cabernet sauvignon vines. He and his wife Sandra picked, pressed and bottled the first vintages of Moss Wood by hand. They soon planted semillon and pinot noir, and eventually chardonnay. In 1979, the freshly graduated Keith Mugford came on as winemaker. Six years later, Keith and Clare Mugford assumed full ownership of the estate and Moss Wood has been synonymous with the Mugford name since. Like many of the other early Margaret River wineries, long-lived, high-quality cabernet sauvignon has brought recognition and success to Moss Wood.
mosswood.com.au

PIERRO

Another MD-turned-winemaker, Dr Mike Peterkin purchased a scrubby block of north-facing slopes in 1979. He produced Australia's first semillon-sauvignon blanc blend in the same year, while making wine for Kevin and Diana Cullen (his in-laws). The initial Pierro wines were made from cabernet sauvignon fruit purchased from Moss Wood, until vineyards of chardonnay, semillon, sauvignon blanc, chenin blanc and pinot noir, along with Bordeaux

Margaret River

Virginia Willcock
Vasse Felix

reds, were planted in the 1980s. The planting of chardonnay on the property was fortuitous as Mike had initially intended to grow riesling, but was offered chardonnay rootstocks at a reduced price – chardonnay has become Pierro's most sought-after wine. *pierro.com.au*

SI VINTNERS

Sarah Morris and Iwo Jakimowicz purchased their tiny plot of land in 2010, after over a decade doing vintages in regions across the world. Having spent so long crafting wine for other people, the couple are clear in their winemaking convictions, and pursue a natural approach, from organically farmed fruit to zero additions (except **sulphur** at bottling). Their property in Rosa Glen, in the northern part of the unofficial subregion of Karridale, is a mature vineyard that has been converted to **biodynamic** farming practices. *sivintners.com*

VASSE FELIX

Vasse Felix is the founding estate of the Margaret River wine region. Overlooking Wilyabrup Brook, Dr Tom Cullity planted the first vineyards with cabernet sauvignon, shiraz, malbec and riesling in 1967. The first vintage, four years later, Dr Cullity called a 'disappointment'. Under the direction of chief winemaker Virginia Willcock, Vasse Felix in the 21st century is anything but. Their portfolio focuses on the production of high-quality cabernet sauvignon, chardonnay, shiraz and sauvignon blanc-semillon blends, and they have recently begun producing sparkling wine; after acquiring a vineyard in Karridale and discovering fruit that didn't completely ripen, Willcock identified it as an ideal site for a blanc de blancs base. Willcock believes in the clear sense-of-place wine from Margaret River evokes. Since 1987, Vasse Felix has been owned by the Holmes à Court family and part of their privately owned company, the Heytesbury Group. *vassefelix.com.au*

VOYAGER ESTATE

Perth agriculturalist Peter Gherardi was another pioneer who took notes from Dr John Gladstones. He purchased a 14-hectare 'pasture' in 1978, which he named Freycinet Estate, and set about planting the gravelly soils with Bordeaux varieties. In 1991, he sold it to businessman Michael Wright, a teetotaller with a fanatic passion for agriculture, who renamed it Voyager Estate. Wright vigorously expanded Voyager up until his passing in 2012. His legacy is a focus on 'environmental balance'. Voyager has been carbon neutral since 2017, will have all its wines certified organic by 2023, and is continually seeking ways to adjust to the changing climate through vineyard management. *voyagerestate.com.au*

WINES OF MERRITT

Originally from South Australia, Nick and Sarah James-Martin make wine from some of the less-common varieties growing in Margaret River. Their label is named after Nick's great-grandparents, Forrester and Prim Merritt. The wines are produced in small quantities and are mostly unfined and unfiltered. Their cabernet franc, sauvignon blanc and chenin blanc fruit comes from across Margaret River, however their vermentino is grown further

---

What we're drinking

While **Si Vintners'** *origins and early wines were largely experimental in style, a renaissance has occurred in recent years with an about-turn to pitching at fine wine culture. Chardonnay has become a serious player in terms of quality, albeit in a more rambunctious, fuller-flavoured, expressive style, while cabernet zeroes in on elegance and refinement. Complex rosé-esque wines and skin-contact whites continue to be refined and excel.* – Mike Bennie

inland and north, on the sandy foothills of Geographe GI.
winesofmerritt.com.au

WOODLANDS

Established in in 1973, Woodlands was one of the first five vineyards to be planted in Margaret River. David and Heather Watson found success early on with their cabernet sauvignon, but began selling off their grapes in the 1990s while they brought up their children. The estate was revitalised when Stuart and Andrew Watson took over production in the early 2000s. Woodlands is made up of two vineyards within 2 kilometres of each other in the Wilyabrup Valley, one of which is certified organic.
woodlandswines.com.au

XANADU WINES

Xanadu Wines was established by Dr John Lagan in 1977. Today it is owned by the Rathbone family, alongside Yering Station (Yarra Valley, p. 121) and Mount Langi Ghiran (Grampians, p. 209). Senior winemaker Glenn Goodall has been on board for over two decades. Xanadu has undergone significant vineyard development to improve the quality of their wines, leading to a win of the coveted **Jimmy Watson Memorial Trophy** for their cabernet sauvignon in 2018. *xanaduwines.com*

And don't forget …
Arthur Wines is a modern take on **fortified wines** (and only fortified wines!) from Rob and Tash Arthur … **Domaine Naturaliste** is a contract-production and consulting facility that began making its own wine in 2012, with proprietor/winemaker Bruce Dukes managing 7 hectares in Wilyabrup of chardonnay, grenache and red Bordeaux grapes … **Glenarty Road** embodies their 'ground to glass' philosophy, which means a focus on regenerative viticulture under the watch of fifth-generation farmers Sasha and Ben McDonald … **Gralyn Estate** opened Margaret River's first cellar door in Wilyabrup in 1978 and pioneered port-style wines in the region, which sit alongside more classic offerings in their range … **La Kooki** is the side project of Cape Mentelle winemaker Eloise Jarvis and Xanadu winemaker Glenn Goodall, who make a range of wines that can at times be 'kooki' (self-admittedly), as well as more serious bottlings … **Lenton Brae**, founded in Wilyabrup in 1982, produces Margaret River staples, served throughout the year in their picturesque lakeside cellar door … **LS Merchants** was founded because Dylan Arvidson 'wanted something more from Margaret River than cab sauv and chardy', making wines with a special focus on grapes like vermentino, mataro and petit verdot … **McHenry Hohnen** was founded by Murray McHenry and David Hohnen (the latter of Cape Mentelle), with three vineyards across Margaret River, all farmed **biodynamically** … **Nocturne** is the side project of Julian Langworthy (Deep Woods) and his wife Alana, making affordable and modern cabernet sauvignon and chardonnay … **Sam Vinciullo**, a member of Australia's new guard, farms his vines without chemicals or irrigation and makes his wines with no additions, including **sulphur** or oak – rare indeed for the region … **Stormflower**, planted to cabernet sauvignon, shiraz, chardonnay, sauvignon blanc, semillon and chenin blanc in the 1990s, was purchased in 2007 by David Martin, co-founder of Little Creatures Brewery, achieving full organic certification in 2016 … **Windows Estate** is a labour-of-love for Chris and Joanne Davies, who farm organically and release small batches of smartly composed chardonnay, chenin blanc, semillon-sauvignon blanc, syrah and cab.

> **What we're drinking**
>
> *I mustn't be sat fireside enough, as fuller bodied reds aren't generally the first thing I reach for. However, there is definitely a right time and a right place for these wines – and were I to find myself rugged up on a cold winter night, **Xanadu Wines'** award-wining cabernet sauvignon would be what I would like in my glass. Buy a dozen and drink one a year; your patience will be rewarded.* – Kavita Faiella

Great Southern

Introduction

Great Southern is remote. Not only is the GI removed from the rest of Australia – it is more than a four-hour drive from Western Australia's capital Perth, and takes over 25 hours along the continent's southern coast to reach the next nearest capital city of Adelaide – it is also spread out and sparsely populated. Most wineries are at least 10 kilometres from the next, often quite a bit more. There are 2545 hectares planted across approximately 20,000 square kilometres in Great Southern – compare this to Margaret River, where over double the amount of vines cover about a fifth of the total area of land.

Great Southern shares its name with the governmental region it occupies; there are nine such regions in Western Australia, largely defined by the industries that employ each. Great Southern is recognised for its livestock, dairy and crop farming. Cereal grain, wool and lamb are commonplace, and the regional centre Albany is known for its fishing industry.

The wine region Great Southern (in contrast to the governmental area, which is larger) runs about 100 kilometres northward from the coast, and about 150 kilometres east to west. It forms a rough parallelogram, as the coastline tapers northward east of Albany. Great Southern is a region oriented by the sea and the mountains, two **aspects** that also figured greatly in the lives of its First Nations.

The area we call Great Southern is within the 52,000 square kilometre Noongar Nation subregion recognised as the 'Wagyl Kaip and Southern Noongar Region'. It is home to the language groups Ganeang, Goreng and Minang. Life typically oscillated between the coast in the summer months and inland in the winter months for these original custodians, the Porongurup mountains being of particular cultural importance. On the coast, the Kalgan River at Miaritch (now Oyster Harbour) was one of the major food sources for the first societies.

Two of Great Southern's viticultural subregions lie along the sea; three are positioned inland, among the mountains. Great Southern is a singular Australian appellation in that its sparse plantings are almost all within these five subregions, not sprinkled throughout the entire geographic area. A small percentage of wines are labelled 'Great Southern', but more often than not, they'll assume the identity of one of the more specific subregions.

Some wonder whether this has stunted the overall brand identity of Great Southern, a region that has yet to garner the international acclaim of many others across the nation. Others wonder if Great Southern is a meaningless designation, when the subregions are so particular and discrete. Regardless, these GIs are home to some extraordinary wines and an even more extraordinary sense that there is near-infinite uncharted territory to explore.

Evolution of Wine

Great Southern saw its wine industry emerge in a similar way to Margaret River, though Dr Harold Olmo's 1956 report (p. 413) was even more effusive about the cool-climate potential of Great Southern. He wrote matter-of-factly that the Western Australian region best suited for 'the production of high-quality light **table wines** [is] the south coastal area along the Frankland River ... Here the summer climate is cool enough to promote slow maturity of the fruit, and the rainfall is high enough to produce a vigorous productive vine on the better alluvial soils.' Dr Gladstones similarly touted the potential of the region in his 1960s articles.

Though there is evidence of vine plantings dating back to the mid-1800s, it wasn't until the 1960s that grape growing really took root in Great Southern (pun intended!). With a failing apple industry in the region, the state government turned an eye toward viticulture, with Olmo's report in mind.

A grape industry committee was established in 1963 and identified a site just west of Mount Barker, owned by Tony and Betty Pearse, as suitable. In 1965, trial vineyards were planted on this site by Bill Jamieson, Western Australia's state viticulturist (what a job), and Dorham Mann, a Swan Valley winemaker whose progeny continue to be an important part of the Western Australian wine industry to this day. Though the 1965 vines didn't take due to a wet season, the 1966 ones did, and these are Great Southern's first and longest-standing vines, now under the care of Forest Hill vineyard.

From these vines, a riesling and a cabernet sauvignon were made in 1972. Perhaps not coincidentally, as state viticulturists were involved in both ventures, these were the same grapes and same vintage that first saw bottlings in Margaret River (at Wilyabrup's Vasse Felix, p. 430).

The histories of the two regions diverge after these initial bottlings. While Margaret River saw fairly immediate population influx and interest, Great Southern only grew in small increments. Perhaps it was the physical remoteness or how large and spread out the area was. Or perhaps it was the overall cooler climate, without the surfing attractions and the ability to ripen lusher, more international styles of chardonnay and cabernet.

But whatever it was, Great Southern saw its pioneer wineries emerge slowly through the 1970s and 1980s. And unlike Margaret River, these were not doctors and lawyers looking to try their hand at viticulture; they were mainly local farmers who added grape growing to diversify their crops.

The Forest Hill vineyard in Mount Barker, first planted in 1965.

Great Southern

HOW TO READ THIS MAP

This map includes the full expanse of this isolated region. The five subregions and their vineyards are mapped against changes in elevation – a driving factor, second only to proximity to the sea, in creating numerous **microclimates** of Great Southern.

1   Alkoomi
2   Brave New Wine
3   Bunn
4   Castelli
5   Castle Rock Estate
6   Duke's
7   Express Winemakers
8   Forest Hill Vineyard
9   Frankland Estate
10 Freehand
11 Galafrey Wines
12 Gilbert
13 Jingalla
14 La Violetta
15 Larry Cherubino Riversdale Vineyard
16 Lowboi
17 Moombaki
18 Oranje Tractor
19 Parish Lane
20 Plantagenet Bouverie Vineyard
21 Plantagenet Rocky Horror 1 Vineyard
22 Plantagenet Rocky Horror 2 Vineyard
23 Plantagenet Wyjup Vineyard
24 Singlefile Wines
25 Swinney Powderbark Vineyard
26 Swinney Wilson's Pool Vineyard
27 West Cape Howe
28 Wignalls Wines
29 Willoughby Park
30 Yilgarnia

Western Australia

434

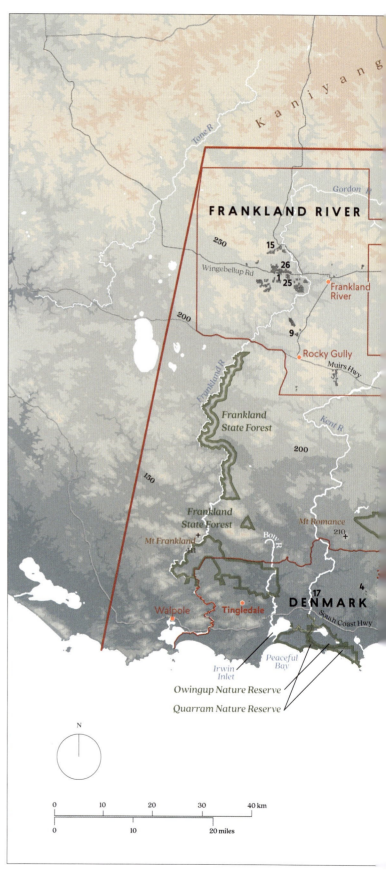

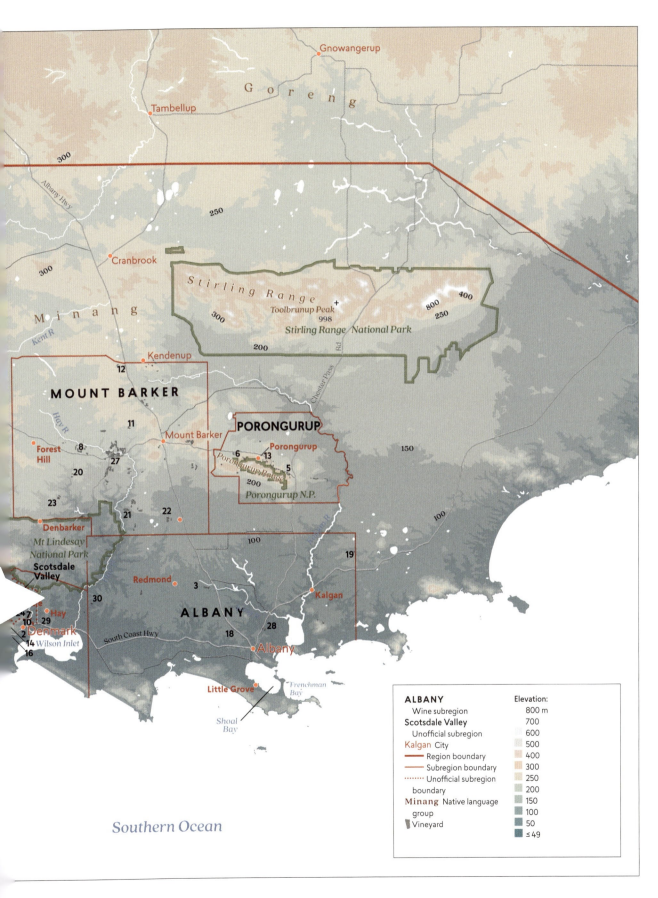

It's hard to talk about Great Southern as a single cohesive GI, historically or geographically, with five distinct subregions and no real plantings or vineyards outside of them. Mount Barker and Frankland River were the subregions that saw most of the early pioneers: Mount Barker had Forest Hill (1966), Plantagenet (1968) and Galafrey (1977); Frankland River had the Roche family (1967), Alkoomi (1971) and Frankland Estate (1988). Porongurup saw its earliest vintner in Castle Rock (1983), and Wignalls (1982) was the first winery in Albany.

The 1990s and early 2000s were a mixed bag for Great Southern – the **Parkerisation** and corporatisation experienced by many regions across the world in this time brought some much-needed investment and interest into the region. But the oaky and extracted style that suited some of Australia's warmer regions did not sit well on the more lithe and nervy wines of Great Southern, despite many attempts to make it work.

These factors combined (and with the exception of just a couple producers, most notably Frankland Estate): Great Southern started to look pretty uncool. Few wines made a splash nationally or found their way onto great wine lists in Sydney, Melbourne, or even Perth. Great Southern was having a bit of an identity crisis.

The late 2000s saw not only an evolution in Great Southern, but also the tides in the wine industry shifting their way. To the latter: cool-climate wines became in vogue, remote and obscure regions were coveted, and value was prized over prestige. And to the former: Great Southern had come into its own.

Great Southern Viticultural Footprint

Total delimited area (km²)	20,440
Total planted area (hectares)	2545
% of delimited area planted	0.125%
Total elevation range	0–1083 masl
Elevation range of plantings	20–350 masl
Number of producers	71

Many young producers – like Brave New Wine, Express Winemakers, La Violetta, Lowboi and Singlefile Wines – have brought in an energy of grape-growing gravitas and winemaking levity that seems at home in the region. Single sites are purchased, labelled and featured from across subregions. Oak has been scaled back. Riesling is celebrated, with dry, textural styles finding their groove (stalwart Frankland Estate still leads this charge). The diversity of climate is embraced, with structured and nimble styles of riesling, shiraz and cabernet sauvignon becoming classic, as well as unique expressions of grenache popping up in warmer pockets – new winery (though mature grower) Swinney has done much to reinvigorate national interest in Great Southern grenache. And mainstream wine styles coexist harmoniously with more adventurous takes, creating palpable excitement for what might come next.

Lay of the Land

When the national GI system was drawn in the 1990s, few subregions were issued. Most GI regions were left whole, without acknowledging any further delineation. Great Southern is the most dramatic example of recognised subregions in Australia, and holds a commanding five of the total 14 subregions.

It's easy to wonder whether these subregions should have been regional GIs in their own right. Most Australian subregions – take Adelaide Hills' Lenswood and Piccadilly Valley, or Hunter Valley's Pokolbin and Upper Hunter – represent a unique growing area, but don't command the brand power that the larger region does. But the subregional GIs of Great Southern seem fairly autonomous: their individual brands (especially Frankland River, but the others as well) command more attention than Great Southern does as a whole. And there isn't much activity (in terms of wineries or vineyards) in between the subregions, which is also an aberration from the norm of how subregions typically function.

The differences between the subregions in Great Southern are also much more drastic than between other intraregional GIs. Soil type is the one constant across the region: in general, lateritic sandy loams formed from degrading gneiss and granite.

Climate is much more variable, and any generalisations about Great Southern as a whole tend to be incorrect for one region or another. Great Southern is often described as a maritime climate, though it would be more accurate to say it is a Mediterranean climate created by maritime influence, and even this is only true of the coastal subregions (Albany and Denmark). These coastal regions enjoy wetter winters than summers, a narrow range of annual temperatures, and few extremes of highs and lows. They trend cooler than Margaret River because the ocean is colder here, without the influence of the warming Leeuwin surface current and with a more direct influence of the Southern Ocean. As you move inland, toward Porongurup, Mount Barker and Frankland River, the climate turns more continental, with greater temperature ranges and lower rainfall.

Great Southern is often described as being cool-climate (starting with Dr Olmo's 1956 assessment), though some climates in the region run more moderate, capable of successfully ripening cabernet sauvignon, shiraz, grenache and mourvèdre. Mediterranean climates are rarely super cold, their lows moderated by the ocean influence.

Altitude and proximity to the coast are the two factors that vary widely across the subregions and create climatic differences. Coastal Albany's range of elevation across the GI is 0–115 metres above sea level, with plantings not breaching 100 metres, and many sitting around 50 metres. Denmark, also on the coast, ranges from 0–220 metres. All Denmark plantings – aside from the lowlands on the eastern end, near Wilson Inlet – sit around or somewhat above the 100-metre mark. Denmark's coastline has seaside cliffs giving way to a more dynamic, forested topography when compared to the flatter and more heavily farmed area of Albany. Denmark has a larger temperature range, thanks to its higher elevation.

Frankland River, Mount Barker and Porongurup are the three inland wine regions, with a considerable rise in elevation from the coast, with vineyards typically sitting between 220 and 350 metres in elevation. Maximum

Great Southern Climate Data

	FRANKLAND RIVER	MOUNT BARKER	PORONGURUP	DENMARK	ALBANY
Annual rain/GSR	617/199.5	726/278	764/333	1085/362	925/520
Warmest month avg. temp.	21.1	20.2	20.2	19.5	19.5

Great Southern Viticultural Footprint

	FRANKLAND RIVER	MOUNT BARKER	PORONGURUP	DENMARK	ALBANY
Total delimited area (km²)	1438	1344	398	1595	1223
Total planted area (hectares)	1354	895	96	85	89
% of delimited area planted	0.942%	0.666%	0.241%	0.053%	0.073%
Total elevation range	200–345 masl	100–495 masl	150–700 masl	0–220 masl	0–115 masl
Elevation range of plantings	220–280 masl	150–285 masl	150–350 masl	25–200 masl	20–100 masl

elevations are often misunderstood in Great Southern, quoted as 700 metres above sea level, which is the highest peak in the Porongurup National Park (and, of course, has no vineyards).

Though irrigation is nearly universal in the arid climate of Australia, many vineyards in Great Southern are **dry-grown**. Conventional wisdom dictated irrigation when vineyards were established, and many who still employ it do so to maximise quality, not quantity. But it's thought that the entire region – and specifically Denmark, Albany and Mount Barker – could exist completely **dry-grown** because of the ample rainfall in these regions. Frankland River and Porongurup experience less consistent rainfall, and irrigation can sometimes be a necessary prophylactic against the stress of dryness.

Riesling and cabernet sauvignon often get touted as the premier grapes of Great Southern, but, perhaps surprisingly, 30% of the region's annual harvest is devoted to shiraz. In fact, with Margaret River's focus on chardonnay and Bordeaux grapes, and the heat of Swan Valley impeding taut expressions of the grape, Great Southern may be the best region in Western Australia for shiraz, producing it successfully in each of its climate zones.

The second-most planted grape in Great Southern is cabernet sauvignon, followed by sauvignon blanc, chardonnay, semillon, riesling and pinot noir. Other grapes grown in the region include pinot gris, malbec, sangiovese, tempranillo, grenache and mourvèdre. About one-third of plantings are white grapes. Though riesling is only the fourth most planted white grape, its reputation in Great Southern belies these meagre plantings.

These are some overarching truths about Great Southern, but to understand this GI is really to understand its five discrete subregions.

Albany was Western Australia's first colony, and is the administrative centre of Great Southern. It is the southeastern-most subregion in the larger GI, sitting on the coast at low elevation, plantings beginning around 40 metres above sea level. There are just 70 hectares of plantings in Albany, all sloping generally south, east and west (nothing north-facing). Albany is the coolest and least-planted subregion in Great Southern. There are only five producers based here, though many outside of the subregion source from vineyards here.

Denmark sits just west of Albany on the Wilson Inlet, known for pristine beaches, surf and marine wildlife. The western edge of the GI is an eco park known as Valley of the Giants, with flora present from when Australia was attached to Antarctica. The northern edge of Denmark borders the Mount Franklin and Mount Lindesay National Parks and the Denmark Catchment State Forest. Vineyards are nestled alongside the Hay, Denmark and Kent River valleys, which descend from these forested foothills, all within 20 kilometres of the coast. The most concentrated area is Scotsdale Valley, defined by the Denmark River, and home to the region's oldest plantings.

Denmark is marginally warmer and wetter than Albany, and home to more plantings and producers than its eastern neighbour. The topography is also more varied than Albany, with defined valleys and steeper hills. Soils are somewhat richer and more fertile; the relative high vigour is not a problem per se, but needs to

Fair Labour Wine

There's plenty of talk about fair trade coffee and chocolate, but not much about whose labour provided the grapes you drink with dinner. It might not seem obvious, but remarkably, Australia has one of the highest minimum wages of any wine-producing country in the world. Workplace laws mean that wage theft is criminalised, so if a business is caught deliberately underpaying its workers, not only are those wages due, but the offence can be punishable by massive fines and jail time. Labour conditions that Australians tend to take for granted, like free healthcare and paid annual leave for part-time and full-time workers, are starkly unique in the world of wine production. So when you pick up a bottle of Australian wine, the provenance of its production is one of the surer bets worldwide.

Sunset across Frankland Estate.

Great Southern

be taken into account when **shoot thinning**, **leaf pulling**, **pruning** and **clonal decisions** are made. The area is well suited to olive trees and other Mediterranean orchard fruits, which dot the landscapes of many vineyards.

Porongurup is the small subregion just north of Albany. It is named for the 12 kilometre-long mountain range that defines the region. The range is over 1.2 billion years old, and its weathered granite peaks are the oldest known mountains on the Earth's surface (!). Though the mountain range gets up near 700 metres in elevation, most plantings range between 150 and 350 metres above sea level.

Just 60 kilometres inland from the coast, the oceanic-influenced climate largely disappears. Rainfall is lower and daily temperature fluctuations are large: warmer daytimes, but colder nights. The north side of the mountain experiences a nocturnal inversion layer, where warm air rises above cooler air sliding down the mountain slopes. The cold air settles in the valley a good 50–75 metres lower in altitude than the vineyard area, with warm air sitting on top of it. This prevents frost risk and aids in ripening, though it raises evening temperatures, creating less of a **diurnal swing** than Frankland River or Mount Barker.

The largest cluster of vineyards sit almost uniformly on the northern side of the Porongurup range, between the townships of Porongurup and Mount Barker, with a few vineyards and producers scattered throughout the eastern and western portions of the appellation. The eastern half of the appellation is less defined by the Porongurup range; its elevation is the lowest within the GI, where vineyards reach down to the 150 metre mark and have a clear line of sight across a gently descending 50 kilometres of farmland down to the coast.

Only 10 producers are based in Porongurup, though several producers from outside the region source from here, like Brave New Wine, West Cape Howe, Cherubino Wines, Marchand & Burch (owned by Howard Park), La Violetta and Express Winemakers. Riesling tends to get top billing in Porongurup, supported by other cool-climate grapes like pinot noir, chardonnay

and sauvignon blanc. Chiselled styles of shiraz and the cabernets are also seen widely.

A 15-minute drive west of the Porongurup range is Mount Barker, which houses the second-largest vineyard area in Great Southern (after Frankland River). Vineyards are clustered in the central and southern area of the GI, with a few sporadic others in the north. Because the town of Mount Barker is the highest altitude point in the region, the vineyards to the south slope gently south, and the vineyards to the north slope gently north.

Without Porongurup's inversion layer, the **diurnal swing** is high in Mount Barker, with cool nights preserving bright acidity. Of course, frost risk and ripening are also more challenging. Vineyards sit slightly below Porongurup on average, between 150 and 285 metres above sea level. Mount Barker houses a good number of old, **dry-grown** vineyards. These mature plantings tend to represent the classic varieties – riesling, chardonnay, cabernet sauvignon, shiraz – but Mount Barker is also home to some more unexpected grapes, such as vermentino, gewürztraminer and chenin blanc.

Last but certainly not least, Frankland River is the most northwestern of the five subregions, containing over half of Great Southern's total vineyards. It is the warmest and driest of all the subregions and sits at about the same elevation as Mount Barker. Some tout Frankland River as a Mediterranean climate; however its large **diurnal swing** during the growing season and relatively low level of precipitation are more in line with the characteristics of a continental climate.

The area is a catchment for a variety of rivers that make their way to the coast. The eponymous Frankland River of course, as well as the Kent, Gordon and Tone Rivers, all provide pathways for ocean air to make its way north to the valley and furnish its moderating effects. The rivers also deliver enough moisture for botrytis to set in on occasion, and botrytis-influenced riesling, though produced in minority compared to non-botrytised styles, has become a specialty of the region.

Riesling in general has become closely associated with Frankland River – largely thanks to the efforts of Frankland Estate – but the region also makes fuller red wine to great effect. Shiraz, cabernet sauvignon, and even warm-climate grapes like grenache and mourvèdre do well in the region. For a region to have equal success with riesling and grenache is an anomaly in the wine world, and both grapes are at the margin of their potential for growing in Frankland River. Riesling tends to be shaded to protect from the afternoon sun, and grenache is planted in **bush vines**, which create a three-dimensional **canopy** allowing for an open fruit zone and dappled, even light. Grenache is also planted on the warmest gravelly hilltops with a predominantly northern **aspect**, while the best riesling is on heavier soils with southern and eastern **aspects**.

Rob Mann (of Corymbia, p. 427), also the winemaker at Frankland River's Swinney, has summed up the region best, in its ability to be a marginal climate for both cool- and warm-climate grapes, and why those grapes have historically been a focus for the region: 'Certainly it is true of the great wines of the world that they are grown in places on the margins of ripeness for the variety and this is where you can achieve the highlights.'

Hubbub

Branding has always been a problem for Great Southern, despite – or maybe because of – its unique set of circumstances. According to Frankland Estate's Hunter Smith, this uniqueness, both in geographic and viticultural landscape, is part of the challenge: 'I've never seen native trees like this, and it really does stand out as somewhere unique. And the wines do it too, but verbally communicating that uniqueness, without just putting a uniqueness label on it, is something that we've grappled with a little.' Compounding this, the strong identity of each of the subregions sometimes conflicts with an overall identity for Great Southern. No other Australian GI has such distinctive subregions – with very few plantings

in between – operating more like a zone than a regional GI.

The diffuse nature of Great Southern has other ramifications, beyond branding. Smith describes the 'tyranny of distance' that plagues Great Southern, causing labour shortages, a lack of resources, less new talent and few tourism dollars. La Violetta's AJ Hoadley reckons that the potential of the region could rival some of the most applauded in Australia: 'I compare it to when I went to visit Adelaide Hills a couple of years ago, just driving around and thought, oh my God, this is like Denmark, except these guys have got Adelaide 20 minutes' drive away.' The challenge – of attracting tourism to such a remote region, as well as young winemakers, who tend to crave a more urban lifestyle – is real in Great Southern.

The remoteness and underdog mentality of Great Southern has fostered a collaborative winemaking and grape-growing community, though. Great Southern feels collegiate, with young producers and pioneers alike inspired by each other to be better. Each feels the onus to work with (not against) their neighbour to get more facetime for Great Southern as a whole.

The sparseness of Great Southern also radiates the feeling of unmitigated possibility. The general consensus is that many great sites aren't under vine yet, just waiting for the right people to plant the right grapes.

The land, though it may be remote, carries the benefit of producing honest styles of wine that reflect the individuals and the vineyard sites without interference. As Hunter Smith describes, there's a sense of abandon and service to site in Great Southern (a philosophy often touted, but rarely executed, in the great wine regions of the world): 'You can't control anything here, the landscape will swallow you up. Better to work with it, than against it.'

PRODUCERS

MOUNT BARKER

EXPRESS WINEMAKERS

Expressive, rather than rushed, Ryan O'Meara has been making wines with a sense of place under his own label for the past decade. Having cut his winemaking teeth hopping between hemispheres, Ryan was drawn back to the Great Southern by its beauty and exceptional riesling. While working at Forest Hill and watching different expressions of single sites come in, he decided to begin Express Winemakers in 2011. Ryan's wines are adventurous and confident. He makes a riesling fermented in a combination of oak barrel and ceramic egg, matured under flor. There's also a frothy, pink **pét-nat** made from both red and white grapes, and the aptly named Drinking Wine – a light, juicy red recommended to be drunk straight from the fridge.

expresswinemakers.com

FOREST HILL VINEYARD

In 1964, a farm owned by Tony and Betty Pearse was identified as an appropriate site to plant the first vines in Great Southern. An experimental vineyard was planted and the first bunches of riesling and cabernet sauvignon were harvested in 1972. After a successful few years in wine shows across the state, this experimental vineyard became Forest Hill and was soon expanded. Forest Hill was eventually sold to the Holmes à Court family (of Margaret River's Vasse Felix, p. 430), then on to the Lyons family, who own it to this day. Since 2005, Forest Hill has been bottling 'Block' wines, vinified from small parcels of high-quality old-vine fruit.

foresthillwines.com.au

PLANTAGENET

After coming to Australia as a Ten Pound Pom (slang for English migrants who paid £10 for a boat ticket to Australia after World War II), Tony Smith bought his farm as soon as he set eyes on it. The Department of Agriculture, who were trialling vineyards further north at the time, offered him no assistance so, during a very wet winter in 1968, Tony cleared the land and planted vines himself. Local farmers said that grapes would never grow, but the first Plantagenet wines were produced in 1975. Tony continued to plant vineyards, with five sites becoming the cornerstones of production. In the early 90s, one of the oldest Australian family businesses, Lionel Samson & Son, began buying up shares in the winery, eventually completely buying it out at the start of the new millennium (before selling in 2021 to a subset of their family, Tom and Mary Wisdom).

plantagenetwines.com

> **JR — What we're drinking**
>
> The Clare Valley and Eden Valley often get all the credit for riesling in Australia, but the high hills of Western Australia's Great Southern are as, if not more, exciting. The Block 1 Forest Hill Vineyard Riesling from **Forest Hill in Mount Barker** is textured and rich with an electric line of citrusy acid preserving the wine for decades. This one is exciting in its youth, and enchanting when mature. – Jonathan Ross

WEST CAPE HOWE

West Cape Howe was founded in 1997 by four Western Australian families. They have since acquired vineyards across Mount Barker and Frankland River. The winery sits on the Langton vineyard, which was first planted in 1978, and is home to some

of the oldest vines in the area. Their wines are well received at wine shows and have consistently helped to put Great Southern on the map.
westcapehowewines.com.au

FRANKLAND RIVER

ALKOOMI

Merv Lange and his wife Judy inherited a sheep farm from his father. The property was named 'Alkoomi' by his mother, a local Aboriginal word meaning 'a place we chose'. Merv and Judy decided to try their hand at grape growing in the early 70s during a slump in the wool industry. They weren't wine drinkers, but after success with their first wine, made at Plantagenet, they became 'hooked on what was in the bottle' and decided never to sell off their grapes again. Initially planted to riesling, cabernet sauvignon and malbec, the vineyards were quickly expanded. Alkoomi is now run by the third generation of the Lange family, Sandy and her husband Rob.
alkoomiwines.com.au

FRANKLAND ESTATE

In perhaps one of the most isolated wine regions in Australia, Barrie Smith and Judi Cullam began planting vines. Their farm had been used for sheep and wheat, but a trip to France piqued their interest in grape growing. A friend joked that they should call their vineyard Isolation Ridge, such was the remoteness of the property, and it stuck. Barrie had a little experience making wine, having grown up on a vineyard, but it was Judi whose belief in the concept of terroir led them to focus on using the varying soils to their advantage. Frankland Estate was founded by the pair in 1988. Riesling has been a big focus and strength for the estate, but the couple's time in Bordeaux also led them to plant the spread that makes up the Olmo's Reward blend, named after pioneering viticulturist Dr Harold Olmo. Frankland Estate is now run by the couple's children, Hunter and Elizabeth. The winery has been a constant standard bearer in the landscape of Great Southern, and their precise and expressive wines helped put the region on the map.
franklandestate.com.au

SWINNEY

George Swinney came to Western Australia and settled his family property called Franklands on the Frankland River in 1922. The farm

*Judi Cullam
Frankland Estate*

has been occupied by the Swinney family ever since. From a long history of farming, the family decided to diversify in the 90s and plant grapes, culminating in 240 hectares of renowned vineyards. Viticulture is managed by Rhys Thomas, and their grapes fill the bottles of 40 different producers, from the likes of everyone from Brave New Wine to Penfolds. Most of the plantings are dominated by cabernet sauvignon and shiraz, but quite unique are the plots of **untrellised** grenache, tempranillo and mourvèdre **bush vines**, a rarity in Great Southern. Swinney's own wine label is crafted by Rob Mann

---

 What we're drinking

It's non-negotiable that a visit to Great Southern includes a visit to Frankland Estate. Nestled among thatches of Australian bush and scree clinging onto brown dirt sits the wonderfully authentic and historical winery. Taste some of Australia's greatest riesling, now produced in a diversity of styles, marvel at medium weight, spicy, satiny textured reds, and have a cup of tea mid-morning with Judi Cullam. — Mike Bennie

Great Southern

443

What we're drinking

*Very rarely do wines come on the scene and immediately revolutionise what was thought possible of a region. The **Swinney** vineyard has proven itself a mainstay grower of Frankland River fruit, and now the wines produced under the label have become instant classics, recognised as not only some of the finest of the region, but some of the finest of Australia.* — **Jane Lopes**

(see Corymbia, p. 427), a sixth-generation Western Australian winemaker. Since joining the team in 2017, he has developed an outstanding range of sought-after releases and international acclaim. *swinney.com.au*

DENMARK

BRAVE NEW WINE

Brave New Wine are on the brave new frontier of Western Australian winemaking. Born out of boredom with the more traditional fare, Yoko Luscher-Mostert and Andries Mostert decided to make a couple of barrels of wine they'd like to drink. Now their tiny quantities sell out each year. Their wines have spunk and push boundaries, with room for an appreciation of technique and quality fruit. One of their favourites? The Dreamland riesling, wild-fermented in barrel with native botanicals. *bravenewwine.com.au*

LA VIOLETTA

The name La Violetta is derived from an old Piemontese song jubilating intoxication. Founder and winemaker AJ Hoadley made his way across Italy, Washington State and Australia before being drawn to Western Australia by the vast range of high-quality grapes grown. The first La Violetta wine, Das Sakrileg, was released in 2008, and each vintage has solidified the winery's reputation for its creative and well-made wines. Some wines are more serious, like the La Ciornia Shiraz, sourced from a few different Great Southern sites over the years. The Das Sakrileg riesling, on the other hand, is the playful antithesis to the linear and lithe rieslings of WA – wild barrel-fermented, matured on **lees**, blended with a splash of gewürztraminer and 'may undergo partial malolactic fermentation'. AJ gets his hands on top-quality fruit, from zibibbo to tempranillo, and tests the boundaries of what he can do with it. *laviolettawines.com.au*

SINGLEFILE WINES

During a family holiday, enjoying the vineyards of Europe, the idea for Singlefile was hatched. Geologists by trade, Phil and Viv Snowden sold their business, and together with their daughter and son-in-law went in search of the perfect patch of rock in a cool-climate region. They found it in Denmark's Scotsdale Valley. The block was planted to chardonnay, shiraz and merlot in the 1980s, but they have since pulled out the latter to focus on chardonnay and plant pinot noir. Singlefile is named after the geese who waddle single file across the vineyard at dusk. *singlefilewines.com*

AJ Hoadley
La Violetta

What we're drinking

*How could I not love a wine called Klusterphunk? 'Crunchy stalkiness bouncing off chardonnay curves, it's a bunch of good times in your glass' says **Brave New Wine** owner Yoko Luscher-Mostert. This wine is as delightful as the duo who dreamed it up. Warning ... it goes down easy.* — **Kavita Faiella**

PORONGURUP

CASTLE ROCK ESTATE

Angelo and Wendy Diletti acquired their 55-hectare property in the early 80s, with visions of planting premium **table wine** grapes. Riesling and cabernet sauvignon were first planted in 1983, followed a few years later by chardonnay and pinot noir. Winemaker Rob Diletti is well regarded in the commercial wine media for his work at the family estate. Of 370 tonnes of grapes crushed in the winery each year, only 70 is for Castle Rock wines. Rob makes wine for several other wineries in Great Southern, including Oranje Tractor and, before its sale in 2021, Duke's. *castlerockestate.com.au*

DUKE'S

Duke's began in 1999 as a retirement project for Duke and Hilde Ranson, with plantings of riesling, cabernet sauvignon and shiraz on the western side of the Porongurup range. Duke's became known for its Magpie Hill Reserve Riesling, which was named Wine of the Year at the 2019 Halliday Wine Companion Awards, for the 2017 vintage – a big deal for any wine, but for a white wine (and riesling, no less), unheard of. Now truly retiring, Duke and Hilde sold the winery to Ben Cane and Sarah Date in 2022. Ben has made wine for 25 years – in Victoria, Western Australia, Sonoma, Piedmont and Burgundy – and the two are bringing new energy to an already esteemed property. As Duke penned in his final newsletter, 'The vineyard carries on regardless with good weather from above. / But the wine that bears the label, will still be made with love.' *dukesvineyard.com*

LOWBOI

Lowboi is the side project of Guy Lyons, who is winemaker and general manager at Forest Hill in Mount Barker. Guy and his wife bought the Springviews vineyard in 2017. Chardonnay and riesling were planted on this site in 1985, sloping down the southern side of the ancient Porongurup Ranges. They also produce a pristine, spicy grüner veltliner sourced from the Lyons' family farm in Mount Barker. The Lowboi labels feature the work of Noongar artist Ms B. Kelly, who painted landscapes of Great Southern up until her death in 1994. *lowboiwines.com.au*

ALBANY

WIGNALLS WINES

Having sold his veterinarian practice in the early 80s, Dr Bill Wignall founded his winery with a vision many thought was unrealistic. He had studied the climate of Albany and believed it to have a similar summer ripening period to Burgundy, so he decided to plant pinot noir and chardonnay. He ordered some vines from Di Cullen in Margaret River and set about planting 4 hectares, a little over half of which was pinot. He ended up having to double his plantings to keep up with demand. Bill's son and daughter-in-law now run the winery and their range has extended to include some of the more traditional grapes for the area. *wignallswines.com.au*

And don't forget ...
Bunn, with Albany plantings dating back to the 90s, farms **biodynamically** and with no irrigation, releasing cabernet, shiraz and riesling to their loyal fans ... **Freehand**, Matt Eastwell's **lo-fi** Denmark winery, features zero-**sulphur** takes on a range of styles, from **pét-nat** to skin-contact, barrel-aged reds and **fortifieds** ... **Galafrey Wines**, one of the historic estates of Mount Barker, is now under the care of the second generation, who tend to the estate's 1978 plantings of cab, shiraz, merlot, cab franc and pinot noir ... **Oranje Tractor** is another Albany winery leading the environmentalism front, with organic vineyards and regenerative agriculture initiatives, releasing a range of fresh and vibrant wines ... **Trevelen Farm**, a hidden gem, has the northernmost vineyards in all of Great Southern (about 55 kilometres due north of the Mount Barker township), planted to riesling, sauvignon blanc, chardonnay, shiraz, cabernet sauvignon and merlot.

Other Regions of Western Australia

The story of Western Australia's wine industry – long before Margaret River and Great Southern had commercial plantings – begins in the Swan Valley, a region nestled in the eastern plains of the city of Perth. Swan Valley is a subregion GI of the Swan District region, which runs from Perth's southeast for 130 kilometres north to the Moore River National Park. Vineyards were first established in 1830 along the Swan River, just north of today's Perth Airport, at Olive Farm by Thomas Waters, an English botanist. For over 130 years, the Swan Valley was Western Australia's principal source of grapes.

The only other vineyard area in the Swan District, besides Swan Valley, is centred around the town of Gingin (where the chardonnay **clone** takes its name from), about 60 kilometres north of the Swan Valley. The greater area of Gingin sits in a coastal watershed of lakes, rivers and brooks abutting the Darling Scarp, making a variety of agriculture possible on the western edge of Australia's wheat belt.

The Swan Valley is largely defined by the Swan River, and its tributary the Avon River, both pathways for watershed descending from the Darling Scarp. Soils are alluvial mixes of sand and gravels, and drainage varies greatly. The best soils for the production of grapes sit along either side of the river, in the western corridor of the valley, hence the concentration of vines here. The other area highly regarded, according to fourth-generation WA winemaker Rob Mann, is the 'weathered, deep sandy gravel deposits immediately below the Darling Range on the eastern boundary of the Swan Valley'. The Darling Scarp defines these early growing regions east of Perth – an abrupt range that rises 15 kilometres east of Perth, and tops out at 1909 metres, running parallel to the nearby Darling Fault.

Fortified wines, like in many early wine-producing areas, were dominant in the Swan Valley. Verdelho was the key grape, still abundantly planted today. Chenin blanc, chardonnay, riesling, semillon and muscadelle – all present today, contributing to various sparkling, still and **fortified wines** – were once blended to create one of Australia's most celebrated early **table wines**: Houghton's White Burgundy, first produced by second-generation winemaker Jack Mann in the late 1930s.

Flash forward to today, Rob Mann – Jack Mann's grandson and a winemaker himself – and his wife Genevieve have worked in wineries all over the world, but still report favourably on the Swan Valley in this global context: 'The wines that were produced from the Swan Valley are some of the most exciting ones I reckon I've made in my life. I'm so super excited by them,' Rob says. With the correct heat-mitigation techniques in place (shade cloths, row orientation and **canopy management**), the Manns believe that the only thing holding the Swan Valley back from being recognised as a premium wine region is exposure.

Indeed, Swan Valley is enjoying a renaissance beyond the sound bites of its accessibility to Perth and its hot climate. As Australia's modern generation of winemakers and growers seek to reinterpret the nation's wealth of old vines, the Swan Valley has become WA's centre of this energy. Lithe, zippy, sea-breeze scented verdelho, vermentino and chenin blanc lead the pack for white grapes, along with increasingly vibrant interpretations of old-vine grenache, tempranillo, negramoll and tinta cão.

Discussions of viticulture in Western Australia are often confined to three regions: Swan District, Margaret River and Great Southern. The three account for 82% of plantings in the state and nearly 100% of premium wine production. But there are several other areas worth knowing (and also several without much to speak of).

There are three zones in the state that have no further regions defined, and are practically void of any sort of significant viticulture (and are full of overly verbose geographic descriptors!): Central Western Australia, Eastern Plains – Inland and North of Western Australia, and West Australian South East Coastal.

There are two other regions within the Greater Perth zone (along with Swan District) that deserve a mention. The Perth Hills GI stretches 100 kilometres from the Lower Chittering River Valley in the north to the Serpentine River in the south, sharing most of its western border with the inland boundary of Swan District. Over 100 hectares of vineyards are dotted along the west coast-facing slopes between 150 and 300 metres in elevation. Vineyards are at most 30 kilometres from the sea, and the hills collect and help dispense arriving precipitation.

Few producers have grown to any significant commercial scale in Perth Hills, but boutique artisans and growers continue to explore the dynamics of the region. Cooler sites offer delicate examples of chardonnay and sauvignon blanc, while warmer, lower-lying vineyards with a **heat summation index** similar to Portugal's Douro Valley are dedicated to cabernet sauvignon, merlot and shiraz.

South of the city of Perth, the Peel GI contains only 52 hectares of vineyards, stretching over 100 kilometres inland from the coast, and encompassing a broad area including the Dwellingup State Forest over the rise of the Darling Ranges. Wineries' production rarely

Swan Valley is currently enjoying a renaissance beyond the sound bites of its accessibility to Perth and its hot climate.

The Pinnacles Desert is a frequented stop while exploring the warm beaches of Western Australia, just a few hours drive north of Perth along the coast. Here, pink-hued sand is dotted with teardrop pillars of limestone.

The white sands of Yeagarup Beach, along the coast of the Pemberton GI.

extends beyond local consumption, and most focus on catering to wine tourism.

The remaining appellations in Western Australia fall in the South West Australia zone. Margaret River and Great Southern are two of the six regions in this zone.

Geographe GI connects Peel to Margaret River, stretching from the coast to the Darling Plateau and adjacent to a warm, shallow bay of the same name. Its 760 hectares of plantings are clustered in various valleys adjacent to state forests, and in the lowland areas between the Darling Scarp and the coast, from Bunbury to Busselton. The altitude of plantings range from 30 metres above sea level, near the seaside town of Capel, to 300 metres in elevation at the inland reaches of the GI.

Like many modern Australian vineyards, Geographe is home to a broad range of grapes, though you can see the influence from its northern neighbours (in the prominence of tempranillo, verdelho and **fortifieds**), and its southern neighbour (in the focus on cabernet sauvignon, usually with just a touch less structure than those from Margaret River).

The area between Geographe and Great Southern is lovingly known as the Southern Forests and Valleys Region. Twenty different national forests surround verdant valleys with a bounty of produce that includes some of Australia's top truffle terrain, and three wine appellations (north to south): Blackwood Valley, Manjimup and Pemberton (the latter two have banded together to form an official growers association called Southern Forests).

Blackwood Valley and Manjimup, with their continental climates and fertile soils, are less hospitable to fine wine and have few producers of note, though a number of individual vineyards have started to receive some attention from producers outside the region.

The southernmost, Pemberton, with its coastal influence, is the most developed of the three. The region was originally speculated for viticulture in the late 1970s, with its first commercial vineyard planted in 1982. Chardonnay is the most prolific grape across the region's 466 hectares of vineyards, with pinot noir, cabernet sauvignon, merlot, malbec and sauvignon blanc trailing behind. Annual rainfall is high, but less than 25% of it occurs during the growing season. Soils are lateritic gravel sands and loams mixed with a clay subsoil that provides moisture retention, along with the fertile red karri loams found throughout this region. The region's most notable producer, Picardy, was founded in 1993 by the Pannell family, who first put down roots at Moss Wood (p. 429) in Margaret River.

The sun rises above the Darling Scarp, illuminating Circosta vineyard, **bush-vine** grenache planted in the 1950s.

PRODUCERS

SWAN DISTRICT

CORYMBIA
(See Margaret River, p. 427)

HARRIS ORGANIC

Tassie-native Duncan Harris moved to Perth in 1993. While working as an engineer at an automotive research facility by day, Duncan pursued his dream of making wine on the side, buying his property in the Swan Valley in 1998. In 2001, he devoted himself to the winery fulltime. As the name implies, organic viticulture has always been important to Duncan, implemented for its beneficial effect on the environment as well as the wines; he achieved organic certification in 2006. The wines span a wide range, but Duncan has become particularly known for a few styles: a concentrated malbec made from a single row of vines; back-vintage releases of shiraz; a huge spread of **fortifieds**, including a sherry-style 'apera'; and organic brandy, gin and vodka.
harrisorganicwine.com.au

HOUGHTON WINES

Although of incredible historic importance to the region, Houghton has fully divested itself from the Swan Valley in recent years. In 2021, Accolade (who has owned Houghton since 1976, when the conglomerate was still Thomas Hardy & Sons) sold off the Swan Valley winery and land holdings to the Yukich family, who have rebranded them as Nikola Estate. The current Houghton brand focuses its premium wine offerings on fruit from Margaret River and Frankland River, while its affordable 'Stripe' range is Western Australia appellated. *houghton-wines.com.au*

JOHN KOSOVICH

Croatian immigrants the Kosovich brothers planted their first vines in 1922. Their inaugural wines were a sherry-style white and a 'claret'. Ivan Kosovich and his wife Ane ran the winery until 1952, when it was decided that their 15-year-old son, John, would leave school to become the winemaker. In the 1960s, John began making dry whites, adding riesling, chardonnay and verdelho to their plantings. An accident in 1998 meant John's son Arch was left to complete his first vintage alone, with assistance from his father over the phone. The winery was renamed John Kosovich Wines in 2003, in honour of John's 50th vintage.
johnkosovichwines.com.au

MANN

There are two grapes grown on the Mann property in Upper Swan: cabernet sauvignon and its Australian offshoot, cygne blanc. Dorham Mann, son of industry pioneer Jack Mann, assisted in the initial site selection to plant Margaret River's first vines. He went on to head up winemaking at Sandalford before returning to his family vineyard. In 1989, his wife, Sally, noticed a seedling growing next to the vineyard which had very similar leaves to cabernet sauvignon, except the fruit was white. Dorham continued to propagate the vine in secret until they were able to patent and name it a decade later. At Mann, they make tiny batches of **traditional method** sparkling from the two relative varieties, which is aged for two and a half years before release. Cygne blanc is not grown anywhere else in the world.

SANDALFORD

Sandalford's story spans all the way back to 1840, when John Septimus Roe was awarded land by Queen Victoria. Table grapes were first harvested in 1842 from their extensive vineyards, but experiments eventually led John and his family to planting wine grapes. The estate

What we're drinking

Though cool-climate viticulture is often celebrated, some of the most exciting wines are coming out of one of Australia's hottest regions (and you wouldn't know its heat by tasting them): fresh yet bold, Vino Volta's grenaches and chenin blancs are electric. — Jane Lopes

survived through World War II and thrived with the arrival of Italian and Croatian immigrants, who brought knowledge and new techniques to Sandalford. During the 60s and 70s, Dorham Mann, the son of WA wine industry pioneer Jack Mann, led the winemaking team, and encouraged the family to expand their estate into the Margaret River. They bought a property at Wilyabrup and planted vines in 1970. **sandalford.com**

SITTELLA

Beginning with verdelho, shiraz and chardonnay, Simon and Maaike Berns began planting Sittella on their weekends in 1993. Before the turn of the century, their hobby vineyard had become a thriving business with a winery, tasting room, cellar door and restaurant. Their vineyards have been expanded to include varieties, such as tempranillo and petit verdot, to suit hot, dry summers in the Swan Valley. Wines are also made from a small vineyard in Margaret River. **sittella.com.au**

SWAN VALLEY GARAGISTAS

A collective that bills itself as 'minimal intervention winemakers and artisans', Swan Valley Garagistas are a testament to the new energy and revitalisation in the region. The group includes six wineries: Chalari, Chouette, Local Weirdos, Ohkela, Swan Valley Wines and Yume. Their mission statement includes nurturing a sense of place, caring for the land, respecting Indigenous customs and traditions, encouraging creativity, and constantly learning, evolving and collaborating. The wines produced from the set include a wide range of unique styles, including a co-ferment of chenin blanc and tempranillo, passed over grenache skins; a low-ABV 'sticky' pedro ximénez; and **qvevri**-aged grenache paired next to skinsy semillon.

TALIJANCICH

Croatian immigrant Jim Talijancich and his wife Ljubica bought a Swan Valley vineyard and harvested their first vintage in 1932, making **fortified wine** from muscat and shiraz. When Jim unexpectedly died in 1945, his 13-year-old son Peter began working on the vineyard with his mother, keeping production alive for the next generation, James and Hilda Talijancich, to take over the winery in 1998. **Biodynamic** practices are now implemented in the vineyards, with the aim of producing vital and expressive wines: everything from long-aged **fortifieds**, harkening back to Jim's first vintage, as well as **table wines** made from verdelho, graciano and shiraz – all of which can be enjoyed in Talijancich's beautiful tasting room. **taliwine.com.au**

What we're drinking

Swan Valley Garagistas *is the shot in the arm that Swan Valley needed. The collective is set between Swan Valley locals and Perth folk, with a broad range of avant-garde wines, from ultra-successful through to 'work in progress', but with charisma and a derring-do that is unlocking parochial pride in the often-maligned region. The Swan Valley gained a boon with this younger generation hungry to reinvent the region through a similar lens to the Adelaide Hills' Basket Range revolutionaries.* — Mike Bennie

VINO VOLTA

Garth Cliff and Kristen McGann chose to focus on the stars of the Swan – chenin blanc and grenache – when they launched Vino Volta in 2019. They are self-confessed experimentalists, striving to make quaffable wines with complexity and character. With a collective 40 years' experience in the wine industry, Garth and Kristen select from some of the highest-quality old vines in the region. They make four kinds of chenin blanc, including one aged under a veil of flor yeast, and their grenache comes from 30- and 65-plus-year-old vineyards. The duo's style preserves the dignity of pristine old-vine fruit, but packages it for the modern palate. *vinovolta.com.au*

GEOGRAPHE

GREEN DOOR

Perched on the top of Darling Scarp, Green Door came to fruition when Ashley and Kath Keeffe rescued a rundown vineyard in 2006. Grenache and cabernet franc were found in excellent condition, and the plantings were expanded with tempranillo, monastrell (aka mourvèdre), fiano, shiraz and verdelho. Alongside contract winemaker, Vanessa Carson, Ashley uses a variety of winemaking techniques, including fermentation in clay amphora pots. *greendoorwines.com.au*

WILLOW BRIDGE

Willow Bridge is the result of Jeff and Vicki Dewar's investment in the viticultural potential of the Ferguson Valley, planting 60 hectares of vines in the region in 1997 and 1998. The estate is 25 kilometres from the coast, as the crow flies, and sees ripening times similar to the cooler southern portions of Margaret River. Plantings include WA classics like chardonnay, semillon, sauvignon blanc, shiraz, merlot and cabernet sauvignon, as well as small parcels of chenin blanc, viognier, tempranillo and grenache. The wines are affordable and expressive, making a case for more attention to be brought to this under-the-radar wine region. *willowbridge.com.au*

PEMBERTON

PICARDY

Inspired by some of the great wines of the world, Bill Pannell wanted to plant pinot noir in WA. He and his wife Sandra had started Moss Wood (p. 429) in the 1970s – **pruning**, picking and pressing everything by hand – so experience was never an issue. After selling Moss Wood to Keith Mugford, they settled on Pemberton as the place to plant pinot noir and chardonnay, being cooler and higher up than Margaret River. Bill and Sandra were part of a syndicate that bought into Domaine de la Pousse d'Or in the 1980s and accessed many of the best estates in Burgundy for the specific planting material they desired. Bill and Sandra's son Dan is an integral part of the modern Picardy estate, and their offering has expanded to feature Rhône and Bordeaux-style blends. *picardy.com.au*

MANJIMUP

LONELY SHORE

Liam and Holii Carmody established Lonely Shore in 2015, a love letter to pinot noir. Made at the Forest Hill winery (p. 442), where Liam is senior winemaker, they produce small batches of just one wine. The fruit comes from the DeiTos vineyard, an elevated, **dry-grown** site close to Manjimup. It is heady and expressive, awash with lean, savoury pinot fruit. *lonelyshore.com.au*

What we're drinking

Manjimup is a place of immense natural beauty: massive forests, the nearby sea, and black truffles. Lonely Shore's DeiTos Vineyard Pinot Noir seems to capture all of those things. The wine is savoury, crunchy and smoky overlaid with sour raspberry and dark cherry fruits. – Jonathan Ross

And don't forget …

Batista has almost zero internet presence, quietly growing and making some of Australia's most elusive and fine pinot noir from a tiny Manjimup plot … **Battles Wine** is new to the scene and making waves, taking out the gong for Wine Companion Shiraz of the Year with their Perth Hills 2020 Granitis, in addition to their compelling offerings from Great Southern and Margaret River … **Bellarmine Wines** was founded in Pemberton in 2000, with a special focus on riesling made in varying levels of sweetness by gun winemaker Di Miller … **Capel Vale** represents some of the earliest vines in Geographe, with plantings dating back to 1974 … **Fairbrossen** bottles estate-grown Perth Hills wines, with everything from fun-loving **pét-nats** to structured durif and **nouveau** tempranillo … **Ironcloud**, formerly Pepperilly Estate (and still with a label called Pepperilly), grows everything from chardonnay and cabernet to saperavi and touriga, high up in the hills of Geographe … **Mazza** is not only unique to Geographe, but unique in all of Australia, being only planted to Spanish and Portuguese red grapes … **Myattsfield** is pushing forward the case for **regionality** in Perth Hills, with their mature cab, merlot, petit verdot, shiraz and chardonnay vines from the distinct Bickley Valley … **Nikola Estate**, the modern incarnation of the historic Houghton's, purchased in 2019 by the Yukich family, with affordable and classic Swan Valley bottlings … **Olive Farm**, the oldest winery in Western Australia, established in 1829 (and run by the same family since 1933), known for a wide selection of polished wines, from flagship sparkling and cabernet, to quaffable rosé and chenin blanc … **Riverbank Estate**, with a vast spread of different grapes and styles, runs one of the most dynamic cellar doors in the region, offering a restaurant with local Swan specialties and consistent programming to engage visitors … **Swan Valley Wines**, established in 1983, marries tradition and modernism to great effect, preserving old vines and biodiversity and making wines with little intervention in a fresh, drinkable style … **Talisman**, planted in 1999 in the Ferguson Valley (Geographe GI) with the aim of selling off fruit, formed a boutique wine label in recent years with a focus on classic French grapes (plus some zinfandel!) … **Whicher Ridge** combines the talents of long-time winemaker Cathy Howard and viticulturist Neil Howard, who grow sauvignon blanc, viognier, petit verdot, malbec, mourvèdre and cabernet sauvignon at their Geographe vineyard.

QUEENSLAND

Queensland is Australia's second largest state, after Western Australia, occupying the northeast quadrant of the island continent. It is most well known for the Great Barrier Reef and the white sandy beaches of the Gold Coast, as well as tropical rainforests, bushlands, creeks, estuaries, 200 national parks, and nearly 2000 islands off its coast. Queensland is home to a wide array of native flora and fauna, and is a huge tourist destination for Australians and foreigners alike.

Wine seems an odd bedfellow for this landscape, and indeed it mostly is. The terrain that is occupied by vines in Queensland is a narrow band along the western slopes and tablelands of the Great Dividing Range, which provides moderation from the wet, tropical coastal climate and from the dry heat of the desert plains that quickly set in to the east. The Granite Belt hugs the New South Wales border (in fact, it is bordered fully on its east and south by the state) and is much smaller in total size (though larger in total plantings) than Queensland's other GI South Burnett: 1170 square kilometres, compared to the latter's 8340.

South Burnett is a four-hour drive due north of the Granite Belt, directly inland from the coastal town Noosa (known for its great spanner crab). Despite its nearly eight-fold size, only 204 hectares are under vine in South Burnett, compared to 305 in the Granite Belt. Those plantings don't seem large, though in the context of Australian wine regions, they're not skeletal either. Granite Belt is a more densely planted area than many more famous appellations of Australia – like Geelong, Hunter Valley and the Macedon Ranges. And even though South Burnett has planted just 0.02% of its allocated land to the vine, it has a greater density and volume of plantings than both Gippsland and Henty.

South Burnett is on the traditional lands of the Waka Waka Nation. Their lands sit behind the coastal range to the west and along the Burnett River and its tributaries. The Bunya Mountains, at the southern end of the GI, are home to one of the largest gathering sites of Aboriginal people. The bunya pine tree is the world's largest, and both the nut and the tree are considered sacred. First Nations from across today's southern Queensland and New South Wales would meet in these forests for the bunya nut harvest, a tradition that has been going on for thousands of years.

In Lake Barambah, where the eastern shore is populated by many of South Burnett's vineyards today, freshwater eel was plentiful: not only central to the Waka Waka diet, but was (and is) one of the totems of Waka Waka culture. The way the mother eel (Aboriginal culture is a matriarchy, not a patriarchy) spread her eggs along the numerous rivers and creeks is a part of their Dreaming, the spiritual story of how they came to that place: a story that teaches a belonging to and connection

Girraween National Park sits on the outskirts of the Granite Belt GI, southeast of the town of Ballandean. It marks the edge of the granite plateau that rises amid the tablelands of the Great Dividing Range, seen here. Girraween means 'place of flowers' in Dharug, the traditional language of numerous First Nations throughout northern New South Wales and southern Queensland.

to place, and therefore also teaches about the responsibility to care for it.

The Granite Belt GI – formed in the western tablelands of the Great Dividing Range – is the natural transition from Bundjalung Country to Ngarabal and Kambuwal Country. The Kambuwal people neighbour the Waka Waka to the north and the Ngarabal to the south.

Kambuwal and Ngarabal people are known for their impressive ability to adapt to the highland climate's massive temperature swings. They outfitted themselves with possum fur, but also fished warm weather inland fish and cared for lands that enjoyed tropical sun. Further insight into the Kambuwal Nation, whose Country the Granite Belt mostly occupies, can be gleaned from their neighbouring nation to the west, Bigambul. The Bigambul people have an established Native Title Aboriginal Corporation, and in their work to share and continue their culture and history, they also acknowledge that their neighbours, the Kambuwal, would have had similar interests, Dreamtime stories, cultural practices and traditions applied to Country. Adapting to the place, rather than adapting the place to their needs, is core to the Aboriginal Australian psyche – and, increasingly, the outlook of the wine-grower in Queensland.

In terms of premium wine potential, Granite Belt has the upper hand. South Burnett is hot, classified in the top (hottest) tier of the **Winkler Scale**, though in 2020 it exceeded the scale's maximum of 2700°C days – clocking in at a scorching 2894. The growing conditions create a tough enterprise for fine wine, but produce reliable bottlings to satisfy local demand and have even helped generate a popular tourism scene, with local art galleries, natural attractions and artisan food purveyors.

Granite Belt is higher in elevation and cooler than South Burnett, and has proven itself capable of producing excellent (and often quite interesting) wine. The scene is bustling, with over 60 producers today: the area is one to watch in the Australian wine industry. Although its location in Queensland has not advertised it as a serious wine region, the Granite Belt is producing wine that says otherwise: wine that recognises where it's from, and works with the conditions, not against them.

Queensland Geographical Indications

REGION
Granite Belt
South Burnett

Queensland Viticultural Footprint

	GRANITE BELT	SOUTH BURNETT
Total delimited area (km²)	1170	8274
Total planted area (hectares)	305	204
% of delimited area planted	0.260%	0.025%
Total elevation range	604–1298 masl	169–1141 masl
Elevation range of plantings	700–1050 masl	300–500 masl
Number of producers	32	9

Granite Belt Climate Data (°C)

	1960–1990	1991–PRESENT	2020
Heat summation/GDD	● 1747	● 1844	● 2067
Annual rain/GSR	829/578	733/535	552/457
Warmest month avg. temp.	20.7	21.4	23.5

South Burnett Climate Data (°C)

	1960–1990	1991–PRESENT	2020
Heat summation/GDD	● 2564	● 2632	● 2894
Annual rain/GSR	747/555	689/527	456/413
Warmest month avg. temp.	24.3	24.8	26.7

Winkler Scale:

● 850–1111   ● 1112–1389   ● 1390–1667   ● 1668–1944   ● 1945–2222   ● 2223–2700   ● >2700

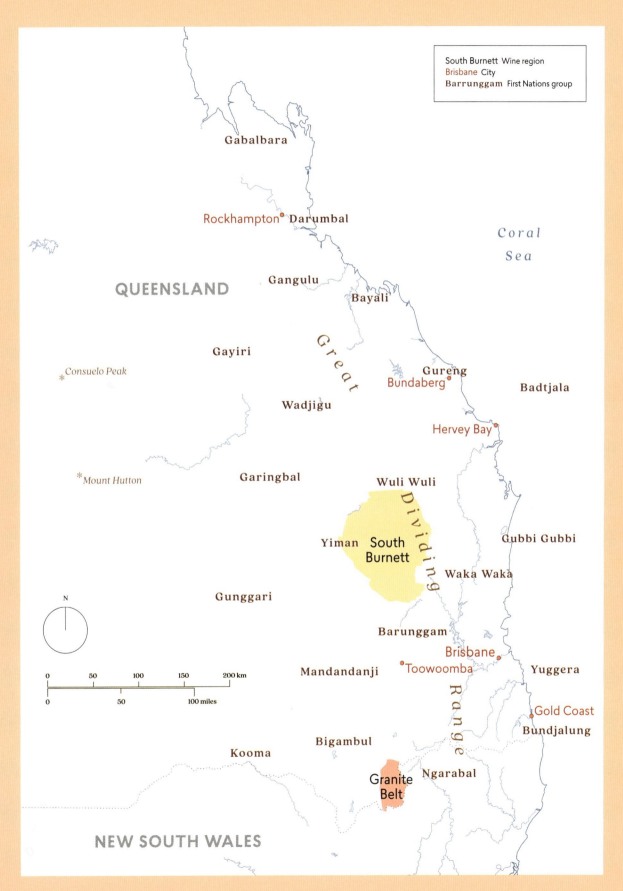

Evolution of Wine

The first grapevine in Queensland was said to be planted in 1859 – a 'White Syrian' grape (most likely muscat) in the Granite Belt. Like states to its south, Queensland had its 'rush' in the late 19th century, but it was tin, not gold, that the miners were looking for. Tin mining brought people and commerce to the area.

It was local parish priest Father Geronimo Davadi who encouraged the tin miners to diversify their industries, projecting the impending economic collapse when the region ran out of tin. Davadi was from the Marche region of Italy, and had already established his own vineyard and nursery, the cuttings from which he offered to locals wanting to plant vines. South Burnett also saw its first vineyards in the late 19th century, with the great-grandfather of Sue Crane (Crane's Winery) planting shiraz in 1898.

Despite these early plantings, the regions remained quiet, though not dormant, for the first half of the 20th century. After each world war, Italian immigrants flocked to Australia, with many ending up in the Granite Belt. Table grapes and stone fruit orchards formed a big industry in these early days; some modern wineries can even trace their origins to these vineyards and orchards planted pre-World War II, like Bungawarra, Ballandean Estate and Rumbalara.

For the Granite Belt, the modern winemaking era began in the mid-1960s when the Ricca family planted the first shiraz vines in the southern end of the region. The Granite Belt was at the early end of the **table wine** revolution in Australia – at this point, only a handful of wine regions were actively planting again, after a harrowing first half of the century for wine.

And the Granite Belt expanded fast, with a handful of other vineyards and wineries being established in the 1960s and 1970s: Biltmore Cellars, Angelo's, Robinson Family Vineyards, Rumbalara and Bungawarra.

In 1970, Dr Bryce Rankine, the principal research scientist for the **AWRI** (Australian Wine Research Institute), visited the Granite Belt. He educated the region on modern technology and encouraged the local winemakers to import new vine material; in 1974 over 140,000 cuttings from more than 25 different grape cultivars and **clones** were brought into Queensland.

South Burnett had a later resurgence, with the first modern commercial production beginning in 1993. In 1997, Clovely Estate was established, which has gone on to be the largest and best-known producer in South Burnett – its wines (**traditional method** blanc de blancs, semillon, barbera and shiraz) being some of the few made in the region that are sold beyond its borders. The South Burnett tourism association lists only nine wineries on its website today.

The energy in the Granite Belt comes from a much greater number of producers. Still, few of them are making entries in the premium wine sector, and even fewer have generated buzz or listings outside of Queensland. But that all seems ready to change. The Granite Belt's biggest disadvantage is its association with hot, tropical Queensland, which has led many to overlook this promising region. But the region's best producers – Ballandean Estate, Bent Road/ La Petite Mort, Golden Grove, Ridgemill and more – are not taking no for an answer, crafting wines that are demanding consideration.

Lay of the Land

The Granite Belt is a plateau created by the Great Dividing Range and the result of a single mass of molten rock that rose to the surface some 240 million years ago, during the Triassic Period. The formation is unique in that, as it slowly reached the surface, pressure did not build causing a violent extrusion, and the magma cooled slowly as it ascended through the earth's crust. The slow cooling resulted in the minerals feldspar, quartz and mica crystallising in an abnormally large fashion. The remaining crust above (about 3 kilometres thick), and portions of the granite itself, have been eroding away for hundreds of millions of years, displacing large volumes of granitic sandy loams – the resulting soils house all the region's vines.

Bent Road farm, winery, and distillery is the Granite Belt's wide-open creative space materialised. Here, proprietors Andrew Scott and Glen Robert peer into one of their 14 imported Georgian **qvevri**, buried clay vessels used to age their La Petite Mort wines.

Granite, as the name implies, is the feature of the region. But it's not just granite soils, says La Petite Mort's Glen Robert: 'there are granite boulders, formations, cliffs and quarries' that define the landscape.

Vineyards are centred through the lowest-lying land, which follows the Severn River and its many tributaries. The greatest confluence in the GI happens at Ballandean, which also happens to be the GI's most densely planted area. Plantings range from just over 700 metres to over 1000 metres above sea level, though vineyards mainly sit between 750 and 900 metres in elevation. The inland altitude provides extreme **diurnal swings**, sometimes varying up to 28°C between day and night in the summer, and even more in the spring and autumn months. While in the summer and autumn this swing is celebrated for retaining freshness and acidity in fruit, it poses some serious frost risk well into spring. Granite, luckily, is known for the ability to retain its temperature, radiating heat well into the evening's chill. (Granite is actually so reflective, that the area is known to experience higher than normal rates of skin cancer.)

While the Granite Belt is often referred to as a cool climate (probably to distinguish it from the perception of Queensland), that is only true when relating its climate to its distance from the equator (the same latitude as Miami, Florida). It is firmly at the top end of Region 3 on the **Winkler Scale**, and sometimes performs like a Region 4 in dry, hot years when the **El Niño** weather pattern occurs.

Most of its rainfall occurs during the growing season and in the form of summer storms. The rain can result in severe hail and/or disrupt important phases in the life cycle of the vine, but it can also be welcomed to mitigate heat stress. Most vineyards are set up with drip irrigation lines, though they are not used in all years. Those in pursuit of quality will not irrigate unless heat stress is an issue. Finding the deepest soils for planting is key to ensuring there is enough available water for the vine throughout the year: 'If you can find a patch of soil with no rock in it,' says Golden Grove's Ray Costanzo, 'you're doing very well ... we lost about 15% of our vineyard to drought just recently, and the ones that died were on those shallower soils.'

Those in the Granite Belt have drawn parallels between it and France's Rhône Valley, in terms of soil and climate. The Granite Belt's granite has greater purity and is closer to the surface, though with greater unpredictability than the Rhône, and with depth of soil having no corollaries to elevation or proximity to the river. And the Granite Belt is much warmer and sunnier than the Rhône Valley. However, the nights are cooler and windier,

The Granite Belt hosts a 'Strange Bird' wine trail (in addition to a more conventional one) that showcases the unique offerings of the region.

Granite Belt

HOW TO READ THIS MAP

Elevation is the Granite Belt's calling card – and what enables it to be suitable for viticulture. Shown here, the elevation of the Granite Belt breaches 1200 metres and provides an extreme **diurnal temperature swing** throughout the year.

1	Balancing Heart	12	Mason Wines
2	Ballandean Estate	13	Mountview
3	Bent Road/La Petite Mort	14	Pyramids Road
4	Boireann Winery	15	Ravenscroft Vineyard
5	Bungawarra	16	Ridgemill Estate
6	Girraween Estate	17	Robert Channon Wines
7	Golden Grove Estate	18	Rumbalara Estate
8	Granite Ridge	19	Savina Lane
9	Jester Hill Wines	20	Summit Estate
10	Just Red	21	Symphony Hill
11	Kominos	22	Tobin Wines

and the vines are under greater stress (a good thing) in the Granite Belt. So, while the comparison might not be all that apt, it doesn't shake out too far in the negative for the Granite Belt. Sixty per cent of the Granite Belt's vineyard surface is dedicated to mainstream grapes like shiraz, cabernet sauvignon, merlot and chardonnay. However, there are over 50 different grapes planted in the region, with notable expressions of fiano, gewürztraminer, muscat, marsanne, roussanne and viognier for whites, and saperavi, tempranillo, nebbiolo, tannat, mourvèdre and graciano for reds. The Granite Belt hosts a 'Strange Bird' wine trail (in addition to a more conventional one) that showcases the unique offerings of the region.

South Burnett's demarcated area ranges from 169 metres in elevation to 1141 metres, though plantings don't top 500 metres. Its latitude is 26 degrees south – the same (in the Northern Hemisphere) as Egypt's Al Farafra Desert, or the Bahamas. Vineyards are concentrated on the eastern edge of the appellation, along the many creeks and tributaries of Lake Barambah. There are a few large contiguous properties planted here. They are the lowest in elevation in the region, sitting between 300 and 320 metres above sea level. The lake is at the bottom of the Wondai State Forest to its southwest. A few other vineyards are scattered south, but remain on the eastern side of the appellation, following along the winding creeks that flow into Lake Barambah downstream. Nothing is planted in the western half of the appellation.

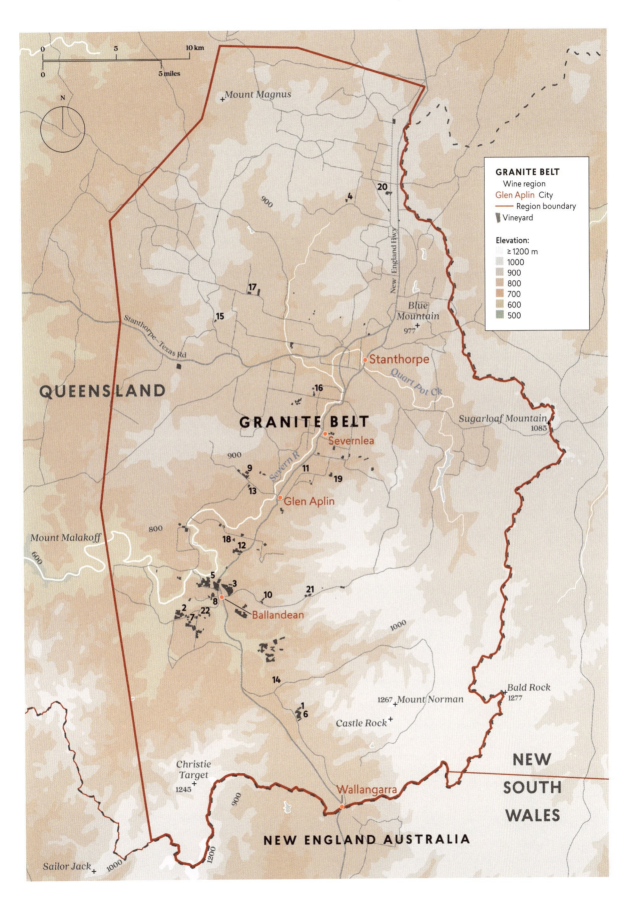

Hubbub

'I dislike the term "Queensland wine",' says Ray Costanzo, a third-generation winemaker in the Granite Belt. 'People associate Queensland with pineapples and sunshine ... But Granite Belt has its own reputation.'

Granite Belt is certainly the area of the most vinous accomplishment and potential in the state. Its reputation is growing (albeit slowly) in national and international acclaim. Within Queensland, many have discovered the wines of the Granite Belt – and it isn't state loyalty that's drawing locals to these wines. In fact, many Queenslanders had previously overlooked the wines and cellar doors of the Granite Belt, opting instead for interstate and international travel. But the COVID 19 pandemic has changed that.

Due to strict biosecurity measures, Queenslanders stayed largely uninfected throughout the pandemic – a goal realised, in part, through the freezing of interstate travel. So holidays previously spent in Victorian and South Australian wine country were rerouted to Queensland's own wine regions, with the effect being a much greater appreciation for the quality and beauty of the Granite Belt. 'They came here,' Costanzo says, describing the pandemic-related influx of Queensland visitors, 'discovered us, and have absolutely fallen in love with the place. And they've come back again. They say, "We should have come here years ago".'

A small-but-loyal sect of Brisbane sommeliers have long supported the wines of the region, and now with consumer demand as well, the capital city has become a hotspot for the wines of Granite Belt. The wines are starting to be

The Show System

Show-judging wines is an integral part of wine culture in Australia. Many of the country's great winemakers are closely involved in the show system, and the process provides an opportunity for networking, benchmarking and a little bit of good old-fashioned, spirited competition. The types of wine shows run from major national endeavours that judge wines from all over the country to microregional ones that focus on a specific GI or style, but the rules are largely the same: wines are tasted partially blind, with only the grape, vintage, and occasionally region known; judges are often winemakers, but also writers, retailers, sommeliers and other wine professionals; they work in small groups to go through hundreds of wines per day, elevating stand-outs to be considered for medals at the end. The results are often lauded: winning wines sell out quickly, bottles trumpet their awards with gold, silver and bronze stickers, and news passes swiftly through the ranks of the industry (and consumers) about which are the must-try wines of the year.

appreciated beyond the boundaries of Queensland as well, with sommeliers and consumers alike in Sydney and Melbourne slowly getting on board with Granite Belt wine. In fact, the response has been so dramatic (coupled with low yields due to drought and bushfire) that many producers are short on Granite Belt fruit. A look at the current releases from a range of producers showcases how purchased Riverland and Murray Darling fruit is a major component of the region's post-pandemic bottlings. Though this foreign produce has helped wineries maintain a steady offering, it does nothing to bolster regional identity, which is still in its formative era.

The Granite Belt has something going for it that few other quality regions do in Australia (or, really, in the world): its relative obscurity means that there are no expectations or identity to live up to. 'There are no rules,' says Glen Robert. 'We are able to define ourselves.'

This has resulted in many of the region's wineries embracing more uncommon grapes – though this wasn't always the case in Granite Belt. Costanzo's father Sam planted many of the region's first alternative grape varieties and, at the time, received flak for it. Ray recounts, 'people were saying, "How are you going to sell tempranillo, when it's really hard to sell cabernet and shiraz?" But he took a risk, did his research, and he planted the right varieties. And it took off.'

Especially with the ever-changing climate of Australia, the winemakers of Granite Belt are being embraced as prescient. Their experimentation with drought-resistant grapes is echoed across Australia now. And their identity as outsiders in the Australian wine industry has provided them the ultimate dexterity to accurately match grape variety to site.

Tempranillo is being touted as the signature grape of Granite Belt, with both Golden Grove and La Petite Mort putting it forward as one of the varieties best suited for the region. 'When you think of tempranillo in Australia, there are no specific GIs that come to mind,' says La Petite Mort's Andrew Scott. 'So I think we have an exciting opportunity to claim the variety as our own.' The high elevation, continental climate and riverside vineyards are in line with what tempranillo is traditionally grown in. And, while granite isn't necessarily the classic soil type for the grape, the combination of sandy loams and harder rock most certainly is.

Though tempranillo is the front runner, the wider Granite Belt seems unwilling to hinge its identity to a single grape. At least not yet. Aglianico, barbera, durif, fiano, malbec, marsanne, nebbiolo, nero d'Avola, tinta barroca, vermentino and viognier all find a place next to more common grapes, such as cabernet sauvignon, chardonnay, merlot, muscat, sauvignon blanc and shiraz. And though this diversity may make the Granite Belt a bit harder to pin down – a bit harder to assign a neat brand to – it certainly makes it one of the most dynamic wine regions in Australia. And, one of the best positioned to evolve and adapt to an uncertain climatic future.

PRODUCERS

BALANCING HEART

Balancing Heart was originally called 'Balancing Rock', purchased by entrepreneur Greg Kentish and renamed in 2020 – both names referencing a precariously balanced granite boulder in the vineyard, which does indeed resemble a heart (the shape more so than the organ). Under the new ownership, there is a renewed interest in hospitality, with luxe cellar door offerings, live music and onsite accommodation at the 'campfire cottage'. Wines include classic and lifted versions of chardonnay, petit verdot, pinot gris, shiraz, verdelho and viognier.
balancingheart.com.au

BALLANDEAN ESTATE

In 1968, Angelo Puglisi planted his first block of shiraz, cementing his identity as the father of Queensland wine. The Puglisi family, now in its second generation running Ballandean Estate, continues to steer the direction of Granite Belt wine. A wide range of wine offerings includes shiraz (the 1968 vines still in production), fiano, nebbiolo, durif, muscat, saperavi and cabernet sauvignon.
ballandeanestate.com

BENT ROAD/LA PETITE MORT

Bent Road and La Petite Mort are two wine labels released by the same four guys: Glen Robert, former scientist and head winemaker/co-owner; Robert Richter, co-owner and viticulturist; Andrew Scott, assistant winemaker and the mind behind La Petite Mort; and horticulturist Andrew Price. They maintain an organic farm at nearly 1000 metres above sea level in the Granite Belt, and purchase fruit from select vineyards in New South Wales and South Australia. Bent Road is the name of the vineyard, and its corresponding wine label came first, offering more classically styled wines. La Petite Mort is their chance to do something 'a little left of centre' – namely, extended skin-contact reds and whites aged exclusively in **qvevri** (clay pots buried underground).
bentroadwine.com.au
lapetitemort.com.au

> **What we're drinking**
>
> If you want to meet **Granite Belt's** biggest cheerleader, then Peter McGlashan is your advocate. McGlashan is an excellent winemaker, firstly, but a strident preacher for the region, delivering detail on weather, soils, varieties and styles, while investing heavily in community action to bring more collegiate broadcast to and from the area. An excellent human, undervalued by and large. The wines are increasingly excellent from **Ridgemill Estate**, elegant chardonnay and spicy, medium-weight shiraz (dare we say syrah?) a forte, while a variety of **nouveau**, skin-fermented and other experimental styles bolster the offering. — *Mike Bennie*

> **What we're drinking**
>
> Could this be Australia's best saperavi? Granted, there aren't a lot to compete with, regardless of popularity. The crew at **Ballandean Estate** nail this wine year after year. The tannin structure is bang on and it is delicious. Perhaps Queenslanders should be planting more of this Georgian grape.
> — *Kavita Faiella*

Ray Costanzo, Golden Grove Estate

to their range of small-batch wines, Ravenscroft also puts out a popular cider made from local Stanthorpe apples. *ravenscroftvineyard.com*

RIDGEMILL ESTATE

Ridgemill Estate was first planted in 1998 by Spanish couple Tom and Cath Jimenez, originally dubbed Emerald Hill. In 2004, Brisbane project manager Martin Cooper purchased the property, continuing the Jimenez's legacy of planting alternative grape varieties – the estate is home to Granite Belt's oldest tempranillo and saperavi vines. Cooper and wife Michelle Feenan have turned the winery into a tourism destination, with a welcoming cellar door and luxury cabins abutting the vines. *ridgemillestate.com*

GOLDEN GROVE ESTATE

Now in the hands of third-generation Ray Costanzo, Golden Grove helped pioneer alternative grape varieties in Granite Belt. Ray's father, Sam, was told to focus on wines made with classic French grapes, which were hard enough to sell in Queensland. But Sam persisted in planting grapes as diverse as vermentino, barbera, tempranillo and sagrantino – a legacy his son continues, and a legacy that has defined the modern Granite Belt era. *goldengroveestate.com.au*

JESTER HILL WINES

Owned by Michael and Ann Bourke, the Jester Hill site dates back to 1993, and is home to a wide range of grapes, including cabernet sauvignon, chardonnay, merlot, petit verdot, roussanne, sauvignon blanc and shiraz. The winery was so-named to capture the mirth, hospitality and history inherent in the role of the jester. The on-theme wine names – Touchstone, Trinculo (both Shakespearean fools), Muckle John, Roland le Fartere (real-life court jesters) – can belie the serious nature of the juice in the bottle, which often aptly captures what the Granite Belt climate is capable of. *jesterhillwines.com.au*

RAVENSCROFT VINEYARD

In 2002 Mark Ravenscroft purchased his 26-hectare property, sitting at 950 metres above sea level. The first vines were planted in 2005, with additions in the following 15 years, among them verdelho, pinotage, pinot gris and albariño. In 2021, the vineyard and winery were purchased by Caitlin and Nick Roberts, with Mark remaining on as 'principal winemaker and mentor'. In addition

ROBERT CHANNON WINES

Robert Channon and his wife Peggy planted in Stanthorpe in 1998. A happy accident put verdelho in their hands (the nursery ran out of the chardonnay they had ordered), which has become one of their most important grapes. James Halliday called Channon 'arguably Australia's foremost producer of verdelho', and one of the winery's bottlings of the grape was served to Queen Elizabeth II on one of her visits to Brisbane. In addition to verdelho, the vineyard is now planted to cabernet sauvignon, chardonnay, pinot gris, pinot noir and shiraz across 20 hectares. *robertchannonwines.com.au*

 New Guard   Environmental Hero   Rising Star   Legend   Regional Stalwart   Must Visit   Cult Following Historic Estate

467

And don't forget ...

4382 Terroir is a collaboration between Rob Davidson (owner of Ballandean's St Judes Cellar Door & Bistro) and consultant winemaker Andy Williams, currently working with Riverland fruit until Rob's new Granite Belt plantings come of age ... **Clovely Estate** represents the best of South Burnett, with food-friendly wines and warm hospitality ... **Heritage Estate** boasts two vineyards of differing altitudes and soil profiles, one at Cottonvale and one at Ballandean, to encapsulate the scope of expressions possible from the Granite Belt ... **Settlers Rise** offers a concise and affordable range, made by **Master of Wine** Peter Scudamore-Smith ... **Symphony Hill**, from three generations of the Macpherson family, produces Granite Belt wines that have impressed for decades ... **Terra di Granito**, a study in granite soils from industry veteran Peter Wise, has a narrow focus (by Granite Belt standards) of riesling, chardonnay, shiraz and cabernet ... **Tobin Wines**, custodian to the Granite Belt's oldest vines (planted in the 60s), is known in particular for polished semillon, merlot and shiraz ... **View Wine** is the house label of Sancerre Estate, a bed and breakfast accommodation in Ballandean, making classics alongside more unusual grapes like gros manseng and alvarinho ... **Witches Falls**, perched on Mt Tamborine, makes wine from a wide range of grapes, including some niche fan favourites like aglianico and tinta barroca, all served on their beautiful grounds.

Conclusion

If you've made it this far, we hope you're walking away with a new-found appreciation for Australian wine, in all its diversity, complexity, nuance and glory. There is nothing that Australia can't do, wine-wise, and its landscape of plantings and bottlings is constantly evolving.

There will surely be cause for a second edition of this book (and third, fourth, fifth ...) in the decades to come, as Australia realises even more of its potential and adapts to meet the changing demands of its climate. We welcome feedback with open arms, and hope that it will be offered with the same attitude we've worked under for this book: with a genuine love for Australian wine and a desire to make it more widely consumed and appreciated on the world stage.

If nothing else, we hope you carry the following ideas with you when thinking about Australian wine:

1. Australia is a widely diverse and high-quality wine-growing nation, worthy of every bit of scholarship, regional distinction and premium price-points bestowed upon the great wine regions of the world.

2. Just like anywhere else you spend money, the wine you buy enables certain businesses to thrive and certain businesses to falter. We urge you to be conscious of the regions, retailers and wineries you're supporting and to purchase wine that aligns with your values.

3. Whenever the time comes for you to part with this book, we hope you keep its pages out of landfill. Donation, libraries, used-book shops and recycling are all viable options.

Thanks for your curiosity about Australian wine. We wish you many good bottles and good times.

Cheers,
Jane & Jonathan

Thanks

A book of this magnitude takes a true community to create.

First, to Jane Willson, without whom this book would not have happened (for so many reasons). Your belief in us, your wisdom, your expertise and your friendship have been the guiding light in this book. We are forever grateful.

Kavita Faiella, our original collaborator: thank you for sticking with us through a pandemic and the birth of Kiaan. Your insight and calm demeanour have helped steer the ship more than you know.

Our eternal gratitude goes to Martin von Wyss, whose gorgeous and rigorously researched maps have set the tone for this book from day one. Thank you for inspiring us to live up to your work.

To Mike Bennie, thank you for joining the team and bringing a renewed sense of energy and passion for Australian wine. We are honoured that you believe in this project and have graced its pages with your beautiful words. Our editor, Dom Sweeney, thank you for finding the perfect balance of respecting our text and guiding it in the right direction. You've been the rock of this editorial process. Hannah Day, a shining light in the Australian wine industry, thank you for coming in at a clutch time and shouldering some of the workload. And Robin Cowcher, it's always a pleasure working with you. Your illustrations have humanised Australian wine and brought its great personalities to life.

We've been truly impressed by the professionalism, talent and enthusiasm of the whole team at Murdoch Books. Justin Wolfers, you brought a great sense of security to the project; we have always felt the manuscript was very safe in your thoughtful and thorough hands. Megan Pigott, your passion is contagious. We knew from the first time meeting you that you understood the vision and knew how to visually express it. Ariana Klepac, thank you for stewarding the later stages of the edit with your careful eye and immense flexibility. And to our designer, Jacqui Porter (of Northwood Green), thank you for your gorgeous concept and meticulous execution. We know it was a bit of a beast!

Lily Cummins, we have long admired your work on the labels of Rasa, and are grateful that you came on board for this book for the beautiful cover and chapter illustrations. We adore the way you have captured the feel of Australia in a surprising, striking and delightful way.

We will always be grateful to our families for their tireless support of us. We also want to thank each other; somehow our marriage and business not only survived this process, but thrived.

And finally, a big thank you to AUSTRALIA! To all the winemakers, viticulturists and sommeliers who donated their time and expertise to help us write this book — thank you! And to every Australian person and place affiliated with wine, thank you for creating an industry that demands a book like this. You constantly inspire us. And we are grateful that you have opened your doors to us. Australia is one of the world's great wine-producing countries, but it's the wine industry's hospitality — to its consumers, suppliers, sellers, writers and each other — that is unparalleled.

Thank you,
Jane & Jonathan

Glossary

Aspect – The way a vineyard is facing. A northerly aspect means a vineyard faces north.

AWRI – The Australian Wine Research Institute. The Australian grape and wine industry's own research organisation, supporting grape-growers and winemakers through scholarship and education.

Barrique – A small barrel, approximately 225 litres in size. New barriques are often used to age some of the most oak-influenced wine in the world, including Burgundy, Bordeaux and Napa cabernet sauvignon.

Biodynamics – A branch of viticulture based on the teachings of Rudolf Steiner. Biodynamics focuses on creating an enclosed ecosystem within a vineyard, using natural preparations to treat it, and timing actions with lunar cycles. Biodynamics is considered a sustainable viticultural solution and one that generally results in an excellent quality of grapes.

Bush vines – Vines that are trained to be free-standing, with no **trellising** system; also known as head training or gobelet training. Some grape varieties have an affinity for this type of training, including gamay, zinfandel and – most notably in Australia – grenache.

Canopy / Canopy management – The canopy describes the leaves and foliage of a grapevine. Canopy management is an integral part of viticulture, as it can help manage sun exposure, moisture accumulation, fruit ripeness and disease control.

Carbonic maceration – A winemaking technique primarily for red wines, whereby grape juice is encouraged to begin fermenting inside the skin of the grape (sometimes naturally, by not crushing the grapes, and sometimes through the addition of CO_2 and sealing of the fermentation vessel). This process can result in lower tannins, brighter colour and primary fruit notes. Additionally, sometimes either a pickled quality or a 'pear drop' aroma is described from wines with a heavy amount of carbonic maceration.

Charmat method – A method of sparkling wine production whereby secondary fermentation occurs in a large pressurised tank, allowing for less **lees**-derived influence than traditional, Champagne-method sparkling wine. This is the classic method used to make the fruity, primary sparkling wines of Prosecco in Italy.

Clones / Clonal selection / Clonal deviation – Grapes have evolved and mutated over the years, creating multiple (sometimes dozens) of clones of the same grape. Clonal selection describes the act of choosing clones to propagate in a vineyard (usually from a nursery). The opposing method is called selection massale, under which a random assortment of clones is selected from a vineyard site, allowing for clonal diversity to thrive, instead of selecting for a specific clone.

Close-planting – See Planting density.

CSIRO – The Commonwealth Scientific and Industrial Research Organisation, an Australian governmental agency responsible for the country's scientific research, with main offices in Canberra.

Diurnal shift / Diurnal swing – The temperature difference between night-time and daytime temperatures.

Dry-farmed – A vineyard that is not farmed with the use of irrigation. In the larger agricultural sense, dry-farming generally refers to areas with little rainfall, which rely on drought-resistant crops and moisture-conserving methods to operate in low-water settings. However, in the wine world, it is largely taken to mean any vineyard that does not require supplemental irrigation.

El Niño – A climate pattern in the Pacific Ocean (along with **La Niña**) that can have a significant impact on weather worldwide. The two are perhaps the strongest of any influence on climate variability in Australia. In El Niño cycles, surface water temperatures become warmer, which can result in Australian vintages of reduced rainfall, warmer temperatures, increased frost risk and greater bushfire likelihood (as in 2002–2003, 2006–2007, 2009–2010 and 2015–2016).

Fortified wine – Describes wine that has been 'fortified' with distilled spirit, either before, during or after fermentation. The result is most often a sweet wine that is higher in alcohol, famously port, sherry and Madeira.

Garrigue – A French term describing the native vegetation on the Mediterranean coast, most often used as a wine descriptor to characterise aromas of mixed Provençal herbs, such as juniper, lavender, rosemary, sage and thyme.

GSM – The classic Aussie blend of grenache, shiraz and mourvèdre, patterned from blends originally found in France's Southern Rhône of those three grapes and others.

Heat Summation Index – A way of categorising wine climates, originally created at the University of California, Davis. Also referred to as the **Winkler Scale**. The system relies on the concept of 'growing degree days', which are calculated by adding the number of degrees the daily average temperature exceeds 10°C for each day within the defined growing season (1 October to 30 April in the Southern Hemisphere). The temperature 10°C is chosen as the threshold as grapevines do not exhibit any growth below this temperature. (See p. 21 for more details.)

High density / High-density planting – See Planting density.

Jimmy Watson Memorial Trophy – An award given each year at the Melbourne Royal Wine Awards (one of the country's most prestigious wine shows) to recognise the best young (one- or two-year-old) dry red wine of the competition. The award is quite coveted, and generally speaks to the current trending styles and production methods.

La Niña – A climate pattern in the Pacific Ocean (along with **El Niño**) that can have a significant impact on weather worldwide. The two are perhaps the strongest of any influence on climate variability in Australia. In La Niña cycles, surface water temperatures become colder and currents more erratic, which can result in Australian vintages of increased rainfall, cooler daytime temperatures, decreased frost risk and greater tropical storm likelihood (like 1998–2001, 2007–2009, 2010–2012 and 2019–2022).

Langton's Classification – A classification updated every five years since 1990 by Langton's, Australia's largest wine retailer and auction house, based on prices, volume of demand and supply at auction. The list ends up being a who's who of Australia's most collected wines. The classification is split into three tiers. The top tier, 'Exceptional', is defined as 'the most highly sought after and prized first growth-type Australian wine on the market'. The middle 'Outstanding' tier is 'benchmark quality wines with a very strong market following'. And the third (though still quite prestigious) 'Excellent' tier is 'high performing

wines of exquisite quality with solid volume of demand'.

Leaf pulling – A **canopy management** technique (of exactly what it sounds like – removing leaves), which can result in improved air circulation and exposure of the fruit to more sunlight.

Lees / Lees work – Lees describe expended yeast cells that result from fermentation. The way in which lees are managed post-fermentation is referred to as lees work or lees handling; this often refers to how often (if at all) lees are 'stirred'. Lees stirring was traditionally used to build body in cool-climate whites, but can also result in cheesy, yeasty lees-derived flavours like parmesan rind, stale beer and nutty brioche.

Lo-fi – A relatively new term used to describe wines that are made with minimal intervention: generally fresh, unoaked styles with little to no **sulphur** additions, no added yeast, no fining or filtration and moderate skin-contact (less than is typical for reds, and more than is typical for whites). The term often goes hand-in-hand with producers who are considered part of the natural wine category, though the latter has a farming component where 'lo-fi' refers more specifically to winemaking techniques.

masl – Metres above sea level.

Mesoclimate – A climatic area defined by influence of elevation, **aspect**, slope or distance from a large body of water. A single vineyard is often considered a mesoclimate, containing various **microclimates** and sitting within a larger macroclimate.

475

Microclimate – Often used generally to describe the unique factors affecting a specific plot of land, it is the smallest and most specific climatic area, sometimes as small as a row of vines.

Mousy / Mousiness – A wine flaw created by the presence of various strains of spoilage bacteria. It is often described as resembling 'hamster cage', 'puppy's breath', 'corn nuts' and 'vomit'. It usually does not present itself aromatically, and is detected late on the palate, sometimes after swallowing. This quality occurs in some, though not all, wines that see minimal or no added **sulphur**.

MVGWTA – McLaren Vale Grape Wine & Tourism Association.

MW / Master of Wine – MW is short-hand for Master of Wine, a prestigious wine qualification bestowed by the Institute of Masters of Wine in the UK. The Master of Wine certification is less service-based and more writing and analytics, attracting more wine writers and winemakers than sommeliers.

No-till farming – A method of farming that has become widely adopted across Australia (viticulture and other agriculture), which avoids tilling/ploughing the soils. Tillage is normally used to aerate the land before sowing crops, but it rapidly depletes soil moisture, degrades micro flora and fauna, and leaves soils vulnerable to erosion, the latter being the leading cause of land degradation in Australia (exacerbated by drought, salinisation and lack of biodiversity).

Nouveau – A term used to describe wine that is fresh and unaged (in either oak or bottle), meant to be consumed young. It derives from France's 'Beaujolais nouveau', which is released mere weeks after harvest.

Nutrient load – Not a commonly used term, but one that has been used in research projects on the Barossa, describing the 'mass of nutrients in a water body', specifically nitrogen and phosphorus. Soils play a key role in making these nutrients available to a vine, and their ability to do so is often referenced.

Oxidative – Describes wines that are made in exposure to oxygen (as opposed to **reductively** made wines, which are made in the absence of oxygen). This is not the same as a wine being oxidised, which is a fault.

Parkerisation – A global phenomenon in which wines became dominated by alcohol, fruit and oak – attributed to the iconic *Wine Advocate* reviewer Robert Parker.

Pétillance – A French word meaning bubbly, sparkling or fizzy. Its use generally implies a softer effervescence than the full pressure of **traditional method** sparkling wine.

Pét-nat – Short for 'pétillant natural', which entails the use of méthode ancestrale sparkling wine production, where wine is transferred to bottle part way through primary fermentation, producing bubbles from a single fermentation (rather than the classic secondary fermentation of **traditional method**). Though not a requirement of méthode ancestrale production,

most pét-nat is undisgorged – the accumulated **lees** remain in the bottle, creating thick turbidity and solids.

Phenolic ripeness – Also known as physiological ripeness, describing the ripeness accumulated in grape skins, seeds and stems – generally indicative of flavour ripeness. Phenolic ripeness is often measured in how it relates to sugar ripeness (whether it arrives sooner or later), the latter an indication of sugar content and potential alcohol in grapes.

Phylloxera – An aphid that feeds on the roots of grapevines. Phylloxera, at one point or another, has devastated most wine regions around the world. The solution is to graft *Vitis vinifera* (the species of nearly all the world's wine production) onto American rootstock, which is resistant to phylloxera.

Piquette – A light and lightly fizzy wine made by adding water to grape pomace (the spent skins, seeds and stems) and fermenting what remains of the sugars. Traditionally piquettes were made by vineyard workers to enjoy a by-product of winemaking that otherwise would go to waste, but it's enjoying a new life as a trendy and affordable sip.

Planting density – A term used to describe how densely planted a vineyard is: how many vines are planted per hectare. The greater the planting density (often referred to as high planting density or close-planting), the fewer bunches per vine and the lower the yield. Especially for pinot noir, a high planting density is considered very beneficial to flavour concentration and quality.

Pruning – A winter viticultural activity, where growth from the previous year is trimmed back to focus fruit production in select shoots.

Quaternary – The current time period, which began 2.6 million years ago.

Qvevri – A clay vessel used for fermenting and ageing wine that is traditional to Georgia. Qvevri are ovular in shape (which helps promote circulation of solids) and are buried underground (which maintains consistent temperatures and stabilises the structure).

Reductive – A term that describes a winemaking environment (intentional or otherwise) that restricts the presence of oxygen. A variety of aromatics can result from a reductive atmosphere for wine. Subtle reduction and the associated aromatics can be desired and are especially prevalent in white (and to a lesser extent red) wines of Burgundy (and increasingly Burgundian grapes made around the world), smelling like flint and gun smoke. Reduction can veer into wine fault territory when wines develop sulphide-based aromas like cabbage, hard-boiled eggs and onion.

Regionality – A term used to describe the quality of being specific to a region; in the world of wine, regionality is connected to the idea of terroir – that the wines of a certain area will exhibit unique characteristics because of shared geographical and climatic features.

Reverse osmosis – A method used in industrial wine production to dealcoholise wine, whereby the flavour components are separated from the alcohol and then reassembled after alcohol has been adjusted or removed.

Shoot thinning – Typically the first **canopy management** technique of the growing system, whereby unfruiting shoots (and sometimes fruiting shoots) are thinned back. This process can also be thought of as the conclusion of the **pruning** process, establishing the coming year's fruiting zone.

Stem inclusion – Also referred to as 'whole bunch', the term speaks to the inclusion of stems in a fermentation; the practice is typically used in select red wine ferments (pinot noir, syrah, grenache and gamay, most notably). Stems can leach alcohol and colour from ferments (often in a positive way) and add savoury, green notes. Stem inclusion often goes hand-in-hand with **carbonic maceration**, as whole bunches go into fermentation uncrushed and juice can begin fermenting within the skins.

Subregionality – See Regionality, but specifically in reference to smaller regions within a larger one.

Sulphur – An organic element naturally occurring in wine that is also added to prevent bacterial spoilage and oxidation.

Table wine – A term used in opposition to **fortified wine**, describing dry, non-fortified wines (i.e. most of what we see in production today!).

Traditional method – Also referred to as méthode champenoise or Champagne method, this is the method of creating sparkling wine traditionally used in Champagne (and considered to result in the highest quality bubbly), whereby the wine undergoes secondary fermentation in bottle.

Trellising – A system used to support the structure of a grapevine, given that most do not have a self-supporting trunk.

Ungrafted vines – Vines that have not been grafted onto American rootstock. Also called 'own-rooted vines', these vines are generally older because they did not have to be replanted due to **phylloxera**. There is an air of superiority to vines that are own-rooted, though there is no scientific research that proves any benefit (besides the often correlative age).

Water-holding capacity – An important physical characteristic of soils, measuring how much water a soil can retain. Clays famously have a higher water-holding capacity than any other soil type, while soils like sand are well known for their quick drainage (low water-holding capacity).

Wine Australia's Climate Atlas – A research project in collaboration with the University of Tasmania, mapping detailed climate projections for individual Australian wine regions in near-, mid- and long-term time frames. The result is an exhaustive scholastic resource, free for anyone to access.

Winkler Scale – See Heat Summation Index.

Bibliography

General Citations

For this book, we consulted the following regularly:

- Wine Australia
- Vinehealth Australia annual reports for Wine Australia
- GI Applications
- Gaia/Greenbrain's vineyard scans
- The regional wine body's website for every Australian wine region
- State/regional tourism association websites
- The website of every producer profiled
- Every available First Nation's website and literature (for Nations that overlap with a wine region, as well as select others)
- The Aboriginal Heritage Councils for each Australian state
- Australian wine media websites, including: Australian Financial Review, James Halliday's Wine Companion, Meininger's Wine Business International, The Age, The Real Review, Wine Business Monthly, and Young Gun of Wine.

Websites / Blogs

Aboriginal Cultural Heritage Register and Information System, Victorian Aboriginal Heritage Register <achris.vic.gov.au/#/dashboard>

Aboriginal Heritage Office <aboriginalheritage.org>

Aboriginal Heritage Tasmania <aboriginalheritage.tas.gov.au>

Agriculture Victoria, Victorian Resources Online <vro.agriculture.vic.gov.au/dpi/vro/vrosite.nsf/pages/vrohome>

Australian Government, Geographical Indications Committee, 2020, *Decision not to make a final determination of Wilyabrup as a Geographical Indication for wine, Statement of reasons* <wineaustralia.com/getmedia/d4467bb9-ab2e-4cc0-b072-22e60c961022/20200803-Statement-of-Reasons.pdf>

Australian Government, Geoscience Australia, Significant Rock Features <ga.gov.au/scientific-topics/national-location-information/landforms/significant-rock-features>

Australian Museum, 12 September 2021, *When Did Modern Humans Get to Australia?* <australian.museum/learn/science/human-evolution/the-spread-of-people-to-australia/>

Best Wines Under $20, 7 April 2012, *How Southcorp and Fosters trashed Australia's greatest icons* <bestwinesunder20.com.au/how-southcorp-fosters-trashed-australias-greatest-wine-brands>

Best Wines Under $20, 12 April 2013, *Where did Murray really get his Chardonnay from?* <bestwinesunder20.com.au/where-did-murray-really-get-his-chardonnay-from>

Boyd, G., January 2007, 'Atypical Greats from Clarendon Hills', *Wine Review Online* <winereviewonline.com/Boyd_on_Clarendon_Hills.cfm>

Clare Museum, SA, 2022, *The Story of Clare's Wineries* <claremuseum.com/1-early-wine-making>

Common Ground <commonground.org.au>

Durrant, J., May 2020, 'Revisiting the forgotten world of Victoria's alpine valleys and ranges: the case for restoring our ancient open woodlands', *Life on Spring Creek*, <lifeonspringcreek.com/2020/05/21/forgotten-world-of-north-east-victorias-ancient-open-woodlands>

Firesticks Alliance <firesticks.org.au>

Franson, P., 18 March 2016, 'Complex History Behind Treasury's Turnaround', *Wines Vines Analytics*, <winesvinesanalytics.com/blog/?cms_preview=true&dataid=166363>

Graham, A., 'What is McLaren Vale's Scarce Earth Program?' *Australian Wine Review*, July 2013 <ozwinereview.com/2013/07/what-is-mclaren-vale-scarce-ear.html>

Hunter Valley Time Line, 2017 <hunterweb.com.au>

Melbourne Royal, *RASV Virtual Museum, Jimmy Watson Memorial Trophy Winners* <melbourneroyal.com.au/media/3348/jimmy-watson-memorial-trophy-winners.pdf>

Murray Lower Darling Rivers Indigenous Nations <mldrin.org.au>

National Landcare Conference, *Wandoon Estate Aboriginal Corporation – VIC* <nationallandcareconference.org.au/project/wandoon-estate-aboriginal-corp-vic>

National Portrait Gallery, 2022, *T.T. Seppelt* <portrait.gov.au/portraits/2012.180/tt-seppelt>

Natural Selection Theory, 2011 <naturalselectiontheory.com>

New South Wales Aboriginal Land Council, *Aboriginal Heritage Information Management System* <alc.org.au/ahims>

North Central Catchment Management Association Victoria, *Kulin People* <nccma.vic.gov.au/sites/default/files/publications/kulin_people_brochure.pdf>

Parks Victoria <parks.vic.gov.au>

PS I Love You, A Petite Sirah Advocacy Organization, 2022 <psiloveyou.org/about/about-petite-sirah>

Queensland Aboriginal and Torres Strait Islander Cultural Heritage Database and Register <aboriginalheritage.tas.gov.au>

Queensland Art Gallery, *The Indigenous People of the Darling Downs* <visualarts.qld.gov.au/content/martens_standard.asp?name=Martens_context_indigenous>

Recognising Kaurna Heritage Through Physical Features of the City, *City of Adelaide Reconciliation* <cityofadelaide.com.au/community/reconciliation/kaurna-place-naming>

Robert Parker's Wine Advocate, 2001–2022, <robertparker.com>

Romsey Australia, 2012, *Volcanoes and Earthquakes* <romseyaustralia.com/volcmap.html>

Rutherglen Historical Society, 2022, *Wine* <rutherglenhistoricalsociety.com.au/wine>

Shanahan, C., October 1994, 'Canberra District wines', *Chris Shanahan: Australian wine & beer judge, writer, and connoisseur*, <chrisshanahan.com/articles/1994/canberra-district-wines>

State Library Victoria, 2019, *Melbourne Intercolonial Exhibition of Australasia 1866–67* <guides.slv.vic.gov.au/interexhib/1866to67>

Taa Wika <taawika.sa.gov.au/public/home>

The Free Library, 2004, *The Coonawarra: a viticultural frontier? Or just a case of sour grapes?* <www.thefreelibrary.com/The+Coonawarra%3A+a+viticultural+frontier%3F+Or+just+a+case+of+sour...-a0134292965>

The Len Evans Tutorial, 2006, *Len Evans – in his own words* <lenevanstutorial.com.au/about/the-story>

Wine Australia, *A Climate Atlas* <wineaustralia.com/climate-atlas>

Wine Australia, *Australian Wine Geographic Indications Map Dashboard* <wineaustralia.maps.arcgis.com/apps/dashboards/bdbab83752814afbace145ef06491358>

Wine Australia, *Vintage Survey Dashboard* <marketexplorer.wineaustralia.com/vintage-survey>

Books

Anderson, K., *Growth and Cycles in Australia's Wine Industry: A Statistical Compendium, 1843 to 2013*, Adelaide: University of Adelaide Press, 2015

Beeston, J., *A Concise History of Australian Wine*, 3rd ed., Sydney: Allen & Unwin, 2001

Birch, W.D., *Volcanoes in Victoria*, Melbourne: Royal Society of Victoria, 1994

Busby, J., *Journal of a Tour Through Some of the Vineyards of Spain and France*, Sydney: David Ell Press, 1979

Caillard, A., *Imagining Coonawarra – The Story of John Riddoch Cabernet Sauvignon*, Melbourne: Hardie Grant, 2020

Caillard, A., *The Rewards of Patience*, Melbourne: Hardie Grant, 2013

Evans, L., 'Theory of Consumption', *The Australian Wine Browser*, ed. Ousback, A., Sydney: David Ell Press, 1979

Gammage, B., *The Biggest Estate on Earth: How Aborigines Made Australia*, Sydney: Allen & Unwin, 2012

Gladstones, J., *Viticulture and Environment: A Study of the Effects of Environment on Grapegrowing and Wine Qualities, with Emphasis on Present and Future Areas for Growing Winegrapes in Australia*, Adelaide: Winetitles, 2002

Halliday, J., *Wine Atlas of Australia.* Berkeley: University of California, 2007

Johnston, B., 'A Brief History of the Canberra District' in *Proceedings of the 7th University House Wine Symposium*, ed. Kirk, K. & Richards, J., Canberra: The Australian National University, 2012, pp. 35–40

Laing, P., *Tasmanian Wines*, Launceston: Bokprint, 1997

Lewis, I.D., *Discover Naracoorte Caves*, Edwardstown: Subterranean Foundation, 1977

Longbottom, M., Pichler, M. & Maschmedt, D., *Unearthing Viticulture in the Limestone Coast*, Coonawarra: Limestone Coast Grape and Wine Industry Council, 2011

McIntyre, J., *Hunter Wine: A history*, Sydney: NewSouth, 2018

Mitchell, T.L., *Three Expeditions Into the Interior of Eastern Australia*, vol. 2, London: T&W Boone, 1839

Olmo, H.P., *A Survey of the Grape Industry of Western Australia*, Perth: Vine Fruits Research Trust Inc., 1956

Pascoe, B., *Dark Emu: Aboriginal Australia and the Birth of Agriculture*, Broome: Magabala Books Aboriginal Corporation, 2018

Robinson, J., Harding, J. & Vouillamoz, J., *Wine Grapes: A Complete Guide to 1,380 Vine Varieties, Including Their Origins and Flavors*, New York: Ecco/HarperCollins, 2012

Smyth, R.B., *The Aborigines of Victoria: with Notes relating to the Habits of the Natives of Other Parts of Australia and Tasmania*, Melbourne, 1878

Steffensen, V., *Fire Country: How Indigenous Fire Management Could Help Save Australia*, Melbourne: Hardie Grant, 2020

Tindale, N., *Aboriginal Tribes of Australia*, Berkley: University of California Press, 1974

Twidale, C.R., *Ancient Australian Landscapes.* Dural: Rosenberg, 2016

Veevers, J.J., *Billion-year Earth History of Australia and Neighbours in Gondwanaland*, Sydney: GEMOC Press, 2000

Walker, T., *Vintage Tasmania: The Complete Book of Tasmanian Wine*, Dilston: Providence Island Tasmania, 2014

Ward, E., *The Vineyards and Orchards of South Australia*, Adelaide: Sullivan's Cove, 1979

Essays / Journals / Articles

'2018 McLaren Vale Port Willunga Aquifer Groundwater Status Report', Department for Environment and Water, Government of South Australia, Adelaide, 16 July 2019

Allen, B., 'Seppeltsfield acquires Bunyip Water', *The Shout*, 7 September 2022

Allen, M., 'Discover Australia's hottest new wine region with a road trip', *Australian Financial Review*, 25 June 2021

Allen, M., 'Don't panic, but natural wine is here to stay', *Australian Financial Review*, 22 August 2019

Allen, M., 'How the three sisters at Brown Brothers revived tarrango', *Australian Financial Review*, 30 September 2022

'Australia's Free Trade Agreement with India – a Small Step Towards Replacing China', *Meininger's Wine Business International*, 21 April 2022

Blake, B.J. & Reid, J., 'Pallanganmiddang: a language of the Upper Murray', *Aboriginal History*, vol. 23, 1999, pp. 15–31

Bramley, R.G.V. & Ouzman, J., 'Underpinning Terroir with Data: On What Grounds Might Subregionalisation of the Barossa Zone Geographical Indication be Justified?', *Australian Journal of Grape and Wine Research*, vol. 28, no. 2, 28 July 2021, pp. 196–207

Bourke, J., 'Forged by Fire: Volcanoes in Victoria' *Australian Geographic*, 17 May 2017

Carmichael, H., 'Hunter River Vineyard Association', *The Maitland Mercury and Hunter River General Advertiser*, 1850

Driscoll, W.P., 'The Beginnings of the Wine Industry in the Hunter Valley', *Newcastle History Monographs*, no. 5, 1969

Dunstan, D., 'Irvine, Hans William (1856–1922)', *Australian Dictionary of Biography*, vol. 9, 1983

Dunstan, D., 'Preece, Colin Thomas (1903–1979)', *Australian Dictionary of Biography*, vol. 16, 2002

Edis, R., 'The Good Earth: Coonawarra Red Dermosol and Cabernet Sauvignon' *The Conversation*, 31 May 2013

Edmond, G., 'Disorder with law: determining the geographical indication for the Coonawarra wine region', *Adelaide Law Review*, vol. 27, no. 1, January 2006

Gladstones, J., 'A conceptual plan for viticultural sub-regions of Margaret River,' Unpublished report to the Margaret River Wine Association, 1999

Gladstones, J., 'The climate and soils of south-western Australia in relation to vine growing', *Journal of the Australian Institute of Agricultural Science*, 1956

Hooke, H., 'Hilltops vineyard back from the brink', *The Real Review*, 16 May 2010

Hooke, H., 'How the wine show system works,' *The Real Review*, 14 February 2018

Hooke, H., 'Red means go in the Vale', *The Real Review*, 6 August 2013

Hooke, H., 'Tumbarumba rises from the ashes', *The Real Review*, 13 August 2020

Hooper, N., 'Chardonnay Pioneer Going Strong,' *Australian Financial Review*, 2 October 1995

Kyte-Powell, R., 'Mornington's rich wine history', *The Real Review*, 19 April 2021

Lacorde, M., 'Assessing the Environmental Characteristics of the Margaret River Wine Region, Australia: Potential New Geographical Indication Sub-Units', *International Journal of Applied Geospatial Research*, vol. 10, no. 3, July 2019, pp. 1–24

Lewis, J., 'Bob Oatley's Rosemount company began in the Upper Hunter', *Newcastle Herald*, 19 Jan 2016

McLaren Vale Grape Wine and Tourism Association, 'Districts of The McLaren Vale Wine Region', *McLaren Vale*, 2013

Murphy, D., 'Curse steals another Drayton', *The Sydney Morning Herald*, 18 January 2008

Payne, S., 'Wine Country: Coonawarra', *Gourmet Traveller*, 2021

Pickard, C., 'Natural Winemakers are Disrupting Australian Wine with Unfiltered Passion', *Wine Enthusiast*, 12 February 2020

Pierre, M. '"France of the southern hemisphere": transferring a European wine model to colonial Australia', Université Michel de Montaigne – Bordeaux II, University of Newcastle, 2020

Port, J., 'AWRI reacts to plagiarism claims', *Meininger's Wine Business International*, 15 October 2020

Port, J., 'Name-calling shakes up the valley', *The Age*, 18 September 2007

Port, J., 'On the outer', *The Sydney Morning Herald*, 7 November 2007

Pygott, M., 'Has climate change occurred in the Barossa Valley over the last fifty years and if so, how have vine growers adapted to any changes?' *The Institute of Masters of Wine*, 2016

Quinn, S., 'The sparkling isle', *Meininger's Wine Business International*, 5 December 2014

'Reynella Farm the Residence of Mr. John Reynell', *The South Australian Advertiser*, 26 May 1862

Robinson, J., 'South Australia's unknown second wine region', *Jancis Robinson*, 9 April 2005

Robinson, S. & Sandercock, N., 'A Barossa Grounds Project', *Barossa Grape & Wine Association*, 2014

Roch, M. & Werner, M., 'Clare Valley Rocks: The Earth Beneath our Vines', *Clare Valley Wine and Grape Association*, Adelaide, July 2016

Ryan, N., 'Great Hunter wines with a dash of McLaren Vale', *The Australian*, 2 July 2019

Skinner, W., 'Fermenting Place: Wine Production and Terroir in McLaren Vale, South Australia', *University of Adelaide*, September 2015

Smith, M., 'Quest for superb Pinot from suburbs', *Tasmanian Times*, 6 February 2019

Steiman, H., 'Promising Australian Partnership Ends Bitterly', *Wine Spectator*, 23 March 2006

Tille, P., Stuart-Street, A. & Gardiner, P., *Geology, soils and climate of the Margaret River wine region*, Department of Primary Industries and Regional Development, Perth, 2020

Venning, C.M., 'The Impact of Weather on the Cost of Production of Wine Grapes', *University of Southern Queensland*, 2017, pp. 1–29

Walker, A., 'A History of the Tasmanian Wine Industry', *University of Tasmania*, April 2012

'Welcome Back to Best's Wines', *Wine Business Monthly*, 7 Sept 2022

White, T., 'Red crosses', *Australian Financial Review*, 8 Dec 2001

Wright, C., 'Making Grenache Great Again', *Fleurieu Living Magazine*, 4 Dec 2020

Maps

Australian Institute for Aboriginal and Torres Strait Islander Studies, 2022, *Map of Indigenous Australia* <aiatsis.gov.au/explore/map-indigenous-australia>

Favenc, E., *The Explorers of Australia and Their Life-Work*, 'Stuart and Hume and Hovell Expeditions', Melbourne: Whitcombe & Tombs Limited, 1908

Margaret River Survey Co., McMullen Nolan Group, 2012, 'Margaret River Viticultural Sub-Regions As Proposed by John Gladstones 1999'

Olliver, J., 'Districts of the McLaren Vale Wine Region', ed. Hook, J., McLaren Vale Grape Wine and Tourism Association, 2013

Map Data

The maps in this book are based on Digital Topographic Data <ga.gov.au/scientific-topics/national-location-information/topographic-maps-data/digital-topographic-data> by Geoscience Australia which are © Commonwealth of Australia and are provided under a Creative Commons Attribution 4.0 International Licence and are subject to the disclaimer of warranties in section 5 of that licence. These data were viewed and retrieved 2020–2022.

Abatzoglou, J.T., Dobrowski, S.Z., Parks, S.A. & Hegewisch, K.C., 2018, Terraclimate, a high-resolution global dataset of monthly climate and climatic water balance from 1958–2015, Scientific Data <climatologylab.org/terraclimate.html> (Barossa, Western Victoria, Tasmania North and South)

Department of Primary Industries and Regional Development, Western Australia, April 2018, *Soil Landscape Mapping – Systems (DPIRD-064)* <catalogue.data.wa.gov.au/dataset/soil-landscape-mapping-systems> (Margaret River)

All vineyard footprint data via satellite imagery provided by Green Brain <greenbrain.ag>

Natural Earth <naturalearthdata.com>

Raymond, O.L., Liu, S., Gallagher, R., Zhang, W. & Highet, L.M., 'Surface Geology of Australia 1:1 million scale dataset 2012 edition', *Geoscience Australia*, 1 January 2012 <pid.geoscience.gov.au/dataset/ga/74619>

World Wine Regions <worldwineregions.com>

Interviews / Lectures

Shepherd, T., 'Lectures on the Horticulture of NSW', Sydney: Mechanics School of Arts, 1835

WINeFare, 'The Australian Wine Renaissance', 2021

Original Interviews

For this book, Jane, Jonathan and Kavita conducted interviews (either by video conference, phone call, or email) with the following people:

- Loïque Allain, Dilworth & Allain
- Sue Bell, Bellwether Wines
- Gareth Belton, Gentle Folk
- Tessa Brown & Jeremy Schmölzer, Vignerons Schmölzer & Brown
- Tim Byrne & Niki Nikolovski, Babche
- John Carty, University of Adelaide
- Julian Castagna, Castagna
- Kim & Tennille Chalmers, Chalmers Wines
- Jim Chatto, Chatto Wines
- Samantha Connew, Stargazer
- Joshua Cooper, Joshua Cooper Wines
- Ray Costanzo, Golden Grove Estate
- Dan Coward, Alkina Wines
- Rollo Crittenden, Crittenden
- Sarah Crowe, Yarra Yering
- Vanya Cullen, Cullen
- Andy Cummins, Rasa Wines
- Michael Dhillon, Bindi
- Fiona Donald, Seppeltsfield
- Michael & Andrew Downer, Murdoch Hill
- William Downie, William Downie
- Peter Dredge, Meadow Bank/Dr. Edge
- Jacqui Durrant, The Wheeler Centre
- Nick & Gary Farr, By Farr
- Emma Farrelly, State Buildings
- Steve Flamsteed, Giant Steps
- Mac Forbes, Mac Forbes
- Adam Foster, Syrahmi
- Peter Fraser, Yangarra
- Peter Gago, Penfolds
- Penny Grant, Shaw+Smith
- Gary Green, Mt Yengo Wines
- Dylan Grigg, Vinya Vella

- Jeffrey Grosset, Grosset
- Charlotte Hardy, Charlotte Dalton Wines
- Riley Harrison, Harrison Wines
- Matt Harrop, Curly Flat/Silent Way
- Ken Helm, Helm Wines
- Prue Henschke, Henschke
- Michael Hill Smith, Shaw+Smith
- AJ Hoadley, La Violetta
- Matt Holmes, Bannockburn
- Jonny Hughes, Mewstone
- Andrew & Leighton Joy, Pyren Vineyard
- Cath Kidman, Wynns Coonawarra Estate
- Rick Kinzbrunner, Giaconda
- Tim Kirk, Clonakilla
- Erinn Klein, Ngeringa
- David LeMire, Shaw+Smith
- Gilli & Paul Lipscombe, Sailor Seeks Horse
- Genevieve & Rob Mann, Corymbia
- Louella Mathews, Bibo/The Somm & The Winemaker
- Bryan Martin, Ravensworth
- Colin McBryde, Adelina/Some Young Punks
- Kate McIntyre, Moorooduc
- Alex McKay, Collector Wines
- Emily McNally, Jasper Hill
- Sam Middleton, Mount Mary
- Rowly Milhinch, Scion
- Colleen Miller, Mérite
- Evan Milne, Stock on Hand
- Barry Morey, Sorrenberg
- Elizabeth Morris, Pennyweight
- Fred Morris, Campbells
- Ray Nadeson, Lethbridge
- Drew Noon, Noon Wines
- Emma Norbiato, Calabria Family Wines
- Jayden Ong, Jayden Ong
- Steve Pannell, S.C. Pannell
- Nic Peterkin, L.A.S. Vino
- Jen Pfeiffer, Pfeiffer Wines
- Ben Portet, Dominique Portet
- Sierra Reed, Reed Wines
- Iain Riggs, Brokenwood
- Louisa Rose, Yalumba
- Charlie Seppelt, Paralian Wines
- Shashi & Rohit Singh, Avani
- Hunter Smith, Frankland Estate
- Nick Spencer, Nick Spencer Wines
- Patrick Sullivan, Patrick Sullivan
- James Thomas, Heroes Vineyard
- Belinda Thomson, Crawford River
- Ben & Nicole Thomson, Best's Great Western
- Bruce, Chris and Jane Tyrrell, Tyrrell's
- Angus Vinden, Vinden Wines
- Nadja Wallington, ChaLou
- Mark Walpole, Fighting Gully Road
- Tom Ward, Swinging Bridge
- Virginia Willcock, Vasse Felix
- Corrina Wright, Oliver's Taranga

Producers in Jane and Jonathan's Imports Portfolio, Legend

- Attwoods
- Babche
- Bird on a Wire
- Chalmers Wines
- Corymbia
- Domaine A
- Dominique Portet
- Fighting Gully Road
- Giaconda
- Henskens Rankin
- La Petite Mort
- Mérite
- Minimum
- Moorilla
- Mt Yengo Wines
- Murdoch Hill
- Ngeringa
- Patrick Sullivan
- Pyren Vineyard
- Rasa
- Reed Wines
- Sailor Seeks Horse
- Seppeltsfield
- Silent Way
- Stargazer
- Syrahmi
- Vino Volta
- William Downie

Index

This index has been designed to assist you on your Australian wine journey, including wine regions, grapes, production methods, climate, soil and key historical figures. Further historical information, First Nations groups, geographical features, along with a myriad of people, places, stories and products are described in detail within each region, and an index of each producer referenced can be found on page 489.

A

ACT (unofficial subregion) 79
Adelaide Hills (region) 336–55
aglianico 217, 239, 246, 329, 465, 468
Albany (subregion) 436–8, 445
albariño 42, 50, 128, 132, 144, 225, 467
alicante bouschet 42, 50
aligoté 78, 176, 426
Alpine Valleys (region) 217, 240–1, 244, 246, 250
alvarinho 237, 468
amphora-aged wine 89–90, 162, 216, 223, 225, 373, 428, 452
  see also ceramic egg fermentation, qvevri
apera (sherry-styled wines) 223, 322, 450
  see also sherry
aperitivo 404
arinto 50, 237, 375
arneis 68, 97, 125, 244, 247, 281, 351
assyrtiko 329, 333
Australian Geographical Indication System (GI system) 19–20
AWRI (The Australian Wine Research Institute) 64, 375, 460, 474
azal 211

B

Ballarat (region) 163, 248–9
barbera 42, 48, 84, 90, 106, 121, 191, 224, 244, 247, 329, 335, 355, 377, 384, 460, 465, 467
Barossa (region) 20, 96, 284, 288–318, 358, 476
Barossa Grounds (unofficial subregion) 299, 302–5
Beechworth (region) 212–25, 250
beer 84, 89, 402, 405
bela 375
Bellarine Peninsula (unofficial subregion) 138, 140–1, 144–6, 148–50
Bendigo (region) 238–9, 246, 250
Big Rivers (region) 93
biodiversity 179, 210, 231, 261, 279, 392, 416, 453, 476
biodynamics 63, 68, 70, 74, 87–8, 128, 132, 136, 154, 159, 162, 165, 167, 169, 177–9, 192, 199, 210, 216, 222–4, 246, 277, 280, 297, 302, 310, 313, 316, 331, 333, 338, 345, 348–9, 352, 355, 362, 368, 374, 378, 395, 402, 404–5, 415–16, 426, 428, 429–31, 445, 451, 474
blanc de blancs 68, 116, 274, 276, 430, 460
blanc de noirs 150
blaufränkisch 267, 279, 355
Blewitt Springs (unofficial subregion) 363, 366–8, 370, 372–3, 376, 378
Bordeaux varieties 67–8, 70, 119, 120–1, 124, 176, 266, 333, 338, 350, 354, 393, 396–7, 427, 429–30, 431, 438, 452

botrytis 95–6, 150, 372, 396, 416, 440
bourboulenc 378
brachetto 121, 244
brandy 195–6, 316, 382, 450
Broke Fordwich (subregion) 39, 42
Brunello 216–17
Burgundy 37, 45, 107, 124, 141, 148, 162, 195–6, 228, 294, 337, 427, 446
Busby, James 31–2, 53, 148, 213, 358
bush vines 67, 191, 297, 302, 367, 370, 378, 441, 443, 474
bushfires 22, 38, 43, 64, 70, 84, 97, 131, 220, 234, 273, 284, 401, 405, 412, 465, 475

C

cabernet franc 67–8, 75, 86, 88, 120, 177, 179, 190, 208, 210, 224, 281, 324, 344, 351, 366, 375, 384, 395–6, 401, 405, 430, 440, 445, 452
cabernet sauvignon 42, 46–7, 54, 58, 62–3, 66, 68–70, 73–4, 78–9, 82–3, 86–8, 90, 97, 104–5, 106–8, 112, 116–17, 119–21, 123, 125, 132, 133, 139, 144, 153, 155, 163, 165, 176–7, 179, 181, 192, 197, 204, 208, 210–11, 213, 220, 223–4, 228–9, 238–40, 246–7, 250, 258–9, 275, 280, 288–9, 302, 305, 311–12, 314, 318, 320–4, 329, 332, 334–5, 338, 340, 344–5, 358–9, 362, 366, 368, 371, 373–4, 376, 378, 381–4, 389, 392–7, 399–402, 404–5,

413–15, 417, 420–1, 424–31, 433, 436–8, 440–3, 445, 447–8, 450, 452–3, 462, 465–8, 474

canaiolo 244

Canberra District (region) 26, 72–5, 78–9, 82–4, 86–90

carbonic maceration 312, 351, 355, 420, 474, 477

carbon-neutral wineries 23, 47, 69, 119, 134, 239, 428, 430

Carbunup (unofficial subregion) 417, 420

carignan 288, 316, 332, 357, 375

Central Ranges (region) 52–70

ceramic egg fermentation 78, 442

Chablis 37, 195–6, 228, 263, 372

chambourcin 92–3, 97, 245

Champagne method *see* méthode champenoise, sparkling wine, traditional method

chardonnay 30, 37, 42, 47–50, 53–5, 62–3, 66–70, 73–5, 78–9, 82–3, 87–90, 97, 104, 106–7, 109, 112, 114, 116–25, 132–6, 140, 144–5, 148–50, 152, 154, 158–9, 162–5, 168–9, 172, 176–9, 181, 197, 199, 204, 208–11, 213, 216, 220, 222–5, 229, 236–41, 247–50, 259–61, 263, 266–7, 274–81, 295–6, 302, 314, 317–18, 329, 333, 336–8, 340–1, 344–5, 350–5, 359, 362, 368, 371, 375–7, 382, 395, 399–400, 402, 404, 415, 420–1, 424–6, 428–31, 433, 438, 440, 444–8, 450–3, 462, 465–8

charmat method 240, 474

chasselas 105, 213

chenin blanc 42, 68, 109, 112, 176, 220, 351, 370–2, 420, 427, 429–31, 440, 446, 451–3

cider 119, 267, 280, 467

cienna 245, 247

cinsault 42, 84, 119, 288, 297, 308, 314–16, 371, 374

clairette 119, 372, 378

Clare Valley (region) 284, 320–35, 355

Clarendon (unofficial subregion) 337, 363, 366–8, 370, 373, 378

climate 19, 21–2, 26, 30, 32, 37–9,

42–3, 54, 58–60, 62–4, 79–80, 82–4, 92, 100, 108–9, 114–15, 124–5, 128, 131, 140–1, 144–5, 149, 152, 155, 158–9, 168–9, 180, 182–3, 188–9, 198–9, 202–4, 207, 216–17, 228, 230, 234, 239, 254, 260–3, 266, 272–3, 284, 298–9, 302–4, 308, 324, 331, 340–1, 344–5, 349, 356, 363, 366–8, 385, 388–9, 392, 399, 401–2, 408, 414, 416–17, 433, 436–8, 440, 446, 456, 458, 461, 465, 474–7

climate change 22–3, 38–9, 43, 64, 84, 114–15, 128, 131, 159, 180, 188–9, 191, 198, 207, 220, 234, 261, 273, 308, 331, 340–1, 349, 363, 371, 389, 392, 397, 414

El Niño 284, 461, 474–5

La Niña 141, 284, 416, 474–5

macroclimate 198, 475

mesoclimates 42, 62, 141, 475

microclimates 79, 83, 109, 125, 128, 141, 155, 198–9, 202, 266, 272, 299, 345, 424, 475–6

see also bush fires, drought, floods, hail, Heat Summation Index, Winkler Scale

Coonawarra (region) 295, 333, 355, 380–97

cortese 377

corvina 89

counoise 86, 378

Cowra (region) 26, 52, 54–5, 58, 62–4, 69–70

crouchen 106, 334

CSIRO (Commonwealth Scientific and Industrial Research Organisation) 128, 245, 247, 474

cygne blanc 450

D

Denmark (subregion, WA) 437–8, 444–5

dessert wines 266, 334
    see also sweet wines

dolcetto 106, 163, 345, 400

doradillo 358

drought 39, 54, 64, 169, 172, 229, 273, 298, 324, 373, 388, 401, 461, 465, 476

dry-farmed 54, 128, 131, 141, 145, 169, 172, 178–9, 181, 188, 208, 223, 267, 273, 302, 304–5, 308, 313, 316–17, 329, 335, 378, 399, 438, 440, 452, 474

durif 225, 228–9, 236–7, 245, 453, 465–6

E

East Coast (unofficial subregion, TAS) 263–4, 276, 280–1

East Gippsland (unofficial subregion) 169, 172

Evans, Len 33, 37, 45, 50, 67

F

fiano 42, 50, 84, 86, 90, 121, 125, 190–1, 239, 244, 246, 318, 329, 333, 335, 351, 354, 362, 371, 373–4, 376–7, 399, 405, 420, 429, 452, 462, 465–6

Fleurieu Peninsula (region) 351, 354, 401, 404

floods 38, 43, 97, 254

flor 89, 128, 132, 442, 452

fortified wines 32, 46, 48, 53, 63, 70, 90, 97, 106, 123, 139, 153, 195–6, 213, 216, 223, 226, 228–30, 236–7, 245, 247, 290–2, 294, 309, 314, 316–17, 322, 335, 358, 382, 396, 400, 404, 413, 431, 445–6, 448, 450–1, 475
    see also port, sherry

Frankland River (subregion) 20, 426, 436–8, 440–4

friulano 135, 178, 192, 246

frontignac 376, 404

G

gamay 42, 69, 78, 90, 104, 109, 117, 119, 121, 136, 140, 144, 150, 158, 163–4, 176, 216, 224, 236–7, 263, 267, 275, 277, 279, 352, 474, 477

garganega 88, 244

Geelong (region) 138–50

Geographe (region) 448, 452–3

gewürztraminer 66, 90, 97, 133, 139, 158, 176, 211, 240, 250, 261, 263, 279,

483

329, 351, 427, 440, 444, 462

GI system *see* Australian Geographical Indication System

gin 117, 210, 354, 450

Gippsland (region) 20, 136, 166–79

Gladstones, Dr John 124, 413, 416–21, 424, 427, 430, 433

Glenrowan (region) 225, 244–5, 247

glera 240, 247

   see also prosecco

gouais 236, 289, 357

graciano 42, 88, 244, 288, 316, 378, 397, 451, 462

Grampians (region) 100, 194–9, 202–4, 207, 209–11

Granite Belt (unofficial subregion) 456, 458, 460–2, 464–8

Great Southern (region) 14, 432–45, 447–8

Great Western (subregion) 195–9, 202, 207, 209, 211, 250

grechetto 97

Greenock (unofficial subregion) 302–4, 310

grenache 66, 68, 79, 84, 90, 100, 119, 163, 189, 191–2, 210, 249, 259, 288, 295, 297, 303–5, 308, 310–18, 321, 329, 332, 334, 337, 351, 354, 356–9, 362, 366–8, 370–4, 375–8, 404–5, 431, 436–8, 441, 443, 451–2, 474–5, 477

grenache blanc 112, 311, 372, 375

grenache gris 316

gros manseng 97, 468

grüner veltliner 50, 74, 79, 82, 88, 163, 179, 204, 263, 279–81, 344, 355, 402, 445

GSM 112, 210, 310, 317–18, 358, 475

Gundagai (region) 72, 75, 78, 82–4, 90

H

hail 38, 43, 58, 63, 144, 263, 273, 461

Halliday, James 33, 37, 46, 73, 106–7, 116, 359, 405, 467

Hastings River (region) 92–3

Heat Summation Index 21–2, 83, 154, 217, 298, 324, 447, 475

see also Winkler Scale

Heathcote (region) 64, 100, 180–92, 220

Henty (region) 100, 194–9, 203–4, 207, 210–11

Hermitage 31, 46, 195, 213, 217, 239, 248, 292

High Eden (subregion) 298, 302, 305, 316

Hilltops (region) 72–3, 75, 82–4, 89–90

Hock 195, 228, 322

Hunter Valley (region) 26, 30–50, 53

J

Jimmy Watson Memorial Trophy 78, 87, 89–90, 136, 276, 311, 313, 317, 359, 382–3, 395, 400, 428, 431, 475

K

Kangaroo Island (region) 284, 399, 401, 405

Karridale (unofficial subregion) 417, 420, 429–30

King Valley (region) 116, 222, 240–1, 244, 247, 250

Kosher wines 47

L

lagrein 158, 162, 402

Lake George (unofficial subregion) 73–4, 82, 86–8

Langhorne Creek (region) 351, 399, 400–1, 404–5

Langton's Classification 26, 37, 78, 145, 167, 173, 207, 216, 296, 311–13, 315, 329, 374, 383, 394–5, 475

lees 68, 222, 274, 276–7, 444, 474–6

Len Evans Tutorial 37, 45

Lenswood (subregion) 338, 340–1, 344–5, 351–3, 355

lo-fi 70, 118, 133, 179, 250, 281, 316, 318, 445, 475

   see also minimal intervention

Loire 107

low intervention *see* lo-fi, minimal intervention

Lower Hunter (unofficial subregion) 39

Lower Yarra (unofficial subregion) 108–9, 112

M

Macedon Ranges (region) 100, 152–65, 249

malbec 63, 67, 107, 120, 153, 158, 208, 228, 244, 281, 311, 321, 329, 332, 335, 357, 381, 384, 395, 405, 413, 420, 426–7, 430, 438, 443, 448, 450, 453, 465

malvasia 192, 246, 267, 279

mammolo 323

Manjimup (region) 448, 452–3

Margaret River (region) 383, 412–31, 433, 447

marsanne 84, 88, 104–5, 107, 116, 119, 121, 164, 181, 223, 225, 229, 236, 240, 249, 314, 316–17, 362, 462, 465

marzemino 121

Master of Wine 134, 280, 308, 338, 353, 363, 376, 384, 468, 476

mataro 288, 310–12, 315–17, 321, 329, 332, 355, 357–8, 371–2, 375, 378, 431

McLaren Vale (region) 116, 314, 344–5, 353, 356–78, 400, 404

mencía 112, 121, 371, 374–7

merlot 42, 50, 62–3, 68, 70, 75, 88, 106–7, 116, 119–20, 132, 133, 144, 158, 179, 204, 224–5, 239, 246, 281, 318, 329, 340, 344, 355, 366, 371, 378, 381, 384, 392, 394–5, 397, 399, 400, 402, 404–5, 420, 428, 444–5, 447–8, 452–3, 462, 465, 467–8

méthode champenoise 474, 477

   see also traditional method

minimal intervention 121, 164, 223, 349, 355, 377, 415, 451, 475

   see also lo-fi

monastrell 372, 452

mondeuse 88, 249

montepulciano 84, 96, 312, 371, 377, 399, 405

Moorabool Valley (unofficial subregion) 138–41, 144–6, 148–50, 203

Mornington Peninsula (region)
122–36

moscato 250, 312

moscato giallo 135

Mount Barker (subregion, WA) 428,
433, 436–8, 440, 442–3, 445

Mount Benson (region) 385, 402, 405

mourvèdre 84, 100, 119, 189, 191,
239, 249, 288, 297, 305, 314, 317,
345, 358, 372, 378, 437–8, 441, 443,
452–3, 462, 475
see also mataro, monastrell

Mudgee (region) 26, 52–5, 58–9,
62–4, 66–7, 70

müller-thurgau 70

Murray Darling (region) 26, 244–5,
248

Murrumbateman (unofficial
subregion) 72, 74, 78, 82, 84,
86–90

muscadelle 228, 236, 245, 247, 446

muscat 54, 226, 228–9, 236–7, 244,
247, 288, 297, 314–16, 357, 372, 451,
460, 462, 465–6

muscat blanc à petits grains 228,
308, 351

muscat, brown 245

muscat of Alexandria 321, 329

muscat rouge à petits grains 228

N

Nagambie Lakes (subregion) 20, 189,
239–40, 249

natural wines 261, 316, 338–9, 344,
348–9, 351–3
see also lo-fi, minimal intervention

nebbiolo 82, 90, 97, 104, 107, 109,
116–18, 121, 165, 178–9, 188, 191,
197–8, 203, 211, 220, 223–4, 239,
244, 247, 249–50, 311, 329, 340, 344,
353, 355, 462, 465–6

negramoll 446–7

negroamaro 121, 335, 373

nero d'Avola 90, 96, 191, 225, 333–4,
371–3, 399, 404–5, 465

New England Australia (region) 92,
97

nielluccio 323

see also sangiovese

no-till farming 169, 172, 476

Northeast (unofficial subregion, TAS)
263–4

Northwest (unofficial subregion, TAS)
263

nouveau wines 70, 86, 198, 297, 316,
397, 426, 453, 466, 476

O

Olmo, Dr Harold 413, 433, 437, 443

Options game 45

Orange (region) 26, 52, 54, 58–9,
62–4, 66–70

orange wines 50, 89, 176, 348
see also skin-contact

organic farming 47, 50, 54, 63, 67,
69–70, 89, 119, 121, 128, 132, 135–6,
140, 145–6, 148, 154, 159, 162, 164,
169, 176, 191, 208, 210–11, 216, 222–4,
246–7, 250, 261, 302, 310, 313–14,
316–17, 331–3, 338, 341, 345, 348–52,
354–5, 362, 368, 374–5, 395, 404–5,
415–16, 426, 428, 430–1, 445, 450,
466, 475

O'Shea, Maurice 33, 48, 196

Otway hinterland (unofficial
subregion) 138, 140–1, 144–6, 148–9

P

palomino 216, 308, 357

Parker, Robert 181–2, 192, 236, 296,
311–12, 359, 414, 476

pecorino (grape) 97

pedro ximénez 106, 228, 316–17, 357,
381, 451

peloursin 228–9

Pemberton (region) 426, 448, 452–3

Perricoota (region) 93

pét-nats 50, 66, 70, 78, 89, 107, 168,
176, 249–50, 261, 280, 339, 349, 351,
353, 377, 404–5, 426, 442, 445, 453,
476

petit verdot 63, 179, 208, 312, 431,
453, 466–7

petite sirah 228–9

phylloxera 43, 53, 100, 106, 114, 123,

131, 139, 140, 149, 153, 189, 195, 209,
228, 234, 236, 239, 244, 247, 249,
286, 290–1, 308, 357, 476–7

Piccadilly Valley (subregion) 337–8,
340–1, 344–5, 350, 353–4

picolit 178, 192, 247

picpoul noir 378

pigato 323
see also vermentino

pinot bianco 178, 192

pinot blanc 117, 121, 163, 279

pinot grigio 124, 135, 178–9, 238, 244,
247, 278, 355

pinot gris 66, 70, 83, 90, 119, 122,
124–5, 134–6, 144–5, 150, 158, 177,
204, 240–1, 247, 249, 261, 263, 263,
266, 274, 277, 279–81, 329, 351–2,
355, 357, 377, 397, 402, 405, 438,
466–7

pinot meunier 68, 83, 109, 123, 133,
136, 139, 199, 209, 247, 250, 274–5,
277, 337, 352, 377

pinot noir 48, 50, 62, 66–9, 73, 75,
78–9, 82–3, 87–90, 93, 97, 100,
104–7, 109, 112, 114, 116–25, 129,
131–6, 139–40, 144–5, 148–9, 152–3,
154–5, 158–9, 162–9, 176–9, 191, 194,
197, 199, 204, 209–11, 216–17, 223–5,
237, 240–1, 247–50, 259–61, 263–4,
266–8, 273–81, 333, 336–8, 340–1,
344–5, 348, 350–5, 371, 381, 395,
401–2, 428–9, 438, 440, 444–5,
448, 452–3, 467, 477

pinotage 467

Pipers River (unofficial subregion)
262–4, 275

piquette 50, 66, 250, 349–50, 354,
374, 404, 476

Pokolbin (subregion) 31–3, 37, 39,
42–3, 46–7, 49–50

Porongurup (subregion) 436–8, 440,
445

port 229, 237, 313, 431, 475

preservative-free wine 54, 375
see also sulphur

prosecco 83, 240, 244, 250
see also glera

Pyrenees (region) 116, 194, 196–8,
203–4, 207–8, 211

Q

Queensland (region) 456–468
qvevri 162, 451, 466
   see also amphora-aged wine

R

refosco 165, 246
regenerative farming 23, 47, 131, 216,
   223, 239, 276, 318, 332, 338, 352, 431,
   445
Rhône varieties 70, 120, 249, 452
ribolla gialla 279
riesling 37, 62, 66–8, 74, 78–9, 82–4,
   86–90, 97, 100, 125, 133–5, 136, 140,
   144–5, 149–50, 153, 158, 163–4, 179,
   188, 194, 196–7, 199, 204, 209–10,
   216–17, 225, 240–1, 244, 247, 249,
   259–61, 263, 266, 268, 274–81,
   288–90, 295, 297, 302, 311, 313–18,
   320–4, 329, 332–5, 337–8, 340–1,
   350, 354–5, 371–2, 375, 377, 395,
   397, 402, 413–14, 427–30, 433, 436,
   438, 440–6, 450, 453, 468
Riverina (region) 93, 95–7
Riverland (region) 245, 398–9, 404–5
rolle *see* vermentino
rondinella 89
rosé 50, 67, 84, 90, 116–17, 155, 237,
   250, 274, 276, 297, 310–11, 350, 354,
   395, 430, 453
roussanne 84, 86, 88, 106, 119, 121,
   216, 223, 225, 239, 249–50, 314, 332,
   362, 374–5, 378, 462, 467
roussillon 228, 357
rubienne 245
Rutherglen (region) 96, 100, 223,
   226–37, 245

S

sagrantino 97, 224, 371–2, 378, 467
sangiovese 66, 79, 83, 88–90, 191,
   216–17, 220, 223, 239, 244, 246–7,
   249–50, 320, 329, 334, 340, 344–5,
   352–3, 373, 378, 405, 420, 438
saperavi 246, 344, 350, 405, 453, 462,
   466–7

sauternes 228
sauvignon blanc 63, 68, 83, 86, 90,
   97, 104, 107, 116–17, 120, 125, 144,
   149, 158, 176–7, 204, 208, 210–11,
   224, 238, 240, 250, 263, 266, 274–5,
   277, 279, 281, 336, 338, 340–1,
   344–5, 351–2, 355, 359, 371, 396–7,
   401–2, 405, 420, 426, 429–31, 438,
   440, 445, 447–8, 452–3, 465, 467
savagnin 125, 128, 132, 355
schioppettino 246
sciacarello 334
semillon 30, 32–3, 37, 39, 42, 45–50,
   63, 66, 88, 93, 96–7, 140, 144, 177,
   188, 210, 224, 288, 296–7, 308,
   310–12, 314–18, 329, 339, 353, 371–2,
   402, 405, 420, 426, 428–31, 438,
   446, 451–2, 460, 468
semillon gris 310
Seppeltsfield (unofficial subregion)
   290, 297–8, 302–3, 312–13, 315–16
Sevenhill (unofficial subregion) 326,
   328, 332
sherry 228, 475
   see also apera (sherry-styled wines)
shiraz 30–3, 37, 39, 42, 46–50, 54,
   58, 62–3, 66, 68, 70, 78–9, 82–4,
   86–90, 96, 104–5, 106–7, 109, 112,
   116, 118–21, 125, 134–5, 139, 144–5,
   148–9, 153, 155, 163–4, 177, 180–3,
   188–92, 194, 196–8, 202–4, 207–11,
   216, 220, 222–5, 228–9, 237–8,
   239–40, 244–5, 246–50, 259–60,
   266, 276–7, 288–90, 292, 294–7,
   299, 302–5, 308, 310–18, 320–4,
   329, 332–7, 340, 344–5, 350–1,
   354–9, 362, 366–70, 372–6, 378,
   381–2, 384, 392–6, 400–5, 413, 420,
   426, 429–31, 436–8, 440, 443–5,
   447, 450–3, 460, 462, 465–8, 475
shiraz vs. syrah 32, 106
   see also syrah
Shoalhaven Coast (region) 72, 92–3,
   97
show judging 37, 464
skin-contact 23, 46, 66, 70, 89, 97,
   135, 168, 198, 238, 280, 297, 310,
   312, 315–16, 323, 333–4, 339, 351,

354, 372, 377, 397, 402, 405, 426,
   429–30, 445, 451, 466, 475, 477
   see also orange wines, skin-
   macerated
skin-macerated 107, 134, 281
   see also skin-contact
soil 19, 22, 39, 49, 59, 62, 78–9, 82,
   108, 112, 128, 149, 155, 158, 241, 268,
   288, 299, 303–4, 324, 331, 363, 381,
   385, 395–6, 410, 420–1, 424, 438,
   448, 461, 476–7
   acidic 39, 63, 79, 108, 112, 128, 172,
      385
   alkaline 42, 230, 303
   alluvial 39, 42, 63, 141, 144, 169, 230,
      367–8, 433, 446
   basalt 42, 63, 79, 100, 128, 141, 155,
      169, 183, 199, 262, 385, 388
   Black Dog soils 230–1, 245
   black soil 141, 199, 368
   blue soil 344
   brown soil 62–3, 302–3, 368, 388,
      417
   buckshot soils 141, 199, 224
   chert 183
   clay 39, 42, 58, 63, 79, 82, 112, 128,
      144, 149, 169, 172, 199, 202–3,
      223–4, 230, 239, 298–9, 302–4,
      313, 328–9, 340, 344, 366–8, 385,
      388, 401, 413, 448, 477
   dolerite 262, 326
   dolomite 326, 328
   feldspar 460
   Fordwich Sill 42, 47, 50
   Forest Grove soils 417
   gneiss 416, 437
   granite 79, 100, 108, 112, 155, 183,
      191, 217, 220, 222–3, 262, 302, 385,
      388, 416, 437, 440, 460–1, 465–6,
      468
   granitic soil 63, 112, 117, 169, 172,
      189, 202, 222–4, 299, 460
   granodiorite 100, 217
   gravel 141, 169, 183, 199, 203, 223,
      239, 313, 329, 367–8, 413, 417, 446,
      448
   grey soil 112
   iron 42, 169, 183, 388

ironstone 58, 141, 183, 199, 203, 303, 313, 340, 344, 367, 385, 417

limestone 62, 74, 79, 88, 141, 144, 199, 284, 303, 313, 328–9, 368, 385, 388, 396, 401–2

loam 39, 42, 58, 63, 112, 128, 141, 169, 172, 199, 202–3, 223, 230–1, 298–9, 302–3, 313, 328–9, 340, 344, 367–8, 385, 388, 398, 401–2, 417, 437, 448, 460, 465

marine sediments 128, 145, 183, 217, 367, 385

marly soils 141, 328

mica 460

mudstone 112, 145, 183, 202–3, 217, 225

quartz 58, 203, 217, 220, 230–1, 340, 344, 366, 460

quartzite 262, 302, 328, 368

red soil 39, 42, 62, 82, 97, 112, 128, 141, 155, 169, 172, 177, 183, 199, 203, 220, 230–1, 302–3, 313, 326, 328–9, 344, 367–8, 385, 388, 398, 413, 417, 448

sandstone 145, 155, 158, 183, 202–3, 217, 262, 284, 299, 326, 344, 366, 368

sandy soil 39, 42, 47, 58, 63, 79, 112, 117, 128, 141, 144, 146, 149, 169, 172, 183, 202, 230–1, 239, 297–9, 303–4, 313, 329, 340, 366–8, 385, 388, 398, 417, 430–1, 437, 446, 448, 460, 465, 477

schist 262, 344

sediments 79, 100, 112, 128, 144, 172, 326

shales 144, 155, 158, 183, 202–3, 217, 231, 284, 326, 328, 340, 344, 366

siliceous soil 183, 202

silts/silty 42, 62, 366–7

siltstone 112, 145, 328, 366, 368

slate 326, 328–9

terra rossa 326, 328, 366, 382–3, 385, 388, 402

volcanic soil 39, 42, 58, 62–3, 67–8, 79, 88, 97, 112, 128, 141, 155, 169, 172, 177, 183, 199, 230–1, 239, 262, 284, 326, 328, 385, 402

zircon 14

South Burnett (unofficial subregion) 456, 458, 460, 462, 468

South Gippsland (unofficial subregion) 167, 169, 172, 176–8

Southeast (unofficial subregion, TAS) 263, 266

Southern Highlands (region) 72, 93, 97

Southern New South Wales (region) 72–90

sparkling wines 37, 46, 66–8, 75, 78, 82–3, 87–90, 97, 100, 107, 112, 116, 121, 140, 150, 154–5, 165, 178, 195, 197–8, 209, 222, 236, 241, 250, 259–61, 263–4, 272, 274–7, 279, 281, 286, 291, 294, 309, 312–14, 335, 337, 341, 350, 355, 367, 375, 396, 430, 446, 450, 453, 474, 476
   see also traditional method

spirits 50, 97, 196, 316, 402, 475
   see also brandy, gin, vodka

stem inclusion 250, 280–1, 295, 420, 477

Strathbogie Ranges (region) 100, 240, 246

sulphur 323, 348, 430, 477
   low-to-no-sulphur wines 23, 47, 70, 162, 165, 249, 280, 316, 318, 323, 338–9, 348, 351–2, 354, 431, 445, 475–6

sultana 245, 247

sumoll 247

Sunbury (region) 238, 248

Surf Coast (unofficial subregion) 138, 141, 144–6, 150

sustainability 19, 23, 50, 63, 97, 119, 133–4, 141, 150, 162, 176, 210, 231, 234, 239, 249–50, 261, 308, 318, 331, 333, 341, 349, 362, 368–9, 373–4, 428, 430, 450, 475
   see also biodiversity, biodynamics, organic farming, no-till farming, regenerative farming

Sustainable Winegrowing Australia 362, 369, 375, 377, 397, 399, 415, 474

Swan District (region) 446–7, 450–2

Swan Hill (region) 245

Swan Valley (subregion) 427, 438, 446, 450–1, 453

sweet wines 37, 47, 63, 67, 95, 106–7, 123, 228, 234, 292, 314–5, 329, 337, 475
   see also dessert wines

sylvaner 281

syrah 90, 106, 116–19, 132, 136, 162, 164, 176–7, 179, 191, 210, 222, 225, 228–9, 238–9, 249–50, 277–9, 281, 315–16, 318, 345, 351, 353–4, 359, 372, 375, 377, 428, 431, 466, 477
   see also shiraz

T

table wines 33, 53, 73, 97, 100, 105, 124, 181, 196, 223, 226, 228–30, 237, 292, 294, 309, 322, 358, 396, 413, 433, 445–6, 451, 460, 477

Tamar Valley (unofficial subregion) 260, 263–4, 274, 276, 279–80

tannat 97, 462

tarrango 245, 247

Tasmania (region) 247, 254–81, 353

tempranillo 42, 68–9, 79, 84, 88–90, 112, 192, 216, 223, 225, 229, 244, 250, 329, 345, 353, 371, 374–5, 377–8, 384, 395, 405, 420, 427, 429, 438, 443–4, 447–8, 451–3, 462, 465, 467

teroldego 88

tinta barroca 399, 465, 468

tinta cão 371, 447

tinta roriz 237

Tokay 228

Topaque 228

touriga nacional 50, 88, 245, 247, 329, 372, 377–8, 400, 453

traditional method 66, 87–8, 116, 121, 209, 250, 274, 315, 337, 450, 460, 474, 476–7
   see also méthode champenoise

traminer 334

Treeton (unofficial subregion) 417, 420

trousseau 280, 316

Tumbarumba (region) 72, 75, 83–4, 89–90

tyrian 245

U

ugni blanc 316, 332
Upper Hunter Valley (subregion) 39, 42, 436
Upper Yarra (unofficial subregion) 104, 108–9, 112, 117
uva di troia 377

V

verdelho 31–2, 42, 47–50, 63, 70, 240, 289, 345, 357, 377, 400, 404, 446, 448, 450–2, 466–7
verduzzo 244, 246–7
vermentino 42, 78, 84, 318, 320, 334, 362, 371, 378, 399, 405, 430–1, 440, 446, 465, 467
vermouth 70, 250, 317
viognier 66, 68, 78, 82, 86, 88–90, 100, 133, 144, 148, 192, 198, 203, 216–17, 220, 238–9, 246, 249, 316, 344, 359, 362, 405, 452–3, 462, 465–6
vodka 450

W

Wallcliffe (unofficial subregion) 417, 420
Watervale (unofficial subregion) 322, 326, 328, 332, 333–5
Werribee (region) 248–9
West Gippsland (unofficial subregion) 167, 169, 172, 176
Western Victoria (region) 141, 194–211
whole bunch *see* stem inclusion
Wilyabrup (unofficial subregion) 417, 420–1, 424, 426, 428–31, 451
Wine Australia's Climate Atlas 39, 477
Winkler Scale 21–2, 63, 82–3, 125, 230, 298, 324, 399, 403, 458, 461, 475, 477
   see also Heat Summation Index
Wrattonbully 380–97
Wyndham, George 31, 46, 92

Y

Yallingup (unofficial subregion) 417, 420, 428
Yarra Valley (region) 104–21, 220
Yass 73, 82–3, 90
Yellow Tail 55, 95–6, 383

Z

zibibbo 354, 444
zinfandel 67, 84, 259, 426, 453, 474
zweigelt 355

Index of Producers

4382 Terroir (QLD) 468

A

A. Rodda Wines (VIC) 213, 222
Accolade Wines 124, 136, 259, 312,
   323, 355, 374, 383, 395, 414, 450
   see also BRL Hardy Limited,
      Thomas Hardy & Sons
Adelina (SA) 320, 322, 332
Agricola (SA) 302, 318
Alkina (SA) 310
Alkoomi (WA) 436, 443
All Saints Estate (VIC) 227, 230, 236
Allies Wines (VIC) 125, 136
Alpha Box & Dice (SA) 345, 367, 372
Amherst Winery (VIC) 211
An Approach to Relaxation (SA) 318
Angove (SA) 362, 366–7, 398–9, 404
Angullong (NSW) 70
Anim (TAS) 261, 268, 280
A.P. Birks Wendouree (SA) 332
Aphelion (SA) 362, 368, 372
Apogee (TAS) 274
Apsley Gorge Vineyard (TAS) 280
A.R.C. (VIC) 125, 168, 176
Arcadia (VIC) 225
Arthur Wines (WA) 431
Ashton Hills (SA) 338, 341, 350
Athletes of Wine (VIC) 159, 165
Attwoods (VIC) 140, 248
Audrey Wilkinson (NSW) 33, 46
Avani (VIC) 128, 132

B

Babche (VIC) 140, 144, 146, 148
Baileys of Glenrowan (VIC) 244, 247
Balancing Heart (QLD) 466
Balgownie Estate (VIC) 239, 250
Ballandean Estate (QLD) 460, 466

Ballinaclash (NSW) 83, 90
Balnaves of Coonawarra (SA) 382,
   384, 394
Bannockburn Vineyards (VIC)
   138–40, 146, 148
Barossa Valley Estate (SA) 318
Basket Range Wine (SA) 338, 340,
   344, 349–50
Bass Phillip (VIC) 166–9, 173, 176
Bass River (VIC) 167, 179
Bassham Wines (SA) 405
Batista (WA) 453
Battles Wine (WA) 453
Bay of Fires (TAS) 259, 261, 264, 274
Bekkers (SA) 367, 370, 372
Bellarmine Wines (WA) 453
Bellbrae Estate (VIC) 145, 150
Bellebonne (TAS) 274
Bellvale (VIC) 179
Bellwether (SA) 380–1, 384, 394
Ben Haines (VIC) 116, 197, 207
Benson and the Mooch (NSW) 70
Bent Road (QLD) 97, 460, 466
Bertrand Bespoke (VIC) 250
Best's Great Western (VIC) 195–6,
   198, 207, 209
Bicknell FC (VIC) 121
Billy Button Wines (VIC) 244, 246
Bindi (VIC) 152, 154–5, 159, 162
Bird in Hand (SA) 355
Bird on a Wire (VIC) 116
BK Wines (SA) 339, 350
Black & Ginger (VIC) 198, 211
Bleasdale (SA) 400, 404
Blind Corner (WA) 426
Bloodwood (NSW) 54, 67
Bochara (VIC) 211
Bondar (SA) 362, 368, 372–3
Borachio (SA) 339, 344, 348, 355
Bowen Estate (SA) 394
Brash Higgins (SA) 362, 368, 371, 373

Brave New Wine (WA) 436, 440,
   443–4
Bremerton Wines (SA) 405
Brian (TAS) 22, 261, 280
Briar Ridge Vineyard (NSW) 50
Brindabella Hills (NSW) 74, 79, 90
BRL Hardy Limited 75, 78, 86, 88, 182,
   259, 274, 374, 414
   see also Accolade Wines, Hardys,
      Thomas Hardy & Sons
Brokenwood (NSW) 33, 37, 42, 46
Brown Brothers (VIC) 182–3, 188–9,
   197, 213, 216, 241, 244–5, 247, 259,
   280
Brown Magpie (VIC) 145, 150
Buller Wines (VIC) 237
Bunn (WA) 445
Burrundulla Vineyards (NSW) 64, 70
Bush Track Wines (VIC) 250
By Farr (VIC) 138–40, 145–6, 148

C

Calabria Family Wines (NSW) 95–6
Campbells (VIC) 227, 231, 236
Canobolas-Smith (NSW) 54, 67
Cape Jaffa (SA) 405
Cape Mentelle (WA) 414–15, 420,
   426, 431
Capel Vale (WA) 453
Casella Family Brands (NSW) 55,
   95–6, 226, 236, 247, 314, 383
Castagna (VIC) 216–17, 222
Castle Rock Estate (WA) 436, 445
Cavedon Wines (VIC) 244, 250
Centennial Vineyards (NSW) 97
Chalmers (VIC) 182, 188–90, 244–5
ChaLou (NSW) 52, 64, 67–8
Chambers Rosewood (VIC) 227, 231,
   236
Chandon Australia (VIC) 116, 241

Charles Melton (SA) 295, 310
Charlotte Dalton (SA) 339, 350–1, 401, 404–5
Château Comme Ci Comme Ça (SA) 339, 355
Château Tanunda (SA) 290, 303, 310
Chatto (TAS) 45, 272, 274–5
Cherubino Wines (WA) 426, 440
Chris Ringland (SA) 296, 310–11
Circe Wines (VIC) 136, 207
Cirillo (SA) 297, 305, 311
Clarendon Hills (SA) 359, 366–7, 373
Clonakilla (NSW) 74, 78, 82–3, 86, 89
Clos Clare (SA) 335
Cloudburst (WA) 426–7
Clovely Estate (QLD) 460, 468
Clover Hill (TAS) 275
Clyde Park Vineyard (VIC) 140, 149
Cobaw Ridge (VIC) 154, 159, 162
Coldstream Hills (VIC) 106–7, 116
Collector Wines (NSW) 78, 82–3, 86–7
Commune of Buttons (SA) 339, 344, 349, 351
Coolangatta Estate (NSW) 93, 97
Coppabella of Tumbarumba (NSW) 83, 89
Coriole (SA) 359, 362, 367, 373
Corymbia (WA) 427
Courabyra (NSW) 83, 90
Craiglee (VIC) 238, 248
Craigmoor (NSW) 53–4, 64, 66, 70
Crawford River Wines (VIC) 197–8, 204, 210
Crittenden Estate (VIC) 124–5, 128, 132–3
Cullen Wines (WA) 414–15, 417, 421, 427–8
Cumulus (NSW) 70
Curly Flat (VIC) 154, 159, 162–3

D

Dal Zotto Wines (VIC) 244, 247
Dalrymple Vineyards (TAS) 275
Dalwhinnie (VIC) 197–8, 204, 207–8
Dalwood Estate (NSW) 31–3, 46
Dappled Wine (VIC) 121

d'Arenberg (SA) 358, 362, 367, 373–4, 376
Dawson James (TAS) 280
De Bortoli (NSW, VIC) 83, 95–7, 107, 116–17, 182, 226
De Iuliis (NSW) 37, 42, 46
De Salis (NSW) 68
Deep Woods (WA) 414, 417, 428
Delamere Vineyards (TAS) 259–60, 275
Delinquente (SA) 399, 404
Denton (VIC) 112, 117
Derwent Estate (TAS) 259, 280–1
Deviation Road (SA) 355
Dhiaga (VIC) 250
Dilworth & Allain (VIC) 154, 159, 163
Din (VIC) 177
Dirt Candy (NSW) 37, 46
Dirty Three Wines (VIC) 168–9, 179
DogRock (VIC) 211
Domaine A (TAS) 259, 275
Domaine Naturaliste (WA) 431
Domaine Simha (TAS) 261, 281
Domenica Wines (VIC) 222–3
Dominique Portet (VIC) 112, 117
Dormilona (WA) 428
Dr. Edge (TAS) 261, 275, 277
Dr Folk (VIC) 167, 169, 177
Drayton's Family Wines (NSW) 33, 42, 47
Duke's (WA) 445
Dune (SA) 378

E

Eastern Peake (VIC) 249
Eden Road (NSW) 74, 78, 82–3, 87–90
Edenflo (SA) 297, 318
Eight at the Gate (SA) 384, 397
Elderton (SA) 295, 310–11
Eldorado Road (VIC) 225
Eldridge (VIC) 124, 136
Elgee Park (VIC) 123, 125, 133
Elsewhere Vineyard (TAS) 281
Eminence Wines (VIC) 250
Empire of Dirt (VIC) 140, 144, 149
Entropy (VIC) 168, 176–7
Eperosa (SA) 297, 299, 311

Ephemera Wines (VIC) 121
Even Keel (VIC) 135
Express Winemakers (WA) 436, 440, 442

F

Fairbrossen (WA) 453
Farmer & the Scientist (VIC) 192
Fighting Gully Road (VIC) 213, 216, 223
First Creek (NSW) 48–50
Flametree (WA) 428
Flaxman Wines (SA) 318
Fleet (VIC) 125, 168–9, 177
Fogarty Wine Group 47, 208, 259, 281, 414, 428
Forest Hill Vineyard (WA) 433, 436, 442
Foster's 107, 135, 188, 259, 382, 414
    see also Southcorp, Treasury Wine Estates
Fowles Wine (VIC) 240, 246
Fox Creek Wines (SA) 359, 368, 378
Frankland Estate (WA) 436, 440, 443
Freddy Nerks (SA) 345, 355
Frederick Stevenson (SA) 316, 318
Freehand (WA) 445
Freeman Vineyards (NSW) 83, 89
Freycinet (TAS) 259, 276
Frogmore Creek (TAS) 259, 281

G

Galafrey Wines (WA) 436, 445
Garagiste (VIC) 125, 133
Gembrook Hill (VIC) 117
Gemtree (SA) 362, 368, 374
Gentle Folk (SA) 339, 349, 351
Geoff Weaver (SA) 341, 355
Geyer Wine Co (SA) 311–12
Ghost Rock (TAS) 281
Giaconda (VIC) 213, 216, 223
Giant Steps (VIC) 117, 247
Gibson Wines (SA) 318
Gilbert Family Wines (NSW) 66
Gippsland Wine Company (VIC) 179
Gisborne Peak (VIC) 165
Glaetzer Wines (SA) 312

Glaetzer-Dixon Family Winemakers (TAS) 276
Glenarty Road (WA) 431
Golden Grove Estate (QLD) 460, 465, 467
Good Intentions (SA) 402, 405
Goodman Wines (VIC) 121
Gralyn Estate (WA) 414, 417, 431
Granite Hills (VIC) 153, 158, 163
Grant Burge Wines (SA) 295, 312
Green Door (WA) 452
Greenock Creek (SA) 295–6, 302–4, 312
Grey Sands Vineyard (TAS) 281
Grosset (SA) 320, 322, 324, 328–9, 331, 333
Grove Estate (NSW) 69
Gundog Estate (NSW) 50
Guroo (SA) 405

H

Haddow & Dineen (TAS) 281
Hahndorf Hill (SA) 338, 355
Hanging Rock Winery (VIC) 154, 165
Hardys (SA) 78, 84, 345, 358, 374, 401–2
see also BRL Hardy Limited
Harkham (NSW) 37, 47
Harris Organic (WA) 450
Harrison Wines (SA) 375
Hart & Hunter (NSW) 50
Head Wines (SA) 318
Heathcote Estate (VIC) 192
Heathcote Winery (VIC) 181, 192
Heemskerk (TAS) 258–9, 276–7
Helm Wines (NSW) 74, 78, 82–3, 87
Henschke (SA) 290, 294, 296, 299, 302, 312–13, 341
Henskens Rankin (TAS) 276
Hentley Farm Wines (SA) 313
Heritage Estate (QLD) 468
Heroes Vineyard (VIC) 140, 145–6, 149
Hickinbotham Vineyard (SA) 366, 378
Highbank (SA) 384, 394–5
Hochkirch Wines (VIC) 198–9, 210–11
Hoddles Creek (VIC) 121

Holm Oak (TAS) 281
Holyman (TAS) 279–80
Home Hill (TAS) 281
Houghton Wines (WA) 446, 450, 453
House of Arras (TAS) 259, 264, 276–7
Howard Park (WA) 414, 421, 428, 440
Howard Vineyard (SA) 355
Huntington Estate (NSW) 66
Hurley Vineyard (VIC) 133

I

Indigo Vineyard (VIC) 225
Inkwell (SA) 362, 368, 375
Ironcloud (WA) 453
Irvine (SA) 318
Islander Estate Wines (SA) 405

J

Jackson Family Wines 117, 378
Jacob's Creek (SA) 95, 313, 400
Jamsheed (VIC) 250
Jansz Tasmania (TAS) 259, 264, 276–7
Jasper Hill (VIC) 181–2, 188–90
Jauma (SA) 339, 351–2, 362
Jayden Ong (VIC) 118
Jester Hill Wines (QLD) 467
Jilly (NSW) 92, 97
Jim Barry Wines (SA) 320, 328–9, 333
Johansen Wines (NSW) 83, 90
John Duval Wines (SA) 315, 318
John Kosovich (WA) 450
Jones (VIC) 227, 237
Josef Chromy Wines (TAS) 281
Joshua Cooper Wines (VIC) 154, 159, 164
Journey Wines (VIC) 121
Juniper Estate (WA) 414, 429

K

Kaesler Wines (SA) 318
Kalleske (SA) 318
Katnook Estate (SA) 382, 395
Kay Brothers Amery Vineyard (SA) 357, 378
Keith Tulloch (NSW) 47
Kerri Greens (VIC) 125, 133

Kilikanoon (SA) 322–3, 328, 335
Knappstein (SA) 322–3, 335, 338, 341
Koerner (SA) 322–3, 332–3
Konpira Maru (VIC) 238, 244, 247
Koomilya (SA) 367, 378
Kooyong (VIC) 124, 133

L

La Kooki (WA) 431
La Petite Mort (QLD) 97, 460, 465–6
La Violetta (WA) 436, 440, 444
Lake Breeze (SA) 400, 404
Lake George Winery (NSW) 74, 82, 87–8
Lake's Folly (NSW) 33, 47
Langmeil (SA) 305, 313
Lark Hill (NSW) 74, 78, 82, 87–8
L.A.S. Vino (WA) 412, 429
Latta Vino (VIC) 249
Lauren Langfield (SA) 355
Leconfield (SA) 397
Leeuwin Estate (WA) 414–16, 420, 429
Lenton Brae (WA) 414, 417, 431
Leo Buring (SA) 37, 295, 297, 313, 328
Leogate Estate (NSW) 50
Lethbridge Wines (VIC) 140, 146, 149–50, 197
Levantine Hill (VIC) 121
Lightfoot & Sons (VIC) 172, 179
Limus (SA) 402, 405
Lindeman's (NSW) 33, 37, 42, 47, 294–5, 402
Linear Wines (NSW) 78, 90
Lithostylis (VIC) 167, 169, 177
Little Reddie (VIC) 165
Logan (NSW) 66
Lonely Shore (WA) 452
Longview (SA) 338, 355
Lowboi (WA) 436, 445
Lowe Wines (NSW) 67
Lowestoft (TAS) 281
LS Merchants (WA) 431
Lucy M (SA) 339, 348, 352
Luke Lambert (VIC) 107, 117–8
Lyons Will (VIC) 154, 159, 164

M

M.Chapoutier (VIC) 182, 188, 203, 207–8
Mac Forbes (VIC) 107–8, 112, 118–19, 240
Mada Wines (NSW) 78, 90, 125
Made by Monks (TAS) 261, 281
Main Ridge Estate (VIC) 123, 125, 133
Maipenrai (NSW) 90
Maison Lapalus (VIC) 250
Majella (SA) 382, 384, 395
Mallaluka Wines (NSW) 78, 90
M&J Becker (NSW) 37, 50
Mann (WA) 450
Marco Lubiana (TAS) 277
Margan Wines (NSW) 37, 42, 47–8
Marius Wines (SA) 378
Mayford Wines (VIC) 244, 250
Mazza (WA) 453
McAlister Vineyards (VIC) 167, 172, 179
McHenry Hohnen (WA) 431
McLeish Estate (NSW) 50
McWilliam's (NSW) 43, 48, 75, 82–3, 95, 97
Meadowbank Estate (TAS) 259, 261, 277
Medhurst (VIC) 45, 119
Meerea Park (NSW) 50
Merindoc (VIC) 192
Mérite (SA) 384, 393, 395
Metala (SA) 405
Mewstone Wines (TAS) 260–1, 268, 277
Minimum Wines (VIC) 250
Ministry of Clouds (SA) 362, 368, 375
Mitchell (SA) 328, 335
Mitchelton (VIC) 191, 249, 338
Mitolo (SA) 362, 368, 378
Moët & Chandon 107, 116, 414
Mollydooker (SA) 359, 367, 375–6
Momento Mori (VIC) 168, 177
Montalto (VIC) 136
Montrose (NSW) 66
Moondarra (VIC) 167, 169, 177–8
Moorilla (TAS) 258–9, 264, 277
Moorooduc Estate (VIC) 124–5, 134, 177
Moppity Vineyards (NSW) 89

Morris (VIC) 96, 226–7, 231, 236
Moss Wood (WA) 414–15, 417, 421, 429
Mount Avoca (VIC) 197, 204, 211
Mount Horrocks (SA) 322, 328–9, 331, 334
Mount Langi Ghiran (VIC) 196, 198, 202, 207, 209
Mount Majura (NSW) 74–5, 78–9, 88
Mount Mary (VIC) 106, 112, 119
Mount Pleasant (NSW) 33, 37, 42, 48, 97, 259
Mountadam (SA) 302, 318
Mt Yengo Wines (NSW) 19, 48
Mulline (VIC) 140, 150
Murdoch Hill (SA) 338, 341, 344, 352
Myattsfield (WA) 453

N

Nashdale Lane Wines (NSW) 54, 68
Nazaaray (VIC) 128, 136
Neldner Road (SA) 302, 314
Ngeringa (SA) 338, 345, 349, 352–3
Nicholson River (VIC) 167, 172, 179
Nick O'Leary Wines (NSW) 78–9, 83, 88–9
Nick Spencer Wines (NSW) 78, 82–3, 90
Nikau Farm (VIC) 177
Nikola Estate (WA) 453
Nocturne (WA) 431
Noon (SA) 362, 376, 400
North (VIC) 159, 164

O

Oakdene (VIC) 144, 150
Oakridge Wines (VIC) 119
Ocean Eight (VIC) 134
Ochota Barrels (SA) 316, 339, 348, 353, 362
O'Leary Walker (SA) 322, 335
Olive Farm (WA) 446, 453
Oliver's Taranga (SA) 367, 371, 376
Onannon (VIC) 125, 136
One Block (VIC) 118
Oranje Tractor (WA) 445
Orbis (SA) 378

Orlando (SA) 55, 289–90, 292, 295, 313
Ossa Wines (TAS) 281
Ottelia (SA) 397

P

Paradigm Hill (VIC) 134
Paralian Wines (SA) 362, 376–7
Paringa Estate (VIC) 124, 134–5
Parker Coonawarra Estate (SA) 397
Patrick of Coonawarra (SA) 397
Patrick Sullivan (VIC) 168–9, 178
Paul Osicka (VIC) 188, 190–1
Pauletts (SA) 335
Penfolds (SA) 32–3, 46, 53, 75, 83, 291–2, 294–6, 303, 305, 313–4, 356, 376, 382–4, 398, 443
Penley Estate (SA) 395–6
Pennyweight (VIC) 216–17, 223
Pepper Tree Wines (NSW) 50
Petaluma (SA) 55, 337–8, 341, 355, 382–3
Peter Lehmann (SA) 96, 295, 299, 310–11, 314
Pewsey Vale Vineyard (SA) 289–90, 295, 297, 302, 314
Pfeiffer (VIC) 230, 234, 236–7
Philip Shaw Wines (NSW) 54, 68
Philippa Farr Wines (VIC) 179
Piano Piano (VIC) 225
Picardy (WA) 448, 452
Pierro (WA) 414, 421, 429–30
Pieter van Gent (NSW) 64, 70
Pikes (SA) 322, 334
Pipan Steel (VIC) 250
Pipers Brook Vineyard (TAS) 258–60, 264, 274, 278
Pirie (TAS) 274, 280–1
Pizzini (VIC) 244, 247
Place of Changing Winds (VIC) 154, 159, 164
Plantagenet (WA) 436, 442
Polperro (VIC) 135
Pooley Wines (TAS) 259, 278
Poppelvej (SA) 378
Powell & Son (SA) 302, 314, 318
Pressing Matters (TAS) 281
Principia (VIC) 136

Printhie Wines (NSW) 68
Proud Primary Produce (VIC) 121
Provenance Wines (VIC) 150
Punch (VIC) 121
Punt Road (VIC) 119
Pyren Vineyard (VIC) 198, 204, 207–8

Q

Quealy Winemakers (VIC) 124, 135

R

R. D'Meure (TAS) 261, 281
Raïdis (SA) 397
Rasa (SA) 297, 314, 316
Ravenscroft Vineyard (QLD) 467
Ravensworth (NSW) 78, 82–3, 89
Redman (SA) 382, 384, 396
Reed (VIC) 125, 140, 150, 316
Renzaglia (NSW) 70
Ricca Terra (SA) 399, 404–5
Ridgemill Estate (QLD) 460, 466–7
Rieslingfreak (SA) 297, 314–5
Rikard Wines (NSW) 68–9
Riposte (SA) 355
Riverbank Estate (WA) 453
Robert Channon Wines (QLD) 467
Robert Stein Vineyard (NSW) 54, 67
Rockford (SA) 295, 302, 310–11, 315
Rosnay Wines (NSW) 69–70
Ross Hill Wines (NSW) 69
Ruggabellus (SA) 297, 302, 315

S

Sabi Wabi (NSW) 37, 50
Sailor Seeks Horse (TAS) 260, 278–9
Sally's Paddock (VIC) 197, 203, 208
Salo (VIC) 121
Saltram (SA) 290, 295, 318
Sam Vinciullo (WA) 431
Sami-Odi (SA) 297, 315
Samuel's Gorge (SA) 362, 368, 378
Sandalford (WA) 414, 450–1
Savaterre (VIC) 216, 224
S.C. Pannell (SA) 362, 367, 370, 377
Scion (VIC) 234, 237
Scotchmans Hill (VIC) 144, 150

Sentio (VIC) 224, 244
Seppelt Wines Great Western (VIC)
    182–3, 196–8, 207, 209, 289, 290–1
Seppeltsfield (SA) 289–90, 297,
    303–4, 308, 315–16, 376
Serrat (VIC) 121
Settlers Rise (QLD) 468
Sevenhill (SA) 321, 335
Seville Estate (VIC) 112, 121, 134
Shadowfax (VIC) 140, 181, 197, 249
Shaw+Smith (SA) 11, 260, 338, 340–1,
    344, 349, 353, 370
Shobbrook Wines (SA) 316
Sholto Wines (NSW) 78, 90
Shut the Gate (SA) 335
Si Vintners (WA) 430
Sigurd (SA) 297, 318
Silent Way (VIC) 154, 159, 164–5
Silkman Wines (NSW) 48–9
Simão & Co (VIC) 237
Sinapius (TAS) 260, 264, 279
Singlefile Wines (WA) 436, 444
Sittella (WA) 451
Skillogalee (SA) 322–3, 328, 334
Smallfry (SA) 297, 316
Smith & Hooper (SA) 384, 397
Somos (SA) 362, 377
Sonnen (TAS) 261, 281
Sorrenberg (VIC) 216, 224
Soumah (VIC) 121
South Gippsland Wine Company
    (VIC) 179
Southcorp 42, 55, 75, 90, 106, 124,
    182, 382, 414
    see also Foster's, Treasury Wine
    Estates
Spinifex (SA) 297, 299, 316
Spring Vale Vineyards (TAS) 281
Staindl (VIC) 128, 136
Stanton & Killeen Wines (VIC) 227,
    231, 237
Stargazer (TAS) 45, 261, 279
Stefano Lubiana (TAS) 259, 279–80
Stoney Rise (TAS) 259, 264, 275,
    279–80
Stonier Wines (VIC) 123–4, 135–6,
    338
Stormflower (WA) 431
SubRosa (VIC) 198, 211

Summerfield (VIC) 197, 204, 211
Sutton Grange (VIC) 239, 246
Swan Valley Garagistas (WA) 451
Swan Valley Wines (WA) 453
Swinging Bridge Wines (NSW) 69
Swinney (WA) 414, 436, 441, 443–4
Symphony Hill (QLD) 468
Syrahmi (VIC) 188, 191

T

Tahbilk (VIC) 239–40, 249
Talijancich (WA) 451
Talisman (WA) 453
Tamar Ridge (TAS) 259, 280
Tamburlaine (NSW) 70
Tapanappa (SA) 341, 353–4, 382–4,
    401
TarraWarra Estate (VIC) 121
Taturry (VIC) 136
Taylor's (SA) 322, 335
Tellurian (VIC) 188, 191
Ten Minutes by Tractor (VIC) 124, 136
Terra di Granito (QLD) 468
Terre à Terre (SA) 354, 384, 396
Tertini Wines (NSW) 97
The Other Right (SA) 339, 354
The Standish Wine Company (SA)
    296, 316
The Stoke (SA) 405
The Story Wines (VIC) 198, 210, 244
The Vintner's Daughter (NSW) 78,
    90
The Wine Farm (VIC) 168–9, 178–9
Thick as Thieves (VIC) 121, 244
Thistledown (SA) 299, 354
Thomas Hardy & Sons 75, 291–2, 357,
    374, 398, 450
Thomas Wines (NSW) 37, 49
Thousand Candles (VIC) 120
Tim Smith (SA) 318
Timo Mayer (VIC) 107, 120
Tobin Wines (QLD) 468
Tolpuddle Vineyard (TAS) 260, 280,
    353
Toolangi (VIC) 121
Topper's Mountain (NSW) 92, 97
Torbreck Vintners (SA) 296, 304, 311,
    316–17

Traviarti (VIC) 224
Travis Tausend (SA) 339, 345, 355
Treasury Wine Estates 47, 90, 106–7, 116, 119, 124, 135, 181, 198, 209, 259, 276, 313, 316–17, 367, 382–3, 393, 397, 400, 405, 414
see also Foster's, Southcorp
Trevelen Farm (WA) 445
Tulloch Wines (NSW) 42, 49
Tumblong Hills (NSW) 75, 83, 90
Turkey Flat (SA) 317
Turon (SA) 355
Two Tonne Tasmania (TAS) 260, 264, 280
Tyrrell's (NSW) 33, 37, 42–3, 46, 49, 53, 93, 182

U

Unico Zelo (SA) 345, 354, 399
Usher Tinkler Wines (NSW) 37, 42, 50
Utzinger (TAS) 281

V

Vanguardist (SA) 317
Vasse Felix (WA) 414–15, 417, 420–1, 430, 433
View Wine (QLD) 468
Vignerons Schmölzer & Brown (VIC) 212, 216, 224–5, 244
Vinden Wines (NSW) 37, 42–3, 50
Vinea Marson (VIC) 182, 188–9, 191–2
Vinelea (VIC) 225
Vino Volta (WA) 452
Vinya Vella (SA) 318
Virgin Hills (VIC) 153, 165
Voyager Estate (WA) 414, 430

W

Wallington Wines (NSW) 52, 70
Wanted Man (VIC) 192
Wantirna Estate (VIC) 106, 112, 120
Warner Vineyard (VIC) 225, 250
Warrenmang (VIC) 197, 211
Weathercraft (VIC) 225
Wendouree (SA) 191, 320–2, 328–9, 331–2, 350

West Cape Howe (WA) 440, 442–3
Whicher Ridge (WA) 453
Whispering Brook (NSW) 50
Whisson Lake (SA) 338, 354
Whistling Eagle (VIC) 188, 192
Wild Duck Creek (VIC) 181, 188, 192
Wilimee (VIC) 154, 159, 165
William Downie (VIC) 169, 178
Willow Bridge (WA) 452
Willow Creek Vineyard (VIC) 136
Willunga 100 (SA) 368, 378
Windowrie (NSW) 70
Windows Estate (WA) 417, 431
Wines by KT (SA) 322, 334
Wines of Merritt (WA) 430–1
Wirra Wirra (SA) 338, 357, 359, 362, 368, 376–8
Witches Falls (QLD) 468
Wolf Blass (SA) 295, 317, 400
Woodlands (WA) 414, 417, 421, 431
Worlds Apart (SA) 297, 339, 354
Wynns Coonawarra (SA) 68, 382, 396–7

X

Xanadu Wines (WA) 414, 431
Xavier Goodridge (VIC) 168, 179

Y

Yabby Lake Vineyard (VIC) 124, 136
Yalumba (SA) 289–90, 292, 294, 297, 299, 304, 317–18, 384
Yangarra (SA) 362, 367, 370–1, 378
Yarra Yering (VIC) 45, 106, 112, 120–1
Yarrabank (VIC) 121
Yering Station (VIC) 105, 116, 121
Yeringberg (VIC) 104, 106, 112, 121

Conversion Charts

AREA

HECTARE (ha)	ACRE (ac)
0.10	0.25
0.50	1.24
1	2.47
5	12.36
10	24.71
25	61.78
50	123.55
75	185.33
100	247.11
150	370.66
200	494.21
500	1235.53
1000	2471.05
1500	3706.58
2000	4942.11
4000	9884.22
5000	12355.27
10000	24710.54
15000	37065.81
20000	49421.08

SQUARE KILOMETRE (km^2)	SQUARE MILE (m^2)
1	0.39
5	1.93
10	3.86
25	9.65
50	19.31
75	28.96
100	38.61
150	57.92
200	77.22
500	193.05
1000	386.1
1500	579.15
2000	772.2
4000	1544.4
5000	1930.5
10000	3861
15000	5791.5
20000	7722

LENGTH

METRE (m)	FOOT (ft)
1	3.28
5	16.4
10	32.81
25	82.02
50	164.04
75	246.06
100	328.08
200	656.17
500	1640.42
1000	3280.84
1500	4921.26
2000	6561.68

KILOMETRE (km)	MILE (mi)
1	0.62
5	3.11
10	6.21
25	15.53
50	31.07
100	62.14
200	124.27
500	310.69
1000	621.37
2000	1242.74

MILLIMETRE (mm)	INCH (in)
10	0.39
25	0.98
50	1.97
75	2.95
100	3.94
200	7.87
300	11.81
400	15.75
500	19.69
1000	39.37
1500	59.06
2000	78.74

WEIGHT

METRIC TONNE (t)	IMPERIAL TON (T)
1	0.98
5	4.92
10	9.84
25	24.61
50	49.21
75	73.82
100	98.42
150	147.63
200	196.84
500	492.10
1000	984.21
1500	1476.31
2000	1968.41
4000	3936.83
5000	4921.03

KILOGRAM (kg)	POUND (lb)
1	2.20
5	11.02
10	22.05
25	55.12
50	110.23
75	165.35
100	220.46
150	330.69
200	440.92
500	1102.31
1000	2204.62
1500	3306.93
2000	4409.25
4000	8818.49
5000	11023.12

TEMPERATURE

(For Winkler scale conversions, see p. 21)

CELSIUS (°C)	FAHRENHEIT (°F)
-5	23
-1	30.2
-0.50	31.1
0	32
0.50	32.9
1	33.8
5	41
10	50
15	59
20	68
25	77
30	86
35	95
40	104

VOLUME

LITRE (L)	IMPERIAL GALLON (imp gal)	US GALLON (gal)
1	0.22	0.26
5	1.1	1.32
10	2.2	2.64
25	5.5	6.6
50	11	13.21
75	16.5	19.81
100	22	26.42
200	44	52.83
500	110	132.09
1000	219.97	264.17
1500	329.95	396.26
2000	439.94	528.34
4000	879.88	1056.69
5000	1099.85	1320.86

Published in 2023 by Murdoch Books, an imprint of Allen & Unwin

Murdoch Books Australia
Cammeraygal Country
83 Alexander Street
Crows Nest NSW 2065
Phone: +61 (0)2 8425 0100
murdochbooks.com.au
info@murdochbooks.com.au

Murdoch Books UK
Ormond House
26–27 Boswell Street
London WC1N 3JZ
Phone: +44 (0) 20 8785 5995
murdochbooks.co.uk
info@murdochbooks.co.uk

For corporate orders and custom publishing, contact our business development team at salesenquiries@murdochbooks.com.au

Publisher: Jane Willson
Editorial Manager: Justin Wolfers
Head of Creative: Megan Pigott
Designer: Northwood Green
Editors: Dom Sweeney and Ariana Klepac
Illustrator: Robin Cowcher
Artist: Lily Cummins
Indexer: Helena Holmgren
Production Director: Lou Playfair

Text © Jane Lopes and Jonathan Ross 2023
The moral right of the authors has been asserted.
Maps © Martin von Wyss 2023
Illustrations © Robin Cowcher 2023
Artworks © Lily Cummins 2023
Design © Murdoch Books 2023
Photographs: 409 by Frances Andrijich © Wine Australia; 439, 449 by Frances Andrijich © Frances Andrijich; 231 by Ewen Bell © Wine Australia; 160–161, 235 by Rob Blackburn © Visit Victoria; 129, 151 by Parker Blain © Wine Australia; 393 by Steve Bourne © Steve Bourne; 16 by John Carnemolla © Alamy; 309 by Andre Castellucci © South Australian Tourism Commission; 147 by Mark Chew © Visit Victoria; 457 by Maxime Coquard © Tourism Australia; 285 by Duy Dash © South Australian Tourism Commission; 321, 357 by Jampal Dawa © Tourism Australia; 337 by Andrew Downer © Andrew Downer; 193 by Pip Foster © Pip Foster; 181 by Shaun Guest © Shaun Guest; 205, 251 by David Hannah © Visit Victoria; 174–175 by Gavin Hansford © Visit Victoria; 370 by Declan Hartley-Brown © South Australian Tourism Commission; 319 by Hill-Smith Family Estates © Hill-Smith Family Estates; 433 by Holii & Ash © Holii & Ash; 381 by Brendan Homan © South Australian Tourism Commission; 73 by Tony Karacsonyi © Tourism Australia; 153 by Lisa Kimmorley © Lisa Kimmorley; 289 by Sven Kovac © Yalumba; 189 by Georgia Laughton © Georgia Laughton; 34–35, 44, 79, 91, 294 by Kimberley Low © Wine Australia; 258 by Moorilla Winery © Moorilla Winery; 139 by Niki Nikolovski © Niki Nikolovski; 267 by Andy Nowell © Wine Australia; 76–77 by Camille Nuttall © Tourism Australia; 15 by PDerrett © iStock; 270–271 by Prime Perspectives © Tourism Australia; 101, 159 by Kyla-Jane Rickard © Kyla-Jane Rickard; 255 by Emilie Ristevski © Tourism Tasmania; 186–187, 242–243 by Ben Savage © Visit Victoria; 123 by SHERPA © Visit Victoria; 167, 173 (left), 173 (right) by Tim Grey Photography © Tim Grey Photography; 27 by Daniel Tran © Tourism Australia; 213 by Mark Walpole © Fighting Gully Road; 4–5, 31, 36, 39, 51, 53, 54, 56–57, 59, 63, 65, 71, 85, 93, 94, 105, 109, 113, 130, 137, 195, 196, 203, 206, 214–215, 221, 227, 239, 261, 291, 293, 305, 306–307, 325, 329, 330, 345, 346–347, 369, 379, 390–391, 399, 400, 403, 413, 421, 422–423, 425, 461, 465, 469, 471 by Wine Australia © Wine Australia; 360–361 by Milton Wordley © Jackson Wine Estates Australia

Every reasonable effort has been made to trace the owners of copyright materials in this book, but in some instances this has proven impossible. The authors and publisher will be glad to receive information leading to more complete acknowledgements in subsequent printings of the book and in the meantime extend their apologies for any omissions.

Murdoch Books and all the contributors for this book acknowledge the Traditional Owners of the Country on which we live and work. We pay our respects to all Aboriginal and Torres Strait Islander Elders, past and present.

All rights reserved. No part of this publication may be reproduced, stored in a retrieval system or transmitted in any form or by any means, electronic, mechanical, photocopying, recording or otherwise, without the prior written permission of the publisher.

ISBN 978 1 92261 672 2

 A catalogue record for this book is available from the National Library of Australia

A catalogue record for this book is available from the British Library

Colour reproduction by Splitting Image Colour Studio Pty Ltd, Wantirna, Victoria

Printed by C&C Offset Printing Co. Ltd., China

10 9 8 7 6 5 4 3 2 1

Jane Lopes is a sommelier, author and importer, having worked at New York's Eleven Madison Park, Nashville's The Catbird Seat, Chicago's The Violet Hour, and most recently as the wine director at Melbourne's Attica, before passing the prestigious master sommelier exam in 2018. Lopes published her first book, *Vignette: Stories of Life and Wine in 100 Bottles*, in 2019. In 2020, Lopes co-founded Legend, an Australian wine imports company, with husband Jonathan Ross, to help bring the great wines they'd experienced in Australia to the US. @janeymaxine

Jonathan Ross is a sommelier and wine importer whose career in restaurants has included posts at New York's Eleven Madison Park, Oceana and Anthos, and as the beverage director for Australia's Rockpool Dining Group. Ross passed the prestigious master sommelier exam in 2017, has curated wine offerings for Qantas Airlines, and founded the boutique wine label Micro Wines. In 2020, Ross returned to the US, eager to spread the word of the world-class wine he'd worked with in Australia, and co-founded Legend Imports in 2020 with his wife Jane Lopes. @dj_gramenon

When **Mike Bennie** isn't wandering vineyards on the four corners of the globe, he is a widely published Sydney-based wine and drinks writer, journalist and presenter. Mike is one of the most internationally known commentators in this space. He is also a co-founder and partner in the landmark P&V Wine + Liquor Merchants, a shop and education space devoted to artisan fermented, brewed and distilled products, and co-director of the landmark Rootstock Sydney wine and food festival. @mikebennie101

After 10 years abroad developing wine programs for some of the world's most revered resorts and heading up the wine program for Hong Kong's Press Room Group, **Kavita Faiella** has returned to Sydney to oversee marketing for Shaw+Smith, Tolpuddle Vineyard, MMAD Vineyard and The Other Wine Co. She is a Len Evans scholar and a graduate of the Wine Australia Future Leaders program. @kavita.faiella

Hannah Day is a Melbourne-based writer turned cabaret artist turned sommelier turned winery hand with a fierce and unquenchable fascination for wine – drinking it, sharing it, talking about it and writing about it. @ohhannahday

Obsessed with the geography of wine, **Martin von Wyss** is a cartographer and publisher of award-winning maps for *National Geographic*, academic and trade publishers, and his own vW Maps. Martin's web-based World Wine Regions atlas (worldwideregions. com) reveals the world's 2500 wine appellations, from Albania to Venezuela, and his Melbourne bottle shop and wine bar, Cardwell Cellars, stocks wines from regions near and far. @vwmaps

'The wine book that the Australian wine industry deserves. Insightful, intelligent and in-depth ... An instant classic.' **NEIL PERRY, chef, restaurateur and author of** *Everything I Love to Cook*

'*How to Drink Australian* is INCREDIBLE. The most comprehensive book on the best Australian wines. It's not an easy feat to bring together so much information, diving deep into the intricacies of the great regions, producers and terroirs of Australia. A must have on every wine lover's book shelf.' **RAJAT PARR, sommelier, winemaker and author of** *The Sommelier's Atlas of Taste*

'A refreshing take on Australian wine. Colour, facts, figures, personalities – all masterfully and sensitively interconnected.' **PETER GAGO, Penfolds chief winemaker**

'As an American sommelier, Australia was really one of those places that I thought was mostly full of funny critters and over-hyped wines. That is, until I met Jane and Jon – they showed me that this is a land of terroir and growers who rival many of their European counterparts. This book further solidified me falling in love with this wild continent so rich with history and a new generation of wines. An important read for both wine geeks and novices alike!' **VICTORIA JAMES, sommelier and author of** *Wine Girl*

'Capturing all the complexities of wine in contemporary Australia is a massive job, but Jane and Jon and their team of collaborators have absolutely nailed it: *How to Drink Australian* is an exhaustive, insightful, invaluable new guide to what's going on right now in the vineyards and cellars – and, crucially, the hearts and minds – of winegrowers right across this dynamic country.' **MAX ALLEN, author of** *The Future Makers: Australian Wines for the 21st Century*

'As someone who has followed the Australian wine scene since 1992, it is about time for this great book by Jane Lopes and Jonathan Ross. So much has changed, not just in the past 30 years – the last 10 alone have been revelatory. To have them walk us through these changes and these wine regions, is so timely.' **BOBBY STUCKEY, sommelier, restaurateur and author of** *Friuli: Food and Wine*